THE CZECH & SLOVAK REPUBLICS

THE ROUGH GUIDE

G000069742

THE ROUGH GUIDES

OTHER AVAILABLE ROUGH GUIDES

AMSTERDAM • BARCELONA • BERLIN • BRAZIL • BRITTANY & NORMANDY
BULGARIA • CALIFORNIA & WEST COAST USA • CANADA • CRETE
CYPRUS • EGYPT • EUROPE • FLORIDA • FRANCE •GERMANY • GREECE
GUATEMALA & BELIZE • HOLLAND, BELGIUM & LUXEMBOURG • HONG KONG
HUNGARY • IRELAND • ISRAEL • ITALY • KENYA • MEDITERRANEAN WILDLIFE
MEXICO • MOROCCO • NEPAL • NEW YORK • NOTHING VENTURED • PARIS
PERU • POLAND • PORTUGAL • PRAGUE • PROVENCE • PYRENEES
SAN FRANCISCO • SCANDINAVIA • SICILY • SPAIN • THAILAND • TUNISIA
TURKEY • TUSCANY & UMBRIA • USA • VENICE • WEST AFRICA
WOMEN TRAVEL • ZIMBABWE & BOTSWANA

FORTHCOMING
AUSTRALIA • ST PETERSBURG

Rough Guide Credits

Series editor: Mark Ellingham
Text editor: Kate Berens
Editorial: Martin Dunford, John Fisher, Jack Holland, Jonathan Buckley, Greg Ward,
  Richard Trillo, Jules Brown
Production: Susanne Hillen, Andy Hilliard, Gail Jammy, Vivien Antwi, Melissa Flack
Accounts: Celia Crowley

Special thanks to David and Mira for hospitality in Karlovy Vary and Prague, Petr, Pavla and Zdeněk for the Jeseníky trip, Al for going back against his best intentions, and of course, Kate, Louise, Nat, Nancy, Stan, Gren, Juliet, Jan and Andy, and the folks in Wetherby.

And thanks to all those at **Rough Guides**, in particular Kate Berens, but also Jack Holland, John Fisher and Jules Brown for previous editing, and Gareth Nash, Andy Hilliard, Gail Jammy, Susanne Hillen and Vivien Antwi for their patience during production.

Published by Rough Guides Ltd, 1 Mercer Street, London WC2H 9QJ.
Distributed by Penguin Books, 27 Wrights Lane, London W8 5TZ
New edition of *Czechoslovakia: The Rough Guide*, first published by Harrap Columbus 1991 and
reprinted by Rough Guides Ltd 1992.

Typeset in Linotron Univers and Century Old Style to an original design by Andrew Oliver
Printed by Cox & Wyman, Reading, Berks

Illustrations in Part One and Part Four by Ed Briant.
Basics illustration by Tommy Yamaha. Contexts illustration by Sally Davies.

480pp. includes index

British Library Cataloguing in Publication Data
A catalogue record for this book is available from the British Library.

ISBN 1-85828-029-X

THE CZECH & SLOVAK REPUBLICS

THE ROUGH GUIDE

Written and researched by

ROB HUMPHREYS

THE ROUGH GUIDES

HELP US UPDATE

We've gone to a lot of effort to ensure that this new edition of *The Czech and Slovak Republics: The Rough Guide* is up-to-date and accurate. However, things are changing at an extraordinary speed in both republics, and what were formerly little-known areas are becoming increasingly popular – any suggestions, comments or corrections would be much appreciated.

We'll credit all contributions, and send a copy of the next edition (or any other *Rough Guide* if you prefer) for the best letters. Please write to:

Rob Humphreys, The Rough Guides, 1 Mercer Street, London WC2H 9QJ.

Thanks to the following people, who helped with the previous edition, and contributed to the production of this second edition with their letters and comments:

M. Griffiths, M. Hejzlar, J. Lunn, F. C. M. Jones, A. Fricker, J. Waring, L. Eveleigh, V. Cooke, Mrs G. Hopkins, J. Wilson, B. Welch, A. Gibson, L. Hudson, R. Rowe, R. Sansome, B. Dorf, S. Ridgway, B. Rodgers, W. P. Keats, D. Benton, R. Travers, J. J. Poprac, T. Marlow, B. Reifsnider, C. Sutherland, H. Dickner, J. Hutts, A. Paling and S. Evans, K. J. Chinn, E. J. Warans, T. Simpson, J. Weber, W. M. Warren, J. Jooby, J. Lightfoot, A. Orzoff, A. Harrison, L. Harris, J. Graham, M. Thorpe, C. Albertson, F. Hall, G. Neudeck, R. Deaver, R. O'Hara, E. Griffiths, J. T. Riley, C. Gillett, R. Sully, D. M. Larson, C. T. Walker, C. Marcer, A. Reiners, S. R. McCombie, D. Greene, B. S. Towner, A. Hoskin, J. Knox, I. Gasse, A. Brown, C. Hilton, L. J. Nemec, T. Buchdahl-Tintner, H. Brigitte, D. Lock, Y. Marascalchi, L. J. Cowell, C. White, J. Stone, R. A. Blackie, D. Charter and B. Harrison, P. Horák, M. Nelson and C. Edwards, R. Farquhar, H. Downey, H. Owen-Reece, M. Lindsay, M. Millar, J. Marrone, G. Hemken, D. S. Cox, G. M. Prince, P. Smyth, J. Plant, J. Perowne, A. Robinson, N. Werle, M. Fedor, R. R. Gonsalves, M. Hodder, M. Holman, M. C. Graham, J. Randall, J. Hague, R. Dowthwaite, H. Hagan, M. Searle, N. Thompson, M. Walshe, J. Phillimore, M. Spafford, R. Cox, R. and P. Smith, Mr & Mrs C. George, H. Davies, P. Tucker, P. Shackleton and S. Cox, B. Vohryzek, Dr P. O' Sullivan, S. Forrest, C. Eida, C. and A. Kenny, T. Young, P. Yale, G. Bevan, T. Gordon, J. Wilson, I. Forbes and B. Wright, S. Gill, L. Nias and Jonathan Bousfield.

CONTENTS

Introduction xiii

| PART ONE | BASICS | 1 |

Getting There from Britain 3
Getting There from North America 7
Red Tape and Visas 9
Health and Insurance 10
Costs, Money and Banks 11
Information and Maps 12
Getting Around 14
Accommodation 18
Eating and Drinking 21

Communications: Post, Phones and Media 27
Opening Hours and Public Holidays 29
Castles, Churches and Museums 30
Festivals and Entertainment 32
Sport 35
Trouble and the Police 36
Disabled Travellers 37
Women and Sexual Harassment 38
Directory 38

| PART TWO | THE CZECH REPUBLIC | 41 |

■ 1   Prague and Around 43

■ 2   South Bohemia 144

■ 3   West Bohemia 171

■ 4   North Bohemia 199

■ 5   East Bohemia 222

■ 6   South Moravia 248

■ 7   North Moravia 291

| PART THREE | THE SLOVAK REPUBLIC | 313 |

■ 8   Bratislava and West Slovakia 315

■ 9   The Mountain Regions 351

■ 10   East Slovakia 387

| PART FOUR | CONTEXTS | 419 |

The Historical Framework 421
Books 438
Language 445

An A–Z of Czech and Slovak Street Names 449
Glossaries 452
Index 455

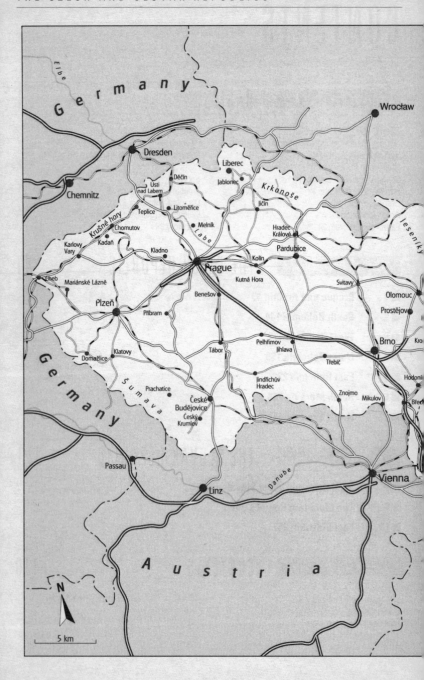

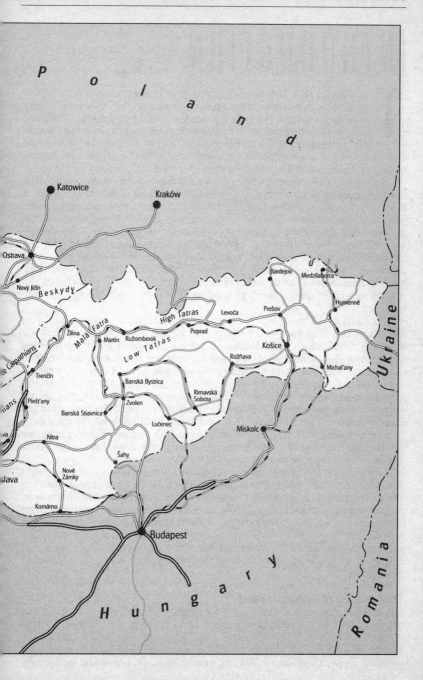

INTRODUCTION

The **Czechs and Slovaks** have rarely been in full control of their historical destiny. The Nazis carved up their country in 1938, only twenty years after its foundation; the Iron Curtain descended just ten years later; and in 1968, Warsaw Pact tanks trampled on the country's dreams of "socialism with a human face". Even the recent break-up of the country went ahead against the will of the majority of the population, without a proper referendum, cooked up by the intransigent leaders of the two main political parties.

Yet the events of November 1989 – the **Velvet Revolution** – were probably the most unequivocally positive of all the anti-Communist upheavals in Eastern Europe. True to their pacifist past, the Czechs and Slovaks shrugged off forty-one years of Communist rule without so much as a shot being fired. In the parliamentary elections the following summer the Communists were roundly defeated, and Václav Havel, a playwright of international renown with an impeccable record of resistance against the previous regime, was chosen as president. The euphoria and unity of those first few months evaporated more quickly than anyone could have imagined, and just three years after the revolution, against most people's predictions, the country split into two separate republics.

In contrast to the political upheavals that have plagued the region, the Czech and Slovak republics have suffered very little physical damage over the last few centuries. Gothic castles and Baroque chateaux have been preserved in abundance, town after town in Bohemia and Moravia has retained its old medieval quarter, and even the wooden architecture of Slovakia has survived beyond all expectations. Geographically speaking, the two republics are the most diverse of all the former Eastern Bloc states. Together they span the full range of central European cultures, from the old German towns of the west to the Hungarian and Rusyn villages in East Slovakia. In physical terms, too, there's enormous variety: Bohemia's rolling hills, lush and relentless, couldn't be more different from the flat Danube basin, or the granite alpine peaks of the High Tatras, the beech forests of the far east, or the coal basins of the Moravian north.

For the visitor, the Czech and Slovak republics are fascinating to travel in right now. More accessible today than at any time since the 1930s, the major **cities** are now buzzing with a cultural and commercial diversity, and fail to conform to most people's idea of Eastern Europe. At the same time, the remoter regions are more reminiscent of the late 1940s than the mid-1990s, and, outside Prague, neither republic is quite geared up for consumptive Western-style tourism. Inevitably, the **pace of change** means that certain sections of this book are going to be out of date even as you read them, such is the volatility and speed of the current transformation.

The break-up of Czechoslovakia

The sharpest division in the country before 1989 was between Party member and non-Party member; nowadays, the most acute problems are between **ethnic groups** – Czech and Slovak, Slovak and Hungarian, Slav and Romany. The Czechs who inhabit the western provinces of Bohemia and Moravia are among the most Westernised Slavs in Europe: urbane, agnostic, liberal and traditionally quite well-off. The Slovaks of the newly independent republic of Slovakia are, by contrast, fervently Catholic, and, for the most part, deeply conservative. The peasant way of life here is slowly dying out, but the traditional codes of conduct, which accompany such an agrarian society, remain embedded in Slovak culture.

Despite decades of peaceful coexistence, the Czech–Slovak divide remained one of the distinctive features of the country. Czechs and Slovaks rarely mixed socially, they visited one another's republics only as tourists and knew little about each other's ways, relying instead on hearsay and prejudice. Despite the constant rumblings of discontent in Slovakia, few people, Slovak or Czech, predicted the imminent **break-up of Czechoslovakia**. Throughout the summer of 1992, numerous attempts were made by the Czech and Slovak federal governments to reach a compromise that would preserve the federation, while giving the Slovaks a degree of autonomy to satisfy their national aspirations. For whatever reasons, no agreement emerged from the hours of talks.

Events were soon overtaken by the elections of June 1992. A sweeping victory by the nationalists in Slovakia and the right-wing in the Czech Lands quickly propelled the country towards disintegration. The new Czech administration, intent on pushing through free market economic policies inimicable to the Slovaks, and a Slovak government that had pledged itself to declare Slovak sovereignty, finally agreed to disagree, and on January 1, 1993, after seventy-four years of turbulent history, Czechoslovakia ceased to exist.

Although now officially two separate countries, it will be some time before the personal, political, economic and cultural ties of the old federation are unravelled. In any case, international pressure, and the prospect of EC membership in the not too distant future, will help to ensure that neither side acts rashly. Predictions of a post-Yugoslav scenario are, for the most part, unfounded, though the fears of Slovakia's Hungarian minority must be addressed if conflict is to be entirely avoided. Both republics have witnessed an upsurge in nationalism and racism, often directed against the large Romany population they share – these, too, must be kept in check if the misgivings of the international community are to be put aside.

Where to go and when

Almost entirely untouched by the wars of this century, the Czech capital, **Prague**, is justifiably one of the most popular destinations in Europe. Poised at the centre of **Bohemia**, the westernmost province, Prague is also the perfect base from which to explore the surrounding countryside. Both the gentle hills and forests of **South Bohemia**, one of central Europe's least-populated regions, and the famous **spa towns of West Bohemia** – Karlovy Vary, Mariánské Lázně and Františkovy Lázně – are only a couple of hours' drive from Prague. Pine-covered **mountains** form Bohemia's natural borders, and the weird **sandstone "rock cities"** in the north and east of the region are some of its most memorable landscapes.

Moravia, the eastern province of the Czech republic, is every bit as beautiful as Bohemia, though the crowds thin out here significantly. The largest city, **Brno**, has its own peculiar pleasures – not least its interwar functionalist architecture – and gives access to the popular Moravian karst region, plus a host of other nearby castles and chateaux. The north of the region is often written off as an industrial wasteland, but **Olomouc** is a charming city, more immediately appealing than Brno, and just a short step away from the region's highest mountains, the **Jeseníky**.

Although the Slovak capital of **Bratislava** can't compare with Prague, it does have its virtues, not least its compact old town, and its position on one of Europe's great rivers, the Danube. Slovakia also boasts some of Europe's highest mountains outside the Alps: these have long formed barriers to industrialisation and modernisation, preserving and strengthening regional differences in the face of Prague's centralising efforts. Medieval mining towns like **Banská Štiavnica** and **Kremnica** still smack of their German origins, and the cathedral capital of the east, **Košice**, was for centuries predominantly Hungarian. In the **Orava** and **Liptov** regions, many of the wooden-built villages, which have traditionally been the focus of Slovak life, survive to this day. **Carpatho-Ruthenia**, in the far east bordering Poland and the Ukraine, has a timeless, impoverished feel to it, and is dotted with wooden Uniate churches and monuments bearing witness to the heavy price paid by the region during the liberation of World War II.

In general the **climate** is continental, with short, hot summers and bitterly cold winters. Spring and autumn are often both pleasantly hot and miserably wet, all in the same week. Winter can be a good time to come to Prague: the city looks beautiful under snow and there are fewer tourists to compete with. Other parts of the country have little to offer during winter (aside from skiing), and most sights stay firmly closed between November and March.

Taking all this into account, the **best months to come** are May, June and September, thereby avoiding the congestion that plagues the major cities and resorts in July and August. Prague in particular suffers from crowds all year round, though steering clear of this high season will make a big difference. In other areas, you may find yourself the only visitor whatever time of year you choose to go, such is the continuing isolation of the former Eastern Bloc countries.

	Jan	Feb	March	April	May	June	July	Aug	Sept	Oct	Nov	Dec
AVERAGE TEMPERATURES (°C)												
Prague	-1	0	4	9	14	17	19	18	14	9	4	0
Brno	-2	-1	3	8	13	16	18	17	14	8	3	-1
Bratislava	-1	0	5	10	15	18	20	19	16	10	4	0
Banská Štiavnica	-3	-2	2	7	12	15	18	17	13	8	2	-1
Košice	-3	-2	3	9	14	17	19	18	14	9	3	-1

Note that these are **average daily temperatures**. At midday in summer, Bratislava can be blisteringly hot. Equally, in most mountainous regions it can get extremely cold and wet at any time of year.

PART ONE

THE

BASICS

GETTING THERE FROM BRITAIN

By far the most convenient way to get to either the Czech or Slovak republic is by plane. It takes just under two hours to reach Prague (compared with over 24hr by train), and there are direct flights from London daily throughout the year. At the time of writing there were no non-stop flights to the Slovak capital, Bratislava.

BY PLANE

Czechoslovak Airlines (ČSA) and *British Airways (BA)* both run daily (and sometimes twice daily) **scheduled flights** from London to Prague. Prices are identical for both airlines, and the cheapest ticket is an Apex return, which currently costs £235 between April and September; £10 more for a weekend flight, £30 less over the winter period. The usual Apex fare restrictions apply: reservations must be made at least fourteen days in advance and there's a refund of fifty percent on tickets cancelled before the fourteen-day deadline. Tickets are valid for three months and can be booked direct from either airline or through most high-street travel agents.

Charter flights to Prague are thin on the ground, only occasionally making it into the "bucket shop" adverts of the various London freebie magazines, *Time Out*, *The Evening Standard* and the quality Sunday papers. During the summer of 1992, *Excalibur Airways* ran a weekly charter service, available through *Campus Travel*, with one-ways from as little as £69, and returns from £129. Otherwise, you'll be pushed to find a

return fare of much less than £150, and in peak season flights are often booked up weeks in advance. It might be worth considering flying to a neighbouring European city like Berlin, Munich or Vienna, for which return fares can be under £100, though of course you'll have to add on the cost of your onward travel.

PACKAGE DEALS AND CITY BREAKS

The only tour operator which specialises in simple flight and accommodation **package deals** to the Czech and Slovak republics is *ČEDOK* (see box below for address), the old state tourist monopoly, whose all-inclusive packages are much better value than their fairly exorbitant accommodation-only deals. The cheapest deal is the City Break, with a return flight from London, plus two nights' accommodation for around £100; better value are the six-night deals at around £300 per person. With either of these packages, there's no compulsion to go on any organised tours once you're there, but, should you wish to, each activity will cost extra.

Other companies which do packages to the Czech and Slovak republics tend to be either accommodation-only or specialist operators. A list of the main agents can be found in the box below.

BY TRAIN

Taking the train is arguably the most pleasurable way of getting to the former Czechoslovakia. The journey **from London to Prague** takes just over 24 hours. Departures are from Victoria Station daily at around 8–11am, arriving in Prague the following morning. There are two main routes, with a couple of minor variations, but all involve changing at least once along the way.

THE ROUTES

The main route is **via the ferry to Ostend**, Brussels, Cologne, Frankfurt and Nuremberg, entering the Czech republic by the Schirnding/Cheb border crossing. You can opt for an hour-long wait at Nuremberg from 11pm to midnight; two very quick changes at Cologne and Frankfurt earlier in the evening (and a 7DM supplement for the German portion); or taking the ***Jetfoil* to Ostend** (an extra £6–9), with an hour at both Cologne and Stuttgart (a slightly longer, but, in fact, faster route).

AIRLINES AND OPERATORS

AIRLINES

British Airways, 156 Regent St, London W1 (☎081/897 4000).

Czechoslovak Airlines, 12a Margaret St, London W1 (Reservations ☎071/255 1898).

AGENTS AND OPERATORS

Campus Travel/Eurotrain, 52 Grosvenor Gardens, London SW1 (☎071/730 3402); and other branches. *Youth/student specialist.*

ČEDOK, 17–18 Old Bond St, London W1 (☎071/629 6058). *The old Czechoslovak state travel agents; flights, accommodation and package deals.*

Czech Travel Ltd, 21 Leighlands Rd, South Woodham Ferrers, Essex CM3 5XN (☎0245/328647). *B&B and self-catering flats and houses for rent all over the Czech and Slovak republics.*

Czechbook Agency, 52 St John's Park, London SE3 (☎081/853 1168). *Cheap private and self-catering accommodation in Prague.*

Czech-in Ltd, 63 Market St, Heywood, Rochdale OL10 1HZ (☎0706/620999). *Self-catering flats and houses for rent all over the Czech and Slovak republics.*

Czechscene, 63 Falkland Rd, Evesham, Worcs WR11 6XS (☎0386/442782). *B&B and self-catering flats for rent in central Bohemia.*

Martin Randal Travel, 10 Barley Mow Passage, London W4 4PH (☎081/994 6477). *Specialist cultural guided tours of Bohemia and Moravia.*

New Millennium, 20 High St, Solihull, West Midlands B91 3TB (☎021/711 2232). *Very cheap ten-day coach and half-board deals to South Moravia.*

STA Travel, 86 Old Brompton Rd, London SW7 (☎071/937 9921).
    117 Euston Rd, London NW1
    25 Queen's Rd, Bristol
    33 Sidney St, Cambridge
    36 George St, Oxford
    75 Deansgate, Manchester.
Independent travel specialists; discount flights.

TK Travel, 14 Buckstone Close, London SE23 (☎081/699 8065). *B&B and self-catering flats available in Prague.*

Travelscene, 11–15 St Ann's Rd, Harrow, Middlesex HA1 (☎081/427 4445). *Three- and five-night holidays in Prague.*

Another option (though one that takes eight hours longer) is to travel **via Paris**, which means changing stations in Paris from the Gare du Nord to the Gare de l'Est (one stop on metro line 4 or 5). The advantage is that, thereafter, it's direct from Paris to Prague.

All the above routes are fairly comfortable provided you've reserved a seat; do so well in advance in summer. You may also want to reserve a **couchette bed** for the final, overnight leg of the journey (around £9 one way).

TICKETS AND PASSES

A **standard rail ticket** from London (bookable through some high-street travel agents or at London's Victoria Station) will currently set you back £238 return (via Ostend), £222 return (via Paris) or £219 (via the Hook of Holland and Berlin): tickets are valid for two months and allow one stopoff en route. If you're under 26, however, or plan to travel extensively by train, there are other options than simply buying a return ticket.

The best-known is the **InterRail pass** (currently £180 a month if you're under 26; £260 a month, or £180 for 15 days if you're not), available from British Rail or travel agents: the only restriction is that you must have been resident in Europe for at least six months. From 1993, however, the system is due to be significantly altered and prices may be thirty percent higher. If you're just heading for the Czech and Slovak republics, it's not necessarily a good deal anyway – rail travel within the two countries is extremely cheap, so you may not really get your money's worth.

The alternative for under-26s is a discounted **BIJ** ticket from *Eurotrain* (through *Campus Travel/USIT*) or *Wasteels*. These can be booked for journeys from any British station to any major station in Europe; they remain valid for two months and allow as many stopovers as you want along a pre-specified route (which can be different going out and coming home). The current return fare to Prague is £158 (via Ostend) or £186 (via Paris). If you travel overnight on the Hook of Holland ferry you'll be charged an extra £12 each way and get some lousy connections.

BY COACH

The cheapest way to get to the former Czechoslovakia is by **coach**. There's a direct service from London to Prague three times a week, leaving from Victoria Coach Station at 7pm and arriving around 21 hours later at Praha-Florenc bus terminal. It is operated by *Kingscourt Express*, who have offices in London and Prague; tickets currently cost £45 single and £83.50 return. *Eurolines* also run coaches to Prague, leaving London at 7pm every Friday and Monday and arriving at the inconvenient hour of 10.30pm the following day; tickets currently cost £65 single and £109 return. Times and frequencies are liable to change, so always check first.

The journey is long but quite bearable – just make sure you take along enough to eat, drink and read, and a small amount of Belgian and German currency for coffee etc. There are stops for around fifteen minutes every three hours or so, and the routine is broken by the Dover–Ostend ferry (included in the cost of the ticket).

BY CAR – THE FERRIES

Driving to the Czech or Slovak republic is not the most relaxing option – even if you're into non-stop rally motoring, it'll take the best part of two days – but with two or more passengers it can

work out relatively inexpensive. The cheapest and quickest Channel crossings are the **ferry** or **hovercraft** links between **Dover** and Calais, and **Ramsgate** and Dunkirk. Ferry **prices** vary according to the time of year, and, for motorists, the size of your car. The Dover–Calais run, for example, starts at about £70 one-way for a car, two adults and two kids, but roughly doubles in high season. Foot passengers should be able to cross for just under £25 single.

The most direct route from Calais/Dunkirk to Prague is via Brussels, Cologne, Frankfurt and Nuremberg, entering the Czech republic at the **Waidhaus–Rozvadov** border crossing: a distance of over 1000km. Another possibility is to head east from Cologne through Hessen via Erfurt and Chemnitz (formerly Karl Marx Stadt), and enter at the **Reitzenhain/Pohraniční** border crossing.

HITCHING

If you're **hitching** to Prague, your best bet is to catch the ferry to Ostend and follow the busier route via Cologne and Nuremberg. Buying a train/ferry ticket as far as Ostend will save you the hassle of hitching out of London and on to the Belgian autoroutes. At all events, you should organise a lift while you're still on the ferry. Hitching in Belgium, Germany and the Czech and Slovak republics will seem like a doddle compared to anywhere in Britain, but again don't bank on getting there in less than two days. For all trips overland you should take a few Belgian francs and some Deutschmarks for the journey.

GETTING THERE FROM NORTH AMERICA

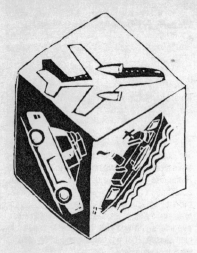

The quickest and easiest way to reach the Czech and Slovak republics from the US or Canada is to fly to Prague. In the summer months, the national airline, ČSA, has four non-stop flights every week out of New York, three a week from Montréal, and dozens of one- and two-stop flights from other North American cities via major European centres.

However, because the former Czechoslovakia is only now becoming well established as a tourist destination, flights there from North America are still comparatively expensive, and you may be better off buying a transatlantic flight to Paris, London, Frankfurt or Vienna and making your way overland. Furthermore, because the tourist infrastructure is not as efficient as that of western Europe, even the most independent-minded traveller may want to consider some form of package tour, in which flights and some or all of your accommodation is arranged for you in advance – though for this you'll pay considerably more than you would on the ground.

Names and addresses of agents specialising in travel to the Czech and Slovak republics, and details for all the various options are given below. Unless specified otherwise, prices quoted are for round-trip tickets and include all applicable taxes.

FLIGHTS FROM THE US

If you're flying out of New York, the **non-stop** service offered by *ČSA*, which costs around $800 in low season and rises to $978 in summer, is probably your best bet. Starting from other US cities, airlines offering **flights to Prague** include *Delta* (via Frankfurt and Vienna), *Lufthansa* (via Frankfurt), *SAS* (via Copenhagen), *TWA* (via Amsterdam) and *American* (via London or Zurich). **Apex fares**, almost all of which allow a maximum stay of 21 days, are pretty much identical, with low season rates starting at around $800 from New York, $1100 from West Coast cities; in summer fares rise to $1000 from the eastern US, $1200 from the west. If you want to stay longer than three weeks, the next level of ticket is good for visits of up to six months but costs around $150 more.

Full-time students and anyone under 26 can take advantage of the excellent deals offered by *Council Travel*, *STA* and other **student/youth travel agencies.** These fares are for flights on major carriers like *British Airways* or *Air France*, and even in the peak summer season cost as little as $700 from the East Coast, $950 from the West Coast. For example, *Council Travel* offers round-trip tickets to Prague on the Belgian-run *Sabena Airways*, flying from New York via Brussels, for $636. A further advantage to these student fares is that they allow you to **stop over en route** for little or no extra charge, something you can't do on an Apex ticket. If you don't meet the student/youth agents' requirements, you can still save some money by buying your tickets through **discount agencies** like *Travel Avenue* (formerly *McTravel*), 180 N Jefferson Street, Chicago IL (☎1-800/333-3335).

If you're flexible about your travel plans, or have waited until the last minute to buy your ticket, the best deals are available through **seat consolidators** like *TFI Tours*, 34 W 32nd St, New York NY (☎212/736-1140 or ☎1-800/825-3834). For the best prices, scan the ads in the back pages of the Sunday travel sections of *The New York Times* or your local paper, and phone around. Because these tickets are basically impossible to change once you've paid for them, be sure about your dates and ask about the rout-

NORTH AMERICAN AGENTS AND OPERATORS

COUNCIL TRAVEL IN THE US

*Head Office:*205 E 42nd St, New York, NY 10017 (☎212/661-1450).

12 Park Place South, Atlanta, GA 30303 (☎404/377-9997).

2486 Channing Way, Berkeley, CA 94704 (☎510/848-8604).

729 Boylston St, Suite 201, Boston, MA 0211 (☎617/266-1926).

1384 Massachusetts Ave, Suite 206, Cambridge, MA 02138 (☎617/497-1497).

1153 N Dearborn St, 2nd floor, Chicago, IL 60610 (☎312/951-0585).

1093 Broxton Ave, Suite 220, Los Angeles, CA 90024 (☎310/208-3551).

35 W 8th St, New York, NY 10011 (☎212/254-2525).

1138 13th St, Boulder, CO 80302 (☎303/447-8101).

312 Sutter St, Suite 407, San Francisco, CA 94108 (☎415/421-3473).

1501 University Ave SE, Room 300, Minneapolis, MN 55414 (☎612/379-2323).

2000 Guadalupe St, Suite 6, Austin, TX 78705 (☎515/472-4931).

1314 Northeast 43rd St, Suite 210, Seattle, WA 98105 (☎206/632-2448).

3300 M St NW, 2nd floor, NW Washington, DC 20007 ☎202/337-6464

STA IN THE US

273 Newbury St, Boston, MA 02116 (☎617/266-6014).

7202 Melrose Ave, Los Angeles, CA 90046 (☎213/937-5781).

82 Shattock Sq, Berkeley, CA 94704 (☎510/841-1037).

48 E 11th St, Suite 805, New York, NY 10003 (☎212/986-9470).

166 Geary St, Suite 702, San Francisco, CA 94108 (☎415/391-8407).

TRAVEL CUTS IN CANADA

Head Office: 187 College St, Toronto, Ontario M5T 1P7 (☎416/979-2406).

12304 Jasper Ave, Edmonton, AL T5N 3K5 (☎403/488-8487).

1516 Duranleau St, Granville Island, Vancouver V6H 3S4 (☎604/687-6033).

Student Union Building, University of British Columbia, Vancouver V6T 1W5 (☎604/228-6890).

60 Laurier Ave E, Ottawa K1N 6N4 (☎613/238-8222).

96 Gerrard St E, Toronto M5B 1G7 (☎416/977-0441).

Université McGill, 3480 rue McTavish, Montréal H3A 1X9 (☎514/398-0647).

1613 rue St Denis, Montréal H2X 3K3 (☎514/843-8511).

NOUVELLES FRONTIÈRES

In the US

12 E 33rd St, New York, NY 10016 (☎212/779-0600).

6363 Wilshire Blvd, Suite 200, Los Angeles, CA 90048 (☎213/658-8955).

209 Post St., Suite 1121, San Francisco, CA 94108 (☎415/781-4480).

In Canada

800 bd de Maison Neuve Est, Montréal, Québec H2L 4L8 (☎514/288-9942).

176 Grande Allée Ouest, Québec, G1R 2G9 (☎418/525-5255).

ing of the flight – many involve lengthy stopovers and multiple changes of plane. They can be excellent value, however, with peak-season fares starting as low as $650 from New York, $850 from Los Angeles or Seattle.

FLIGHTS FROM CANADA

In contrast to the usual story, getting **flights from Canada** to Prague is no problem. *ČSA* fly non-stop three times a week from Montréal for just over CDN$1000, though it can be hard to arrange an inexpensive connection from elsewhere in the country. Outside Montréal, your best bet is *Lufthansa*, who fly direct from major Canadian airports to Prague via Frankfurt. Fares start at CDN$1000 from Toronto, CDN$1250 from Vancouver in low season, rising to CDN$1200/ 1550 in summer. **Students** and those under 26 can sometimes find cheap flights through *Travel Cuts*.

PACKAGE TOURS

Since the situation regarding tourism is still very changeable, along with everything else in the former Eastern Bloc, **travel agencies specialising in Eastern Europe**, such as *Travel Travel*, 10 E 39th St New York NY (☎212/545-0737) and *Sir Bentley*, 17280 Newhope St, Fountain Valley CA (☎714/559-6946 or ☎1-800/675-0559) are excellent sources of up-to-date advice, as well as being the best way to find out about any other cheap flight deals that might be available. They can also arrange for accommodation and travel to other parts of the Czech and Slovak republics, as can **package tour** companies like *Fugazy International*, 770 US-1, North Brunswick NJ (☎1-800/828-4488) and *ČEDOK*, 10 E 40th St, New York NY (☎212/689-9720 or ☎1-800/8891), the old Czechoslovak state tourist monopoly, which still offers the broadest range of all-inclusive (and generally quite expensive) tours.

VIA EUROPE

Since direct flights to Prague are quite a bit more expensive than flights to other European cities (at the time of going to press there were no non-stop flights to Bratislava), it may be worth your while to fly to another country and make your way overland from there. Munich, Berlin and Frankfurt are the closest major European cities to Prague: you can get there by train from either in well under twelve hours. Vienna and Budapest are the best placed for Bratislava: both are under six hours' train ride away. Paris (21hr by train) and London (25hr by ferry and train) are equally cheap but more distant gateways.

"**Open-jaw**" **fares**, which enable you to fly into one city and out of another, usually split the difference between standard Apex round-trip fares. For example, you can fly from San Francisco into Berlin, then fly out of Prague two weeks later, for around $1200 in peak season. A similar flight from New York could cost well under $1000. See "Getting There From Britain", p.3, for a more complete rundown of trans-European options.

AIRLINES SERVING PRAGUE

Air France ☎1-800/237-2747
American ☎1-800/433-7300
British Airways ☎1-800/247-9297
ČSA ☎212/682-5833
Delta ☎1-800/241-4141
KLM ☎1-800/777-5553

Lufthansa ☎1-800/645-3880
SAS ☎1-800/221-2350
Sabena ☎1-800/955-2000
TWA ☎1-800/892-4141
United ☎1-800/538-2929

RED TAPE AND VISAS

British, Irish, US and most EC nationals need only a full passport to enter the Czech and Slovak republics for up to three months. New Zealand, Australian and Canadian citizens still need a visa (valid for thirty days), available from a Czech/Slovak embassy or consulate – usually on the day – or at the border crossings with Germany and Austria. There is no longer a minimum exchange requirement. If you need a visa extension, the local police office will issue one without too much fuss for around 100kčs.

If you need to stay longer than three months, you'll have to fill in the application form known (in Czech) as *a povolení k pobytu*, attach six photos and pay a fee of 100kčs. It's best to try this at the head passport office at Olšanská 2, Žižkov, Prague. Many people avoid this bureaucratic nightmare by simply leaving the country for a few days when their time runs out and getting a new date upon re-entry, but the legality of this is somewhat doubtful. If you cross over into a neighbouring country for this purpose, make sure that your passport gets stamped (which isn't done routinely) and re-enter at least a couple of days later by a different border post.

CUSTOMS AND ALLOWANCES

Since the events of 1989, **border controls** have relaxed considerably. Export controls, however, are still quite restrictive, if infrequently enforced. Officially you're only allowed to export 500kčs worth of taxable goods (£10/$18 at the current exchange rate) duty-free, after which you're supposed to pay twenty percent tax. In practice, you'll rarely encounter problems unless you're found exporting large amounts of high-quality Bohemian crystal and glassware. If you pay for the goods in hard currency, and keep the receipt, you'll avoid any possible hassle.

Duty-free allowances from the Czech and Slovak republics into EC countries are different from the normal EC allowances: you can export 250 cigarettes, two litres of wine and one litre of spirits. These allowances may change in the future, so check with customs before you leave.

CZECH/SLOVAK EMBASSIES AND CONSULATES

UK and Eire 28 Kensington Palace Gardens, London W8 4QX (Mon–Fri 10am–1pm; ☎071-727 3966).

Australia 169 Military Rd, Dover Heights, Sydney, NSW 2030 (☎02-371 8878).

Austria Penzinger Strasse 11–13, 1140 Vienna (☎1-894 3741).

Belgium 152 Avenue A. Buyl, 1050 Brussels (☎02-647 5898).

Canada 50 Rideau Terrace, Ottawa, Ontario K1M 2A1 (☎514-849 4495).

France 15 Avenue Charles Floquet, 75 007 Paris (☎47 34 29 10).

New Zealand 12 Anne St, Wadesdown, PO Box 2843, Wellington (☎04-723 142).

USA 3900 Linnean Ave N.W., Washington DC 20008 (☎202-363 6315).

HEALTH AND INSURANCE

On production of a passport all foreign nationals can get free emergency medical care, with a nominal charge for certain drugs or medicines. No inoculations are required for the Czech and Slovak republics; health standards are coming under increasing criticism, however.

HEALTH PROBLEMS

With much of the country blighted by decades of ecological abuse, there have been well-founded criticisms about the quality of the water, milk, meat and vegetables in the Czech and Slovak republics. More specifically, if you have respiratory problems, you should avoid going to parts of North Bohemia, North Moravia or Prague during the winter months when sulphur dioxide levels regularly reach three or four times World Health Organisation safety levels.

PHARMACIES, DOCTORS AND HOSPITALS

If you should become ill, it's easiest to go to a *lekárna*. Pharmacists are willing to give advice (though language may well be a problem), and able to dispense many drugs available only on prescription in other western countries. They usually keep normal shopping hours (ie 8am–1pm & 2–5pm), but several are open 24 hours: the most central in Prague is at Na příkopě 7.

INSURANCE

If it's not an emergency but you can't hold out until you return home, you're going to have to pay for any medical care you receive, and, depending on the treatment necessary, you might find yourself running up a considerable bill.

Some form of **travel insurance** is therefore pretty essential, enabling you to claim back the cost of any treatment and drugs, and covering your luggage/tickets in case of theft. **In Britain**, travel insurance schemes (from around £20 a month) are sold by all travel agents: *ISIS* policies, from any of the youth/student travel companies listed in "Getting There", or branches of *Endsleigh Insurance* (in London at 97 Southampton Row, WC1; ☎071/436 4451) are among the cheapest.

US AND CANADIAN CITIZENS

In the **US and Canada**, insurance tends to be much more expensive, and may be medical cover only. Before buying a policy, check that you're not already covered by existing insurance plans. **Canadians** are usually covered by their provincial health plans; holders of **ISIC cards** and some other student/teacher/youth cards are entitled to $3000 worth of accident coverage and sixty days ($100 per day) of hospital in-patient benefits for the period during which the card is valid. **Students** will often find that their student health coverage extends through the vacations and for one term beyond the date of last enrollment. Bank and charge **accounts** (particularly *American Express*) often have certain levels of medical or other insurance included, and travel insurance may also be included if you use a major credit or charge card to pay for your trip. **Homeowners' or renters'** insurance often covers theft or loss of documents, money and valuables while overseas, though conditions and maximum amounts vary from company to company.

Only after exhausting the possibilities above might you want to contact a specialist travel insurance company; your travel agent can usually recommend one. Travel insurance policies are quite comprehensive, anticipating everything from charter companies going bankrupt to delayed or lost luggage, by way of sundry illnesses and accidents. **Premiums** vary widely, from the very reasonable ones offered primarily through student/youth agencies (*STA*'s policies range from about $50–70 for 15 days to $500–700 for a year, depending on the amount of financial cover), to those so expensive that the cost for anything more than two months of cover will probably equal the cost of the worst possible combination of disasters. Note also that very few insurers can make on-the-spot payments in the event of a major expense or loss; you will usually be reimbursed only after going home.

None of these policies insures against **theft** of anything while overseas. (Americans have been easy pickings for foreign thieves – a combination of naivety on the part of the former, and an all-Americans-are-rich attitude among the latter – and companies were going broke paying claims.) North American travel policies apply only to items **lost** from, or **damaged** in, the custody of an identifiable, responsible third party – hotel porter, airline, luggage consignment, etc. Even in these cases you will have to contact the local police to have a complete report made out for your insurer. If you are travelling via London it might be better to take out a British policy (though making any claim may prove more complicated).

COSTS, MONEY AND BANKS

Right now, the Czech and Slovak republics are still incredibly cheap for westerners. The only exception is accommodation, which is comparable with the rest of Europe. That said, price differentiation across the country is now quite marked: prices in the centre of Prague are creeping ever upwards, while the far east of Slovakia is still as inexpensive as ever.

Sudden price rises are still quite common, but roughly speaking, if you're camping and stick to pubs for your eating, you could get by on as little as £5–10/$9–18 a day. If you intend to stay in private accommodation or hotels, and eat fancier meals, then you'll need more like £15–20/$26–35 a day. In fact, you'd be hard pushed to spend over £20/$35 a day even if you set your mind to it, unless, that is, you spend your time exclusively in the big cities.

Accommodation will be your largest daily expense, with hostels and private accommoda-tion both charging at least £10/$18 a night. All other basic costs like **food**, **drink** and **transport** remain very cheap, a good meal washed down with a couple of beers in a local *pivnice* or restau-rant still costing as little as £2–3/$3–5 a head – and even in the top-class establishments prices rarely go much over £10–15/$18–26 a head.

MONEY AND THE EXCHANGE RATE

The **currency** in the former Czechoslovakia is the crown or *koruna* (indicated in this book as kčs), which is divided into 100 heller or *haléř* (indi-cated as h). Coins come in the denominations 5h, 10h, 20h, 50h, 1kčs, 2kčs, 5kčs and 10kčs; notes as 10kčs, 20kčs, 50kčs, 100kčs, 500kčs and 1000kčs. A whole new series of notes replacing the old workerist ones is being gradually intro-duced, so any 1000kčs notes issued before 1985 are now invalid. Production has also stopped on the new bile-green 100kčs note, introduced as recently as the summer of 1989 and sporting a picture of Klement Gottwald, Czechoslovakia's first Communist President. At the time of writing, there was no separate Slovak currency, though this would seem a likely development.

In January 1991, the crown was drastically devalued by around 100 percent. Since then, it has remained pretty steady against the major western currencies, though it still can't be bought or sold entirely freely on the foreign exchange markets. The **exchange rate** is currently around 50kčs to the pound sterling, 30kčs to the US dollar. It is still technically illegal to import or export crowns, though if you keep your exchange receipts, you can convert any surplus crowns back into western currency.

TRAVELLERS' CHEQUES & CREDIT CARDS

Probably the safest and easiest way to carry your funds is in **travellers' cheques**; sterling, US dollars or Deutschmarks are all equally acceptable. If you hold an account with a British bank you can apply for Eurocheques and a Eurocheque card. With this you can write cheques in crowns in some shops and hotels, as well as withdrawing cash from most banks or exchange outlets. You pay a small commission plus a flat fee every time you write a cheque, and perhaps a set charge for the cheque card.

Credit cards like *Visa*, *Master Card* (*Access*) and *Amex* are accepted in most hotels, upmarket restaurants and some of the flashier shops. Only a few banks in Prague will advance cash on your plastic, while five-star hotels will only do this for residents; all transactions are subject to withdrawing a minimum of the equivalent of £50/$80. It's a good idea to keep at least some hard currency in **cash** for emergencies, as it will be accepted almost anywhere (this is not the case for Scottish bank notes). If you lose your credit card, ring the Prague credit card hotline – ☎236 66 88.

CHANGING MONEY

Most Czech and Slovak **banks** should be prepared to change travellers' cheques (occasionally with reluctance for certain less well-known brands), accept Eurocheques, and give cash advances on credit cards – look for the window marked *směnárna/zmenáreň*. Commissions at banks are fairly reasonable, but the queues and the bureaucracy can mean a long wait. Quicker, but more of a rip-off in terms of commission, are the exchange outlets which crop up here and there in the bigger towns. **Banking hours** are Monday to Friday 7.30am–noon and 1.30–3.30pm.

With the banks offering virtually the same rates as the streets, the attraction of the **black market** is pretty slim for westerners. Before the currency reform, it was a universal and fairly harmless pursuit, occasionally interrupted by a plain-clothes policeman, but nowadays it really doesn't seem worth the risk – you'll have to change a large amount to make any great profit out of the deal, and the likelihood of receiving dodgy Polish zloty notes is high.

INFORMATION AND MAPS

The old state tourist board, ČEDOK, produces and gives away various maps, pamphlets and special interest leaflets. Visit one of their offices before you leave home and stock up, especially on the lists of campsites, hotels etc, as well as details of the latest regulations and changes likely to affect the traveller.

INFORMATION OFFICES

Prague and Bratislava both have tourist offices (*PIS* in Prague and *BIS* in Bratislava) specifically set up to give information to foreign visitors. Otherwise *ČEDOK*, the old state-controlled travel agency, has branches in most towns, generally open Monday to Friday 9am to noon and 1 to 5pm, plus Saturday mornings in larger places. Originally conceived as a travel agency for Czechs and Slovaks to book their organised tours round the Eastern Bloc, *ČEDOK* offices usually have a modicum of maps, brochures or information about the town you're actually in, but their staff are notoriously underpaid, unmotivated and unhelpful. In larger cities there should be at least one person who speaks faltering English, and in the smaller towns someone may speak German. Really, the only reason for going to *ČEDOK* is to book a hotel room – though they often cover only the more expensive ones, and only occasionally deal with private rooms. A nominal fee is charged for this service. The addresses of local offices are given throughout the guide.

ČEDOK OFFICES ABROAD

UK and Eire 17–18 Old Bond St, London W1 (☎071/629 6058).

USA and Canada 10 E 40th St, New York NY 10157 (☎212/689-9720).

Netherlands Leidsestraat 4, Amsterdam (☎20-220 101).

Germany Kaiserstrasse 54 6000 Frankfurt-am-Main (☎69-232 975).

Denmark Vester Farimagsgade 6, 1606 Copenhagen V (☎01-120121).

Sweden Sveavägen 9–11, 11157 Stockholm (☎8-207290).

The lack of basic tourist information in almost every town is one of the most glaring (and previously deliberate) omissions of the previous regime as regards tourism. Foreigners were effectively discouraged from embarking on individual travel in the country and rounded up into organised tours. Hopefully, this will change in the near future as locally organised tourist offices start to emerge, and the republics wake up to the income to be derived from tourism . . . and tourists.

MAPS

The regional and city maps in this guide should be fine for most purposes, but if you crave a bit more detail, all kinds of maps are available **in the Czech and Slovak republics** themselves (though subject to the usual shortages). You can buy them, often very cheaply, from bookshops (*knihkupectví*) and some hotels — just ask for a *plán města* (town plan) or *mapa okolí* (regional map) followed by the name of the town or region. Gazeteered **town maps** with local bus, tram and trolleybus routes marked on, are available for most towns and cities.

ADDRESSES AND TOWN NAMES

The street name is always written before the number in **addresses**. The word for street (*ulice/ulica*) is either abbreviated to *ul.* or simply missed out altogether – Celetná ulice, for instance, is commonly known as Celetná. Other terms often abbreviated are *náměstí/námestie* (square), *třída/trieda* (avenue), and *nábřeží/nábrežie* (embankment), which become *nám.*, *tř./tr* and *nábř/nábr* respectively.

Bear in mind when using a Czech or Slovak **index** that "Ch" is considered a separate letter, and comes after "H" in the alphabet. Similarly, "Č","Ď","Ľ","Ř","Š" and "Ž" are all listed separately, immediately after their non-accented cousins.

Many towns and villages in the Czech and Slovak republics were once (or still are) inhabited by **German** (or **Hungarian**) minorities. In these places we have given the German (or Hungarian) names in brackets after the Czech or Slovak, for example Mariánské Lázně (Marienbad).

Of the **road maps** of the country, the new 1:200,000 *Autoatlas Československa* is the best, written in four languages including English, and marking all campsites and petrol stations. You can get portions of the same map in the *Poznávame československo* series of seventeen 1:200,000 maps covering the country, which mark all castles, museums and other sights (though not campsites) as well as giving a brief, dry English account of the major towns and villages. The same 1:200,000 maps under the title *automapa* list hotels, camp-

---

MAP SUPPLIERS

USA

The Complete Traveler 199 Madison Ave, New York, NY 10016 (☎212/685-9007).

Rand McNally Mapstore 150 E 52nd St, New York, NY 10022 (☎212/758-7488).

French and European Publications 115 Fifth Ave, New York, NY 10003 (☎212/673-7400).

Map Link 529 State St, Santa Barbara, CA 93101 (☎805/963-4438).

BRITAIN

Stanford's 12–14 Long Acre, London WC2E 9LP (☎071/836 1321). *Excellent specialist map and general travel shop.*

The Map Shop 15 High St, Upton-on-Severn, Worcs WR8 0HJ (☎06846/31 46). *Mail order service.*

sites (including diagrams helping you find them) and so forth, instead of the sight-seeing information, and are well worth considering if you're intending to camp in out-of-the-way places.

For **hiking**, the 1:100,000 *Soubor turistických map* series marks the complex network of coloured footpaths that weave their way across the country. Certain very popular regions are treated to 1:50,000 maps, but whichever one you get, make sure you make the right choice between the *letná mapa* (summer map) and the *zimní mapa* (winter map), which concentrates on pistes, ski-lifts and other such matters. Czech maps have their keys in four languages including English, but the Slovak ones present a few problems, the key being in five languages: Slovak, Hungarian, Polish, Russian and German – but not English.

GETTING AROUND

The most relaxing way of travelling around the Czech and Slovak republics is by train. The system, which has changed little since it was bequeathed to the country by the Habsburgs in 1918, is often breathtakingly beautiful, but also extremely slow. If you're in a hurry, the buses are nearly always faster. Bus and train timetables can be found in the "Travel Details" section at the end of each chapter.

TRAINS

Trains go just about everywhere, and the antiquated rolling stock is a pleasure to travel in. The restaurant cars, on inter-city services, are still relatively cheap, and run with a shabby semblance of Austrian formality. Many of the stations recall the nineteenth-century civic pride that accompanied the building of the original tracks. In Slovakia, where the system is less developed, a lot of the journeys are worth making for the scenery alone: try the Banská Bystrica–Diviaky line or the Brezno–Margecany trip in the Low Tatras. As state subsidies are phased out costs are bound to increase; a second-class single from Prague to Kosice (the longest journey you're likely to make) currently costs around the equivalent of £5/$8.

The state railways, *Československé státní dráhy* (*ČSD*), run two main **types of train**: *rychlík/rýchlik* trains are the faster ones which stop only at major towns. They cost very little, but still almost twice as much as an *osobný vlak* or local train, which stops at every single station on the line and averages about 30km an hour. Other fast trains go by the name of *expres* or *spěšný*. It's better to avoid the international expresses which, although theoretically fast, often get delayed at border crossings.

TICKETS AND RESERVATIONS

A **ticket** (*jízdenka/lístok*) can be bought at the station (*nádraží/stanica*) before or on the day of departure. Write down all the relevant information on a piece of paper and hand it to the clerk to avoid any linguistic misunderstandings – rectifying any mistakes involves a lengthy bureaucratic process and costs you ten percent of the ticket price.

If you simply say the destination, it will be assumed that you want a second-class single (*jednoduchá*) on an *osobný vlak*. If you want a return ticket (*zpáteční*), or you're travelling on a faster train (*rychlík*), you must say so. First-class carriages (*první třída/prvá trieda*) exist on all fast trains; tickets are fifty percent more expensive but should guarantee you a seat on a busy train if you've forgotten to buy a *místenka* or reservation (see below). If you should end up in the wrong carriage, you'll be fined upwards of 100kčs on the spot.

All the Czech and Slovak terms in this section appear in italics. Where only one term is given, it is the same in either language; otherwise the Czech term is followed by the Slovak.

There are half-price **discount fares** for children under twelve, and you can take two children under five for free (providing they don't take up more than one seat). There are even some "crèche carriages" on the slower trains, for the exclusive use of mothers (sic) with children under five.

All international through-trains, and any other services marked with an "R" surrounded by a box, require a **seat reservation** (*místenka/ miestenka*). For those marked with an "R" not in a box, reservations are recommended but not obligatory: it's advisable to get one if you're travelling at the weekend on one of the main routes. The *místenka* costs very little, but you must get it at least an hour before your train leaves, and after you've purchased your ticket.

INFORMATION AND TIMETABLES

With very few English-speakers employed on the railways, it can be extremely difficult getting **train information** without some knowledge of Czech or Slovak. The larger stations have a simple airport-style flip-over arrivals and departures board, which includes information on delays under the heading *zpoždění/zdržanie*. Other stations have poster-style displays of arrivals and departures, the former on white paper, the latter on yellow, with fast trains printed in red. Lastly, the smallest stations have a couple of simple boards under the heading *směr/smer*, followed by the destination, and a list of departure times.

In addition to the above, all but the smallest stations have a comprehensive display of **timings and route information** on rollers. These timetables may seem daunting at first, but with a little practice they should become increasingly decipherable. First find the route you need to take on the diagrammatic map and make a note of the number printed beside it; then follow the timetable rollers through until you come to the appropriate number. The only problem now is language since everything will be written in Czech or Slovak. Arrivals are *příjezd/príchod* (*příj./prích.* in short form) and departures are *odjezd/odchod* (*odj./odch.* in short form). A platform or *nástupiště/nástupište* is usually divided into two *kolej/kolaj* on either side. Some of the more common notes at the side of the timetable are *jezdí jen v/chodí len v* (only running on), or *nejezdí v/nechodí v* (not runnning on), followed by a date or a symbol: a cross or an "N" for a

The train system is currently in deep financial crisis, and, at the time of going to print, there was much talk in the press of drastically increased ticket prices and reduced services, including the axing of anything up to one hundred and fifty lines as of May 1993. Check the timetables displayed in all stations for the current state of play.

Sunday; a big "S" for a Saturday; two crossed hammers for a workday; "A" for a Friday and so on. Small stations may simply have a board with a list of departures under the title *směr* (direction) followed by a town.

If you're going to be travelling on the trains a lot, it might be an idea to invest in a *ČSD* **timetable** (*jízdní řád/cestovný poriadok*), which comes out every May (and often sells out soon afterwards). There's one for each region and a very heavy bumper national edition, available from bookshops and tobacconists.

BUSES

Since the reduction of state subsidies on the railways, **buses** (*autobus*) have become an even more attractive alternative to the trains. Most routes are still run by the state bus company, *Československá státní automobilová doprava* (*ČSAD*). Private companies do exist, most notably *ČEBUS*, though for the moment, their services are confined to the more popular, long-distance routes such as Prague–Brno–Bratislava. *ČSAD* buses go almost everywhere, and from town to town they're often faster than the train. Bear in mind, though, that in rural areas timetables are often designed with the working and/or school day in mind. That means up and out at 6am and back at around 3pm during the week, and completely different services at weekends.

In many towns and villages, the **bus station** is adjacent to the train station, though you may be able to pick up the bus from the centre of town, too. The bigger terminals, like Prague's Florenc, are run with train-like efficiency. Often you can book your ticket in advance, and it's essential to do so if you're travelling at the weekend or early in the morning on one of the main routes. For most minor routes, simply buy your ticket from the driver. If you have any large items of **luggage**, you'll have to put them in the boot and pay the driver a couple of crowns for the privilege.

Bus **timetables** are even more difficult to figure out than train ones, as there are no route maps at any of the stations. Each route is listed separately, so you may have to scour several timetables before you discover when the next bus is. Make sure you check on which day the service runs, since many run only on Mondays, Fridays or at the weekend (see the "Trains" section for key phrases).

Minor bus stops are marked with a rusty metal sign saying *zastávka*. If you want to get off, say *já chci vystoupit/ja chcem vystúpit*, "the next stop" is *příští zastávka/ďalšia zastávka*. It's probably not worth buying any of the hefty *ČSAD jízdní řád/cestovný poriadok* (regional bus timetables), though you might feel the need to buy volume 11, which details the *medzinárodné a diaľkové linky* (international and long-distance services).

URBAN TRANSPORT

Urban public transport is generally excellent, with buses (*autobus*), trolleybuses (*trolejbus*) and sometimes also trams (*tramvaj/električka*) running from dawn until around midnight in most major towns (and all night in the three big cities of Prague, Brno and Bratislava). Ticket prices vary from place to place (currently 2–4kčs for an adult; reduced rates for those aged 10–16; under-10s travel free) but are universally cheap. In Prague, Brno and Bratislava, various **passes** are available (see the "Getting Around" sections of the relevant city accounts).

With a few exceptions, such as Mariánské Lázně and Olomouc, you must buy your **ticket** (*lístek/lístok*) before getting on board. Tickets, which are standard for all types of transport, are available from newsagents, tobacconists and the yellow machines at major stops, and are validated in the punching machines once you're on board. There are no conductors, only plain clothes **inspectors** who will fine anyone caught without a ticket 100kčs or more.

TAXIS

Taxis, which come in all shapes and sizes, are cheap and plentiful. Supply far exceeds demand at the moment, so competition is often fierce. Horror stories abound in Prague: tourists are seen as easy prey by some taxi drivers; if the meter isn't switched on, ask the driver to do so – *zapněte taxametr, prosím*; and if you suspect you've been overcharged, asking for a receipt –

prosím, dejte mi potrzení. – should have the desired effect. Watch out for cabs which display signs like *TAXL* or *FAXI* – as long as it isn't *TAXI*, they can legally set their own rates.

DRIVING AND HITCHING

With just one in five Czechs and Slovaks owning a vehicle and most of those used only at the weekend, traffic outside the big cities is extremely sparse. Road conditions are generally not bad, though there's only one complete motorway to speak of. The only place where you might encounter difficulties is in the bigger cities and towns, where the lane system is confusing, tramlines hazardous and parking a nightmare.

Most foreign driver's licences are honoured in the Czech and Slovak republics – including all EC, US and Canadian ones – but an **International Driver's Licence** (available from the *AA* or *RAC*) is an easy way to set your mind at rest. If you're bringing your own car, you are legally required to carry the vehicle's registration document; if it's not in your name, you must have a letter of permission signed by the owner and authorised by the *AA*, *RAC* or official body (this does not apply if you're renting a car). Check with your insurance company before leaving home whether you need a **green card**, as without one you may only get third party cover. You're also required to carry a red warning triangle, a first-aid kit and a set of replacement bulbs, and to display a national identification sticker.

RULES OF THE ROAD

Rules and regulations are pretty stringent – a legacy of the old police state – though less strictly adhered to by the locals nowadays. On-the-spot fines are still regularly handed out, ranging from a pathetic 20kčs to over 200kčs. The basic rules are driving on the right; compulsory wearing of seatbelts outside built-up areas; and children under twelve must travel in the back. It's against the law to have any alcohol in your blood when you're driving. Also, don't overtake a tram when passengers are getting on and off if there's no safety island for them, and give way to pedestrians crossing the road at traffic lights, if you're turning right or left. As in other continental countries, a yellow diamond sign means you have right of way; a black line through it means you don't.

Speed limits are 110kph on motorways (and if you travel any faster you *will* be fined), 90kph on other roads and 60kph between 5am and

11pm in all cities, towns and villages; after that you can, theoretically, tear through town at 90kph. In addition, there's a special speed limit of 30kph for **level crossings** (you'll soon realise why if you try ignoring it). A large number of level crossings have no barriers, simply a sign saying *pozor* and a series of lights: a single flashing light means that the line is live; two red flashing lights mean there's a train coming.

FUEL AND GARAGES

Petrol (*benzín*) comes in two types: *super* (96 octane) and *special* (90 octane); diesel (*nafta*) is also available but two-stroke fuel (*mix*), which powers the old east German Trabants and Wartburgs, is being phased out. Remember that petrol stations aren't as frequent as in western Europe and many are closed at lunchtimes and after 6pm (though 24-hour ones can be found in Prague). **Lead-free** petrol (*natural*) is available from most major petrol stations, but these start to thin out drastically the further east you go (*ČEDOK* may have up-to-date information). The price of petrol is cheaper than in much of western Europe, currently around 18kčs a litre (£0.36/$0.60).

If you have **car trouble**, dial ☎154 at the nearest phone and wait for assistance. For peace of mind it might be worth taking out an insurance policy like the *AA* Five-Star scheme, which will pay for any on-the-spot repairs and, in the case of emergencies, ship you and all your passengers back home free of charge.

Since every other car in the former Czechoslovakia is a Škoda, and most of the rest are Ladas and Trabants, obtaining **spare parts** for any other vehicles can be a tricky business. Small Fiats, Renault 12s and German models are probably slightly better catered for than most, but there are still only a few western-marque garages in Prague and virtually none in the countryside (see the box below for details). If it's simply a case of a flat tyre, however, you can go to the nearest *pneuservis*.

CAR RENTAL

To rent a car, you'll need to be 21 years of age and have been driving for at least a year, and, if you book from abroad, you're looking at over $25 per day for a small car (cheaper by the week, and with special rates at the weekend). The big companies all have offices in Prague, Brno and Bratislava, but you'll get a far better deal if you go to a local agent when you get here.

INTERNATIONAL CAR RENTAL RESERVATIONS

UK:
Avis ☎081/848 8733
Budget ☎0800/181 181
Europcar ☎081/950 5050
Hertz ☎081/679 1799

US:
Avis ☎1-800/331-1212
Budget ☎1-800/527-0700
Hertz ☎1-800/654-3131

HITCHING

Hitching is widely practised throughout both republics. Despite the low cost of public transport, it's still too much for many people and there's usually a long line of hitchers on the roads out of major cities. The main problem is the scarcity of vehicles, so to hit what rush hour there is, you'll have to set out early – and that means 6–8am. Although many Czech and Slovak women hitch, usually in pairs, women travelling alone should exercise the usual caution about which lifts to accept. The main roads in the border regions with Germany and Austria are particularly dodgy for women hitchers, since these are areas favoured by Czech and Slovak prostitutes. "Where are you heading?" is *kam jedete?* and if you want to get out of the car, just say *já chci vystoupit/ja chem vystúpiť.*

MOTORBIKES, CYCLING AND HIKING

The Czech and Slovak republics would be great for **motorcycling**, if it weren't for the prohibitive **speed limits** for bikes – devised with domestic machines in mind, the biggest of which are the Jawa 350s that the police still ride. In towns and villages the limit is 60kph but out on the open roads, and even on motorways, the limit is 80kph. Unless you ride a Jawa, or an MZ, be prepared for crowds of curious onlookers to surround your bike in every town and village. Helmets are compulsory, as is some form of eye protection (goggles or visor) for the driver; you should use dipped headlights at all times. At the time of writing, it was still not possible to rent motorbikes or mopeds in either republic.

Cycling is catching on fast in the Czech and Slovak republics, and the rolling countryside, though hard work on the legs, is rewarding viewing. Facilities for **bike rental** are improving, and the increasing number of new bike shops makes repairs possible, and spare parts easier to get hold of. Taking a bike on the train is not usual behaviour in Czechoslovakia, but it's easy enough to persuade the guard on a local train to let you on, perhaps for a small fee.

Walking is a very popular pastime. Young, old or indolent, they all spend their weekends following the dense network of paths that covers not just the hills and mountains but the whole countryside – some even within the city boundaries of Prague. All the trails are colour-coded with clear markers every 200m or so, and signs indicating how long it'll take you to reach your destination. The walks around Prague are usually fairly easy-going, but it can be wet and muddy underfoot even in summer, and, particularly if you venture into the mountains proper, you'll need some fairly sturdy boots. There are no hiking guides in English, but it's a good idea to get hold of a *soubor turistických map*, which details all the marked paths in the area (see "Information and Maps"). The most enthusaistic hikers – curiously enough known as "tramps" – dress up in quasi-army gear, camp in the wilds, play guitar and sing songs round the campfire.

PLANES AND BOATS

Domestic flights run by *ČSA* and the Slovak airline, *Slov-Air*, link all major cities in both republics. Though not exactly cheap, particularly when compared with the train or bus, they can prove useful if time is short and you want to get to the east of the country quickly. Prague to Košice (via Bratislava), for example, works out at about £40 single fare (you must pay in hard currency), nearly three times the price of the train, but reduces the journey time from twelve hours to two. If you do decide to fly, make sure you book well in advance – demand is high, and flights to places like Poprad in the High Tatras are booked solid in the high season. Further details can be obtained from *ČSA* offices in most large towns.

The opportunity for travelling by **boat** is pretty limited, but there are a few services worth mentioning. From Prague, boats run by *ČSAD* (the state bus company) sail all the way down to Orlík, with a change of vessel at each of the dams on the way. There's also a summer service on Lake Lipno in South Bohemia. German boats chug down the Labe (Elbe) between Děčín and Dresden, although information and tickets can be difficult to obtain from the Czech end. Finally, there's a service from Bratislava to Vienna or Budapest between May and September. **Tickets** cost roughly £20 return and must be paid for in hard currency. The trip to Vienna tends to be heavily booked up in advance by tour groups, and if you're heading for Budapest you'll need to get a Hungarian visa before you set off. It might be easier to settle for the domestic service between Bratislava and Komárno, which operates daily from April to September and costs very little.

ACCOMMODATION

For the moment at least, finding a place to spend the night can be the most difficult part of travelling in the former Czechoslovakia. Visitors from abroad have traditionally been shepherded into the state hotels, where prices for foreigners (*cizinci/cudzinci*) are nearly three times those charged to Czechs and Slovaks. Unfortunately this attitude still prevails, and there are very few ways to escape it; the country has only a limited number of youth hostels and the private room network is still patchy. However, many of the problems outlined below are slowly being eliminated.

ACCOMMODATION PRICES

Hotels listed in the guide are given a symbol which corresponds to one of **seven price categories**:

① Under 500kčs   ② 500–750kčs   ③ 750–1000kčs   ④ 1000–1500kčs

⑤ 1500–2000kčs   ⑥ 2000–3000kčs   ⑦ 3000kčs and upwards

If you're going to one of the big cities at a time when demand for beds will be great (from late spring to late summer, and over the Christmas holidays), it might put your mind at rest if you arrange accommodation before you arrive. Most people book their accommodation through ČEDOK offices abroad, who'll arrange as many nights as you like in as many different towns as you like. The snag is that they only book the more expensive hotels (£40 a night and upwards in Prague). Thankfully, cheaper accommodation specialists are beginning to emerge (see box on p.4 for a list of current operators). Another alternative, if you speak at least some German, is to use the listings in the guide to ring or fax a hotel and book yourself.

HOTELS

The republics' **hotels** are in a state of flux at the moment. The new hotels that are being built are almost exclusively in the luxury category, often joint-ventures with western firms. The cheaper hotels have been sold off in the recent state auctions, and the vast majority are currently undergoing modernisation; a handful have been returned to their former owners under the "restitution" law.

Previously classified from A to C, according to the facilities they provided and the price they charged, most hotels have now switched to using the star system. Whichever scale is used, it should be taken with a large pinch of salt, since conditions and prices can vary greatly within each category. For the moment at least, hotels are still charging foreigners two to three times what Czechs and Slovaks pay in an effort to reflect the real disparity in incomes.

For the most part, hotels tend to be drab, concrete affairs. There are, of course, exceptions, but the interiors of even the older buildings have often been routinely modernised. Most hotel rooms are sparsely furnished, with just a washbasin and the obligatory Tesla radio permanently tuned to the state radio station. Hot water and heating can be erratic – it's either boiling

and you can't turn the thing off, or else it's unremittingly cold. In the top hotels, of course, you can be fairly certain of pristine service and consistently overheated rooms.

Breakfast isn't normally included unless you're paying a lot for your room. If it is, you'll be given a voucher covering a specific amount of money, which you hand in to the waiter as payment. Almost without fail, hotels also have a restaurant and/or a bar.

PRIVATE ROOMS

Since 1989, there has been a huge increase in the number of **private rooms** available, and most of them are kept to a high standard in terms of cleanliness. Before agreeing to part with any money, however, ask whether you'll be sharing bathroom, cooking facilities etc with the family or not – Czech and Slovak hospitality can be somewhat overwhelming, although meals other than breakfast are not generally included in the price. For **people travelling alone**, private rooms are definitely the best bet, since prices are invariably charged per person. Single rooms can be hard to find in hotels, and are generally only slightly less than the price of a double.

YOUTH HOSTELS AND STUDENT ACCOMMODATION

There are a number of **youth hostels** in both republics, which are useful if you're travelling alone, or looking for a very cheap bed. Although some will rent out blankets and sheets, it's as well to bring your own sleeping bag. A handful of official hostels-cum-hotels are run by Cestovní kancelář mládeže (CKM), which is affiliated to the International Youth Hostel Federation (IYHF). It's not necessary to have a card to stay at these, but at around 1000kčs a double they're no great bargain – and the reductions for members are significant (if you can get a place). In addition to the CKM hostels, other unofficial hostels are beginning to appear. Standards and prices vary, but you can pay as little as 50kčs per night.

A more reliable alternative to the youth hostels in the big university towns is **student accommodation**, which is let out cheap to travellers in July and August. The beds, usually in dormitories, cost about 50kčs per person for students, double that for non-students. Again, they're heavily booked up in advance by groups, but they'll try their best to squeeze you in. Curfews operate in many hostels and they tend to be pretty early (around 10–11pm). Addresses change each year, so to find out the current address, go straight to *CKM*, which has offices in most major towns (listed in main text of the guide), or drop in at the head office in Prague (Žitná 12, Nové Město, Praha 2; ☎02/29 45 87).

Rock-bottom accommodation comes in the form of *turistická ubytovna*, ridiculously cheap and basic **dormitory hostels** with few facilities beyond a bunk bed, toilet and cold shower. Normally, there are one or two in every town and village, but they're often owned by one of the old state corporations to house immigrant workers or for workers' vacations; nevertheless it's worth enquiring about them at the local *ČEDOK*.

CAMPING AND OTHER OPTIONS

Campsites, known as *autokempink*, are plentiful all over the Czech and Slovak republics. Although some are huge, ostentatious affairs with shops, swimming pools, draught beer and so on, most are just a simple stretch of grass with loos and cold showers. Many sites feature **bungalows** (*chata*), sometimes reserved for certain organisations, but often for rent for anything upwards of £5/$8 for two people. The flashiest bungalows are really small chalets, while the most primitive are little more than rabbit hutches.

The more basic campsites, called *tábořiště / táborisko*, are only marked on the 1:100,000 hiking maps. They open in the height of summer only, providing just *ad hoc* toilets and a little running water. Very few sites are open all year round, and most don't open until May at the earliest, closing mid- to late September. Even though prices are inflated for foreigners, costs are still reasonable; two people plus car and tent weigh in at around £1–2/$1.50–3.50. The nicest thing about camping in the Czech and Slovak republics is that campfires are allowed, and guitar-playing sessions go on until well into the night.

Before 1989, **camping rough** was strictly illegal, although most young Czechs, Slovaks and East Germans paid little or no attention to that. The problem for foreigners was that they had to register with the police for every night in the country. With the lifting of visa restrictions, it has become easier to camp rough. Obviously if you're in a camper van, you're very unlikely to get hassled.

MOUNTAIN HUTS

In the mountains of the Krkonoše and the High Tatras, there are a fair number of **mountain huts** (*bouda* or *chata*) scattered about the hillsides. Some are little less than hotels and cost upwards of £5/$8 a double, but the more isolated ones are simple wooden shelters costing as little as £2/$3 per person. None are accessible by road, but many are only a few miles from civilisation. Ideally, these should be booked in advance (through *ČEDOK* in Vrchlabí for the Krkonoše, or *Slovakoturist* in Nový Smokovec for the High Tatras) but at the moment this can only be done from inside the country – a lengthy and bureaucratic process. If you turn up before 6pm at the more isolated ones, you may strike lucky but don't bank on it – best to take a tent with you just in case.

EATING AND DRINKING

There are several ways of eating out in the Czech and Slovak republics: you can go to a *restaurace/reštaurácia* or *vinárna/vináreň* and have a full meal; you can have something cheaper, more basic (though equally filling) and in less formal surroundings at a *pivnice/pivnica*, *hostinec* or *hospoda*; or, at the budget end of the scale, you can eat very cheaply indeed at one of the stand-up *bufets* or fast-food places.

BREAKFAST, SNACKS AND TAKEAWAYS

Most Czechs and Slovaks get up so early in the morning (often around 5 or 6am) that they don't have time to start the day with anything more than a quick cup of coffee. As a result, the whole concept of **breakfast** as such is alien to the Czechs and Slovaks. Most hotels will serve the "continental" basics, but it's cheaper and more enjoyable to go hunting for your own.

Pastries (*pečivo*) are available from most bakeries (*pekářství/pekárna*), but rarely in bars and cafés, so you'll most likely have to eat them on the go. The traditional pastry (*koláč*) is more like sweet bread, dry and fairly dense with only a little condiment to flavour it, such as almonds (*oříškový/orieskový*), poppy seed jam (*mákový*), prune jam (*povidlový*) or a kind of sour-sweet Slovak curd cheese (*tvarohový*). Recently, French- and Viennese-style bakeries have started to appear in the big cities, selling croissants (*loupáky*) and lighter cream cakes.

Czech and Slovak **bread** (*chléb*) is some of the tastiest around when fresh. The standard loaf is *šumava*, a dense mixture of wheat and rye, which you can buy whole, in halves (*půl*) or quarters (*čtvrtina*). *Česky chléb* is a mixture of rye, wheat and whey, with distinctive slashes across the top; *kmínový chléb* is the same loaf packed full of caraway seeds. *Moskva* is a Slovak favourite, despite the name – a moist, heavy, sour dough loaf that lasts for days. Rolls come in two varieties: *rohlík*, a plain white finger roll, and *houska*, a rougher, tastier round bun.

The ubiquitous street **takeaway** is the hot dog or *párek/párok*, a dubious-looking frankfurter (traditionally two – *párek/párok* means a pair), dipped in mustard and served with a white roll (*v rohlíku*). A Czech speciality all year round is *smažený sýr/vyprážaný syr* – a slab of melted cheese (and, more often than not, ham) fried in breadcrumbs and served with a roll (*v housce*). If it's *plněný* or *se šunkou*, then you can be certain it's got ham in it, and it generally comes with a large dose of the local tartare sauce – a lot less piquant than its western counterpart. The greasiest option of the lot is *bramborák*, a thin potato pancake with little flecks of bacon or salami in it. Finally, there's *langoše*, a Hungarian invention – a deep-fried doughy base smothered in garlic. In the autumn, you'll find freshly cooked corn-on-the-cob (*kukuřice/kukurica*) sold on the streets.

BUFETS AND FAST FOOD

Stand-up **bufets** (see below) are open from as early as 6am and offer everything from light snacks to full meals. They're usually self-service (*samoobsluha*) and non-smoking, and occasionally have rudimentary seats. The cheapest of the wide range of meat sausages on offer is *sekaná*, bits of old meat and bread squashed together to form a meat loaf – for connoisseurs only. *Guláš* is popular – stew that may bear little relation to the original of that name – usually *Szegedínský* (pork with sauerkraut) but sometimes *special* (with better meat and a creamier sauce). If you're prepared to risk it, you could try some roast chicken.

Less substantial fare boils down to *chlebíčky* – artistically presented **open sandwiches** with differing combinations of gherkins, cheese, salami, ham and aspic – and great mountains of

salad (*salát/šalát*), bought by weight (200 grammes is a medium-sized portion). *Feferonkový salát* is a mildly hot pepper and pea salad, while *vajíčkový salát* is a rich egg and mayonnaise dish. Others, like *vlašský/talianský* (Italian) and *francouský* (French) *salát* are, in reality, Czech/Slovak affairs with varying amounts of salami, ham, potato and mayonnaise.

Western-style **fast food** has yet to hit the country in a really big way, but *McDonalds* are set to reverse that trend, with its first two outlets recently opened in Prague. In the meantime there are sort of cross-breed *bufets* serving traditional Czech/Slovak fare, plus *hamburgery* (as the locals call them), pizzas and other "international" dishes. Other staple fast-food snacks include *hranolky/zemiaky* (chips/French fries) or *krokety* (croquettes), served with tartare sauce. Czech/Slovak crisps (*chips*) are lightly salted, greasy and generally stale.

COFFEE, TEA AND CAKES

Like the Austrians and Hungarians who once ruled over them, the Czechs and Slovaks have a grotesquely sweet tooth, and the coffee-and-cake hit is part of the daily ritual. **Coffee** is drunk black and described rather hopefully as *turecká* (Turkish) – it's really just hot water poured over coffee grains. Downmarket *bufet*s sell *ledová káva*, a weak, cold black coffee, while at the other end of the scale *Vídeňská káva* (Viennese coffee) is a favourite with the older generation, not quite as refined as the Austrian original, but still served with an adequate dollop of whipped cream. Espresso coffee (*presso*) is becoming trendy in the big cities, though it rarely matches up to the Italian version. Whatever you do, avoid *kapucín*, which is rarely like the cappuccino it purports to be.

Tea is drunk weak and without milk, although you'll usually be given a glass of boiling water and a tea bag so you can do your own thing. **Milk** itself is rarely drunk on its own, though it can be bought in supermarkets – but bearing in mind that some seventy percent of it is unfit for human consumption, it might be wiser to stick to the UHT type. The country used to produce vast quantities of delicious **yoghurts** and sour milks, which, if you can still find them, you should buy in preference to the sugary western stuff that has flooded the market recently; *bílý jogurt* is natural yoghurt, but look out for *kefír* or *biokys*, the thick and thin respectively of the sour milks.

The *cukrárna/cukáreň* is the place to go for cake-eating. There are two main types of cake: *dort*, like the German *Tort*, consist of a series of custard cream, chocolate and sponge layers, while *řez* are lighter square cakes, usually containing a bit of fruit. A *věneček*, filled with "cream", is the nearest you'll get to an eclair; a *větrník* is simply a larger version with a bit of fresh cream added. One speciality to look out for is *rakvička*, which literally means "Granny's little coffin", an extended piece of sugar with cream, moulded vaguely into the shape of a coffin.

Whatever the season, Czechs and Slovaks have to have their daily fix of **ice cream** (*zmrzlina*), dispensed from little window kiosks in the sides of buildings. In a *cukrárna* there's generally more choice, but it's at the outlets advertising *italská/talianská zmrzlina* (actually nothing like Italian ice cream) that the longest queues form.

FULL MEALS

For a **full meal**, you can go anywhere from a local *pivnice* to a regular *restaurace/reštaurácia* or late-night *vinárna/vináreň*. It's as well to remember that Czechs and Slovaks eat their main meal of the day at lunchtime, between noon and 2pm. Traditionally, they only have cold meats and bread later on, but obviously the posher restaurants make more of the evening.

If your main concern is price, the local beer-swilling *pivnice/pivnica*, *hospoda* or *hostinec* are the ones to go for. Nearly all of them will serve hot meals from mid-morning until 2 or 3pm, and some continue serving until 8 or 9pm. A *vinárna* (wine bar) – though not necessarily its kitchen – will sometimes stay open after 11pm.

Away from the big hotels, the **menu** (*jídelní lístek/jedálny lístok*), which should be displayed outside, is often in Czech/Slovak only, and deciphering it without a grounding in the language can be quite a feat. Just bear in mind that the right-hand column lists the prices, while the far left column usually gives you the estimated weight of every dish in grammes; if what you get weighs more or less, the price will alter accordingly.

Some restaurants still insist, with varying degress of coercion, that you leave your coat and bags in the **cloakroom** (*šatna/šatňa*). It's another leftover of Habsburg airs and graces, but also provides a meagre employment for the pensioners who generally run them. A modest form of **tipping** exists, generally done by rounding up the bill to the nearest few crowns.

A FOOD AND DRINK GLOSSARY (IN CZECH/SLOVAK)

Basics

snídaně/raňajky	Breakfast	*chléb/chlieb*	Bread	*ovoce/ovocie*	Fruit
oběd/obed	Lunch	*maslo*	Butter	*cukr/cukor*	Sugar
večeře/večera	Supper/	*houska*	Round roll	*sůl/soľ*	Salt
	dinner	*pohlík*	Finger roll	*pepř/čierne*	Pepper
nůž/nôž	Knife	*chlebíček*	Open	*korenie*	
vidlička	Fork		sandwich	*ocet/ocot*	Vinegar
ižíce/lyžica	Spoon	*med*	Honey	*hořčice/horčica*	Mustard
talíř/tanier	Plate	*mléko/mlieko*	Milk	*tartarská omáčka*	Tartare sauce
šálek/šálka	Cup	*vejce/vajcia*	Eggs	*křen/chren*	Horseradish
pohár	Glass	*pečivo*	Pastry	*rýže/ryža*	Rice
předkrmy/predkrmy	Starters	*maso/mäso*	Meat	*knedlíky/knedle*	Dumplings
polévka/polievka	Soup	*pyby*	Fish	*jidla na*	Main dishes
zákusky/Múčnik	Dessert	*zeleniny*	Vegetables	*objednávku*	to order

Soups, fish and poultry

boršč	Beetroot soup	*kachna/kačica*	Duck	*pstruh*	Trout
bramborová/	Potato soup	*kapr/kapor*	Carp	*rajská/*	Tomato soup
zemiaková		*kapustnica*	Sauerkraut and	*paradajková*	
čočková/	Lentil soup		meat soup	*sardinka*	Sardine
šošovicová		*kuře/kurča*	Chicken	*zavináč*	Herring/
fazolová/fazuľová	Bean soup	*kuřecí/kuracia*	Thin chicken		rollmop
hovězí/hovädzia	Beef soup		soup	*zeleninová*	Vegetable
hrachová	Pea soup	*makrela*	Mackerel		soup

Meat dishes

drštky/drňky	Tripe	*kýta/stehno*	Thigh	*šunka*	Ham
čevapčiči	Spicy meat	*ledvinky/obličky*	Kidneys	*telecí/teľacie*	Veal
	balls	*salám/saláma*	Salami	*vepřové/bravčové*	Pork
hovězí/hovädzie	Beef	*sekaná*	Meat loaf	*vepřové řízek/*	Breaded pork
játra/pečeň	Liver	*skopové/baranina*	Mutton	*bravčový rezeň*	cutlet or
jazyk	Tongue	*slanina*	Bacon		schnitzel
klobásy	Sausages	*svíčková/*		*žebírko/rebierko*	Ribs
kotleta	Cutlet	*sviečkovica*	Sirloin		

Vegetables

brambory/zemiaky	Mushrooms	*Karot*	Cauliflower	*ředkev/reďkovka*	Radish
cibule/cibuľa	Potatoes	*květák/karfiol*	Pickled gherkin	*řepná buľva/*	Beetroot
česnek/cesnak	Onion	*kyselá okurka*	Sauerkraut	*cukrová repa*	
čočka/šošovica	Garlic	*kyselé zelí/*		*Hranolky*	Chips
fazole/fazuľa	Lentils	*kyslá kapusta*	Ratatouille	*špenát*	Spinach
houby/huby	Beans	*lečo/liečo*	Carrot	*zelí/kapusta*	Cabbage
hrášky	Peas	*okurka/uhorka*	Cucumber	*žampiony/*	Mushrooms
chřest/špargľa	Asparagus	*rajče/rajčína*	Tomato	*šampiony*	

Fruit and cheese

banán	Banana	*oříšky/oriešky*	Peanuts
borůvky/borievky	Bilberries	*ostružiny/černica*	Blackberries
broskev/broskyňa	Peach	*oštěpek*	Heavily smoked curd
bryndza	Goat's cheese in		cheese
	brine	*parenyica*	Rolled strips of lightly
citrón	Lemon		smoked curd cheese
druh citrusu	Grapefruit	*pomeranč/pomoranč*	Orange
hermelín	Czech brie	*pivny sýr*	Cheese flavoured
hrozný	Grapes		with beer
hruška	Pear	*pozinky/hrozienky*	Raisins
jablko	Apple	*švestky/slivky*	Plums
kompot	Stewed fruit	*třešeň/čerešna*	Cherry
jahody	Strawberries	*tvaroh*	Fresh curd cheese
maliny	Raspberries	*urda*	Soft, fresh
mandle	Almonds		whey cheese
meruňka/marhuľa	Apricot	*vlašské ořechy/*	
niva	Semi-soft crumbly	*orechy*	Walnuts
	blue cheese	*uzený sýr/údený syr*	Smoked cheese

Common terms

čerstvý	Fresh	*nakládaný*	Pickled
domácí	Home-made	*(za)pečený*	Baked/Roast
dušený/dusený	Stew/casserole	*nadívaný*	Stuffed
grilovaný	Roast on the spit	*slatký*	Sweet
kyselý/kyslý	Sour	*smažený/vyprážený*	Fried in breadcrumbs
m.m.	With butter	*syrový/surový*	Raw
na kmíně/na ražni	With caraway seeds	*uzený/údený*	Smoked
na roštu/na rasci	Grilled	*vařený/varený*	Boiled
nadívaný	Stuffed	*znojmský*	Served with gherkins

Drinks

čaj	Tea	*mléko/mlieko*	Milk
destiláty	Spirits	*pivo*	Beer
káva	Coffee	*suché víno*	Dry Wine
koňak	Brandy	*svařené víno*	Mulled Wine
láhev/fľaša	Bottle	*vinný střik*	White wine with soda
led	Ice	*víno*	Wine
minerální (voda)	Mineral (water)	*na zdraví/nazdravie*	Cheers!

CZECH AND SLOVAK CUISINE

Forty years of intensive centralisation has produced a nationwide cuisine, mostly derived from the Germanic-influenced Bohemian cuisine, with a predilection for big slabs of meat served with lashings of gravy, dumplings and pickled gherkins, not to mention a good helping of pickled cabbage.

Don't, however, judge Czech and Slovak food by the mediocre fare served up in most restaurants. At home the same dishes are prepared with a flair and imagination unknown to most state-trained chefs. If you don't get the opportunity to eat in someone's house, be prepared for some pretty stodgy servings of meat and one veg. On the plus scale, Prague ham is justly famous and Czech beer is among the best in the world*.

* Even Hitler was tempted enough to break his lifelong vow of vegetarianism and teetotalism and tuck into some Prague ham and Pilsen beer when he and his troops marched into the capital in March 1939.

Slovak food is traditionally spicier and more varied – a hangover from Hungarian rule. It's also possible to eat the real thing amongst the half-million strong Hungarian-speaking community of Bratislava and southern Slovakia.

Most menus start with the **soups** (*polévky/ polievky*), one of the region's culinary strong points and mainly served at lunchtimes. Posher restaurants will have a serious selection of starters such as *uzený/údený jazyk* (smoked tongue), *tresčí játra* (cod's liver) or perhaps *kaviárové vejce* (a hard-boiled egg with caviar on top). *Šunková rolka* is another favourite, consisting of ham topped with whipped cream and horseradish, but you're more likely to find yourself skipping the starters, which are often little more than a selection of cold meats.

Main courses are overwhelmingly based on **meat** (*maso/mäso*), usually pork or beef. The Czechs are experts on these meats, and although the quality could often be better, the variety of sauces and preparative techniques beats traditional Anglo-American cooking hands down. The difficulty lies in decoding names such as *klašterny tajemství* ("mystery of the monastery") or even a common dish like *Moravský vrabec* (literally "Moravian sparrow", but actually roast pork).

Fish (*ryby*) are generally listed, along with chicken and other fowl like duck, under a separate heading. Trout and carp (the traditional dish at Christmas) are cheaply and widely available, and although their freshness may be questionable, they are usually served, grilled or roasted, in delicious buttery sauces.

Most main courses are served with potatoes, pickled cabbage and/or **dumplings** (*knedliky/ knedle*), which, though German in origin and name, are now the mainstay of Bohemian cooking. The term itself is misleading for English-speakers, since they resemble nothing like the English dumpling – more like a heavy white bread. *Houskové knedliky* come in large flour-based slices (four or five to a dish), while *bramborové knedliky/zemiakové knedle* are smaller and made from potato and flour. Occasionally, you may be treated to *ovocné knedliky* (fruit dumplings), the king of Czech dumplings. **Fresh salads** are a new concept in most restaurants, and rarely rise above lettuce, tomato or cucumber, often swimming in a slightly sweet, watery dressing.

With the exception of *palačinky* (pancakes) filled with chocolate or fruit and cream, **desserts**, where they exist at all, can be pretty unexciting. Even the ice cream in restaurants isn't up to the standards of the street stuff, so go to a *cukrárna* if you want a dose of sugar.

VEGETARIANS

The Czech and Slovak republics are no place for **vegetarians** or health freaks; meat consumption here is one of the highest in the world – around half a kilo a day per head. On top of that, most of the animals are factory-farmed and often seriously ill by the time they're slaughtered, rendering large parts of the carcass unfit for human consumption. Inefficiencies of agricultural production mean that, even in this rich and fecund land, you'll be offered very few fresh vegetables as a compensation.

If you eat fish but not meat you won't have too hard a time. Most Czech and Slovak menus feature a fish dish, usually trout or carp. Many also have a section called *bezmasa* (literally "without meat") but this often simply means the dish is not entirely based around a slab of burnt flesh, for example *omeleta se šunkou* (ham omelette). Regular standbys are *knedliky s vejce* (dumplings and egg) or *omeleta s hrášem* (pea omelette), both of which most chefs will knock up for you without too much fuss. Another possibility is, of course, pizza, an approximation of which is becoming increasingly popular.

Vegans will have little or no choice in restaurants, aside from certain pizzas; even dishes like beans or lentils regularly turn up with an egg plonked in the middle. Falafel is beginning to appear in Prague, and, in addition, a number of health-food shops have opened across the region which sell soya-based produce.

VEGETARIAN PHRASES

As serious meat-eating nations, most Czechs and Slovaks simply can't conceive of anybody going through even a small portion of their life without eating meat (unless they're critically ill or clinically insane). So simply saying you're a vegetarian or that you don't eat meat or fish may instil panic and/or confusion in the waiter – it's often better to ask what's in a particular dish you think looks promising.

The phrases to remember are *jsem vegeterián/vegeteriánka. máte nejaké bezmasa?* (I'm a vegetarian. Is there anything without meat?); and for emphasis, you could add *nejím maso nebo ryby* (I don't eat meat or fish).

ALCOHOLIC DRINKS

Alcohol consumption in the Czech and Slovak republics has always been high, and in the decade following the events of 1968 it doubled. A whole generation found solace in drinking, mostly beer. It's a problem which seldom spills out onto the streets; violence in pubs is uncommon and you won't see that many drunks in public. That said, it's not unusual to see someone legless in the afternoon, on their way home from work.

BEER

At the last count Czechoslovakia was second in the world league table of beer consumption, behind the Germans, Czech **beer** ranking among the best in the world. It may not boast the variety of its western neighbour, but is the true home of most of the lager drunk around the world today.

It was in the Bohemian city of Plzeň (Pilsen) that the first **bottom-fermented** beer was introduced in 1842, after complaints from the citizens about the quality of the top-fermented predecessor. The new brewing style quickly spread to Germany, and is now blamed for the bland rubbish that is served up in the English-speaking world as lager or Pils.

Whether due to lack of technological know-how or through positive choice, brewing methods in the republics have remained stuck in the old ways, eschewing chemical substitutes. The distinctive flavour of Czech beer comes from the famous Bohemian hops, Žatec (Saaz) Red, still hand-picked and then combined with soft local water and served with a high content of absorbed carbon dioxide – hence the thick, creamy head. Even if you don't think you like lager at all, you must try at least a *malé pivo* (0.3 litre). The average jar is medium strength, usually about 1050 specific gravity or 5 percent alcohol (12° to the Czechs who use their own peculiar Balling scale).

The most famous Czech beer is **Pilsner Urquell**, know to the Czechs as *Plzeňský Prazdroj*, the original bottom-fermented Pils from Plzeň (Pilsen), a city 80km southwest of Prague. Plzeň also boasts the **Gambrinus** brewery, thus producing two out of the three main Czech export beers. The other big Bohemian brewing town is České Budějovice (Budweis), home to **Budvar**, a mild beer for Bohemia but still leagues ahead of *Budweiser* beer, the German name for *Budvar* that was adopted by an American brewer in 1876. All three Czech beers are widely available in both republics.

The biggest brewery in the region, however, is in the Smíchov suburb of Prague where **Staropramen** is produced, a typical Bohemian brew with a mild hoppy flavour. Prague also produces some of the country's best strong, special beer: **Flek**, a dark caramel concoction brewed and served exclusively at a pub called *U Fleků* in Prague's Nové Město since 1399, and **Braník**, a light malty beer from south Prague, creamy even by smooth Bohemian standards. Other Bohemian beers worth sampling are the award-winning bitter **Velkopopovický kozel**, and the smooth, hoppy **Krušovice** beer. In Moravia, the love of beer is somewhat tempered by the south and east Moravian partiality to wine, but the breweries of Brno and Ostrava have some good light and dark beers of their own. The Slovaks, by contrast, have no great tradition of beer drinking, but union with the Czech Lands in 1918 has gradually changed things – since 1945 their beer consumption has increased tenfold.

WINE AND SPIRITS

Neither Czech nor Slovak **wine** will ever win over as many people as Czech beer, but since the import of French and German vines in the fourteenth century, the region has produced a modest selection of medium-quality wines. Since few are exported, and the labelling is notoriously imprecise – most wines are made by large farm co-operatives and sold under brand names – it's difficult to give a very clear picture. Suffice to say that most domestic wine is pretty drinkable and rarely more than about £1–2/$1.70–3.50 a bottle, while the best wine can only be had from the private wine cellars, hundreds of which still exist.

The biggest producers and consumers by far are the Slovaks, whose two main wine regions are along the hot southern edge of the republic. The vineyards of the Small Carpathians stretch right down to the suburbs of Bratislava, while those of the Slovak Tokaj are right next to the main Hungarian wine-producing region of the same name, and produce a passable dry white known as **Furmint**. South Moravia boasts some fine white wines, grown under identical conditions as those of the Austrian Weinviertel. Bohemia's wine-growing region consists of only 1000 acres around the town of Mělník, but it produces at least one good red, **Ludmila**, and a couple of whites. **Burčak**, a misty wine that contains little or no alcohol, is drunk in the autumn soon after the harvest.

All the usual **spirits** are on sale and known by their generic names, with rum and vodka leading the sales. Domestic brands originate mostly from Slovakia and east Moravia, like *hanácká*, a vodka from the Haná region around Olomouc. The home-production of brandies is a national pastime, resulting sometimes in almost terminally strong brews. The most famous of the lot is *slivovice*, a plum brandy originally from the border hills between Moravia and Slovakia but now available just about everywhere, though the home-made stuff is best. You'll probably come across *borovička* at some point, a popular firewater from the Slovak Spiš region, made from pine trees; *myslivec* is a rough brandy with an ardent following. There's also a fair selection of intoxicating **herbal concoctions**. *Fernet* is a dark-brown bitter drink, known as *bavorák* (meaning Bavarian beer) when it's mixed with tonic, while *becherovka* is a supposedly "healthy" herbal spirit from the Bohemian spa town of Karlovy Vary, with an unusual taste quite unlike any other spirit.

SOFT DRINKS

Unfortunately, aside from the country's plentiful mineral water, **soft drinks** in the Czech and Slovak republics are pretty nasty. As well as the ubiquitous *Coke* and *Pepsi*, there's *Perla*, a sugary lemon drink, and *Topic*, reputedly made with grapes and herbs; *Vinea* is a slightly subtler version. If you ask for a lemonade (*límonáda*), you're just as likely to get orangeade, and vice versa if you ask for *oranž*.

Unless you long for a cross between cherryade and dandelion and burdock, avoid the variety of vivid fizzy drinks that go under the promising name of *džus* (pronounced "juice"). Fresh fruit juice has only recently become available. The safest bet for those without a sweet tooth is to ask for *soda* or *tonic*. *Minerální voda* (mineral water) is everywhere, always carbonated, and a lot more "tasty" than western brands. Try *Mattoni* for a milder option.

WHERE TO DRINK

Even the most simple *bufet* serves draught beer, but the **pivnice/pivnica** or pub (which closes around 10 or 11pm) is the place where most heavy drinking goes on. It's common practice to share a table with other drinkers; *je tu volno?* (Is this seat free?) is the standard question. Waiter-service is the norm, so sit tight and a beer should come your way. When you decide you want to leave, simply say *zaplatím, prosím* (literally "I'll pay, please"), and your tab will be totted up.

Since *pivnice* (and the more local *hospoda* or *hostinec*) are traditionally male preserves, women tend to head instead for the more mixed atmosphere of the country's restaurants or **vinárna/vináreň** (wine bars). A *vinárna* generally has slightly later opening hours, often doubling as an upmarket restaurant or nightclub. The younger generation tend to hang out more in the **kavárna/kaviáreň** (café) or ubiquitous continental bars around town.

COMMUNICATIONS: POST, PHONES AND MEDIA

POST

Most **post offices** (*pošta*) are open from 7 or 8am to 5 or 6pm every day except Sundays. They're pretty baffling institutions with separate windows for just about every service. Look out for the right sign to avoid queueing unnecessarily: *známky* (stamps), *dopisy* (letters) or *balky* (parcels).

Outbound mail is reasonably reliable, with letters or postcards taking around five working days to reach the UK, a week to ten days to reach North America. You can also buy **stamps** from newsagents and kiosks, as well as post offices, though often only for domestic mail.

Poste restante (pronounced as five syllables in Czech and Slovak) services are available in major towns, but remember to write *Pošta 1* (the main office), followed by the name of the town. Get the sender to write their name and address on the back so that mail can at least be returned if something goes wrong. If you're passing through the capital at some point, it might be safer to have mail sent to your embassy, but write and tell them beforehand that you intend to do this.

PHONES

Public **phones** in either republic are far from reliable. There are usually instructions in English, but despite the graphic description, you may still encounter problems. The yellow phones take 1kčs coins only, and are only good for **local calls**. Theoretically, you simply pick up the receiver and dial the number with your crown poised in the slot. To call outside the local area code, you must find one of the elusive grey phone boxes which take 1, 2 and 5kčs coins. When you run out of money, you'll hear a recorded message urging you in Czech or Slovak to put more in.

More sophisticated phones that give back any unused coins are beginning to appear in Prague, as are **card phones**. Phonecards (*telecarty*), currently available in 50 and 150kčs denominations, can be bought at post offices. The **dialling tone** is a short followed by a long pulse; the **ringing tone** is long and regular; **engaged** is short and rapid; the standard Czech/Slovak response is *prosím*; and the word for extension is *linka*. If you have any problems, ring ☎0135 and ask for an English-speaking operator.

It's also theoretically possible to make **international calls** from the grey phone boxes, but few people do. It's a lot less hassle to seek out one of the new card phones, or simply go to the telephone exchanges situated in most major post offices. Write down the town and number you want, leave a deposit of around 200kčs and wait for your name to be called out. Keep a close watch on the time since international calls are extremely expensive at whatever time of the day or night you ring. You can also make calls from most hotels, although their surcharge is usually pretty hefty. It might be easier in the long run to ask for a **collect call** – which will cost the recipient less than it would cost you. Dial ☎0132 and ask for an English speaker or say *na účet voleného*.

DIALLING CODES

To the Czech/Slovak republic
From Britain ☎010 42
From USA and Canada ☎011 42
From Australia and New Zealand ☎0011 42

From the Czech/Slovak republic
UK ☎0044
Eire ☎00353
Australia ☎0061
New Zealand ☎0064
USA and Canada ☎001

Telegrams can be sent from any post office or by phone (though not from phone boxes) by dialling 127. **Telex** and **Fax** machines are gradually arriving in many big hotels (charges are as for western Europe), and if you want a **photocopy** (*xerox*), ask at a hotel before joining the long queue in town.

NEWSPAPERS AND MAGAZINES

For years, **foreign newspapers** were restricted to old copies of the *Morning Star*, and its fraternal equivalents. All that has changed, and it's now possible to get most of the quality British papers, as well as the *International Herald Tribune*, in Prague and Bratislava. They're generally a day old, though one that you can buy on the day of issue is the European edition of *The Guardian*, printed in Frankfurt (it arrives on the streets of Prague around mid-morning, Bratislava by midday).

By far the most respected **daily newspaper** is *Lidové noviny*, which started life as a monthly Czech *samizdat* under the Communists. Under Havel's presidency it was generally considered to be "close to the castle", that is to say pro-Havel; many of its regular contributors, like Havel himself, were involved in the human rights organisation Charter 77. The slickly produced centre-right *Telegraf* is the latest of the "independents" to be launched; most of the rest of the Czech and Slovak press is run along party political lines. *Rudé právo* (*Pravda* in Slovakia), once the official mouthpiece of the Communist Party, with a guaranteed readership of around one million, has survived against all the odds, though it now describes itself as a "left-wing daily".

In the three big cities of Prague, Brno and Bratislava, commuters hide London-style behind the entirely forgettable local **evening papers**, usually called *Večerník* ("Evening") or something similar. As far as **magazines** go, western glossies grab the attention of most of the nation more effectively than their domestic competitors, with the exception of the Czech edition of *Playboy*, whose success has taken place against the background of a huge nationwide increase in **porn** magazines and books.

TV AND RADIO

Until recently, the only good thing to be said about Czechoslovak state television was that, since federalisation in 1969, it had consistently broadcast in Czech *and* Slovak. This commitment to **bilingual broadcasting** was so strictly adhered to that, in the course of an ice hockey match, the first half would be commentated in Czech and the second in Slovak. For the last twenty years this, more than anything else, has helped nurture a generation for whom the differences between the two nations, at least linguistically, are an irrelevance.

Since 1989, the Slovaks and Czechs have begun to dismantle the old system. Shortly after the 1992 elections, the Slovaks made the final break with Czech TV in Prague. Both sides now have programmes exclusively in their own language. State-run channels in either republic are pretty bland, with keep-fit classes and classical concerts still taking up much of peak-time viewing. All foreign films and serials are dubbed and everything shuts down well before midnight. A third, 24-hour channel, *OK3*, has recently joined in: a seemingly arbitrary mix of *CNN* and sundry satellite channels of varying quality. *CNN* is currently broadcast from midnight to 8am, from 9 to 10am and again from noon to 2pm.

As far as **radio** goes, most cafés and bars tune into the new FM music stations that have recently appeared. The most popular in the Czech Lands is *Europe II*, which dishes out bland Euro-pop; in Slovakia, it's *Rock FM.*, in a similar vein. You can pick up the **BBC World Service** fairly easily now from most major cities in either republic, on a variety of FM wavelengths around the 100Mhz mark. Be warned: most FM stations give out pretty weak signals, so don't expect to get much once you've left the immediate vicinity.

OPENING HOURS AND PUBLIC HOLIDAYS

Shops in both republics are generally open Monday to Friday from 9am to 5pm, though most supermarkets stay open later. Smaller shops tend to close for lunch for an hour sometime between noon and 2pm. Those shops that do open on Saturday generally close at noon or 1pm; and none will be open on Sunday. Pubs and restaurants tend to close between 10 and 11pm, with food often unobtainable past 9pm. Over the weekend, they close for one or two days out of Saturday, Sunday or Monday.

Official national holidays were always a potential source of contention with the old regime, and may be set to change again in Slovakia following independence. Even the final **May Day** celebrations that took place in Prague in 1989 were marred by "anti-socialist elements"; people unrollling banners which called for democracy and *glasnost*. For the moment, the 100-year tradition of the event, and the public holiday, look set to stay, as do the other *slavné májové dny*

(Glorious May Days): **May 5**, the beginning of the Prague Uprising in 1945, and VE Day. In 1992 the Czechs and Slovaks decided to break with the Soviet tradition of celebrating VE Day on May 9, one day later than the west, and join their western allies on **May 8**. Apart from these, none of the Communist national holidays remain.

NATIONAL HOLIDAYS

January 1
Easter Monday
May 1
May 5
May 8
July 5 (Introduction of Christianity)
July 6 (Death of Jan Hus)
October 28 (Foundation of the Republic)
December 24
December 25
December 26

CASTLES, CHURCHES AND MUSEUMS

The Czech and Slovak republics boast something like two thousand castles, ranging from piles of thirteenth-century rubble to the last vain attempts produced earlier this century by the old aristocracy. Many have been converted for modern use – into old people's homes, trade union holiday retreats and even training centres for the secret police; some have been returned to their former owners. The country's churches and monasteries are similarly blighted by years of structural neglect, and more recently, by art thefts; most now lock their doors outside worshipping hours. Museums and galleries, by contrast, thrived under the Communists, filled to the gunnels with propaganda. Some have bitten the dust, others have changed out of all recognition, but most are now more interesting to visit.

CASTLES AND GUIDED TOURS

The basic **opening hours** for castles and other historical buildings are Tuesday to Sunday 8 or 9am to noon or 1pm, then 2 to 4pm or later. From the end of October to the beginning of April, most castles are closed. In April and October, opening hours are often restricted to weekends and holidays only.

Whatever the time of year, if you want to see the interior of the building, nine times out of ten you'll be compelled to go on a guided tour (nearly always in Czech or Slovak, occasionally German) that can last an hour or more. Some places insist on a minimum number of people (five is the absolute bottom line) before they begin a tour, unless you can successfully beg your way in. Ask for an *anglický text*, an often unintentionally hilarious English resumé of the castle's history. More than likely you'll to be asked to wear special furry overshoes (*papučky*) which protect and polish the floors at the same time. Tours almost invariably set off on the hour, and the last one leaves an hour before the final closing time. Entrance tickets cost very little – rarely more than 50kčs – hence no prices are quoted in the text. Special rates for foreigners are being introduced at certain sights; no proof is needed to claim student status, which usually cuts the price in half.

CHURCHES AND MONASTERIES

The vast majority of religious orders were closed down by the Emperor Joseph II in the eighteenth century; the rest fell prey to the Communists. The old **monasteries** became schools, factories and prisons. Many orders have now returned to their former residences; a few remain as museums, which keep similar hours to the country's castles. Getting into **churches** can present more of a problem. The really important churches operate in much the same way as museums, occasionally charging an entry fee, particularly for their crypts or cloisters; while opening hours for the smaller ones are often brief and erratic.

Way back in the fifteenth century, the vast majority of the population of Bohemia and Moravia were Protestant or Hussite, and the Slovaks converted to the Lutheran doctrine a century later. But the ferocity of the Counter-Reformation was unequalled in both the Czech Lands and Slovakia, and nowadays both regions are predominantly **Roman Catholic**, with the most ardent followers in Slovakia and the least committed populations in Bohemia. Hundreds of Baroque churches litter the countryside, but they're usually kept locked due to the enormous number of art thefts that have taken place. The only time you can guarantee their being open is just before and after services in the early morning (around 7 or 8am) and/or evening (around 6 or 7pm) – times are often posted outside the main doors. Otherwise, it's worth asking around for the local *kňaz* (priest) or *kaplan*, who's usually only too happy to oblige with the key (*klíč*). In the Czech Lands, widespread agnosticism and the punitive policies of the last regime (self-confessed believers were not allowed to join the Party or take up teaching posts) have left many churches in a terrible state of disrepair. This is not the case in Slovakia – not because the activities of the state were any less harsh, but because the church-going population was more determined to maintain its religious tradition.

In the north and east of Slovakia, there's a small number of Orthodox (*Pravoslavný*) believers and a much larger contingent who belong to the **Uniate Church** (*Grécko-katolický*), an obscure branch of Roman Catholicism whose small wooden churches, packed with icons and

Byzantine paraphernalia, appear just like Russian Orthodox churches to the uninitiated. You'll find a much more thorough account of the Uniates and their churches in the section on Carpatho-Ruthenia in Chapter Ten. Suffice to say that the buildings are fascinating, especially their dark and poky interiors, but they are kept firmly locked with little indication of what time the next service will be held.

The former Czechoslovakia's once considerable Jewish population has been whittled down to an official figure of around 2000, over half of whom live in Prague, one of the few places where regular worship still takes place. Very few of the now disused **synagogues** have been saved from collapse, though there are some notable exceptions like Mikulov in South Moravia and Trenčín in West Slovakia.

MUSEUMS AND GALLERIES

Czechoslovakia's **museums** used to be stronger on quantity than quality, and exclusively Czech or Slovak labelling only made matters worse. This is changing slowly, as tourism becomes more important, and many places do have *anglický text* on offer. Occasionally you'll come across a real gem – the local museums in Slovakia often boast amazing collections of folk art – but, generally speaking, many of the local museums are far from riveting and school groups are often the only visitors. There are three main types, plus one other now extinct: a **národní muzeum** or national museum, which exists only in the two capitals, Prague and Bratislava, and is normally an unremarkable archaeological and art collection gathered from the region, often accompanied by a liberal sprinkling of stuffed animals from around the globe. A **krajské muzeum** or regional museum traces the local history through arts, crafts and old photos, while a **městské muzeum** or town museum is more provincial still. Finally, every town was obliged to have a museum of "working-class history" – either as a separate entity or tacked on to the end of the regional or town museum – which amounted to little more than a lengthy eulogy of the Communist Party and a quasi-historical justification for the status quo. Some of these have now

simply been closed down, but others have been reorganised and rewritten in a brave attempt to come to terms with recent history.

The big cities boast the best **art galleries**, though even Prague's National Gallery collections pale in comparison with those of most major Western European cities. The impact of Socialist Realism was as heavy here as elsewhere in the Soviet Empire, and the results can still be seen in the country's provincial art galleries. Before the war, Czechoslovakia was at the forefront of the European avant-garde, but only recently have works from this period been put on show, except previously during the occasional one-off exhibition. Many of the country's best artists – people like Kupka and Mucha – worked abroad, and little attempt was made by the last regime to buy back the works of such "degenerates", which, as a result, now grace the galleries of Paris and New York. Nevertheless, exhibitions of new artists are constantly doing the rounds, and some of the country's better artists, previously banned, are now once more able to put on shows.

Opening hours for museums and galleries tend to be from 9am to 4pm or later, usually without a break at lunch. Many stay open all year round or switch from a Tuesday–Sunday summer routine to Monday–Friday during the winter. Full opening hours are detailed in the guide. Ticket prices are still negligible (rarely more than 20kčs) – and claiming you're a student will cut costs in half. As with hotels, some of the more touristy places may charge a special rate (anything up to five times as much) for foreigners, but, again, it's rarely more than 50kčs.

CLOSED FOR TECHNICAL REASONS

A regular feature of travelling around the region is for museums, galleries and chateaux to be temporarily "closed for technical reasons", or, more permanently, "closed for reconstruction". Notices are rarely more specific than that, but the widespread shortage of staff and funds is often the reason behind the closure. It's impossible to predict what will be closed when, but it's as well to make alternative plans when visiting galleries, museums and castles, just in case.

FESTIVALS AND ENTERTAINMENTS

There are remarkably few national annual events, and aside from the usual religious-oriented celebrations and mass pilgrimages, most annual shindigs are arts and music-based festivals, confined to a particular town or city. In addition, there are also folkloric events in the nether regions which take place in the summer only, the Strážnice folk festival in Moravia being by far the most famous.

Freed from the straitjacket of Communist censorship, and state control of the arts, popular culture has diversified considerably in the last few years. Theatre, jazz and rock in particular are enjoying something of a renaissance. The position of sport and classical music – both actively encouraged and subsidised by the old regime – is slightly different.

FESTIVALS, FAIRS AND OTHER ANNUAL EVENTS

The *Strážnice Folk Festival* is the biggest and most prestigious of the many annual **folk festivals**, with groups from all over the Czech and Slovak republics performing. Other ones worth looking out for are the *Chod Festival* in Domažlice every August and the *Folk Dance Festival* held in July in Východná in Slovakia.

The 1980s witnessed a revival of **pilgrimages** (*pouť* or *púť*), usually centred around the cult of the Virgin Mary. The biggest gathering is on the first weekend in July at Levoča, in the Spiš region of East Slovakia, when up to 250,000 people descend on the small pilgrimage church above the town. Lesser celebrations go on in the region for the following two months.

For the Orthodox and Uniate churches, which predominate in the east of the country, **Easter** (in Czech *velikonoce*, in Slovak *Veľká noc*) is much more important than Christmas, and the processions and services can be elaborate and lengthy affairs that are well worth catching. For the rest of the country, it's a good excuse for a party, and also the age-old sexist ritual of whipping girls' calves with braided birch twigs, tied with ribbons (*pomlazka*) – objects which you'll see being furiously bought and sold from markets in the runup to Easter Sunday. To prevent such a fate, the girls are supposed to offer the boys a coloured easter egg. What may once have been an innocent bucolic frolic has now become another excuse for Czech and Slovak men to harass any woman who dares to venture onto the street during this period.

As in the West, **Christmas** (*Vánoce/Vianoce*) is a time for over-consumption and family gatherings and, therefore, a fairly private occasion. On December 4, the feast day of Saint Barbara, cherry tree branches are bought as decorations, the aim being to get them to blossom before Christmas. On the eve of December 6, numerous trios, dressed up as *svaty Mikuláš* (Saint Nicholas), an angel and a devil, tour round the neighbourhoods, the angel handing out sweets and fruit to children who've been good, while the devil dishes out coal and potatoes to those who've been naughty. The Czech/Slovak Saint Nicholas has white hair and a beard, and dresses not in red but in a white priest's outfit, with a bishop's hat.

With a week or so to go, large barrels are set up in the streets from which huge quantities of live *kapr* (carp), the traditional Christmas dish, are sold. Christmas Eve (*Štědrý večer*) is traditionally a day of fasting, broken only when the evening star appears, signalling the beginning of the Christmas feast of carp, potato salad, schnitzel and sweet breads. Only after the meal are the children allowed to open their presents.

FESTIVALS DIARY

APRIL
Mid-April Kroměříž: home-grown Jazz Festival.
Late April–early May Brno: International Trade Fair.

MAY
May 12–June 2 Prague Spring International Music Festival.
Mid-May Zlín: International Childrens' Film Festival.

JUNE
Mid-June Mariánské Lázně: International Festival of Mime.
End June–early July Strážnice: International Folk Festival.
Mid-June Litomyšl: National Opera Festival.
June Gombasek: Hungarian Folk Festival.
June Svidník: Ukrainian (Rusyn) Folk Festival.

JULY
Early July Chrudim: Puppet Festival.
First weekend in July Levoča: Marian Pilgrimage.

July Karlovy Vary: International Film Festival.
July Východná: International Folk Festival.
July Detva: Folk Festival.

AUGUST
Mid-Aug Domažlice: Chod Folk Festival.
Mid-Aug Valtice: Baroque Music Festival.
End Aug Strakonice: International Bagpipers' Festival.
End Aug Brno: International Grand Prix motorcycling event.

SEPTEMBER
Early Sept Kroměříž: Chamber Music Festival.
Early Sept Žatec:Hop (and beer) Festival.
Late Sept–early Oct Teplice: Beethoven Music Festival.
Late Sept–early Oct Brno: International Music Festival.
Sept Bratislava: International Jazz Festival.

OCTOBER
Early Oct Pardubice: Grand steeple-chase event.
Early Oct Košice Marathon.

Birthdays are much less important in the Czech and Slovak republics than **saint's name days**, which fall on the same day each year. Thus popular names like Jan or Anna are practically national celebrations, and an excuse for everyone to get drunk since you're bound to know at least somebody with those names.

The ritual slaughter of the pig, known as *zabíjačka*, still takes place in parts of Bohemia and Moravia (as in Bavaria) towards the end of January, traditionally a time when all other winter provisions are exhausted. Every single bit of the animal is prepared as food for the feast that accompanies the event.

There's not much of the festive spirit about it, but the **International Trade Fair** held in Brno every April/May is more interesting than it sounds – as well as being set in a virtual museum of prewar avant-garde architecture. Following 1948, the Trade Fair became a showcase for shoddy COMECON goods, but the last few years have seen it successfully shake off its reputation for Cuban cigars and cheap Romanian stereos.

MUSIC

Folk songs lie at the heart of all Czech and Slovak music: people strike up traditional songs and contemporary folk tunes at the slightest excuse, especially in the countryside. A living tradition still exists in some of the more remote mountain regions of Slovakia: elsewhere professional and amateur groups keep the music alive. Styles of music vary from the more familiar Bohemian dances to the Carpathian shepherd songs of Slovakia, but the richest tradition is in Moravia, which bridges the gap between the two styles. *Dudy* (bagpipes), or *gajdy* in the Moravian dialect, are still used in the western part of the country, while the *cimbalom* (a kind of zither), and *fujara* (half flute, half bassoon), the traditional instrument of the shepherd, begin to appear further east.

The nation's great wealth of folk tunes have found their way into much of the country's **classical music**, of which the Czechs are justifiably proud, having produced four composers of considerable stature – Smetana, Dvořák, Janáček and

Martinů – and the more liberal can even claim Mahler as a fifth. The Slovaks, too, can boast some impressive musical connections: Komárno is the birthplace of Franz Lehár, the Hungarian composer, while Bratislava is the home town of Johann Nepomuk Hummel. The Czechs have also produced a host of singers, like the late Ema Destinnová, and virtuoso violinists, the latest of whom play with the prestigious Suk Quartet who regularly perform outside the country.

All three big cities have **music festivals**, which give most of their space over to national composers. Smaller towns have annual festivals often dedicated to composers, for instance Smetana (Litomyšl), Beethoven (Teplice), and Chopin (Mariánské Lázně). Throughout the year, it's easy to catch works by Czech or Slovak composers, since the repertoires of most regional companies are ardently nationalistic. Most opera houses and concert halls are closed in July and August; as compensation, watch out for the summer concerts held in many of the country's countless castles.

Jazz (or *džez* as it is sometimes written) has an established tradition, particularly in the Czech republic, despite the best efforts of the Nazis and the Communists to suppress it, though venues are almost entirely confined to Prague, except for occasional one-off gigs in the other big cities. The *Bratislava Jazz Days* are held annually in September, followed closely by Prague's *International Jazz Festival* in October, one of the best eastern Europe has to offer.

When it comes to **rock and pop music**, the majority of the indigenous product is divided evenly between western muzak and heavy metal, but these two trends ignore the more interesting side of Czech and Slovak music – the protest songs that grew out of the 1960s and the punk-influenced sound of *The Plastic People of the Universe* and their various imitators. As yet, very little of this type of music is on disc, but check the fly-posters for up-and-coming gigs, which cover the whole spectrum from highly accomplished folk/jazz performers to crass derivations of *Motorhead*.

CINEMA

Cinemas (*kino*) are cheap and rudimentary, and can be found in almost every town and village in the Czech and Slovak republics, showing all the major international films as well as the home-produced ones. The majority of foreign films are dubbed into Czech or Slovak (indicated by a small white square on the poster), but a few are shown with subtitles. The month's film listings are usually fly-posted up around town or outside each cinema. Titles are always translated into Czech or Slovak, so you'll need to have your wits about you to identify films like *Umělcova smlouva* as *The Draughtsman's Contract* (though the film's country of origin is always shown – *VB* means it's British, *USA*, American).

Prague's Barrandov Studios produced a string of innovative films in the 1960s, known collectively as the Czech New Wave, which included **Miloš Forman**, perhaps the country's best-known director. The industry's strength has always been in comedy, satire, and history as farce, as in *Obchod na korce* (*The Shop on the High Street*) by Ján Kadár, set in the Slovak Nazi puppet state in World War II. **Jiří Menzel** made his name in similar vein with the film *Ostře sledované vlaky* (*Closely Observed Trains*), set in the final stages of the last war, an antidote to the endless overblown stories of heroism.

One of the fields in which the Czechs and Slovaks excel is animation, with **Jan Švankmajer** having established a considerable international following with his disturbing version of *Alice in Wonderland* and most recently with his bitter statement on *The Death of Stalinism in Bohemia*, commissioned by the BBC. Sadly, it's well-nigh impossible to catch a showing, though should you be fortunate enough, language is unlikely to be a problem. The **International Film Festival** held in Karlovy Vary every July has established a good reputation now: in even-numbered years it's international; in odd-numbered years it's a student festival – both are open to the public.

THEATRE

Theatre is cheap in the Czech and Slovak republics, and most towns with a population of over 20,000 have at least one permanent venue with the month's programme pinned up outside and elsewhere around town. The serious stuff goes on in the *kamenná divadla* or "stone theatres", mostly opulent opera houses built by the Habsburgs in the late nineteenth century. Aside from the odd British or American touring company, there's precious little in English, although ticket prices are cheap, and the venues often interesting enough in themselves – the Czechs and Slovaks go as much for the interval promenade as for the show itself. The smaller fringe companies have been particularly badly hit by the withdrawal of state subsidies and the recent drop in audiences. In Prague, there's a strong tradition of mime, from the classical variety put on by the late Ladislav Fialka and his troupe, to more experimental stuff from international stars like Boris Polívka.

With over fifteen permanent **puppet theatres**, Czech and Slovak puppetry is big business. Of the traditional forms of puppetry, only the Spejbl & Hurvínek Theatre in Prague survives; the rest have introduced live actors into their repertoire, making the shows less accessible if you don't speak the language. However, this trend has produced innovative and highly professional companies like Hradec Králové's *Drak* who have toured extensively throughout Europe and now rarely use puppets in their shows. If you want to see a performance, look out for the words *loutkové divadlo*, or in Slovak, *babkové divadlo*.

SPORT

Czechoslovakia is probably most famous for its world-class tennis players and for its national ice hockey team. But the sport which actually pulls the biggest crowds is football (soccer). Getting tickets to watch a particular sport is easy (and cheap) enough on the day – even the really big matches rarely sell out. Actually taking part is more difficult – Czechs and Slovaks belong to local clubs and there are very few facilities for the general public.

FOOTBALL

Football's *první liga* or national league and the *Československý pohár* (the knock-out competition) are dominated by the number one team *Sparta Praha*, who supplied a large proportion of the national squad for the 1990 World Cup Finals in Italy, including the competition's top-goal scorer Tomáš Skuhravý (now playing in Italy). Games are played on a Sunday afternoon; tickets for a major domestic or international match cost less than £1/$1.70.

The local **style of play** is difficult to pinpoint, but a battle of wits is definitely preferred to the English style of direct attacking or the Latin preference for individual flair. Working-class towns such as the mining town of Ostrava produce some of the country's better sides like *Baník Ostrava* and *Vítkovice*. Clubs are still organised in the traditional "socialist" manner: sides sporting the prefix *Dukla* are picked from the army, those with the initials *RH* (*Rudá hvězda* – Red Star) are made up of full-time policemen (probably the most unpopular clubs in the country), and other initials are derived from various old state indus-

tries. The recent breakup of the country looks likely to cause a major shake-up in the national league. For the moment, however, Czech and Slovak teams will continue to play against each other.

ICE HOCKEY

Ice hockey runs football a close second as the most popular sport. It's not uncommon to see kids playing their own form of the game in the street, rather than kicking a football around. The national league is dominated by *Sparta Praha* but the Moravian army team *Dukla Jihlava* and *VSŽ Košice*, the East Slovak steelworkers' side, are equally well respected. Games are fast and physical, cold but compelling viewing, taking place on Tuesday and Friday at around 6pm. The season starts at the end of September and culminates in the annual World Championships, when the fortunes of the national side are subject to close scrutiny, especially if pitched against the Russians. A double victory against them in 1969 precipitated riots in towns across the country, culminating in the torching of the *Aeroflot* (Soviet Airlines) offices in Prague.

TENNIS AND OTHER SPORTS

Tennis was one of Czechoslovakia's most successful exports of the 1980s, although the country holds no major international events and its national Davis Cup team rarely gets anywhere. Martina Navrátilová, now nearing the end of her magnificent career, has been the most consistent Czech player on the circuit, although she became a naturalised American some years ago. On the men's side Ivan Lendl has been a towering figure in world tennis throughout the 1980s, even though a Wimbledon title has consistently eluded him. He too has had his day, and the country badly lacks a young generation of players to take their place in the world ranking. Any home-grown talent there is will be on display in the Czech/Slovak Open, held every August in Prague.

Table-tennis is taken very seriously in the Czech and Slovak republics, although the last time the country won the European Championships was back in the 1970s. **Motor sports** are also popular, particularly motocross and speedway, for which the country's two-stroke Jawas are justifiably famous. The Brno Motorcycle Grand Prix is on the world circuit and takes place every August, attracting thousands of leather-clad bikers from all over Europe.

SKIING AND ROCK CLIMBING

The Czechs and Slovaks may not produce any world-class skiers but with much of the country covered in a thick blanket of snow for three months of the year, **skiing** is a popular and necessary skill which most people learn at school. The main ski resorts are in Slovakia but there are also facilities in parts of Bohemia and Moravia. ČEDOK are the major agents for skiing holidays – see the "Getting There" sections for more details. If you go independently, you'll need to take your own equipment with you as renting it is difficult. Prices for the lifts are very low when compared with the West, but then poor facilities and long queues make up for it.

There are some great opportunities for **rock climbing** in Bohemia and Slovakia. North and east of Prague there are concentrated areas of limestone and basalt rocks: the most popular is the Český ráj, just 80km northeast of the Czech capital; equally good is the České Švýcarsko region, which borders with Saxony, or the Adršpach rocks near the Silesian border. In Slovakia, the Slovenský raj offers smaller-scale sandstone opportunities, whereas the Malá Fatra and the Tatras themselves are in a different league – higher altitudes and longer, more arduous climbs. You'll need to take your own equipment wherever you go, and take the usual precautions on all climbs.

TROUBLE AND THE POLICE

Despite their recent name change, the police force – the former Communist police (Veřejná bezpečnost or VB), now known simply as Policie/Polícia – are still extremely unpopular, certainly among the younger generation, and they know it. Their participation in the November 17 masakr destroyed what little credibility they had managed to hold on to over the last forty years of Communist control.

Public confidence in their competence has also suffered a severe blow due to the dramatic rise in the level of **crime** since 1989. The murder rate has quadrupled, and prostitution is rife in Prague and parts of North Bohemia. However, you shouldn't be unduly paranoid: the crime rate is still very low, especially when compared with other European or North American countries.

There are just two main types of police nowadays: the *Policie* and the municipal police. The *Policie/Polícia*, in khaki-green uniforms (hence their nickname – *žáby* or "frogs") with red lapels and a red band on their caps are the national force, with the power of arrest, and are under the control of the respective Ministries of Interior. They drive around in clapped-out green and white Škodas and Ladas. If you do need the police, though – and above all if you're reporting a serious crime – you should always go to the municipal police, run by the local authorities, and known as *Cerné šerií* (Black Sheriffs) because of their all-black uniforms.

In addition, there are various private police forces, most notably supplied by the American firm *Pinkertons*, employed mostly by hotels and banks, and they are often very officious, though in reality they are little more than glorified security guards. They are allowed to carry guns, but have no powers of arrest, and you are not legally obliged to show them your ID.

AVOIDING TROUBLE

Almost all the problems encountered by tourists in the Czech and Slovak republics are to do with **petty crime** – mostly from cars and hotel rooms – rather than more serious physical confrontations. Sensible precautions include making photocopies of your passport, and leaving passport and tickets in the hotel safe; and noting down travellers' cheque and credit card numbers. If you have a car, don't leave anything in view when you park it; take the radio with you if you can. Vehicles are rarely stolen, but luggage and valuables left in cars do make a tempting target and rental cars are easy to spot.

In theory, you're supposed to carry some form of **identification** at all times, and the police can stop you in the street and demand it. In practice, they're rarely bothered if you're clearly a foreigner (unless you're driving). In any case, the police are now so deferential that they tend to confine themselves to socially acceptable activities like traffic control and harassing Romanies.

If you are unlucky enough to have something stolen, you need to **go to the police** to report it, not least because your insurance company will require a police report. It's unlikely that there'll be anyone there who speaks English, and even less likely that your belongings will be retrieved but, at the very least, you should get a statement detailing what you've lost for your insurance claim. Try the phrase *pravě mi ukradl někdo* – "I have just been robbed".

DISABLED TRAVELLERS

In the past, very little attention was paid to the needs of the disabled anywhere in Czechoslovakia. Attitudes are slowly changing, but there is still a long way to go, and the chronic shortage of funds for almost anything is not helping matters.

ČEDOK claims to be able to arrange holidays suitable for the disabled, but most people's experiences have proved otherwise. A shortlist of organisations which should be able to provide some help and advice are listed in the box below.

Transport is a major problem, since buses and trams are virtually impossible for wheelchairs and trains are only slightly better (though there are special carriages designed to take wheelchairs on certain trains). At the time of writing, none of the car rental companies could offer vehicles with hand controls anywhere in the Czech and Slovak republics. If you're driving overland, most cross-Channel ferries now have adequate facilities, as do *British Airways* for those who are flying.

CONTACTS FOR DISABLED TRAVELLERS

Holiday Care Service 2 Old Bank Chambers, Station Rd, Horley, Surrey RH6 9HW (☎0293/774 535). *Information on all aspects of travel.*

Jewish Rehabilitation Hospital 3205 Place Alton Goldbloom, Québec H7V 1R2 (☎514/688-9550). *Guidebooks and travel information.*

Kéroul 4545 ave. Pierre de Coubertin, CP 1000, Montréal, Québec H1V 3R2 (☎512/252-3104). *Travel for mobility-impaired people.*

Metatur Štefanikova 48, Smíchov, Prague (☎55 10 64). *Only organisation in Prague which* campaigns for the disabled. English-speakers available, and can arrange trips in Czechoslovakia.

Mobility International USA PO Box 3551, Eugene, OR 97403 (☎503/343-1248). *Information, access guides, tours and exchange programmes.*

RADAR (*The Royal Association for Disability and Rehabilitation*) 25 Mortimer St, London W1N 8AB (☎071/637 5400). *Travel information.*

Travel Information Center Moss Rehabilitation Hospital, 1200 W. Tabor Rd, Philadelphia, PA 19141 (☎215/329-5715, x2233). *Access information.*

WOMEN AND SEXUAL HARASSMENT

Despite the sloganeering of the Communist regime, women are still treated as second-class citizens in the former Czechoslovakia, and not even a vaguely feminist women's

movement exists. Ironically, part of the reason for this is the adverse effect of the official campaigns for women's equality, which forced women to take jobs, usually at the bottom of the pay ladder. What women's organisations there are tend to focus on single issues such as the environment.

As far as **sexual harassment** is concerned, things are, if anything, marginally less intimidating than in western Europe, although without the familiar linguistic and cultural signs, it's easier to misinterpret situations. Attitudes in Prague are much more liberal than in most rural areas, where women travelling alone can still expect to encounter stares and comments. Single women should nonetheless avoid certain areas in Prague and the border towns of North Bohemia, where it will be assumed by many men that you are a prostitute. Hitchhiking is a risk, as it is anywhere, and although it's quite common to see Czech and Slovak women hitching, they at least have the advantage of a common language.

DIRECTORY

BOTTLES The republics have yet to become fully paid-up members of the throw-away culture and most drinks still come in bottles with a deposit on them. Shops and supermarkets will refund bottles bought elsewhere providing they stock the relevant type. Otherwise, there are now bottle banks scattered around most towns and cities.

CIGARETTES Loosely packed and lethal, their only virtue is their cheapness. The poseurs smoke the top of the domestic range, *sparta* – paradoxically named after the country's leading football team. The most popular brand is *petra*, while the cheapskates smoke *mars* or the filterless *start*. *Marlboro* lead the western brands, with *Peter Stuyvesant* running a close second – all at standard continental prices. Domestic rolling tobacco, and cigarette papers, are worth avoiding, especially now that *Duma* is fairly widely available. Matches are *sirky* or *zápalky*.

CONTRACEPTIVES Condoms (*preservativ*) are now available in most major cities from the machines marked *Men's Shop, Easy Shop* or some such euphemism. They're also on sale from pharmacies everywhere.

ELECTRICITY is the standard continental 220 volts AC: most European appliances should work as long as you have an adaptor for European-style two-pin round plugs. North Americans will need this plus a transformer.

FILM Western brands of colour film are now widely available. And n both republics, it's still very cheap and quick to get your black-and-white film developed and printed.

GAY AND LESBIAN Homosexuality isn't illegal in the former Czechoslovakia, though attitudes remain conservative. Prague is more relaxed but even here there's no great "scene" as such, with just a few bars and clubs that have become an established part of Prague nightlife (see p.121). Since 1989, an organisation for gays and lesbians has started up – *Lambda Praha*, c/o Jan Lány, Pod Kotlářkou 14, Smíchov, Prague. They publish a monthly paper called *Lambda*, and run a gay/lesbian helpline (evenings only; ☎57 73 88) usually with at least one English-speaker on call.

KIDS/BABIES Being a Catholic region, the attitude towards kids and babies is much more positive than in the UK and North America. Hotels and private landlords are generally very accommodating, but you'll rarely see any children in restaurants. Kids under five go free on trains; five- to twelve-year olds pay half-fare; public transport is free for under-tens. Disposable nappies are not widely available, nor is convenience food for babies. Some private landlords will baby-sit by prior arrangement.

LANGUAGE SCHOOLS A number of month-long beginners' courses are held regularly in Prague, Karlovy Vary, Brno, Olomouc and Bratislava. Average cost is £300/$500 for the month, which includes half-board and accommodation. For further details (and possible financial assistance) contact the British Council.

LAUNDRY Self-service launderettes don't exist, except in Prague. You can get clothes servicewashed or dry-cleaned in a couple of days at a *čistírna*.

LEFT LUGGAGE Most bus and train stations have lockers and/or a 24-hour left luggage office, which officially only take bags under 15kg. If your bag is very heavy, say *promiňte, je těšký* and offer to carry it yourself – *já to vezmu*. To work the lockers, find an open one, put the correct change in the slot on the inside of the door and set the code (choose a number you can easily remember and make a note of it), then shut the door and make a note of the locker number. To get the door open again, set the code on the outside and wait a few seconds before trying the door. The lockers are usually checked every night, and the contents of any still occupied are taken to the 24-hour left luggage office.

RACISM It is a sad fact that racism is a casual and common phenomenon and the half-million Romanies and much smaller Vietnamese communities bear the brunt of the nation's ignorance and prejudice. Another alarming development is the rise of right-wing extremism and the skinhead movement. There are now an estimated 2000 skinheads in Prague alone, and attacks on Romanies, Vietnamese and foreign black tourists are on the increase. Consequently, anyone even remotely dark-skinned can expect to arouse, at the very least, a great deal of curiosity.

TAMPONS Tampons (*tampóny*) and sanitary towels (*vložky*) are cheap and easy to get hold of, though if you're heading for the more remote areas, it's best to bring your own.

TIME The former Czechoslovakia is generally one hour ahead of Britain and nine hours ahead of EST, with the clocks going forward as late as May and back again some time in September – the exact date changes from year to year.

TOILETS Public toilets (*záchod* or *WC*) are few and far between. In most, you can buy toilet paper (by the sheet) from the attendant, whom you will usually have to pay as you enter, the amount depending on the purpose of your visit. It's generally acceptable to use the toilets in restaurants and hotels; another place worth trying are metro stations. Standards of hygiene are low.

METRIC WEIGHTS AND MEASURES

1 ounce = 28.3 grammes	1 inch = 2.54 centimetres (cm)
1 pound = 454 grammes	1 foot = 0.3 metres (m)
2.2 pounds = 1 kilogramme	1 yard = 0.91 m
1 pint = 0.47 litres	1.09 yards = 1m
1 quart = 0.94 litres	1 mile = 1.61 kilometres (km)
1 gallon = 3.78 litres	0.62 miles = 1km

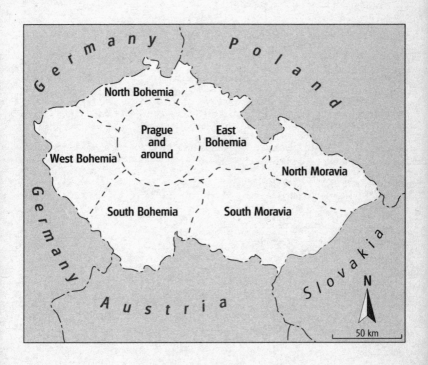

CHAPTER ONE

PRAGUE AND AROUND

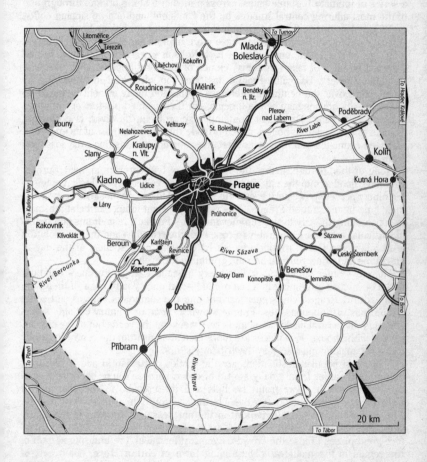

P rague is one of the least "Eastern" European cities you could imagine. Architecturally, and in terms of city sights, it is a revelation: few other cities, anywhere in Europe, look so good – and no other European capital can present six hundred years of architecture so completely untouched by natural disaster or war. Culturally, it is closer in many ways to Paris than Moscow, and after four decades of Soviet-imposed isolation the city is now keen to re-establish its position as the political and cultural centre of *Mitteleuropa*.

One of Prague's most appealing characteristics is that its artistic wealth is not hidden away inside grand museums and galleries, but displayed in the streets and squares. Its town-planning took place in medieval times, its palaces and churches were decorated with a rich mantle of Baroque, and the whole lot has escaped the vanities and excesses of postwar redevelopment. Prague's unique compactness allows you to walk from the grandeur of the city's castle district, via a series of intimate Baroque lanes, across a medieval stone bridge, through one of the most alluring central squares on the continent, and end up sipping coffee on Wenceslas Square, the modern hub of the city, in under half an hour.

That's not to say Prague doesn't have more than its fair share of problems. As long ago as the 1920s, one visitor – E. I. Robson – warned "you must not be deterred by piles of fallen masonry, clouds of dust and impenetrable forests of scaffolding poles". Basically, Prague has been too successful in preserving its architecture over the centuries: there are simply too many ancient buildings to maintain – its houses may be photogenic, but their painted plasterwork requires constant repainting. The major contemporary problem, however, is **pollution**. Thanks to the coal-fired boilers which provide the city with most of its energy, it has been estimated that Prague now receives one hour's sunshine a day less than it should.

None of this, though, deters the thousands of tourists from all over Europe, who have flooded into the city since the country's "Velvet Revolution". A staggering ninety percent of western visitors to what used to be Czechoslovakia spend all their time in and around Prague. This relatively recent influx can be an obstacle to appreciating the city in the summer months – Prague's restaurants and hotels in particular are failing miserably to cope with the crowds – and the best solution is to follow the Czech routine: rise early, eat your biggest meal of the day at lunchtime and drink yourself into the ground in the evening.

The city's outer suburbs look like every other in Eastern Europe – half-built high-rise estates swimming in a sea of mud – but once you're clear of them, the area **around Prague** shifts gear straight into the somnolent villages and softly rolling hills of Bohemia. Most Praguers own a *chata*, or country cottage, somewhere in these rural backwaters, and every weekend the roads out of the city are packed with Škodas. Few places are more than an hour from the centre by public transport, making most an easy day trip for visitors.

The most popular destinations are the castles of **Karlštejn** and **Konopiště**, though both suffer from a daily swarm of coach parties. You're better rewarded by heading north, away from the hills and the crowds, to the chateaux of **Veltrusy** and **Nelahozeves** (Dvořák's birthplace), or to the wine-town of **Mělník**. The wooded hills around **Křivoklát** in the northeast, or **Kokořín** in the southwest, both around 40km from Prague, are too far for most day-trippers, and therefore good places to lose the crowds. Even further afield, the undisputed gem of the region is the medieval silver-mining town of **Kutná Hora**, 60km east of Prague.

An historical background

The Czechs have a legend for every occasion and the founding of their capital **Prague** (Praha) is no exception. Some time in the seventh or eighth century AD the Czech prince, Krok, moved his people south from the plains of the river Labe (Elbe) to the rocky knoll that is now Vyšehrad (literally "high castle"). His youngest daughter, Libuše, a woman endowed with the gift of prophecy, fell into a trance one day and pronounced that they should build a city "whose glory will touch the stars", at the point in the forest where they found an old man constructing the threshold of his house. He was duly discovered on the Hradčany hill, overlooking the Vltava, and the city was named *Praha,* meaning threshold. Subsequently, Libuše was compelled to take a husband, a man called Přemysl (which means ploughman), allegedly the founder of the Přemyslid dynasty which ruled Bohemia until the fourteenth century.

So much for the legend. Historically, though, Hradčany and not Vyšehrad was where the first Slav settlers established themselves. The Vltava was relatively shallow at this point, and it probably seemed a safer bet than the plains of the Labe. The earliest recorded **Přemyslid** was Prince Bořivoj, the first Christian ruler of Prague, baptised in the ninth century by the Slav apostles Cyril and Methodius. It was his grandson, Prince Václav, who was to become the dynasty's most famous member – the Good "King" Wenceslas of the Christmas carol and the modern Czech patron saint.

Under the Přemyslids the city prospered, benefiting from its position on the central European trade routes. Merchants from all over Europe came to settle here, and in 1234 the first of Prague's historic towns, the Staré Město, was founded. In 1257, King Otakar II founded the Malá Strana on the slopes of the castle, as a separate quarter for Prague's German merchants, but he failed in his attempt to become Holy Roman Emperor and the Přemyslid dynasty died out in 1306. The crown was handed over by the Czech nobles to the Luxembourgs, and it was under Charles IV of Luxembourg, who did succeed in being elected Emperor, that Prague enjoyed its **golden age**. In just thirty years Charles transformed Prague into one of the most important cities in fourteenth-century Europe, establishing institutions and buildings that still survive today – a university, a cathedral, a host of monasteries and churches – and founding an entire new town, Nové Město, to accommodate the influx of students.

His son, Václav IV, was no match for such an inheritance, and the city was soon in crisis. Following the execution of the radical reformist preacher Jan Hus in 1415, the whole country became engulfed in **religious wars**, with Prague experiencing some of the most bitter struggles. Not until the Polish Jagiellonian dynasty succeeded to the throne later that century, was a degree of prosperity and religious tolerance restored. Surprisingly enough, it was a Habsburg, **Rudolf II**, who gave the city its second golden age, inviting artists (and alchemists) from all over Europe, and filling the castle galleries with the finest art.

However, trouble broke out again between the Protestant nobles and the Catholic Habsburgs in 1618, this time culminating in a decisive defeat for the Protestants at the Battle of Bílá hora (White Mountain), on the outskirts of the city. Then followed the period the Czechs refer to as the **dark ages**, when the full force of the Counter-Reformation was brought to bear on the city's people: Czechs were forced to conduct their affairs in German, and were persecuted for their religious beliefs. Paradoxically, though, the spurt of Baroque rebuilding during the Counter-Reformation lent Prague its most striking architectural aspect, and from this period date the majority of the city's impressive palaces.

The next two centuries saw Prague's importance gradually whittled away within the Habsburg Empire. Two things dragged it out of the doldrums. The first was the **industrial revolution** of the mid-nineteenth century, which brought large numbers of Czechs in from the countryside to work in the factories, and led the city to expand beyond its medieval boundaries for the first time.

The second was the Czech **národní obrození**, the contemporary national revival movement, which gave Prague a number of symbolically significant monuments, like its proud National Theatre. More importantly, the *národní obrození* led to the foundation of the **First Republic** in 1918, once again putting Prague at the centre of the country's political events. Architecturally, the city's position was consolidated too, as the inter-war period embellished Prague with a rich mantle of Bauhaus-style buildings.

After World War II, which it survived remarkably unscathed and industrially intact, Prague disappeared completely behind the Iron Curtain. Internal centralisation only increased the city's importance – it hosted the country's show trials, and at one time boasted the largest statue of Stalin in the world. The city briefly re-emerged on to the world stage during the cultural blossoming of the **Prague Spring** in 1968, but following the Soviet invasion, Prague vanished from view for another twenty-one years. However, there was one more upheaval to come. In November 1989, a peaceful student demonstration in Prague, brutally broken up by the police, triggered off the **Velvet Revolution** which eventually toppled the government. Today, the mood of optimism which followed the revolution has evaporated, as the price of the last forty years' economic mismanagement makes itself felt, but there is still a great sense of newfound potential in the capital. Paranoia and fear, at least, are things of the past and there's a new sense of openness here which makes any visit rewarding.

PRAGUE

With a population of just one and a quarter million, **Prague** is one of the smallest capital cities in Europe. It originally developed as four separate, self-governing towns and a walled ghetto, whose individual identities and medieval street plans have been preserved, more or less intact, to this day. Almost everything of any historical interest lies within these central districts, the majority of which are easy to master quickly on foot – only in the last hundred years has Prague spread beyond its ancient perimeter.

The city's most obvious orientational axis is the **River Vltava** (known as the Moldau in German), which divides the capital into two unequal halves. The steeply inclined left bank is dominated by **Hradčany**, which contains the most obvious sights – the castle itself, the cathedral, the royal palace and gardens, as well as a cluster of museums and galleries. Squeezed between the castle hill and the river, **Malá Strana** – around 150 acres of twisting cobbled streets and secret walled gardens – is home to some of the city's finest Baroque palaces.

Over the river, on the right bank, the city's twisting matrix of streets is at its most confusing in the original medieval hub of the city, **Staré Město** whose great showpiece is its main square, Staroměstské náměstí. Enclosed within the boundaries of Staré Město is the Jewish quarter, or **Josefov**, with six surviving synagogues and a medieval cemetery. **Nové Město**, whose wide boulevards make up the city's commercial and business centre – most famously Wenceslas Square – lies to the south and east of Staré Město. Further afield lie various **suburbs**, most of which were developed only in the last hundred years or so – the single exception being **Vyšehrad**, one of the original fortress settlements of the newly arrived Slavs in the last millennium.

Arrival and information

The major points of arrival are all fairly central, with the obvious exception of the airport, and from even the most obscure train and bus terminals there are fast city transport connections to the the centre.

By air

Prague's airport, **Ruzyně** (☎36 77 60 or 36 78 14), is 15km northwest of the city, and pretty unimpressive, with few of the high-tech facilities you'd expect from a European capital city's main point of entry. There are, however, 24-hour exchange facilities and, should you need them, accommodation agencies and car rental outlets. The airport is linked to the city by a regular, cheap and direct **bus service** (every 20–30min, 7.30am–7pm; journey time 10min), run by *ČSA*, which drops you at the *ČSA* offices on Revoluční, on the edge of Staré and Nové Město; to obtain a ticket simply pay the driver. There's a city bus connection, too: bus #119 (every 15–20min, 4.30am–11.30pm; journey time 20min), which ends its journey outside the Dejvická metro station at the end of metro line A. Alternatively, there are **taxis** which cost roughly 250kčs to Hradčany, or 350kčs to somewhere more central; make sure the driver turns on the meter, or, if in doubt, agree on a price before getting in.

When leaving, always allow plenty of time to **get to the airport**. Don't get off the city bus until the last stop – the first building saying *Praha letiště* (Prague Airport) is an outbuilding, and a good 2km from the international terminal. There's an airport restaurant in which to fritter away your surplus time and crowns, but the duty-free shop only takes fully convertible currencies.

By train

Arriving by **train** from the west, you're most likely to end up at the Art-Nouveau **Praha hlavní nádraží**, on the edge of Nové Město and Vinohrady. Downstairs in the modern part there are exchange and information offices (a branch of the

---

PRAGUE ADDRESSES

The wholesale **renaming of streets** has just about run its course in Prague, and although no indication is given as to the old name, most maps and street signs have now been changed, so there shouldn't be any confusion. In order to help locate addresses more easily, we have used the names of the city **districts** as they appear on street signs, for example Hradčany, Josefov etc. Prague's postal districts, which also appear on street signs, are too large to be much help in orientation, since the centre of town lies almost entirely within Prague 1.

In the old town, many houses have retained their original medieval **house signs**, a system that is still used today, though predominantly by *pivnice*, restaurants and *vinárna*, for example *U černého vola* (The Black Bull). In the 1770s, the Habsburgs, in their rationalising fashion, introduced a numerical system, with each house in the city entered onto a register according to a strict chronology, and later, the conventional system of progressive **street numbering** was introduced; so don't be surprised if seventeenth-century pubs like *U medvídků* (The Little Bears) have, in addition to a house sign, two numbers: in this case 345 and 7; the former Habsburg number written on a red background the latter modern number on blue.

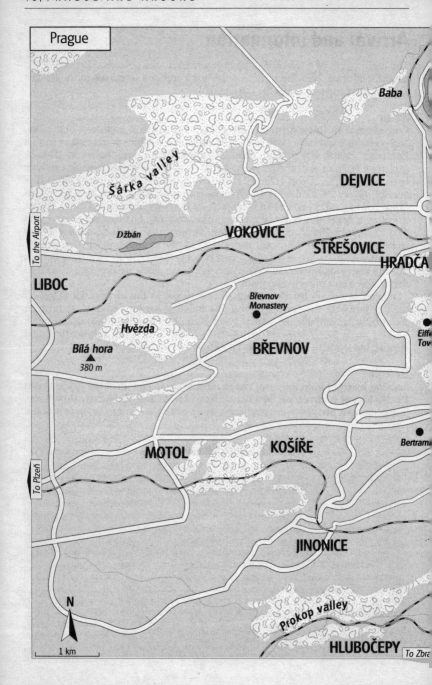

Prague

Baba

Šárka valley

DEJVICE

Džbán

VOKOVICE

STŘEŠOVICE

HRADČA

To the Airport

LIBOC

Břevnov
Monastery

Hvězda

Eiff
Tov

Bílá hora
380 m

BŘEVNOV

MOTOL

KOŠÍŘE

Bertram

To Plzeň

JINONICE

N

Prokop valley

1 km

HLUBOČEPY   To Zbr

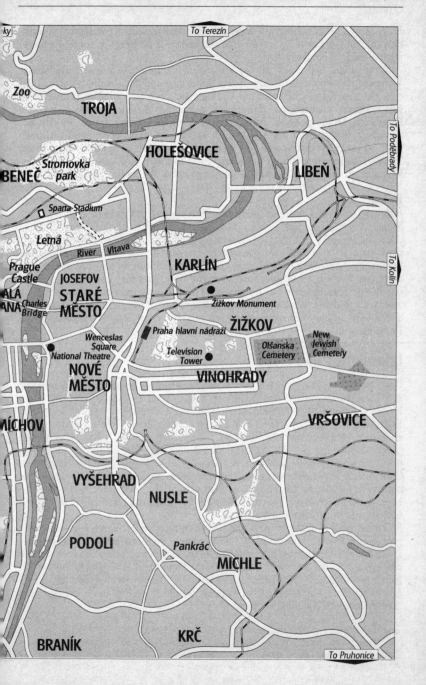

PIS), as well as a 24-hour left luggage office and various accommodation agencies. It's only a five-minute walk into the centre from here, or there's a metro station inside the railway station.

International expresses passing through from Berlin/Warsaw to Budapest/Vienna often stop only at **Praha-Holešovice**, in an industrial suburb north of the city centre, at the end of metro line C. Domestic trains may wind up at the central **Masarykovo nádraží** on Hybernská, a couple of blocks east of náměstí Republiky. Other possible arrival points for slow, *osobný* trains are **Praha-Smíchov** (trains from the southwest), served by metro Smíchovské nádraží; **Praha-Vysočany** (trains from the east) – take tram #3 to Masarykovo nádraží; **Praha Dejvice** (trains from the west), close to metro Hradčanská; and **Praha-Vršovice** (trains from the south) – take tram #24 to Wenceslas Square.

By bus

Prague's main bus terminal is **Praha-Florenc**, on the eastern edge of Nové Město (metro Florenc), where virtually all international and long-distance domestic services terminate. It's a seemingly chaotic place, and finding the right platform can be a real struggle. There are few tourist facilities, besides left luggage, but the main train station, Praha hlavní nádraží, is only one metro stop away (see above). For destinations around Prague, you may need to head out to one of the more obscure bus terminals, all of which are easy enough to reach by metro. To find out which one you want, ask at any of the *PIS* offices in town, or check the comprehensive (and extremely complicated) timetables at Praha-Florenc.

Information and maps

Once in Prague, the main tourist office is the **Prague Information Service** or *PIS* (*Pražská informační služba*), whose main branch is at Na příkopě 20, Nové Město (Mon–Fri 8am–7/8pm, Sat 8am–3.30pm). The staff speak at least four languages among them, including English, and will be able to answer most enquiries, except on the subject of accommodation (for which see "Accommodation", below). *PIS* also distributes some useful free publications, worth picking up while you're there: *The Month in Prague*, an English-language leaflet listing the major events, concerts and exhibitions; a separate broadsheet of cinema listings; and a fairly basic orientation map (they sell more comprehensive ones, too). There are additional offices in the main train station, Praha hlavní nádraží, and on Staroměstské náměstí.

Getting hold of a proper **map** of the city is a top priority. The one to buy is the *plán města* (currently sporting a yellow cover) produced by *Kartografie Praha* (24kčs), available at most information offices, kiosks and bookshops around the city – it marks all the tram, bus and metro lines. Details of **what's on** can be found in the quality English-language weekly, *Prague Post*, or the fortnightly *Prognosis*, aimed at a somewhat younger readership. For more on this, see "Entertainments", later in the chapter.

The phone code for Prague is ☎02

Getting Around

The centre of Prague, where most of the city's sights are concentrated, is reasonably small and best covered on foot. At some point, however, in order to cross the city quickly or reach some of the more widely dispersed attractions, you'll need to use the city's cheap and efficient public transport system, which comprises the metro and a network of trams and buses.

Tickets and passes

On all the city's public transport, a single **ticket** (*lístek*) currently costs 4kčs for an adult; 1kčs for those aged 10–16; under-10s travel free. Tickets, which are standard for all forms of public transport, must be bought beforehand either from one of the yellow ticket machines, found inside metro stations and at some bus and tram stops, or from a *tabák*, street kiosk or newsagent.

Except when changing lines on the metro, you must use a separate ticket each time you change tram or bus, punching it in one of the archaic little devices at hand. Buy as many tickets in advance as you think you'll need, to avoid the problem of hoarding change for the machines, or finding a machine that actually works. To avoid any hassle, and to save money, most Praguers buy monthly or quarterly **passes** (which is why you see so few of them punching tickets). If you're here for a few days, it's worth getting hold of a **tourist pass** (*turistická síťová jízdenka*), valid from one to five days and currently costing 30–80kčs; no photos or ID are needed. There's nothing to stop people from freeloading on the system, since there are no barriers. However, plain-clothes inspectors make spot checks and will issue an on-the-spot fine of 100kčs and upwards to anyone caught without a valid ticket or pass.

Metro

The futuristic Soviet-built **metro** is fast, smooth and ultra-clean, running daily from 5am to midnight with trains every two minutes during peak hours, slowing down to every six minutes by late in the evening. Its three lines (with a fourth planned) intersect at various points in the centre and the route plans are easy to follow – we've provided one on p.52. The stations are fairly discreetly marked above ground with the logo as on the map, in green (line A), yellow (line B) or red (line C). The constant bleeping at metro entrances is to enable blind people to locate the escalators.

In contrast to the trams and buses, you don't have to use a fresh ticket each time you change lines, though you must complete your journey within an hour (it would be difficult not to). Few people are in a hurry, though, and the escalators are a free-for-all, with no fast lane. Once inside the metro, it's worth knowing that *výstup* means exit and *přestup* means connection.

Trams and buses

The **tram** system, in operation since 1891, navigates Prague's hills and cobbles with remarkable dexterity – the present Škoda trams were designed in the 1950s, but are due to be replaced soon. After the metro, trams are the fastest and most efficient way of moving around, running every ten to twenty minutes throughout the day – check the timetables posted at every stop (*zastávka*), which list only the departures times from that specific stop.

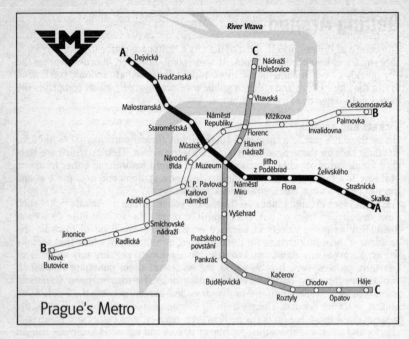

River Vltava

Prague's Metro

Some lines operate only during rush hour (Mon–Fri 5–8am & 1–3pm), while others run seven days a week (5am–midnight). Night trams (#51–58) run from 11.30pm to 4.30am, and all of them pass by Lazarská in Nové Město. Tram #22, which runs from Vinohrady to Hradčany, is a good way to get to grips with the lie of the land, and is a cheap method of sightseeing. On summer weekends, genuine vintage trams (#91 and #92) make special sightseeing journeys across the city's cobbles (though without commentary); tickets are a little bit more expensive and must be purchased on board.

You'll rarely need to use Prague's **buses**, which for the most part keep well out of the centre of town. If you're intent upon visiting some of the more obscure suburbs, though, you may need to use them: their hours of operation are similar to those of the trams, and route numbers are given in the text where appropriate.

Taxis, cars and bikes

Taxis, which come in all shapes and sizes, are cheap and plentiful. There's a minimum charge of 6kčs, and after that it's currently 8kčs or more per kilometre, depending on the time of day. Supply far exceeds demand at the moment, so competition is fierce. There are numerous taxi ranks in the centre of town, notably on Wenceslas Square, Národní and náměstí Republiky. **Cabs** can also be called on the following numbers: ☎35 03 20, ☎35 04 91, ☎20 29 51 and ☎20 39 41.

Tourists are seen as easy prey by some taxi drivers; if the meter isn't switched on, ask the driver to do so – *zapněte taxametr, prosím*; and if you suspect you've been overcharged, asking for a receipt – *prosím, dejte mi potrzení* – should have the desired effect. Watch out for cabs which display signs like *TAXL* or *FAXI* – as long as it isn't *TAXI*, they can legally set their own rates.

Driving in Prague really isn't a sensible option, since much of the city centre is pedestrianised, so parking is severely restricted (and fairly dear) in the historical quarters, and the one-way system is fiendishly difficult to master. If you want to rent a car to explore other parts of the country, try *Esucar*, Husitská 58, Žižkov (☎691 22 44), who rent out vehicles at a fraction of the cost of the major Western firms like *Avis*, Opletalova 33, Nové Město (☎22 23 24), or *Europcar*, Pařížská 26, Nové Město (☎231 02 78).

Facilities for **bike rental** are improving all the time in Prague, though with its cobbled streets and tramlines, it's not an ideal environment for cycling. However, if you're heading off into the countryside, try the following: *Cyklo Centrum*, 27–29 Karlovo náměstí, Nové Město; *Půjčovna kol*, Národní 38, Nové Město; or any number of outlets around Wenceslas Square and Staroměstské náměstí.

Accommodation

Prague's hotel problem is notorious. Not only are there still just 10,000 hotel beds in the city – many of them currently unavailable due to reconstruction work – but they are extremely expensive for what you get. As a result, most tourists now stay in private accommodation, easy enough to arrange either from abroad, or on arrival in Prague. There are several accommodation **agencies** at the airport, the main train station, and elsewhere in Prague (see overleaf for addresses).

Private accommodation

The (almost) endless supply of **private rooms** in Prague means it's not really necessary to book in advance – although it can be worth doing to save time, and for some peace of mind, especially if you're arriving in July or August, or late in the evening (see p.4 for list of relevant travel agencies). If you arrive without a room reservation, the easiest thing to do is head for one of the **booking offices** at the airport or main train station. If the queues are horrendous, as they can be in peak season, and it's not too late in the evening, then try one of the other agencies in town (see below for a list).

Alternatively, if you hang around at the station, airport or outside one of the agencies, you're almost certain to be approached by a tout. Most offers are genuine, but make sure you ask for a receipt before you pass over any money. In any case, you should always check exactly how far out of the centre you're going to be and how close to public transport (and preferably have a look at the room), before committing yourself.

Accommodation agencies

Agentura B & B, 28 října 9, Nové Město (☎26 82 20; daily 8/9am–6/7pm). Private rooms from 350kčs per person.

AVE Ltd, offices at the airport and the main train station (☎236 56 60; daily summer 6am–11pm, winter 6am–4pm). Private rooms from 350kčs upwards.

ČEDOK, Panská 5, Nové Město (☎212 71 11; April–Nov Mon–Fri 9am–10pm, Sat 8.30am–6pm, Sun 8.30am–4.30pm; Dec–March Mon–Fri 9am–8pm, Sat & Sun 8.30am–2pm). Deals with the top end of the hotel market only.

Hello Ltd, Gorkého náměstí 3, Nové Město (☎22 42 83; daily 9am–10pm). Hostels for 250kčs per person; private rooms from 350kčs; private apartments from 600kčs per person.

IFB, Václavské náměstí 38, Nové Město (☎26 03 33; Mon–Fri 9am–1pm & 2–6pm, Sat 9am–4pm). Private rooms from 500kčs per person, plus some hotels.

Pragotur, U Obecního domu 2, Staré Město (☎232 22 05; April–Oct Mon–Fri 8am–10pm, Sat 8am–8pm, Sun 8am–3pm; March, Nov & Dec Mon–Fri 8am–8pm, Sat 8am–6pm, Sun 8am–3pm; Jan Mon–Fri 8am–6pm; Feb Mon–Fri 8am–8pm, Sat 8am–6pm). Deals with the lower end of the hotel market and will also book private rooms from 350kčs per person.

Prague B & B Association, Rosa Luxemburgové 3, Smíchov (☎54 93 44). Private rooms from 300kčs, and apartments from 500kčs, plus a cheap summer hostel.

Toptour, Rybná 3, Staré Město (☎232 10 77; Mon–Fri 9am–8pm, Sat & Sun 10am–7pm). Private rooms from 500kčs per person, and self-contained apartments from 1000kčs a night.

Hotels

Hotels in Prague are expensive, and, with a few notable exceptions, nondescript. Nevertheless, since demand still far exceeds supply, they are booked up solid months in advance during the summer. So, unless you're here off-season, there's really no point in trekking around any of the hotels listed below on the off chance. Besides, Prague's cheaper hotels are scattered throughout the city, with virtually none in the older quarters of Hradčany, Malá Strana and Staré Město.

If you're determined to stay in a hotel, you'll need to book well in advance, especially during the high season (Easter to October, and the two weeks around Christmas and New Year). ČEDOK in London (see *Basics* for address) can do this for you, but their choice of hotels is limited, and prices start at around £40 for a double. ČEDOK in Prague has a wider selection, but still doesn't handle the bottom end of the market. As yet, the only method of ensuring a cheap hotel room is to contact the hotel yourself by letter, phone or fax – a time-consuming and often frustrating business.

Around náměstí Republiky

The hotels within spitting distance of náměstí Republiky tend to be fairly extortionate, with a much cheaper, run-down cluster just a couple of blocks east, near the Wilsonova flyover – where the Těšnov train station used to be.

Atlantic, Na poříčí 9, Nové Město (☎231 85 12). Modern, and therefore a cut above its neighbours in terms of both facilities and price. ⑥

■ ACCOMMODATION PRICES

The hotel lists below are divided according to area; within each section the lists are arranged alphabetically. After each entry you'll find a symbol which corresponds to one of seven **price categories**:

   ① Under 500kčs   ② 500–750kčs   ③ 750–1000kčs   ④ 1000–1500kčs

     ⑤ 1500–2000kčs   ⑥ 2000–3000kčs   ⑦ 3000kčs and upwards

All prices are for the cheapest **double room** available, which usually means without private bath or shower in the less expensive places. For a **single room**, expect to pay around two-thirds the price of a double.

Note that some of the hotels listed below are currently closed, undergoing extensive modernisation – others, at present open, will no doubt follow in the near future. This is bound to result in higher prices when they reopen; the prices quoted below should, therefore, be taken only as a guideline.

Axa, Na poříčí 40, Nové Město (☎232 72 34); metro Sokolovská. Just five minutes' walk from náměstí Republiky, and a favourite with young German tour groups. ②

Botel Albatros, nábřeží Ludvika Svobody, Nové Město (☎231 36 34). Double cabins for rent on a moored boat at the end of Revoluaní. Not quite as romantic or cheap as you might expect, but the best of the city's three floating "botels". ⑥

Central, Rybná 8, Staré Město (☎232 43 51). One of the very few hotels in Staré Město – no work of art, but true to its name and surprisingly cheap. ④

Hybernia, Hybernská 24, Nové Město (☎22 04 31). At the time of writing, as gloomy as ever, but no doubt soon to fall under the onslaught of the developers. ④

Merkur, Těšnov 9, Nové Město (☎231 68 40). Few mod cons here as yet, and so, for the moment, one of the few cheap central hotels in Prague. ③

Opera, Těšnov 13, Nové Město; ☎231 56 09. Moderately priced nineteenth-century hotel and remarkably pleasant considering it's right by the flyover. ④

Paříž, U Obecního domu 1, Staré Město (☎232 20 51). A mostly quite modern interior to this turn-of-the-century hotel, superbly located off náměstí Republiky and therefore over £100 double. ⑦

Ungelt, Štupartská 1, Staré Město (☎232 04 71). Unbelievably well positioned, exclusive little hotel in the backstreets of the old town, but over £100 double since its recent modernisation. ⑦

Around Wenceslas Square

There's no question that these hotels are right in the centre of things, though it's worth bearing in mind that Wenceslas Square (Václavské náměstí) doubles as Prague's red-light district and nightclub zone by night.

Evropa, Václavské náměstí 25 (☎236 52 74). Without doubt, the most beautiful hotel in Prague, sumptuously decorated in Art Nouveau style (except for the rooms themselves). Surprisingly, it's not the most expensive, but it's incredibly difficult to get a room here, since ČEDOK don't deal with them and they claim not to take bookings more than fourteen days in advance – and yet they're always full. ⑥

Juliš, Václavské náměstí 22 (☎235 28 85). Tired-looking 1930s functionalist hotel, halfway down Wenceslas Square, which was known as the *Tatran* under the Communists and has only recently reverted to its original name. ④

Southern Nové Město

Only a metro stop or two from the centre of things, though in parts blighted by heavy traffic flow.

Morát, Václavská 5 (☎29 42 51); metro Karlovo náměstí. A very basic place just off Karlovo náměstí , with few facilities – and therefore a prime candidate for reconstruction. ③

Hlavkova, Jenytynská 1 (☎29 21 39). Spartan but clean hotel one block south of Resslova. Large breakfast included in price of room. ④

Koruna, Opatovická 16 (☎29 39 33). Hidden in the backstreets three blocks south of Národní. ④

The suburbs

All the hotels listed below are out of the main historical centre, but no more than twenty minutes away by public transport.

Juventus, Blanická 10, Vinohrady (☎25 51 51); metro náměstí Míru. One of the few cheap Vinohrady haunts still functioning at the time of going to press. ②

Libeň, Rudé armády 37, Libeň (☎82 82 27); metro Palmovka. Not your usual tourist locale, but very convenient for Prague's Hare Krishna restaurant (see p.119). ②

Zotavovna, Sokolovská, Karlín; metro Invalidovna. Within minutes of the centre of town by metro; must be booked through *Pragotur*. ④

Moravan, U Uranie 22, Holešovice (☎80 29 05); metro Nádraží Holešovice. Not a jolly part of town, but within easy reach of the Stromovka park. ②

International, Podbaba, Dejvice (☎331 91 11); tram #20 or #25. Classic, pompous 1950s Stalinist hotel with plenty of dour social realist friezes and large helpings of marble – go now, before they modernise it. ⑥

Balkán, Svornosti 28, Smíchov (☎54 07 77); metro Anděl. One of the cheapest functioning hotels in Prague; recently privatised but still reassuringly run-down. ②

U Blaženký, U Blaženký 1 (☎53 82 66); metro Anděl. Nice hilltop location, just up from the Mozart Museum, and with a good cheap restaurant. ④

Hostels

Prague has very few **hostels**, official (*IYHF*) or otherwise. Those that do exist generally cost about two-thirds the price of a private room – around 250kčs a night – though one or two are very cheap. All hostels are heavily oversubscribed during the summer, so phone ahead where possible to save a fruitless journey; none of them requires a membership card. To find out the latest on the Prague hostel and dorm scene, go to the *CKM* agency at Žitná 9, Nové Město (☎236 27 98; Mon–Sat 8am–6pm).

Děkanka, Děkanská vinice I #5, Pankrác (☎643 19 06); open mid-June–mid-Sept; metro Pankrác. Rock-bottom price for a "cot" on a gym floor – run by *Prague B & B Association* (see "Accommodation Agencies" on p.53).

Dukla Karlín, Malého 1, Karlín (☎22 20 09); metro Florenc. Situated in the insalubrious locale of the Praha-Florenc bus station. Reception opens at 6pm and you'll be turfed out at 8am the next morning – a definite last resort.

Hotel Praha, Žitná 42, Nové Město; metro Karlovo náměstí. Billed as "the cheapest hotel in Prague", this place charged just 50kčs for a camp bed on a gym floor in the summer of 1991. Open July & Aug only; reception 6–11am & 5–11pm.

Juniorhotel "B & B", Jankovcova 163, Holešovice; metro Nádraží Holešovice. Private youth hostel in a sort of scout hut by the river Vltava – sounds scenic but isn't. Dorm beds 250kčs.

Ubytovna Raketa, Havlíčkova 2, Nové Město. A cheap dorm-style hostel near náměstí Republiky.

Na Vlachovce, Rudé armády 217, Kobylisy; tram #5, #17 or #25; open May–Sept. Cheap two-sleeper giant beer barrels – heaven or hell depending on your tastes.

Campsites

Prague abounds in **campsites** and most are relatively easy to get to by public transport. Facilities, on the whole, are rudimentary and badly maintained, but the prices reflect this. Note that most Prague campsites close down from the end of October to the end of March.

Troja, Trojská 157, Troja (☎84 28 33); bus #112 roughly hourly, or tram #5, #17 or #25 then a short walk, from metro Nádraží Holešovice; open mid-April to Sept. Good location, 3km north of the city centre, on the road to the Troja chateau. In addition to this official site, a whole series of campsites have sprung up on Trojská, ranging from people's back gardens to just two properly equipped sites.

Aritma Džbán, Nad lávkou 3, Vokovice (☎36 85 51); tram #20 or #26 from metro Dejvická; open all year. 4km west of the centre, near the Šárka valley. Tent camping only.

Kotva Braník, U ledáren 55, Braník (☎46 13 97); tram #3 or #17 along the right bank of the Vltava; open April–Oct. 6km south of the city.

Caravancamp Motol, Plzeňská, Motol (☎52 47 14); tram #4, #7 or #9 from metro Anděl; open April–Sept. 5km west of the city centre.

Hradčany

HRADČANY's raison d'être is its castle, or **Hrad**, built on the site of one of the original hill settlements of the Slav tribes who migrated here in the seventh or eighth century AD. The Přemyslid prince, Bořivoj I, erected the first castle here sometime in the late ninth century, and since then, whoever occupied the Hrad has exercised authority over the Czech Lands. Consequently, unlike the city's other districts, Hradčany has never had a real identity of its own – it became a royal town only in 1598 – existing instead as a mere appendage, its inhabitants serving and working for their masters in the Hrad. The same is still true now. For although the odd café or *pivnice* survives in amongst the palaces (and even in the Hrad itself), there's very little real life here beyond the stream of tourists who trek through the castle and the civil servants who work either for the president or in the multifarious ministries whose departmental tentacles spread right across Hradčany.

Stretched out along a high spur above the River Vltava, Hradčany shows a suitable disdain for the public transport system. There's a choice of **approaches** from Malá Strana, all of which involve at least some walking. From Malostranská metro station, most people take the steep short cut up the Staré zámecky schody, but there are more opportunities for stopping and admiring the view along the stately Zámecké schody, which leaves you gasping at the castle gates. The alternative to all this climbing is to take tram #18 or #22 from Malostranská metro, which tackle the hairpin bends of Chotkova with ease, and deposit you either outside the Royal Gardens to the north of the Hrad, or if you prefer, outside the gates of the Strahov monastéry, at the faŕ western edge of Hradčany.

Prague Castle (Pražský hrad)

Unless otherwise stated, the opening hours for sights within Prague Castle are April–Oct Tues–Sun 9am–5pm; Nov–March Tues–Sun 9am–4pm; you have to buy a separate entry ticket for each one. Entry to St Vitus Cathedral is free; the castle courtyards and streets are open until late in the evening. There's an information office on the north of the cathedral at Vikářská 37 (opening hours as above), and a post office in the third courtyard, open daily 8am–8pm.

Viewed from the Charles Bridge, **Prague Castle** (popularly known as "the Hrad") stands aloof from the rest of the city, protected not by bastions and castellated towers, but by its palatial Neoclassical facade – an "immense unbroken sheer blank wall", as Hilaire Belloc described it – breached only by the great mass of St Vitus Cathedral. It's *the* picture-postcard image of Prague, though for the Czechs the castle has been an object of disdain as much as admiration, its alternating fortunes mirroring the shifts in the nation's history. The golden age and the dark ages, Masaryk's liberalism and Gottwald's terror – all of these emanated from the Hrad. When the first posters appeared in December 1989 demanding "*HAVEL NA HRAD*" (Havel to the Castle), they weren't asking for his reincarceration. Havel's occupancy of the Hrad was the sign that the reins of government had finally been wrested from the Communist regime.

This site has been successively built on since the first castle was erected here in the ninth century, but two **architects** in particular bear responsibility for the present outward appearance of the Hrad. The first is **Nicolo Pacassi**, court archi-

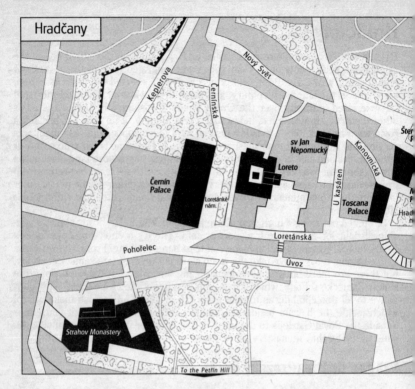

tect to the Empress Maria Theresa, whose austere restorations went hand in hand with the deliberate run down of the Hrad until it was little more than an administrative barracks. For the Czechs, his grey-green eighteenth-century cover-up, which hides a variety of much older buildings, is unforgivable. Less apparent, though no less controversial, is the hand of **Josip Plečnik**, the quirky Slovene architect who was commissioned by T. G. Masaryk, president of the newly founded Czechoslovak Republic, to restore and modernise the castle in the 1920s.

The first and second courtyards

The **first courtyard** (první nádvoří), which opens on to Hradčanské náměstí, is guarded by Ignaz Platzer's *Battling Titans* – two gargantuan figures, one on either gate pier, wielding club and dagger and about to inflict fatal blows on their respective victims. Below them stand a couple of impassive presidential sentries, no longer kitted out in the paramilitary khaki of the last regime, but sporting new blue uniforms that deliberately recall those of the First Republic. They were designed by the Oscar-winning costume designer for Miloš Forman's film *Amadeus*, and chosen by Havel himself. The hourly **changing of the guard** is a fairly subdued affair, but every Sunday at noon there's a much more elaborate parade, accompanied by a brass ensemble which appears at the first-floor windows to play local rock star Michal Kocáb's slightly comical, gentle modern fanfare.

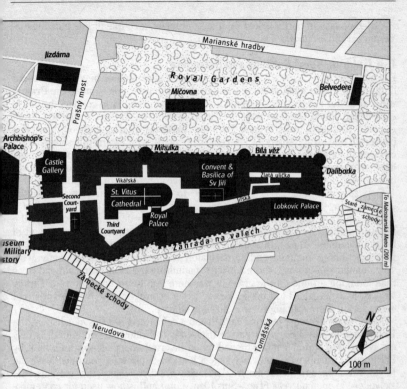

To reach the **second courtyard** (druhé nádvoří), you must pass through the early Baroque Matthias Gate, originally a freestanding triumphal arch, now set into one of Pacassi's blank walls. Grand stairways on either side lead to the presidential apartments in the south wing, and to the **Spanish Hall** (Španělský sál) and **Rudolf Gallery** (Rudofova galerie) in the north wing – two of the most stunning rooms in the entire complex, sadly used only for state occasions (and, of course, the filming of *Amadeus*). Once you've entered the rectangular courtyard, there's no escape from the monotonous onslaught of Pacassi's plastering and the smooth granite paving added in the 1960s. It's an unwelcoming and impersonal space, relieved only by Anselmo Lurago's Chapel of the Holy Cross, which cowers in one corner. Its richly painted interior used to house the treasury (klenotnice), a macabre selection of medieval reliquaries, but recently it's been rather brutally converted into a dull private gallery.

In the north wing, the **Castle Gallery** (Obrazárna Pražského hradu; Tues–Sun 10am–6pm) occupies what were once the royal stables and contains European paintings from the sixteenth to the eighteenth centuries. The collection was begun by Rudolf II, the Habsburgs' most avid art collector but, sadly, the best of what he amassed was either taken as booty by the marauding Saxons and Swedes, or sold off by Rudolf's successors – a fact which explains the bizarre inclusion of photographs of much better paintings from other European galleries. The best of what's left includes *The Assembly of the Olympian Gods*, a vast, crowded canvas of portly naked figures by Rubens, a couple of fine paintings by Veronese, and a *Flagellation* by Tintoretto.

The Jízdárna, Royal Gardens and Belvedere

From the second courtyard, it's worth making a short detour beyond the official limits of the castle walls. Passing through the north gate, you come to the **Prašný most** (Powder Bridge), first erected in the sixteenth century to connect the newly established Royal Gardens with the Hrad. Beyond the bridge, to the left, Jean-Baptiste Mathey's plain French Baroque **Jízdárna** (Riding School) has been converted into an art gallery (Tues–Sun 10am–6pm), which currently serves as the city's main exhibition space for twentieth-century Czech art. The temporary installations are consistently impressive, but any hopes of a permanent collection will have to wait until the new premises in Holešovice are complete (see p.111).

Opposite the Jízdárna is the entrance to the **Royal Gardens** (Královská zahrada; May–Sept only), founded by Emperor Ferdinand I on the site of a former vineyard. Burned down by the Saxons and Swedes, and blown up by the Prussians, the gardens were only saved from French attack by the payment of thirty pineapples. Today, this is one of the best-kept gardens in the capital, with fully functioning fountains and immaculately cropped lawns. Consequently, it's a very popular spot, though more a place for admiring the azaleas and almond trees than lounging around on the grass. It was here that tulips brought from Turkey were first acclimatised to Europe, before being exported to the Netherlands, and every spring there's an impressive, disciplined crop.

At the end of the gardens is Prague's most celebrated Renaissance legacy, the **Belvedere** or Royal Summer Palace (Belvedér or Královské letohrádek), a delicately arcaded summerhouse topped by an inverted copper ship's hull, built by Ferdinand I for his wife, Anne; to inspect it at close quarters, you must leave the Royal Gardens and head down Mariánské hradby. Unlike the gardens, the Belvedere is open all year (Tues–Sun 10am–6pm) and is now used for contemporary exhibitions, the artists chosen by the president. At the centre of the palace's miniature formal garden is the **Singing Fountain** (Zpívající fontána), built shortly after the palace, and named for the musical sound of the drops of water falling in the metal bowls below. From the garden terrace, you can enjoy an unrivalled view of Prague Castle's finest treasure – the cathedral.

St Vitus Cathedral

St Vitus Cathedral (katedrála svatého Víta) takes up so much of the third courtyard that it's difficult to get an overall impression of this chaotic Gothic edifice. Its asymmetrical appearance is the product of a long and chequered history, for although the foundation stone was laid in 1344, the cathedral was not completed until 1929 – exactly one thousand years after the foundation of the first church within the Hrad.

The inspiration for the medieval cathedral came from Charles IV, who, while still only heir to the throne, had not only wangled an independent archbishopric for Prague, but had also managed to gather together the relics of Saint Vitus. Impressed by the cathedral at Narbonne, in 1344 Charles commissioned the Frenchman **Matthias of Arras** to start work on a similar structure. Matthias died in 1352, with the cathedral barely started, and Charles summoned **Peter Parler**, a precocious 23-year-old from a family of great German masons, to continue the work. For the next 46 years, Parler imprinted his slightly flashier, more inventive

SonderGotik (Unusual Gothic) style on the city, but the cathedral got no further than the construction of the choir and the south transept before his death in 1399.

Little significant work was carried out during the next four centuries and the half-built cathedral became a symbol of the Czechs' frustrated aspirations of nationhood. Not until the Czech national revival or *národní obrození* of the nineteenth century did building begin again in earnest, with the foundation, in 1861, of the **Union for the Completion of the Cathedral**. A succession of architects, including Josef Mocker and Kamil Hilbert, oversaw the completion of the entire west end, and, with the help of countless other Czech artists and sculptors, the building was transformed into a treasure-house of Czech art. The cathedral was finally given an official opening ceremony in 1929, though work, in fact, continued right up to World War II.

The sooty Prague air has made it hard now to differentiate between the two building periods. Close inspection, however, reveals that the **western facade**, including the twin spires, is the rigorous if unimaginative work of the neo-Gothic restorers (their besuited portraits can be found below the rose window), while the eastern section – best viewed from the Belvedere – shows the building's authentic Gothic roots. The south door or **Zlatá brána** (Golden Gate), decorated with a heavily restored fourteenth-century mosaic of the Last Judgement, is also pure Parler. Oddly then, it's above the south door that the cathedral's tallest steeple reveals the most conspicuous stylistic join: Pacassi's Baroque topping resting absurdly on a Renaissance parapet of light stone, which is itself glued onto the blackened body of the original Gothic tower.

THE INTERIOR

The cathedral is the country's largest church and once inside, it's difficult not to be impressed by the sheer height of the nave. Of the 22 side chapels, the grand **Chapel of sv Václav** (St Wenceslas, patron saint of Bohemia), by the south door, is easily the main attraction. Although officially dedicated to Saint Vitus, spiritually the cathedral belongs as much to the Přemyslid prince, Václav (of "Good King" fame, see box below), who was killed by his pagan brother, Boleslav the Cruel. Ten years later, in 939, Boleslav repented, converted, and apparently transferred his brother's remains to this very spot. Charles, who was keen to promote the cult of Wenceslas in order to cement his own Luxembourgeois dynasty's rather tenuous claim to the Bohemian throne, had Peter Parler build the present chapel on top of the original grave; the lion's head **door-ring** set into the north door is said to be the one to which Václav clung before being killed. The chapel's rich, almost Byzantine decoration is like the inside of a jewel casket: the gilded walls are inlaid with over 1372 semiprecious Bohemian stones (corresponding to the year of its creation), set around ethereal fourteenth-century frescoes of the *New Heavenly Jerusalem*, while the tragedy of Wenceslas unfolds above in the later paintings of the Litoměřice school.

Though a dazzling testament to the golden age of of Charles IV's reign, it's not just the chapel's artistic merit which draws visitors. A door in the south wall gives access to a staircase leading to the coronation chamber (only rarely open to the public) which houses the **Bohemian crown jewels**, including the gold crown of Saint Wenceslas, studded with some of the largest sapphires in the world. The door is secured by seven different locks, the keys kept by seven different people, starting with the president himself – like the seven seals of the holy scroll from The Book Of Revelation.

The perfect Baroque answer to the medieval chapel of sv Václav is the **Tomb of St John of Nepomuk**, plonked in the middle of the ambulatory in 1736. It's a work of grotesque excess, designed by Fischer von Erlach's son, and sculpted entirely in silver with free-flying angels holding up the heavy drapery of the balda-chin. Where Charles sought to promote Wenceslas as the nation's preferred saint, the Jesuits, with Habsburg backing, replaced him with the Czech martyr, John of Nepomuk (Jan Nepomucký), who had been arrested, tortured, and then thrown – bound and gagged – off the Charles Bridge in 1393 on the orders of Václav IV, allegedly for refusing to divulge the secrets of the queen's confession. A cluster of stars was said to have appeared over the spot where he drowned, hence the halo of stars on every subsequent portrayal of the saint.

The Jesuits, in their efforts to get him canonised, exhumed his corpse and produced what they claimed to be his living tongue (it was in fact his very dead brain). In 1729, he duly became a saint, and, on the lid of the tomb, back-to-back with the martyr himself, a cherub points to his severed tongue, sadly no longer the "real" thing. The true reason for John of Nepomuk's death was simply that he was caught up in a dispute between the archbishop and the king over the appoint-ment of the abbot of Kladruby, and backed the wrong side. The Vatican finally admitted this in 1961, some 232 years after his canonisation.

At the centre of the choir, within a fine Renaissance grill, cherubs irreverently lark about on the sixteenth-century marble **Imperial Mausoleum**, commis-sioned by Rudolf II and containing his grandfather Ferdinand I, his Polish grand-mother, and his father Maximilian II, the first Habsburgs to wear the Bohemian crown. Rudolf himself rests beneath them, in one of the two pewter coffins in the somewhat cramped **Royal Crypt** (the entrance is beside the Royal Oratory; there's a small entry charge). A good number of other Czech kings and queens are buried here, too, reinterred this century in incongruously modern 1930s sarcophagi, among them the Hussite King George of Poděbrady, Charles IV and, sharing a single sarcophagus, all four of his wives.

Of the later additions to the church, the most striking is František Bílek's **wooden crucifix**, on the north side of the transept, which breaks free of the neo-Gothic strictures that hamper other contemporary works inside. Also worth some

GOOD KING WENCESLAS

As it turns out, there's very little substance to the story related in the nineteenth-century Christmas carol, *Good King Wenceslas*, by J. M. Neale. For a start, **Václav** was only a duke, and never a king (though he did become a saint); the St Agnes fountain, by which "yonder peasant dwelt" wasn't built until the thirteenth century; in fact, he wasn't even that "good", except in comparison with the rest of his family.

Born in 907, Václav inherited his title at the tender age of thirteen. His Christian grandmother, Ludmilla, was appointed regent in preference to Dragomíra, his pagan mother, who murdered Ludmilla in a fit of jealousy the following year. On coming of age in 925, Václav became duke in his own right, and took a vow of celi-bacy, intent on promoting Christianity throughout the dukedom. Even so, the local Christians didn't take to him, and when he began making conciliatory overtures to the neighbouring Germans, they persuaded his pagan younger brother, Boleslav the Cruel, to do away with him. On December 28, 929, two days after the Feast of Stephen, Václav was stabbed to death by Boleslav at the entrance to a church just outside Prague.

attention are the cathedral's modern **stained-glass** windows. Beautiful though their effect is, it's entirely out of keeping with Parler's original concept of almost exclusively clear glass windows. The most unusual windows are those by František Kysela, which look as though they have been shattered into hundreds of tiny pieces, a technique used to greatest effect in the rose window over the west door with its kaleidoscopic *Creation of the World* (1921). In keeping with its secular nature, two of the works from the time of the First Republic were paid for by financial institutions: the *Cyril and Methodius* window, in the third chapel in the north wall, was commissioned from Alfons Mucha by the *Banka Slavie*; while on the opposite side of the nave, the window on the theme *Those Who Sow in Tears Shall Reap in Joy* was funded by a Prague insurance company.

The Royal Palace

Across the third courtyard from the cathedral's south door, the **Royal Palace** (Královský palác) was home to the princes and kings of Bohemia from the eleventh to the sixteenth centuries. It's a sandwich of royal apartments, built one on top of the other by successive generations, but left largely unfurnished and unused for the last three hundred years. The original Romanesque palace of Soběslav I now forms the cellars of the present building, above which Charles IV built his own Gothic chambers; these days you enter at the third and top floor, built at the end of the fifteenth century.

Immediately past the antechamber (now the ticket office) is the bare expanse of the massive **Vladislav Hall** (Vladislavský sál), the work of Benedikt Ried, the German mason appointed by Vladislav Jagiello as court architect. It displays some remarkable, sweeping rib-vaulting which forms floral patterns on the ceiling, its petals reaching almost to the floor. It was here that the early Bohemian kings were elected, and since Masaryk in 1918 every president has been sworn into office in the hall. In medieval times, the hall was also used for banquets and jousting tournaments, which explains the ramp-like **Riders' Staircase** in the north wing.

From the southwest corner of the hall, you can gain access to the Ludvík Wing. The rooms themselves are pretty uninspiring but the furthest one, the **Bohemian Chancellery**, was the scene of Prague's **second defenestration** (see p.101 for details of the first). After almost two centuries of uneasy coexistence between Catholics and Protestants, matters came to a head over the succession to the throne of the Habsburg archduke Ferdinand, a notoriously intolerant Catholic. On May 23, 1618, a posse of over one hundred Protestant nobles, led by Count Thurn, marched to the Chancellery for a showdown with Jaroslav Martinic and Wilhelm Slavata, the two Catholic governors appointed by Ferdinand I. After a "stormy discussion", the two councillors (and their personal secretary, Philipp Fabricius) were thrown out of the window. As a contemporary historian recounted: "No mercy was granted them and they were both thrown dressed in their cloaks with their rapiers and decoration head-first out of the western window into a moat beneath the palace. They loudly screamed "*ach, ach, oweh!*" and attempted to hold on to the narrow window-ledge, but Thurn beat their knuckles with the hilt of his sword until they were both obliged to let go." There's some controversy about the exact window from which they were ejected, although it's generally agreed that they survived to tell the tale, landing in a medieval dung heap below, and – so the story goes – precipitating the Thirty Years' War.

The rooms up the stairwell to the left of the Riders' Staircase are bare and basically rather dull. Head instead down the Riders' Staircase to the **Gothic and Romanesque chambers** of the palace, equally bare, but containing a couple of interesting models showing the castle at various stages in its development, plus copies of the busts by Peter Parler's workshop, including the architect's remarkable self-portrait; the originals are hidden from view in the triforium of the cathedral.

The Basilica and Convent of sv Jiří

The only exit from the Royal Palace is via the Riders' Staircase, which deposits you in Jiřské náměstí. Don't be fooled by the uninspiring red Baroque facade of the **Basilica of sv Jiří** (St George) which dominates the square; inside is Prague's most beautiful Romanesque building, meticulously scrubbed clean and restored to recreate something like the honey-coloured stone basilica that replaced the original tenth-century church in 1173. The double staircase to the chancel is a remarkably harmonious late Baroque addition and now provides a perfect stage for chamber music concerts. The choir vault contains a rare Romanesque painting of the *New Heavenly Jerusalem*, while to the right of the chancel, only partially visible, are thirteenth-century frescoes of the **burial chapel of sv Ludmila** (St Ludmilla), grandmother of Saint Wenceslas, who was killed by her own daughter in 921 (see box above), thus becoming Bohemia's first Christian martyr and saint.

Next door is Bohemia's first monastery, the **Convent of sv Jiří**, founded in 973 by Mlada, sister of the Přemyslid prince Boleslav the Pious, who became its first abbess. Like most of the country's religious institutions, it was closed down and turned into a barracks by Joseph II in 1782, and now houses the National Gallery's **Old Bohemian Art Collection** (Tues–Sun 10am–6pm). The exhibition is arranged chronologically, starting in the crypt with a remarkable collection of Gothic art, which first flourished here under the patronage of Charles IV.

The **earliest works** are almost exclusively symbolical depictions of the Madonna and Child, the artists known only by their works and locations, not by name. The first named artist is **Master Theodoric**, who painted over 100 panels for Charles IV's castle at Karlštejn (see p.139); just six are on display here, their larger-than-life portraits overflowing onto the edges of the panels.

On the next floor, the first work is the tympanum from the Týn church (see p.80) – originally coloured and gilded – by Peter Parler's workshop, whose mastery of composition and depth heralded a new stage in the development of Bohemian art. The following room contains mostly paintings by the **Master of Třeboň**, whose work shows even greater variety of balance and depth, moving ever closer to outright portraiture. The last room on this floor is devoted to a series of superb woodcuts by **Master I P**.

The transition from this to the next floor, where you are immediately thrown into the overtly sensual and erotic **Mannerist paintings** of Rudolf II's reign, comes as something of a shock. Soon, however, the restraining influence of Baroque is felt, and the collection begins to wane under the sheer volume and mediocrity of the likes of Bohemia's Karel Skréta and Petr Brandl, whose paintings and sculptures fill chapels and churches across the Czech Lands. Aside from the works of Jan Kupecký and the statues of Matthias Bernhard Braun, this might well be the moment to head for the gallery's little coffee bar on the ground floor.

Zlatá ulička and the Lobkovic Palace

Around the corner from the convent is the **Zlatá ulička** (Golden Lane), a blind
alley of miniature sixteenth-century cottages in dolly-mixture colours, built for
the 24 members of Rudolf II's castle guard, though the lane takes its name from
the goldsmiths who followed (and modified the buildings) a century later. By the
nineteenth century, this had become a kind of palace slum, attracting artists and
craftsmen, its two most famous inhabitants being Jaroslav Seifert, the Nobel
prize-winning Czech poet, and Franz Kafka. Kafka's youngest sister, Ottla, rented
no. 22, and during a creative period in the winter of 1916 he came here in the
evenings to write short stories. Finally, in 1951, the Communists kicked out the
remaining residents and turned most of the houses into souvenir shops for
tourists.

The tower at the far end of the lane, **Daliborka** (April–Oct 9am–5pm), is dedicated to its first prisoner, the young Czech noble, Dalibor, accused of supporting
a peasants' revolt at the beginning of the fifteenth century. According to Prague
legend, he learnt to play the violin while imprisoned here, and his playing could
be heard all over the castle – a tale that provided material for Smetana's opera,
Dalibor. If you're keen to see the inside of one of the castle towers, you'll have to
backtrack to **Mihulka**, the tower just off Vikářská, which runs along the north
side of the cathedral, famous as the place where Rudolf's team of alchemists were
put to work trying to discover the philosopher's stone.

THE LOBKOVIC PALACE

If your grounding in Czech history is still a bit sketchy, the hotchpotch historical
collection in the **Lobkovic Palace** (Tues–Sun 9am–5pm), towards the bottom of
Jiřská, is a good introduction to the subject. The exhibition actually begins on the
top floor, but by no means do all the objects on display deserve attention. The
prize exhibits are the copies of the Bohemian crown jewels (the originals are
hidden away above the Chapel of sv Václav in the cathedral), an interesting
sixteenth-century carving of *The Last Supper*, originally an altarpiece from the
Bethlehem Chapel, and the sword of the famous Prague executioner, Jan Mydlář,
who could lop a man's head off with just one chop.

From Hradčanské náměstí to the Strahov monastery

The monumental scale and appearance of the rest of Hradčany, outside the
castle, is a direct result of the **great fire of 1541**, which swept up from Malá
Strana and wiped out most of the old dwelling places belonging to the serfs,
tradesmen, clergy and masons who had settled here in the Middle Ages. With the
Turks at the gates of Vienna, the Habsburg nobility were more inclined to pursue
their major building projects in Prague instead, and, following the Battle of Bílá
hora in 1620, the palaces of the exiled (or executed) Protestant nobility were up
for grabs too. The newly ensconced Catholic aristocrats were keen to spend
some of their expropriated wealth, and over the next two centuries, they turned
Hradčany into a grand architectural showpiece. As the Turkish threat subsided,
the political focus of the Empire gradually shifted back to Vienna and the building
spree stopped. For the last two hundred years, Hradčany has been frozen in time,
and, two world wars on, its buildings have survived better than those of any other
central European capital.

Hradčanské náměstí

Hradčanské náměstí fans out from the castle gates, surrounded by the over-sized palaces of the old Catholic nobility. For the most part, it's a tranquil space that's overlooked by the tour groups marching through, intent on the Hrad. The one spot everyone does head for are the ramparts in the southeastern corner, which allow an unrivalled view over the reddish-brown rooftops of Malá Strana, past the famous dome and tower of the church of sv Mikuláš and beyond, to the spires of Staré Město.

Until the great fire of 1541, the square was the hub of Hradčany, lined with medieval shops and stalls but with no real market as such. After the fire, the developers moved in; the **Martinic Palace** at no. 8 was one of the more modest newcomers, built in 1620 by one of the councillors who survived the second defenestration. Its rich sgraffito decoration, which continues in the inner court-yard, was only discovered during restoration work in the 1970s, and was part of the reason it was featured as Mozart's house in the film *Amadeus*. Mathey's rather cold, formal **Toscana Palace** was built on a more ambitious scale, replacing the row of butchers' shops that once filled the west end of the square.

The powerful Lobkovic family replaced seven houses on the south side of the square with the over-the-top sgraffitoed pile at no. 2, known as the **Schwarzenberg Palace** after its last aristocratic owners, and now housing the **Museum of Military History** (Vojenské muzeum; May–Oct Tues–Sun 9.30am–4.30pm). The Czechs and Slovaks have a long history of supplying top-class weap-onry to world powers (most recently in the form of Semtex to the Libyans and tanks to the Syrians); it's no coincidence that one of the two Czech words to have made it into the English language is pistol (*pistole* in Czech). Among the endless uniforms and instruments of death – all of which are pre-1914 – you'll find an early Colt 45 and the world's largest mortar (courtesy of Škoda).

On the opposite side of the square, just outside the castle gates, stands the sumptuous Rococo **Archbishop's Palace** (Archbiskupský palác), seat of the archbishop of Prague since the beginning of the Roman Catholic church's suze-rainty over the Czechs, following the Battle of Bílá hora. The elusive interior is open to the public only on Maundy Thursday – the Thursday before Easter; the last incumbent was Archbishop Tomášek (known affectionately as "Frantši"), who was well into his nineties when he died in 1992.

Šternberk Palace – the European Art Collection

A passage down the side of the Archbishop's Palace leads to the early eighteenth-century **Šternberk Palace** (Tues–Sun 10am–6pm), now the main building of the National Gallery, housing its **European Art Collection** (ie non-Czech) – which, though rich enough for most tastes, is relatively modest in comparison with those of other European capitals. The collection is divided into three sections: the **first floor** kicks off with Florentine religious art, most notably a series of exquisite miniature triptychs by Bernardo Daddi. Also worth checking out are the side rooms containing Orthodox icons from the Balkans to northern Russia. The section ends with a series of canvases by Breughel the Younger, and *Haymaking* by Breughel the Elder.

The **second floor** contains one of the most prized paintings in the whole collection, the *Festival of the Rose Garlands* by Albrecht Dürer, depicting, among others, the Virgin Mary, the Pope, the Holy Roman Emperor, and even a self-portrait of Dürer himself (top right). There are other outstanding works here, too: a whole series of portraits by the Saxon master, Lucas Cranach – including the striking, almost minimalist *Portrait of an Old Man* – and a mesmerising *Head of Christ* by El Greco. Rubens' colossal *Murder of St Thomas* is difficult to miss, with its pink-buttocked cherubs hovering over the bloody scene, and a couple of dogs clearing up the mess.

At this point, you are suddenly propelled straight into the world of **twentieth-century art**, beginning with Klimt's mischievous *Virgins*, a mass of naked bodies and tangled limbs painted out in psychedelic colours. Although none of the artists here is Czech, many of them had close connections with Bohemia: Egon Schiele's mother came from Český Krumlov, the subject of a tiny autumnal canvas; while the handful of works by Oskar Kokoschka date from his brief stay here in the 1930s, when the political temperature got too hot in Vienna. Perhaps the most influential artist on show is Edvard Munch, whose one canvas, *Dance at the Seaside*, hardly does justice to the considerable effect he had on a generation of Czech artists after his celebrated exhibition in Prague in 1905.

By far the most popular section of the gallery is the **"French" art section** across the courtyard on the ground floor, featuring anyone of note who hovered around Paris in the fifty years from 1880 onwards. There are few famous master-pieces here, but it's all high quality stuff. Among those represented are Gauguin, Monet, Pissarro, Seurat, Van Gogh, Cézanne, Toulouse-Lautrec, Dufy and Matisse. Several works by Rodin are scattered around the room, particularly appropriate given his ecstatic reception by Czech sculptors at the beginning of this century, following his Prague exhibition in 1902. And there's a surprisingly good collection of Picassos, including several paintings and sculptures from his crucial early Cubist period (1907–08). At the end of this section there's a shop selling postcards, posters, books and coffee.

From Nový Svět to Loretánské náměstí

At the other end of Hradčanské náměstí, Kanovnická heads off towards the north-west corner of Hradčany. Nestling in this shallow dip, **Nový Svět** (meaning "New World", though not Dvořák's) provides a glimpse of life on a totally different scale from Hradčanské náměstí. Similar in many ways to the Zlatá ulička in the Hrad, this cluster of brightly coloured cottages, which curls around the corner into Černínská, is all that's left of Hradčany's medieval slums, painted up and sanitised in the eighteenth and nineteenth centuries. Despite having all the same ingredients for mass tourist appeal as Zlatá ulička, it remains remarkably undisturbed, save for a few kitsch ateliers and swish wine bars.

Up the hill from Nový Svět, Loretánské náměstí is dominated by the phenome-nal 150-metre-long facade of the **Černín Palace** (Černínský palác), decorated with thirty Palladian half-pillars and supported by a swathe of diamond-pointed rustication. For all its grandeur – it's the largest palace in Prague, for the sake of which two whole streets were demolished – it's a miserable, brutal building, commissioned in the 1660s by Count Jan Humprecht Černín, one-time imperial ambassador to Venice and a man of monumental self-importance. After quarrelling with the master of Italian Baroque, Gianlorenzo Bernini, and disagreeing with Prague's own Carlo Lurago, Count Černín settled on Francesco Caratti as his architect, only to have the building panned by critics as a tasteless mass of stone. The grandiose plans, which were nowhere near completion when the count died, nearly bankrupted future generations of Černíns, who were eventually forced to sell the palace in 1851 to the Austrian state, which converted it into a barracks.

Since the First Republic, the palace has housed the Ministry of Foreign Affairs, and during the war it was the Nazi *Reichsprotektor*'s residence. On March 10, 1948, it was the scene of Prague's third – and most widely mourned – defenestration. Only days after the Communist coup, **Jan Masaryk**, the only son of the founder of the Czechoslovak Republic, and the last non-Communist in Gottwald's cabinet, plunged forty-five feet to his death from the top-floor bathroom window of the palace. Whether it was suicide (he had been suffering from bouts of depression, partly induced by the country's political path) or murder will probably never be satisfactorily resolved, but for most people Masaryk's death cast a dark shadow over the newly established regime.

The facade of the **Loreto** (Loreta; Tues–Sun 9am–noon & 1–5pm), immediately opposite the Černín palace, was built by the Dientzenhofers, a Bavarian family of architects, in the early part of the eighteenth century, and is the perfect antidote to Caratti's humourless monster: all hot flourishes and twirls, topped by a tower which lights up like a Chinese lantern at night – and in the daytime clanks out the hymn *We Greet Thee a Thousand Times* on its twenty seven Dutch bells.

The facade and the cloisters are, in fact, just the outer casing for the focus of the complex, the **Santa Casa**, founded by Kateřina Lobkovic in 1626 and smothered in a mantle of stucco depicting the building's miraculous transportation from the Holy Land. Legend has it that the Santa Casa (Mary's home in Nazareth), under threat from the heathen Turks, was transported by a host of angels to a small village in Dalmatia and from there, via a number of brief stopoffs, to a small laurel grove (*lauretum* in Latin, hence *Loreto*) in northern Italy. News of the miracle spread across the Catholic lands, prompting a spate of copy-cat shrines, and during the Counter-Reformation, the cult was actively encouraged in an attempt to broaden the popular appeal of Catholicism. The Prague Loreto is one of fifty to be built in the Czech Lands, each of the shrines following an identical design, with pride of place given to a lime-wood statue of the *Black Madonna and Child*, encased in silver.

You can get some idea of the Santa Casa's serious financial backing in the **treasury** on the first floor of the west wing, much ransacked over the years but still stuffed full of gold. The padded ceilings and low lighting create a kind of giant jewellery box for the master exhibit, a tasteless Viennese silver monstrance studded with 6222 diamonds, standing over three feet high and weighing nearly two stone. It was constructed in 1699 to a design by Fischer von Erlach, on the posthumous orders of one of the Kolovrat family who had made the Loreto sole heir to her fortune.

The Strahov Monastery

West of Loretánské náměstí, Pohořelec, an arcaded street-cum-square, leads to the chunky remnants of the zigzag eighteenth-century fortifications that mark the edge of the old city, as defined by Charles IV back in the fourteenth century. Close by, to the left, is the **Strahov Monastery** (Strahovský klášter), founded in 1140 by the Premonstratensian order. Having managed to evade Joseph II's 1783 dissolution of the monasteries, it continued to function until shortly after the Communists took power, when, along with all other religious establishments, it was closed down and most of its inmates thrown into prison. Following the events of 1989, the monks have returned, so the future of the monastery as a tourist sight is now somewhat uncertain.

The monastery's two **libraries** are the main reason for visiting Strahov; the entrance for both is back in the main courtyard to the left. The first room you come to is the later of the two, the Philosophical Hall (Filosofický sál), built in some haste in the 1780s, in order to accommodate the books and bookcases from Louka, a Premonstratensian monastery in Moravia that failed to escape Joseph's decree. The walnut bookcases are so tall they touch the library's lofty ceiling, which is busily decorated with frescoes by the Viennese painter Franz Maulpertsch on *The Struggle of Mankind to Know Real Wisdom*. The other main room is the low-ceilinged Theological Hall (Teologický sál), its wedding-cake stucco framing frescoes on a similar theme, executed by one of the monks seventy years earlier.

If you leave the monastery through the narrow doorway in the eastern wall, you enter the gardens and orchards of the **Strahovská zahrada**, from where you can see the whole city in perspective. The gardens form part of Petřín Hill, and the path to the right contours round to the miniature Eiffel Tower (see p.74).

Malá Strana

More than anywhere else, **MALÁ STRANA**, the "Little Quarter", conforms to the image of Prague as the ultimate Baroque city. It was here that Miloš Forman chose to shoot many of the street scenes in *Amadeus*, judging that its picturesque alleyways resembled Mozart's Vienna more than Vienna itself. And it's true; the streets have changed very little since Mozart walked them, as he often did on his frequent visits here between 1787 and 1791. Unlike Hradčany, its main arteries are filled with city life during the day; while around practically every corner, narrow cobbled streets lead to some quiet walled garden, the perfect inner-city escape.

Many visitors never stray from the well-trodden paths that link the Charles Bridge with Hradčany, thus bypassing most of Malá Strana. This is easy to do, given that the whole town takes up a mere 150 acres of land squeezed between the river and the Hrad, but it means missing out on one of the greatest pleasures of Malá Strana – casually exploring its hilly eighteenth-century backstreets.

Malostranské náměstí and around

The main focus of Malá Strana has always been the sloping, cobbled **Malostranské náměstí**, across which hurtle trams and cars, as well as a procession of people – some heading up the hill to the Hrad, others pausing for coffee and cakes at the *Malostranská kavárna*, whose tables and chairs spill out on to the square.

Dominating and dividing the square, as it does the whole of Malá Strana, is the church of **sv Mikuláš** (St Nicholas), easily the most magnificent Baroque building in the city, and one of the last great structures to be built on the left bank, begun in 1702. For Christoph Dientzenhofer, a German immigrant from a dynasty of Bavarian architects, this was his most prestigious commission and is, without doubt, his finest work. For the Jesuits, it was their most ambitious project yet in Bohemia, the ultimate symbol of their stranglehold on the country. When Christoph died in 1722, it was left to his son Kilian Ignaz Dientzenhofer, along with Kilian's son-in-law, Anselmo Lurago, to finish the project, which they did

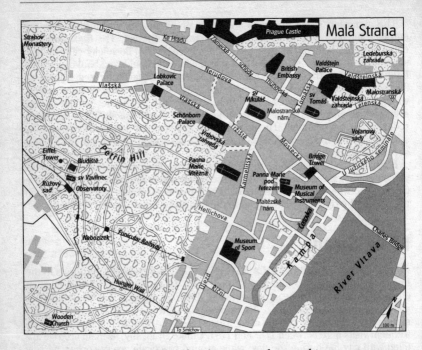

with a masterful flourish, adding the giant copper dome and tower – now among the most characteristic landmarks on Prague's left bank. Sadly for the Jesuits, they were able to enjoy the finished product for just twenty years, before they were banished from the Habsburg Empire in 1773.

Nothing about the relatively plain west facade prepares you for the overwhelming High Baroque **interior**. The fresco in the nave, by Jan Lukáš Kracker, is one of the largest paintings in Europe, covering an area of over 1500 square metres and portraying some of the more fanciful miraculous feats of Saint Nicholas. Even given the overwhelming proportions of the nave, the dome at the far end of the church, built by the younger Dientzenhofer, remains impressive, thanks, more than anything, to its sheer height. Leering over you as you gaze up at the dome are Ignaz Platzer's two terrifyingly oversized and stern Church Fathers, leaving no doubt as to the gravity of the Jesuit message.

Nerudova, Tržiště and Vlasská

The most important of the streets leading up to the Hrad from Malostranské náměstí is **Nerudova**, named after the Czech journalist and writer Jan Neruda (1834–91), who lived for a while at *U dvou sluncù* (The Two Suns), a former inn at the top of the street. His tales of Malá Strana immortalised bohemian life on Prague's left bank, and inspired countless other writers, not least the Chilean Nobel prize-winner, Pablo Neruda, who took his pen-name from the lesser-known Czech. Historically, this is Prague's artists' quarter, and although few of the present inhabitants are names to conjure with, the various private galleries and craft shops that have sprouted up over the last few years continue the tradition.

The houses that line the steep climb up to the Hrad are typically restrained, many retaining their medieval barn doors, and most adorned with their own peculiar house signs. Halfway up the hill, Nerudova halts at a crossroads; the cobbled hairpin of Ke Hradu is the path the royal coronation procession used to take; continuing west, along Úvoz (The Cutting), takes you to the Strahov monastery. On the south side of Úvoz, the houses come to an end, and a view opens up over Malá Strana's red Baroque roofs, while to the north, narrow stairways squeeze between the towering buildings of Hradčany, emerging on the path to the Loreto chapel.

Running (very) roughly parallel to Nerudova is **Tržiště**, which sets off from the south side of Malostranské náměstí. Halfway up on the left is the **Schönborn Palace**, now the American Embassy, whose entrance, and renowned gardens, are nowadays watched over by closed-circuit TV and machine-gun toting GIs – a far cry from the dilapidated palace in which Kafka rented an apartment in March 1917, and where he suffered his first bout of tuberculosis.

As Tržiště swings to the right, bear left up **Vlašská**, home to yet another **Lobkovic Palace**, now the German Embassy, which witnessed the first rumblings of the 1989 revolutions. In the summer of that year, several thousand East Germans (a mere fraction of the six million or so who used to visit Czechoslovakia each year) climbed over the garden wall and entered the embassy compound to demand West German citizenship, which had been every German's right since partition. The neighbouring streets were jam-packed with abandoned Trabants, while the beautiful palace gardens became a muddy home to the refugees. Finally the Czechoslovak government gave in and organised special trains to take the East Germans over the Federal border, cheered on their way by thousands of Praguers, and thus prompted the exodus that eventually brought about *Die Wende*.

The palace itself is a particularly refined building, best viewed from the **gardens** around the back, which were laid out in the early nineteenth century by Václav Skalník, who went on to landscape the spa at Mariánské Lázně. They're usually open to the public but, given the hammering they took in 1989, are likely still to be undergoing major botanical surgery.

The Valdštejn Palace and gardens

To the north of Malostranské náměstí, the **Valdštejn Palace** takes up the whole of the eastern side of Valdštejnské náměstí as well as the entire length of Valdštejnská. As early as 1621, Albrecht von Waldstein (known to the English as Wallenstein, and to the Czechs as Albrecht z Valdštejna) started to build a palace which would reflect his status as commander of the Imperial Catholic armies. By buying, confiscating, and then destroying twenty-five houses around the square, he succeeded in ripping apart a densely populated area of Malá Strana to make way for one of the largest and, quite frankly, most unappealing Baroque palaces in the city – at least from the outside.

The Ministry of Culture is now firmly ensconced in the palace, with just one wing, containing, ironically enough, the **Comenius Museum** (Pedagogické muzeum; Tues–Sun 10am–noon & 1–5pm), accessible to the public. This is a small and none too exciting exhibition on Czech education and, in particular, the influential teachings of Jan Amos Komenský (1592–1670) – often anglicised to John Comenius – who was forced to leave his homeland after the victory of the

Catholic armies under Valdštejn, eventually settling in Protestant England. To get to the exhibition, go through the main gateway and continue straight across the first courtyard; the museum is on your right.

If you've no interest in pedagogical matters, the formal **Valdštejnská zahrada** (Valdštejn gardens; May–Sept daily 9am–7pm) are a good place to take a break from the city streets. The focus of the gardens is the gigantic Italianate *sala terrena*, a monumental arch which stands at the end of an avenue of sculptures, the originals of which were taken off as booty by the Swedes in 1648. On the opposite side of the gardens, the palace's former **riding school** has been converted into a gallery, which puts on exhibitions of fine art and photography. Access to the gardens is via a concealed entrance on Letenská; you can get to the riding school from the courtyard of the nearby Malostranská metro station.

There are a number of other Baroque palace **gardens** on the slopes below the castle, and all except the Polish Embassy's Fürstenberská zahrada are, theoretically at least, open to the public. The **Černínská zahrada** is the best-loved – a jumble of balustrades, terraces and (dried-up) fountains – closely followed by the **Ledeburská zahrada**. You may find that in practice you can't get into any of them – if you're thwarted, try instead the **Vojanovy sady**, securely concealed behind a ring of high walls off U lužického semináře. It's a public park rather than a palace garden, with sleeping babies, weeping willows and the occasional open-air art happening.

From Karmelitská to Kampa

Karmelitská is the busy cobbled street that runs south from Malostranské náměstí along the base of Petřín Hill, towards the industrial suburb of Smíchov, becoming Újezd at roughly the halfway point. On the corner of Karmelitská and Tržiště, at no. 25, is the entrance to one of the most elusive of Malá Strana's many Baroque gardens, the **Vrtbovská zahrada**, founded on the site of the former vineyards of the Vrtba Palace. Laid out on Tuscan-style terraces dotted with ornamental urns and statues of the gods by Matthias Bernhard Braun, the gardens twist their way up the lower slopes of Petřín Hill to an observation terrace, from where there's a spectacular rooftop perspective of the city.

Further down, on the same side of the street, is the rather plain church of **Panna Marie Vítězná**, which was begun in early Baroque style by German Lutherans in 1611, and later handed over to the Carmelites after the Battle of Bílá hora. The main reason for coming here is to see the *pražské Jezulátko* or *Bambino di Praga*, a high-kitsch wax effigy of the infant Jesus enthroned in a glass case illuminated with strip-lights, donated by one of the Lobkovic family's Spanish brides in 1628. Attributed with miraculous powers, the *pražské Jezulátko* became an object of international pilgrimage equal in stature to the Santa Casa in Loreto, similarly inspiring a whole series of replicas. It continues to attract visitors (as the multilingual prayer cards attest) and boasts a vast personal wardrobe of expensive swaddling clothes, regularly changed by the local prelate.

From the trams and traffic fumes of Karmelitská, it's a relief to cut across to the calm restraint of **Maltézské náměstí**, one of a number of delightful little squares between here and the river. It takes its name from the Order of the Knights of St John of Jerusalem (better known by their later title, the Maltese Knights), who founded the nearby church of **Panna Marie pod řetězem** in 1160. The original Romanesque church was pulled down by the Knights themselves in the fourteenth century, but only the chancel and towers were success-fully rebuilt by the time of the Hussite Wars. The two severe Gothic towers are still standing and the chancel is now thoroughly Baroque, but the nave remains unfinished, an open, grassy, and generally inaccessible space.

Just to the south, music wafts across **Velkopřevorské náměstí**, another pretty little square where the Prague Conservatoire and the **Museum of Musical Instruments** (Hudební Muzeum; April–Oct Tues–Sun 10am–6pm) occupy what used to be the Knights' Grand Priory. The museum faces an uncertain future, and its mixed bag of exhibits may well be locked away until a new home is found for them. Around the corner, on the opposite side of the square, sitting pretty in pink, is the **Buquoy Palace**, built for a French family and appropriately enough now the French Embassy.

In these unlikely surroundings, along the garden wall of the Grand Priory, Prague's youth set up what has become known as **John Lennon's mock-grave**. Following the violent death of the Beatle and lifelong pacifist in 1980, graffiti from the inane to the profound was scrawled on the wall in honour of Lennon. Inevitably the wall also developed into a forum for grievances against the state; and a running battle between the police and the graffiti artists still continues despite the events of 1989.

Kampa

The two or three streets that make up **Kampa**, the largest of the central islands, contain no notable palaces or museums; just a couple of old mills, an exquisite main square, and a serene riverside park – in other words, plenty enough diver-sion for a lazy summer afternoon. The island is separated from the left bank by Prague's "Little Venice", a thin strip of water called **Čertovka** (Devil's Stream), which used to power several mill-wheels until the last one ceased to function in 1936. In contrast to the rest of the left bank, the fire of 1541 had a positive effect on Kampa, the resulting flotsam effectively stabilising the island's shifting shore-line. Nevertheless, Kampa was still subject to frequent flooding right up until the Vltava was dammed in the 1950s.

MOZART IN PRAGUE

Mozart made the first of several visits to Prague in 1787, staying with his friend and patron Count Thun in what is now the British Embassy (Thunovská 14). A year earlier, his opera *The Marriage of Figaro*, which had failed dismally to please the opera snobs in Vienna, had been given a rapturous reception at Prague's *Nostitz Theater* (now the Stavovské divadlo, see p.83); and on his arrival in 1787, Mozart was already flavour of the month, as he wrote in his diary: "Here they talk about nothing but Figaro. Nothing is played, sung or whistled but Figaro. Nothing, noth-ing but Figaro. Certainly a great honour for me!". Encouraged by this, he chose to premiere his next opera, *Don Giovanni*, later that year, in Prague rather than Vienna. He arrived with an incomplete score in hand, and wrote the overture at the Dušeks' Bertramka Villa in Smíchov (see p.113), dedicating it to the "good people of Prague". In 1791, the year of his death, *La Clemenza di Tito*, commissioned for the coronation of Leopold II as King of Bohemia – and apparently written on the coach from Vienna to Prague – was premiered here. Although Mozart was buried in Vienna as a little-known pauper, in Prague four thousand people turned out for his memorial service, held in Malá Strana's church of sv Mikuláš to the strains of his *Requiem Mass*.

For much of its history, the island was the city's main wash house, a fact commemorated by the church of sv Jan Na Prádle (St John at the Wash House) on Říční, near the southernmost tip of the island. It wasn't until the sixteenth and seventeenth centuries that the Nostitz family, who owned Kampa, began to develop the northern half of the island; the southern half was left untouched, and is today laid out as a public park. To the north, the oval main square, **Na Kampě**, once a pottery market, is studded with slender trees and cut through by the Charles Bridge, to which it is connected by a double flight of steps.

Petřín Hill

The scaled-down version of the Eiffel Tower is the most obvious landmark on **Petřín Hill**, the largest green space in the city centre. The tower is just one of the exhibits built for the 1891 Prague Exhibition, whose modest legacy includes the **funicular railway** (lanová dráha) which climbs up from a station just off Újezd. The original funicular was powered by a simple but ingenious system whereby two carriages, one at either end of the steep track, were fitted with large watertanks that were alternately filled at the top and emptied at the bottom. The new electric system, built in the 1960s, runs every ten to fifteen minutes until around 11.30pm – tickets are the same as for the rest of the public transport system. As the carriages pass each other at the halfway station of Nebozízek, you can get out and visit the restaurant of the same name, where the food and views are spectacular day and night.

At the top of the hill, it's possible to trace the southernmost perimeter wall of the old city – popularly known as the **Hunger Wall** (Hladová zeď) – as it creeps eastwards back down to Újezd, and northwestwards to the Strahov Monastery. Instigated in the 1460s by Charles IV, it has been much lauded (especially by the Communists) as a great public work which provided employment for the burgeoning ranks of the city's destitute inhabitants (hence its name); in fact, much of the wall's construction was paid for by the expropriation of Jewish property.

Follow the wall northwest and you come to the aromatic **Růžový sady** (rose garden), laid out in front of Petřín's **observatory** (Hvězdárna; hours vary considerably month by month), which offers a range of telescopes for use by the city's amateur astronomers. On the other side of the wall is Palliardi's twin-towered church of **sv Vavřinec** (St Lawrence), from whence derives the German name for Petřín Hill – Laurenziberg. Dotted along the nearby paths are the Stations of the Cross, culminating in the sgraffitoed Calvary Chapel, just beyond the church.

Opposite the church are a series of buildings from the 1891 Exhibition, starting with the diminutive **Eiffel Tower** (Rozhledna; daily 11am–11pm), a hexagonal interpretation – though a mere fifth of the size – of the tower which shocked Paris in 1889, and a tribute to the city's strong cultural and political links with Paris at the time; naturally, the view from the public gallery is terrific in fine weather. The next building along is an idealised neo-Gothic bastion, its interior converted into a **Maze** (Bludiště; April–Oct daily 9am–6pm) with convex and concave mirrors inside, a stroke of infantile genius by the exhibition organisers. The maze also contains an action-packed, life-sized diorama of the Prague students' and Jews' victory over the Swedes on the Charles Bridge in 1648.

From the tower, the path contours round to the northwest, giving great views over Petřín's palatial orchards and a sea of red tiles until it ducks under the perimeter wall of the Strahov Monastery (see p.68).

Staré Město

STARÉ MĚSTO, literally the "Old Town", is Prague's most central, vital ingredient. People live, work and sleep here; many of the capital's best markets, shops, restaurants and pubs are located in the area; and during the day a gaggle of shoppers and tourists fills its narrow streets. The district is bounded on one side by the river, on the other by the arc of Národní, Na příkopě and Revoluční, and at its heart is the **Staroměstské náměstí**, Prague's showpiece main square, easily the most magnificent in central Europe.

Merchants and craftsmen began settling in what is now Staré Město as early as the tenth century, and in the mid-thirteenth century it was granted town status, with jurisdiction over its own affairs. The fire of 1541, which ripped through the quarters on the other side of the river, never reached Staré Město, though the 1689 conflagration made up for it. Nevertheless, fewer houses were built and destroyed here than by the nobles who colonised the left bank, and apart from the Jesuits' powerhouse, the Klementinum, and the largely reconstructed Jewish Quarter that sits within the old town (see p.86), the medieval street plan remains intact. But like so much of Prague, Staré Město is still, on the surface, overwhelmingly Baroque, built literally on top of its Gothic predecessor to guard against the floods which plagued the town.

The Charles Bridge (Karlův most)

The **Charles Bridge** – which for over four hundred years was the only link between the two halves of Prague – is by far the city's most familiar monument. It's an impressive piece of medieval engineering, aligned slightly askew between two mighty Gothic gateways, but its fame is due almost entirely to the magnificent Baroque statues, additions to the original structure, that punctuate its length. Individually, only a few of the works are outstanding, but taken collectively, set against the backdrop of the Hrad, the effect is breathtaking.

The bridge was begun in 1357 to replace an earlier structure after this was swept away by one of the Vltava's frequent floods in 1342. Charles IV commissioned his young German court architect, Peter Parler, to carry out the work, which was finally completed in the early fifteenth century. For four hundred years thereafter it was known simply as the Prague or Stone Bridge – only in 1870 was it officially named after its patron. Since 1950, the bridge has been closed to vehicles, and is now one of the most popular places to hang out, day and

---

THE KRÁLOVÁ CESTA

In their explorations of Staré Město, most people unknowingly retrace the **králová cesta**, the traditional route of the coronation procession from the Prašná brána to the Hrad, established by the Přemyslids, and followed, with a few minor variations, by every Bohemian king until Emperor Ferdinand I in 1836, the last of the Habsburgs to bother having himself crowned in Prague. It's also the most direct route from the Charles Bridge to the main square, Staroměstské náměstí, and therefore a natural choice. However, many of the real treasures of Staré Město lie away from the *králová cesta*, so if you want to escape the crowds, it's worth heading off into the quarter's silent, twisted matrix of streets, and simply following your nose.

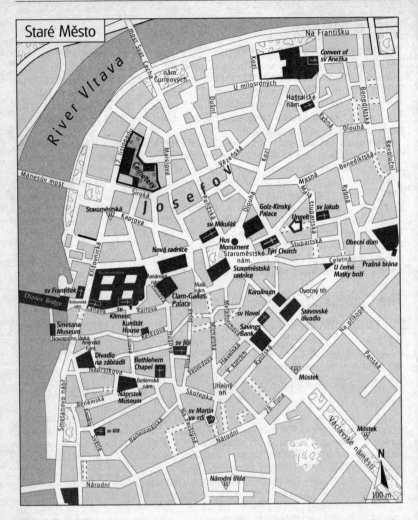

Staré Město

night; apart from the steady stream of sightseers, the niches created by the bridge-piers provide space for souvenir hawkers, buskers, punks and politicos.

A bronze **crucifix** has stood on the bridge since its construction, but its gold-leaf Hebrew inscription, "Holy, Holy, Holy Lord", was added in 1696, paid for by a Prague Jew who was ordered to do so by the city court, having been found guilty of blasphemy before the cross. The first of the sculptures wasn't added until 1683, when a bronze statue of **St John of Nepomuk** appeared, as part of the Jesuits' persistent campaign to have him canonised (see p.62); this later inspired hundreds of copies, which adorn bridges throughout central Europe. On the base, there's a bronze relief depicting his martyrdom, the figure of John now extremely worn through years of being touched for good luck. The statue was such a success with the church authorities that another twenty one saintly statues were added between 1698 and 1713. These included works by Prague's leading Baroque sculptors, led by Matthias Bernhard Braun and Maximilian Brokoff; the Max brothers unimaginatively filled in the remaining piers in the mid-nineteenth century. The original sculptures, mostly crafted in sandstone, have weathered badly over the years and are gradually being replaced by copies.

On the Malá Strana side, two unequal **bridge towers**, connected by a castellated arch, form the entrance to the bridge. The smaller, stumpy tower was once part of the original Judith Bridge (named after the wife of Vladislav I, who built the twelfth-century original); the taller tower, crowned by one of the pinnacled wedge-spires more commonly associated with Prague's right bank, can be climbed for a bird's-eye view (daily 10am–5/6pm). On the Staré Město side is arguably the finest bridge tower of the lot, its eastern facade still encrusted in Gothic cake-like decorations from Peter Parler's workshop. The severed heads of ten of the Protestant leaders were displayed here following the executions on Staroměstské náměstí in 1621, and, in 1648, it was the site of the last battle of the Thirty Years' War, fought between the besieging Swedes and an ad hoc army of Prague's students and Jews, which trashed the western facade of the bridge tower.

Křížovnické náměstí to Malé náměstí

Pass under the Staré Město bridge tower and you're in **Křížovnické náměstí**, an awkward space hemmed in by its constituent buildings, and a dangerous spot for unwary pedestrians. Hard by the bridge tower is a nineteenth-century cast-iron statue of **Charles IV**, erected on the 500th aniversary of his founding of the university, and designed by a German, Ernst Julius Hähnel, in the days before the reawakening of Czech sculpture.

The two churches on the square are both quite unusual. The half-brick church of **sv František** was built by Jean-Baptiste Mathey for the Order of the "Knights of the Cross with a Red Star", the original gatekeepers of the old Judith Bridge, who were at the zenith of their power in the seventeenth century, when they supplied most of the archbishops of Prague. The single dome plan and rich marble furnishings inside are both untypical in Prague. Over the road is the church of **sv Salvátor**, its facade prickling with blackened saints which are lit up enticingly at night. Built between 1578 and 1602, sv Salvátor marks the beginning of the Jesuits' rise to power and, like many of their churches, is designed along the lines of the Gesù church in Rome. It's worth a quick look, if only for the frothy stucco work and delicate ironwork in its triple-naved interior.

Along Karlova

Running from Křížovnické náměstí all the way to Malé náměstí is the narrow street of **Karlova**, packed with people winding their way towards Staroměstské náměstí, their attention divided between checking out the waffle stalls and souvenir shops, and not losing their way. At the first bend in Karlova, you come to the **Vlašská kaple** (Italian Chapel), which served the community of Italian masons, sculptors and painters who settled in Prague during the Renaissance period, and is still, strictly speaking, the property of the Italian state.

As they stroll down Karlova, few people notice the **Klementinum**, the former Jesuit College on the north side of the street, which covers an area second in size only to the Hrad. In 1556, Ferdinand I summoned the Jesuits to Prague to help bolster the Catholic cause in Bohemia, giving them the church of sv Kliment (see below), which Dientzenhofer later rebuilt for them. Initially the Jesuits proceeded with caution, but once the Counter-Reformation set in, they were put in control of the whole university and provincial education system. From their secure base at sv Kliment, they began to establish space for a great Catholic seat of learning in the city by buying up the surrounding land, demolishing over 32 old town houses, and, over the next two hundred years, gradually building themselves a palatial headquarters. In 1773, soon after it was completed, the Jesuits were turfed out of the country and the Klementinum handed over to the university authorities.

Nowadays the Klementinum houses the National Library's collection of over five million volumes, but much of the original building has been left intact. The **entrance** is inconspicuously placed just past the church of sv Kliment; it's easy enough just to walk past the caretakers – they'll probably allow you in anyway, but are unlikely to speak anything except Czech. Once inside, there are several ornate corridors worth checking out, but the chief attraction is the old **Music Library** (Hudební oddělení) on the first floor, filled with leather tomes, ancient globes and lovely frescoes. At roughly the centre of the Klementinum complex is the **observatory tower** from where seventeenth-century Prague's most illustrious visiting scientist, Johannes Kepler, did his planet-gazing. A religious exile from his native Germany, Kepler was court astronomer to Rudolf II, and lived at no. 4 Karlova for a number of years, during which time he drew up the first laws on the movement of the planets.

The church of **sv Kliment** (St Clement) itself can also be visited: its opening hours are erratic – the entrance is alongside the Vlašská kaple – but if you do get in, you'll find a spectacular set of frescoes depicting the life of Saint Clement (whose fate was to be lashed to an anchor and hurled into the Black Sea), and a unusual modern screen added by its new owners, the eastern rites Uniate Church (*Řecko-katolický*).

Malé náměstí

After a couple more boutiques, hole-in-the-wall bars and a final bend in Karlova, you emerge onto **Malé náměstí**, a square originally settled by French merchants in the twelfth century. It's best known for the russet-red, neo-Renaissance **Rott Haus**, previously an ironmongers' shop belonging to the Rott family – a building that immediately catches the eye, smothered in agricultural scenes and motifs inspired by the Czech artist Mikuláš Aleš. The original house sign of three white roses has been preserved on the central gable. Malé náměstí was home to the first pharmacy in Prague, opened by a Florentine in 1353, and the tradition is continued today by the *lékárna* at no. 13, which boasts chandeliers and a restored Baroque interior. Two doors up, there's no fear of missing the *American Hospitality Centre*, set up within months of the Velvet Revolution.

Staroměstské náměstí

East of Malé náměstí is **Staroměstské náměstí** (Old Town Square), easily the most spectacular square in Prague, and the traditional heart of the city. Most of the brightly coloured houses look solidly eighteenth-century, but their Baroque facades hide considerably older buildings. From the eleventh century onwards, this was the city's main marketplace, known simply as Velké náměstí (Great

Square), to which all roads in Bohemia led, and where merchants from all over Europe gathered. When the five towns that made up Prague were united in 1784, it was the square's town hall that was made the seat of the new city council, and for the next two hundred years the square was the scene of the country's most violent demonstrations and battles. For a long time now, the square has been closed to traffic, the cafés have spread out their tables and the tourists have poured in to watch the town hall clock chime and to drink in this historic showpiece.

The most recent arrival in the square is the colossal **Jan Hus Monument**, a turbulent sea of blackened bodies – the oppressed to his right, the defiant to his left – out of which rises the majestic moral authority of Hus himself, gazing into the horizon. For the sculptor Ladislav Šaloun, a maverick who received no formal training, the monument was his life's work, commissioned in 1900 when the Viennese Secession was at its peak, but strangely old-fashioned by the time it was completed in 1915. It would be difficult to claim that it blends in with its Baroque surroundings, yet this has never mattered to the Czechs, for whom its significance goes far beyond aesthetic merit.

Its unveiling on July 6, 1915, the 500th anniversary of the death of Hus, was accompanied by boisterous nationalist outbursts. Draped in swastikas by the invading Nazis in March 1939, and in black by Praguers in August 1968, when the Soviets marched in, it has always been a powerful symbol of the Czech nation. The inscription along the base is a quote from *The Will of Comenius*, one of his later followers, and includes Hus' most famous dictum, *Pravda vítězí* (Truth Prevails), which has been the motto of just about every Czech revolution since then.

The Staroměstská radnice

It wasn't until the reign of King John of Luxembourg (1310–46) that Staré Město was allowed to build its own town hall, the **Staroměstská radnice**. Short of funds, the citizens decided against an entirely new structure, buying a corner house on the square instead and simply adding an extra floor; later on, they added the east wing, with its graceful Gothic oriel and obligatory wedge-tower. Gradually, over the centuries, the neighbouring merchants' houses to the west were incorporated into the building, so that now it stretches all the way across to the richly sgraffitoed **Dům U minuty**, which juts out on to the square.

On May 8, 1945, three days into the Prague Uprising, the Nazis still held on to Staroměstské náměstí, and in a last desperate act set fire to the town hall – one of the few buildings to be irrevocably damaged in the last war. The tower was rebuilt immediately, but of the rest of the neo-Gothic **east wing**, which stretched almost as far as the church of sv Mikuláš, only a crumbling fragment remains; the rest of it is marked by a small stretch of grass. Set into the paving nearby are twenty seven **white crosses** commemorating the Protestant leaders who were condemned to death on the orders of the Emperor Ferdinand II, following the Battle of Bílá hora. They were publicly executed in the square on June 21, 1621: twenty-four enjoyed the nobleman's privilege and had their heads lopped off; the three remaining commoners were hung, drawn and quartered.

Today, the town hall's most popular feature is its fifteenth-century *orloj* or **Astronomical Clock** – every hour, a crowd of tourists and Praguers gather in front of the tower to watch a mechanical performance by the clock's assorted figures. The Apostles shuffle past the top two windows, bowing to the audience, while perched on pinnacles below are the four threats to the city as perceived by the medieval mind: Death carrying his hourglass and tolling his bell, the Jew with his moneybags, Vanity admiring his reflection, and a turbaned Turk shaking his head. Beneath the moving figures, four characters representing virtues stand motionless throughout the performance. Finally, a cockerel pops out and flaps its wings to signal that the show's over; the clock then chimes the hour.

The powder-pink facade on the south side of the town hall now forms the **entrance** to the whole complex (daily March–Oct 8am–6pm; Nov–Feb 8am–5pm). As long as at least five people turn up, a thirty-minute guided tour of the four rooms that survived the last war sets off every hour, when the clock has finished striking. Despite being steeped in history, there's not much of interest here, apart from a few decorated ceilings, striped with chunky beams, and a couple of Renaissance portals. You'll probably get more enjoyment from climbing the tower – with access for the disabled – for the panoramic sweep across Prague's spires.

The church of sv Mikuláš and the Golz-Kinský Palace

The destruction of the east wing of the town hall in 1945 rudely exposed Kilian Ignaz Dientzenhofer's church of **sv Mikuláš** (Tues, Wed & Fri 10am–1pm, Thurs 2–5pm), built in just three years between 1732 and 1735. Dientzenhofer's hand is obvious: the south front is decidedly luscious – painted in brilliant white, with Braun's blackened statuary popping up at every cornice – promising an interior to surpass even its sister church of sv Mikuláš in Malá Strana, which Dientzenhofer built with his father immediately afterwards (see p.69). Inside, however, it's a curious mixture. Although caked in the usual mixture of stucco and fresco, the church has been stripped over the years of much of its ornament and lacks the sumptuousness of its namesake on the left bank. This is partly due to the fact that Joseph II closed down the monastery and turned the church into a storehouse, and partly because it's now owned by the very "low", modern, Hussite Church.

The largest secular building on the square nowadays is the Rococo **Golz-Kinský Palace**, designed by Kilian Ignaz Dientzenhofer and built by his son-in-law Anselmo Lurago. In the nineteenth century it became a German *Gymnasium*, which was attended by Kafka (whose father ran a haberdashery shop on the ground floor). The palace is perhaps most notorious, however, as the venue for the fateful speech by the Communist prime minister, Klement Gottwald, who walked out on to the grey stone balcony one snowy February morning in 1948, flanked by his Party henchmen, to address the thousands of enthusiastic supporters who packed the square below. It was the beginning of *Vítězná února* (Victorious February), the bloodless coup which brought the Communists to power and sealed the fate of the country for the next forty-one years. The top floor now houses the National Gallery's specialist exhibitions of graphic art, but the entire palace was recently purchased by the Kafka Society who plan to turn it eventually into a vast museum and library dedicated to Kafka.

The Týn Church and dům U kamenného zvonu

Staré Město's most impressive Gothic structure, the mighty **Týn Church** (Panna Marie před Týnem), whose two irregular towers rise like giant antennae above the arcaded houses which otherwise obscure its facade, is a building of far more confidence than sv Mikuláš. Like the nearby Hus monument, the Týn Church, begun in the fourteenth century, is a source of Czech national pride. In an act of proud defiance, George of Poděbrady, the last Czech and the only Hussite King of Bohemia, adorned the high stone gable with a statue of himself and a giant gilded *kalich* (chalice), the mascot of all Hussite sects. The church remained a hotbed of Hussitism until the Protestants' crushing defeat at the Battle of Bílá hora, after which the chalice was melted down to provide a newly ensconced statue of the Virgin Mary with a golden halo, sceptre and crown.

Despite being one of the main landmarks of Staré Město, it's well-nigh impossible to appreciate the church from anything but a considerable distance, since it's boxed in by the houses around it, some of which are actually built right against the walls. At the moment, its opening hours are restricted to the evening mass around 6pm, so you may well find it closed; to reach the entrance, take the third arch on the left, which passes under the Venetian gables of the former Týn School.

Given the church's significance, it's sad that the **interior** is mostly dingy, unwelcoming and in need of repair, with little of the feel of the original Gothic structure surviving the church's ferocious Catholicisation. One exception is the fine north portal and canopy, which bears the hallmark of Peter Parler's workshop; the fifteenth-century pulpit also stands out from the dark morass of black and gold Baroque altarpieces, its panels enhanced by some sensitive nineteenth-century icons. The pillar on the right of the chancel steps contains the marble tomb of Tycho de Brahe, the famous Danish astronomer who arrived in Prague wearing a silver and gold false nose, having lost his own in a duel in Denmark. Court astronomer to Rudolf II for just two years, Brahe laid much of the groundwork for Johannes Kepler's later discoveries – Kepler getting his chance of employment when Brahe died of a burst bladder after one of Petr Vok's notorious binges in 1601.

Until recently, the **Dům U kamenného zvonu** (House at the Stone Bell), which adjoins the Golz-Kinský Palace, was much like any other of the merchant houses that line Staroměstské náměstí – covered in a thick icing of Baroque plasterwork and topped by a undistinguished roof gable. In the 1970s, however, it was stripped down to its Gothic core, uncovering the original honey-coloured stonework and simple wedge roof, and it now serves as a superb central venue for modern art exhibitions, lectures and concerts.

Celetná and north to the convent of sv Anežka

Celetná, whose name comes from the bakers who used to bake a particular type of small loaf (*calty*) here in the Middle Ages, leads east from Staroměstské náměstí direct to the Prašná brána, one of the original gateways of the old town. It's one of the oldest streets in Prague, lying along the former trade route from the old town market square, as well as on the *králová cesta*. Its buildings were smartly refaced in the Baroque period, and their pastel shades are now crisply maintained. Most of Celetná's shops veer towards the chic end of the Czech market, making it a popular place for a bit of window-shopping, but the spruced-up surroundings are only skin-deep. Dive down one of the covered passages to the left and you're soon in Staré Město's more usual, dilapidated backstreets.

Two-thirds of the way along Celetná, at the junction with Ovocný trh, is the **Dům U černé Matky boží** (House at the Black Madonna), one of the best examples of Czech Cubist architecture (for more on which, see p.106), built in 1911–12 by Josef Gočár. It was a short-lived style, whose most surprising attribute, in this instance, is its ability to adapt existing Baroque motifs: Gočár's house sits much more happily amongst its eighteenth-century neighbours than, for example, the functionalist Baťa shoe-shop opposite – one of Gočár's later designs from the 1930s.

Celetná ends at the fourteenth-century Prašná brána, beyond which is náměstí Republiky (see "Nové Město", p.91), at which point, strictly speaking, you've left Staré Město behind. Sticking to the old town for the moment, head north into the backstreets which conceal the bubbling, stucco facade of the Franciscan church of **sv Jakub**, on Malá Štupartská. Its massive Gothic proportions – it has the longest nave in Prague after the cathedral – make it a favourite venue for organ recitals, Mozart masses and other concerts. After the great fire of 1689, Prague's Baroque artists remodelled the entire interior, adding huge pillasters, a series of colourful frescoes and over twenty side altars. The most famous of these is the tomb of the Count of Mitrovice, in the northern aisle, designed by Fischer von Erlach and Prague's own Maximilian Brokoff.

The Convent of sv Anežka

Further north through the backstreets, the **Convent of sv Anežka** (St Agnes), Prague's oldest surviving Gothic building, stands within a stone's throw of the river as it loops round to the east. It was founded in 1233 as a convent for the Order of the Poor Clares, and named after Agnes, youngest sister of King Václav I, who left her life of regal privilege to become the convent's first abbess. Agnes herself was beatified in 1874 to try to combat the spread of Hussitism amongst the Czechs, and there was much speculation about the wonders that would occur when she was officially canonised, an event which finally took place on November 12, 1989, when Czech Catholics were invited to a special mass at St Peter's in Rome. Four days later the Velvet Revolution began: a happy coincidence, even for agnostic Czechs.

The convent itself was closed down in 1782, and fell into rack and ruin. It was squatted for most of the next century, and although saved from demolition by the Czech nationalist lobby, its restoration only took place in the 1980s. The convent now houses the National Gallery's **nineteenth-century Czech art collection** (Tues–Sun 10am–6pm), and if the art inside is not always of the highest quality, it is at least interesting in terms of the Czech *národní obrození*, while the building itself is also worth inspecting.

The well-preserved cloisters are filled with unremarkable Bohemian glass, porcelain and pewter dating from the nineteenth century; the fine art is housed in the three remaining chapels and continues on the first floor. The predominant trend in Czech painting at this time was the depiction of events of national significance: favourite themes – on display in several works here – ranged from legendary figures such as Břetislav and Jitka to the real-life tragedy of the Battle of Bílá hora. Far superior to these in technique is the work of Josef Václav Myslbek, the grand master of Czech sculpture, whose simple statue of Saint Agnes from his *Monument to St Wenceslas* (see p.95) is the gallery's outstanding exhibit.

Upstairs, the rooms are dominated by the Romantic landscapes of Antonín Mánes, Josef Navrátil and Antonín Chittussi, which lovingly recreate the rolling hills of Bohemia. In the same vein, though they were to be more influential on later generations of Czech artists, are the portraits and landscapes of Josef Mánes, who took an active part in the 1848 disturbances in Prague and consistently espoused the nationalist cause in his paintings. The final room is given over to the graphics of Mikuláš Aleš, whose designs can be seen in the sgraffito on many of the city's nineteenth-century buildings.

Southern Staré Město

The southern half of Staré Město is a triangular wedge bounded by the *králová cesta* and the curve of Národní and Na příkopě, which follow the course of the old fortifications. There are no showpiece squares like Staroměstské náměstí here, but the complex web of narrow lanes and hidden passageways, many of which have changed little since medieval times, make this an intriguing quarter to explore.

From Ovocný trh to Uhelný trh

Heading southwest from the Dům U černé Matky boží on Celetná, you enter **Ovocný trh**, site of the old fruit market, its cobbles recently restored along with the lime-green and white **Stavovské divadlo** (Estates Theatre), which lies at the end of the marketplace. Built in the early 1780s by Prague's large and powerful German community, the theatre is one of the finest Neoclassical buildings in Prague, reflecting the enormous self-confidence of its patrons. It is also something of a mecca for Mozart fans, since it was here rather than in the hostile climate of Vienna that the composer chose to premiere both *Don Giovanni* and *La Clemenza di Tito* (for more on Mozart's time in Prague, see p.73). This is, in fact, the only opera house in Europe which remains intact from Mozart's time, a major factor in Miloš Forman's decision to film the concert scenes for his Oscar-laden *Amadeus* here.

On the north side of the Stavovské divadlo is the **Karolinum** or Charles University, named for its founder Charles IV, who established it in 1348 as the first university in this part of Europe. Although it was open to all nationalities, with instruction in Latin, it wasn't long before differences arose between the German-speaking students, who were in the majority, and the Czechs, who, with Jan Hus as their rector, successfully persuaded Václav IV to curtail the privileges of the Germans. In protest, the Germans upped and left for Leipzig, the first of many ethnic problems which continued to bubble away throughout the university's six-hundred-year history until the forced expulsion of Germans after World War II. The new main entrance is a peculiarly ugly red-brick curtain wall by Jaroslav Fragner, set back from the street and inscribed with the original Latin name *Universitas Karolina*. Only a couple of small departments and the rectorate are now housed here, with the rest spread over the length and breadth of the city. The heavily restored Gothic vaults of the south wing are now used as a public **art gallery** for contemporary Czech art.

The junction of Melantrichova and Rytířská is always teeming with people pouring out of Staroměstské náměstí and heading for Wenceslas Square. Clearly visible from Melantrichova is Prague's last surviving **open-air market** – a poor relation of its Germanic predecessor, which stretched all the way from Ovocný trh to Uhelný trh. Traditionally a flower and vegetable market, it runs the full length of the arcaded Havelská, and sells everything from celery to CDs. The stalls on V kotcích, the narrow street parallel to Havelská, sell mainly clothes. Both markets run west into **Uhelný trh**, which gets its name from the *uhlí* (coal) that was sold here in medieval times.

THE FORMER GOTTWALD MUSEUM

One block west of the Stavovské divadlo, at no. 29 Rytířská, is the former **Prague Savings Bank**, a large, pompous neo-Renaissance building designed in the 1890s by Osvald Polívka, before he went on to erect some of Prague's most flamboyant Art-Nouveau structures.

For over thirty years it housed the museum all Praguers loved to hate – dedicated to **Klement Gottwald**, the country's first Communist president. A joiner by trade, a notorious drunkard and womaniser by repute, he led the Party with unswerving faith from the beginnings of Stalinism in 1929 right through to the show trials of the early 1950s. He died shortly after attending Stalin's funeral in 1953 – either from grief or, more plausibly, from drink.

Remarkably, his reputation survived longer than that of any other East European leader. While those whom he had wrongfully sent to their deaths were posthumously rehabilitated, and the figure of Stalin denigrated, Gottwald remained sacred, his statue gracing every town in the country for the last forty-odd years. As recently as October 1989, the Communists were happily issuing brand new 100kčs notes emblazoned with his bloated face, only to have them withdrawn from circulation a month later, when the regime toppled.

Not surprisingly, the museum has closed and the building is once again a savings bank. It's worth a peek inside; go upstairs to the left and check out the main hall.

Sv Martin ve zdi and Bartolomějská

South of Uhelný trh, down Martinská, the street miraculously opens out to make room for the twelfth-century church of **sv Martin ve zdi** (St Martin-in-the-Walls), originally built to serve the Czech community of sv Martin, until it found itself the wrong side of the Gothic fortifications when they were erected in the fourteenth century. It's still essentially a Romanesque structure, adapted to suit Gothic tastes a century later, and thoroughly restored at the beginning of this century by its present owners, the Czech Brethren, who added the creamy neo-Renaissance tower. For them, it has a special significance as the place where communion "in both kinds" (ie bread and wine), one of the fundamental demands of the Hussites, was first administered to the whole congregation in 1414.

Around the corner from sv Martin ve zdi is the gloomy lifeless street of **Bartolomějská**, dominated by a tall, grim-looking building on its south side, which served as the main interrogation centre of the universally detested secret police, the *Statní bezpečnost*, or *StB*. Although now officially disbanded, the *StB* continues to be one of the most controversial issues of the post-revolutionary period. As in the rest of Eastern Europe, the accusations and revelations of who exactly collaborated with the *StB* have caused the downfall of a number of leading politicians right across the political spectrum. Up until the 1950s, the building was occupied by Franciscan nuns, a small number of whom have recently returned to try and exorcise the building, in order to continue where they left off some forty years ago.

Betlemské náměstí

After leaving the dark shadows of Bartolomějská, the calm of **Betlémské náměstí** comes as a welcome relief. The square is named after the **Bethlehem Chapel** (Betlémská kaple), whose high wooden gables face on to the square. This was founded in 1391 by the leading Czech reformists of the day, who were denied the right to build a church, so proceeded instead to build the largest chapel in Bohemia, with a total capacity of 3000. Sermons were delivered not in the customary Latin, but in the language of the masses – Czech. From 1402 to 1413, **Jan Hus** preached here, regularly pulling in more than enough commoners to fill the chapel. Hus was eventually excommunicated for his outspokenness, found guilty of heresy and burnt at the stake at the Council of Constance in 1415.

The chapel continued to attract reformists from all over Europe for another two centuries – the leader of the German Peasants' Revolt, **Thomas Müntzer**, preached here in the sixteenth century – until the advent of the Counter-Reformation in Bohemia. Inevitably, the chapel was handed over to the Jesuits, who completely altered the original building, only for it to be demolished after they were expelled by the Habsburgs in 1773. What you will see (when it finally reopens after its most recent renovation) is a scrupulous reconstruction of the fourteenth-century building by Jaroslav Fragner, using the original plans and a fair amount of imaginative guesswork. The reconstruction work was carried out after the war by the Communists, who were keen to portray Hus as a Czech nationalist and social critic as much as a religious reformer, and, of course, to dwell on the revolutionary Müntzer's later appearances here.

At the western end of the square stands the **Náprstek Museum** (Náprstkovo muzeum; Tues–Sun 10am–noon & 1–6pm), whose founder, Vojta Náprstek, was inspired by the great Victorian museums of London while in exile following the 1848 revolution. On his return, he turned the family brewery into a museum, initially intending it to concentrate on the virtues of industrial progress. Náprstek's interests gradually shifted, however, and the museum now displays just his American, Australian and African collections; the original exhibits are now in the Technical Museum (see p.111).

The Church of sv Jiljí

Between Betlémské náměstí and Staroměstské náměstí lies a confusing maze of streets, passageways and backyards, containing few sights as such, but nevertheless a joy to explore. One building that might catch your eye is the church of **sv Jiljí** (St Giles), on Husova, whose outward appearance suggests another Gothic masterpiece, but whose interior is decked out in the familiar white and gold excess of the eighteenth century. The frescoes by Václav Vavřinec Reiner (who's buried in the church) are full of praise for his patrons, the Dominicans, who took over the church after the Protestant defeat of 1620. They were expelled, in turn, after the Communists took power, only to return following the events of 1989.

To the waterfront

Heading west from Husova along Řetězová and Anenská brings you eventually to the waterfront. On Anenské náměstí, just before you reach the river, is the **Divadlo na zábradlí** (Theatre at the Balustrade). In the 1960s, this became the centre of Prague's absurdist theatre scene, with Havel himself working first as a stage-hand and later as resident playwright.

The gaily decorated neo-Renaissance building at the very end of Novotného lávka, on the river front itself, was once the city's waterworks but now houses a café-theatre and, on the first floor, the **Smetana Museum** (10am–5pm; closed Tues), of specialist interest only. Smetana, despite being a German-speaker, was without doubt the most nationalist of all the great Czech composers, taking an active part in the 1848 revolution and much of the later *narodní obrození*. Towards the end of his life he went deaf, and eventually died of syphilis in a mental asylum. Outside, beneath the large weeping willow that droops over the embankment, the statue of the seated Smetana is unfortunately placed, with his back towards one of his most famous sources of inspiration, the River Vltava (Moldau in German).

Josefov

It is crowded with horses; traversed by narrow streets not remarkable for cleanliness, and has altogether an uninviting aspect. Your sanitary reformer would here find a strong case of overcrowding.

Walter White, "A July Holiday in Saxony, Bohemia and Silesia" (1857)

Less than half a century after Walter White's comments, all that was left of the former ghetto of **JOSEFOV** were six synagogues, the town hall and the medieval cemetery. At the end of the nineteenth century, a period of great economic growth for the Empire, it was decided that Prague should be turned into a beautiful bourgeois city, modelled on Paris. The key to this transformation was the "sanitisation" of the ghetto, a process begun in 1893, which reduced the notorious malodorous backstreets and alleyways of Josefov to rubble and replaced them with block after block of luxurious five-storey mansions. The Jews, Gypsies and prostitutes were cleared out and the area became a desirable residential quarter, rich in Art Nouveau buildings festooned with decorative murals, doorways and sculpturing – the beginning of the end for a community which had existed in Prague for almost a millennium.

In any other European city occupied by the Nazis in World War II, what little was left of the old ghetto would have been demolished. But although Prague's Jews were transported to the new ghetto in Terezín, by a grotesque twist of fate Hitler chose to preserve the ghetto itself as the site for his planned "Exotic Museum of an Extinct Race". With this in mind, Jewish artefacts from all over central Europe were gathered here, and now make up one of the richest collections of Judaica in Europe – and one of the most fascinating sights in Prague.

A brief history

Jews probably settled in Prague as early as the tenth century in what is now Malá Strana. From the outset they were subjected to violent pogroms, and harsh, often arbitrary persecution, through laws restricting their choice of profession, their movements and dress. The first dress codes were introduced under Vratislav II (1061–92) and required Jews to wear a yellow cloak; later, it was enough to wear a yellow circle, but some form of visible identification remained a constant feature of ghetto life.

In 1096, at the time of the first crusade, the first recorded pogrom took place, though it wasn't until the thirteenth century (300 years before the word "ghetto" was coined in Venice) that Jews were actually herded into a **walled ghetto** within Staré Město, cut off from the rest of the town and subject to a curfew. Prague's Jews effectively became the personal property of the king, protected by him when the moment suited, used as scapegoats when times were hard. During one of the worst pogroms, in 1389, 3000 Jews were massacred over Easter, some while sheltering in the Old-New Synagogue – an event which is still commemorated there every year on Yom Kippur.

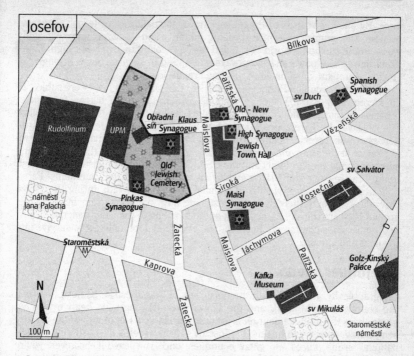

In contrast to the rest of Europe, the reign of Rudolf II (1576–1612) was a time of economic and cultural prosperity for the community. The Jewish mayor, **Mordecai Maisl**, Rudolf's minister of finance, became one of the richest men in Bohemia and the success symbol of a generation; his money bought the Jewish quarter a town hall, a bath house, pavements and several synagogues. This was the golden age of the ghetto: the time of **Rabbi Löw**, who, according to Jewish legend, created the famous "golem" (a precursor of Frankenstein's monster), and David Gans, the Jewish chronicler, both of whom are buried in the old cemetery.

It was the enlightened **Emperor Joseph II** (1780–90) who did most to lift the restrictions on Jews. His 1781 Toleration Edict ended the dress codes, opened up education to all non-Catholics, and removed the gates from the ghetto – the community paid him homage by officially naming the ghetto Josefov, or Josefstadt. It was not until 1848, however, that Jews were granted equal status as citizens and permitted to settle outside the ghetto. Gradually, the more prosperous Jewish families began to move to other districts of Prague, leaving behind only the poorest Jews and strictly Orthodox families, who were rapidly joined by the underprivileged ranks of Prague society: Gypsies, beggars, prostitutes and alcoholics. By 1890, only twenty percent of Josefov's population was Jewish, yet it was still the most densely populated area in Prague.

The ending of restrictions, and the destruction of most of the old ghetto, increased the pressure on Jews to assimilate, a process which brought with it its own set of problems. Prague's Jews were predominantly German- or Yiddish-speaking, and therefore seen by the Czech nationalists as a Germanising influence. By 1900 two-thirds of Prague's German population were Jewish. Tensions between the country's German-speaking minority and the Czechs grew steadily worse in the run-up to World War I, and the Jews found themselves caught in the firing line – "like powerless stowaways attempting to steer a course through the storms of embattled nationalities", as one Prague Jew put it.

After Hitler occupied Prague on March 15, 1939, the city's Jews were subject to an increasingly harsh set of regulations, which saw them barred from most professions, placed under curfew, and compelled once more to wear the yellow Star of David. In November 1941, the first transport of Prague Jews set off for the new ghetto in Terezín, 60km northwest of Prague. Of the estimated 55,000 Jews in Prague at the time of the Nazi invasion, over 36,000 died in the camps; many survivors emigrated to Israel and the USA. Of the 8000 who registered as Jewish in the Prague census of 1947, a significant number joined the Communist Party, only to find themselves victims of Stalinist anti-Semitic wrath during the 1950s. Nowadays, it's extremely difficult to estimate how many Jews remain in Prague: around 1000 are registered, and most of them belong to the older generation. Just two synagogues continue to function, and even they look unlikely to survive into the next millennium.

The former ghetto

Geographically, Josefov lies to the northwest of Staroměstské náměstí, between the church of sv Mikuláš and the Vltava river. Through the heart of the old ghetto runs the ultimate bourgeois avenue, **Pařížská**, a riot of turn-of-the-century sculpturing, spikes and turrets. It's Josefov's main street, a lively stretch of international airline offices and glitzy boutiques; once you leave it, however, you're immediately in the former ghetto, now one of the most restful parts of the old town.

The Old-New Synagogue and the Jewish Town Hall

Halfway down Pařížská, on the left, are the steep, jagged brick gables of the **Old-New Synagogue** (Staronová synagóga or Altneuschul), the oldest functioning synagogue in Europe. Begun in the second half of the thirteenth century, it's one of the earliest Gothic buildings in Prague and still the religious centre for Prague's Orthodox Jews. Since Jews were prevented by law from becoming architects, the synagogue was most probably constructed by the Franciscan builders working on the convent of sv Anežka. Its five-ribbed vaulting is unique for Bohemia; the extra rib was added to avoid any hint of a cross.

To get to the **main hall**, you must pass through one of the two low vestibules from which women are allowed to watch the proceedings. Above the entrance is an elaborate tympanum covered in the twisting branches of a vine tree, its twelve bunches of grapes representing the tribes of Israel. The low glow from the chandeliers is the only light in the hall, which is mostly taken up with the elaborate

All the "sights" of Josefov are run by the **State Jewish Museum** and you need a separate ticket for each one. Due to the unprecedented number of tourists visiting Josefov, you must now enter the cemetery with a guide. Opening hours for all sights are April–Oct 9am–5pm; Nov–March 9am–4.30pm; closed Sat.

wrought-iron cage enclosing the *bimah* in the centre. In 1357, Charles IV allowed the Jews to fly their own municipal standard, a moth-eaten remnant of which is still on show. The other flag – a tattered red banner – was a gift to the community from Emperor Ferdinand III for helping fend off the Swedes in 1648. On the west wall is a glass cabinet, shaped like Moses' two tablets of stone and filled with tiny personalised light bulbs, each one lighting up on the anniversary of a person's death (there's even one for Kafka).

Just south of the synagogue is the **Jewish Town Hall** (Židovnická radnice), one of the few such buildings to survive the Holocaust. Founded and funded by Maisl in the sixteenth century, it was later rebuilt as the creamy-pink Baroque house you now see, housing a kosher lunchtime restaurant. The belfry, permission for which was granted by Ferdinand III, has a clock on each of its four sides, plus a Hebrew one stuck on the north gable which, like the Hebrew script, goes "backwards".

The Old Jewish Cemetery

The main reason most people visit Josefov is to see the **Old Jewish Cemetery** (Starý židovský hřbitov), called *Beth Chaim* in Hebrew, meaning "House of Life". Established in the fifteenth century, it was in use until 1787, by which time there were an estimated 100,000 buried here, one on top of the other, as many as twelve layers deep. The oldest grave, dating from 1439, belongs to the poet Avigdor Karo, who lived to tell the tale of the 1389 pogrom. Get there before the crowds, and the cemetery can be a poignant reminder of the ghetto, its inhabitants subjected to inhuman overcrowding even in death. The rest of Prague recedes beyond the sombre lime trees and cramped perimeter walls, the haphazard headstones and Hebrew inscriptions casting a powerful spell.

Immediately on your left as you leave the cemetery is the **Obřadní síň**, a grim neo-Renaissance house that was the site of the original Jewish Museum, founded in 1906. It's now devoted to a harrowing exhibition of children's drawings from the Jewish ghetto in Terezín (see p.206).

The museum-synagogues

Opposite the entrance to the cemetery is the **Klaus Synagogue** (Klausová synagóga), a late seventeenth-century building, originally founded by Mordecai Maisl in what was then a notorious red-light district of Josefov. The first floor is now used for the interesting temporary exhibitions put on by the State Jewish Museum; the rest contains a display of Jewish prints and manuscripts (the world's first Jewish printing house was founded in Prague in 1512).

On the south side of the cemetery, the **Pinkas Synagogue** (Pinkasova synagóga) juts out at an angle from the cemetery wall. Closed since 1968, allegedly due to problems with the masonry, it's recently been re-opened; access is from Široká. It was built for the powerful Pinkas family, and has undergone countless restorations over the centuries. In 1958, a chilling memorial to the 77,297 Czech and Slovak Jews killed during the Holocaust was unveiled inside – a simple *menorah* (candelabra) set against the carved stone backdrop of a complete list of the names of those who perished. It was destroyed at some point in the last twenty years – by damp, according to the Communists. Whatever the reason, there are plans now to reconstruct the memorial with the aid of old photographs, though work won't finish until the end of 1993.

On the far side of the town hall it was once part of is the **High Synagogue** (Vysoká synagóga), whose rich interior stands in complete contrast to its dour, grey facade. The huge vaulted hall is now used to display a mere fraction of the hundreds of Jewish textiles, dating from the sixteenth to the early twentieth century, that were gathered here by the Nazis for their infamous museum.

Across Pařížská, on Dušní, is the **Spanish Synagogue** (Španělská synagóga), closed "for electrical rewiring" since 1980, and used for storage in the meantime – a great shame, since this is one of the most ornate synagogues in Josefov, rebuilt at the turn of the century in a Moorish style recalling its fifteenth-century roots, when it was founded by Sephardic Jews fleeing the Spanish Inquisition.

The neo-Gothic **Maisl Synagogue** (Maislova synagóga), set back from the neighbouring houses on Maislova, has recently reopened after a lengthy restoration. Founded and paid for entirely by Mordecai Maisl, in its day it was without doubt one of the most ornate synagogues in Josefov. Nowadays, it is almost entirely bare apart from the rich offerings of its glass cabinets, which contain a selection of gold and silverwork, *hanuka* candlesticks, *torah* scrolls and other religious paraphernalia.

Around náměstí Jana Palacha

As Kaprova and Široká emerge from Josefov, they meet at the newly christened **náměstí Jana Palacha**, previously called náměstí Krasnoarmejců (Red Army Square) and embellished with a flowerbed in the shape of a red star, in memory of the Soviet dead who were temporarily buried here in May 1945. It was probably this, as much as the fact that the building on the east side of the square is the Faculty of Philosophy, where Palach was a student, that prompted the new authorities to make the first of the street name changes here in 1989 (there's a bust of Palach on the corner of the building). By a happy coincidence, the road which intersects the square from the north is called 17 listopadu (17 November), originally commemorating the students' anti-Nazi demonstration of 1939, but now equally good for more recent events.

The north side of the square is taken up by the **Rudolfinum** or Dům umělců (House of Artists), designed by Josef Zítek and Josef Schulz. One of the proud civic buildings of the nineteenth-century *národní obrození*, it was originally built to house an art gallery, museum and concert hall for the Czech-speaking community. In 1918, however, it became the seat of the new Czechoslovak parliament, only returning to its original artistic purpose in 1946; in the last couple of years it's been sandblasted back to its original woody-brown hue, and is now one of the capital's main art and concert venues.

UPM – the Decorative Arts Museum

A short way down 17 listopadu from the square is the **UPM**, or Uměleckoprůmyslové muzeum (Tues–Sun 10am–6pm), installed in another of Schulz's worthy nineteenth-century creations, richly decorated in mosaics, stained glass and sculptures. Literally translated as a "Museum of Decorative Arts", this hardly does justice to what is one of the most fascinating museums in the capital. From its foundation in 1885 through to the end of the First Republic, the UPM received the best that the Czech modern movement had to offer – from Art Nouveau to the avant-garde – and judging from previous catalogues and the various short-term exhibitions mounted in the past, its collection is unrivalled.

ON KAFKA'S TRAIL

Franz Kafka was born on July 3, 1883, above the *Batalion* schnapps bar on the corner of Maislova and Kaprova (the original building has long since been torn down), and spent most of life in and around Josefov. His father was an upwardly mobile small businessman from a Czech-Jewish family of kosher butchers (Kafka himself was a vegetarian), his mother from a wealthy German-Jewish family of merchants. The family owned a haberdashery shop, located at various premises on or near Staroměstské náměstí. In 1889, they moved out of Josefov and lived for the next seven years in the beautiful Renaissance Dům U minuty, next door to the Staroměstská radnice, during which time Kafka attended the *Volksschule* on Masná (now a Czech primary school), followed by a spell at an exceptionally strict German *Gymnasium* on the third floor of the Golz-Kinský Palace.

At eighteen, he began a law degree at the German half of Charles University, which was where he met his lifelong friend and posthumous biographer and editor, Max Brod. Kafka spent most of his working life as an insurance clerk, until he was forced to retire through ill health in 1922. Illness plagued him throughout his life and he spent many months as a patient at the innumerable spas in *Mitteleuropa*. He was engaged three times, twice to the same woman, but never married, finally leaving home at the age of thirty-one for bachelor digs on the corner of Dlouhá and Masná, where he wrote the bulk of his most famous work, *The Trial*. He died of tuberculosis in a Viennese sanatorium on June 3, 1924, at the age of forty, and is buried in the New Jewish Cemetery in Žižkov (see p.108).

Kafka's birthplace is commemorated by a gaunt-looking modern bust. Next door, there is a small **Kafka Museum** (Tues–Sat 10am–6pm), which retells his life simply but effectively with pictures and quotes (in Czech, German and English). It's run by the Kafka Society, who are planning to open a much bigger museum and cultural centre in the Golz-Kinský Palace on Staroměstské náměstí, sometime in the future.

Unfortunately, the permanent exhibition consists of just a sample from each of the main artistic periods from the Renaissance to the 1930s, giving only the vaguest hints at the wealth of exhibits stored away in the museum's vaults. Worse still, the top floor, which covers the period from the 1880s to the 1930s, had been closed for a number of years at the time of writing. As a consolation, the museum's ground and first floors are used for some of the best temporary exhibitions in Prague, mostly taken from its twentieth-century collections. There's also a **public library** in the building (Mon noon–6pm, Tues–Fri 10am–6pm; closed July & Aug), specialising in catalogues and material from previous exhibitions.

Nové Město

NOVÉ MĚSTO is the largest of Prague's four towns and the city's main commercial and business district. Although it comes over – architecturally speaking – as a sprawling late nineteenth-century bourgeois quarter, it was actually founded in 1348 by Charles IV as an entirely new town, intended to link the southern fortress of Vyšehrad with Staré Město to the north. Large market squares, wide streets, and a level of town-planning far ahead of its time were employed to transform Prague into the new capital city of the Holy Roman Empire. However, this quickly became the city's poorest quarter after Josefov, renowned as a hotbed of Hussitism and radicalism throughout the centuries. In the second half of the nine-

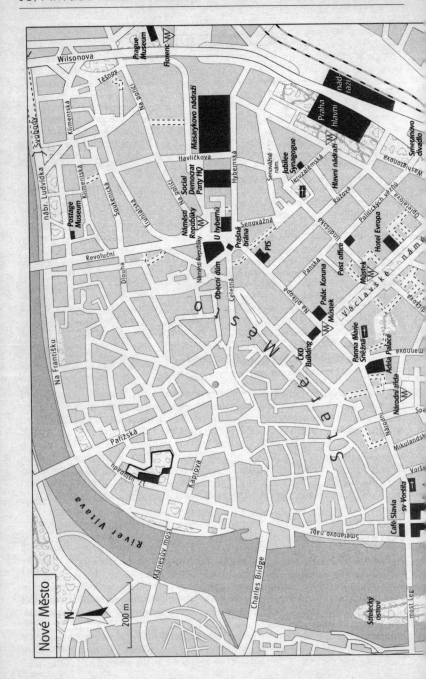

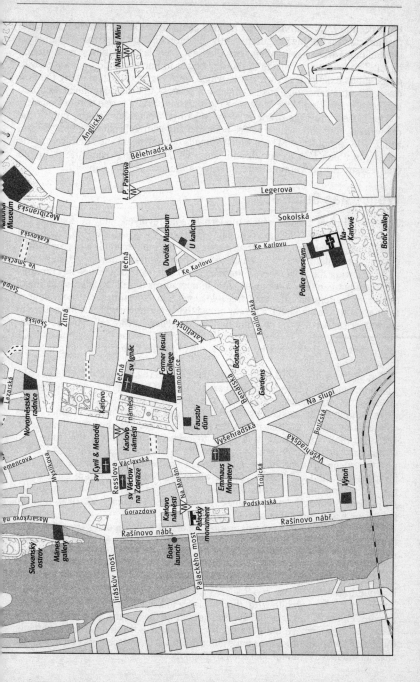

Náměstí Minu

Anglická

Bělehradská

I. P. Pavlova

Legerova

Sokolská

Mezibranská

Národní Museum

Krakovská

Ve Smečká

Ke Karlovu

U kalicha

Dvořák Museum

Ke Karlovu

Na Karlově

Botič valley

Police Museum

Apolinářská

Štěpá

Ječná

Žitná

Školská

Ječná

Kateřinská

Former Jesuit College

sv Ignác

Benátská Botanical Gardens

Na slupi

Lazarská

Novoměstská radnice

Karlovo náměstí

U nemocnice

Faustův dům

Botičská

emencova

Myslíkova

sv Cyril & Metoděj

Karlovo náměstí

Vyšehradská

Vyšehradská

Vratoň

Ressiova

Václavská

sv Václav na Zderaze

Na Moráni

Emmaus Monatery

Trojická

Masarykovo ná

Gorazdova

Karlovo náměstí

Podskalská

Rašínovo nábř.

Slovanský ostrov

Mánes gallery

Jiráskův most

Rašínovo nábř.

Boat launch

Palackého most

Palacký monument

teenth century, the authorities set about a campaign of slum clearance similar to that inflicted on the Jewish quarter; only the churches and a few important historical buildings were left standing, but Charles' street layout survived pretty much intact. The leading architects of the day began to line the wide boulevards with ostentatious examples of their work, which were eagerly snapped up by the new class of status-conscious businessman – a process that has continued well into this century, making Nové Město the most architecturally varied part of Prague.

The easiest **starting point** in Nové Město is Wenceslas Square, hub of the modern city and somewhere you're bound to find yourself returning to again and again. The rest of Nové Město, which spreads out northeast and southwest of the square, is much less explored, and unusually for Prague, using the tram and metro systems to get around here will save some unnecessary legwork.

Wenceslas Square

The natural pivot around which modern Prague revolves, and the focus of the events of November 1989, is **Wenceslas Square** (Václavské náměstí), more of a wide, gently sloping boulevard than a square as such. It's scarcely a conventional – or even convenient – space in which to hold mass demonstrations, yet night after night following the November 17 *masakr* (see p.98), over 250,000 people crammed into the square, often enduring subzero temperatures to call for the resignation of the Party leaders and demand free elections. On November 27, the whole of Prague came to a standstill, a bigger crowd than ever converging on the square to show their support for the two-hour nationwide general strike called by the opposition umbrella group, Občanské fórum (Civic Forum). It was this last mass mobilisation that proved decisive: by noon the next day, the Communist old guard had thrown in the towel.

The square's history of protest goes back to the revolutionary events of 1848, which began with a large outdoor mass held here. On the crest of the nationalist disturbances, the square – which had been known as Koňský trh (Horse Market) since its foundation as such by Charles IV – was given its present name. It was only appropriate, then, that it was here that the First Republic was declared in 1918. In 1948, the square was filled to capacity once more, this time with Communist demonstrators in support of the February coup. In August 1968, it was the scene of some of the most violent confrontations between the Soviet invaders and the local Czechs, during which the National Museum came under fire (according to the Czechs, the Soviet officer in charge mistook it for the Parliament building). And, of course, it was here on January 16, 1969, that Jan Palach set fire to himself in protest at the invasion.

Despite the square's medieval origins, its oldest building dates from the eighteenth century, and the vast majority are much younger. As the city's money moved south of Staré Město during the industrial revolution, so the square became the architectural showpiece of the nation, and is now lined with self-important six- or seven-storey buildings, representing every artistic trend of the last hundred years, from neo-Renaissance to Social Realism. Even if you've no interest in modern architecture, there's plenty to keep you occupied in the shops, arcades, cinemas, theatres and general hubbub of the square. This is also the one place in Prague where life goes on after midnight – the hotels and nightclubs throbbing away – though the pimps and prostitutes have recently been moved on, after an intensive clean-up operation by the police.

Up the square

The northern end of the Wenceslas Square, around Můstek, the city's most central metro station, is a popular place to meet up before hitting town, and, without doubt, the busiest part of the square. It's dominated by a hulking wedge of sculptured concrete and gold, the **Palác Koruna**, built in 1914 by one of Jan Kotěra's many pupils and employing a rare mixture of heavy constructivism and gilded ornamentation. The rather half-hearted post-modernism of the **ČKD dům**, directly above the main entrance/exit to Můstek, is no architectural match for it, though it does contain no fewer than three cafés, including one on the roof (under reconstruction at the time of writing) with an unbeatable view straight up the square.

On the right-hand side of the square, as you look up, are two functionalist buildings designed by Ludvík Kysela in the late 1920s, billed at the time as the ultimate glass curtain-wall buildings. Along with the Hotel Juliš (see below), they represent the perfect expression of the optimistic mood of progress and modernism that permeated the interwar republic. The building on the right was erected by the chocolate firm, Lindt; while the **Dům obuv** (House of Shoes), on the left, was built for the Czech shoe magnate, Tomáš Baťa, one of the greatest patrons of avant-garde Czech art. It was recently returned to the family, along with a number of their shoe factories, and is now, once more, a Baťa shoe shop.

Twenty-five years earlier, Czech architecture was in the throes of its own version of Art Nouveau, one of whose earliest practitioners was Jan Kotěra. The **Peterkův dům**, a slender essay in the new style, was his first work, undertaken at the age of 28. Kotěra, a pupil of the great Otto Wagner, came from the restrained Viennese school of Secession, and very soon moved on to a much less flamboyant constructivism. The square's earliest example of Czech functionalism, a few doors further up at no. 22, is the **Hotel Juliš**, designed by Pavel Janák, who had already made his name as one of the leading lights of the short-lived Czech Cubist (and later Rondo-Cubist) movement (see p.106).

Further up on the same side of the square is the **Melantrich** publishing house, whose first floor is occupied by the offices of the Socialist Party newspaper, *Svobodné slovo* (The Free Word). For forty years, the Socialist Party was a loyal puppet of the Communist government, but on the second night of the November 1989 demonstrations, the newspaper handed over its well-placed balcony to the opposition speakers of Občanské fórum (Civic Forum). Melantrich House faces probably the most famous and most beautiful building on the entire square, the Art-Nouveau **Hotel Evropa**, built in 1903–04. It represents everything the Czech modern movement stood against: chiefly, ornament for ornament's sake, not that this has in any way dented its popularity. The café terrace has always had a reputation for low-key cruising and a great deal of posing, but it's worth forgoing the sunlight for the interior, which is as sumptuous as it was when the hotel first opened.

The Wenceslas Monument and the National Museum

A statue of Saint Wenceslas (sv Václav) has stood at the top of the square since 1680 but the present **Wenceslas Monument**, by the father of Czech sculpture, Josef Václav Myslbek, was not finally unveiled until 1912, after thirty years on the drawing board. The Czech patron saint sits astride his mighty steed, surrounded by smaller-scale representations of four other Bohemian saints – his mother Ludmilla, Procopius, Adalbert and Agnes – added in the 1920s. It was at the foot of the statue that the new republic of Czechoslovakia was declared in 1918, while World War I was still raging on the western front. In 1968, and again in 1989, the monument was used as a national political noticeboard, constantly festooned in posters, flags and slogans; even now, it remains the city's favourite soap box venue.

A few metres below the statue, on January 19, 1969, the 21-year-old student Jan Palach set himself alight in protest against the continuing occupation of his country by the Soviets. His example was emulated four days later by another four people around the country, and, on February 25 – the anniversary of the Communist coup – by a fifth, Jan Zajíc. The spot is now occupied by the small, impromptu **martyrs' shrine**, with photos, candles and messages commemorating the deaths of all those who died at the hands of the Communist state.

At the top, southern end of Wenceslas Square sits the broad, brooding hulk of the **National Museum** (Mon & Fri 9am–4pm, Wed, Thurs, Sat & Sun 9am–5pm), built by Josef Schulz. Deliberately modelled on the great European museums of Paris and Vienna, it dominates the view up the square like a giant golden eagle with outstretched wings. Along with the National Theatre (see below), this is one of the great landmarks of the nineteenth-century Czech *národní obrození*, sporting a monumental gilt-framed glass cupola, worthy clumps of sculptural decoration and narrative frescoes from Czech history.

Unless you're a geologist or a zoologist, you're unlikely to be excited by most of the exhibits – room after room of stuffed animals and endless display cases full of rocks – but it's worth taking at least a quick look at the ornate marble entrance hall, and the **Pantheon** of Czech notables at the top of the main staircase. Arranged under the glass-domed hall are some forty-eight busts and statues of distinguished Czech men (plus a couple of token women and Slovaks), including the universally adored T. G. Masaryk, the country's founding president, whose statue was removed by the Communists from every other public place (there's a brief A–Z of leading Czechs, past and present, on p.449). Since the revolution, the appeal of the museum's temporary exhibitions (on such themes as Masaryk himself) has increased dramatically, so it's always worth checking to see what's on.

Wilsonova

At the southern end of Wenceslas Square is some of the worst blight that Communist planners inflicted on Prague; above all, the six-lane highway that now separates Nové Město from the residential suburb of Vinohrady to the east and south, and effectively cuts off the National Museum from Wenceslas Square. Previously known as Vitězného února (Victorious February) after the Communist coup, the road was renamed **Wilsonova** in honour of US President Woodrow Wilson (a personal friend of the Masaryk family), who effectively gave the country its independence from Austria-Hungary in 1918.

The former stock exchange building alongside the National Museum, only completed in the 1930s but rendered entirely redundant by the 1948 coup, was another victim of postwar "reconstruction". The architect Karel Prager was given the task of designing a new "socialist" **Federal Assembly** building on the same site, without destroying the old bourse: he opted for a supremely unappealing bronze-tinted plate-glass structure, supported by concrete stilts and sitting uncomfortably on top of its diminutive predecessor. The breakup of the federation means it's likely to become the new Czech parliament in the near future.

Next to the Parliament building, the **Smetanovo divadlo** (Smetana Theatre), the grand opera house built by the Viennese duo Helmer and Fellner, looks stunted and deeply affronted by the traffic which now tears past its front entrance. It was opened in 1888 as the *Neues Deutsches Theater*, shortly after the Czechs had built their own National Theatre on the waterfront. Always second fiddle to the Stavovské divadlo, though equally ornate inside, it was one of the last great building projects of Prague's once all-powerful German minority. The velvet and gold interior is still as fresh as it was when the Bohemian-born composer Gustav Mahler brought the traffic to a standstill, conducting the premiere of his Seventh Symphony.

The last building on this deafening freeway is **Praha hlavní nádraží**, Prague's main railway station, and one of the final glories of the dying Empire, designed by Josef Fanta and officially opened in 1909 as the *Franz Josefs Bahnhof* (though the emperor himself never bothered to visit the city in his entire reign). Trapped in the overpolished subterranean modern section, it's easy to miss the station's surviving Art-Nouveau parts. The original entrance on Wilsonova still exudes imperial confidence, with its wrought-iron canopy and naked figurines clinging to the sides of the towers; on the other side of the road, two great glass protrusions signal the new entrance in the Vrchlického sady.

The Golden Cross

The so-called *zlatý kříž* or **"golden cross"**, Prague's commercial centre and proba-bly the most expensive slice of real estate in the capital, is made up of Wenceslas Square and **Národní** and **Na příkopě**, Prague's busiest shopping streets and promenades, lined with banks, boutiques and bookshops. Their boomerang curve – following the course of the old moat, which was finally filled in in 1760 – marks the border between Staré Město and Nové Město (strictly speaking, the dividing line runs down the middle of the street). Ranged around here are a variety of styl-ish edifices, including the city's most flamboyant Art-Nouveau buildings.

Jungmannovo náměstí

Heading west from the northern end of Wenceslas Square along 28 října (October 28 – the foundation of the former republic), it's only a short way before you reach **Jungmannovo náměstí**. The square takes its name from Josef Jungmann (1772–1847), a prolific writer, translator and leading light of the *národní obrození*, whose pensive, seated statue was erected here in 1878.

The chunky charcoal-coloured **Adria Palace**, on the south side of the square, was designed in the 1920s by Pavel Janák and Josef Zasche. Janák was a leading figure in prewar Czech Cubism, but after the war he attempted to create a national style of architecture appropriate for the new republic. The style was dubbed "Rondo-Cubism", though few of the projects actually got off the ground, and most of its protagonists soon moved on to embrace the international modern movement of the likes of Le Corbusier and Bauhaus.

Originally built for the Italian insurance company *Reunione Adriatica di Sicurità*, the palace's basement was until very recently a studio theatre for the multimedia **Laterna magika** (Magic Lantern) company. In 1989, it became the underground nerve centre of the Velvet Revolution, when Civic Forum found temporary shelter here shortly after their inaugural meeting on the Sunday following the November 17 demonstration. Against a stage backdrop for

Dürenmatt's *Minotaurus*, the Forum thrashed out tactics in the dressing rooms and gave daily press conferences in the auditorium during the crucial fortnight before the Communists relinquished power. Since then, *Laterna magika* has moved to the much more spacious Nova scéna (see below) and the *Divadlo za branou II* is now based here instead. Upstairs, there's a good café-terrace from which to observe life on the square below.

On the other side of the Jungmann statue is one of Prague's most endearing Cubist legacies, Vlastislav Hofman's unique **Cubist streetlamp** (and seat) from 1912. Close by are the iron gates of the church of **Panna Marie Sněžná** (St Mary-of-the-Snows), once one of the great landmarks of Wenceslas Square, when it towered over the backs of the old two-storey houses that lined the square, but now barely visible from any of the surrounding streets. If the gates are shut, try going through the unpromising courtyard back near the Jungmann statue.

Like most of Nové Město's churches, the Panna Marie Sněžná was founded by Charles IV, who envisaged a vast coronation church on a scale comparable with the St Vitus Cathedral, on which work had just begun. Unfortunately, the money ran out shortly after completion of the chancel; the result is curious – a church which is short in length, but equal to the cathedral in height. The hundred-foot-high vaulting – which collapsed on the Franciscans who inherited the half-completed building in the seventeenth century – does little to stave off claustrophobia, further compounded by an overbearing Baroque altar which touches the ceiling. To get an idea of the intended scale of the finished structure, take a stroll through the small gardens, to the south of the church.

Národní

The eastern end of Národní is taken up with shops, galleries and clubs, all of which begin to peter out as you near the river. Three-quarters of the way down on the right-hand side is an eye-catching duo of Art-Nouveau buildings designed by Polívka in 1907–08. The first, at no. 7, was built for the **pojišťovna Praha** (Prague Savings Bank), hence the beautiful mosaic lettering above the windows advertising *život* (life insurance) and *kapital* (loans), as well as help with your *důchod* (pension) and *věno* (dowry). Next door, the slightly more ostentatious **Topičův dům**, headquarters of *Československý spisovatel*, the official state publishers, provides the perfect accompaniment, with a similarly ornate wrought-iron and glass canopy.

THE MASAKR – NOVEMBER 17 1989

On the night of Friday, November 17, 1989, a 50,000-strong, officially sanctioned student demo, organised by the students' union, *SSM* (League of Young Socialists), worked its way down Národní with the intention of reaching Wenceslas Square. Halfway down the street they were confronted by the *bílé přílby* (white helmets) and *červené barety* (red berets) of the hated riot-police. For what must have seemed like hours, there was a stalemate as the students sat down and refused to disperse, some of them handing flowers out to the police. Suddenly, without any warning, the police attacked and what became known as the **masakr** (massacre) began – no one was actually killed, though it wasn't for want of trying by the police. Under the arches of Kaňka's house (Národní 16), there's a small symbolic bronze relief of eight hands reaching out for help, a permanent shrine in memory of the hundreds who were hospitalised in the violence.

At the western end of Národní, overlooking the Vltava, is the gold-crested **National Theatre** (Národní divadlo), proud symbol of the Czech nation. Refused money by the Austrian state, Czechs of all classes dug deep into their pockets to raise funds for the venture themselves. The foundation stones, gathered from various historically significant sites in Bohemia and Moravia, were laid in 1868 by the historian and politician, František Palacký, and the composer, Bedřich Smetana; the architect, Josef Zítek, spent the next thirteen years on the project. In August 1881, just two months after the opening night, fire ripped through the building, destroying everything except the outer walls. But within two years the whole thing was rebuilt – even the emperor contributed this time – under the supervision of Josef Schulz (who went on to design the National Museum), and it opened once more to the strains of Smetana's opera *Libuše*. The grand portal on the north side of the theatre is embellished with suitably triumphant allegorical figures, and, inside, every square inch is taken up with paintings and sculptures by leading artists of the *národní obrození*. Tickets are relatively cheap but most productions are in Czech, so unless there's an opera or ballet on, content yourself with a quick peek at the decor.

Standing behind the National Theatre, and in dramatic contrast with it, is the theatre's new extension, the ultra-modern glass box of the **Nová scéna**, designed by Karel Prager, the leading architect of the Communist era, and completed in 1983. It's one of those buildings most Praguers love to hate, described by one Czech as looking like "frozen piss" – not that this seems to put off the swarms of theatregoers who choose to eat in its restaurant before the show.

The famous **Café Slavia**, opposite the theatre, has been a favourite haunt of the city's writers and artists (and, inevitably, actors) since the days of the First Republic. The Czech avant-garde movement, *Devětsil*, led by Karel Teige, used to hold meetings here in the 1920s, recorded for posterity by the Nobel prize-winner Jaroslav Seifert in his *Slavia Poems*. It's been carelessly modernised since those arcadian days but remains as popular as ever, with Czechs as much as tourists.

Na příkopě

Heading the other way from the northern end of Wenceslas Square, you can join the crush of bodies ambling down **Na příkopě** (literally "On the moat"). The street was once lined on both sides with grandiose buildings, like the former *Haas* department store at no. 4, built in 1869–71 by Theophil von Hansen, the architect responsible for much of the redevelopment of the Ring in Vienna. Many of the finest buildings, though – like the *Café Corso* and the *Café Francais*, once the favourite haunts of Prague's German-Jewish literary set – were torn down and replaced during the enthusiastic construction boom of the interwar republic. The Art-Nouveau **U Dorflerů**, at no. 7, from 1905, is one of the few survivors along this stretch, its gilded floral curlicues gleaming in the midday sun.

Further along, there are another couple of interesting buildings at nos. 18 and 20, designed by Polívka for the *Zemská banka* and connected by a kind of Bridge of Sighs suspended over Panská. It's worth nipping inside the **Živnostenka banka**, on the left, built in the 1890s in neo-Renaissance style, to appreciate the financial might of Czech capital in the last decades of the Austro-Hungarian Empire. On the right is the **Státní banka**, built some twenty years later, an arresting blend of the competing styles of the day – Art-Nouveau and nineteenth-century historicism. Yet more financial institutions, this time from the dour 1930s, line the far end of Na příkopě, as it opens up into náměstí Republiky.

Náměstí Republiky

Náměstí Republiky is an unruly space, made more so since the construction of its metro station and the ugly brown *Kotva* department store. The oldest structure on the square is the **Prašná brána** (Powder Tower), one of the eight medieval gate-towers that once guarded Staré Město. A small historical exhibition inside (April & Oct Sat, Sun & holidays 10am–5pm; May–Sept Sat, Sun & holidays 10am–6pm) traces the tower's architectural metamorphosis, up to its present remodelling by the nineteenth-century restorer, Josef Mocker. Most people, though, ignore the displays, and climb straight up for the modest view from the top.

Attached to the tower, the **Obecní dům** (Municipal House) is by far the most exciting Art-Nouveau building in Prague, one of the few places that still manages to conjure up the atmosphere of Prague's turn-of-the-century café society. Conceived as a cultural centre for the Czech community, it's probably the finest architectural achievement of the *národní obrození*, designed by Osvald Polívka and Antonín Balšánek, and extravagantly decorated inside and out with the help of almost every artist connected with the Czech Secession. From the lifts to the cloakrooms, just about all the furnishings remain as they were when the building was completed in 1911, and the cheapest way of soaking up the cavernous interior – peppered with mosaics and pendulous brass chandeliers – is to sit around the fountain at the far end of the spacious *kavárna*.

It's worth wandering upstairs, too, for a look at the central **Smetanova síň**, the city's largest concert hall, where the opening salvo of the Prague Spring Festival – traditionally a rendition of Smetana's *Ma vlast* (My Country) – takes place in the presence of the president. Recently, there have been **guided tours** of the building, showing off its abundant treasures (which include paintings by Alfons Mucha, Jan Preisler and Max Švabinský, among others); check at the *PIS* for the current times. Otherwise, the restaurant and café are open from 7am to 11pm, and there's a chance you may be able to just stroll into the other parts of the building.

Around Karlovo náměstí

The streets south of Národní and Wenceslas Square still run along the medieval lines of Charles IV's town plan, though they're now lined with grand nineteenth-century buildings. Of the many roads which head down towards Karlovo náměstí, **Vodičkova** is probably the most impressive, running southwest for half a kilometre from Wenceslas Square. You can catch several trams (#3, #14, #24) along this route, though there are a handful of buildings worth checking out on the way. The first, **U Nováků**, is impossible to miss, thanks to Jan Preisler's mosaic of bucolic frolicking (its actual subject, *Trade and Industry*, is confined to edges of the picture), and Polívka's curvilinear window frames and delicate, ivy-like ironwork. Originally built for the *Novák* department store in the early 1900s, for the last sixty years it has been a cabaret hall, restaurant and café all rolled into one.

Halfway down the street, at no. 15, the *McDonald's* "restaurant", opened in March 1992, must qualify as a landmark of sorts. Directly opposite is an imposing neo-Renaissance school, covered in bright-red sgraffito patterning, which was founded in 1866 as the **Minerva** girls' school, the first in Prague. At the beginning of this century, the school became notorious for the antics of its pupils, the "Minervans" – most famously Milená Jesenská, the epistolary lover of Franz Kafka – who shocked bourgeois Czech society with their experimentations with fashion, drugs and sexual freedom.

Karlovo náměstí

As Lazarská, meeting point of the city's night trams, leads off to the right, Vodičkova curves left towards Prague's biggest square, **Karlovo náměstí**, created by Charles IV as Nové Město's cattle market (Dobytčí trh). Unfortunately, its once impressive proportions are no longer so easy to appreciate, obscured by a tree-planted public garden and cut in two by the busy thoroughfare of Ječná.

The Gothic **Novoměstská radnice**, at the northern end of the square, was once a town hall to rival that of Staré Město. After the amalgamation of Prague's separate towns in 1784, however, it was used solely as a criminal court and prison. It was here that Prague's **first defenestration** took place on July 30, 1419, when the radical Hussite preacher Jan Želivský and his penniless religious followers stormed the building, mobbed the Catholic councillors and burghers and threw several of them out of the town hall windows onto the pikes of the Hussite mob below. Václav IV, on hearing the news, suffered a stroke and died just two weeks later. So began the long and bloody Hussite Wars (for details of Prague's two other defenestrations, see p.63 and 68).

Towards the river: Resslova

West off Karlovo náměstí, **Resslova** is a noisy extension of Ječná, heading towards the Vltava. A short way down is the eighteenth-century church of **sv Cyril and Metoděj**, the main base of the Orthodox church in the Czech republic since the 1930s, but originally constructed for the Roman Catholics by Bayer and Dientzenhofer. Amid all the traffic, it's extremely difficult to imagine the scene here on June 18, 1942, when seven of the Czechoslovak secret agents involved in the most dramatic assassination of World War II (see box below) were besieged in the church by over 300 members of the SS and Gestapo. For most of the night the Nazis fought a pitched battle, trying explosives, flooding and any other method they could think of to drive the men out of their stronghold in the crypt. Eventually, all seven agents committed suicide rather than give themselves up. There's a plaque at street level on the south wall commemorating those who died; in the crypt itself, which is rarely open, a small exhibition with photos details the incident.

The islands and the embankments

Magnificent turn-of-the-century mansions line the Vltava's right bank, almost without interruption, for some two kilometres from the Charles Bridge south to the rocky outcrop of Vyšehrad. It's a long walk, even just along the length of **Masarykovo** and **Rašínovo nábřeží**, though there's no need to do the whole lot in one go: you can hop on a tram (#3, #7 or #17) at various points, drop down from the embankments to the waterfront itself, or escape to one of the two islands connected to them, **Střelecký** and **Slovanský ostrov**.

The islands

Slovanský ostrov (commonly known as Žofín), accessible via Mánes, came about as a result of the natural silting of the river in the eighteenth century. By the late nineteenth century it had become one of the city's foremost pleasure gardens, where, as the composer Berlioz remarked, "bad musicians shamelessly make abominable music in the open air and immodest young males and females

THE ASSASSINATION OF REINHARD HEYDRICH

The assassination of Reinhard Heydrich in 1942 was the only attempt the Allies ever made on the life of a leading Nazi. It's an incident which the Allies have always billed as a great success in the otherwise rather dismal seven-year history of the Czech resistance. But, as with all acts of brave resistance during the war, there was a price to be paid. Given that the reprisals meted out on the Czech population were entirely predictable, it remains a controversial, if not suicidal, decision to have made.

The target, **Reinhard Tristan Eugen Heydrich**, was a talented and upwardly mobile anti-Semite (despite rumours that he was partly Jewish himself), a great organiser and a skilful concert violinist. He was a late recruit to the Nazi Party, signing up in 1931, after having been dismissed from the German Navy for dishonourable conduct towards a woman. However, he swiftly rose through the Party ranks to become, in the autumn of 1941, Protector of the puppet state of *Böhmen und Mähren* – effectively, the most powerful man in the Czech Lands. Although his rule began with brutality, it soon settled into the tried and tested policy which Heydrich liked to call *Peitsche und Zucker* (literally, "whip and sugar").

On the morning of May 27, 1942, as Heydrich was being driven by his personal bodyguard in his open-top Mercedes from his manor house north of Prague to his office in Hradčany, three Czechoslovak agents (parachuted in from England) were taking up positions in the northern suburb of Libeň. As the car pulled into Kirchmayer Boulevard (now V Holešovičkách), one of them, a Slovak called Gabčík, pulled out a gun and tried to shoot. The gun stuck but Heydrich's bodyguard, rather than driving out of the situation, slowed down and attempted to shoot back. At this point, another agent, Kubiš, threw a grenade at the Mercedes. The blast injured Heydrich and stopped the car, but failed to harm his bodyguard, who immediately jumped out and began chasing Gabčík down the street, shooting. Gabčík pulled out a second gun, shot the bodyguard dead and hopped on board an approaching tram.

Back at the Mercedes, Kubiš had been badly injured himself and, with blood pouring down his face, jumped on his bicycle and rode into town. Heydrich, seemingly only slightly wounded, flagged down a delivery van and hitched a lift to the nearest hospital. However, he died eight days later from shrapnel wounds and was given full Nazi honours at his Prague funeral; the cortège passed down Wenceslas Square, in front of a crowd of thousands – the Nazis made attendance compulsory. Revenge was quick to follow. The day after Heydrich's funeral, the village of **Lidice** (see p.141) was burnt to the ground.

The plan to assassinate Heydrich had been formulated in the early months of 1942 by the Czechoslovak government-in-exile in London, without consultation with the Czech Communist leadership in Moscow, and despite fierce opposition from the resistance within Czechoslovakia. Since it was clear that the reprisals would be horrific, the only logical explanation for the plan is that this was precisely the aim of the government-in-exile's operation – to forge a solid wedge of resentment between the Germans and Czechs. In this respect, if in no other, the operation was ultimately successful.

indulge in brazen dancing, while idlers and wasters . . . lounge about smoking foul tobacco and drinking beer". On a good day, things seem pretty much unchanged from those heady times. Concerts, balls, and other social gatherings take place here, and there are rowing boats for hire from May to October.

Closer to the other bank, and accessible via the most Legií (Legion's Bridge) by the National Theatre, **Střelecký ostrov**, or Shooters' Island, is where the army held their shooting practice, on and off, from the fifteenth until the nineteenth century. Later, it became a favourite spot for a Sunday promenade and is still popular, especially in summer. The first *Sokol* festival took place here in 1882; the first May Day demonstrations in 1890, and, one hundred years on, having been used and abused by the Communists for propaganda purposes, the traditional low-key *Májales* celebrations have returned.

Along the embankment

Most of the buildings along the waterfront are private apartments, and therefore inaccessible. One exception to this, and an architecturally atypical building for this part of Prague, is the striking white functionalist mass of the **Mánes Gallery** (Tues–Sun 10am–6pm), halfway down Masarykovo nábřeží. Designed in open-plan style by Otakar Novotný in 1930, it spans the narrow channel between Slovanský ostrov and the waterfront, close to the onion-domed Šítek watertower. The gallery is named after Josef Mánes, a traditional nineteenth-century land-scape painter and Czech nationalist, and puts on some of the more unusual exhibitions in Prague; there are two cafés, and an upstairs restaurant, suspended above the channel.

At **Palackého náměstí**, the buildings along the embankment retreat for a moment to reveal an Art-Nouveau sculpture to rival Šaloun's monument in Staroměstské náměstí (see p.79): the **Monument to František Palacký**, the great nineteenth-century Czech historian, politician and nationalist, by Stanislav Sucharda. Like the Hus Monument, which was unveiled three years later, this mammoth project – fifteen years in the making – had missed its moment by the time it was finally completed in 1912, and found universal disfavour. The critics have mellowed over the years, and nowadays it's appreciated for what it is – an energetic and inspirational piece of work. Ethereal bronze bodies, representing the world of the imagination, shoot out at all angles, contrasting sharply with the plain stone mass of the plinth, and, below, the giant seated figure of Palacký himself, representing the real world.

Vyšehradská and Ke Karlovu

Behind Palackého náměstí, off **Vyšehradská**, the twisted concrete spires of the **Emmaus monastery** (Emauzy) are an unusual modern addition to the Prague skyline. The monastery was one of the few important historical buildings to be damaged in the last war, in this case by a stray American bomb. The cloisters contain some extremely valuable Gothic frescoes, but since the return of the monks from their forty-year exile, it's become increasingly difficult to gain access to them. Heading south from here, Vyšehradská descends to a junction, where you'll find the entrance to the city's **botanical gardens** (Botanická zahrada; daily 10am–4/5/6pm), laid out in 1897 on a series of terraces up the other side of the hill; though far from spectacular, they're one of the few patches of green in this part of town.

On the far side of the gardens, Apolinářská runs along the south wall and past a grim red-brick maternity hospital before joining up with Ke Karlovu. Head left up here and the first street off to the right is Na bojišti, which is usually packed with tour coaches. The reason for this is the **U kalicha** pub, on the right, which was immortalised in the opening passages of the consistently popular comic novel *The Good Soldier Švejk*, by Jaroslav Hašek. In the story, on the eve of the Great War, Švejk (*Schweik* to the Germans) walks into *U kalicha*, where a plain-clothes officer of the Austrian constabulary is sitting drinking and, after a brief conversation, finds himself arrested in connection with the assassination of Archduke Ferdinand. Whatever the pub may have been like in Hašek's day (and even then, it wasn't his local), it's now unashamedly oriented towards reaping in the Deutschmarks, and about the only authentic thing you'll find inside is the beer.

Further down Ke Karlovu, set back from the road behind wrought-iron gates, is the russet country house **Vila Amerika** (Tues–Sun 10am–5pm), one of the most successful secular works of Kilian Ignaz Dientzenhofer. Finished in 1720, it now houses a museum devoted to **Antonín Dvořák**, easily the most famous of all Czech composers, who for many years had to play second fiddle to Smetana in the orchestra at the National Theatre, where Smetana was the conductor. When in his forties, Dvořák received an honorary degree from Cambridge before leaving for the "New World", and his gown is one of the very few items of memorabilia to have found its way into the museum's collection, along with the programme of a concert given at London's Guildhall in 1891. But there's compensation for what the display cabinets may lack in the tasteful period rooms, the composer's music wafting in and out of them, and the tiny garden dotted with Baroque sculptures.

The Police Museum and Na Karlově church

There's a metro station (I. P. Pavlova) not far from Vila Amerika, but if you've got a few hundred metres more left in you, continue south down Ke Karlovu. At the end of the street, the former Augustinian monastery of Karlov is now the **Police Museum** (Muzeum Policie; Tues–Sun 10am–5pm; closed July & Aug), formerly the Museum of the Security Forces. With the barbed wire and border patrols all but disappeared, and the police at the nadir of their popularity, the new exhibition concentrates on road and traffic offences, and the force's latest challenges: forgery, drugs and murder. It's not what it used to be, but it's still mildly amusing, with several participatory displays, including a *Scalextric* race track, road-crossing practice, and a quiz on the Highway Code (in Czech).

Attached to the museum is **Na Karlově** church, founded by Charles IV (of course), designed in imitation of Charlemagne's tomb in Aachen, and quite unlike any other church in Prague. If it's open, you should take a look at the dark interior, which was remodelled in the sixteenth century by Bonifaz Wohlmut. The stellar vault has no central supporting pillars – a remarkable feat of engineering for its time, and one which gave rise to numerous legends about the architect being in league with the devil.

From outside the church, there's a great panorama south across the Botič valley, to the twin delights of the skyscraper *Hotel Forum* and the low-lying **Palác kultury** (Palace of Culture), originally used for Party Congresses and now the country's biggest concert venue; to the right of the Palác kultury is Vyšehrad (see opposite). The nearest metro (Vyšehrad) is across Nuselské most; alternatively, you can walk down to the the the bottom of the valley and catch a tram (#7, #18 or #24).

Vyšehrad

At the southern tip of Nové Město, around 3km south of the city centre, the rocky red-brick fortress of **VYŠEHRAD** (literally "High Castle") has more myths attached to it per square inch than any other place in Bohemia. According to Czech legend, this is the place where the Slav tribes first settled in Prague, where the "wise and tireless chieftain" Krok built a castle, and whence his youngest daughter Libuše went on to found *Praha* itself. Alas, the archaeological evidence doesn't bear this claim out, but it's clear that Vratislav II (1061–92), the first Bohemian ruler to bear the title "king", built a royal palace here, to get away from his younger brother who was lording it in the Hrad. Within half a century the royals had moved back to Hradčany, into a new palace, and from then on Vyšehrad began to lose its political significance.

Charles IV had a system of walls built to link Vyšehrad to the newly founded Nové Město, and decreed that the *králová cesta* begin from here; these fortifications were destroyed by the Hussites in 1420, but the hill was settled again over the next two hundred years. In the mid-seventeenth century, the Habsburgs turfed everyone out and rebuilt the place as a fortified barracks, only to tear it down in 1866 to create a public park. The Czech *národní obrození* movement became interested in Vyšehrad when only the red-brick fortifications were left as a reminder of its former strategic importance, rediscovering its history and its legends, and gradually transforming it into a symbol of Czech nationhood.

For all its national historical significance, Vyšehrad today offers a pretty unremarkable set of buildings, and it's worth visiting mainly as an afternoon escape from the human congestion of the city, or in the evening to watch the sun set behind the Hrad.

The fortress

There are several approaches to the **fortress**, depending on where you arrive in Vyšehrad. From the Vyšehrad metro station, walk west past the modern Palác kultury, and enter through the Leopoldová brána; if you've come by tram #3, #7 or #21, all of which pass along the waterfront, you can either wind your way up Vratislavova and enter through the Cihelná brána, or take one of the two steep stairways leading up through the trees to a small side entrance in the west wall.

The last approach brings you out right in front of the blackened sandstone church of **sv Petr and Pavel**, rebuilt in the 1880s in dull neo-Gothic style on the site of an eleventh-century basilica. The twin openwork spires are the fortress's most familiar landmark; the church itself has been closed since archaeologists began to search for the remains of the eleventh-century royal palace here some years ago.

The Vyšehrad Cemetery

One of the first initiatives of the *národní obrození* movement was to establish the **Vyšehrad Cemetery** (Vyšehradský hřbitov; daily May–Sept 8am–7pm; March, April & Oct 8am–6pm; Nov–Feb 9am–4pm), which spreads out to the north and east of the church. It's a measure of the part that artists and intellectuals played in the foundation of the nation, and the regard in which they are still held, that the most prestigious graveyard in the city is given over to them: no soldiers, no politicians, not even the Communists managed to muscle their way in here.

Sheltered from the wind by its high walls, and lined on two sides by arcades, it's a small cemetery, filled with well-kept graves, many of them designed by the country's leading sculptors.

To the uninitiated only a handful of figures are well-known, but for the Czechs the place is alive with great names (there's a useful plan of the most notable graves at the entrance nearest the church). **Dvořák**'s grave, under the arches, is one of the more showy ones, with a mosaic inscription, studded with gold stones, glistening behind wrought-iron railings. **Smetana**, who died twenty years earlier, is buried in comparatively modest surroundings near the Slavín monument (see below). The Spring Music Festival begins with a procession from his grave to the Obecní dům, on the anniversary of his death.

The focus of the cemetery, though, is the **Slavín monument**, a big bulky stele, covered in commemorative plaques and topped by a sarcophagus and a statue representing Genius. It's the communal resting place of over fifty Czech artists, including the painter Alfons Mucha, the sculptors Josef Václav Myslbek and Ladislav Šaloun, the architect Josef Gočár, and the opera singer Ema Destinová.

The rest of the fortress

The rest of the deserted fortress makes for a pleasant afternoon stroll; you can walk almost the entire length of the ramparts, which give some superb views out across the city. The small museum of historical drawings in one of the bastions and the exhibition in the new deanery are both pretty dull, though you might want to head for the latter to buy some postcards. The **rotunda of sv Martin** – one of a number of Romanesque rotundas scattered across Prague – is the sole survivor of the medieval fortress, originally built by Vratislav II in the eleventh century but heavily restored by the nineteenth-century nationalists. Time is probably better spent lounging on the patch of grass to the south of the church, where you'll come across the gargantuan legendary statues by Myslbek that used to grace the city's Palackého most.

Czech Cubism in Vyšehrad

Even if you harbour only a passing interest in modern architecture, it's worth seeking out the cluster of **Cubist villas** below the fortress in Vyšehrad. Whereas Czech Art-Nouveau was heavily influenced by the Viennese Secession, it was Paris rather than the imperial capital that provided the stimulus for the short-lived but extremely productive Czech Cubist movement. In 1911, the *Skupina výtvarných umělců* or *SVU* (Group of Fine Artists) was founded in Prague, and quickly became the movement's organising force. **Pavel Janák** was the *SVU*'s chief theorist, **Josef Gočár** its most illustrious exponent, but **Josef Chochol** was the most successful practitioner of the style in Prague.

Cubism is associated mostly with painting, and the unique contribution of its Czech offshoot was to apply the theory to furniture (most of which now resides in the vaults of the UPM, see p.90) and **architecture**. In Vyšehrad alone, Chochol completed three buildings, close to one another below the fortress, using prismatic shapes and angular lines to produce the sharp geometric contrasts of light and dark shadows characteristic of Cubist painting. Outside the Czech Lands, only the preparatory drawings by the French architect Duchamp-Villon for his *Maison Cubiste* (never undertaken) can be considered remotely similar.

The most impressive example of Czech Cubist architecture, brilliantly exploiting its angular location, is the apartment block **nájemný obytný dům** at Neklanova 30, which dates from 1913. Further along Neklanova at no. 2, Antonín Belada built the street facade **uliční průčelí**, and around the corner is the most ambitious project of the lot – Chochol's **Kovařovicova vila**, which backs onto Libušina. The front, on Rašínovo nábřeží, is presently concealed behind some overenthusiastic shrubs, but it's still possible to appreciate the clever, slightly askew layout of the garden, designed right down to its zigzag garden railings. Further along the embankment is Chochol's largest commission, the **rodinný trojdům**, a building complex with room enough for three families.

The Suburbs

By the end of his reign in 1378, Charles IV had laid out his city on such a grand scale that it wasn't until the industrial revolution hit Bohemia in the midnineteenth century that the first **suburbs** began to sprout up around the boundaries of the medieval town. A few were rigidly planned, with public parks and grid street plans; most grew with less grace, trailing their tenements across the hills, and swallowing up existing villages on the way. The majority still retain an individual identity, which makes them worth checking out on even a short visit to the city.

Vinohrady

Southeast of Nové Město is the well-to-do nineteenth-century suburb of **VINOHRADY**, home over the years to many of the country's most notable personages. Although these days it has a run-down air about it, it's still a desirable part of town to live in, boasting two spacious parks – the **Riegrovy sady**, to the north, and the **Havlíčkovy sady**, to the south – and a fabulous array of turn-of-the-century mansions. In terms of conventional sightseeing, Vinohrady is definitely a low priority, but there are a few places here (and in neighbouring Žižkov) worth visiting, most of them quick and easy to reach by metro.

If Vinohrady has a centre, it's **náměstí Míru** (metro náměstí Míru), a leafy square centred on the neo-Gothic church of sv Ludmila. From here, block after block of decaying tenements, each covered in its own individual garment of sculptural decoration, form a grid-plan of grand bourgeois avenues stretching eastwards to the city's great cemeteries (see below).

Vinohrady's other main square, **náměstí Jiřího z Poděbrad** (metro Jiřího z Poděbrad), halfway between náměstí Míru and the cemeteries, contains Prague's most celebrated modern church, **Nejsvětější Srdce Páně** (Most Sacred Heart of Our Lord), built in 1928 by Josip Plečník, the Slovene architect responsible for much of the remodelling of the Hrad. It's a marvellously eclectic and individualistic work, employing a sophisticated potpourri of architectural styles: a classical pediment, a Gothic rose window, and a great slab of a tower with a giant transparent face, as well as the bricks and mortar of contemporary constructivism. Plečník also had a sharp eye for detail; look out for the little gold crosses inset into the brickwork like stars, on the inside and out, and the celestial orbs of light suspended above the heads of the congregation.

Žižkov

Unlike Vinohrady, **ŽIŽKOV** is a traditionally working-class area – and was a Communist Party stronghold even before the war, earning it the nickname "Red Žižkov". Nowadays it's home to a large proportion of Prague's Romany community and other less privileged sections of Czech society. The main reason for venturing into Žižkov is to visit its two landmarks – one ancient (Vítkov hill) and the other modern (the television tower) – and the city's main cemeteries, on the borders of Žižkov and Vinohrady.

The Žižkov television tower

At over 100m, the **Žižkov television tower** (Televizní vysíláč) is the tallest (and the most unpopular) building in Prague. Close up, though, it's difficult not to be impressed by this truly intimidating piece of futuristic architecture, its smooth grey exterior giving no hint of humanity. In the course of its construction, the Communists saw fit to demolish part of a nearby Jewish cemetery, that had served the community between 1787 and 1891; a small section survives to the northwest of the tower.

Begun in the 1970s in a desperate bid to keep out West German television, the tower has only become fully operational within the last few years, and now boasts a café four metres below ground, a restaurant on the fifth floor, and a **viewing platform** (výhlídka; daily 9am–10pm) on the eighth floor. For a not inconsiderable 50kčs, you can take the lift up there, though given the tower's position in a thoroughly uninspiring part of town, the view is not among the city's best. To get to the tower, take the metro to Jiřího z Poděbrad and walk northeast a couple of blocks.

The cemeteries

Approaching from the west, the first and the largest of Prague's vast cemeteries – each of which is bigger than the entire Jewish quarter – is the **Olšany cemetery** (Olšanské hřbitovy; metro Flora), originally created for the victims of the great plague epidemic of 1680. The perimeter walls are lined with glass cabinets, stacked like shoe-boxes, containing funereal urns and mementoes, while the graves themselves are a mixed bag of artistic achievements, reflecting the funereal fashions of the day as much as the character of the deceased. The cemetery is divided into districts and crisscrossed with cobbled streets; at each gate there's a map, and an aged janitor ready to point you in the right direction at the mention of a name.

To the east of Olšany cemetery, and usually totally deserted, is the **war cemetery** (Vojenský hřbitov); the entrance is 200m up Jana Želivského, on the right (metro Želivského). Its centrepiece is the monument to the Soviet liberation of 1945, surrounded by a small, tufty meadow dotted with simple white crosses. Nearby, the graves of Czechs who died fighting for the Habsburgs on the Italian front in World War I are laid out in a semicircle.

Immediately south of the war cemetery is the **New Jewish Cemetery** (Nový židovský hřbitov; April–Aug 8am–5pm; Sept–March 8am–4pm; closed Fri & Sat), founded in the 1890s, when the one by the Žižkov television tower was full. It's a melancholy spot, particularly so in the east of the cemetery, where large empty allotments wait in vain to be filled by the generation who perished in the Holocaust. In fact, the community is now so small that it's unlikely the graveyard will ever be full. Most people come here to visit **Franz Kafka**'s grave, 400m east along the south wall and signposted from the entrance (for more on Kafka, see p.91). He is buried, along with his mother and father (both of whom outlived him), beneath a plain headstone; the plaque below commemorates his three sisters who died in the camps.

Žižkov hill

Žižkov hill (also known as Vítkov) is the thin green wedge of land that separates Žižkov from Karlín, another industrial district to the north. From its westernmost point, which juts out almost to the edge of Nové Město, can be gained what' is probably the definitive panoramic view over the city centre. It was here, on July 14, 1420, that the Hussites enjoyed their first and finest victory at the **Battle of Vítkov**, under the inspired leadership of the one-eyed general, Jan Žižka (hence the name of the district). Ludicrously outnumbered by something like ten to one but fanatically motivated, Žižka and his Táborite troops thoroughly trounced Emperor Sigismund and his papal forces.

The giant granite **Žižkov monument** was built between the wars as a memorial to the new nation, though its pompous brutality was just as well suited to its post-war use as a Communist mausoleum: presidents Gottwald, Zápotocký and Svoboda were all buried here, along with the Unknown Soldier and various Party hacks. Žižkov was an ideal resting place, lying as it does in the heart of "Red Žižkov", from where the Communists drew so much of their working-class support; in 1990, however, the bodies were reinterred elsewhere to protect them from desecration.

To get to the monument, take the metro to Florenc, walk under the railway lines, and then up the steep lane U památníku. On the right as you climb the hill is the post-1914 section of the **Military Museum** (Vojenské muzeum; Tues–Sun April–Oct 8.30am–5pm; Nov–March 9.30am–4.30pm), guarded by a handful of unmanned tanks, howitzers and armoured vehicles. Before 1989, this place was a glorification of the Warsaw Pact, pure and simple; its recent overhaul has produced a much more evenly balanced account of both world wars.

Holešovice and Bubeneč

The districts of **HOLEŠOVICE** and **BUBENEČ**, tucked into a huge U-bend in the Vltava, have little in the way of magnificent architecture, but they make up for it with two huge areas of green: to the south **Letná**, where Prague's greatest gatherings occur, and to the north the **Stromovka park**, bordering the Výstaviště fairgrounds.

A small piece of Hradčany

For convenience, we've included in this chapter the small patch of Hradčany that lies to the northeast of the castle. The easiest way to this part of town is to take the metro to Hradčanská and head up Tychonova to the leafy avenue of Marianské hradby. To the left, past the Belvedere, is the **Chotkovy sady**, Prague's first public park, founded in 1833 by the ecologically minded city governor, Count Chotek. The atmosphere here is a lot more relaxed than in the nearby Royal Gardens, and you can happily stretch out on the grass and soak up the sun, or head for the south wall, which enjoys an unrivalled view of the bridges and islands of the Vltava. At the centre of the park there's a bizarre grotto-like memorial to the nineteenth-century Romantic poet Julius Zeyer, an elaborate monument from which life-sized characters from Zeyer's works, carved in white marble, emerge from the blackened rocks amid much drapery.

Across the road from the park, hidden behind its overgrown garden at Mieckiewiczova 1, the **Bílkova vila** (mid-May to Sept Tues–Sun 9am–5pm) honours one of the most unusual Czech sculptors, František Bílek. Born in 1872 in a part of South Bohemia steeped in the Hussite tradition, Bílek lived a monkish life, spending years in spiritual contemplation, reading the works of Hus and other Czech reformers. The villa was built in 1911 to Bílek's own design, intended as both a "cathedral of art" and the family home. Even so, at first sight, it's a strangely mute red-brick building, out of keeping with the extravagant Symbolist style of Bílek's sculptures: from the outside, only the front porch, supported by giant sheaves of corn, and the sculptured figures in the garden – the fleeing Comenius and followers – give a clue as to what lies within.

Inside, the brickwork gives way to bare stone walls lined with Bílek's numerous religious sculptures – giving the impression you've walked into a chapel rather than an artist's studio. In addition to his sculptural and relief work in wood and stone, often wildly expressive, there are also ceramics, graphics and a few mementoes of Bílek's life. His work is little known outside his native country, but his contemporary admirers included Franz Kafka, Julius Zeyer, and Otakar Březina, whose poems and novels provided the inspiration for much of Bílek's art.

Letná

Cross over the bridge at the eastern end of the Chotkovy sady, and you'll find yourself on the flat green expanse of the **Letná plain**, traditional assembly point for invading and besieging armies. It was laid out as a public park in the mid-nineteenth century, but its main post-1948 function was as the site of the May Day parades. For these, thousands of citizens were dragooned into marching past the south side of the city's main football ground, the Sparta stadium, where the old Communist cronies would take the salute from a giant red podium.

On November 26, 1989, the park was the scene of a more genuine expression of popular sentiment, when over 750,000 people gathered here to join in the call for a general strike against the Communist regime. Unprecedented scenes followed in April 1990, when a million Catholics came to hear Pope John Paul II speak on his first visit to an eastern European country other than his native Poland.

Letná's – indeed Prague's – most famous monument is one which no longer exists. The **Stalin monument**, the largest in the world, was once visible from almost every part of the city: a thirty-metre-high granite sculpture portraying a procession of people being led to Communism by the Pied Piper figure of Stalin, popularly dubbed "the bread queue". Designed by Otakar Švec, who committed suicide before it was unveiled, it took 600 workers 500 days to erect the 14,000-ton monster, which was revealed to the cheering masses on May 1, 1955. This was the first and last popular celebration to take place at the monument. Within a year, Krushchev had denounced his predecessor and, after pressure from Moscow, the monument was blown to smithereens by a series of explosions spread over a fortnight in 1962.

All that remains above ground is the statue's vast concrete platform, on the southern edge of the Letná plain, now a favourite spot for skateboarders and another good viewpoint, with the central stretch of the Vltava glistening in the afternoon sun. If you're in need of some refreshment, head for the café at the nearby **Hanavský pavilón**, originally built for the 1891 Prague Exhibition in a flamboyant style which anticipated the arrival of Art Nouveau a few years later.

Holešovice museums

At present Holešovice boasts just one fully functioning museum, the **Museum of Technology** (Tues–Sun 10am–5pm) on Kostelní, which contains an impressive technological collection, plus a host of old planes, trains and automobiles, and an upper gallery of motorbikes. The showpiece is the hangar-like main hall, packed with machines from Czechoslovakia's industrial heyday between the wars, when the country's Škoda cars and Tatra limos were really something to brag about. Upstairs, there are displays tracing the development of early photography, and a collection of some of Kepler and Tycho de Brahe's astrological instruments. Below ground, a mock-up of a coal mine offers guided tours every other hour, kicking off at 11am.

The **Museum of Modern and Contemporary Czech Art** is at present no more than a plan, despite constant rumours that it is to open imminently. The 1928 Trade Fair building being restored for the purpose – ten minutes' walk northeast of the Museum of Technology, at the corner of Dukelských hrdinů and Veletržní (tram #5, #12, #17 or #19) – is a magnificent seven-storey glass curtain-wall design that's in many ways Prague's ultimate functionalist masterpiece. It certainly did Le Corbusier's head in, as he himself admitted in 1930: "When I first saw the Trade Fair building in Prague I felt totally depressed, although I did not approve of the building wholeheartedly. However, I did realise that the large and convergent structures I had been dreaming of really existed somewhere, while at the time I had just built a few small villas".

Výstaviště and Stromovka park

Five minutes' walk north up Dukelských hrdinů takes you right to the front gates of the **Výstaviště**, a motley assortment of buildings, originally created for the 1891 Prague Exhibition, that have served as the city's main trade fair arena and funfair ever since. The Communist Party held its rubber-stamp congresses here from 1948 until the late 1970s, and more recently several brand new permanent structures were built for the 1991 Prague Exhibition. The canopy over the main entrance, off U Sjezdového paláce, is one of these – a modern echo of the flamboyant glass and iron **Průmyslový palác** at the centre of the complex.

The park is at its busiest on summer weekends, when hordes of Prague families descend to down hot dogs, drink beer and listen to traditional brass band music. Apart from the annual fairs and lavish special exhibitions, there are a few permanent attractions, such as the city's **planetarium** (Mon–Thurs 8am–noon & 1–6pm, Fri 8am–noon, Sat & Sun 10am–6pm; hours can vary); the **Maroldova panoráma** (daily 9am–5pm), a giant diorama of the 1434 Battle of Lipany (see *Contexts* for the significance of this battle); and the **Dětský svět**, a funfair and playground for kids. Another permanent fixture that will hopefully be restored in the not too distant future is the panoramic cinema screen, near the diorama.

To the west is the *královská obora* or royal enclosure, more commonly known as **Stromovka park**. Originally a game park for the noble occupants of the Hrad, it's now Prague's largest and leafiest public park. From here, you can wander northwards to Troja and the city's zoo (see below), following a path that leads under the railway, over the canal, and on to the Císařský ostrov (Emperor's Island) – and from there to the right bank of the Vltava.

Troja

Though still well within the municipal boundaries, the suburb of **TROJA**, across the river to the north of Holešovice and Bubeneč, has a distinctly provincial air. Its most celebrated sight is its **chateau** (Trojský zámek; April–Sept Tues–Sun 9am–5pm; bus #112 from metro Nádraží Holešovice), perfectly situated against a hilly backdrop of vines. Despite a recent renovation and rusty red repaint, its plain early Baroque facade is no match for the action-packed, blackened figures of giants and titans who battle it out on the chateau's monumental balustrades. To visit the **interior**, you'll have to join one of the guided tours. The star exhibits are the gushing frescoes depicting the victories of the Habsburg Emperor Leopold I (1657–1705) over the Turks, which cover every inch of the walls and ceilings of the grand hall. Alternatively, you can simply take a wander through the chateau's pristine French-style formal **gardens** (open all year), the first of their kind in Bohemia.

On the other side of U trojského zámku, which runs along the west wall of the chateau, is the city's capacious but dilapidated **zoo** (zoologická zahrada; daily April 7am–5pm; May 7am–6pm; June–Sept 7am–7pm; Oct–March 7am–4pm), founded in 1931 on the site of one of Troja's numerous hillside vineyards. Despite its rather weary appearance, all the usual animals are on show here, and kids, at least, have few problems enjoying themselves. Thankfully, a programme of modernisation is currently under way, though only the new lion and tiger building, to the south, has so far been completed. In the summer, you can take a "ski-lift" (lanová dráha) from the duck pond to the top of the hill, where the zoo's prize exhibits – a rare breed of miniature horse known as Przewalski – hang out.

Bílá hora and Hvězda

Spread across the hills to the northwest of the city centre are the leafy, garden suburbs of **Dejvice** and **Střešovice**, peppered with once-swanky villas, built between the wars for the upwardly mobile Prague bourgeoisie and commanding magnificent views across the north of the city. A couple of kilometres southwest of Dejvice, trams #8 and #22 terminate close to the once entirely barren limestone summit of **Bílá hora** (White Mountain). It was here, on November 8, 1620, that the first battle of the Thirty Years' War took place, sealing the fate of the Czech nation for the following three hundred years. In little more than an hour, the Protestant forces under Count Thurn and the "Winter King" Frederick of Palatinate were roundly beaten by the Catholic troops of the Habsburg Emperor Maximilian. As a more or less direct consequence, the Czechs lost their aristocracy, their religion, their scholars and, most importantly, the remnants of their sovereignty.

To get to the hill from the tram stop, walk west, take the first road on the right, Nad višňovkou, and then turn right when you see the small monument (*mohyla*). There's nothing much to see now, apart from the monument and a pilgrims' church, just off Nad višňovkou. This was erected by the Catholics to commemorate the victory, which they ascribed to the timely intercession of the Virgin Mary – hence its name, **Panna Marie Vítězná** (St Mary the Victorious).

A short distance to the northeast of Bílá hora is the hunting park of **Hvězda** (obora Hvězda), scene of a last-ditch counterattack launched by the Moravian

Brethren during the battle. Nowadays it's one of Prague's most beautiful and peaceful parks, with soft, green avenues of trees radiating from a bizarre star-shaped building (hvězda means "star") that was designed by the Archduke Ferdinand of Tyrol for his wife in 1555. Fully restored in the 1950s, it now houses a **museum** (Tues–Sat 9am–4pm, Sun 10am–5pm) devoted to the reactionary writer Alois Jirásek (1851–1930), who popularised old Czech legends during the *národní obrození*, and the artist Mikuláš Aleš (1852–1913), whose drawings were likewise inspired by Czech history. There's also a small exhibition on the Battle of Bílá hora (see above) on the top floor. It's the building itself, though – decorated with delicate stucco work and frescoes – that's the greatest attraction; it makes a perfect setting for the chamber music concerts occasionally staged here. To get back into town, take tram #1, #2 or #18 from Heyrovského náměstí, near the main entrance to the park.

Smíchov and Zbraslav

SMÍCHOV is for the most part an old nineteenth-century working-class suburb, much like Žižkov, though to the west, as it gains height, it harbours another of Prague's sought-after villa quarters. To the north, it borders with Malá Strana, and in fact takes in a considerable part of the woods of Petřín, south of the Hunger Wall.

As long ago as 1838, the Dušek's **Bertramka Villa** (April–Sept Tues–Fri 2–5pm, Sat & Sun 10am–noon & 2–5pm; Oct–March Tues–Fri 1–4pm, Sat & Sun 10am–noon & 1–4pm; metro Anděl), halfway up Mozartova, was turned into a shrine to Mozart, who stayed here on several occasions towards the end of his life. Very little survives of the house he once knew, because of a fire on New Year's Day 1871 – not that this has deterred later generations of Mozart lovers from flocking here (for more on Mozart's links with Prague, see p.73). These days, what the museum lacks in memorabilia, it makes up for in Rococo ambience and the occasional Mozart recital. To get to Bertramka, take the metro to Anděl, walk a couple of blocks west up Plzeňská, then left up Mozartova.

Zbraslav

One of the best art museums in Prague is in the little-visited village of **ZBRASLAV**, 10km south of the city, though now within the municipal boundaries (bus #241, #243, #255, *ČSAD* bus, or local train from metro Smíchovské nádraží). The Přemyslid king Otakar II built a hunting lodge here, which was later turned into a Cistercian monastery and now houses the National Gallery's **collection of modern Czech sculpture** (Tues–Sun 10am–6pm). The sculptures are imaginatively strewn about the chambers, courtyards and gardens of the Baroque buildings. The ground floor is filled with the work of Josef Václav Myslbek (1848–1929), who laid the groundwork for the remarkable outpouring of Czech sculpture in the first half of this century. There are also some outstanding works by the likes of Ladislav Šaloun, who was responsible for the Hus Monument, unveiled in 1912; Stanislav Sucharda, who sculpted the Palacký Monument, completed three years later; and Otto Gutfreund, whose Cubist creations predate those of Picasso et al. Last but not least in the gardens is *The Motorcyclist*, by Otakar Švec, the only extant work by the man responsible for the Stalin Monument.

Eating and drinking

Every restaurant, *pivnice* and *vinárna* in Prague has either closed down or been privatised in the last year or so, so it's not surprising that **eating and drinking** is a bit unpredictable at the moment, with enormous variations in price and quality. A few authentic ethnic eateries have started up, though traditional Czech food still predominates. New western-style outfits are also beginning to appear, charging prices that westerners find very reasonable but few Czechs can afford. Meanwhile, the number of cheap Czech *pivnice* has considerably reduced, particularly downtown.

The biggest mistake most first-time visitors make is to confine their eating and drinking to the obvious sightseeing areas, where prices are generally much higher, quality often a low priority, and, in summer, spare tables a real find. It's worth venturing, instead, into the southern section of Nové Město, which hides a number of good-value restaurants; or to suburbs like Vinohrady, just ten minutes' travel from the centre.

In the **high season**, Prague can be unbearably crowded, and its restaurants rarely manage to cope. There are, however, a number of ways around the problem: reserve a table in advance; eat your main meal at lunchtime (as most Praguers do), when the rest of the city's tourists are busy sightseeing; or try somewhere a bit further from the centre. If you're intent on **drinking** plenty of Bohemia's world-class beers, bear in mind that, with precious few exceptions, Prague's *pivnice* close between 10 and 11pm.

Breakfast, snacks and fast food

Unless a continental **breakfast** is included in the price of your accommodation, you're going to find it difficult to know exactly what to eat for breakfast and where to eat it. The Czechs get up so early, they rarely bother with more than a gulp of grainy black coffee, and perhaps a slice of bread and salami. A few of the newer **bakeries** offer croissants, sundry pastries and coffee all under the same roof, but most don't. Sandwiches (*sendvič*) are starting to catch on, and there are various new **fast-food places** to try out (not all of them *McDonald's*). If you get up much later than 10am, you might as well join Prague's working population for lunch.

Hradčany and Malá Strana

Golden Bun, Mostecká 3. Burgers, kebabs and falafel. Open daily until 8.30pm.

Saté, Pohořelec 4. Convenient fast-food place with a vaguely Indonesian bent, but small portions and zero atmosphere. Open daily 10am–8pm.

U labutí (The Swan), Hradčanské náměstí 11. The cheap snack bar, not the posh *vinárna* in the same building, with outside tables in summer. Open Mon–Sat 10am–6pm.

Staré Město and Nové Město

Arbat, Na příkopě 29, Nové Město. Before *McDonald's*, this bland but extremely popular hamburger outlet was the only fast-food place in town – it remains to be seen how it handles the competition. Open daily 7.30am–11pm.

Bonal, Staroměstské náměstí 4, Staré Město. Flash Czech-German joint venture selling sandwiches, pastries and some of the best coffee in Prague. Stand-up only. Open daily 9am–9pm.

Country Life, Melantrichova 15, Staré Město. Cramped, popular stand-up buffet within a health food shop, which dishes out vegan snacks – though you'll have to buy a lot of them to fill yourself up. Mon–Thurs 8.30am–7pm, Fri 8.30am–2pm, Sun noon–6pm.

Frank's Bistro, Na můstku (right by the bottom end of Wenceslas Square). A convenient but uninspiring stomach filler, run by an LA expatriate, serving pizza, pasta and other snacks. Open daily 7am–10pm.

McDonald's, Vodičková 15, Nové Město and Václavské náměstí *Pilsner Urquell*. Open daily 8am–11pm. Their main virtue is that they sell draught *Pilsner Urquell*.

Palace, Panská 12 (on corner with Jindřišská), Nové Město. Situated in the basement of the most expensive hotel in Prague, this is no place to linger (there are no tables, only counters), but a good spot to binge on fresh produce and the self-service salad bar. Open daily 6–11am & noon–midnight.

Poříčská pekárna, Na poříčí 30, Nové Město. One of the new-style Viennese bakeries, selling coffee and pastries. Open Mon–Fri 7am–7pm, Sat until 1pm.

Rybárna, Václavské náměstí 43, Nové Město. Stand-up buffet with fish in batter and fishy salads on offer. Open daily until 8pm.

Cafés and bars

Prague can no longer boast a **café society** to rival the best in Europe, as it could at the beginning of this century, though a few of the classic haunts survive. Nevertheless, many Praguers still spend a large part of the day smoking and drinking in the city's cafés, particularly in the summer, when the tables spill out onto the streets and squares. At all the places picked out below, the emphasis is more on drinking than eating, and in many the only food on offer will be cakes.

Malá Strana

Café de Colombia, Mostecká 3. French radio, Colombian coffee, but very few tables under its Gothic vaults. Open daily noon–midnight.

Malostranská kavárna, Malostranské náměstí 28. A time-honoured café founded in 1874 in a late eighteenth-century palace. Despite the changes, it's still a good place to meet for coffee and cakes, inside or on the summer terrace, if you can get a table. Open daily 7am–11pm.

Rubín, Malostranské náměstí 9. Arty cellar café with the occasional live music or theatre show. Open 3pm–1am.

Staré Město and Nové Město

A Scéna, (also known as *Lávka*), Novotného lávka, Staré Město (below the Smetana Museum). Tiny, trendy and lively riverside café, with tables outside in summer. Superb view of the castle; occasional theatre and music gigs inside. Open daily noon–2am.

Beránkova-Osvěžovna, Masarykovo nábřeží (two doors down from the *Becher Club*) Nové Město. The first of two plain cafés behind the national theatre. Go for the hot chocolate. Open daily until 11.30pm.

Café Bunkr, Lodecká 2, Nové Město. Posey (but cheap) café attached to the club of the same name. Open daily until 5am.

Hotel Evropa, Václavské náměstí 25, Nové Město. *The* place to be seen on Wenceslas Square. If you want to appreciate the sumptuous Art-Nouveau decor, take breakfast inside. Open daily 10am–11.30pm.

Mánes, Masarykovo nábřeží 250, Nové Město. Pristine white functionalist café, above the gallery, with a view on to the island. The entrance is round the side from the gallery.

Obecní dům, náměstí Republiky, Nové Město. The *kavárna*, with its famous fountain, is in the more restrained south hall of this huge Art-Nouveau complex. Ask for the cake trolley. Open daily 7am–11pm.

Paris-Praha, Jindřišská 7, Nové Město. Small, chic café selling *Gauloise* singles; with a French delicatessen next door. Open Mon–Fri 8.30am–7pm, Sat 8.30am–1pm.

Paříž, U obecního domu 1, Staré Město. The prices are sky-high for Prague, but there's a certain faded elegance about this hotel *kavárna*. Open daily until 1am.

Slavia, Národní 1, Nové Město. An enduring and endearing Prague institution, this place has recently changed hands but is due to re-open sometime in 1993 (see p.99). Open 8am–midnight.

U zelené lipy (The Green Lime Tree), Melantrichova 12, Staré Město. Convenient, smoky caffeine stop en route from Staroměstské náměstí to Wenceslas Square. Open daily 10am–11pm.

Restaurants, pivnice and vinárna

For a full meal, you can go to a *restaurace*, a *pivnice* or a *vinárna*. A *pivnice* is primarily a beer hall for serious (predominantly male) drinkers, but most of them also serve food, and some even have separate (generally more mixed) dining areas (*jídelna*). *Restaurace* span the range from glorified *pivnice* to extremely posh affairs, run by tuxedoed waiters with Viennese airs and graces. A *vinárna* is traditionally a more intimate affair, perhaps with a little live music, a long wine list, and late opening hours. Having said all that, the differences between all three can be very vague indeed.

Most places serve traditional Czech food – beef or pork and dumplings or potatoes – though there are a number of new restaurants offering **international cuisines** – mainly Chinese and Italian – which make a change from the calorific local fare. The Czechs eat their main meal of the day at lunchtime (when you'll be offered the widest choice of dishes), and most kitchens stop taking orders around 10pm. At all but the cheapest *pivnice*, it's recommended that you **reserve a table** in advance, especially in the high season: either ring the number provided, or call in earlier in the day.

As prices continue to rise, we have classified the following listings in comparative terms. Expect to pay no more than £3/$5 a head for a full meal with drinks in a cheap place; around £5/$8 per head in a moderately priced restaurant; and upwards of £7/$12 in an expensive one. While £7/$12 for a meal is hardly expensive to a westerner, it still is for most Czechs – you're unlikely to be sharing your table with any locals. Bear in mind, too, that the full repercussions of privatisation have yet to take effect, and that many of the places listed below may close down or double their prices overnight.

Hradčany and Malá Strana

Hradčany and Malá Strana are two of the nicest parts of the city in which to spend the evening. However, they also contain some of Prague's most exclusive (and expensive) restaurants and *vinárna*, so do check the prices before committing yourself.

Baráčnická rychta, Na tržiště 22 (down a narrow passageway off Nerudova), Malá Strana. A real survivor – a small backstreet *pivnice* squeezed in between the embassies, with a cheap and filling restaurant attached. Open daily 11am–11pm. Cheap.

Český rybářský svaz (Czech Fishermen's Club), U Sovových mlýnů (☎53 02 23), Malá Strana. Worth the trouble to get to – it's hidden away in the park on Kampa island. The manager has an appropriately sailor-like beard, and the fish is fresh from the Sázava river. Open Mon–Sat 1–9pm. Cheap.

Nebozízek (Little Auger), Petřínské sady 411 (☎53 79 05), Malá Strana; funicular from Újezd to first stop. Adventurous Czech cuisine and incredibly attentive service; the view is fantastic. Open daily 11am–6pm & 7–11pm. Moderate.

U černého vola (The Black Bear), Loretánské náměstí 1, Hradčany. Does a brisk business providing the popular light beer *Velkopopovický kozel* in huge quantities to thirsty local workers; its future is uncertain, however. Open 9.30am–9pm. Cheap.

U čerta (The Devil's), Nerudova 4 (☎53 09 75), Malá Strana. Good steaks, some veggie dishes, and not the rip-off you'd expect, given its prime location on the *králová cesta* up to the castle, but expect it to be fairly full. Open daily noon–3pm & 6–11pm. Moderate.

U kocoura (The Cat), Nerudova 2, Malá Strana. The last surviving pub on Nerudova, which was bought by the Beer Party in January 1992 to prevent it, too, from disappearing. Serves some of the best *Pilsner Urquell* in town; the food doesn't stretch much beyond sausages. Open daily until 11pm. Cheap.

U Lorety, Loretánské náměstí 8, Hradčany (☎53 13 95). Right next door to the Loreto chapel, and facing the monster Černín Palace, this is an excellent place to eat outside in summer. Familiar Czech menu, but served with more than the usual flair. Open daily noon–11pm. Moderate.

U malířů (The Artist's), Maltézské náměstí 11, Malá Strana (☎53 18 83). A converted sixteenth-century house that used to belong to an artist called Jiří Šic (pronounced "Shits"). Now one of the best (and most expensive – upwards of 2000kčs a head) restaurants in Prague, run by a French catering company who use fresh produce flown in daily from Paris. Open Mon–Sat 11.30am–3.30pm & 7pm–2am. Extremely expensive.

Staré Město and Josefov

Staré Město has probably the highest concentration of eating places in Prague. Prices, even in the *pivnice*, tend to be higher than elsewhere, so if you're on any kind of budget, it's best to stay away from the more obvious tourist spots like Karlova, Staroměstské náměstí and Celetná.

Bellevue, Smetanovo nábřeží 18 (☎235 95 99). The view of the Charles Bridge and Prague Castle is outstanding, and the food's not bad either. Anywhere that serves fresh vegetables and crispy French fries is a cut above most Prague outfits. Open daily 11am–11pm. Expensive.

Košer jídelna, Maislova 18. Indifferent self-service kosher restaurant in the Jewish town hall, frequented mostly by Prague's dwindling Jewish community. Open 11.30am–1pm. Moderate.

Krušovická pivnice, Široká 20. Once one of the best *pivnice* in Prague; nowadays spoilt by the pretentious decor and its proximity to Josefov. Nevertheless, it still serves *Krušovice* beer, one of Bohemia's finest lagers. Cold food only. Open daily 10am–10pm. Cheap.

Pivnice ve skořepce, Skořepka 1 (☎22 80 81). Unfriendly staff, but if you manage to get a table they serve huge helpings of pork, chicken and duck, and litre mugs of *Gambrinus*. Open Mon–Fri 11am–10pm, Sat 11am–8pm. Cheap.

Pizzeria Mikuláš, Benediktská 16 (☎231 57 27). Stuck in a backstreet off Revoluční, which no doubt contributes to the fact that this is one of the best pizza places in Prague; try the *krabí* (crab). Open Mon–Sat 11.30am–10pm. Cheap.

Reykjavik, Karlova 20 (no reservations accepted). The owners really are Icelandic, though the cuisine – is pretty international. The soups and starters are definitely worth going for, but the best feature is the wonderful variety of fresh(ish) fish, flown in from you know where. Open daily 11am–11pm. Expensive.

U dvou koček (The Two Cats), Uhelný trh. Rowdy *Pilsner Urquell* pub, best known nowadays as a hang-out for pimps and prostitutes. Open Mon–Sat 10am–11pm. Cheap.

U králova dvora (The King's Court), Královorska. Refreshingly untacky, roomy café-restaurant behind the Obecní dům, where you've a good chance of getting a table. Standard Czech dishes on offer. Open daily 10am–11pm. Moderate.

U medvídků (The Little Bears), Na Perštýně 7. Another Prague institution going back to the thirteenth century. Nowadays, the food is not great, and the beer, *Budvar* (the original Budweiser) it is not always what it should be, but it is central, unpretentious and roomy. Open Mon–Sat 11am–11pm. Cheap.

U Rudolfa, Maislova 5 (☎232 26 71). A small *vinárna* in the Jewish Quarter serving tasty meat dishes, grilled in front of you by the chef. If there are no free tables, you can eat at the bar. Open daily 10am–10pm. Moderate.

U supa (The Vulture), Celetná 22. Lively fourteenth-century pub serving cheap Czech meals and very strong, dark *Braník* beer, either inside or on the cobbles of its cool, vaulted courtyard. Open Mon–Sat 11am–9pm. Cheap.

U sv Salvátora, Staroměstské náměstí. Fairly quiet pleasant *vinárna*, despite its location, serving food and reasonably priced wine until late. Open 11am–1am. Cheap.

U zátiší (Still Life), Liliova 1 (☎26 51 07). Exquisitely prepared international cuisine with fresh vegetables and regular non-meat dishes, all served in *nouvelle cuisine* sized portions by professional waiters. Set menus 350–500kčs. Open noon–3pm & 6–11pm. Expensive.

U zlatého tygra (The Golden Tiger), Husova 17. Beery *pivnice* frequented by Prague's literary crowd, including the pub's permanent resident, writer and bohemian, Bohumil Hrabal. Its future is currently uncertain. Open Mon–Sat 3–11pm.

Nové Město

Nové Město covers quite a large area, and you'll need to use public transport to get to some of the recommendations listed below. As a general rule, the prices along the "golden cross" of Národní, Na příkopě and Wenceslas Square will be higher than elsewhere.

Arco, Hybernská 16. Don't expect period furnishings (yet) from the café which gave its name to the "Arconaut Circle" (Kafka, Kisch, Brod et al). Open until 11pm. Cheap.

Branický sklípek, Vodičkova 26. One of the few places where you can down the lethal *Braník 14°* brew. Open daily until 11pm. Cheap.

Crazy Daisy, Vodičkova 9 (☎235 00 21). Misleading American name and trendy bistro-bar decor for what is really just a better-than-average Czech restaurant. Fish and veggie dishes available, not to mention blueberry pie. Open daily 10am–11pm. Moderately priced.

Na rybárně (The Fishmonger's), Gorazdova 17. Wonderful fish restaurant in a cosy cellar, tucked away in the backstreets behind Havel's riverside flat. Good *Pilsner Urquell* on tap. Open Mon–Fri 4pm–1am. Cheap.

Obecní dům, náměstí Republiky. Forget about the prices (which are ridiculous) and the plastic plants, the palatial Art-Nouveau decor is infinitely more satisfying than any Czech meal. Open daily until 11pm. Expensive.

Peking, Legerova 64 (☎29 35 31); metro I. P. Pavlova. Passable Chinese food, and triple-glazing to keep out the noise of the traffic. Open Mon–Sat until 11pm. Moderately priced.

U bubeníčků (The Drummer Boy), Myslíkova 8. Great place to down a few beers and eat some simple Czech cuisine, after visiting the Mánes gallery. Open daily until 11pm. Cheap.

U Fleků, Křemencova 11. Famous medieval *pivnice* where the unique dark 13° beer, *Flek*, has been exclusively brewed and consumed since 1499. Despite seats for over five hundred, you may still have to fight for a bench. The food is perfectly OK, but it's best to go during the day. Open daily 9am–11pm. Cheap.

U Pinkasů, Jungmannovo náměstí 15. Famed as the first *pivnice* in Prague to serve *Pilsner Urquell* (which it still does). Despite its proximity to Wenceslas Square, it still manages to keep a few Czech regulars. Open daily until 11pm. Cheap.

U zpěváčků (The Choir Boy), Na struze 7. The *vinárna* stays open late and is famous for the spaghetti dish that makes up its entire menu; the *pivnice*, round the corner, is a completely different scene (and closes much earlier) – a smoky workers/musicians' pub with an ironic line in Marxist-Leninist tracts, and the local *Staropramen* on tap. *Vinárna* open Mon–Sat 5pm–2am, Sun 5pm–midnight; *pivnice* open daily 11am–10pm. Cheap.

Viola, Národní 7 (☎26 67 32). Small, nominally Italian restaurant with a wide range of steaks and pasta dishes, topped with indifferent sauces. Also puts on cabaret and live bands. Open daily noon–midnight. Moderate.

Vltava, Rašínovo nábřeží (☎29 49 64). A tasty and little-known fish restaurant right by the water's edge, below the main road. Open daily 11am–10pm. Moderate.

The suburbs

Most of the following are easily accessible from downtown, but you should reserve a table to avoid a wasted journey.

CG-čínský restaurace, Janáčkovo nábřeží 1, Smíchov (☎54 91 64); tram #4, #7, #14 or #16. Genuine Chinese cuisine, hence the high prices, popularity and obligatory reservations. Open daily 11.30am–midnight. Expensive.

China-restaurant, Francouzská 2, Vinohrady (☎25 26 43); metro náměstí Míru. Stunningly unimaginative name for what is one of Prague's best ethnic restaurants. Good Chinese food, prepared and served by an all-Chinese staff. Open daily 11am–11pm. Expensive.

Dlouhá zeď (The Great Wall), sídliště Pankrác, Michle; metro Pankrác, then one stop south-west on bus #188. Huge Chinese-run restaurant, in the middle of a housing estate, which serves seriously delicious Chinese food. The menu is long, but the portions are small, so you need to order plenty of dishes. Open Tues–Sun 11am–3pm & 5.30–11pm. Moderate.

Mateo, Arbesovo náměstí 15, Smíchov; tram #6, #9 or #12. A real find in Prague – a whole variety of fresh salads, plus pasta and other meaty and non-meaty Italian-style dishes. Open Mon–Fri 9am–9pm.

Orient, Bělehradská 14, Nusle (☎43 09 13); tram #6 or #11 from metro I. P. Pavlova. A real treat down in the seemingly unpromising Botič valley. Good-value, authentic Chinese food, with a great selection of desserts, too. Open daily 11am–3pm & 5–11pm. Moderate.

Pizzeria West, náměstí bratří Synků 511, Nusle (☎434 502); tram #6 or #11 from metro I. P. Pavlova. One of Prague's better pizzerias, run by some very friendly Macedonian Slavs. Try the *Scandinavská* topped with caviar and sardines. Open daily 10.30am–10.30pm. Cheap.

Principe, Anglická 23, Vinohrady (☎25 96 14); metro náměstí Míru. A new Italian restaurant with the airs, graces and prices of the real thing. The food is pretty special for Prague, too, but it's not difficult to blow 750kčs or more per person here. Open noon–2.30pm & 6–11.30pm. Expensive.

Rebecca, Olšanské náměstí 8, Žižkov; tram #5, #9 or #26 from metro Hlavní nádraží. Tiny non-stop bistro serving meat and pasta dishes, plus sundry other snacks. Open daily 9am–8pm & 9pm–7am. Cheap.

Toscana, Vinohradská, Vinohrady (one block west from metro Flora). Popular new pizza place featuring a *Quattro Formaggi* topped with real Gorgonzola. Open noon–10pm; closed Fri & Sat. Cheap.

U Góvindy, Na hrázi 5, Libeň; metro Palmovka. Newly opened Hare Krishna (*Haré Kršna* in Czech) restaurant serving organic veggie slop. Operates a pay-what-you-can system. Open Mon–Fri noon–6pm. Cheap.

Entertainments

For many Praguers, **entertainment** is confined to an evening's drinking in one of the city's beer-swilling *pivnice*. But if you're looking for something a bit different, there's plenty to keep you from night-time frustration. To find out **what's on**, check out the listings sections of the English-language weekly *Prague Post*, or, for more comprehensive coverage, the fortnightly *Prognosis*. Alternatively, with a bit of Czech you can scour the exhaustive Czech weekly listings broadsheet, *Program*. Another source is the monthly *Přehled*, which gives a full rundown of classical music, theatre and opera performances.

Clubs and live venues

Although there's infinitely more choice than there was prior to 1989, Prague still has nothing like the number of **clubs** you'd expect from a European capital. The dance craze has yet to hit Prague in any significant way; pure dance clubs are the exception away from the tacky meat markets around Wenceslas Square. The **live music** scene is a bit more promising, and quite a few nightclubs double as live music venues, although Czech reggae or skinhead punk may not suit everyone's tastes.

One good thing about going clubbing in Prague is that, compared to the west, it's phenomenally cheap. Admission to live gigs or nightclubs is rarely more than 50kčs, and drinks are only slightly more expensive than usual. And, if you can handle it, a few places stay open until 5 or 6am.

Concert venues

Major western bands only rarely include Prague in their European tours, as tickets here have to be sold at a fraction of their price in the west. Nevertheless, acts like The Rolling Stones, Frank Zappa and Guns 'n' Roses have all made it here, and played at one or another of the venues listed below.

Lucerna, Vodičkova 36, Nové Město (☎235 26 48). Grand old turn-of-the-century ballroom with dripping balconies, now the favoured venue for largish Czech gigs and the trendier imported acts (Siouxsie and the Banshees played here in 1992).

Stadión Sparta, Milady Horákové, Holešovice; metro Hradčanská. Prague's main football stadium, and by far the most popular venue for the really big western acts.

Palác kultury, 5 května 65, Nusle; metro Vyšehradská (☎417 27 41). Prague's largest indoor venue for big-name, mainstream acts, classical concerts and much else besides.

Clubs and gigs

As well as DJs, there are gigs by Czech bands almost every night in the city's clubs and discos. Clubland is a fickle world – places open and close, or go in and out of favour – and the licensing laws are causing problems for some venues, so bear all this in mind if you check out any of the following.

Bar Club, Hybernská 10, Nové Město. Incredibly uninspiring name for one of the city's best nightspots. A very mixed crowd, including many of Prague's African students, goes down to the basement ballroom for the club's nightly "Reggae Sound System" – loud, proud and very early 1980s. Open until 5am; closed Wed & Sun.

Borát, Újezd 18, Malá Strana; tram #6, #9 or #22 from metro Národní třída. A dark and dingy post-punk den which sprawls across three floors of a knackered old building close to the funicular railway. Open daily until 6am.

Bunkr, Lodecká 2, Nové Město (☎231 45 35). Flavour of the month when it first opened, *Bunkr* is, as you might guess, a converted wartime bunker, painted black, and fitted with the longest bar (and slowest service) in Prague. Open until 5am; live music from 9pm.

Classic Club, Pařížská 4, Staré Město. Mainstream dance music, plus an hour or so of 1960s classics for the older crowd who frequent the place. Open until 2am.

Futurum, Zborovská 7, Smíchov; tram #4, #14 or #16 from metro Karlovo náměstí. Soft metal disco. Open until 5am.

Junior klub na Chmelnici, Koněvova 219, Žižkov (☎82 85 98). The main venue for domestic indie bands. Doubles as an alternative theatre venue, too.

Klub na petynce, Radimova 2, Břevnov (☎35 28 18); bus #108, #174 or #235 from metro Hradčanská. Standard indie venue, so expect bands like Gregory Peccary and the Yo Yo Band. Gigs (and the odd seminar) start around 7.30pm – check it's not a seminar.

Mamma klub, Elišky Krásnohorské 7, Staré Město. Popular with local students and tourists, with some serious dancing going down for once.

Rock Café, Národní 22, Nové Město. Tries hard to evoke the underground, but is considered passé in the fickle world of Prague clubbing, since it made its name in the early days of post-Communist euphoria. Open daily until 3am; live music from 10.30pm.

Strahov 007, Strahov stadium, Spartakiádní; tram #8 or #22. Student club with regular thrashy gigs by the local talent; wear black. Open Thurs & Fri until 11pm or later.

Ubiquity, Na příkopě 22, Nové Město. By far the biggest club in Prague, with a team of English DJs, several dancefloors and Mexican food on offer. The central location means it attracts more tourists than most. Open daily 9pm–5am.

Jazz

Despite a long indigenous tradition, Prague today has just a handful of good jazz clubs, and audiences remain predominantly foreign. With little money to attract foreign acts, however, the artists are almost exclusively Czech, and do the entire round of venues each month. The one exception to all this is the annual **international jazz festival** in October, which regularly attracts big names from abroad.

Agharta Jazz Centrum, Krakovská 5, Nové Město (☎22 45 58). New jazz club in a side street off the top end of Wenceslas Square. Open daily 8pm–midnight.

Jazz Art Club, Vinohradská 40, Vinohrady (☎25 76 54); short walk from metro Muzeum. Open Tues–Sun until 2am.

GAY AND LESBIAN NIGHTLIFE

For the latest on Prague's still very low-key gay and lesbian nightlife, you'll need to get hold of the Czech listings weekly *Program*, the gay magazine *SOHO*, or the Czech monthly gay and lesbian broadsheet *Lambda*. In the meantime, the addresses listed below were, with varying degrees of openness, part of the "gay scene" at the time of writing, though most catered for gay men rather than lesbians.

Pubs, Bars and Cafés

Evropa
Václavské náměstí 29, Nové Město.
Kabinet Houdek
Rytířská 18, Staré Město.

Rostov
Václavské náměstí 21, Nové Město.
U dubu
Belgická 9, Vinohrady.

Discos

Červený mlýn
Sokolovská 67, Karlín.
Homolka
Zahradníčkova 16, Motol.

T-Club
Jungmannovo náměstí 17, Nové Město.
U Petra Voka
Na bělidle 40, Smíchov.

Contacts

Gay Service
Olduichova 40, Vyšehrad (☎692 63 59).
Lambda
Pod Kotlářkou 14, Smíchov (☎52 73 88).

SOHO Revue
Vinohradská 46, Vinohrady (☎25 78 91).

Malostranská beseda, Malostranské náměstí 21, Malá Strana (☎53 90 24). Venue with a varied booking policy but often features jazz acts. Music from 8pm.

Press Jazz Club, Pařížská 9, Staré Město (☎53 18 35). Large, unprepossessing former conference hall, with poor acoustics, but you're pretty well guaranteed a seat, and the acts are as good (or bad) as anywhere else. Open until 2am.

Reduta, Národní 20, Nové Město (☎20 38 25). Prague's best-known jazz club, so reserve a table in advance if you want to be sure of a seat. Open Mon–Sat until midnight.

Classical music, opera and ballet

Classical concerts take place throughout the year in Prague, but by far the biggest annual event is the *Pražské jaro* (Prague Spring), the country's most prestigious **international music festival**. It traditionally begins on May 12, the anniversary of Smetana's death, with a performance of *Ma vlast*, and finishes on June 2 with a rendition of Beethoven's Ninth Symphony. The main venues are listed below, but keep an eye out for concerts in the city's churches and palaces, gardens and courtyards. Bear in mind that some (though by no means all) theatres and concert halls are **closed in July and August**.

The cost of **tickets** can vary enormously: most are extremely inexpensive, but prices for some events, such as opera at the Stavovské divadlo, are beginning to approach western levels. The major venues all have their own box offices, and in addition to these there are now several **ticket agencies** throughout the city. The most comprehensive, *Sluna*, has outlets in the Alfa arcade on Wenceslas Square and Černá růže arcade on Panská; the *PIS* on Na příkopě also sells tickets for most events. Don't despair if everything is officially sold out (*výprodano*), as standby tickets are often available at the venue's box office on the night.

Stavovské divadlo (formerly the Tylovo divadlo), Ovocný trh, Staré Město (☎22 86 58). Prague's oldest opera house, looking superb after its recent renovation, puts on a mixture of opera, ballet and straight theatre (with simultaneous headphone translation available).

Smetanovo divadlo, Wilsonova, Nové Město (☎26 97 46); metro Muzeum. A sumptuous nineteenth-century opera house built by the city's German community, and now the number-two venue for opera and ballet.

Smetanova síň, Obecní dům, náměstí Republiky, Nové Město (☎232 98 38). Fantastically ornate Art-Nouveau concert hall where the Prague Spring Festival kicks off, and is also home to the Czech Philharmonic Orchestra (ČF).

Theatre

Theatre has always had a special place in Czech culture, one which the events of 1989 only strengthened. Not only did the country end up with a playwright as president, but it was the capital's theatres that served as information centres during those first few crucial weeks.

Predictably enough, the economic situation is making things very difficult for Prague's theatres; audiences nowadays are often small and/or overwhelmingly made up of visitors. Most plays in Prague are performed in Czech, but mime, puppetry and "black theatre" are still strongly represented, and are thriving on the international audiences.

Traditional theatres

Divadlo DISK, Karlova 8, Staré Město (☎26 53 77). During term time, this is the main venue for the city's drama students' productions, while in summer it's given over to "black theatre".

Divadlo za branou II, Národní 40, Nové Město (☎26 00 33). Theatre showing the multimedia extravaganza that went down so well at the Montréal EXPO 58. It's been going ever since and is a bit too obviously tourist-oriented for some.

Národní divadlo, Národní 2, Nové Město (☎20 53 64). Prague's grandest nineteenth-century theatre puts on a wide variety of plays, opera and ballet. Worth visiting for the decor alone.

Nová scéna, Národní 40, Nové Město (☎20 62 60). Prague's most modern and versatile stage puts on mostly straight theatre, with the occasional opera or ballet, and is now the main stage for the multimedia *Laterna magika*.

Semafor, Alfa arcade, Václavské náměstí, Nové Město (☎26 14 49). Another multimedia venture founded in the 1960s, now catering mostly for Prague's foreign visitors.

Black theatre, mime and puppetry

Branické divadlo pantomimy (Braník Pantomime Theatre), Branická 63, Braník (☎46 05 07); tram #3 or #17, stop Modřanská. Puts on an adventurous mixture of mime and panto-mime featuring Czech and foreign troupes. Hosts an international festival of mime every June.

Divadlo minor, Gorkého Senovážné náměstí 28, Nové Město (☎22 51 41). Children's puppet shows most days; adult shows on Wed evenings.

Divadlo na zábradlí, Anenské náměstí 5, Staré Město (☎236 04 49). Havel's old haunt back in the 1960s, now home base for the Ladislav Fialka troupe, founded by the great-grandfather of Czech mime who died in 1991. Shows straight theatre as well as mime.

Divadlo Spejbla a Hurvínka, Římská 45, Vinohrady (☎25 16 66). Features the indomitable puppet duo, Spejbl and Hurvínek, created by Josef Skupa earlier this century and still going strong at one of the few puppets-only theatres in the country.

Národní divadlo marionet (National Marionette Theatre), Žatecká 1, Josefov (☎232 34 29). Kids' matinees and adult evening shows using traditional all-string marionettes. Also listed under *Divadélko říše loutek*.

Studio Gag, Národní 25, Nové Město (☎26 54 36). Mime artist Boris Hybner's legendary slapstick studio theatre.

Film

More than half the **films** shown in Prague cinemas are American productions, usually around nine months' old and dubbed into Czech. *Prague Post* and *Prognosis* publish a list of films to be shown in their original language; in Czech publications *české titulky* (meaning Czech subtitles) are the words to look for. Most of the city's central main screens are either on or just off Wenceslas Square. The **cinemas** listed below are all that's left of Prague's once vast array of film clubs and art house cinemas. Keep a look out, too, for films shown at the various national cultural institutions around town too.

Alfa, Václavské náměstí 28, Nové Město. A sadly under-used 70mm screen that is, without doubt, the best place to see new releases.

Dlabačov, Bělohorská 24, Střešovice (☎311 53 28); tram #8 or #22. Twice daily, at around 5 and 8pm, you can come here to watch classic films such as *Butch Cassidy and the Sundance Kid*.

Miš Maš, Veletržní 61, Holešovice; tram #1, #8, #25 or #26. Newly opened art house cinema screening recently released art films.

Pražský filmový klub, Sokolovská, Karlín (☎231 57 05); metro Florenc. This place shows some seriously offbeat and unusual material from the archives. You need to become a member (for a nominal fee).

Sports

Prague is almost entirely surrounded by hills, woods and rivers, which means it's easy to do a day's **hiking** while based in the city. Sports facilities are more of a problem, with only a few easily accessible for tourists. If you want to check **forthcoming sports events** get hold of *Program* or ask at a *PIS* office.

Soccer

The top **soccer** team, **Sparta Praha**, play at the Sparta stadium by the Letná plain (a five-minute walk from metro Hradčanská); international matches are played there too. The other local teams are the army team, **Dukla Praha**, whose stadium is in Dejvice, just below the Baba housing development (tram #20 or #25 from metro Dejvická); **Slavia Praha**, who play in Vršovice, just off U Slavie (tram #4, #7, #22 or #24); and **Bohemians**, whose ground is nearer to town, off Vršovická (tram #6, #7 or #24). **Tickets** for all matches are extremely cheap, and can be bought at the ground on match day (even Sparta have only sold out twice in the last twenty-odd years). The season runs from September to December and March to June, and matches are usually held on a Sunday afternoon.

Ice hockey

Ice hockey is the country's second most popular sport (the national side came third in the 1992 Winter Olympics), and, like their football namesake, **Sparta Praha** are one of the most successful teams. Their *zimní stadión* (winter stadium) is next door to the Výstaviště exhibition grounds in Holešovice (tram #5, #12 or #17). **Tickets** can be bought from the stadium on match day, and again cost very little. Matches are fast, physical, and can take anything up to three hours; they take place on Tuesday, Friday and sometimes Sunday afternoon.

Horse racing

Prague's main racecourse is at **Velká Chuchle**, 5km or so south of the city centre; take bus #129, #172, #241, #243, #244, #255 or *osobní* train from Smíchovské nádraží. Steeplechase and hurdles take place from May to October on Sunday afternoons; trots all year round on Thursdays. There's also a smaller trot course on **Císařský ostrov**, north of the Stromovka park (May–Oct only).

Kids' Activities

There are plenty of playgrounds in Prague, ranging from the *Dětský svět* at the **Výstaviště** fairground (p.111) to the swings and slides of countless suburban parks. In summer, the streets are alive with buskers and **street performers**, particularly at the bottom of Wenceslas Square, on Staroměstské náměstí, and of course, on the Charles Bridge. Another good place to head for is **Petřín Hill** (see p.74); take the funicular to the top for a spectacular view of Prague, followed by a visit to the Bludiště (Mirror Maze) and a climb up the miniature Eiffel Tower.

If none of the above is suitable, there are several **puppet theatres** in Prague (details on p.123), and the *American Hospitality Centre* on Malé náměstí shows **children's films** (in English) on Saturday mornings. Trams can be fun – try #22, which goes round some great hairpins, or the vintage trams #91 and #92 (Sat & Sun in summer only). And if all else fails, there's the badly underfunded **zoo** with all the usual beasts and birds, plus a children's train, swings and slides (see p.112).

Listings

Airlines *Aeroflot*, Pařížská 5, Staré Město (☎26 08 62); *Air France*, Václavské náměstí 10, Nové Město (☎26 01 55); *Alitalia*, Revoluční 5, Nové Město (☎231 05 35); *British Airways*, Štěpánská 63, Nové Město (☎236 03 53); *ČSA*, Revoluční 1, Nové Město (☎21 46); *KLM*, Václavské náměstí 39, Nové Město (☎26 43 62); *Lufthansa*, Pařížská 5, Josefov (☎232 74 40); *SAS*, Štěpánská 61, Nové Město (☎22 81 41).

American Express, Václavské náměstí 54, Nové Město (Mon–Fri 6.30am–8pm, Sat 6.30am–1pm).

Banks Most banks are open Mon–Fri 7.30am–noon & 1.30–3.30pm; at other times you'll have to rely on the exchange outlets, which charge much higher commission; there's a 24hr exchange bureau at the airport.

Books in English *Bohemian Ventures*, náměstí Jana Palacha 2, Staré Město. A student bookshop on the ground floor of the Philosophical Faculty, specialising in English-language books. *Cizojazyčná literatura*, Na příkopě 27, Nové Město, stocks a large contingent of Kafka and Agatha Christie, plus postcards, posters, maps and guides.

British Council, Národní 10, Nové Město (☎250 0986; library open Mon–Fri 9am–3pm; closed July & Aug).

Car rental *Avis/Pragocar*, Opletalova 33, Nové Město (☎34 10 97); *Budget*, Národní 17, Nové Město (☎232 29 16); *Europcar*, Pařížská 26, Nové Město (☎231 02 78); *Hertz, Hotel Palace*, Panská 12, Nové Město (☎236 16 37). All the above, except *Esucar*, also have offices at the airport.

Car repairs *Austin Rover*, Jeseniova 56, Žižkov (☎27 23 20); *BMW, Ford, Mercedes & VW*, Severní XI, Spořilov (☎76 67 52); *Fiat*, Na stráži, Krč (☎42 66 14); *Renault*, Ďablická 2, Kobylisy (☎88 82 57). **24-hour breakdown**, Limuzská 12, Malešice (☎77 34 55).

Church services in English on Sunday mornings: *Anglican*, sv Kliment, Klimentská, Staré Město at 11am; *Ecumenical*, Cirkev Bratrská, Vrázova 4, Smíchov at 11.15am; *Roman Catholic*, sv Josef, Josefská, Malá Strana at 10.30am.

Dentists Emergency dentist (7pm–7am), Vladislavova 22, Nové Město.

Department Stores *Bílá labuť*, Na poříčí 23, Nové Město; *Kotva*, náměstí Republiky 8, Nové Město; *Máj*, Národní 26, Nové Město; *Syp*, Šénova 2232, Chodov; metro Chodov.

Embassies/consulates *Belgium*, Valdštejnská 6 (☎54 40 51); *Britain*, Thunovská 14, Malá Strana (☎53 33 47); *Canada*, Mickiewiczova 6, Hradčany (☎32 69 41); *CIS* (the former Soviet Union), Pod kaštany 1, Bubeneč (☎38 19 40); *Denmark*, U Havlíčkových sadů, Vinohrady (☎25 47 15); *France*, Velkopřevorské náměstí 2, Malá Strana (☎53 30 42); *Finland*, Dřevná 2, Smíchov (☎20 55 41); *Germany*, Vlašská 19 (☎53 23 51); *Hungary*, I. V. Mičurina 1, Hradčany (☎36 50 41); *Italy*, Nerudova 20, Malá Strana (☎53 06 66); *Norway*, Na Ořechovce, Dejvice (☎35 66 51); *Poland*, Valdštejnská 8, Malá Strana (☎53 69 51); *Sweden*, Úvoz 13, Malá Strana (☎53 33 44); *USA*, Tržiště 15, Malá Strana (☎53 66 41).

Emergencies Ambulance ☎158; Police ☎155; Fire service ☎150.

Health food *Bio-Market*, Mostecká 3, Malá Strana (Mon–Sat 7am–10pm, Sun 10am–6pm); *Country Life*, Melantrichova 15, Staré Město (Mon–Thurs 8.30am–7pm, Fri 8.30am–2pm, Sun noon–6pm).

Hospitals 24hr casualty at *Záchranná služba*, Dukelských hrdinů, Holešovice.

International calls can be made from the 24hr telephone exchange at the main post office on Jindřišská, or alternatively from any of the new cardphones. English-speaking operator ☎0135.

Lost Property Bolzanova 5, Nové Město (☎24 84 30).

Markets Flea markets at Bubenské nábřeží, Holešovice (Mon–Sat; metro Vltava) and Stadión Sparta, Milady Horákové, Holešovice (Sat & Sun; metro Hradčanská); food, flowers and sundry goods at Havelská, Staré Město (Mon–Sat).

Pharmacies 24hr chemist at Na příkopě, Nové Město (☎22 00 81).

Post office Main office/*poste restante* at Jindřišská 14, Nové Město (limited 24hr service); parcels over 1kg at Plzeňská 139, Smíchov.

Records Pop, rock and jazz CDs from *Bonton*, Malostranské náměstí 31, Malá Strana; Czech classical and traditional folk from *Dedika*, Celetná 32, Staré Město.

Radio *BBC World Service* (101.1 MHz); *Europe II* (88.2 MHz) plays Euro-pop; *Radio 1* (91.9 MHz) plays rock from east and west, and has short English-language bulletins at 10am and 3.30pm on weekdays.

AROUND PRAGUE

Few capital cities can boast such extensive unspoilt tracts of woodland so near at hand as Prague. Once you leave the half-built high-rise estates of the outer suburbs behind, the traditional provincial feel of Bohemia (Čechy) immediately makes itself known. Towns and villages still huddle below the grand residences of their former lords, their layout little changed since medieval times.

To the north, several such chateaux grace the banks of the Vltava, including the wine-producing town of **Mělník**, on the Labe (Elbe) plain. Beyond Mělník lie the wooded gorges of the **Kokořínsko** region, too far for a day trip, but perfect for a weekend in the country. One of the most obvious day-trip destinations is to the east of Prague: **Kutná Hora**, a medieval silver mining town with one of the most beautiful Gothic churches in the country.

Further south, there's a couple of chateaux worth visiting along the **Sázava valley**; while nearby, two more, **Průhonice** and **Konopiště**, are set in exceptionally beautiful and expansive grounds – with a car, you could take in all four in a day. Southwest of Prague, a similar mix of woods and rolling hills surrounds the popular castle of **Karlštejn**, a gem of Gothic architecture, dramatically situated above the River Berounka. There are numerous possibilities for walking in the region around Karlštejn, and, further upstream, in the forests of **Křivoklátsko**. West of Prague, near Kladno, there are two places of pilgrimage: **Lány** is the resting place of the founder of the modern Czechoslovak state, and summer residence of the Czech president; and **Lidice**, razed to the ground by the SS, recalls the horror of Nazi occupation.

Transport throughout Bohemia is fairly straightforward, thanks to a comprehensive network of railway lines and regional bus services, though connections can be less than smooth, and journeys slow. If you're planning to try and see more than one or two places outside Prague, however, or one of the destinations more difficult to reach, it might be worth considering renting a car.

North along the Vltava

One of the quickest and most rewarding trips out of the capital is to follow the Vltava as it twists northwards across the plain towards the River Labe at Mělník. This is the beginning of the so-called **záhrada Čech** (Garden of Bohemia), a flat and fertile region whose cherry blossoms are always the first to herald the Bohemian spring, and whose roads in summer are lined with stalls overflowing with fruit and vegetables. But the real reason to venture into this flat landscape is to visit the chateaux that lie along the banks of the river, all easily reached from Prague by public transport.

Around Kralupy

The Nobel prize-winning poet Jaroslav Seifert didn't beat around the bush when he wrote that **KRALUPY NAD VLTAVOU** "is not a beautiful town and never was". It paid an unusually heavy price in the last war, bombarded from the air, and postwar industrial development has left it with "smokestacks . . . like phantom trees, without branches, without leaves, without blossoms, without bees". Now, Kralupy's oil refineries and chemical plants have spread across both sides of the river, but it's still worth making the 45-minute train journey from Prague, as just a few kilometres to the north, on either side of the Vltava, are two fine chateaux: Nelahozeves on the left bank, and Veltrusy on the right – again both accessible by train.

Nelahozeves

Shortly after pulling out of Kralupy, the train passes through a short tunnel and comes to rest at Nelahozeves zastávka, the first of two stations in the village of **NELAHOZEVES**. Above the railway sits the village's plain, barracks-like **chateau** (April–Oct Tues–Sun 9am–5pm), recently given a new lease of life by a sgraffito facelift. The chateau was built by a group of fairly undistinguished Italian builders for one of the lackeys of the Habsburg Emperor Ferdinand I, and now, stripped of its furniture, it serves as an art repository for European paintings from the collections of three great aristocratic families: the Pernštejns, the Rožmberks and the Lobkovics. The best stuff, sadly, is either in Prague galleries or on permanent loan elsewhere, leaving little to gloat over here, but there are some good portraits spanning the centuries, and you can get something to eat in the chateau restaurant.

The country's most famous composer, **Antonín Dvořák** (1841–1904), was born and bred under the shadow of the chateau, at the house (no. 12) next door to the post office. Dvořák was originally apprenticed to a butcher, but on the recommendation of his schoolmaster, was sent to the Prague Organ School instead. Throughout a successful career, he continued to draw inspiration from his homeland. If there's someone around at the house (officially open 9am–noon & 2–5pm; closed Mon & Fri), you can have a quick look at the great man's rocking-chair, and various other personal effects.

Veltrusy

The industrial suburbs of Kralupy stop just short of the gardens of the chateau of **Veltrusy** (Tues–Sun March, April & Sept 9am–noon & 1–4pm; May–Aug 8am–noon & 1–5pm), over the bridge from the second of the stations in Nelahozeves (one stop on from Nelahozeves zastávka). The classic Baroque symmetry of Veltrusy makes for an altogether more satisfying experience than the chateau at Nelahozeves, its green shutters and henna-dyed wings pivoting round a bulbous, green-domed building that recalls earlier country houses in France or Italy. It was built in the early eighteenth century as a plaything for the upwardly mobile Counts of Chotek, its 290 acres of surrounding woodland perfect for a little light hunting.

If you fancy staying, there's a very good **campsite** (April to mid-Nov) just outside the chateau grounds – a great spot for watching the barges on the Vltava, but no place for a dip given the pollutants that pour into the river further upstream. On the road to the campsite and chateau, several houses offer cheap **private rooms**.

Mělník

Occupying a commanding site at the confluence of the Vltava and Labe rivers, **MĚLNÍK**, 33km north of Prague, lies at the heart of Bohemia's tiny wine-growing region. The town's history goes back to the ninth century, when it was handed over to the Přemyslids as part of Ludmilla's dowry on her marriage to Prince Bořivoj. And it was here, too, that she introduced her heathen grandson Václav (later to become Saint Wenceslas) to the joys of Christianity. Viticulture became the town's economic mainstay only after Charles IV, aching for a little of the French wine of his youth, introduced grapes from Burgundy (where he was also king).

The old town

Mělník's greatest monument is its Renaissance **chateau** (Tues–Sun March, April & Sept 9am–4pm; May–Aug 8am–noon & 1–5pm), perched high above the flat plains and visible for miles around. The present building, covered in the familiar sgraffito patterning, houses the local museum, and more of the apparently unending collection of old masters that belonged to its last aristocratic owners, the Lobkovic family – displayed in magnificently proportioned rooms, which also provide great views out over the plain.

Below the chateau, vines cling to the south-facing terraces, as the land plunges into the river below. From beneath the great tower of Mělník's onion-domed church of **sv Petr and Pavel**, next door to the chateau, there's an even better view of the rivers' confluence, and the subsidiary canal, at one time so congested with vessels that traffic lights had to be introduced to prevent accidents. The remainder of the old town is pleasant enough for some casual strolling, though pretty small – not much more than an arcaded main square, and an old medieval gateway.

Practicalities

Beyond Nelahozeves, the main line from Prague veers northwest, away from Mělník, which means that there's no direct train service here from Prague. There is, however, a regular bus service, which takes around an hour; to reach the older part of town from the **bus station**, simply head up Krombholcova in the direction of the big church tower. If your next destination is Liběchov or Litoměřice, you have the choice of either the bus or the train; the **train station** is further still from the old town, a couple of blocks northeast of the bus station, down Jiřího z Poděbrad.

If you're hoping to stay, there are **private rooms** available on Legionářů, to the north of the old town, and on Palackého náměstí, off the main square; plus the modern hotel, *Ludmila* (☎0206/25 78; ③), 1.5km down the road to Prague. As for **food and drink**, the chateau restaurant is as good (and cheap) a place as any to sample some of the local wine (and enjoy the view): the red *Ludmila* is the most famous of Mělník's wines, but if you prefer white, try a bottle of *Tramín* to accompany the fresh trout (thankfully not pulled out of the Vltava or Labe below). If the tour groups are monopolising the chateau restaurant, you'll have to be content with the basic food and *Krušovice* beer served at the *Zlatý beránek* on the main square in the old town, or *U sv Václava* at Svatováclavská 22, a new *vinárna* beside the main entrance to the chateau. The *Zámecká pivnice*, opposite, was temporarily closed at the time of writing.

Liběchov

Seven kilometres north and ten minutes by train from Mělník – just out of sight of the giant coal-fired power station that provides most of Prague's electricity – is the rhubarb-and-custard coloured **chateau** (Tues–Sun 9am–noon & 1–3.30pm) at **LIBĚCHOV** (Liboch). Even without the sickly colour scheme, it's a bizarre place: formal and two-dimensional when viewed from the French gardens at the front, but bulging like an amphitheatre around the back by the entrance. Inside is another surprise, a **museum of Asian and Oriental cultures** featuring endless Buddhas, Mongolian printing equipment, Balinese monster gear and Javanese puppets – all of which make for a fascinating half-hour tour. The main dining hall, now full of Asian musical instruments, is curious, too, smothered in its original barley-sugar decor with little sculpted jesters crouching mischievously in the corners of the ceiling.

For all the chateau's excesses, the **village** itself is little more than a *hostinec* and a bend in the road, but straggling up the valley are the remains of what was once an attractive spa resort for ailing Praguers. Many of the old *Gasthäuser* are still standing, including the *Pension Stüdl* where Kafka spent the winter of 1918. It was here that he met and became engaged to Julie Wohryzek, daughter of a Jewish shoemaker from Prague – a match vigorously opposed by his father. Kafka was prompted to write his vitriolic *Letter to His Father*, which he passed on to his mother, who wisely made sure it never got any further.

The only working pension nowadays is the private *Hotel Aveco*, Pod kostelíčkem 20 (☎0206/971 156; ④), off the road to Dubá. On the other side of the trickling River Liběchovka, there's a **campsite** (mid-April to Sept), a possible starting point for hikes into the Kokořín region (see below).

Kokořínsko

Northeast of Mělník, you leave the low plains of the Labe for a plateau region known as **Kokořínsko**, a hidden pocket of wooded hills which takes its name from the Gothic castle rising through the treetops at its centre. The sandstone plateau has weathered over the millennia to form sunken valleys and bizarre rocky outcrops, which means there's a lot of scope for some gentle hiking here. With picturesque valleys such as the Kokořínský důl, dotted with well-preserved, half-timbered villages and riddled with marked paths, it comes as a surprise that the whole area isn't buzzing all summer.

At the centre of the region is the village of **KOKOŘÍN**, whose dramatic setting and spectacular fourteenth-century **castle** (April & Oct Sat & Sun 9am–4pm; May–Aug Tues–Sun 8am–5pm; Sept Tues–Sun 9am–5pm) greatly inspired the Czech nineteenth-century Romantics. The castle is a perfect hideaway, ideal for the robbers who used it as a base after it fell into disrepair in the sixteenth century. Not until the end of the nineteenth century did it get a new lease of life, from a jumped-up local landowner, Václav Špaček, who bought himself a title and refurbished the place as a family memorial. There's precious little inside and no incentive to endure the half-hour tour, as you can explore the ramparts and climb the tallest tower on your own.

Unless you've got your own transport, Kokořínsko is not really feasible as a day trip from Prague. In summer, there's one direct **bus** a week from Prague's Praha-Holešovice bus station (leaving at around 7.45am); otherwise, take the regular buses to Mělník and change there. Alternatively, you could catch the local train from Mělník to MŠENO, from where it's a three-kilometre walk west to Kokořín on the green-marked path. Finding **accommodation** shouldn't be too much of a problem; there's the *Hotel Dolina* in Kokořín (☎0206/26; ③), a cluster of campsites at KOKOŘÍNSKÝ DŮL, a couple of kilometres down the valley, and private rooms in KANINA, 2km further east.

East of Prague

The scenery **east of Prague** is as flat as it is around Mělník, a rich blanket of fields spreading over the plain as far as the eye can see. Two places you might consider heading for are **Mladá Boleslav**, where Škoda cars are produced, and **Přerov nad Labem**, an open-air museum of the kind of folk architecture that was common in Bohemia less than a century ago. **Poděbrady** and **Kolín** are not likely to be high on most people's itineraries, but make convenient stopoff points when heading east.

Přerov nad Labem

The **open-air museum** of rural architecture at **PŘEROV NAD LABEM** was the first of its kind in Central Europe when it was founded in 1895 (it is called a *skansen*, after the first such museum, founded in a Stockholm suburb in 1891). Later, in the 1950s and 1960s, *skansens* became quite a fad, as collectivisation and urbanisation wiped out traditional rural communities, along with their distinctive folk culture and wooden architecture. During the summer Přerov's *skansen* is busy with tour groups from Prague, wandering through the various half-timbered and stone buildings, some brought here plank by plank from nearby villages, some from Přerov itself. Particularly evocative is the reconstructed eighteenth-century village school, with a portrait of the Austrian Emperor taking pride of place amid the Catholic icons and a delicate paper theatre that was used in drama lessons.

To get to the village, take one of the slow buses from Prague to Poděbrady and get off at the crossroads just after the turn-off to Mochov – the village of Přerov is a kilometre's walk north.

Mladá Boleslav

Trains from Praha-Vysočany take an hour and a half to reach **MLADÁ BOLESLAV** (Jungbluzzau), where Laurin & Klement set up a bicycle factory in the mid-nineteenth century. They went on to produce the country's first car in 1905, and soon afterwards merged with the Škoda industrial empire. The factory has produced all of Škoda's cars since that time, and currently churns out the latest model, the *Favorit*. (The true home of the Škoda empire is its heavy engineering plant at Plzeň, see p.171.)

The main reason for coming here is to visit the **Škoda Museum** (Mon–Fri 7am–6pm, Sat 9am–1pm), which exhibits over 25 old Škodas and Laurin & Klements in its showroom. The exhibition starts off, as the factory itself did, with an L & K bicycle and a couple of motorbikes. There are also several vintage vehicles and a 1917 fire engine, but the vast majority of the cars date from the 1920s and 1930s – big, mostly black, gangster-style motors. The museum is on třída

Václava Klementa, northeast of the town centre, and not at all well signposted. Diagonally opposite the museum, and handy for orientation, is a park with a palatial neo-Baroque *Gymnasium* at the far end. There's a wonderfully provincial Art-Nouveau theatre close by, brightly painted in white, gold and blue.

The **old town** lies to the east of the River Jizera, in a tight bend of one of its tributaries, the Klenice. It has little going for it besides its fading Renaissance **radnice**, and the **castle** tucked into the southernmost part of town, now the local museum and exhibition space. However, if you're looking for somewhere to **eat**, the *Jihočeská hostinec*, beside the castle entrance, has a big fish restaurant, *Rýbářská*, with an amazing menu that includes pike, eel and plaice. The *Hotel Věnec*, also on the main square (☎0326/24 93; ②), currently offers cheap **rooms**.

Poděbrady

If spa towns evoke images of turn-of-the-century hotels, then **PODĚBRADY** is going to come as something of a disappointment. Its spa waters were only discovered in this century, its chessboard street plan contains no great treasures, and the town owes its previous existence, for better or worse, to its strategic position on the east–west trade route.

Poděbrady's only real claim to fame is as the birthplace of **George of Poděbrady** (Jiří z Poděbrad to the Czechs), the one and only Hussite King of Bohemia (and the last real Czech), whose copper green equestrian statue stands in the main square, náměstí Jiřího. But apart from the statue, there's scarcely a trace of George anywhere: although he was born in the **chateau** (May–Oct Tues–Sun 9am–5pm), which fronts on to the main square (and backs on to the

---

ŠKODA: THE CARS AND JOKES

For Czechs, the **Škoda industrial empire** is a great Czech achievement and a source of national pride. It's doubly ironic, then, that the word *škoda* means "shame" or "pity" in Czech – a marketing own-goal were it not the name of the founding father of the Czech car industry, **Emil Škoda**. The last Škoda model produced under the Communists was very favourably received, even in the west (whence a large proportion of its components derive), and is in great demand from the new Czech bourgeoisie. In 1989, there was a three-year waiting list, despite a retail price of over 90,000 Czech crowns (over twice the average yearly salary). In one of the most controversial deals in the current privatisation programme, Volkswagen now have a majority stake in the firm.

Škoda cars have, however, long been the laughing stock of western European car buffs. A few sample groaners:

Customer to garage mechanic: "Have you got a petrol cap for a Škoda?"; Garage mechanic to customer: "It's a fair swap".

Q: *What do you call a Škoda convertible?* A: *a skip.*

Q: *What's the difference between a Jehovah's Witness and a Škoda?* A: *You can close the door on a Jehovah's Witness.*

Q: *How do you double the value of your Škoda?* A: *Fill up the petrol tank.*

Q: *Why do Škodas have heated rear windows?* A: *To keep your hands warm as you're pushing it along. . .*

river), the present structure was built a hundred years after his death and houses only the minutest of historical exhibitions.

The **spa** itself, laid out earlier this century, is pleasant enough, and its waters are perennially popular judging by the queue of locals at the concrete rotunda on Riegrovo náměstí, a couple of blocks northeast of the main square. Fifteen thousand patients a year pass through Poděbrady, and around teatime most of them can be seen promenading through the town's park, inspecting the window displays of Bohemian crystal and admiring the fully functioning floral clock. For a glimpse of the town's halcyon days, in the last years of the Empire, check out the local **museum** at Palackého 68 (Feb–April Mon–Fri 9am–noon & 1–4pm; May–Oct Tues–Sun 9am–5pm), two minutes' walk from the castle.

Despite its limitations, Poděbrady is a convenient stop on the road to Prague, less than an hour by train from the city. Its two **hotels**, both on Riegrovo náměstí, regularly have vacancies, though only the *Hubertus* (☎0324/38 27; ①) is currently functioning. Alternatively, there's a **campsite** (May to mid-Sept) a little further upstream from the castle. With visitors of one kind or another all summer, there's a fair selection of films and classical concerts on offer in town, not to mention some good **eating** options: the *Bílá Růže* by the river, for Czech food; *Bašta U krále Jiřího*, for dark *Braník* beer; or, for something different, the pizzeria in the *Savoy* on the main square.

Kolín

In addition to its railway sidings and industrial plants, **KOLÍN** – 16km south of Poděbrady along the Labe – has actually managed to preserve its central medieval core. One of numerous towns in Bohemia founded by German colonists in the thirteenth century, its streets are laid out in chessboard fashion, so finding the cobbled main square, Karlovo náměstí, should present few problems. There's a wonderfully imposing Renaissance **radnice**, covered in sgraffito and decorated with four rose-coloured panels from the last century, and four unusual Baroque gables on the west side, but the rest of the square is unspectacular.

Kolín's most significant monument is its fantastic Gothic church of **sv Bartoloměj**, in the southeast corner of the old town, up Karlova. Built in part by Peter Parler, the genius behind Prague's Gothic masterpieces – St Vitus Cathedral and the Charles Bridge, to name but two – the nave is suffused with an unusually intense blue light from the modern stained-glass windows, which disturbs the otherwise resolutely medieval ambience.

Like many towns in Bohemia and Moravia, Kolín had a significant **Jewish community** up until the Holocaust. The ghetto was situated in the southwest corner of the old town, in what is now Na Hradbach and Karoliny Světlé, and even today has a run-down feel to it. There's even a seventeenth-century synagogue, accessible through the passageway at no. 12 Na Hradbach, but it's in a state of disrepair, and seemingly a long way off from becoming the concert hall it is planned to be.

If you need **to stay overnight**, the *Hotel Savoy*, Rubešova 61 (☎0321/220 22; ①), which overlooks the bridge over the Labe, is remarkably cheap, or there's a choice of pensions: *Pension pod věží* on Parléřova, or *U Rabinu*, on Karoliny Světlé (☎0321/244 63; ③). Kolín also happens to be closely associated with **František Kmoch** (1848–1912), king of Bohemian oom-pah-pah music, and every June a brass band festival is held on the main square in his honour.

Kutná Hora

For two hundred and fifty years or so, **KUTNÁ HORA** (Kuttenberg) was one of the most important towns in Bohemia, second only to Prague. At the end of the fourteenth century its population was equal to that of London, its shantytown suburbs straggled across what are now green fields, and its ambitious building projects set out to rival those of the capital itself. Today, Kutná Hora is a small provincial town with a population of just over 20,000, but the monuments dotted around it, and the remarkable monastery and ossuary in the suburb of **Sedlec**, make it one of the most enjoyable day trips from Prague.

A brief history

Kutná Hora's road to prosperity began in the late thirteenth century with the discovery of **silver deposits** in the surrounding area. German miners were invited to settle and work the seams, and in around 1300, Václav II founded the royal mint here and sent for Italian craftsmen to run it. Much of the town's wealth was used to fund the beautification of Prague, but it also allowed for the construction of one of the most magnificent churches in central Europe and a number of other prestigious Gothic monuments in Kutná Hora itself.

While the silver stocks remained high the town was able to recover its former prosperity, but at the end of the sixteenth century the mines dried up and Kutná Hora's wealth and importance came to an abrupt end – when the Swedes marched on the town during the Thirty Years' War, they had to be bought off with beer rather than silver. The town has never fully recovered, shrivelling to less than a third of its former size, its fate emphatically sealed by a devastating fire in 1770.

The Town

The small, unassuming houses that line the town's medieval lanes give little idea of its former glories. The same can be said of the main square, **Palackého náměstí**, now thoroughly provincial in character.

A narrow alleyway on the south side of the square leads to the leafy Havlíčkovo náměstí, off which lies the **Vlašský dvůr** (Italian Court), originally conceived as a palace by Václav II, and for three centuries the town's bottomless purse. It was here that Florentine minters produced the Prague Groschen (*pražské groše*), a silver coin widely used throughout central Europe until the nineteenth century. The building itself has been mucked about with over the years, most recently – and most brutally – by nineteenth-century restorers, who left only the chestnut trees, a fourteenth-century oriel window (capped by an unlikely looking wooden onion dome) and the statue of a miner unmolested. The original workshops of the minters have been bricked in, but the outlines of their little doors and windows are still visible in the courtyard. The short **guided tour** (daily every half-hour 10am–6pm) of the old chapel, treasury and royal palace gives you a fair idea of the building's former importance.

Outside the court is a statue of the country's founder and first president, T. G. Masaryk, twice removed – once by the Nazis and once by the Communists – but now returned to its pride of place. Before you leave, take a quick look in the court gardens, which climb down in steps to the Vrchlice valley below. This is undoubtedly Kutná Hora's best profile, with a splendid view over to the church of sv Barbora (see below).

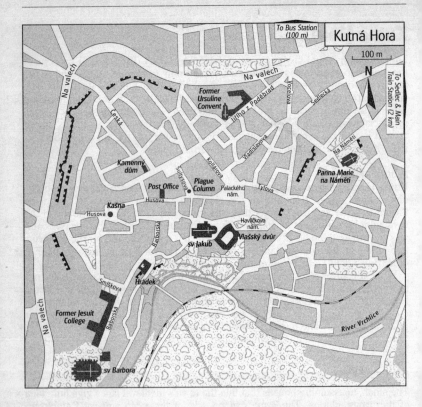

Behind the Vlašský dvůr is **sv Jakub**, the town's oldest church, begun a generation or so after the discovery of the silver deposits. Its grand scale is a clear indication of the town's quite considerable wealth by the time of the fourteenth century, though in terms of artistry it pales in comparison with Kutná Hora's other ecclesiastical buildings. The leaning tower is a reminder of the precarious position of the town, the church's foundations prone to subsidence from the disused mines below. If you want to see some of these, head for the **Hrádek**, an old fort which was used as a second mint and now serves as the **Silver Mining Museum** (Muzeum a středověké důlní dílo; April–Oct Tues–Sun 8am–noon & 1–5pm). Here you can pick up a white coat, miner's helmet and torch, and visit some of the medieval mines that were discovered beneath the fort in the 1960s.

The church of sv Barbora

Kutná Hora's church of **sv Barbora** (Tues–Sun summer 8am–noon & 1–5pm; winter 9am–noon & 1–4pm) is arguably the most beautiful church in central Europe. Not to be outdone by the great monastery at Sedlec (see below) or the St Vitus Cathedral in Prague, the miners of Kutná Hora began financing the construction of a great Gothic cathedral of their own, dedicated to Saint Barbara, the patron saint of miners and gunners. The foundations were probably laid by Parler in the 1380s, but work was interrupted by the Hussite wars, and the church remains unfinished, despite a flurry of building activity at the beginning of the sixteenth century by, among others, Benedikt Reith.

The approach road to the church, Barborská, is lined with a parade of gesticulating Baroque saints and cherubs that rival the sculptures on the Charles Bridge; on the right-hand side is the palatial former **Jesuit College**. The church itself bristles with pinnacles, finials and flying buttresses which support its most striking feature, a roof of three tent-like towers, culminating in unequal needle-sharp spires. Inside, cold light streams through the plain glass windows, illuminating a playful vaulted nave whose ribs form branches and petals stamped with coats of arms belonging to Václav II and the local miners' guilds. The wide spread of the five-aisled nave is remarkably uncluttered: a Gothic pulpit – half wood, half stone – creeps tastefully up a central pillar, and black and gold Renaissance confessionals lie discreetly in the north aisle. On the south wall is the Minters' Chapel, decorated with fifteenth-century wall frescoes showing the Florentines at work, while in the ambulatory chapels are some fascinating paintings – unique for their period – of local miners at work.

The rest of the town

There are a few minor sights worth taking the time to seek out in the rest of the town. On Rejskovo náměstí, the squat, many-sided **Kašna** (fountain) by Matouš Rejsek strikes an odd pose – anything less like a fountain would be hard to imagine. At the bottom of the sloping Šultyskovo náměstí is a particularly fine **Morový sloup** (Plague Column), giving thanks for the end of the plague of 1713; while just around the corner from the top of the square is one of the few Gothic buildings to survive the 1770 fire, the **Kamenný dům**, built around 1480 and covered in an ornate sculptural icing. This used to contain an unexceptional local museum, which has now been moved a couple of blocks down Poděbradova, to Kilian Ignaz Dientzenhofer's unfinished **Ursuline convent**. Only three sides of the convent's ambitious pentagonal plan were actually finished, its neo-Baroque church being added in the late nineteenth century while sv Barbora was being restored.

Sedlec

Buses #1 and #4 run 3km northeast to **SEDLEC**, formerly a separate village but now a suburb of Kutná Hora. Adjoining Sedlec's defunct eighteenth-century Cistercian monastery (now the largest tobacco factory in Europe) is the fourteenth-century church of **Panna Marie**, imaginatively redesigned in the eighteenth century by Giovanni Santini, whose speciality was melding Gothic with Baroque. Here, given a plain French Gothic church gutted during the Hussite wars, Santini set to work on the vaulting, adding his characteristic sweeping stucco rib patterns, relieved only by the occasional Baroque splash of colour above the chancel steps. For all its attractions, however, the church seems to be permanently covered in scaffolding, and closed except for the occasional service.

Cross the main road, following the signs, and you come to the monks' graveyard, where an ancient Gothic chapel leans heavily over the entrance to the macabre subterranean **kostnice** or ossuary (Tues–Sun summer 8am–noon & 1–5pm; winter 9am–noon & 1–4pm), full to overflowing with human bones. When holy earth from Golgotha was scattered over the graveyard in the twelfth century, all of Bohemia's nobility wanted to be buried here and the bones mounted up until there were over 40,000 complete sets. In 1870, worried about the ever-growing piles, the authorities commissioned František Rint to do something creative with them. He rose to the challenge and moulded out of bones four giant bells, one in each corner of the crypt, designed wall-to-ceiling skeletal decorations, including the Schwarzenberg coat of arms, and, as the centrepiece, put together a chandelier made out of every bone in the human body. Rint's signature (in bones) is at the bottom of the steps.

Kačina

Nothing quite so ghoulish confronts you at the early eighteenth-century chateau of **Kačina**, a five-kilometre hike from the Kutná Hora hlavní nádraží, or a much shorter walk if you catch one of the buses heading out to the suburb of Nový Dvory. It's a colossal Neoclassical affair, the facade stretching for over 200m across the lawn. For the owners, the up-and-coming Chotek family (who also owned Veltrusy), the chateau grounds came first, and planting began a full fifteen years before a stone was laid. Appropriately enough, the chateau now acts as home to a museum of agriculture (April–Sept Tues–Sun 8am–5pm), but it's the wide expanse of parkland that draws carloads of Czechs here throughout the summer.

Practicalities

The simplest way to get to Kutná Hora is to take a **bus** from the Praha-Florenc or Praha-Želivského terminals (1hr 30min). Fast **trains** from Prague's Masarykovo nádraží take around an hour (there's only one in the morning); slow ones take two hours; trains from Praha hlavní nádraží involve a change at Kolín. The main **railway station** (Kutná Hora hlavní nádraží) is a long way out of town, near Sedlec; bus #2 or #4 will take you into town, or there's an occasional shuttle train service to Kutná Hora město, not far from the centre of town.

The town has a highly efficient system of orientation signs, and at almost every street corner a pictorial list of the chief places of interest keeps you on the right track. Having said that, the train station signposted is not the main one; and signs even point the way to the *turistická ubytovna* (tourist hostel), which was under reconstruction at the time of writing. The *pokladna* (ticket office) in the Vlašský dvůr also serves as a tourist information point, and can arrange reasonably priced **private rooms**. Otherwise, the only **hotels** are the modern *Mědínek*, on Palackého náměstí (☎0327/2741 or 2743; ③), and a small, very cheap private hotel on Barborská (①).

As for **eating and drinking**, Kutná Hora was in dire need of a good restaurant at the time of writing. If *U Anděla*, the cheap *pivnice* near the Kamenný dům, closes, as looks increasingly likely, you'll be left with only the *Mědínek* for nourishment until somewhere new appears. If it's just a hot drink you want, the *kavárna v zahradě*, at the bottom of Palackého náměstí, has tables outside and stays open until 10pm.

Průhonice and the Sázava valley

A short train ride **southeast** of Prague is enough to transport you from the urban sprawl of the capital into one of the prettiest regions of central Bohemia, starting with the park at **Průhonice**. Until the motorway to Brno and Bratislava ripped through the area in the 1970s, the roads and railways linking the three big cities followed the longer, flatter option, further north along the Labe valley. As a result, commerce and tourism passed the **Sázava Valley** by, and, with the notable exception of **Konopiště**, it remains undeveloped, unspoilt and out of the way.

Průhonice

Barely outside the city limits, and just off the country's one and only motorway, **PRŮHONICE** throngs with Czech weekenders during the summer season. For the great majority, it's the 625-acre **park** (April–Oct only) they come to see and not the **chateau**, a motley parade of neo-Renaissance buildings, most of them closed to the public anyway. The park is a botanical and horticultural research centre, so the array of flora is unusually good here. Though few do, it's worth paying a passing visit to the chateau's **art gallery**, which features a permanent collection of twentieth-century Czech paintings and sculpture, including a hefty series of canvases by the Czech Cubists.

There's a regular *ČSAD* **bus** service from the Praha-Chodov bus terminal to Průhonice, or else you could conceivably walk the 4km cross-country from metro Háje. Being so near Prague, it's a popular place to **stay the night**: the choice is between the flash new *Pension Charlie* on Hlavní (☎75 06 83; ③) and the tatty old hotel, *Tulipán*, on the road to the motorway (☎75 95 30; ②). If you're after something to **eat**, look no further than *U zámku*, the local *hostinec* by the chateau entrance.

Sázava and Český Šternberk

Rising majestically above the slow-moving waters of the river Sázava, the **Sázava monastery** (April & Sept Sat & Sun 9am–4pm; May–Aug Tues–Sun 8am–noon & 1–5pm) was founded by the eleventh-century Prince Oldřich, on the instigation of a passing hermit called **Prokop** (St Procopius), whom he met by chance in the forest. The Slavonic liturgy was used at the monastery and, for a while, Sázava became an important centre for the dissemination of Slavonic texts. Later, a large Gothic church was planned, and this now bares its red sandstone nave to the world, incomplete but intact. The chancel was converted into a Baroque church and, later still, the Tieg family bought the place and started to build themselves a modest chateau. Of this architectural hotchpotch, only the surviving Gothic frescoes – in the popular "Beautiful Style", but of a sophistication unmatched in Bohemian art at the time – are truly memorable. The village itself thrived on the glass trade, and the rest of the monastery's long guided tour concentrates on the local glassware.

Without your own transport, it'll take a good hour and a half by bus or train to cover the 55km from Prague to Sázava. Of the two, the **train** ride (change at ČERČANY) is the more visually absorbing, at least by the time you join the branch line that meanders down the Sázava valley. There's a **campsite** (June to mid-Sept) by the river, and a **hotel**, *Na Růžku*, on the road to Benešov (☎0328/ 915 50; ①), should you need a place to stay.

Český Šternberk

Several bends in the Sázava river later, the great mass of the **castle** at ČESKÝ ŠTERNBERK (April & Oct Sat & Sun 9am–4pm; May–Aug Tues–Sun 8am–5pm; Sept Tues–Sun 9am–5pm) is strung out along a knife's edge above the river – a breathtaking sight. Unfortunately, that's all it is, since apart from its fiercely defensive position, not much remains of the original Gothic castle. Add to that the dull guided tour, the castle's popularity with coach parties, and the full two-hour journey by train or bus from Prague (again, change trains at Čerčany), and you may decide to skip it altogether.

Konopiště

Other than for its proximity to Prague, the popularity of **Konopiště** (April, Sept & Oct Tues–Sun 9am–noon & 1–4pm; May–Aug Tues–Sun 8am–noon & 1–5pm) remains a complete mystery. From the beginning of the season to the last day of October, coach parties from all over the world home in on this unexceptional Gothic castle, stuffed with dead animals and dull weaponry. The only interesting thing about the place is its historical associations: King Václav IV was imprisoned for a while by his own nobles in the castle's distinctive round tower, and Archduke Franz Ferdinand lived here with his wife, Sophie Chotek, until their assassination in Sarajevo in 1914. The archduke's prime interest seems to have been the elimination of all living creatures foolish enough to venture into the castle grounds: between the years 1880 and 1906, he killed no fewer than 171,537 birds and animals, the details of which are recorded in his *Schuss Liste* displayed inside.

There's a choice of two equally tedious **guided tours**: the shorter forty-minute tour of the *Zámecké sbírky* takes you past the stuffed bears, deer teeth and assorted lethal weapons; the tour of the *Zámecké salony* is less gruesome but ten minutes longer. There are occasionally tours in English, French and German, too, so ask at the box office before you sign up. Much the best reason to come to Konopiště, though, is to explore its 555-acre **park**, which boasts several lakes, sundry statuary, an unrivalled rose garden and a deer park.

As Konopiště is only 45km from Prague you shouldn't have to stay the night, though there is a **campsite** (May–Sept) and **motel** not far from the castle car park. The castle is a fifteen-minute walk or short bus ride west from the railway station at BENEŠOV.

Jemniště

Castle enthusiasts are better advised to visit the simple Baroque **chateau** (April, Sept & Oct Tues–Sun 9am–noon & 1–4pm; May–Aug Tues–Sun 8am–noon & 1–5pm) hidden in the woods above the nearby village of **JEMNIŠTĚ**. To get there, you'll need to change trains at Benešov, getting off at POSTUPICE, twenty-five minutes down the line, and then walking fifteen minutes from there. It's worth the effort because the chateau is rarely visited (it should come as no surprise if you're the only taker for the brief guided tour), yet contains an impressive collection of seventeenth-century pictorial maps and plans and a small selection of Empire furniture.

Along the Berounka river

The green belt area to the **west of Prague** has its fair share of rolling hills, but spend more time here and you'll find it's easily the most varied of the regions around the city, and consequently one of the most popular escapes for urban Czechs. The **River Berounka** carves itself an enticingly craggy valley up to Charles IV's magnificent country castle at **Karlštejn**, the busiest destination of all, and continues further upstream, to the castle of **Křivoklát**.

Around Karlštejn

Trains for **KARLŠTEJN** leave Praha-Smíchov station roughly every hour, and take about forty minutes to cover the 28km from Prague. One kilometre from the station, and across the river, is a small T-shaped village (now part of Karlštejn village but originally the separate hamlet of Budňany), strung out along one of the tributaries of the Berounka – pretty, but not enough to warrant a coach park the size of a football pitch. It's the **castle** (Tues–Sun March, April & Oct–Dec 9am–noon & 1–4pm; May–Sept 8am–noon & 1–6pm), occupying a defiantly unassailable position above the village, which draws in the mass of tourists. Designed in the fourteenth century by Matthias of Arras for Emperor Charles IV, as a giant safe-box for the imperial crown jewels and his large personal collection of precious relics, it quickly became Charles' favourite retreat from the vast city he himself had masterminded. Women were strictly forbidden to enter the castle, and the story of his third wife Anna's successful break-in (in drag) became one of the most popular Czech comedies of the nineteenth century.

The castle was ruthlessly restored in the nineteenth century and now looks much better from a distance. Inside, the centuries of neglect and the restoration work have taken their toll. Guided tours last around half an hour, and begin from the main inner courtyard. Most of the rooms visited contain only the barest of furnishings, the empty spaces taken up by uninspiring displays on the history of the castle. However, the top two chambers make the whole trip worthwhile – unfortunately, only the emperor's residential **Mariánská věž** is open to the public at the moment. It was here that Charles shut himself off from the rest of the world, with any urgent business passed to him through a hole in the wall of the tiny ornate chapel of **sv Kateřina**.

A wooden bridge leads on to the highest point of the castle, the Velká věž, where the castle's finest treasure, the **Holy Rood Chapel** (Kaple svatého kříže), has been closed now for over ten years. Traditionally, only the Emperor, the archbishop and the electoral princes could enter this guilded treasure-house, whose six-metre-thick walls contain 2200 semiprecious stones and 128 painted panels, the work of Master Theodoric, Bohemia's greatest fourteenth-century painter (a small selection of Master Theodoric's panels are exhibited in Prague's convent of sv Jiří, see p.64). The imperial crown jewels, once secured here behind nineteen separate locks, were removed to Hungary after an abortive attack by the Hussites, while the Bohemian jewels are now stashed away in the cathedral in Prague.

Walks around Karlštejn and the Český kras

There are some great possibilities for **hiking** in the countryside around Karlštejn. From **ŘEVNICE**, two stops on the train before Karlštejn – the unlikely village in which Martina Navrátilová spent her tennis-playing childhood – several marked paths cover the stiff climb through the forests of the Hřebeny ridge. Armed with a *Praha okolí* map, these are easy enough to follow; you can pick up a bus back to Prague from Mníšek on the other side of the hills.

From **SRBSKO** (one stop on from Karlštejn), a red-marked path winds its way through the woods to **sv Jan pod Skálou**, whose dramatically situated monastery was until recently a secret police training camp. This is also the place where the country's remaining aristocrats were imprisoned following the 1948 coup. Again, you can catch a bus back to Prague easily enough from VRÁŽ, a kilometre or so to the north.

Another option from Srbsko is to take the yellow-marked path west into the Český kras (Bohemian Karst). The geology of this region has fascinated scientists since the early nineteenth century, but the one set of caves open to the public, the **Koněpruské jeskyně** (daily April–Oct), 3km west of Srbsko, lay undiscovered until 1950. Nowadays they're not so easy to miss, thanks to the Hollywood-style giant white lettering on the hillside above. Much more fascinating than the dripstone decorations, however, was the simultaneous discovery of an illegal mint in the upper level of the caves. A full set of weights, miners' lamps and even the remains of food were found here, dating back to the second half of the fifteenth century. To reach the caves other than by foot, you'll need to catch one of the infrequent **buses** from the soap-producing town of BEROUN (50min by train from Praha hlavní nádraží).

Křivoklátsko

The beautiful, mixed woodland that makes up the UNESCO nature reserve of **Křivoklátsko**, further up the Berounka, is just out of reach of the day-trippers, making it an altogether sleepier place than the area around Karlštejn. The agonised twists (*křivky*) of the Berounka cast up the highest crags of the region, which cluster round the castle of **Křivoklát** (Tues–Sun April, Sept & Oct 9am–4pm; May–Aug 8am–noon & 1–5pm) – somehow elevated above everything around it.

With such a perfect location in the heart of the best hunting ground in Bohemia, Křivoklát naturally enjoyed the royal patronage of the Přemyslids, whose hunting parties were legendary. From the outside it's a scruffy but impressive stronghold, dominated by the round tower where the Irish alchemist Edward Kelley found himself incarcerated after falling out with Rudolf II, and in an attempt to escape, leapt to his death. The one-hour guided tour takes in most of the castle's good points, including the Great Hall and the chapel, both of which date back to the thirteenth century and have an austere beauty quite at odds with the castle's reputation as a venue for bacchanalian goings-on.

Practicalities

Virtually all journeys by **train** from Prague to Křivoklát require a change at Beroun. **Buses** from the Praha-Dejvice terminal run frequently only at weekends, and take around an hour and a half. Křivoklát castle is the region's only real sight, though you could happily spend days exploring the surrounding countryside on the network of well-marked footpaths. However, unless you're staying at one of the two **campsites** (June–Sept), a short walk up the river near ROZTOKY, you'll have to hole up in RAKOVNÍK (30min beyond Křivoklát on the train), a deeply provincial town with just one posh **hotel** and a good local beer to recommend it.

Around Kladno

As you approach **KLADNO**, just under 30km west of Prague, it's difficult to miss the low blue barracks of the *Poldí* steelworks on the edge of town, which used to provide employment for almost the entire town but are currently running at a third of normal capacity. It was here in 1921 that the Czech Communist Party was founded, and Kladno's miners and steelworkers were rewarded with some of the best wages in the country after the 1948 coup. Nowadays, it typifies the problems and contradictions of the post-Communist situation: what will happen to a town of over 70,000 people whose livelihood depends on an industry that's both economically and ecologically unsound?

The only reason to come here is to catch one of the **buses** that leave around midday for **Lány** (see below), though you can avoid Kladno altogether by taking the slow train to Chomutov from Prague's Masarykovo nádraží and getting out 3km northeast of Lány at STOCHOV. If you're heading for **Lidice**, take the bus to Kladno from Praha-Dejvice, and get off at the turn-off to the village.

Lidice

The small mining village of **LIDICE**, 18km northwest of Prague, hit the world headlines on June 10, 1942, at the moment when it ceased to exist. On the flimsiest pretext, it was chosen as the scapegoat for the assassination of the Nazi leader Reinhard Heydrich (see p.102). All 184 men from the village were rounded up and shot by the SS, the 198 women were sent off to Ravensbrück concentration camp, and the 98 children either went with their mothers, or, if they were Aryan enough, were packed off to "good" German homes, while the village itself was burnt to the ground.

Knowing all this as you approach Lidice makes the modern village seem almost perversely unexceptional. At the end of the straight tree-lined main street, 10 června 1942, there's a dour concrete memorial with a small but horrific **museum** (daily April–Sept 8am–4pm; Oct–March 8am–5pm) that continually shows a short film about Lidice, including footage shot by the SS themselves as the village was burning. The spot where the old village used to lie is just south of the memorial, now merely smooth green pasture punctuated with a few simple symbolic reminders: the foundations of the old school, a wooden cross and a common grave.

After the massacre, the "Lidice shall live" campaign was launched and villages all over the world began to change their name to Lidice. The first was Stern Park Gardens, Illinois, soon followed by villages in Mexico and other Latin American countries. From Coventry to Montevideo, towns twinned themselves with Lidice, so that rather than "wiping a Czech village off the face of the earth" as Hitler had hoped, the Nazis created a symbol of anti-fascist resistance.

There's no place, nor reason, to stay and most people come here as a day trip from Prague on one of the regular buses from Praha-Dejvice.

Lány

On summer weekends, Škoda-loads of Czech families, pensioners and assorted pilgrims make their way to **LÁNY**, a plain, grey village on a hill by the edge of the Křivoklát forest, 12km beyond Kladno. They congregate in the town's pristine cemetery to pay their respects to one of the country's most important historical figures, Tomáš Garrigue Masaryk, the country's founding father and president from 1918 to 1935.

The Masaryk plot is separated from the rest of the cemetery (*hřbitov*) by a little wooden fence and flanked by two bushy trees. Tomáš is buried alongside his American wife, Charlotte Garrigue Masaryková, who died some fifteen years earlier, and their son Jan, who became Foreign Minister in the post-1945 government, only to die in mysterious circumstances shortly after the Communist coup (see p.68). After laying their wreaths, the crowds generally wander over to the presidential summer **chateau**, with its blue-liveried guards, on the other side of the village. Its rooms are strictly out of bounds, but the large English gardens, orangerie and deer park, which were landscaped by Josip Plečnik, are open to the public at weekends and on public holidays.

TGM

Tomáš Garrigue Masaryk – known affectionately as TGM – was born in 1850 in Hodonín, a town in a part of Moravia where Slovaks and Czechs lived harmoniously together. His father was an illiterate Slovak peasant who worked for the local bigwig, his mother a German, while Tomáš himself trained as a blacksmith. From such humble beginnings, he rose to become professor of philosophy at the Charles University, a Social Democrat MP in the Viennese *Reichskrat*, and finally the country's first, and longest-serving, president. A liberal humanist through and through, Masaryk created what was, at the time, probably the most progressive democracy in central Europe, featuring universal suffrage, an enviable social security system and a strong social democratic thrust. At the time of his death in 1937, Czechoslovakia was one of the few democracies left in Central Europe, "a lighthouse high on a cliff with the waves crashing on it on all sides", as Masaryk's less fortunate successor, Edvard Beneš, put it. The whole country went into mourning – a year later the Nazis marched into Sudetenland.

After the 1948 coup, the Communists began to dismantle the myth of Masaryk, whose name was synonymous with the "bourgeois" First Republic. All mention of him was removed from textbooks, street names were changed and his statue was taken down from almost every town and village in the country. However, during liberalisation in 1968, his bespectacled face and goatee beard popped up again in shop windows, and his image returned again in 1989 to haunt the beleagured Communists.

travel details

Trains

From Prague (hlavní nádraží) to Poděbrady (6 daily; 1hr 10min); Kolín (up to half-hourly; 1hr 10min); Benešov (27 daily; 50min–1hr 15min).

From Prague (Masarykovo nádraží) to Kladno (up to 19 daily; 50min); Kralupy/Nelahozeves (13 daily; 45min/1hr); Kutná Hora (19 daily; 55 min–2hr); Mladá Boleslav (4 daily;

1hr 20min).

From Prague (Smíchov) to Řevnice/Karlštejn/Beroun (up to half-hourly; 30min/35min/45min)

From Prague (Holešovice) to Kolín (13 daily; 40min).

From Prague (Vysočany) to Mladá Boleslav (8 daily; 1hr 30min).

From Prague (Vršovice) to Zbraslav (at least hourly; 30min)

From Beroun to Křivoklát (12 daily; 45 min).

From Čerčany to Sázava/Český Šternberk (12 daily; 40min/1 hr 15min).

From Mělník to Liběchov (11 daily; 10min).

Buses (ČSAD only)

From Prague (Florenc) to Kutná Hora (afternoon & evening only, up to 7 daily; 1hr 15min); Mladá Boleslav (up to 24 daily; 1hr 15min–1hr 30min); Lidice/Kladno (up to hourly; 55min).

From Prague (Holešovice) to Mělník (up to hourly; 1hr); Kokořín (April–Sept Fri & Sat only; 1hr 10min–1hr 25min).

From Prague (Opatov) to Průhonice (Mon–Fri 6 daily, weekends up to 14 daily; 15min)

From Prague (Želivského) to Kutná Hora (up to 7 daily; 1hr 30min); Sázava (up to 8 daily; 1hr 15min).

From Prague (Roztyly) to Český Šternberk (2 daily; 2hr).

CHAPTER TWO

SOUTH BOHEMIA

South Bohemia (Jižní Čechy), more than any other region, conforms to the popular myth of Bohemia as a bucolic backwater of rolling hills and endless forests. A century of conspicuous industrialisation and the destruction from two world wars have pretty much passed it by; the only city to speak of is the regional capital, **České Budějovice**, which makes up for its urban sprawl with a good-looking old town (and a beer of no less standing). The rest of the countryside is dotted with a series of exceptionally beautiful medieval walled towns, known collectively as the **"Rose Towns"** after the emblems of the two most powerful families, the red rose of the Rožmberks, and the black rose of the lords of Hradec. Both dynasties died out at the beginning of the seventeenth century, and their prize possessions have been in almost terminal decline ever since, despite the subsequent rise of the Bavarian-based Schwarzenbergs.

Český Krumlov is by far the most popular of the Rose Towns; others, like **Pelhřimov** and **Třeboň**, are equally well preserved, if not quite as picturesquely located. The latter lies in an uncharacteristically flat part of the region, known as **Třeboňsko**, a unique ecosystem of medieval fishponds which still supply much of the country's Christmas carp. Bohemia's chief river, the **River Vltava**, spends much of its life in South Bohemia, and provides the setting for the region's most popular **castles**, some almost monastic in their simplicity, like **Zvíkov**, and others literally choking on aristocratic decadence, such as **Orlík, Hluboká** and **Rožmberk**.

To the south, the **Šumava**, which forms the natural border with Austria and Germany, is one of the most unspoiled mountain ranges in the country. The German-speaking foresters and traders who settled on the northern slopes have left their mark on the Bohemian towns and villages in that area. Following the postwar expulsions, the local population is now greatly reduced, their number augmented by a seasonal influx of walkers, fishermen, canoeists and inland beach-niks, drawn by the region's natural beauty – probably the least affected by acid rain.

ACCOMMODATION PRICES

Each place to stay in this chapter has a symbol which corresponds to one of seven **price categories**:

   ① Under 500kčs   ② 500–750kčs   ③ 750–1000kčs   ④ 1000–1500kčs
     ⑤ 1500–2000kčs   ⑥ 2000–3000kčs   ⑦ 3000kčs and upwards

All prices are for the cheapest **double room** available, which usually means without private bath or shower in the less expensive places. For a **single room**, expect to pay around two-thirds the price of a double.

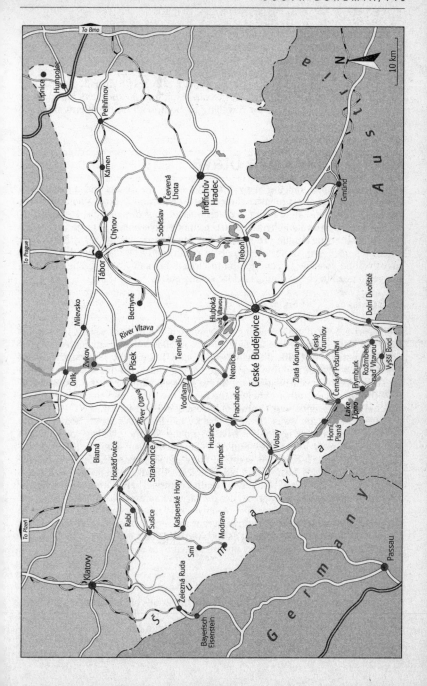

Regional **transport** in South Bohemia isn't as bad as might be expected, given the overwhelmingly hilly, rural nature of the terrain. Travelling by train allows you to experience more of the countryside, and even parts of the Šumava are served by a scenic one-track railway which winds its way from Český Krumlov, along the shores of Lake Lipno and then north to Prachatice. Buses go virtually everywhere, though they're almost invariably less frequent and more expensive, but quicker. There are also opportunities for travelling by **boat**, both on the Vltava and Lake Lipno.

Up the Vltava and Otava

South from Prague and the Slapy dam, there are two castles and a small town worth making the effort to visit. The castles – **Orlík** and **Zvíkov** – both overlook the River Vltava and are difficult to reach without your own vehicle; **Písek** is infinitely more approachable by bus or train. Another possibility is to go part of the way by **boat**; from Prague (Tues–Sun) you can go as far as the Slapy dam (3hr), where it's necessary to switch vessels to reach the Orlík dam (another 3hr). It may even be possible to continue on to Orlík (1hr) and Zvíkov castles (45min), but you'd need to check timings before setting out.

Orlík

If you arrive by boat, thus avoiding the scourge of the *souvenyry* stands that punctuate the walk from the bus terminal, you're unlikely to be disappointed by your first impressions of **Orlík** (literally "eagle's nest"), a creamy nineteenth-century castle which juts out into this wide stretch of the Vltava. No doubt the view was a great deal more spectacular before the valley was dammed in the 1960s; nowadays the water laps rather tamely at the foot of the castle, and concrete has been injected into its foundations to prevent it from being swept away.

Since the castle was handed back to its aristocratic owners, the Schwarzenbergs, you no longer have to queue for the privilege of joining a guided tour (every 10min Tues–Sun April, Sept & Oct 9am–noon & 1–4pm; May–Aug 8am–noon & 1–5pm). As some of the region's greatest self-propagandists, the Schwarzenbergs turned this old Gothic fort into a pseudo-Gothic money-waster in the second half of the nineteenth century. There's nothing among the faience, weaponry and Schwarzenberg military memorabilia to hint at its 700-year history, and even the gardens were only laid out last century. Unless you're drawn by the moderately priced restaurant, *U Toryka* (named after the current Count's pet fox terrier), or the lakeside **campsite**, 2km downriver, the best plan is to catch the late-afternoon ferry upriver to Zvíkov as soon as you can.

Zvíkov

Fourteen kilometres upstream, hidden amid the woods of an isolated rocky promontory at the confluence of the Vltava and the Otava, is the bare medieval husk of **Zvíkov** (April & Sept Sat & Sun 9am–noon & 1–4pm; May–Aug Tues–Sun 8am–noon & 1–5pm), its simplicity a welcome relief after the "romantic interiors" of Orlík. You can wander at will amid the light stone buildings, left to rack and ruin by the Rožmberks as long ago as the 1500s. A small dusty track passes under three gatehouses before leading to the central courtyard, which boasts a simple early Gothic two-storey arcade, reconstructed in the nineteenth century from the few bays that still stood. Even the meagre offerings in the museum are more than compensated for by the absence of tour groups, the cool stone floors and the wonderful views over the water. If you require further incentive, the chapel has faded fifteenth-century frescoes "where nimbed souls in underpants float uncomfortably through a forest", as one critic aptly described it.

Písek

The only guaranteed methods of covering the 20km from Zvíkov to **PÍSEK** are waiting for the afternoon bus at ZVÍKOVSKÉ PODHRADÍ, a couple of kilometres up the road from the castle, or walking 6km south to the train station at VLASTEC. A one-horse rural market town, Písek gets its name from the gold-producing sand (*písek*) of the Otava. Gold fever has waxed and waned in the town over the centuries (an annual gold-panning championship is now held every summer on the river at nearby Slaník), but if recent prospecting discoveries prove correct, the gold under the ground at nearby Mokrsko will be enough to repay the country's entire foreign debt (around $6 billion) – providing, that is, the government prevails over the region's strong environmental lobby.

The town experienced its last gold rush in the thirteenth century, but the Thirty Years' War demolished Písek's prosperity, and all that remains of that period is a **medieval stone bridge**, which predates even the Charles Bridge in Prague, and which likewise accrued a fine selection of beatific Baroque statuary during the Counter-Reformation. Looking south down the river, the ancient remnants of Písek's castle look as though they're about to slip gracefully into the water; north, a monotony of concrete socialist constructions hopefully will. A pleasant stroll can be had up Hálkova from the cramped main square, which brings you to the Putimská brána, the only remaining bastion, adjoined by a number of quiet backstreets. These lead to a small vegetable **market** which takes place under the aegis of the 74-metre onion-domed *hláska* (watchtower) of the Dominican church.

TEMELÍN – CHERNOBYL OF THE FUTURE?

The towers of **Temelín**, which rise up beside the main road from Písek to České Budějovice, are a chastening sight. Built to a Soviet design similar to the one used at Chernobyl, Temelín was designed to be the largest nuclear power station in the world – reason enough to give the town a wide berth. Many of its constituent parts have never been built or tested before, and a long campaign of protest by local and international groups (including the draping of a hundred-foot "STOP ČSFRNOBYL" banner from one of the cooling towers by Greenpeace) persuaded the new government to postpone the opening of the power station, and establish a commission of enquiry. However, with so much money already spent, and so much of the country devastated by the effects of its coal-produced energy, there is enormous pressure to bring at least part of the reactor into operation soon, if only to sell the electricity to rich western neighbours and earn badly needed hard currency.

Practicalities

Písek is low-key and quiet enough to make a night's stay an attractive possibility. The nicest hotel is the *Otava*, Chelčického 8 (☎0362/28 61; ②), smothered in a pictorial history of the town by the nineteenth-century Romantic painter (and local student) Mikuláš Aleš. Less spectacular are the *Bílá růže*, Šrámkova 169 (☎0362/49 31; ③), and the *U tří korun* (☎0362/44 41; ①), on the main square.

In the novel by Jaroslav Hašek, the *Good Soldier Švejk* made his fictional appearance at Písek in a blizzard, handcuffed to a lance-corporal in the Austrian constabulary "for comfort", before moving on to Tábor on the next train. Should you wish to do the same, the **bus** and **train stations** are both south of town, at the end of Nádražní (bus #1 from the main square).

Tábor

For all its grand medieval history, **TÁBOR**, 88km south of Prague, is the quietest of places today, especially the old quarter, devoid of traffic and with precious few shops within its walls. Aside from the very real attractions of the staré město's back alleys, and the rich Renaissance motifs which have survived on many of the houses, the main square and the Hussite Museum are the only specific "sights" in town. Nevertheless, Tábor played such an important part in Czech history that it still manages to pull in the crowds, centuries after its glory days have passed.

A brief history

Founded in 1420 by religious exiles from Prague, Tábor was the spiritual and strategic centre of the Hussites' social and religious revolution, which swept through Bohemia in the first half of the fifteenth century. It gave its name to the radical wing of the reformist Hussite movement, the **Táborites**, whose philosophy, that all people should be equal on earth as in heaven, found few friends among the church hierarchy and feudal-minded nobility of the time, Hussite or Catholic. Under constant threat of physical attack, they developed into a formidable fighting force (Tábor literally means "fortified camp"), declaring war on the Catholic church and remaining undefeated until 1452, when the town was taken by a force led by the moderate Hussite King George of Poděbrady. Two centuries later, the town rose up again in support of the rebellion against the Catholic Habsburgs, and was one of the last to be captured in 1621 after the Protestant defeat at the Battle of Bílá hora. Anti-authoritarianism persists here, and despite the efforts of the Jesuits and others, Tábor still boasts the smallest percentage of Catholics in the country.

The Town

To reach the staré město, walk west from the train or bus **station** through the park by the town's army barracks. En route, you'll pass an unusual and passionate **statue of Jan Hus** by local turn-of-the-century sculptor, František Bílek. It was one of Kafka's favourite works of art, a view not shared by the rest of the citizens of Kolín, where the statue used to reside, who had it transferred here by popular request. For the old town, continue past the statue down třída 9 května until you reach the busy square, náměstí Fr. Křižíka, which straddles the ridge between the new and old towns, then head up Palackého.

Centuries of inactivity have turned the **staré město**, with its vast maze of narrow medieval streets designed to confuse the enemy, into dusty dilapidated back alleys. No fewer than twelve streets lead onto the central square, **Žižkovo náměstí**, the only place that hints at Tábor's former glory, with its brightly coloured houses and wide variety of gables and gargoyles, rebuilt after the fires of the fifteenth and sixteenth centuries. It was here in 1420 that the Táborites threw theological caution to the wind and set up a religious commune under the principle of *není nic mé a nic tvé, než všecko v obec rovně mají* ("nothing is mine, nothing is yours, everything is common to all"). Large urns were set up in the square and anyone – male or female – wishing to live in the commune had first to place all their possessions in the urns, after which they were given work on a daily rota. Men and women were granted equal rights, there was a complete ban on alcohol, and from the stone table which still stands outside the radnice, communion was given to the people "in both kinds" – as opposed to the Catholic practice of reserving the wine (the blood of Christ) for the priesthood. The Hussites had this last symbolic act emblazoned on their flag – a red chalice on a black background – which, like the rousing religious war songs they sang before going into battle, struck fear into the crusaders from thirty nations who came against them.

The former radnice sports three steeply stepped gables and, inside, a huge rib-vaulted banquet hall, now the venue for the town's **Museum of the Hussite Movement** (Tues–Sun 9am–5.30pm), which dwells on the military prowess of the Táborites, including the medieval "tank" invented by the Táborites' brilliant, blind military leader Jan Žižka, whose statue (traditionally depicted with one eye

THE PIKARTS AND ADAMITES

When news of Tábor reached the rest of Europe, all manner of foreign heretics gravitated to this small Bohemian town, and it became something of a haven for unorthodox religious sects. One of the most numerous were the so-called **Pikarts**, who, as their name suggests, came from Picardy in France. The Pikarts took the Táborite heaven-on-earth philosophy one step further, preaching that "the perfect soul does not need to practise acts of virtue". This liberal message was beyond the pale for the more puritanically inclined Táborites, and the Pikarts were expelled from Tábor and forced to set up in the nearby castle of Příběnice (now in ruins) on an island in the Lužnice. Their leader, Martin Húska, was eventually captured and taken to Roudnice castle where he was tortured and burnt to death.

The Pikarts may have raised a few eyebrows in Tábor but they were nothing compared to the **Adamites**, who came to the fore in Příběnice. To become an Adamite, it was necessary to undergo a period of harsh asceticism after which you were "born again". The new soul could then indulge in whatever he or she desired – theft, perjury, sex – with impunity. This gave way to ritual nudism and "love-feasts", as one shocked (and fascinated) contemporary chronicler recalls – "wandering through the forests and hills, some of them fell into such an insanity that men and women threw off their clothes and went naked . . . from the same madness they supposed that they were not sinning if they had intercourse with one another". When rumours of such activities reached the Táborites, Žižka sent an expedition against them, taking the prisoners to Klokoty (see below) and personally seeing to the burning of fifty of them before handing over another twenty-five to his fellow townsfolk.

still functioning) tops the square in front of the church. The museum also gives access to a small section of the huge network of **underground passages** which formed part of the town's fortification system – guided tours are arranged for groups only, though if it's any consolation, the passages are not all they're cracked up to be. As for the rest of the town, its hotchpotch of backstreets, enlivened by the occasional decorative flourish, are perfect for aimless wandering – there's a great view of the surrounding countryside from the town's southern walls along Na parkánech. If you want more direction to your strolling, head off by bus or train to one of the local destinations detailed in the "Around Tábor" section below.

Practicalities

Fast trains from Prague take under two hours to reach Tábor, so, at a pinch, you could actually come here on a day trip. However, if you'd prefer to stay, Tábor has several **hotels** to choose from, the best equipped being the *Bohemia* on Husovo náměstí (☎0361/228 27; ③) near the train station, mostly double rooms with a bathroom, and all with TVs; the high-rise *Palcát*, on třída 9 května (☎0361/229 01; ④), and is similarly priced but in need of modernisation; and the *Slovan*, also on třída 9 května (☎0361/236 97; ①), much cheaper and, in many ways, better. For **private rooms** (①–③) go to *Info central* on náměstí Fr. Křižíka; the *Bican* B&B on Hradební is also worth a try. If it's **food** you want, away from the uniform hotel restaurants there's Chinese-inspired food at *Orient* on Žižkovo náměstí, pizza and pasta at *Pizza Napoli* on Husovo náměstí, or Czech food at the *Třeboňská pivnice* on Budějovická.

All the **campsites** are well out of the centre. Very few buses run to the *Malý Jordán* (mid-June to mid-Sept), situated north of the town, in the woods between Lake Jordán – formed by the oldest dam in Europe, and the spot where the Táborites used to baptise their children – and its smaller sister lake; but it's a pleasant three-kilometre walk by marked track along the lakeside. There's a bigger site, *Knížecí rybník* (open all year), also by a lake, which is a short walk from SMYSLOV train station, 6km (and one stop on the Pelhřimov line) to the east of Tábor.

Around Tábor

Tábor's history is undeniably rich, but it's difficult not to feel a slight disappointment at the dusty, neglected feel of the old town. With an afternoon to spare, several trips are possible around Tábor, all of them an easy walk or short train journey from the town.

Klokoty

Closest to Tábor is the pilgrimage church of **KLOKOTY**, once a separate village, now a suburb of the town, just a kilometre or so west of the centre; walk down Klokotská from the main square, and turn right up Sady, just by the brewery and Bechyně gate, then continue northwest across the fields. An ensemble of nine green onion domes rises above the pristine whitewashed walls, making this small church and cloister one of the most endearing and least pompous of Bohemia's Counter-Reformation monasteries. Sadly there's no admission, but there's a great view across the woods and over to Tábor.

The Chýnov Caves

The dry **Chýnov Caves** (Chýnovská jeskyně) are a three-kilometre walk across the fields from CHÝNOV train station (three stops east of Tábor). Amid gentle meadows and orchards, the entrance to the caves consists of a fifty-metre plunge down narrow, precipitous steps into the earth, to the sounds of Bach's *Toccata in D minor*. The whole experience is a lot more like real potholing than the larger caves in Moravia and Slovakia, and consequently is not recommended for claustrophobes. Tours last thirty minutes (Tues & Wed 10am–5pm, Thurs & Fri 10am–4pm, Sat & Sun 9am–5pm).

Milevsko

Halfway along the branch line from Tábor to Písek, **MILEVSKO** has a couple of interesting sights if you're passing through. The most unusual one is the town's former **synagogue**, on Sokolovská, used by the local Hussite congregation since the last war. Completed in 1919, its Neoclassical facade is disrupted by a double staircase which used to lead to the women's gallery, and the distinctive Cubist prisms in the tympanum. The town's sturdy twelfth-century **Basillica of sv Jiljí**, just off the main Tábor–Plzeň road, used to attract a stream of royal and ecclesiastical admirers until the Hussites wrecked it. Despite repairs and later additions, it's currently in a desperate state. The nearby monastery houses a small **museum** (Tues–Sun 9am–5pm) charting the history of the town, with details on such things as the price of a fifteenth-century chicken.

Bechyně

Every hour and a half, a dinky red electric train – the Empire's first narrow-gauge service when it was built in 1902 – covers the 24km journey from Tábor to the small soporific spa and pottery-producing town of **BECHYNĚ**. As you enter the town, both rail and road cross a spectacular viaduct over the Lužnice gorge, known locally as the "Rainbow". The old town teeters on the edge of the gorge, ten minutes' walk southwest of the station. At the far side of the main square, which has long since lost its function as a marketplace, is the Rožmberks' Renaissance **chateau**, for the most part either falling down or closed to the public, though several painted courtyards are accessible, and you can stay the night here (see below). The **Franciscan monastery**, next door, is now a school, but the church is open on Sundays for mass, and the gardens host summer concerts and afford excellent views of the gorge.

Other places worth exploring are the **Alšova jihočeské galérie** and the **Pottery Museum** (Muzeum keramiky; Tues–Sun 9am–5pm), in what used to be the town brewery, which both have impressive collections of locally produced ceramics. The **Firefighting Museum** (Hašické muzeum; Tues–Thurs 9am–1pm, Fri–Sun 2–5pm) in Široká, on the north side of the square, is interesting less for its contents than for the fact that it is housed in the town's former **synagogue** – there's a well-kept **Jewish cemetery** just beyond the old town walls on Michalská (key from *Helena*, the hairdressers, at no. 314).

The **last train back to Tábor** leaves at around 10pm; the last bus much earlier. If you wish to stay the night, head for the chateau, where you can take breakfast in one of the Rožmberk dining rooms (☎0361/961 143; ②), or at *U draka*, near the station on K lázním (☎0361/960 81; ①), before resorting to the *Panská*, Libušina 54 (☎0361/961 119; ③).

East to Kámen, Pelhřimov and beyond

There's a sporadic branch line service between Tábor and Pelhřimov, but you'll have to take the bus to reach the one-street village of **KÁMEN** (meaning "Rock"), whose castle was once a fortified staging-post between these two strongly pro-Hussite walled towns. It's worth a detour since in 1974, after centuries of neglect, the castle was reopened – somewhat incongruously – as the **Museum of the International Motorcycle Federation** (April & Oct Sat & Sun 9am–4pm; May–Aug Tues–Sun 8am–5pm; Sept Tues–Sun 9am–5pm). Some wonderful old Czech bikes are on display, from the very first Laurin & Klement Model TB from 1899 – not much more than a bicycle with a petrol tank tacked on – to the heyday of stylish Czech biking between the wars. Other machines include ČZs and Jawas, which may have cut some ice back in the 1940s when they were designed, but now only exacerbate the country's environmental problems. To trace the sad demise of the Czech motorcycle industry, you have to join the short guided tour of the castle before reaching the machines.

Pelhřimov

If you're heading east into Moravia and need a place to stay, the tiny medieval town of **PELHŘIMOV** is only 16km further along the road. Barely 200m across, the walled town still retains two sixteenth-century tower gates, on which two rams tirelessly butt each other on the hour, some beautiful Renaissance houses, and, just off the main square, a sixteenth-century chateau, now the local **museum** (Tues–Fri 9am–4pm, Sat & Sun 10am–noon). On the main square itself, it's surprisingly easy to miss a minor masterpiece of Cubist architecture by Pavel Janák, who in 1913 adapted the Baroque house at no. 13 without forsaking the intentions of the original. If you're on the Cubist trail, head 200m west of the square down Strachovská to no. 331, and check out Janák's **Drechselův dům** in once-bold red and yellow, its most attractive feature being the garden canopy; appropriately enough, it now serves as a real estate office. If you've time to kill, the seat of the sgraffitoed town council hosts the occasional temporary exhibition (Mon–Fri 2–5pm, Sat 9–11.30am).

If it's open, the *Hotel Slávie*, overlooking the old square (☎0366/22 98; ①), is the best situated of the town's cheap **hotels**; otherwise, try the *Grand* on Palackého (☎0366/42 37; ①), or the *Rekrea*, on Slovanského bratrství (☎0366/42 37; ②). Alternatively, the tourist information office on the square can organise **private rooms**. Arrive here one weekend in the middle of June and you'll be confronted with the rather unlikely spectacle of Pelhřimov's **"Festival of Records and Curious Performances"**, during which Czech eccentrics attempt to enter the *Guinness Book of World Records*, by whatever means necessary. 1992 saw several new records set, including 157 people on one tractor, and a man with 82 socks on one foot, though the guy lobbing goat droppings into toilet bowls got nowhere.

Lipnice nad Sázavou

Another twenty-odd kilometres northeast, just beyond Humpolec and the Prague–Brno motorway, in the midst of some really lovely Bohemian countryside, is the village of **LIPNICE NAD SÁZAVOU**. Here, Bohemia's

JAROSLAV HAŠEK

Stories about Hašek's life – many propagated by the author himself – have always been a mixture of fact and fiction, but at one time or another he was an anarchist, dog-breeder, lab assistant, bigamist, cabaret artist and People's Commissar in the Red Army. He alternately shocked and delighted both close friends and the public at large with his drunken antics and occasional acts of political extremism. When, towards the end of his life, he made his home in the *Česká koruna* pub in Lipnice, he wrote happily, "Now I live bang in the middle of a *pivnice*. Nothing better could have happened to me". Few friends attended his funeral, and none of his family, with the exception of his eleven-year-old son, who had met his father only two or three times. In a final act of contempt, the local priest would only allow his body to be buried alongside the cemetery wall, among the unbaptised and suicide victims. Before long, however, Hašek's *Good Soldier Švejk* had become the most famous (fictional) Czech of all time, culminating in Hašek's "canonisation" by the Communist regime – his works even being published by the military publishers, *Naše Vojsko* (Our Army).

ultimate bohemian, the writer **Jaroslav Hašek**, died on January 3, 1923, his most famous work still unfinished. The village has changed little over the intervening years; the pub he lived, drank and died in is still going strong, and the castle, ruined even in Hašek's day, is still mostly rubble. A flattering bust of the author has been erected on the way up to the castle, and his gravestone is a little less ignominious these days. Beside the castle, in the house where he died, the **Memorial to Jaroslav Hašek** (Tues–Sun April–Sept 8am–noon & 1–4.15pm; Oct–March 8am–noon & 1–3pm) is respectfully vague about the many contradictions in Hašek's life, not least the alcoholism which eventually cost him his life.

If you want to pay homage to Hašek at Lipnice, roughly five buses a day make the 10km trip from Humpolec, though once here you'll have to backtrack to Pelhřimov or Humpolec to find a bed for the night, unless you stay at the **campsite** just east of the village (mid-May to Sept).

Třeboňsko

The **Třeboňsko** region, with the town of Třeboň at its heart, is unlike the rest of South Bohemia – characterised not by rolling hills but by peat bogs, flatlands and fishponds. This monotonous, unhealthy marshland, broken only by the occasional Gothic fortress, was moulded into an intricate system of canal-linked ponds (totalling over 6000) as early as the fifteenth century, ushering in profitable times for the nobles who owned the land. The fish industry still dominates the region, and around September the ponds are drained to allow the fish to be "harvested". Larger ponds, like the Rožmberk, are drained only every other year and for three days people from the surrounding district gather to feast, sing and participate in what is still a great local event, and one worth seeking out if you're anywhere nearby. Wildlife also thrives on the soggy plains and in 1977 UNESCO declared a large area – from Soběslav south as far as the Austrian border – a nature reserve.

Jindřichův Hradec

JINDŘICHŮV HRADEC (Neuhaus) is a small sleepy town built amongst Třeboňsko's fish ponds. Hemmed in by walls and water, it's typical of the region – blessed with a glorious medieval past, untouched by modern conflicts, and very, very quiet. However, the town betrays no sense of its antiquity as you approach from the bus and train stations to the north, ten minutes' walk along Nádražní. On the north side, the town walls have long since been replaced by a park, and you simply drift into the old quarter, which was ripped apart by a fire in 1801, thus robbing the place of much of its rich medieval dressing.

The main square, **náměstí Míru**, displays a fine Trinity column and a subdued array of wealthy merchants' houses, nowadays sporting mostly Empire facades, though the rest of the town's crusty buildings, huddled round the castle walls, recall an earlier feudal era. Rybniční leads down from the square to a bridge that divides the Vaygar fish pond in two, creating a small harbour. From here, the thirteenth-century **chateau** is picturesquely mirrored in the water, its grim fort-like exterior giving no hint of the exuberant renovations carried out inside by Italian architects in the sixteenth century. Of the chateau's highlights – the slender Renaissance loggia, the striking garden rotunda known as the "Rondel", and the fourteenth-century frescoes – only the triple-tiered arcading in the main courtyard is currently accessible to the public; the rest looks like being closed for some time.

With no tour groups visiting the chateau, there's hardly anyone exploring the flaking alleyways to the north of the old town at the top of Komenského. Most of Jindřichův Hradec's ecclesiastical buildings are out of bounds but the local **museum** (Tues–Sun 8.30am–5pm) is set in the old Jesuit seminary. One room is devoted to Ferenc Rákóczi II, leading light of the Hungarian War of Independence (1703–11), who studied here, while another honours the composer Bedřich Smetana, who seems to have moved from one brewery to another; born in one in Litomyšl (see p.246), he lived in another here, below the castle, from 1831 to 1835.

Places **to stay**, if you're taken by the slow pace of life, are all located on the main square: the two old state hotels, the *Grand* (☎0331/32 46; ②) and the *Vaygar* (☎0331/22 33; ②); and the *Pension Corina* (☎0331/269 34; ④), a newly opened private venture, has clean modern doubles with TV and shower.

Červená Lhota

In the middle of nowhere, off the main road between Soběslav and Jindřichův Hradec, the pink sugar-lump castle of **Červená Lhota** is reflected perfectly in the still waters which surround it. It *is* a remarkable sight – a Gothic waterfort converted into a Renaissance retreat for the rich – and one which appears on almost every tourist handout, but, without your own transport, its isolated location makes it a nightmare to reach on public transport. Given this, and the unremarkable nature of the chateau's interior, it's really only for dedicated fans of Karl Ditters von Dittersdorf (the composer died here in 1799).

Třeboň

Right in the midst of some of the region's largest fishponds, the spa town of **TŘEBOŇ** (Wittingau) is as medieval and minute as they come. The houses lining the long, thin main square, Masarykovo náměstí, make an attractive parade, but the **Bílý koníček** (White Horse) hotel, built in 1544, steals the show with a stepped gable of miniature turrets. The entire staré město is made up of just three more streets, a fourteenth-century monastery and a chateau. Three gateways (including the impressive double south gate, next to the local brewery), and the entire ring of walls, have survived from the sixteenth century, though many houses suffered badly during the last great fire of 1781.

Out of all proportion to the rest of the town is the huge Renaissance **chateau** built by Petr Vok, a colourful character, notoriously fond of sex, drugs and alchemy, friend of the mad Emperor Rudolf II, legendary thrower of parties, and the last heir of the Rožmberk family. The chateau, daubed in blinding white sgraffito and taking up almost a fifth of the town, is a pretty clumsy affair; the greater part of it is now used as a hospital, though several of the grander rooms remain open to the public (April & Oct Sat & Sun 9am–4pm; May–Aug Tues–Sun 8am–4pm; Sept Tues–Sun 9am–4pm). There's an "English park", equal in size to the old town, adjacent to the chateau, and laid out for the town's spa patients to stroll in.

South of the town is the Svět pond, beside which stands the local **fishery** on Novohradská, which handles the region's huge fish harvest, and most importantly its *kapr* (carp) culling. **Carp**, not turkey, is the centrepiece of the Christmas meal in the Czech Lands, traditionally sold live and wriggling from town squares across the country, and transferred to the family bathtub until the big day.

The Schwarzenberg mausoleum

Head south out of Třeboň in the direction of Borovany, and you'll pick up signs to the **Schwarzenberg mausoleum** (Schwarzenberská hrobka; Tues–Sun April & Oct 9am–3.30pm; May–Aug 8am–4.30pm; Sept 9am–4.30pm). It's a strangely subdued, out-of-the-way site for a family so fond of ostentatious displays of wealth, hidden among the silver birch trees south of the Svět pond. The building itself is equally strange, a seemingly brand-new neo-Gothic building with a bare chapel above and a dark crypt below. Třeboň was the first Bohemian town to be bought up by the Bavarian-based Schwarzenberg family in 1660 who, having sided with the Habsburgs in the Counter-Reformation, became the unofficial heirs of ousted or defunct Czech aristocrats like the Vítkovci and Rožmberks. By 1875, the family owned more estates in Bohemia than anyone else, and decided to "honour" Třeboň by establishing the family mausoleum in the town. After 1945 the family's possessions were expropriated and, along with all their fellow German-speakers, they were thrown out of the country. Today, the most famous descendant is probably Count Karl von Schwarzenberg, a former emigré and one of Havel's closest advisors during his presidency.

Practicalities

There are two **hotels** on the main square in the old town: the aforementioned *Bílý koníček* (☎0333/22 48; ④) is small and often full; the *Zlatá hvězda* (☎0333/26 61; ④), opposite, is an equally attractive possibility. **Camping** (and swimming) take place at the *Domanín* campsite (mid-May to Sept), south of the fishpond, near the mausoleum. The local fish restaurant is the *Šupina*, signposted from the main square in the direction of the lake; otherwise you could try your luck at one of the hotels or, better still, if you're camping and cooking your own food, buy fresh fish from the *rybárna* (fishmonger) under the arcades in Březanova.

Třeboň is on the main train line from Prague to Vienna, so it's possible to **cross into Austria** by catching one of the four daily expresses – the train station is five minutes east of the old town. **Motorists** must cross the border further northeast at NOVÁ BYSTŘICE. Alternatively, frequent **buses** run west to České Budějovice or east to Jindřichův Hradec from the station located five minutes west of the old town.

České Budějovice and around

The flat urban sprawl of **ČESKÉ BUDĚJOVICE** (Budweis) comes as something of a surprise after the small-town mentality of the rest of South Bohemia; so too do the chic boutiques and pricey hotels. But first impressions are deceptive, for at its heart it's a laid-back city, no more cosmopolitan than anywhere else in the region – stuck in a Central European backwater, contact with the outside world is still restricted to Bavarians and provincial Austrians. Yet since its foundation by King Otakar II in 1265 as a German merchants' colony, the town has been a self-assured place, convinced of its own importance. Its wealth, based on medieval silver mines and its position on the old salt route from Linz to Prague, was wiped out in the seventeenth century by the twin ravages of war and fire. But perhaps because it remained a loyal Catholic town in a hotbed of Hussitism, the Habsburgs lavishly reconstructed most of České Budějovice in the eighteenth century. The result may not be the "Bohemian Florence" of the tourist brochures, but the staré město, at least, has been carefully preserved in the face of two centuries of rapid industrial growth. Besides, its renown nowadays is due to its local brew *Budvar*, better known abroad under its original German name, *Budweiser*. Needless to say, although lighter than the average Bohemian lager, it bears little resemblance to the bland American *Bud*.

Accommodation

Given České Budějovice's popularity with neighbouring Austrians and Germans, **hotel rooms** can be difficult to find even out of season. To find out what's on offer, go to the first floor of the excessively plush *ČEDOK* offices on the main square, or try the hotels themselves, which are usually more inclined to suddenly discover vacancies. There are no particularly cheap options in the centre, so you might as well head straight for the *Zvon* (☎038/353 61; ③–⑤), just down from the *ČEDOK* office, or the Gomel (☎038/279 49; ④) on Pražská for something a bit more downmarket, there's the *Grand* on Nádražní (☎038/365 91; ③). Alternatively, you could enquire about **private rooms** at either *ČEDOK* or *CTS*, Krajinská 1.

In July and August rooms are available in **student hostels**, and it's worth trying even if you haven't booked in advance. First go to *CKM*, Osovobzeni 14 (☎038/361 38), and find out the addresses for the current year's hostels and (if *CKM* say they're full) then go to the hostels themselves and beg. The only guaranteed cheap sleep is to bring your own tent and **camp**, or rent the **bungalows** at the highly recommendable *Dlouhá louka* site (April–Oct; red bus #6 from the museum, or #16 from the station), or out at Hluboká nad Vltavou (see below).

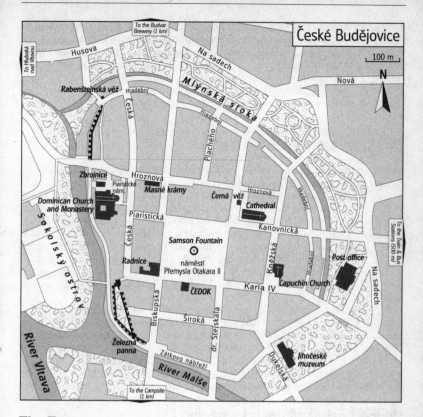

The Town

At the western end of Lannova třída you hit Na sadech, the busy ring road flanked by small parks which encloses the staré město in place of the old town walls. From here, the medieval grid plan leads inevitably to the town's showpiece, the magnificent **náměstí Přemysla Otakara II**, one of Europe's largest squares. The buildings are elegant enough, testifying to the last three centuries of German burgher power (it wasn't until the 1890s that the first Czech was able to buy one of the valuable houses here), but it's the square's arcades and the octagonal **Samson's Fountain** – once the only tap in town – that make the greatest impression. It was German merchants, too, who paid in silver and salt for the 72-metre status symbol, the **Černá věž** (Black Tower), one of the few survivors of the 1641 fire, which leans gently to one side of the square; its roof gallery (April–June & Sept–Nov Tues–Sun 9am–5pm; July & Aug daily 9am–5pm) provides a superb view of the staré město. The streets immediately off the square – Krajinská, Česká and Kněžská – house the odd *cukrárna* (cake and coffee shop) and chic new shops to cater for the German-speaking tourists.

When the weather's fine people tend to promenade by the banks of the Malše, where parts of the original town walls have survived along with some of České

Budějovice's oldest buildings, like the fifteenth-century prison tower, named for its most infamous torture instrument, **Železná panna** (literally "Iron Maiden"). All that is left of the bishop's palace is his serene **garden** (May–Sept daily 8am–6pm), accessible through a small gateway in the walls, a little further on. At the second bridge, a right turn down Hroznová will lead you round into Piaristické náměstí, where the rough-looking, thoroughly medieval **zbrojnice** (one-time arsenal) stands, its stepped gables proof of its former importance as centre of the town's salt trade.

Drinking, eating and nightlife

Drinking is obviously an important activity in České Budějovice, though serious *Budvar* drinkers will be disappointed to learn that the grim brewery gates on U Trojice (bus #2, #4, #6 or #12) are firmly closed to the public – though you can at least be sure of getting the real thing at the grimy modern restaurant next door. The liveliest (and most touristy) place in town is *Masné krámy* on Krajinská, formerly a sixteenth-century covered meat market, which now serves huge quantities of *Budvar*, and a little food, all day until 10pm; another good *pivnice*, which doesn't, however, suffer from the same crowds, is *U Vaticánů* on Lannova třída. If you're looking for an early jar, try the station's faded 1908 *restaurace,* where the beer flows freely from 6am – if you don't believe it, look at the tab of the person sitting next to you.

As for **eating**, picnic fodder can be assembled at the big **supermarket** on Lannova třída, or at the fruit and veg market on Piaristické náměstí. **Sit-down meals** are much of a muchness at the big hotels. For something different, the **fish restaurant**, *U železné panny*, on Široká (Mon–Sat until 10pm) serves carp and trout fresh from the ponds northwest of town. **Nightlife** is still thin on the ground: the locals seem to opt for hanging around the hotel lobbies or tipping each other into the fountain – neither exactly a fun night out.

Up the Českobudějovická pánev

Regular buses run from České Budějovice to **HLUBOKÁ NAD VLTAVOU** (Frauenberg), 8km northwest across a flat basin of soggy land known as the **Českobudějovická pánev**. A Přemyslid stronghold was founded above the village as early as the thirteenth century, but it was sequestered from its Protestant Czech owners in 1622 for their part in the anti-Habsburg rebellion, and given to the *arriviste* Schwarzenberg family, who, during the course of the nineteenth century, spent some of their considerable fortune turning it into the Disneyland **chateau** (Tues–Sun April & Oct 9am–4pm; May–Aug 8am–5pm; Sept 9am–5pm) that pulls in the crowds today. The result – a more or less deliberate copy of Windsor Castle – is both impressive and excessive. In 1945, when all the German estates were nationalised, the Schwarzenbergs decamped with most of the loot, but the odds and ends they left behind at their numerous other castles have been brought here, making the interior similarly over-the-top. The forty-minute guided tours, occasionally in German or English, run every ten minutes.

If the surrounding mock-Tudor fails to move you, it's possible to seek sanctuary in the former **Riding School**, which now exhibits Gothic religious art and the occasional interesting contemporary exhibition. Alternatively, head off into the chateau's very beautiful English grounds, where South Bohemia's wild boars are reputed to roam. Other distractions include occasional displays of falconry (Tues–Sun at 4pm). Should you wish **to stay** overnight here, rather than fight for rooms in České Budějovice, there's the *Parkhotel* (☎038/965 281; ②) in the village, and, further out, the *Baborka Sporthotel* (☎038/965 411; ②); 5km to the north, in KŘIVONOSKA, there's a **campsite** (mid-May to Sept).

It's a stiff climb up to the chateau from the main square, where the **buses** unload passengers. If you're arriving by **train**, two out-of-the-way stations (nominally) serve the village: Hluboká nad Vltavou station, 3km southwest on the Plzeň line; and Hluboká nad Vltavou-Zámostí station, 2km east on the main line to Prague.

Holašovice

If you've got your own transport, it's worth making a quick detour to the village of **HOLAŠOVICE**, 12km west of České Budějovice. There's no specific "sight" here – it's a working village – but the entire settlement stands far and away as the most perfect example of **Baroque folk architecture**, unique to this part of Bohemia. The stone-built farmhouses (including the one and only *hostinec*) date from the first six decades of the nineteenth century, and face onto the original village green. Every house on the square follows the same basic design though the decorative detail of the barn doors and gables are unique to each one. There are other nearby villages displaying similar architectural treats – like ZÁBOŘÍ and DOBČICE – but none compete with the consummate effect of Holašovice.

Kratochvíle

Further west, 2km outside NETOLICE, **Kratochvíle** (Kurzweil) is without doubt the most charming Renaissance chateau in Bohemia. It stands unaltered since its rapid six-year construction by Italian architects between 1583 and 1589, commissioned by the last generation of Rožmberks to while away the time – the literal meaning of *kratochvíle*. The attention to detail is still clearly visible in the exquisite stucco work and painted vaults, but the rest of the place is now given over to the **Museum of Animated Film** (Tues–Sun April & Sept 9am–noon & 1–4pm; May–Aug 8am–noon & 1–5pm; Oct 9am–noon & 1–5pm), which is aimed primarily at a young, domestic audience, with original puppet "actors" and drawings from well-known kids' cartoons like *Boris*. That said, it's a thoughtfully laid out exhibition, which demonstrates all the painstaking processes involved in making animation, and should interest anyone from 3 to 93 – no Jan Švankmajer, sadly.

There's nowhere to stay in Netolice – other than at the **campsite** (May–Sept), southwest of the town centre – but it's only a forty-minute bus ride from České Budějovice. The last 2km to Kratochvíle are probably best covered on foot.

The foothills of the Šumava

An alternative to heading up the Českobudějovická pánev is to aim for the large bulge of forest, known as the **Blanský les**, to the southwest of České Budějovice. Its highest point is **Mount Kleť** (1083m), which stands slightly apart from the rest of the Šumava range, and looks all the more impressive for it, towering above the Vltava basin to the north. From the summit, aside from the obligatory TV tower, on a clear day you can see the undulating forested peaks of the Šumava laid out before you. To reach the top, you can either hop into one of the single-seat chairlifts (Tues–Sun hourly), or opt for the stiff but enchanting four-kilometre hike through the woods. To get there from České Budějovice or Český Krumlov, catch a train to the idyllic rural station at HOLUBOV and walk the last 2km to Krasetín, where the chairlift starts.

There's little **accommodation** in this neck of the woods, aside from a few private bed and breakfast places, but there is a **campsite** in ZLATÁ KORUNA (Goldenkron), a tiny village on the Vltava, whose leafy main square is built inside the fortifications of an old **Cistercian monastery** (Tues–Sun 8am–noon & 1–5pm). Founded in the thirteenth century by King Otakar II, it suffered badly at the hands of the Hussites, but parts of the original medieval structures survive. In one building there's a worthy museum on Czech literature, but the main focus of interest is the vaulted chapterhouse from 1280, and the Gothic church, built in part by Peter Parler's masons, and one of the first to employ ribbed vaulting without any accompanying capitols. Zlatá Koruna is easy enough to reach on the train from České Budějovice or Český Krumlov.

Český Krumlov

Squeezed into a tight S-bend of the Vltava, in the foothills of the Šumava, ČESKÝ KRUMLOV (Krumau) is undoubtedly one of the most exquisite towns in South Bohemia. Rose-brown houses tumble down steep slopes to the blue-green river below, creating a magical effect whose beauty has hardly changed in the last three hundred years. UNESCO is currently trying to save it from gradual disintegration and has turned much of the town into a medieval building site. Consequently, only the castle gets any serious attention from the crowds, leaving the town's warren of narrow streets – which are the real attraction – relatively undisturbed.

The Town

The town's **history** is dominated by the great seigneurs of the region, the Rožmberks and the Schwarzenbergs. Thanks to special privileges won after the Battle of Leipzig in 1813, the Schwarzenbergs were permitted to keep a private army of twelve soldiers dressed in Napoleonic uniform (who also doubled as the castle's private orchestra). Every morning at 9am, one of the liveried guards would sound the bugle from the thirteenth-century round tower. In 1945, Krumau awoke abruptly from this semi-feudal coma when the Schwarzenbergs and the majority of the town's inhabitants, who were also German-speaking, were booted out. Now a thoroughly Czech town, its economy relies more and more heavily on the steady flow of German and Austrian tourists.

For centuries, then, the focal point of the town has been the omnipresent **Krumlov Castle** (Tues–Sun April & Oct 9am–noon & 1–4pm; May–Aug 8am–noon & 1–5pm; Sept 9am–noon & 1–5pm) in the Latrán quarter, as good a place as any to begin a tour. The first courtyard belongs to the older, lower castle but it's the smaller sgraffitoed courtyards of the upper castle, added in the fifteenth century, which contain the treasures – though much of the Schwarzenbergs' best stuff has been taken off to Hluboká. The fifty-minute tour doles out rich helpings of feudal opulence: the Rococo excesses of the blue and pink marble chapel are followed by the garishly decorated *Maškarní sál* (ballroom).

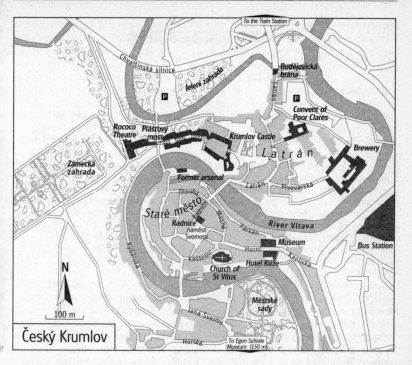

Český Krumlov

The highlight of the tour, the castle's ornate eighteenth-century **Rococo theatre**, is on the other side of the covered Plášťový most – a minor Bridge of Sighs with a superb view over the town. Although frequently, and unpredictably, closed, its restoration should be finally completed by 1994. This is one of the few eighteenth-century theatres in the world to retain so much of its original scenery and wardrobe. An ingenious system of flies and flats meant that a typical comic opera of the kind the theatre specialised in could have more than forty scene changes without interrupting the action. Another covered walkway puts you high above the town in the unexpectedly expansive and formal **terraced gardens** (open all year), whose tranquillity is disturbed only by the annual Drama Festival, performed in the gardens' modern, revolving open-air theatre.

The shabby houses leaning in on **Latrán** lead to a wooden ramp-like bridge which connects with the staré město. There's a compelling beauty at work in the old town, whose precarious existence is best viewed from the circling River Vltava. Turn right down Dlouhá, where the houses glow red at dusk, and continue on to the slip of land which houses the town's former arsenal. From here, if the river's not swollen, you can walk across the gangplanks of the footbridge to Rybářská, which then follows the left bank to the southernmost bridge, taking you back into the old town.

Alternatively, head straight up the soft incline of Radniční to the main square, looking backwards and upwards to the castle. On one side of the square a long, white Renaissance entablature combines two and a half Gothic houses to create the former **radnice**, while on the other, the high lancet windows of the St Vitus

---

SCHIELE IN KRUMAU

Sometime in the spring of 1911, the Austrian painter **Egon Schiele** decided to leave Vienna and spend some time in Krumau, his mother's home town. During his brief sojourn here, Schiele painted a number of intense townscapes of Krumau, like *Houses and Roofs near Krumau* and *Dead City*, in which he managed to make even the buildings look sexually anguished. At the time he was not a commercial artist, and was forced to shuffle from rooming house to rooming house with his seventeen-year-old lover, Wally Neuzil, a model handed down to him by Gustav Klimt. Finally he succeeded in buying a studio, a crumbling Baroque cottage by the river at Plešivec 343, south of the old town.

Schiele and his weird bohemian companions, Erwin Osen and the dancer Moa Mandu, caused more than a little controversy in this resolutely petit-bourgeois town – hiring young local girls for nude modelling and painting Wally naked in the orchard were just some of his more famous *faux pas* – and, forced to leave before the year was out, he vowed never to return. Under the Communists, the town made no attempt to advertise Schiele's brief but productive stay; only now is his studio being repaired and turned into a small museum due to open sometime in 1993 – in the meantime it serves as a private gallery for local artists (daily 10am–6pm).

Church rise vertically above the ramshackle rooftops. Continuing east off the square, down Horní, the beautiful sixteenth-century Jesuit college now provides space for a driving school, and the *Hotel Růže*. Opposite, the local **museum** (Tues–Fri 9am–6pm, Sat & Sun 11am–6pm) puts on small temporary exhibitions relating to the history of the town (see box above), a reconstructed seventeenth-century shop interior, and a model of the 2000-seater theatre, built to stage the Passion Plays, that used to exist at nearby Hořice until the Communists stamped out the tradition.

Practicalities

The **railway station** is ten minutes' walk north of the old town, down a precipitous set of steps, while the **bus station** is closer to the heart of town, on the right bank – either way, the best method of exploring Český Krumlov is on foot. As for **orientation**, the town is divided into two separate quarters by the twisting snake of the River Vltava: the circular staré město on the right bank and the Latrán quarter on the hillier left bank.

Before losing yourself in the town's maze of streets, it's best to find some **accommodation**. The *Hotel Růže*, on Horní (☎0337/22 45; ④), originally built by the Rožmberks to house their guests, and the *Krumlov*, on the main square (☎0337/22 55; ③), are both beautiful old hotels in the staré město; the *Vyšehrad* (☎0337/23 11; ②), near the train station, is cheaper, modern and ugly. If, as is likely, all three hotels are full, you should find few problems getting hold of a **private room** (①) from *CTS* at Látran 67; they also offer boat trips, canoe rental etc. For campers, there's always the primitive **campsite**, 2km south on the road to Větřní. As far as **eating** goes, the choice has improved considerably over the past few years: there's an excellent, if pricey, vegetarian restaurant, *U dvou marií*, with a riverside terrace, on Parkán, or, if it's not too packed, try *U hroznu* on the main square, or *U města vidně* by the Budějovická brána, where Schiele once stayed.

The Šumava

The dense pine forests and peat bogs of the **Šumava** region stretch for miles along the Austrian and German borders southwest of Český Krumlov, part of a much larger whole spreading across into Bavaria to form one of the last wildernesses in Central Europe. The original inhabitants of this sparsely populated region were German foresters who scraped a living from the meagre soil – their Austrian lilt and agricultural poverty separating them from their "civilised" Sudetenland brothers in western and northern Bohemia. Up to the declaration of the First Republic in 1918, the economic armlock of the all-powerful Schwarzenberg and Buquoy dynasties kept the region in a permanent semifeudal state. Even in the nineteenth century, peasants had to have permission from their landlords to marry, and their customary greeting to the local squire was *Brotvater* (literally "Breadfather").

Following the expulsion of the German-speakers in 1945, all links with the past were severed, yet the Šumava has remained underpopulated despite financial incentives for Czechs to move here. Compared to the rest of the former Sudetenland, it was poor, provincial and out of the way, and during the Cold War, had the added misfortune of lying alongside one of the most sensitive stretches of the East–West border, driving the military to close off large areas of forest along the south shore of Lake Lipno. Much of this land has been relinquished, the border dismantled, and cross-border contact re-established, all of which is beginning to revive the area.

Aside from the region's one truly medieval town, **Prachatice**, the majority of visitors come here for the scenery, which is among the most unspoilt in the country – thanks to the lack of heavy industry, and, compared to the rest of Bohemia, minimal acid rain. Most tourists crowd round the northern shore of the artificial **Lake Lipno**, creating their own peculiar brand of beach culture, while others head for the hills – less impressive than on the Austrian and German side, where they rise up dramatically, but also less touristy. If you're considering **hiking**, two maps, available at most bookshops, cover the area from southeast to northwest: *Šumava–Prachaticko* and *Šumava–Klatovsko*. The three most scenic ways of **getting around** the region are the Český Krumlov–Volary branch train line, the boat service across Lake Lipno and, of course, walking; often more convenient are the local buses – though at weekends you may find it necessary to hitch – or, of course, your own car.

Rožmberk nad Vltavou and Vyšší Brod

Buses from Český Krumlov follow the Vltava valley to the pretty village of **ROŽMBERK NAD VLTAVOU** (Rosenberg), its subtle charm completely upstaged by the fortress towering above it. As the name suggests, its *raison d'être* in the thirteenth century was as the headquarters of the powerful and single-minded Rožmberk family, regional supremos until their extinction in 1611. Nowadays, though, the castle speaks little of that family, but volumes instead of the later French owners, the Buquoys, who stuffed the dull, mannerless rooms with heavy neo-Gothic furnishings and instruments of torture. Czech tour groups fall over one another for a place on the 45-minute **guided tours**, which leave every fifteen minutes (April & Oct Sat & Sun 9am–noon & 1–4pm; May–Sept

Tues–Sun 9am–noon & 1–5pm), but one look at the cooped-up gibbon in the forecourt will give you a suitable foretaste of what's to come. Alternatively, you can **rent boats** down in the village, and appreciate the castle from the river instead.

Upriver to the south, fifteen minutes by bus, is **VYŠŠÍ BROD** (Hohenfurth), notable for its dazzling white Cistercian monastery, founded by Austrian monks during the thirteenth century. Its proximity to the border and its extreme wealth gave rise to a set of immodest fortifications that withstood two sieges by the needy, heretical Hussites. The essentially Gothic monastery church was, despite its pews, for the exclusive use of the monks, except on religious holidays when the locals were allowed in at the back. In the blue side chapel rests Petr Vok, the last of the Rožmberks, who died of drink and drugs – but was nonetheless given pride of place as the monastery's rich patron. The popular guided tours end with the monastery's main attraction, a 24-carat gold-decorated Rococo library accessible only via a secret door in one of the bookcases.

Practicalities

There's **accommodation** in Vyšší Brod and Rožmberk, and a **campsite** (May to mid-Oct) in the latter, too, but it's not very far by foot or infrequent local bus or train to Lipno nad Vltavou, at the eastern edge of Lake Lipno, where a host of other facilities are available (see below). If you are walking westwards be sure to take the red route to the viewpoint at **Čertova stěna** (Devil's Walls), a giant scree of granite slabs which tumble into the river below.

If you're planning on crossing the border into **Austria**, it's only 7km from Vyšší Brod to the Studánky–Weigelschlag border crossing, and another 7km east to HORNÍ DVOŘIŠTĚ, from where you can cross the border on one of the international expresses which pause there, or you can continue another 8km northeast to the Dolní Dvořiště–Wullowitz border crossing.

Lake Lipno

Just before Lipno nad Vltavou, a dam marks the southeastern end of **Lake Lipno**. On the face of it, there's not much to get excited about. The barrage turns the turbines of a huge underground hydroelectric power station, while the lake's scenic southern shore was for years occupied by the military – who have only recently relinquished their hold. However, the **northern shore** is punctuated by small beach resorts, which have developed rapidly over the last twenty years, mostly created to give workers some well-needed fresh air. The area is popular with Czechs, Germans and Austrians, and the few **hotels** are invariably full, but you're rarely far from a **campsite**, often with cheap bungalows for rent, too. **Buses** link most places, supplemented by trains from Černá v Pošumaví westwards, while *ČSAD* **ferries** run between Lipno nad Vltavou and Horní Planá, stopping at various points on the way. If you're planning to spend some time here it might be worth buying the very detailed *Lipenská přehrada* map.

Aside from LIPNO NAD VLTAVOU – which has just one hotel, the *Lipno* (☎0337/958 117; ①), and a choice of campsites, complete with takeaway stalls playing loud West Coast music – the southeasternmost villages are the least developed and **FRYMBURK**, with its delicate white octagonal spire jutting out into the lake, is arguably the best place to head for, with two low-key campsites just south of the village. At nearby **DOLNÍ VLTAVICE**, on a secluded thumb of land, a small crowd enjoys the grassy "beach" with a view over to the short stretch on the opposite shore belonging to Austria. To get there, it's necessary to change buses at **ČERNÁ V POŠUMAVÍ**, little more than an averagely priced hotel and a collection of campsites, but one of the few places which rents out boats (*lodí*).

There's not much more to **HORNÍ PLANÁ** (Oberplan) – one hotel, the *Smrčina* (☎0337/972 28; ①), a few private rooms, two pubs and a concrete caravan site – but it's the main resort hereabouts, and in summer the village becomes an extension of the beach with pink flesh and beachwear gracing the little square. The Czechs happily soak up the sun, cheek-by-jowl on the almost sandy beach, surrounded by a dubious combination of crazy golf, candy floss and beer. A little cultural distraction can be experienced at the birthplace of the German-speaking writer and painter **Adalbert Stifter** (1805–68), which is now a small memorial to his life and work; his statue stands behind the church, and there's another memorial to him overlooking the waters of the Plešné jezero, which sits below Plechy at the meeting of the German, Austrian and Czech borders.

Forest walks around the lake

The main road from Horní Planá northwest to Volary was, until recently, punctuated at regular intervals by little red signs warning about the impending Iron Curtain; all villages west of the Vltava were closed to road vehicles, with trains the only legal means of transport. The military have now given up their patch, and in addition to the two newly **reopened border crossings** at Strážný (24hr) and Stožec (pedestrians and cyclists only; daily 9am–9pm), there's a new pedestrian-only border crossing at PŘEDNÍ VÝTOŇ, on the opposite side of the lake from Frymburk. A bus makes the journey to the border from Horní Planá twice daily, but all other vehicles are still forbidden from entering the area, partly due to the state of the roads, and partly due to the recent decision to turn the whole area into a nature reserve. Another extremely useful development for walkers is the **new bus service** (mid-July to Aug only) that winds through the villages and does a complete circuit of the lake, starting and finishing at Přední Výtoň.

One of the most interesting **hikes** sets off from Ovesná station, at the top of Lake Lipno, following the yellow-marked route northwest through gigantic boulders and thick forest to Perník (1049m), before dropping down to JELENÍ, where the **Schwarzenberg Canal** emerges from a tunnel. Built at the turn of the eighteenth century in order to transport the Šumava's valuable timber straight to the Danube (less than 40km due south), the canal was, sadly, abandoned as a waterway in 1962. A little further on you reach the *Bären Stein*, marking the spot where the last bear in the Šumava was shot in 1856. The only threat now are 25 lynx which were resettled hereabouts in 1985. Moving on, you should reach the station at ČERNÝ KŘÍŽ in around six hours from Ovesná. Here, the railway divides and you should head north to **VOLARY** (Wallern), a sprawling village with a few traditional wooden Šumava cottages and a handsome Baroque church, but otherwise little reason to pause, unless you chance upon a vacancy at the *Bobík* hotel (☎0338/923 51; ②), or need to change trains for Prachatice or Vimperk.

Prachatice and Husinec

Where the slopes of Libín (1096m) merge into the Otava and Vltava plain lies the amiable little market town of **PRACHATICE** (Prachatitz), known as the "Gateway to the Šumava". Most people come here en route to the Šumava, but it's a beautiful medieval town in its own right, as well as being a useful base for visiting Husinec, birthplace of Jan Hus (see opposite). Founded in 1325, Prachatice flourished in the following century when it controlled the all-important salt trade route into Bohemia. A 1507 fire is responsible for the uniformly sixteenth-century appearance of the town and its famous collection of sgraffito facades.

The Town

A short walk uphill from the bus and train stations brings you to Malé náměstí, the main square/crossroads of the new town, which contains *ČEDOK*, a supermarket complex and a self-service *restaurace* packed with workers, policemen and cheap food. Everything else of use or interest is contained within the walls of the tiny circular **staré město**, reached through the bulky fifteenth-century Pisecká brána, a gateway with a faded mural showing Vílem of Rožmberk on horseback and, above it, in among the battlements, the red rose symbol of the family who acquired the town briefly in 1501.

The gate's double arches open out on the small Kostelní náměstí where old women sell spices and vegetables in the shade of the trees. The Gothic church of **sv Jakub** is the oldest building in town, its steep, rather peculiar red-ribbed roof the town's most obvious landmark. Prachatice is best known to the Czechs for the exquisitely decorative **Literátská škola** to the left, complete with miniature Renaissance battlements, which local heroes Hus and Žižka are said to have attended in their youth, although the bizarre depictions of men clubbing each other to death seem more appropriate to its present incumbents, a family butchers.

At this point the cobbles open out into the old town square, **Velké náměstí**, which gives off a thoroughly Germanic air. Its most striking aspect is the riot of **sgraffito** on the facades of many of the buildings. If you haven't already come across the phenomenon, Prachatice is as good a place as any to get to grips with it. The technique – extremely popular in the sixteenth century and revived in the nineteenth – involves scraping away plaster to form geometric, monochrome patterns or even whole pictorial friezes, producing a distinctive lace-work effect. The most lavish example of this style is without doubt the sixteenth-century **stará radnice**, decorated with copies of Hans Holbein's disturbing, apocalyptic parables; the sgraffito on the nearby nová radnice dates from the nineteenth century. The arcaded **Rumpalův dům**, opposite, is similarly smothered, as is the former **solnice** or salt house, at the far end of the square, through which the town accrued its enormous wealth in the Middle Ages.

Practicalities

Cheap **accommodation** in Prachatice is supplied by the *Národní dům* (☎0338/215 61; ②) and *Zlatá stezka* (☎0338/218 41; ①), both on Velké náměstí; the latter has a slightly better reputation. Alternatively, you can book **private rooms** (①) through *ČEDOK*, or try your luck at Horní 13 in the old town. To get to the primitive **campsite**, 10km south by the lake at KŘIŠŤANOVICE (July & Aug only), there's an infrequent bus service, followed by a 1500-metre walk from the bus stop on the main road. **Eating** (and drinking) is best done in the *Zlatá stezka* or at the livelier pub *U medvědků*, both on Velké náměstí.

Husinec

> *"You may burn the goose* [hus],
> *but one day there will come a swan,*
> *and him you will not burn."*

Martin Luther

Six kilometres north of Prachatice is the unassuming ribbon village of **HUSINEC**, birthplace of **Jan Hus** (see box below), the man whose death in 1415 triggered off the Hussite revolution. In the nineteenth century, when interest in Hus began to emerge after the dark years of the Counter-Reformation, the poet Jan Neruda visited Husinec, and was horrified to see Hus's former home shabby and neglected. No expense has been spared since, with the family house converted into a **museum** (Tues–Sun 8am–noon & 1–5pm), and many of Hus's old haunts in the surrounding region becoming points of pilgrimage over the last century. That said, you're quite likely to be alone in exploring the museum's small exhibition and the one original room, a tiny garret on the top floor. Getting here is easiest on one of the afternoon **buses** from Prachatice; the train station is 3km east of the village.

JAN HUS

The legendary preacher – and Czech national hero – **Jan Hus** (sometimes anglicised to John Huss) was born in Husinec, on the language border of the Czech- and German-speaking districts, around 1369. From a childhood of poverty, he enjoyed a meteoric rise through the education system to become the first Czech Rector of Prague's Charles University in 1403. He was a controversial choice of candidate, since his radical sermons criticising the social conditions of the time had already caused a scandal in Prague the previous year, not least because they were delivered not in Latin, but in Czech, the language of the masses. A mild-mannered and extremely short man, Hus became involved in a dispute with the more conservative German clergy at the university. On this occasion, the king, Václav IV, sided with Hus, but when he began to rail against the sale of indulgences to fund papal wars, Václav had him excommunicated.

Hus was not the first to draw attention to the plight of the poor, nor did he ever actually advocate many of the more famous tenets of the heretical religious movement that took his name – Hussitism. For example, he never advocated giving communion "in both kinds" – bread and wine – to the general congregation, nor did he ever denounce his Catholicism. However, his outspokenness was too much for a church already riven by the Papal Schism, and he was hauled in for questioning by the Council of Constance in 1415. Hus refused to renounce his beliefs and was burned at the stake as a heretic, despite having been guaranteed safe conduct by Emperor Sigismund himself. The Czechs were outraged, and Hus became a national hero overnight, inspiring thousands to rebel against the authorities of the day. In 1965, the Vatican finally overturned the sentence, and the anniversary of his death is now a national holiday.

Volary to Vimperk

The scenic train ride from Volary to Vimperk takes you deep into the Šumava forest, and it's worth breaking the journey at some point to delve further into the woods. One stop is at the primeval **Forest of Boubín**, 3km from Zátoň station – there's camping from mid-May to mid-September, 1.5km from the station. It is forbidden to walk among the pines and firs, some of which are over four hundred years old, but green markers take you around the perimeter and on to a small **deer park**. To get back to the rail line without retracing your steps, follow the blue-marked path from the deer park to the campsite and station at KUBOVA HUŤ (6km).

From May to September trains skirting the south slope of Boubín also stop at the station high above the village of **HORNÍ VLTAVICE**. The two-kilometre scramble down through the forest is worth it for the justly popular **campsite** and *hostinec* below. From Horní Vltavice, a few local buses cover the 13km to the 24-hour Strážný-Kleinphilippsreuth German border crossing; trains continue for 13km to **VIMPERK** (Winterberg), a pleasant enough town where the first printing press in Bohemia was established in 1484. A couple of hotels – try the *Zlatá hvězda* on 1 máje (☎0339/210; ①) – and a campsite at Hájna Hora, make it another possible base for exploring this part of the Šumava.

Strakonice

The rest of the Šumava lies, strictly speaking, in West Bohemia: the mountainous part is only accessible from the east by an infrequent bus service. Sticking with the railway for the moment, another 30km takes you to **STRAKONICE** (Strakonitz), which qualifies as a large industrial town in these parts. Its factories produce an unusual trio of products – Turkish *fez* hats, ČZ motorcycles, and *dudy*, the Bohemian equivalent of bagpipes. There's a **museum** (Tues–Sun 9am–5pm) on these very subjects in the town's extremely large thirteenth-century castle, at the confluence of the Otava and Volyňka. If you're really into *dudy*, there's an **International Bagpipe Festival** held in the castle courtyard every year in the middle of August, which attracts a regular Scottish contingent. The town has several other bizarre sights, like a rather pathetic, partial reconstruction of Stonehenge, and a head from Easter Island, both by local sculptor Pavel Pavel, not to mention a modern wooden ice-hockey stadium, though none is worth more than a passing nod.

From the **train and bus stations**, it's a five-minute walk to the castle – west down Alfonse Šťastného, then right down Bezděkovská. If you're staying the night, head for the *Švanda dudák*, near the castle (☎0342/222 11; ①), or the *Bílý Vlk*, near the junction of Alfonse Šťastného and Bezděkovská (☎0342/225 10; ①), before forking out for the brand new high-rise *Hotel Bavor*, across from the castle (☎0342/227 40; ⑤).

Rabí and Sušice

There are several ruined castles along the banks of the River Otava beyond Strakonice, but by far the most impressive are the vast and crumbling fortifications of **Rabí**, 25km away by train (change at HORAŽĎOVICE). A key fortress in the Hussite Wars, and allegedly the place where the Hussite general Jan Žižka lost his second eye, it was deliberately allowed to fall into rack and ruin for fear of its strategic value should it fall into the wrong hands. Renovation work, aimed at stabilising some of the more dangerously disintegrating bits, has allowed the public to gain access to most of the site now (Jan–Sept Tues–Sun 9am–5pm; Oct Sat & Sun only).

A few stops on from Rabí is **SUŠICE** (Schüttenhofen), which means just one thing to the Czechs – matches. The local *SOLO* match factory is one of the largest in Europe, and dominates the domestic market. Aside from that, there's little evidence of the town's wealthy medieval past, which, like Prachatice's, was based on the salt trade. The exception is the main square, náměstí Svobody, which boasts a handful of striking sgraffitoed Renaissance houses. The most arresting of the lot is the **Voprchovský dům**, with its fantastical gable made up of several tiers of mini-columns, which houses a museum on the Šumava (Tues–Sun 9am–4pm), established as far back as 1880. The exhibits range from local glassware to fifteenth-century woodcarvings and, of course, the match-making industry, but it's the carefully restored interior that makes it worth a visit. The only **hotel** is the *Fialka* on the main square (π0187/243; ①), a disappointment inside given its attractive double facade of Baroque balustrade and Renaissance gable; otherwise, there are **private rooms** available around town, and a **campsite** near the train station.

Up the Otava

Twice daily from Vimperk, more frequently from Sušice, a local bus heads for **KAŠPERSKÉ HORY** (Bergreichenstein), an old mining village on the River Otava, positioned below the ruined castle of Kašperk that was built by Charles IV in order to guard over the local gold mines. There are a couple of **hotels** on the main square – the *Bílá růže* (π0187/92 22 32; ②) is the nicer of the two – and a smart Renaissance radnice embellished with three perfect eighteenth-century gables. The nearby town **museum** (Tues–Sun 9am–5pm) serves as a repository for some wonderful local glassware, ranging from the fourteenth century to turn-of-the-century gear by Johann Loetz, from the neighbouring town of Klášterský Mlýn (Klöstermühle). In the late nineteenth century Loetz won many prizes in Brussels and Paris for his Tiffany-style iridescent glass vases and weird vegetal shapes, many of which inexplicably escaped the auctioneer's hammer and ended up here.

Down in the narrow Otava valley, the nearby village of REJŠTEJN retains a Germanic flavour, but a short bus ride south, along the newly surfaced road, the once isolated hamlet of **SRNÍ** tells a different story. Here, the traditional timber tiles and shingles of the old mountain cottages exist alongside the likes of the multistorey *Hotel Šumava* (π0187/922 22; ③), with more monstrosities in the pipeline.

A cluster of wooden buildings located 6km south at ANTIGL provides **camping** and a useful base for exploring the cool cascades of the **Vydra river gorge**. Most buses continue 3km upstream as far as **MODRAVA**, where the pseudo-Alpine buildings have all but won the day. From here, there's access to some of the wildest, boggy, woody scenery in the Šumava – though you'll have to walk every step of the way.

The northwestern tip of the Šumava

The northwestern tip of the Šumava centres around the ski resort of **ŽELEZNÁ RUDA** (Eisenstein), 2km from the German border and best approached by train from Klatovy (see p.177). The local sights are confined to the ludicrously over-sized wooden onion dome over the nave of the village church – the real reason for being here is to explore the countryside around. There are several hotels in Železná Ruda and nearby Špičák, as well as a smattering of private rooms, so **accommodation** shouldn't be a problem; or you could go for the **campsite** and bungalows two stops back down the track at Hojsova Stráž-Brčálník. The **rail link with Germany** was severed during the Cold War, but has recently been re-established, and six trains a day now run on to the *Bahnhof* in Bayerisch Eisenstein.

From **ŠPIČÁK**, one stop along from Železná Ruda, a series of chairlifts takes you to the top of **Pancíř** (1214m), all year round. Towards the German border, there are two glacial lakes – Černé jezero and Čertovo jezero – which you can reach via the yellow-marked path from the Špičák station. If you're considering walking, the *Šumava-Klatovsko* map is a worthwhile investment.

travel details

Trains

Connections with Prague Tábor (10 daily; 1hr 40min–2hr 20min); České Budějovice (6 daily; 2hr 30min–5hr 20min).

From Tábor to Bechyně (8 daily; 50min); Písek (9 daily; 1hr 30min); Chýnov/Pelhřimov (8 daily; 15min/1hr 30min); České Budějovice (13 daily; 1hr–1hr 40min); Jihlava (3 daily; 2–3hr); Brno (1 daily; 4hr); Gmünd (4 daily; 1hr 30min).

From České Budějovice to Jindřichův Hradec (9 daily; 1hr–1hr 30min); Plzeň (9 daily; 1hr 45min–3hr); Český Krumlov (8 daily; 1hr); Horní Planá/Volary (up to 6 daily; 2hr 15min/2hr 45min); Linz (4 daily; 2hr 30min).

From Volary to Prachatice (8 daily; 50min); Vimperk/Strakonice (6 daily; 1hr/2hr).

Buses (ČSAD only)

Connections with Prague České Budějovice (up to 12 daily; 2hr 25min–3hr); Český Krumlov (up to 3 daily; 3hr 40min); Orlík/Písek (up to 6 daily; 1hr 30min/2hr 10min); Strakonice/Prachatice (up to 4 daily; 2hr/3hr); Volary (up to 2 daily; 3hr 30min).

From Tábor to Bechyně (up to 14 daily; 40min–1hr 15min); Kámen (up to 6 daily; 30min).

From Pelhřimov to Kámen (up to 7 daily; 30min); Humpolec (up to 10 daily; 30min); Jihlava (up to 8 daily; 45min).

From Jindřichův Hradec to Slavonice (up to 8 daily; 1hr 30min); České Budějovice (12 or more daily; 1hr 10min).

From České Budějovice to Hluboká nad Vltavou (20 or more daily; 20min); Holašovice (up to 8 daily; 40min); Prachatice (up to 10 daily; 1hr 15min).

From Český Krumlov to Rožmberk/Vyšší Brod/Lipno nad Vltavou (up to 10 daily; 40min/55min/1hr 15min).

CHAPTER THREE

WEST BOHEMIA

For centuries, the rolling hills of **West Bohemia** (Západní Čechy) have been a buffer zone between the Slav world and the great German-speaking lands. The border regions were heavily colonised by neighbouring Germans from the twelfth century onwards. At first they were welcomed by the Czech Přemyslid rulers, providing urgently needed skilled craftsmen and miners for the Bohemian economy, but when the newcomers began to enrich themselves while maintaining a separate ethnic identity, political complications inevitably followed.

Every momentous event in Bohemian history found the population split along ethnic lines, until finally in 1938 the excesses of the Sudeten German Party provided the impetus for a violent break with the past. In North and West Bohemia the forced removal of the German-speaking population after World War II left vast areas of the countryside and several large towns empty of people. In the years after the war, Czechs and Slovaks were encouraged to resettle the towns and villages, but even now the countryside in particular remains eerily underpopulated.

The economic mainstay of the region for the last century has been the big industrial city of **Plzeň**: home of the Škoda engineering works, centre of the beer industry, and the region's capital. Within easy reach of Plzeň, though, are the monasteries of **Kladruby** and **Plasy**, monuments to the architectural genius of Giovanni Santini, the master of "Baroque-Gothic". Further south, the historic border town of **Domažlice** offers easy access to the colourful **Chod region**.

West Bohemia also contains the big three Czech spa resorts – **Mariánské Lázně**, **Františkovy Lázně** and **Karlovy Vary**. This famous triangle of spas, conveniently scattered along the German border, was the Côte d'Azur of Habsburg Europe, attracting the great names of *Mitteleuropa*. Following the wholesale nationalisation of the spa industry, every factory and trade union received an annual three weeks' holiday at a *lázně dům* (spa pension): a perk aimed at proving the success of socialism. Even now, *Die Kur* is still very popular among central Europeans, but spas are not to everyone's taste. Even at the most active of the lot – Karlovy Vary – the plethoric and elderly predominate. To avoid cure-seekers, head instead for **Cheb** or **Loket**, both beautifully preserved towns and largely crowd-free.

This being one of the most sparsely populated regions in the country, **public transport** is somewhat patchy. However, excellent rail links exist between the major towns, so unless you're heading for the back of beyond, getting around should present few real problems.

Plzeň

PLZEŇ is the largest city in Bohemia after Prague, with a population of 175,000. Parts of the city defy description, such is their state of disrepair, and the skyline is a symphony of smoke and steam, the results of which can be seen in the colour of the tap water. Yet despite its overwhelmingly industrial character, there are

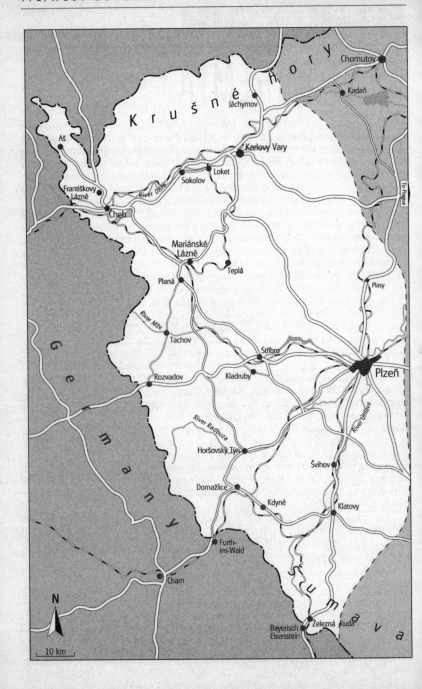

compensations – a large number of students, eclectic architecture and an unending supply of (probably) the best **beer** in the world – all of which make Plzeň a justifiably popular stopoff on the main railway line between Prague and the west.

Some history

Plzeň (or Pilsen as it is still called in the west) was built on beer and bombs. In 1850 it was a small town of 14,000, of whom the vast majority were German; then in 1859 an ironworks was founded and quickly snapped up by the Czech capitalist **Emil Škoda**, under whose control it drew an ever-increasing number of Czechs from the countryside. Within thirty years, the overall population had trebled while the number of Germans had decreased. Although initially simply an engineering plant, it was transformed into a huge armaments factory (second only to Krupps in Germany) by the Austrian government during World War I. Inevitably, it attracted the attention of Allied bombers during World War II. Nowadays, apart from producing the country's rolling stock, it also has the dubious privilege of having manufactured all the dodgy Soviet-designed nuclear reactors for the Warsaw Pact. However, since cancelled orders are now mounting up, and the wisdom of nuclear power is being openly questioned in eastern Europe for the first time, the factory may soon have to switch tack again.

Arrival, orientation and accommodation

Fast trains from Prague take between one and a half and two hours to reach Plzeň, making it just about possible to visit on a day trip. The town's **railway stations** are works of art in themselves: there are numerous minor ones within the city boundaries, but without doubt your likeliest point of arrival is Plzeň hlavní nádraží (main station), east of the city centre. The **bus terminal**, for all national and international arrivals, is on the west side of town. From the bus or the main train station, the city centre is just a short walk away or a few stops on tram #1 or #2.

Finding a vacancy in one of Plzeň's **hotels** presents few problems, though rooms don't come cheap. At the lower end of the market are the faded splendour and Hollywood stairways of the *Slovan*, Smetanovy sady 1 (☎019/335 51; ③), and moving up a bit there's the *Continental*, Zbrojnická 8 (☎019/330 60; ④), or the ugly *Central*, náměstí Republiky 33 (☎019/326 85; ④).

Private rooms are available from *ČEDOK*, Prešovská 10 (Mon–Fri 8am–noon & 2–6pm, Sat 8am–noon), for slightly less per person than the *Slovan*. In July and August, **student hostels** offer cheap dorm accommodation – go to *CKM* on Dominikanská to find out the latest addresses. Bus #20 will drop you at the *Bílá hora* **campsite**, in the northern suburb of the same name, where Plzeňites go to **swim** on summer days.

The City

Stepping out of the main station onto Americká, you're confronted with a variety of bad-taste Communist buildings, some still in the process of completion. Close by, the River Radbuza, one of four rivers running through Plzeň, doesn't bear close inspection, but the historical core of the city, beyond it, certainly does.

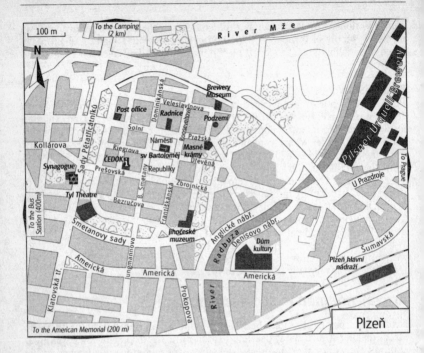

Laid out in chessboard fashion by Václav II in 1295, the old town is still dominated by the exalted heights of the Gothic church of **sv Bartoloměj** (St Bartholomew), stranded awkwardly in the middle of the main square, its bile-green spire extending more than one hundred metres, making it the tallest in the country. The rest of the square – **náměstí Republiky** – presents a full range of architectural styles: some buildings, like the squat, grey *Hotel Central*, as recent as the 1960s, others, like the Italianate **stará radnice** (old town hall), smothered in sgraffito earlier this century, dating from the sixteenth century. Rudolf II based himself next door, at no. 41, for the best part of a year in an effort to avoid the ravages of the 1599 Prague plague.

The vast majority of Plzeň's buildings, however, hail from the city's heyday during the industrial expansion around the turn of the century. In the old town, this produced some wonderful variations on historical themes and Art-Nouveau motifs, particularly to the north and west of the main square. West of Sady Pětatřicátníků, there are still more blocks of late nineteenth-century residential apartments, boasting vestiges of ornate mosaics and sculpturing, now barely visible beneath the black layer of pollution that's eating away at their fanciful facades.

On Sady Pětatřicátníků itself stands the largest surviving **synagogue** in the whole country, its neo-Romanesque facade caked in dirt. The smaller prayer hall inside was in use until very recently, and there are plans now to turn it into a museum on Plzeň's Jewish history along with a concert and exhibition hall. Diagonally opposite is the flamboyant **Tyl Theatre**, named after Josef Kajétan Tyl, the composer of the Czech half of the old Czechoslovak national anthem, who died in Plzeň in 1856.

Beer and the brewery

Whatever its other attractions, the real reason most people come to Plzeň is to sample its famous beer, *Plzeňský Prazdroj* or **Pilsner Urquell** (its more familiar Germanised export name). Beer has been brewed in the town since its foundation in 1295, but it wasn't until 1842 that the famous *Bürgerliches Brauhaus* was built by the German banker Bleichröder, after a near-riot by the townsfolk over the declining quality of their beer. The new brew was a bottom-fermented beer which quickly became popular across central Europe, spawning thousands of paler imitations under the generic name of *Pilsner* – hence the brewers' addition of the suffix *Prazdroj* or *Urquell* (meaning "original"), to show just who thought of it first. The reason for the superiority of Plzeň's beer is said to be the combination of the soft local water and world-renowned Žatec hops.

Joining a guided tour of the **brewery** is now relatively easy, except that no one seems to be quite sure of the exact times. Either turn up at the brewery gates at 12.30pm any day except Wednesday, as the brewery suggests, or ask at *CEDOK*, who tend to tell a different story. Alternatively, if the technological details of brewing don't grab you, try the historical angle at the Brewery Museum instead (see below), and/or go for a glass of the real thing at the *Restaurace Prazdroj* at U Prazdroje 1, next to the brewery's triumphal arch. This was built in 1892 to commemorate the beer's fiftieth birthday – and has appeared on every authentic bottle of *Pilsner Urquell* ever since. Plzeň's annual **beer festival**, incidentally, is held in October.

Plzeň's museums

Plzeň has a fair few museums, the biggest being the copper-topped **Západočeské muzeum** (due to reopen towards the end of 1992). A neo-Baroque extravaganza, it was built in the nineteenth century to help educate the peasants who were flocking to the city; only a few of its mammoth selection of exhibits deserve close attention, notably the art section, which boasts some of the best examples of twentieth-century Czech painting outside Prague. A little to the north, beneath the elongated vaults of the Gothic **Masné krámy** (Butchers' Stalls), the gallery puts on temporary art exhibitions (Tues–Fri 10am–6pm, Sat 10am–1pm, Sun 9am–5pm) and hosts concerts on Sunday mornings.

THE AMERICAN LIBERATION OF PLZEŇ

On May 6, 1945, General Patton's US Third Army liberated Plzeň. Less than 100km of virtually open road lay between the Americans and Prague, by then into the second day of its costly uprising against the Nazis. However, the agreement between the big three Allies at Yalta was that Prague should be liberated by the Soviets, who were, at the time still 200km from Prague, en route from Berlin. Patton offered to march on Prague, and, in fact, on May 7, three US armoured cars reached the outskirts of the city, but the order was to stay put.

Following the 1948 coup, the Communists took down all the monuments, and deleted all references in history books to the American liberation of Plzeň. They even went so far as to say that the Americans had deliberately hung back from Prague, allowing thousands to die in the uprising. Finally, in May 1990, the city was able once again to celebrate the liberation, and with large numbers of US army veterans present, a new memorial was erected on Chodské náměstí, just off Klatovská třída.

At the end of the beautiful, narrow, *fin-de-siècle* Veleslavínova is the most popular of Plzeň's museums, the **Brewery Museum** (Pivovarské muzeum; Tues 1–4.30pm, Wed–Sun 9am–4.30pm), housed in what was originally a Gothic malthouse and later a pub. A more than sufficient consolation for those who fail to get into the brewery itself, its friendly anglophile custodian can furnish you with an English information sheet, and get the old *Würlitzer* organ going while you check out the exhibits: the smallest beer barrel in the world (a mere one-centimetre cube), case after case of kitsch Baroque beer mugs, and much else besides.

Unfortunately, unless you're an automotive engineer you won't get much from the **Škoda Museum**, by the factory on Korandova (Mon–Fri 7am–3.30pm), which has displays on the insides of train engines and suchlike. For an exhibition of old Škoda cars, you'll have to go to Mladá Boleslav (see p.130).

Eating, drinking and entertainment

All the hotels in town have **restaurants** attached to them, but for something more basic – and authentically Czech – you might as well combine your eating with your drinking. Apart from the aforementioned *Restaurace Prazdroj* (see above), you can get *Pilsner Urquell* (and cheap grub) at the *Pivnice na parkánu* (Mon–Fri 10.30am–11pm, Sat 10.30am–midnight), next door to the Brewery Museum, and at *U kanóna*, Rooseveltova 18 (daily 10am–9pm). *Gambrinus*, Plzeň's other beer, is best drunk at *U Žumbery* on Bezručova (currently under restoration). As for cafés, try *U Bedřicha* on B. Smetany (10am–10pm).

Plzeň's wonderful Beaux-Arts **Tyl Theatre** is the city's main venue for opera and ballet. Most other concerts and cultural events take place at the *Dům kultury* on Americká, but in summer the **Festival of Folk Songs** (July) is just one of the events held at the *Přírodní divadlo*, Plzeň's open-air theatre, set in the botanical gardens of Lochotínský park, near the university medical faculty (tram #3 or #4 from outside the Tyl Theatre). Bohemia's longest-running puppet duo, Spejbl and Hurvínek, originated at Plzeň's **puppet theatre**, *Divadlo dětí Alfa* at Americká 17 (entrance is on Jungmannova), which still puts on daily performances plus the occasional film.

Around Plzeň

Within easy reach of Plzeň are two monasteries which bear the hallmark of Giovanni Santini, arguably the most original Baroque architect to work in the Czech Lands. Of the two sights, **Plasy** – north of Plzeň – is the easiest to get to (accessible by train or bus), though **Kladruby** – over 30km west – is without doubt a more rewarding day trip.

Plasy

The **Cistercian monastery** at **PLASY** (Plass) is submerged in a green valley around 25km north of Plzeň. Originally founded in the twelfth century, the present muddle of flaking Baroque outbuildings is the work of two of Prague's leading architects, Jean-Baptiste Mathey and Giovanni Blasius Santini-Aichl. Of the two, **Santini** (1667–1723), the Prague-born son of north Italian immigrants, is the more interesting: a popular architect whose personal, slightly ironic style produced some of the most original works in the country. The brilliant white cloisters harbour palatial pretensions, while the rest of the monastery (Tues–Sun

April & Oct 9am–noon & 1–4pm; May & Sept 9am–noon & 1–5pm; June–Aug 9am–noon & 1–6pm) is now an art gallery, the highlight of whose over-long guided tour is a look at the tall side chapels off the cloisters, whose frescoes create an incredible splash of colour on the ceiling.

Shortly after its Baroque redevelopment, the monastery was dissolved, and in 1826 fell into the hands of **Prince Clarence von Metternich**, the arch-conservative Austrian Chancellor and political architect of the post-Napoleonic European order. Over the road, obscured by willow trees, is the cemetery church transformed by the prince into the family mausoleum. In tune with his politics, its oppressively Neoclassical forms dwarf the commoners' graveyard behind it.

Kladruby

If Plasy fails to move you, the **Benedictine monastery** at **KLADRUBY** (Kladrau) should do the trick. It's an altogether less gloomy affair, once the richest monastery in Bohemia, gutted during the Thirty Years' War and then transformed under Santini's supervision once the Counter-Reformation had set in. The main attraction is the huge monastery church, where the original Romanesque and Gothic elements blend imperceptibly with Santini's idiosyncratic additions. The original lantern tower has been converted into an extravagant Baroque cupola, which filters a faded pink light into the transepts, themselves covered in stars and zigzags mirrored on the cold stone paving below. It's the perfect expression of Santini's so-called Baroque-Gothic style, and a work of consummate skill.

There's a direct bus service from Plzeň to Kladruby; alternatively, you could go as far as **STŘÍBRO** (Mies) by train, and then change on to one of the fairly frequent local buses. Dramatically poised over the Mže (Mies) river, Stříbro was previously the vague frontier post between the German- and Czech-speaking districts, its tidy square sporting arguably the most beautiful Renaissance **radnice** in Bohemia, paid for by the town's long-extinct silver mines. There's no other reason to pause here, unless it's to stay the night at the *Hotel Evropa* (☎0183/24 69; ③) on the main square.

Klatovy and around

Tightly walled in and nervously perched on high ground, **KLATOVY** (Klattau) warns of the approaching border with Germany. The medieval prosperity of the town is still visible in the main square, but it can't compete with the Rose Towns further east. There's enough to keep you occupied for at least a couple of hours, and with Plzeň only an hour away by train it's another possible day trip; or a potential base for exploring the northwest tip of the nearby Šumava region (see p.163).

The Town

Klatovy's best feature is undoubtedly the cluster of tall buildings jostling for position on one side of the cramped town square, náměstí Míru. Tucked in beside the Renaissance radnice, the sixteenth-century **Černá věž** (blackened by past burnings) is the clearest evidence of the town's bygone prosperity – and the need for a lookout post to protect the town. From its pinnacled parapet you can see the forests of the Bavarian border and, across the rooftops, the smaller and later **Bílá věž**.

Next to the Černá věž, Dientzenhofer's white Jesuit church exudes incense and cooled air from its vigorously curvacious interior, though it's more fascinating for its musty **catacombs** (April & Oct Tues–Fri; May–Sept Tues–Sun), where Jesuits and other wealthy locals are preserved in varying stages of decomposition. Next door at *U bílého jednorožce* (The White Unicorn) is a seventeenth-century **apothecary** (May–Oct daily 8am–4pm) that functioned intact until 1964, but has since become a UNESCO registered monument. The bottles and pots are all labelled in Latin, with swirling wooden pillars flanking the shelves, and a unicorn's horn (strictly speaking it's a tusk from an artic narwhal) the pharmacists' mascot, jutting out into the centre. The back room where the drugs were mixed comes complete with horror-movie flasks of dried goat's blood and pickled children's intestines.

Practicalities

The local *ČEDOK* office is opposite the apothecary, dispenses a free brochure and map of town, and can help find you a room in one of Klatovy's cheap **hotels**: the seedy *Beránek*, Pražská 59 (☎0186/223 48; ①); the ugly *Garní* on Voříškova (☎0186/225 14; ①); and the not very aptly named *Centrál*, near the train station (☎0186/200 49; ①). **Private rooms** are available through *Pergolia* on the main square, or from *ČEDOK*, and there's a new pension just beyond the old town on K letišti. Alternatively, there's a rudimentary **campsite** (open mid-June to mid-Sept) by the River Úhlava, a couple of kilometres' bus ride west of the town. One **restaurant** worth recommending is *Zlatý drak*, Viděnská 32, which offers good Chinese-Czech food, dishing out views of the town's towers at the same time.

Švihov

Ruined castles are ten-a-penny in these border regions; the virtue of the one at ŠVIHOV, 11km north of Klatovy, is that it still looks like a proper castle – and it's easy to reach by train, from either Plzeň or Klatovy. It was begun in 1480 by the Rožmberks as a vast concentric structure, with traditional double fortifications creating an inner and outer castle, surrounded by a moat. Suspicious of such an unusually well-fortified stronghold, the Habsburgs ordered the owners to tear down the eastern section, and what remains today is a kind of cross-section of a castle, as if erected for an architectural discussion class. Unfortunately, there's not a lot inside to justify signing up for one of the guided tours (May–Sept Tues–Sun 9am–noon & 1–4pm).

Domažlice and the Chods

Fifteen kilometres from the German border, **DOMAŽLICE** has always been inextricably linked with the Chod people (see box), who had the task of containing the German *Volk*'s inexorable drift eastwards from Bavaria. For centuries the town was the local customs house, but it lost much of its former importance when the border was fixed in 1707, and apart from the **Chod Folk Festival** weekend in August, and a few passing Germans, Domažlice's gentle snoozing goes pretty much undisturbed.

THE CHODS

"The spearhead of the Slavic march into Central Europe" as writer Josef Škvorecký described them, the **Chods** (*Chody*) are one of the few Czech tribes to have kept their identity. Very little is certain about their origin, but their name comes from *chodit* (to walk about), and undoubtedly refers to their traditional occupation as guardians of the frontier. Since the earliest times their proud independence was exploited by a succession of Bohemian kings, who employed them as border guards in return for granting them freedom from serfdom, plus various other feudal privileges.

However, after the Battle of Bílá hora, the Habsburgs were keen to curb the Chods' power, and the whole region was handed over lock, stock and barrel to one of the victorious generals, Wolf Maximilian Lamingen. At first the Chods tried to reaffirm their ancient privileges by legal means, but when this proved fruitless, with the encouragement of one Jan Sladký – better known as Kozina – they simply refused to acknowledge their new despot. Seventy of the rebels were thrown into the prison in Novoměstská radnice in Prague, and Kozina was singled out to be publicly hanged in Plzeň on November 28, 1695, as an example to the rest of the *Chody*.

Although the Empire prevailed, the Chods never allowed the loss of their freedoms to quash their ebullience or their peculiar local dialect, which still survives in the villages. Stubbornly resistant to Germanisation, they carried the banner of Czech national defiance through the dark ages. Even now, of all the regions of Bohemia, Chodsko is closest to its cultural roots, known above all for its rich local costumes, still worn on Sundays and religious holidays, and for its *dudy* (bagpipes), now played only in folk ensembles and at festivals.

The Town

Like many small Bohemian towns, Domažlice starts and ends at its main square, **náměstí Míru**, which extends for 500 metres along a perfect east–west axis. Flanked by uninterrupted arcades under every possible style of gable, the cobbled square seems like a perfect setting for a Bohemian-Bavarian skirmish. Halfway down one side, the thirteenth-century church steeple used to double as a lookout post for the vulnerable town, and ascending its 196 steps provides a bird's-eye view of the whole area. The two streets running parallel, either side of the main square, are scruffier relatives and mark the boundaries of what was the medieval town.

The town's other remaining thirteenth-century round tower is part of the **Chodský hrad**, seat of the Chods' self-government until it fell into the hands of Wolf Maximilian Laminger. The castle museum worthily traces the town's colourful history, but you're more likely to want to spend time in the **Jindřich Jindřich Museum**, northeast of the old town (Tues–Sun 8am–2.30pm) – founded by a local composer, Jindřich Jindřich, who gathered together Chod folk costumes, ceramics and anything else linked to the region. If you can't catch the annual festival, this amazing collection, as well as the mock-up cottage interior, do much to compensate. Under the Communists, there was a pathetic attempt to link the Chods' history as border guards with the activities of the Cold War frontier patrols (they even set up their union headquarters here). One room in particular had displays of neo-Nazi propaganda from Germany alongside a book by Václav Havel – a kind of guilt by juxtaposition. Another museum worth taking a look at is the new **Vintage Car Museum** (Tues–Sun 9.30am–5pm) on Masarykova, the road leading east to the train station.

Practicalities

Arriving at the railway station or the bus terminal, you should avoid **sleeping** at the nearby *Hotel Kalous* (☎0189/23 05; ①), and walk the ten minutes to the main square to check on vacancies at the *Koruna* (☎0189-22 79; ①), and, when it re-opens, the *Vinco* (☎0189/44 63; ①). Just off the square, there are **private rooms** available on Spálená (①), or through *ETM* at Branská 1, to the south. For those with a tent, there's a choice between the riverside *Babylon* **campsite** (May–Sept), 6km south by bus, or the *Hájovna* site (mid-May to mid-Sept), a kilometre or so north of KDYNĚ (20min by train from Domažlice).

If you're heading for Germany, there are now four trains a day to the Bavarian town of FURTH IM WALD, whose *Drachenstich* festival takes places shortly after the Chod folk bash on the second and third Sundays in August.

Horšovský Týn

A lazy afternoon could happily be spent at **HORŠOVSKÝ TÝN** (Bischofteinitz), just 10km north of Domažlice. Its main square, **náměstí Republiky**, is a grassy sloping affair centred on the Church of sv Petr and Pavel, and lined with Gothic houses sporting brightly coloured Baroque facades. At the top end is the quadri-lateral sgraffitoed **castle** (April–Oct Tues–Sun 9am–noon & 1–4pm), transformed by the Lobkovíc family into a rich Renaissance pile. Inside, kitsch china chande-liers equipped with their original Edison bulbs shed light on English Baroque travelling alarm clocks and other bourgeois accessories. Behind the chateau, the vast **Zámecký park** stretches northwards, complete with hidden chapels, a large lake and loads of peacocks. It's a ten-minute walk to the centre from the train station: head east up Nádražní to the main crossroads, then north over the river, and the main square will appear on the right.

Mariánské Lázně

At the end of the eighteenth century, what is now **MARIÁNSKÉ LÁZNĚ** (Marienbad) was unadulterated woodland. It was not until the 1790s that the local abbot, Karel Reitenberger, and a German doctor, Josef Nehr, took the initiative and established a spa here. Within a hundred years **Marienbad*** (as it is best known) had joined the clique of world-famous European spas, boasting a clientele that ranged from writers to royalty. That inveterate spa-man Goethe was among the earliest of the VIPs to popularise the place, and a few generations later it became the favourite holiday spot of King Edward VII, a passion which he shared with his pal, the Emperor Franz Josef. During World War I, even the incorrigibly infirm Franz Kafka spent a brief, happy spell here with Felice Bauer, writing "things are different now and good, we are engaged to be married right after the war".

---

* The title of Alain Resnais' 1961 film *Last Year in Marienbad* is, like the film itself, misleading. The action is shot entirely in a French chateau, though the plot (what there is of it) is based on an incident that may (or may not) have occurred the year before in Marienbad. With a script by *nouveau roman* iconoclast Alain Robbe-Grillet, it's either absolute rubbish or totally seminal, depending on your view.

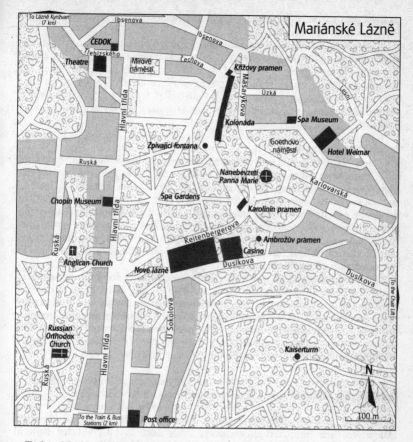

Mariánské Lázně

To Lázně Kynžvart (7 km)
Ibsenova
ČEDOK
Třebízského
Theatre
Mírové náměstí
Ibsenova
Čechova
Masarykova
Křížovy pramen
Úzká
Lesní
Kolonáda
Spa Museum
Zpívající fontana
Goethovo náměstí
Hotel Weimar
Ruská
Nanebevzetí Panna Marie
Karlovarská
Chopin Museum
Hlavní třída
Spa Gardens
Karolínin pramen
Ruská
Reitenbergerova
Ambrožův pramen
Casino
Anglican Church
Nové lázně
Dusíková
Dusíková
To the Chair Lift
U Sokolova
Hlavní třída
Russian Orthodox Church
Ruská
Kaiserturm
N
To the Train & Bus Stations (2 km)
Post office
100 m

Today, Mariánské Lázně is much less exclusive – what was a fat-farm for the rich and famous only two generations ago is now eminently accessible to all and sundry. Meanwhile, the riotous, turn-of-the-century architecture is gradually being restored to its former flamboyance, while the old state spa buildings are beginning to open their doors to the public once again. Above all, the setting, amidst thickly forested hills, remains stunningly beautiful, and the calm and cool air around town is a revelation compared to the more usual traffic-choked streets.

The spa

Mariánské Lázně was the last of Bohemia's famous spa triangle to be built. As far as the eye can see, sumptuous regal buildings rise up from the pine-clad surrounds, most dating from the second half of the nineteenth century, ensuring an intriguing homogeneity in their *fin-de-siècle* opulence. On one side of the main street, **Hlavní třída**, the four-storey luxury mansions are festooned with shapely balconies – built for kings but used by the masses – overlooking the former

Anlagen (spa gardens), which now harbour a modest memorial to the American liberation of the town on May 6, 1945.

Frédéric Chopin stayed at the *Bílá labuť* (The White Swan), the modest three-storey *dům* at no. 47, on his way from Paris to Warsaw. Upstairs in the **Chopin Museum** (Tues–Sun 10–11.30am & 1.30–5pm) you can sink into an armchair and listen to a crackly recording of the composer. A few doors away, there's a shop selling tins of *oplatky*, the sugar- or chocolate-filled wafers for which the spa is famous, and which make the waters you are about to taste infinitely more palatable.

Around the Kolonáda

The focal point of the spa, overlooking the town, is the **Kolonáda**. Easily the most beautiful wrought-iron colonnade in Bohemia, it gently curves like a whale-ribbed nineteenth-century railway station, the atmosphere relentlessly genteel and sober. In summer, Bohemian bands, and occasionally the local symphony orchestra, give daily **concerts**, and German tourists buy up the Bohemian crystal in the upstairs gallery. Access to the colonnade's life-giving faucets is restricted (daily 6am–noon & 4–6pm), though the spa's first and foremost spring, Křížový pramen, which adjoins the northern tip of the colonnade, should eventually be reopened after a lengthy facelift.

At the opposite end of the Kolonáda is the **zpívající fontana**, a computer-controlled dancing fountain, and no great beauty – it does its thing to classical music every two hours from 7am. Beyond, and, more importantly, out of earshot of the fountain, is the Neoclassical colonnade of the **Karolinin pramen**, recently restored to its smooth white former self. This part of town was once patrolled by special spa police who imposed strict fines on those discovered smoking or committing other crimes against health – it's still forbidden to smoke in this part of the spa.

Behind and above the colonnades are yet more giant ochre spa buildings, including the **Hotel Weimar** (now the *Hotel Kavkaz*) in which King Edward VII preferred to stay (there's a well-concealed German Gothic plaque commemorating his visit, above the central balcony). Two doors along is the **Spa Museum** (Tues–Sun 9am–4pm; film shown every other hour in Czech, twice daily in German), occupying the house in which Goethe stayed on his last visit in 1823. The history of the spa's development fills the ground floor; upstairs, along with period furnishings from Goethe's time, there are new historical sections which have become more open about the spa's German roots (and about the American liberation) but are still silent on the postwar expulsions.

The square in which the museum stands is now named after Goethe, a just recompense for the removal of his statue by the retreating Nazis – of which only the granite plinth remains, with a commemorative plaque added after the war, in Czech, Latin and French (but significantly not German). At the centre of the square is the unusual octagonal church of **Nanebevzetí Panna Marie**, decorated inside in rich neo-Byzantine style; further down the hill are two buildings definitely worth checking out. The first is the old **casino** building, now the spa's main social centre, with an old faded dance hall (bands on every night) of *fin-de-siècle* marbled elegance; the next one down is the **Nové lázně**, one of the few places that accepts "out-patients" for a sauna and massage (at a price) – ask for *kabina* 1 or 2, which were fitted out for visiting royalty.

Walking possibilities

Even if you're not booked in for treatment, you should participate in the other spa rituals – drinking the water, wolfing down the wafers and taking the obligatory constitutional. Mariánské Lázně's altitude lends an almost subalpine freshness to the air, even at the height of summer, and **walking** is as important to "the cure" as the various specialised treatments. To this end, the expert nineteenth-century landscape gardener Václav Skalník was employed to transform the valley into an open park, providing an intricate network of paths leading to the many springs dotted around the surrounding countryside.

There are several maps by the Kolonáda, showing the various marked walks around the spa; armed with a *plán města* (available from most hotels, bookshops and newsagents) you can head off on your own. Goethe's favourite walk, up to the *Miramonte* for morning coffee, is retraced by most visitors, though since the café was converted into a *lázně dům* (spa home) for kids, you have to delve deeper into the woods to the *Červená karkulka* café for refreshments. From here, it's not far to the lower town of **Úšovice** whence you can return to town via the Neoclassical Rudolf Spring, where, according to *ČEDOK*, "hypotonic calcareous-magnesium-hydrogen carbonate-ferrugineous acidulous waters" can be experienced.

Back on Hlavní třída, behind the hotel *Atlantik*, there's the strange sight of a small red-brick **Anglican church**, its inwards gutted and windows boarded up, long since abandoned by its royal patrons, but now slowly being restored. Further south, along Ruská, the neo-Byzantine **Russian Orthodox church** (daily Nov & Jan–April 9.30–11.30am & 2–4pm; May–Oct 8.30–11.30am & 2–4.30pm) is in much better shape, and contains a valuable collection of icons, not to mention an iconostasis that's reputedly the largest piece of porcelain in the world. From here, tracks slope up to the town's Catholic and Jewish **cemeteries** (both still in use).

There are several vantage points to head for in order to enjoy a **panoramic view** of the spa: Na Polomu (805m) or the Podhorn (847m), north along the strenuous red-marked paths; or, with considerably less exertion, the old **Kaiserturm** (*rozhledna*), on the hillside southeast of the spa.

Practicalities

On **arrival**, passengers are unloaded from their buses and trains at a suitably discreet distance from the spa. Trolley bus #5 (drop 2kčs into the machine by the driver; 5kčs if you're going to *Hotel Krakanoš*) then covers the 3km up the former Kaiserstrasse to the *Hotel Excelsior*, where the pedestrianised zone of the spa proper begins.

Accommodation

Many of the central **hotels** retain a modicum of their former decadence without being ridiculously expensive; to save a lot of legwork, you could head first for *ČEDOK* on Třebizkého (Mon–Fri 8–11am & 11.30am–4pm), to enquire about vacancies.

Atlantic, Hlavní třída 46 (☎0165/5911). Big turn-of-the-century hotel on the main street through the spa – try and get a room overlooking the park. ②

Evropa, Třebizkého 101 (☎0165/2063). Cheapest rooms in town, and next door to *ČEDOK*. ①

Kavkaz, Goethovo náměstí 9 (☎0165/3141). Fantastic view over the spa – if you feel like splashing out, ask for Edward VII's favourite room. ②–④

Krakonoš, Zádub 53 (☎0165/2624). Officially a "youth hostel", this is actually a hotel, beautifully situated in the hills to the east of town; take bus #12 from Hlavní třída, the chair-lift (*lánovka*) from Dusíkova, or walk up the path from Karlovarská. ① to *IYHF* members and students; ③ to non-members.

Oradour, Hlavní třída 43 (☎0165/4304). Plush hotel, previously owned by the Communist trade union organisation *ROH*. ③

CAMPSITES

Luxor, Velká Hleďsebe (May–Sept). Awkwardly located campsite several kilometres to the west of the train station; take bus #6 to Velká Hleďsebe, then walk 1km south down the Plzeň road.

Start, on Plzeňská (April–Oct). Small campsite and motel, which also offers cheap bungalows. Conveniently located, but a touch noisy.

Eating and drinking

Hlavní třída is punctuated with **cafés and restaurants**, most hinting at a bygone opulence. *Café Polonia* at Hlavní třída 50 offers stucco decoration as rich as its cakes; or you can sit out on the terrace of *Ludvík XIV* (daily 10am–11pm), further up on the same side, and at the *Sadová kavárna*, Poštovní 195. The first-floor restaurant at the *Jalta*, Hlavní třída 42, is reasonably priced, or there's more basic food – and wonderful *Krušovice* beer – at the *Krušovická pivnice*, round the back of the *Hotel Atlantic*. If you're after something different, try and get your mouth round some *vepřové po Ščchuansku* (Szechuan pork) at the *Čínský restaurace*, above the *Atlantic* at Hlavní třída 46. For **late-night spots**, there's the *Hodonínská vinárna* for nourishment, and *Maxim's* on Hlavní třída for dancing (daily 10.30pm–5am).

Lázně Kynžvart and Teplá

If you're looking for a longer excursion out of Mariánské Lázně, spend a leisurely afternoon walking over to **LÁZNĚ KYNŽVART** (Königswart), 8km northwest of town. Now a spa for children, it was for many years the private spa of the Metternich family, who entertained Goethe, Beethoven and Dumas (among others) at their Neoclassical **chateau**, 2km from the railway station. A word of warning: at the time of writing, the chateau (though not the gardens) had been closed for repairs for over ten years, but was long overdue to reopen.

A longer day trip is to **TEPLÁ** (Tepl), 15km east, whose abbots used to own the springs at Mariánské Lázně. The monastery, until recently used as an army barracks, is a kilometre east of town along the Toužim road, though it's easy enough to spot thanks to the plain stone towers of the original twelfth-century monastery church. The rest of the monastery carries the universal stamp of the Baroque Counter-Reformation, courtesy of the Dientzenhofer duo, but the real reason to come here is to see the Neoclassical *Nová knihovna* (New Library). Built in the 1900s, it boasts almost edible stucco decoration, triple-decker bookshelves and swirling black iron balconies framed by white pilasters.

If you're heading for Karlovy Vary next, be sure to take the train, which winds its way slowly but picturesquely, via Teplá, through the **Slavkovský les**, the thick forest that lies between the two spas.

Cheb

For many Western visitors, **CHEB** (Eger), 10km from the German border, is their first taste of the Czech Republic. Although money has been poured into the town, Cheb's postwar haemorrhage has left it with less than a third of its prewar population, and a collective identity crisis of mammoth proportions. Cheb is a beautiful historic town, yet despite incentives offered by successive postwar governments, Czechs have been reluctant to move here. The root of the malaise lies in the authorities' ambivalence to Cheb, simultaneously encouraging its future and denying its past. Nevertheless, its historic centre is worth an afternoon's stopoff – if only to escape the spa towns all around.

The Town

Had you arrived at Cheb's **railway station** any time before 1945, the impression of never having left Germany would have begun right here: by a quirk of railway history, the *Deutsche Bundesbahn* built and ran all the lines heading west out of Eger. It's a none too pleasant ten-minute walk from the ugly postwar station, along **Svobody**, to the old town. As a foreigner, it's difficult not to feel self-conscious strolling through town – there's an almost tangible tension between the town's Romany and Czech populations, and both sides, to a greater or lesser extent, resent the large numbers of German day-trippers.

It's not unusual to heave a sigh of relief – aesthetic at any rate – once you reach the town square, **náměstí krále Jiřího z Poděbrad**, named after one of the few Czech leaders the *Egerländer* ever willingly supported. Established in the twelfth century, but today lined with handsome seventeenth-century houses, this was the old *Marktplatz*, the commercial and political heart of Egerland for eight centuries. After four decades of neglect, commercial life is returning to the square, with several cafés and restaurants now in residence. The batch of half-timbered buildings huddled together at the bottom of the square, known as **Stöckl** (*Špalíček* in Czech), forms an utterly unCzech ensemble – originally a cluster of medieval German-Jewish merchant houses, now housing just a small café.

In the backstreets to the west of the main square, the parade of seventeenth-century German merchants' houses continues unabated. Cheb's medieval **Jewish ghetto** is recalled in the names of the streets – Židovská (Jewish Street) and Zavražděných (Massacre Street), the latter thought to refer to a particularly bloody pogrom in 1350. Beyond this, virtually nothing remains of the community, which came under sustained attack during the 1930s as the SdP rose to prominence in the region. Fascist thugs butchered a pig in the local synagogue shortly before its official opening, and *Kristallnacht* demolished what was left.

Cheb museum and art gallery

Behind Stöckl lurks the **Cheb Museum** (Tues–Sun 8am–noon & 1–4pm), in the former *Stadthaus* where **Albrecht von Waldstein** (better known as *Wallenstein* from Schiller's famous trilogy), Duke of Friedland (Frýdlant) and generalissimo of the Thirty Years' War, was murdered in 1634 by an Irishman on the secret orders of Emperor Ferdinand II. A converted Catholic, Waldstein took it upon himself to raise, fund, and lead the Habsburg Imperial army to victory against the rebellious Protestant nobility, procuring for himself no fewer than sixty estates in

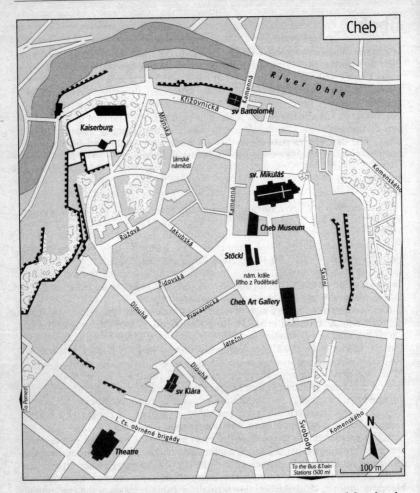

Cheb

River Ohře

Křižovnická

sv. Bartoloměj

Kamenná

Kaiserburg

Jánské náměstí

sv. Mikuláš

Milynská

Kamenná

Komenského

Růžová

Jakubská

Cheb Museum

Stöckl

Židovská

nám. krále Jiřího z Poděbrad

Školní

Dlouhá

Provaznická

Cheb Art Gallery

Jatečni

Dlouhá

sv Klára

I. čs. obrněné brigády

Svobody

Komenského

To Pomezi

Theatre

To the Bus & Train
Stations (500 m)

N

100 m

northeast Bohemia alone. Having routed the Saxons, Bavarians and Swedes, he began negotiating with them on the emperor's behalf, but the suspicion that he intended to set up his own kingdom led Emperor Ferdinand to order his assassination. Within three days, an Englishman, an Irishman and a Scotsman had carried out the imperial decree (and collected the reward), cutting the general down in his nightshirt as he rose from his sickbed. The museum studiously avoids Cheb's more recent history, but 1634 gets close attention and the heavy Gothic woodwork provides an evocative setting for Waldstein's murder, graphically illustrated on the bedroom walls.

Great efforts have been made to establish a new cultural life in the vacuum left by the postwar expulsion of Germans. Nevertheless, the **Cheb Art Gallery** (Tues–Sun 9am–5pm), at no. 16 on the square, focusing as it does on Czech modern art, seems strangely out of context in a town with such rich traditions of its own. Few of the town's predominantly German tourists pay a visit to the temporary exhibitions on the ground floor, nor to the wide-ranging permanent collection of modern Czech art upstairs. Kicking off with the 1890 generation, led by Jan Preisler and Antonín Procházka, there are several memorable paintings depicting Prague cityscapes, including the Belvedere, St Vitus Cathedral and a red and cream city tram. More surprising is the large contingent of Cubist and Fauvist canvases, including a vivid blue *River Otava* by Václav Špála. In place of the usual Socialist Realism, a thought-provoking postwar collection rounds off the gallery.

Beyond the main square

Cheb's two largest buildings, dating from the town's early history, are out of keeping with the red-roofed uniformity of the seventeenth-century *Altstadt*. The church of **sv Mikuláš** has a bizarre multifaceted roof, like the scales of a dinosaur, though since the renowned Austrian architect Balthasar Neumann (who was born here) restored it in the eighteenth century, only the bulky towers remain from the original thirteenth-century building, conceived as a monumental Romanesque basilica.

EGERLAND

Most Germans still refer to Cheb as **Eger**, the name given to the town by the German colonists who settled here from the eleventh century onwards. The settlers were typically hard-working and proud *Volk*, who developed their own folk traditions and peculiar dialect. Aided by its status as a Free Imperial City of the Holy Roman Empire, the town soon came to dominate trade between Bavaria and Bohemia. Shunted around between Babenbergs, Swabians and Přemyslids, Egerland finally accepted the suzerainty of King John of Luxembourg in 1322, in return for certain privileges – and in fact the *Egerländer* remained self-governing until well into the nineteenth century.

Hardly surprisingly then, that the town was at the centre of the (anti-Semitic) **Pan-German Schönerer movement** of the late nineteenth century, which fought desperately against the advance of Czech nationalism, aided and abetted (as they saw it) by the weak and liberal Austrian state. The most famous protest against the 1897 Badeni Decrees, which granted the Czech language equal status with German throughout the Czech Lands, took place in Eger. The establishment of the First Czechoslovak Republic in 1918 was seen as a serious setback by most *Egerländer*, who made no bones about where their real sympathies lay; Eger remained the only town to successfully rebuff all attempts at putting up street names in Czech as well as German.

Thus, in the 1930s, the pro-Nazi **Sudeten German Party** (SdP) found Egerland receptive to its anti-Semitism as much as to its irredentism. Although it's estimated that a quarter of the German-speaking voters stubbornly refused to vote for the SdP, the majority of *Egerländer* welcomed their incorporation into the Third Reich, completed in 1938. At the end of World War II, only those Germans who could prove themselves to have been actively anti-Fascist (Czechs were luckily exempted from this acid test) were permitted to remain on Czechoslovak soil; the others were bodily kicked out, reducing the population of Cheb to 27 percent of its prewar level. The mass expulsions were accompanied by numerous acts of vengeance, and the issue remains a delicate one. Havel's suggestion in his first presidential address that an apology to the Germans was in order was one of the most unpopular statements of his short presidency.

In the northwestern corner of the town walls, by the River Ohře (Eger), is the **Kaiserburg** (Chebský hrad; May–Sept Tues–Sun 9am–noon & 1–5pm), a sprawl of ruins built on, and with, volcanic rock – all that remains of the twelfth-century castle bequeathed by that obsessive crusader, the Holy Roman Emperor Frederick Barbarossa. In among the Baroque fortifications, the Gothic Černá věž (Black Tower) presents an impressive front and offers peeks at Cheb's chimneys and roof-tiles through its tiny windows. Stroll down to the lower storey of the ruined chapel in the northeastern corner and you'll catch a glimpse of the castle of Barbarossa's time, including some beautifully carved Romanesque capitals. A short way along the river, the small Gothic church of **sv Bartoloměj** has been converted (with large helpings of Bulgarian marble) into a spacious setting for a superb collection of fourteenth- and fifteenth-century Bohemian sculpture.

Practicalities

It's easy enough to arrange a place to stay in one of Cheb's cheap and central **hotels**; or else there's a **campsite**, 5km away at Dřenice by the Jesenice lake. *ČEDOK* on Svobody (Mon–Fri 8.30am–4.30pm, Sat 9am–noon) should be able to help with any problems, and will **change money** and travellers' cheques; if they're closed, try the exchange booth in the station (daily 7.30am–10pm).

Hradní dvůr, Dlouhá 12 (☎0166/220 06). Rough around the edges, but situated in the picturesque backstreets of the old town. ②

Hvězda, nám. krále Jiřího 4 (☎0166/225 49). Slightly sleeker, on the main square itself, but no more expensive. ②

Slavie, Svobody 32 (☎0166/332 16). Cheapest option, hence the less than hot showers, and insalubrious locale, halfway between the old town and the station. ②

Eating and drinking

Eating and drinking possibilities have improved greatly now visa-free travel has been introduced between the Czech Lands and Germany, though most places still close down by 10pm. The *Valdštejn* is a relatively expensive new restaurant at no. 35 on the main square, while the *Staročeská*, at the beginning of Kamenná, is a more traditional eating option. The Cheb youth play billiards and drink excellent beer at *U kata*, an otherwise typical Czech *pivnice* on Židovská; and there are now two or three **late-night haunts** to choose from in the old town – *Peklo* is a disco bar opposite *U kata* (open until 2am), and there's a nightclub on the main square.

Františkovy Lázně

"The present Františkovy Lázně has nothing of historic interest", wrote Nagel's Guide in the 1960s, casually writing off a town hailed by Goethe as "paradise on earth". **FRANTIŠKOVY LÁZNĚ** (Franzensbad), 5km north of Cheb and linked by regular trains, may not boast any individual architectural gems but it is *the* archetypal spa town. The early nineteenth century's obsession with symmetry ensured a regular grid plan, barely five streets across, surrounded on all sides by parks and woods. Every conceivable building has been daubed in *Kaisergelb*, a soft ochre colour, set against a backdrop of luscious greenery.

Originally known as *Egerbrunnen*, the spa was founded in 1793 and named Franzensbad after the then Habsburg Emperor. The Neoclassical architecture of

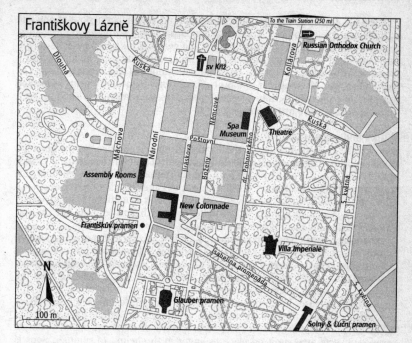

the Empire period finds its way into every building – even the cinema has Doric pilasters. The virtual absence of vehicles and rowdy nightlife make it the most peaceful of the spas, though as patients stagger about and people in white coats run between buildings, it can sometimes resemble a large open lunatic asylum.

The Town

From the recently restored ochre station, the road opens out on to the former *Kurpark*, whose principal path leads diagonally to a white wooden bandstand. This stands at the head of **Národní**, the spa's main boulevard, dotted with potted palms and ornamental trees. Beethoven stayed at no. 7 in 1812, as the German plaque by the entrance recalls; while *U tří lilie*, the eponymous garden café further down, features in a poem by the Czech surrealist Vítězslav Nezval. The diminutive splendour of the *Slovan* hotel's salons is equally perfect for a coffee or something more substantial.

At the opposite end of Národní, the **Františkův pramen** (Franzensquelle) is enclosed under a plain Classical rotunda. While the faithful queue to have their receptacles filled from the dazzling brass pipes, real spa snobs retire to drink from their beakers under the nearby colonnade. Like most spa water, it's pretty unpalatable, on this occasion due to its high salt content. A different kind of faith drives women to touch the feet (and other more specific parts) of a repulsive bronze cherub who sits holding a phallic fish not far from the spring: Františkovy Lázně specialises in the treatment of gynaecological problems and popular myth has it that such a gesture will ensure fertility.

The 1820 church of **sv Kříž** strikes an appropriately imperial pose at one end of Jiráskova, itself another riot of princely mansions with wrought-iron balconies. And don't miss Františkovy Lázně's finest spa pension, *Villa Imperiale*, its corner balconies held up by caryatids, set apart from the other spa buildings and a favourite with visiting Germans. Previous generations of Teutonic guests are on view in the **Spa Museum**, dr. Pohoreckého 8 (daily 9am–4pm), being subjected to gruesome nineteenth-century cures; don't miss the man with a leech on each buttock, held in place by two jam jars.

Walks and excursions

As with all the Bohemian spas, the formal parks quickly give way to untamed woodland, the difference being that in Františkovy Lázně the landscape is almost entirely flat, which is easier on the legs, but shorter on the views. A two-kilometre **walk** through the silver birches will take you to Lake Amerika (in dry weather a mini-train, or *mikrovláčka*, runs every 30min), though swimming is not advisable. On the other side of town, a path marked by red hearts leads to the popular *Zámeček Café*, hidden away amidst the acacia.

On a **longer walk**, you could easily make it to Cheb itself, just over 5km south; follow the red markers down Klostermannova. Alternatively, it's a similar distance northeast to **Soos**, a small area of peatland, pockmarked with **hot gaseous springs**. As you approach the place, the smell of salt emanating from the mini-geysers wafts across from the marsh. A nature trail raised above the bogland allows closer inspection of the springs that gurgle and bubble just above the surface, staining the land with a brown-yellow crust. A unique phenomenon in mainland Europe, the area attracts rare species of flora and fauna – not to mention insects, making it no place to linger in the height of summer. Soos is also accessible by train from Cheb – three stops to Nový Drahov on the Luby u Chebu line.

Practicalities

Františkovy Lázně may not be the busiest spot in Bohemia, but with few **beds** available to non-patients, it can sometimes be difficult to find a place. Try the *Slovan* on Národní (☎0166/94 23 95; ③), or, for half the price, the *Květen*, three doors along (②); if you have any problems, ask at ČEDOK on Národní. There's a good **campsite** with **bungalows** 1500m southwest of the town, by the lake (May–Sept). Both the above-mentioned hotels have reasonable restaurants, or else you could try the *Selská jizba* on the corner of Postovní and Jiráskova.

Karlovy Vary

KARLOVY VARY is the undisputed king of the famous triangle of Bohemian spas. Its guest list of European notables is by far the most illustrious, but what really makes it so special is its wonderful hilly setting – *Belle Époque* mansions pile on top of one another along the steep wooded banks of the endlessly twisting River Teplá. Known throughout the world by its German name **Karlsbad** (Carlsbad in its anglicised form), it was Germans who made up the vast majority of the town's population until their forced expulsion in 1945. Despite this violent uprooting, the spa has survived and continues to attract an international clientele which annually doubles the local population, and is further supplemented in the summer by thousands of able-bodied tourists, the greatest number of whom, are, naturally enough, German.

Tradition grants Charles IV (or rather one of his hunting dogs) with discovery of the springs (hence Karlsbad): in actual fact, the village of Vary (which means "boiling" in Czech) had existed for centuries before Charles' trip, though the king did found a German town here in around 1350, and set a precedent for subsequent Bohemian rulers by granting Karlsbad various privileges. By the nineteenth century its position at the meeting point of two great German-speaking empires, and the much heralded efficacy of its waters, ensured the most impressive visitors' book in Europe.

Arrival and accommodation

The **bus station** and Karlovy Vary dolní nádraží (where trains from Mariánské Lázně arrive) are next door to one another, on the south side of the River Ohře; the **main train station** is to the north of the river. Whichever one you arrive at, you're basically in the more modern, northern part of town, where the shops and hotels are slightly cheaper, providing the otherwise invisible local residents with their daily necessities. The spa proper stretches south along the winding Teplá valley and is closed to motor vehicles, so, like all good spa patients, you'll have to walk.

For **information** (and help with accommodation), *ČEDOK*, in the *Hotel Atlantic*, Tržiště 23, should be able to help, though if it's **spa treatment** you're after, you'll have to go the main spa information centre in the nearby Vřídelní colonnade.

Accommodation

Karlovy Vary can get pretty busy in the summer, especially in July during the film festival (see p.196), so it's best to start looking for **accommodation** early in the day. The taxi hut in the main train station's car park can organise **private rooms**, as can *W Privat*, an office on náměstí Republiky (daily 10am–7pm), near the bus station, and of course *ČEDOK* will gladly do the same (see above for address). If you're **camping**, head for the site near the *Motel Březova* (May–Sept); take bus #7 from behind the *Národní dům* (see below).

Grand Hotel Pupp, Mírové náměstí (☎221 21). They don't come better (nor more expensive) than this outside Prague – but it's worth every *koruna*. ⑦

Atlantic, Tržiště 23 (☎247 15). Equally grand and central, but less than half the price. ④

Juniorhotel Alice, Pětiletky 1 (☎248 48). An official *IYHF* hostel in the woods south of the spa (dorm beds only); take bus #7 from behind the *Národní dům* (see below). ① for *IYHF* members and students; ② for non-members.

Národní dům, Masarykova 24 (☎233 86). Seedy nineteenth-century option, in the northern part of town, full of "character" – go now before they ruin it and put the prices up. ①

Turist, dr Davida Bechera 18 (☎268 37). Same part of town as the above – fewer surprises and more money. ②

The telephone code for Karlovy Vary is ☎017

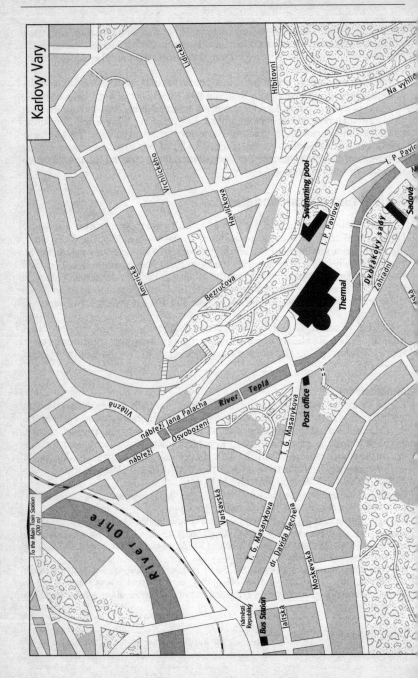

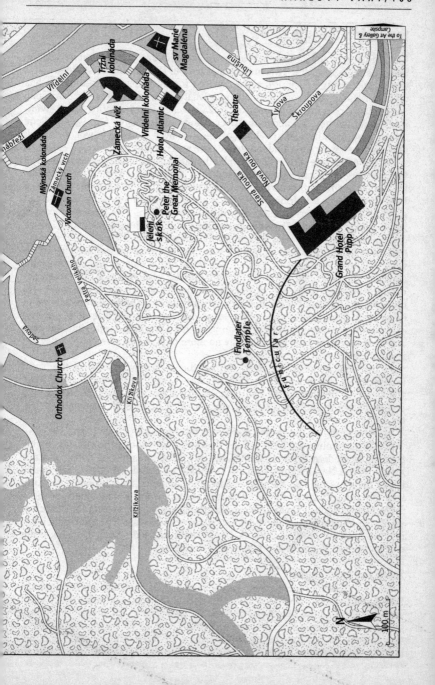

Exploring the spa

Unfortunately, many visitors' first impressions of Karlovy Vary are marred by the unavoidable sight of the **Thermal** sanatorium, an inexcusable concrete scab for whose sake a large slice of the old town bit the dust. Aesthetics aside, its box office is a useful source of information for what's on in town (Mon–Fri 8am–5pm, Sat 9–11am), plus there's an open-air *bazén* attached to it – a spring-water **swimming pool** set high up above the river (Mon–Sat 2–9.30pm, Sun 9am–9.30pm; closed third Mon in month). The poolside view over the town is wonderful, but don't be taken in by the clouds of steam – the water is only tepid.

On the other side of the River Teplá, the late nineteenth-century grandeur of Karlovy Vary begins to unfold along the river banks. Just beyond the *Thermal* is the first of a series of constructions undertaken by the Viennese duo Helmer & Fellner: the **Sadová kolonáda**, a delicate piece of wrought ironwork in white and grey. As the valley narrows, the river disappears under a wide terrace in front of Josef Zítek's graceful **Mlýnská kolonáda** (Mühlbrunnen Colonnade), which contains four separate springs, each one more scalding than the last.

If you've forgotten your cure cup, you can buy the faintly ridiculous *becher* vessels (after the famous Dr Becher, see below) from one of the many souvenir shops, or cut costs and buy a plastic cup. Popular wisdom has it that "when the disorder becomes a disease, doctors prescribe the hot waters of Carlsbad" – in other words, it's strong stuff. In the eighteenth century, the poor were advised to drink up to five hundred cups of the salty waters to cure the disease of poverty. The German playwright Schiller (who came here in 1791) drank eighteen cups and lived to tell the tale, but generally no more than five to seven cups a day are recommended.

At the next bend in the river, the weather-beaten woodwork of the **Tržní kolonáda** – a Helmer and Fellner job, needless to say – has been closed for renovation for a number of years now. Rising above it is the **Zámecká věž** (Schlossberg), the only link with the spa's founder, Charles IV, built on the site of his original hunting lodge.

Most powerful of the twelve springs is the **Sprudel** (*Vřídlo* to the Czechs), which belches out over 2500 gallons of water every hour. The smooth marble floor of the modern **Vřídelní kolonáda** (the old one was melted down for armaments by the Nazis) allows patients to shuffle up and down contentedly, while inside the glass rotunda the geyser pops and splutters, shooting hot water forty feet upwards. Ensuing clouds of steam obscure what would otherwise be a perfect view of Kilian Ignaz Dientzenhofer's Baroque masterpiece, the church of **sv Marie Magdaléna**, pitched nearby on a precipitous site. The light, pink interior, full of playful oval shapes, is a refreshing interlude from the nineteenth-century, almost Victorian air of the rest of the town.

Stará and Nová louka

South of the Sprudel was Karlovy Vary's most famous shopping street, the **Stará louka** (Alte Wiese), described rather mystifyingly by Le Corbusier as "a set of *Torten* (cakes) all the same style and the same elegance". Its shops, which once rivalled Vienna's Kärntnerstrasse, still exude the snobbery of former days, though they have some way to go yet before the *haute couture* posse open up branches here again. The best on offer, for the moment, is tea and cakes on

MARX IN KARLSBAD

A certain Mr Charles Marx from London (as he signed himself in the visitors' book) visited the spa several times towards the end of his life, staying at the *Hotel Germania* (now the *Olympic*) at Zámecký vrch 41, above the Mühlbrunnen Colonnade. He was under police surveillance each time, but neither his daughter Eleanor's letters (she was with him on both trips) nor the police reports have much to say about the old revolutionary, except that he took the waters at 6am (as was the custom) and went on long walks. The Communists couldn't resist the excuse to set up a Karl Marx Museum, just down from the Mühlbrunnen Colonnade, and, somewhat unbelievably, it was the only one of its kind in the entire Communist world, Lenin being the orthodox choice. Needless to say, it no longer exists.

marble tables at the *Elefant Café*, or glassware from the *Moser* shop (everyone who's anyone has had a Moser glass made for them, from Stalin to the Shah, and you can buy the stuff here or direct from the factory showroom in the suburb of Dvory, just off the Cheb road).

At the end of Stará louka is the **Grand Hotel Pupp**, named after its founder, the eighteenth-century confectioner, Johann Georg Pupp. At the turn of the century *Pupp*'s was *the* place to be seen, and became a meeting place for Europe's elite. Despite its lacklustre upkeep and careless modernisation, it can't fail to impress, and the cakes are still made to Mr Pupp's own recipe. On the opposite bank, the former *Kaiserbad* (Lázně no. 1) is another sumptuous edifice, designed like a theatre by the ubiquitous Helmer and Fellner. It's worth checking out the luscious velvet and marble interior, and, if you fancy a spot of spa treatment, this is one place where you don't have to pre-book.

Back round the corner in Nová louka, the richly decorated, creamy white **Vítězslav Nezval Theatre** is another Helmer and Fellner construction. What makes this one special is that the frescoes and the main curtain were executed by a group of painters that included a young **Gustav Klimt**, later to become one of the most famous figures in the Viennese Secession. If you ask at the box office, you should be able to get a glimpse of the auditorium, though the curtain – by far the most interesting work – is rarely fully exposed to the audience. Nevertheless, you can spot Klimt's self-portrait in the bottom right-hand corner, playing the flute, and looking at the audience.

Walking in the hills

Of all the spas, Karlovy Vary's constitutional **walks** are the most physically taxing and visually rewarding. You can let the **funicular** (*lánovka*) take the strain by hopping aboard one of the trains (10am–4pm; every 15min) from behind *Hotel Pupp*, which deposit you at a café and viewpoint. Alternatively, you can climb up through the beech and oak trees to the wooden crucifix above Stará louka, and then on to the spectacular panorama where the **Peter the Great Memorial** commemorates the visiting Russian Tsar and his dozen or so royal hangers-on. In season, you can enjoy the (not so perfect) view northwards from the **Jelení skok** restaurant (Tues–Sun 10am–6pm).

The road below *Jelení skok* slopes down to Zámecký vrch, which the English aristocracy used to ascend in order to absolve their sins at the red-brick **Victorian Church** (Evangelical and Methodist services are still held here).

Clearly visible from here, high on the opposite bank, is the **Imperial**, a huge fortress hotel, built in 1912 to rival *Pupp*'s and flying in the face of the popular Art-Nouveau architecture of the spa. An alternative route back down to the Sadová Colonnade is down Sadová street, on which the Russian aristocracy built their very own onion-domed **Orthodox Church**.

The most popular level walk is along the Puškinova stezka towards Karlovy Vary's main **art gallery** (Tues–Sun 9am–noon & 1–5pm), which contains a small but interesting cross-section of twentieth-century Czech canvases, and a disappointingly limited selection of glassware.

Eating, drinking and entertainment

The main **restaurant** at the *Grand Hotel Pupp* is without doubt the place to eat, not least because of the decor; but it's not cheap, and you must reserve a table. Otherwise, you'll have to make do with the less exclusive *Plzeňská restaurace*, situated in the hotel's modern wing (and dubbed "the crematorium" by the locals). If you'd rather mix with Czechs, Slovaks and Romanies, head for the *Národní dům*'s lively restaurant. A couple of other places to check out are the pizza place *Fortuna*, at Zámecký vrch 14 (Fri & Sat until 2am; rest of the week until midnight), and the vegetarian restaurant (called just that) at I.P. Pavlova 25 (daily 10am–9pm), tucked underneath an unprepossessing block of flats near the *Thermal*. Those thirsty for a draught beer with their food should head for the *Krušovická pivnice*, Masarykova 43. A final word of warning: prices in Karlovy Vary are approaching those in the West, so check the menu before tucking in.

Karlovy Vary is, of course, the home to one of the country's most peculiar drinks, **becherovka**, a herbal liqueur invented by Dr Becher. You can get it in bars and restaurants all over town (and just about anywhere else in the republic). It's an aquired taste – many liken it to cough medicine – and it's supposed to be good for you, though it contains none of the local spring water. Not so good for you, but all part of the spa ritual is **coffee and cakes**, and the faded beauty of the *Elefant* on Stará louka remains a perennial favourite.

Entertainment

> *What I indulged in, what I enjoyed*
> *What I conceived there*
> *What joy, what knowledge*
> *But it would be too long a confession*
> *I hope all will enjoy it that way*
> *Those with experience and the uninitiated.*

Needless to say, Goethe had a good time here. His coy innuendos are a reference to the enduring reputation of spas like Karlovy Vary for providing extra-marital romance. Dancing, after all, was encouraged by the spa doctors as a means of losing weight. These days, it's easy enough to indulge yourself in a similar fashion, at *Pupp*'s and the *Národní dům*, to name but two.

Karlovy Vary's **cultural life** is pretty varied, from classical concerts at the former *Kurhaus* (Lázně #3), and occasionally at *Pupp*'s, to the hysterically bad variety shows at the *Národní dům*. For details of what's going on, ask at the box office (Mon–Fri 8am–5pm, Sat 9–11pm) in the *Thermal* complex. The town also plays host to an **International Film Festival**, held in July; in even-numbered years it's professional, with at least a handful of big names turning up; in odd-numbered years it's a student festival, though no less fun for that. All showings are open to the public, and, again, the place to pick up information is the *Thermal*.

Loket and Jáchymov

Ten kilometres west of Karlovy Vary, **LOKET** (Elbogen) gets its name – *loket* means elbow – from the sharp bend in the Ohře that provides a dramatic setting for this minute, previously very German, hilltop town. The thirteenth-century **castle**, which slots into the precipitous fortifications, should eventually reopen as a **Museum of Porcelain**, displaying wares that have been manufactured in the town for centuries. Also on display, hopefully, will be the meteorite, weighing nearly a ton, that was found at the bottom of a well in 1775. In the meantime, you'll have to be content with wandering Loket's picturesque streets, which form a garland around the base of the castle, sheltering Saxon houses and secluded courtyards like Sklenařská, where the redundant German sign *Glaser Gasse* has been left unmolested.

On the main square, the only **accommodation** available is at the *Bílý kůň* (☎01608/941 71; ②), a sky-blue neo-Gothic hotel, formerly the *Weisses Ross*, where Goethe met his last love, Ulrike von Lewetzow, he in his seventies, she a mere seventeen. Hardly surprisingly, she refused his marriage proposal – his *Marienbader Elegie* describes the event – and, as it turned out, remained unmarried all her long life.

Loket is easily accessible by bus from Karlovy Vary, but by far the most inspiring way of getting there is to take the beautiful blue-marked track from Karlovy Vary, which crosses over to the left bank of the River Ohře at the halfway point, and passes the giant pillar-like rocks of the **Svatošské skály** (Hans Heiling Felsen), which have inspired writers from Goethe to the Brothers Grimm.

The uranium mines at Jáchymov

JÁCHYMOV (Joachimsthal), 20km northeast of Karlovy Vary and only 5km from the German border, will probably never recover from its past. In the early 1950s literally thousands of citizens (many of them former Communist Party members) were rounded up during the country's Stalinist terror and sentenced to hard labour in the **uranium mines** to the north of the town. Underfed and subject to harsh treatment by their jailers, untold numbers died of exhaustion, starvation and leukaemia.

Joachimsthal was founded in the sixteenth century, when silver deposits were discovered. The royal mint established here struck the famous *Joachimsthaler* (eventually giving rise to the *Dollar*, a corrupt form of the abbreviation *Thaler*). In 1896 the Frenchman Henri Bequerel discovered uranium, and it was from Joachimsthal uranium that Marie and Pierre Curie discovered radium earlier this century. The experiment proved as fatal to them as it did to the generations of German miners who worked the pits: even under the First Republic their average life expectancy was 42 years. Although the mine was closed down in 1964, radiation levels far in excess of *WHO* safety levels were recorded in the town in the 1980s, and calls for the immediate evacuation of the village were made by the youth journal *Mladá fronta* even before November 1989. Despite this, the citizens of Jáchymov continue to work in the local tobacco factory and the Marie Curie spa pension, where patients are "cured" by the town's radioactive springs.

travel details

Trains

Connection with Prague Plzeň (18 daily; 1hr 30min–2hr); Mariánské Lázně/Cheb (8 daily; 2hr/ 3hr 30min); Karlovy Vary (5 daily; 3hr 30min); Žatec (5 daily; 2hr); Kadaň (5 daily; 2hr 30min).

From Plzeň (hlavní nádraží) to Plasy (11 daily; 30–45min); Domažlice (up to 15 daily; 1hr–1hr 40min); Klatovy (up to 16 daily; 1hr–1hr 20min); Železná Ruda (up to 8 daily; 1hr 30min–3hr 10min); Stříbro/Mariánské Lázně/ Cheb (14 daily; 30–50min/1hr 15min–1hr 30min/1hr 40min–2hr 20min); Žatec (8 daily; 2hr–2hr 45min); Munich (2 daily; 7hr).

From Domažlice to Klatovy (7 daily; 1hr 10min).

From Mariánské Lázně to Teplá/Karlovy Vary (11 daily; 40min/1hr 50min).

From Cheb to Františkovy Lázně (15 daily; 8min); Karlovy Vary (15 daily; 50min–1hr 10min).

From Karlovy Vary to Kadaň (17 daily; 50min–1hr 10min); Teplice (5 daily; 2hr); Leipzig (1 daily; 4hr 30min).

Buses (ČSAD only)

Connections with Prague Louny/Jáchymov (2 daily; 1hr 15min/3hr); Karlovy Vary (up to hourly; 2hr 20min).

From Plzeň to Karlovy Vary (up to hourly; 1hr 30min); Horšovský Týn (7 daily; 1hr).

From Karlovy Vary to Loket (up to 14 daily; 25min); Jáchymov (up to 18 daily; 50min); Děčín (up to 4 daily; 3hr 45min).

CHAPTER FOUR

NORTH BOHEMIA

North Bohemia (Severní Čechy) has become a byword for the ecological disaster facing the country since the demise of Communism. Its forests have all but disappeared, weakened by acid rain and finished off by parasites, and its citizens are literally choking to death – all due to the brown coal-burning power stations that have provided the region with employment for the last hundred years. Despite this grim reality, parts of North Bohemia remain popular with Czech and German tourists, in particular the eastern half of the region, where the industrial landscape gives way to areas of outstanding natural beauty like **České Švýcarsko**, and towns of architectural finesse, like **Litoměřice**.

Geographically, the region splits conveniently into two, roughly equal halves, divided by the River Labe (Elbe). To the east, where the frontier mountains are less pronounced, two rich German cities developed: **Liberec** (Reichenberg), built on its cloth industry, and **Jablonec** (Gablonz), which relied on jewellery, with smaller mixed settlements in the very north producing Bohemia's world-famous crystal and glass. To the west, the forests of the **Krušné hory** (Erzegebirge or Ore Mountains), as their name suggests, have long been a source of great mineral wealth, providing material for porcelain, and, more latterly, coal.

Historically, the region has been part of Bohemia since the first Přemyslid princes, but from very early on, large numbers of Germans from neighbouring Saxony drifted over the ill-defined border, some taking up their traditional wood-based crafts, others working in the mines that sprung up along the base of the mountains. By the end of the nineteenth century, **factories** and **mines** had become as much a part of the landscape of North Bohemia as mountains and chateaux. Then, with the collapse of the Empire, the new-born Czechoslovak state inherited three-quarters of the Habsburg industry, and at a stroke became the world's tenth most industrialised country.

German and Czech miners remained loyal to the Left until the disastrous slump of the 1930s, when the majority of North Bohemia's German *Volk* put their trust in the pro-Nazi Sudeten German Party or SdP, with disastrous consequences for the country – and for Europe. Allied bombings took their toll during the war, and with the backing of the Big Three (Churchill, Roosevelt and Stalin) at Potsdam, the German population was forcibly (and bloodily) expelled in 1945. In the case of North Bohemia, economic necessity ensured that the region was quickly rebuilt and resettled, but the last forty years of unbridled industrialisation have irrevocably marred the land and lives of North Bohemia.

While the rest of Europe was belatedly tempering sulphur emissions and increasing fuel efficiency, the Czechs were steadily sinking to fortieth place in the world league of industrial powers, and rising to first place for male mortality rates, cancer and still-births. It's easy to blame all these calamities on the factory fetishism of the Communists, but damage to the forests of the Krušné hory was noted even before World War II, and smog levels have irritated the citizens of North Bohemia for the best part of this century. Yet now that the voices of dissent have been unleashed, the outlook is not all bleak – the brown-coal indus-

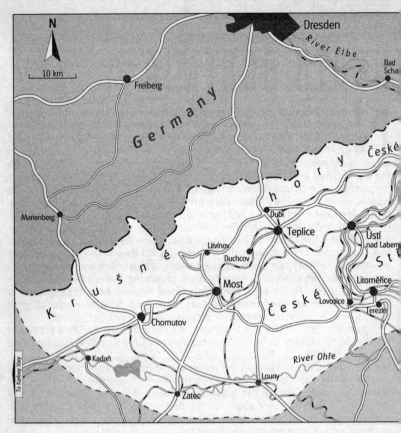

try is gradually being wound down, and alternative forms of energy being sought. The downside to this is that these measures are likely to leave the region with one of the highest unemployment rates in the Czech Republic, something which can only exacerbate the smouldering tensions between the Czechs and Romanies who have shared this polluted home since 1945.

Up the Ohře

There are three walled towns along the **River Ohře** (Eger), foolishly neglected by most travellers eager to reach Karlovy Vary and the spas of West Bohemia. With your own car, all three can be easily covered in a day; by public transport, it's best to concentrate on just one or two towns. If you are driving, be sure to take in one of the best **views** in the entire region, from the ridge shortly after Panenský Týnec, on Route 7; in the foreground, bizarre hillocks rise up like giant mole hills, while behind, the entire range of the Krušné hory is stretched out in all its distant glory (close up it's not so pretty).

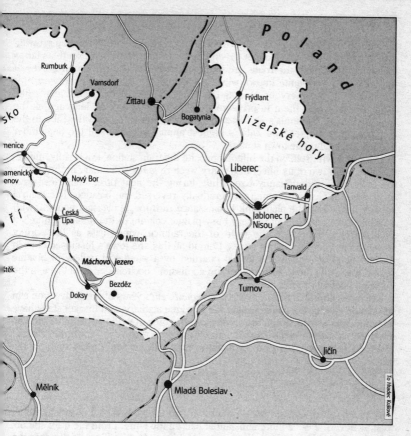

On the map: Rumburk, Varnsdorf, Zittau, Bogatynia, Frýdlant, Poland, Jizerské hory, menice, Nový Bor, amenický enov, Liberec, Tanvald, Česká Lípa, Jablonec n. Nisou, Mimoň, Máchovo jezero, štěk, Bezděz, Doksy, Turnov, Jičín, Mělník, Mladá Boleslav, To Hradec Králové

Louny

LOUNY (Laun) is the first of the medieval fortified towns on the Ohře, its perfect
Gothic appearance all but entirely destroyed by fire in 1517 – all, that is, except the
strikingly beautiful church of **sv Mikuláš**, whose triple pyramidal roof was rebuilt
by the German mason Benedikt Ried and now provides the town with its most
famous landmark (he used a similar design to great effect on sv Barbora in Kutná
Hora; see p.133). Ried died here in 1534, but his work – including his skilful ribbed
vaulting – lives on, and the only problem is getting inside to look at it; unless it's
approaching mass, you'll have to track down the key from the local priest.

If you need a place **to stay**, there are extremely cheap doubles and triples at the
Dům kultury (①), badly signposted behind the modern red-brick building on the
eastern edge of the old town. The local **beer** is served up at *U kalicha*, on Česká,
near the church, and it would be churlish not to mention the **late-night** excitement provided by the *Rock Café*, on the corner of Česká and Jakoubkova (open Fri
& Sat until 1am, the rest of the week 11pm), and the *Satan Club*, just across from
the bus station (disco on Fri & Sat; rest of the week, restaurant until midnight).

Žatec

ŽATEC (Saaz), 24km up the Ohře from Louny, is the centre of the hop-growing region that supports the famous Czech beer industry. From here, south as far as Rakovník (Rakonitz), the roads are hemmed in by endless tall, green groves of hop vines. No one quite knows why Czech hops are the best in the world for brewing beer, but everyone accepts the fact, and even Belgian beer giants like *Stella Artois* import them in preference to their own. Since as long ago as the twelfth century, Bohemia's *Red Saaz* hops have been sent down the Elbe to the Hamburg hop market, and Žatec's biggest annual binge is still the September hop festival held in the town square.

The **old town** itself, on the hilltop opposite the train station, is a scruffy, medieval affair, with two of its fifteenth-century western gates still intact. In those days the town was predominantly Czech but during the next three centuries, wave upon wave of German immigrants gradually reversed the balance. The central square, headed by the plain pink Renaissance **radnice**, is pleasant enough, with arcades down one side and a very busy plague column in the middle. There's a small garden of hops to the right of the radnice, which acts as the perfect advertisement for the town's wares. Behind all this, the town's Jesuitised church (in bad need of a coat of paint) is guarded by a wonderful gallery of beatific sculptures, while the town **brewery** (no admission) occupies pride of place in the thirteenth-century castle.

Life is beginning to return to the main square after years of inactivity – you can sit outside and have a coffee beside the Baroque statuary, and market stalls have begun to appear in between the arcades. At the time of writing, the only functioning **hotel** in town was the *Zlatý lev*, on Oblouková (☎0397/40 78; ①); the *Družba* and the *Zlatý anděl*, both on the main square, will no doubt open again in the future.

Kadaň

Very much in the same mould as the other two towns, **KADAŇ** (Kaaden), 22km west, is nevertheless a more substantial halt on the Ohře. From the train station, you enter the old town through the round whitewashed barbican of the **Žatecká brána**. The town suffered badly during the Thirty Years' War, but has hardly been touched since then, maintaining a dusty air of neglect about its eighteenth-century buildings, as if it has never quite recovered from the postwar expulsions. The most striking sight in town is the prickly white cone of the watchtower, and, on the opposite side of the square, **Katovská** ("Hangman's Street" – his house is below the gate at the end), Bohemia's narrowest street, is barely more than a passage, the light straining to make its way past the maze of buttresses.

At the southern tip of town, Kadaň's partially renovated **castle**, a modest domestic seat, sits over the Ohře, one wing now a **hotel**, *vinárna* and exhibition gallery. From a gate by the side of the castle you can gain access to the best preserved part of the **town walls**. If you need **to stay**, there's also the concrete, high-rise *Zelený strom* (which means "Green Tree"; ①), beyond the west town gate, on Jiráskova.

The North Bohemian brown coal basin

The **North Bohemian brown coal basin** contrives to be even less enticing than it sounds. It forms an almost continuous sixty-kilometre rash of mines, factories and prefabricated towns, from Kadaň to Ústí nad Labem. Seventy-five percent of the country's brown coal (lignite) is mined here, the majority of it from just ten metres below the surface. Huge tracts of land at the foot of the **Krušné hory** have been transformed by giant insect-like diggers that crawl across fields of brown sludge like the last surviving cockroaches in a post-nuclear desert. Around one hundred villages have been bulldozed, the rail and road link east of Chomutov shifted south, and the entire town of Most flattened to make way for the ever-expanding mines.

Not only is the stuff extracted here, but much of it is burnt locally, and brown coal is particularly nasty stuff – far and away the filthiest and most harmful of all fossil fuels. You can't fail to see the lethal yellowish clouds billowing out of the power stations at Tušimice and Prunéřov, both only recently fitted with filters (Tušimice is due to be closed down in 1996), and both less than 5km north and east of Kadaň. Every winter, filter masks are distributed to local school children as the whole valley slowly suffocates in a thick, 24-hour smog of noxious gases.

Most to Duchcov

The only building in **MOST** (Brüx) to survive the town's recent migration was the valuable early sixteenth-century church of **Nanebevzetí Panna Marie**, which was transported in one piece to the edge of the mine, 841 metres away. Designed by Jakob Heilmann of Schweinfurt, a pupil of Benedikt Ried, it is an awe-inspiring sight, perched on the edge of a vast apocalyptic crater. The rest of the town – a desolate collection of prefabricated buildings – lies to the south, on the other side of the motorway.

At **LITVÍNOV** (Leutensdorf), 6km north of Most, the unwelcome bonus of a huge chemical plant just south of the town, coupled with the constant sulphur emissions, creates a bank of cloud that regularly blots out the sun and reduces all light to a grey haze. At the side of the road, special lights switch on above the simple command "RED LIGHT STOP! SWITCH OFF YOUR ENGINE!" when the authorities deem the chemical levels to be too dangerous. Somewhat incredibly, Litvínov still has the leftovers of its nineteenth-century *Ringstrasse*, now boarded up and long since overtaken by the town's new constructions.

At first **DUCHCOV** (Dux), 8km further east, appears no different, encircled as it is by coal mines. But in this unlikely location a grandly conceived Baroque **chateau** (April–Oct Tues–Sun 9am–3pm), designed by Jean-Baptiste Mathey, contains a small exhibition dedicated to the world's most famous bounder, **Giacomo Casanova** (1725–98). Exiled from his native Venice, Casanova took refuge here, at the invitation of Count Waldstein, and whiled away his final, fairly miserable years as a librarian in these staid surroundings, writing his steamy memoirs.

Teplice-Šanov

In the midst of this polluted region lies the traumatised town of **TEPLICE-ŠANOV** (Teplitz-Schönau), the forgotten fourth spa of the once celebrated quartet of Bohemian resorts that included Karlsbad, Marienbad and Franzensbad (see Chapter Three). In the nineteenth century it became "the drawing room of Europe", prompting the likes of Wagner, Liszt and Beethoven to appear on its *Kurliste*. But by the 1880s, the all-too adjacent mining industry had already inflicted its first blow on Teplice's idyllic way of life: the nearby Döllinger mine breached an underwater lake, flooding the natural springs, which have had to be artificially pumped to the surface ever since. The lingering smell of lignite was a characteristic of the town even then, and is now complemented by several additional chemical vapours.

The accumulative cost of this assault on the environment is extremely serious. In winter, as the smog wraps itself round the town for weeks, the sulphur dioxide levels sometimes reach 25 times the *WHO* safety maximum. In addition, Teplice has more than its fair share of social problems: there's a large and vocal skinhead movement here, which has come to blows with the town's Vietnamese and Romany communities on several occasions over the last few years; meanwhile, the roads out of town – in particular the road to Dresden – are currently lined with Czech and Romany prostitutes trying to flag down German customers.

The Town

Arriving at the main train station, **Teplice v Čechách nádraží**, injects a sense of hope in innocent minds, with its rich neo-Renaissance frescoes adorning the vaulted ceiling, though this is soon dispelled by the block after block of silent and peeling nineteenth-century houses between here and the centre. To reach the centre from the station, take either 28 října, or the main street, Masarykova třída, one block south.

At the end of Masarykova, behind the rather brutal Krušnohorské divadlo (an uncharacteristic, late work by Helmer and Fellner), the spa proper begins. Even the old *Kur Garten* – now the **Lázeňský sad** – has a somewhat deseased air about it, despite the lively sounds of birdlife. Nowadays, the modern white concrete box of the **Dům kultury** is the dominant feature of the park, fronted by the **New Colonnade**, a glorified greenhouse made up from some of Bohemia's great glass surplus.

Only when you cross the valley to the brightly coloured Empire houses on Lázeňská (including one where Beethoven once stayed) it's just about possible to make the imaginative leap into Teplice's arcadian past. Beyond lies the town's monumental **chateau**, seat of the Clary-Aldringen family until 1945 when they, and most other *Teplitzer*, took flight from the approaching Red Army. The countless rooms of the chateau are now part of the local museum (Tues–Sun 9am– noon & 1–5pm), with memorials to Beethoven, Pushkin, and (of course) Goethe, wall-to-wall *Biedermeyer* and much else besides.

Outside the main gates of the chateau, the Zámecké náměstí enjoys a flash of gold on Braun's charcoaled plague column, while east of the chateau, a splendid staircase takes you past the twin turrets of the *U Petra* restaurant to the blissful **Zámecká zahrada** (chateau garden), which spreads itself around two lakes, still "enlivened ·with swans", just as Baedeker noted approvingly back in 1905. Teplice's other train station, **Teplice-zámecká zahrada** (for trains to Litoměřice and Liberec), lies beyond the motorway that marks the western border of the park. The surrounding neighbourhood, lined with nineteenth-century burgher houses, gives a much better idea of the town's halcyon days than the radically altered centre.

Šanov

The rest of the spa lies in the eastern part of town, once the separate village of **Šanov** (Schönau), linked by Lipová (Lindenstrasse), which still clings on to its lime trees despite the acid onslaught. Like the bark on the trees, the paint is slowly dropping off the grandiose private villas and spa pensions that characterise this part of the spa. Lipová culminates in the sady Československé armády, overlooked by a large, run-down red-brick Protestant church and peppered with yellowing Neoclassical spa buildings.

If you haven't pre-booked any treatment, you could always go for a **swim** in the sky-blue Art-Nouveau *Thermalní lázně*, just off Lipová on V. Halke (or play crazy golf next door); or else improve your health by climbing the 230 steps to the summit of Letná (accessible from Laubeho náměstí, at the eastern corner of the Lázeňský sad), and enjoy a great **view** over the spa.

Practicalities

Nowadays, it's perfectly possible to stay in **private rooms** in Teplice, like those on Lipová, or in one of the new pensions, like the *Gizela*, at the Šanov end of Vrchlického (☎0417/288 67; ②). Teplice's choice of **hotels** begins with the grim *Hotel de Saxe* (☎0417/266 11; ①) on the corner of Masarykova and Husitská, near the main train station, followed by the more central *Thermia*, also on Masarykova (☎0417/282 21; ②), or the modern, high-rise *Panorama* (☎0417/270 52; ①), east of the centre – bus #18 or #23 from Masarykova. But by far the nicest (and most expensive) place to stay is the *Prince de Ligne* (☎0417/247 55; ⑤), a newly renovated nineteenth-century hotel overlooking Zámecké náměstí.

Moving on from Teplice, the main **bus terminal** and train station (Teplice v Čechách) are next to one another just off Masarykova. For trains to Liberec and Litoměřice (one to each daily), you need to go to Teplice zámecká zahrada, to the west of the chateau garden; slow, scenic trains to Děčín leave from Teplice lesní brána, 1km northwest of the centre – a fifteen-minute walk down Dubská from the town hall, and across the motorway, or bus #20 from the main train station, or the choice of buses #16 and #23 from Benešovo náměstí.

Terezín

The road from Prague to Berlin passes right through the fortress town of **TEREZÍN** (Theresienstadt), just over 30km southeast of Teplice. Purpose-built in the 1780s by the Habsburgs to defend the northern border against Prussia, it was capable of accommodating 14,500 soldiers and hundreds of prisoners. In 1941, the whole town was turned into a **Jewish ghetto**, and used as a transit camp for Jews whose final destination was Auschwitz.

Although the **Main Fortress** (Hlavní pevnost) has never been put to the test in battle, Terezín remains a garrison town. Today, it's an eerie, soulless place, built to a dour eighteenth-century grid plan, its bare streets still ringing with the sounds of soldiers and military police. As you enter, the red-brick fortifications are still an awesome sight, though the huge moat has been put out of action by local gardening enthusiasts.

The Ghetto Museum

The unnerving feel of the place apart, there's just one thing to see here, the **Ghetto Museum** (Muzeum Ghetta; daily 9am–6pm), which was finally opened in 1991, on the fiftieth anniversary of the arrival of the first transports in Terezín. After the war, the Communists had followed the consistent Soviet line by deliberately ignoring the Jewish perspective on Terezín. Instead, the emphasis in the museum set up in the Lesser Fortress (see below) was on the war as an anti-Fascist struggle, in which good (Communism and the Soviet Union) had triumphed over evil (Fascism and Nazi Germany). It wasn't until the Prague Spring of 1968 that the idea of a museum dedicated specifically to the history of the Jewish ghetto first emerged. In the 1970s, however, the intended building was turned into a museum of the Ministry of the Interior instead.

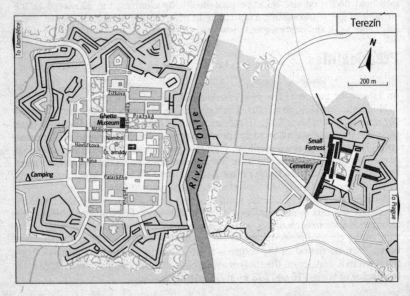

A BRIEF HISTORY OF THE GHETTO

In October 1941, Reinhard Heydrich and the Nazi high command decided to turn the whole of Terezín into a Jewish ghetto. It was an obvious choice: fully fortified, close to the main Prague–Dresden railway line, and with an SS prison already established in the Lesser Fortress nearby. The original inhabitants of the town – fewer than 3500 people*– were moved out, and transports began arriving at Terezín from many parts of the Greater German Reich. Within a year, nearly 60,000 Jews were interned here in appallingly overcrowded conditions, and the monthly death rate rose to 4000. In October 1942, the first transport left for Auschwitz. By the end of the war, 140,000 Jews had been deported to Terezín; fewer than 17,500 remained when the ghetto was finally liberated on May 8, 1945.

One of the perverse ironies of Terezín is that it was used by the Nazis as a cover for the real purpose of the *Endlösung* or "final solution", devised at the Wannsee conference in January 1942. The ghetto was made to appear self-governing, with its own council, its own bank printing ghetto money, its own shops selling goods confiscated from the internees on arrival, and even a café on the main square. For a while, a special "Terezín family camp" was even set up in Auschwitz, to continue the deception. The deportees were kept in mixed barracks, allowed to wear civilian clothes and – the main purpose of the whole thing – to send letters back to their loved ones in Terezín telling them they were OK. After six months "quarantine", they were sent to the gas chambers.

Despite all this, the ghetto population turned their unprecedented freedom to their own advantage. Since the entire population of the Protectorate (and Jews from many other parts of Europe) passed through Terezín, the ghetto had an enormous number of outstanding Jewish artists and scholars. Thus, in addition to the officially sponsored activities, countless clandestine cultural events were organised in the cellars and attics of the barracks; teachers gave lessons to children, puppet theatre productions were held, and literary evenings were put on.

Towards the end of 1943, the so-called *Verschönerung* or "beautification" of the ghetto was implemented, in preparation for the arrival of the International Red Cross inspectors. Streets were given names instead of numbers, and the whole place was decked out as if it were a spa town. When the International Red Cross asked to inspect one of the Nazi camps, they were brought here and treated to a week of Jewish cultural events. The Red Cross visited Terezín twice, once in June 1943, and again in April 1945; both times the delegates filed positive reports.

Now that it's open, this extremely informative and well laid-out exhibition at last attempts to do some justice to the extraordinary and tragic events which took place here between 1941 and 1945, including background displays on the measures which led up to the *Endlösung*. There's also a fascinating video (with English subtitles) showing clips of the Nazi propaganda film shot in Terezín – *Hitler gives the Jews a Town* – intercut with harrowing interviews with survivors.

The Lesser Fortress

On the other side of the River Ohře, east down Pražská, lies the **Lesser Fortress** (Malá pevnost; daily 9am–5pm), built as a military prison in the 1780s, at the same time as the main fortress. The young Bosnian, Gavrilo Princip, who succeeded in shooting the Archduke Ferdinand in 1914, was interned here during World War I. In 1940 it was turned into an SS prison by Heydrich and, after the war, it became the official memorial and museum of Terezín.

There are guides available (usually survivors from Terezín), or else you can simply buy the brief broadsheet guide to the prison in English, and walk around yourself. The infamous Nazi refrain *Arbeit Macht Frei* (Work Brings Freedom) is daubed across the entrance on the left, which leads to the exemplary washrooms, still as they were when built for the Red Cross tour of inspection. The rest of the camp has been left empty but intact, and graphically evokes the cramped conditions under which the prisoners were kept half-starved, badly clothed, and subject to indiscriminate cruelty and execution. The main **exhibition** is housed in the smart eighteenth-century mansion set in the prison gardens, which was home to the Camp Kommandant, his family and fellow SS officers. A short documentary, intelligible in any language, is regularly shown in the cinema that was set up in 1942 to entertain the prison officers.

Practicalities

Terezín is actually easiest to reach from Prague's Florenc **bus** terminal (1hr), or from Litoměřice, just 3km to the north. The nearest train station to Terezín (from which the transports used to leave) is at BOHUŠOVICE, 2km south of the fortress. There's a smart new **restaurant**, *Teresian*, on the main square, which serves simple but good Czech food. It's difficult to imagine a less appealing place to stay, but you may stay at the **campsite** (May to mid-Sept) just west of town; the *Parkhotel* is currently closed, but there's a hotel and rooms in Litoměřice (see below).

Litoměřice

If the idea of lingering in Terezín is unappealing, it might be worth walking or catching the bus 3km north to **LITOMĚŘICE** (Leitmeritz), at the confluence of the Ohře and the Labe rivers. The town has been an ecclesiastical centre since the Přemyslid Spytihněv II founded a collegiate chapter here in 1057. From the eleventh century onwards, German craftsmen flooded into Litoměřice, thanks to its strategic trading position on the Labe, and it soon became the third or fourth city of Bohemia. Having survived the Hussite Wars by the skin of its teeth, it was devastated in the Thirty Years' War. But its most recent upheaval came in 1945, when virtually the entire population (which was predominantly German) was forcibly expelled from the country.

The main reason people come here now is to pay their respects at Terezín, just south of the town (see above); however, Litoměřice is of more than passing interest, since virtually the entire town is a museum to **Octavio Broggio**. Broggio was born here in 1668 and, along with his father Giulio, redesigned the town's many churches following the arrival of the Jesuits and the establishment of a Catholic bishopric here in the mid-seventeenth century. The reason for this zealous re-Catholicisation was Litoměřice's rather too eager conversion to the heretical beliefs of the Hussites and its disastrous allegiance to the Protestants in the Thirty Years' War.

Since 1989, the town has begun to pick up the pieces after forty years of neglect. Restoration work is continuing apace, and the re-establishment here of Bohemia's one and only Catholic seminary has brought some pride back to the town.

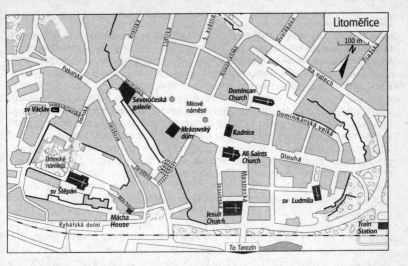

The Town

Stepping out of the train station, you'll notice the last remaining bastion of the old town walls across the road; behind it lies the historical quarter, entered via the wide boulevard of Dlouhá. There's no better place to get an understanding of the town's rich religious heritage than at the hybrid church of **All Saints** at the top of the street. It started life as a Romanesque church and now boasts the only Gothic spire left on the skyline, a beautiful wedge-shaped affair reminiscent of Prague's right bank. Broggio designed the present Baroque facade, though the oppressively low ceiling and dusty furnishings inside are disappointing, with the notable exception of the fifteenth-century panel painting by the Master of Litoměřice.

The town's vast cobbled marketplace, **Mírové náměstí**, once one of the most important in Bohemia, now boasts only a couple of buildings from before the Thirty Years' War. The best known is the **Mrázovský dům**, on the south side of the square at no. 15, whose owner at the time, a devout Hussite, had a huge wooden *kalich* (chalice) – the symbol of all Hussites – plonked on the roof in 1537. The other building that stands out is the arcaded fourteenth-century **town hall**, at the eastern end of the square, rebuilt in Renaissance style and covered in sgraffito decoration. It now serves as the town museum (Tues–Sun 10am–noon & 1–5pm), worth a quick spin round, if only for the coffered sixteenth-century ceiling of the council hall; there's still precious little mention in the exhibition of the 1945 expulsions.

West of the square, the **Severočeská galerie** (Tues–Sun 9am–noon & 2–5pm) occupies a wonderfully rambling sixteenth-century building on Michalská, its inner courtyard draped in ivy and echoing to the trickle of a modern fountain. Exhibitions doing the Bohemian circuit stop off here, supplementing the already handsome permanent collection of Czech works, ranging from sixteenth-century panels by the Master of Litoměřice to a small selection of twentieth-century canvases, and the sculpture terrace round the back.

Cathedral hill

On a promontory 500m southwest of the town centre, the **Cathedral hill**, where the bishop and his entourage once held residence, was originally entirely separate from the town, with its own fortifications. On its northern slope, the small, pasty chapel of **sv Václav** (St Wenceslas) is in many ways the younger Broggio's finest work, grand despite its cramped proportions and location. But the real reason to come out here is to wonder at the former cathedral of **sv Štěpán** (St Stephen), which looks out onto the quiet grassy enclosure of Dómské náměstí. Redesigned by Giulio Broggio (among others) in the seventeenth century, sv Štěpán marked the start of the extensive rebuilding of Litoměřice. The cathedral's interior is full of light touches missing from the later churches, set against the dark wood and gloomy altar paintings from the school of the Saxon master Lucas Cranach. Outside, the freestanding campanile adds a peculiarly Tuscan touch.

A path along the north side of sv Štěpán leads down the cobbled lane of Máchova, where the Czech poet **Karel Hynek Mácha** died in 1836. The corner house at no. 3 – built after Mácha's untimely death – contains a small exhibition (Tues–Sun 10am–5pm) on the life of the poet who, in the true style of the Romantics, died of consumption at the age of 26. His most famous poem, *Máj* (May), was hijacked by the Communists as their May Day anthem. He used to be buried in the local cemetery, but when the Nazis drew up the Sudetenland borders Litoměřice lay inside the Greater German Reich, so the Czechs dug the poet up and reinterred him in the Vyšehrad cemetery in Prague (see p.105). Once you've reached the bottom of the cathedral hill, the stairway of the Máchovy schody will take you back up into town.

Practicalities

From the **train station**, which is also where **buses** terminate, *ČEDOK* is only a short walk up Dlouhá. They can help you find a **room**, though the only hotel at present is the high-rise *Sechezy* (☎0416/24 51; ②), at Vrchlického 10 in the housing estate northeast of town. There's a **campsite** with bungalows (and an open-air cinema), open June to September in the woods between the railway line and the river. The *Hotel Rak* on the main square (no longer in fact a hotel) serves good Czech **food** and beer from Louny in its ground-floor vaults, and also has a new nightclub in the backrooms. Alternatively, there are several new snack bars and bistros on Novobranská.

On from Litoměřice

Moving on from Litoměřice, if you're heading northeast to Liberec (see p.216), or north to the České Švýcarsko (see p.212), you could break the journey at one or more of the places described below.

Northeast towards Liberec

First off, just 6km northeast of Litoměřice, off Route 15, is the village of **PLOSKOVICE**, which hides a crisp, light summer **chateau** (30-min guided tour, April–Oct Tues–Sun 8am–4pm), one of Octavio Broggio's few secular works. The rusting scaffolding that accompanies all Czech renovation jobs is currently still in place, but hopefully the fountains will soon issue forth and the whole place – sometimes frivolous, sometimes tasteless, always fun – and its beautiful walled grounds will flourish once more.

Bypassed by the main road – and, it seems, by all of modernity – for the last three centuries, **ÚŠTĚK** (Auscha) originally grew up around a now-ruined medieval fortress. It's not sufficiently picturesque to go out of your way for (it's 50min by train from Litoměřice), but if you're **camping** (May–Sept) out by the pleasant sandy beached Chlemař lake, behind the railway station, you should definitely wander into town. On one side of the main street there's a line of fourteenth-century burgher houses, which, unusually for Bohemia, still retain their original triangular gables of wood or slate.

Down by the Úštěcký stream to the southwest of the town, in among the geese and hens, there are some fascinating wooden shacks, known as the **ptačí domky** (birds' houses). Perched on top of each other on the highest ledge of the steeply terraced banks, they provided ad hoc accommodation for Jewish families, and the Italian workers who built the town's railway link in the late nineteenth century.

Around Doksy

Thirty kilometres further east, **DOKSY** itself maybe no great shakes, but the sandy shores of the **Máchovo jezero** (for once a natural lake) have been a popular recreational spot since the nineteenth-century Romanticists used to trek out here – the lake is named for Karel Hynek Mácha, its greatest fan. As well as the *Klůček* **campsite** along the southeastern shores of the lake (mid-May to mid-Sept), there's **accommodation** at the *Pasáž* (☎04258/727 31; ①) in STARÉ SPLAVY, northwest of the lake, and at the *Grandhotel* (☎04258/722 07; ②) in Doksy itself.

Some 8km southeast of here, and clearly visible for miles around, is the ruined hilltop castle of **Bezděz** (April–Oct Tues–Sun 9am–4pm). One of the most important castles in Bohemia until its destruction in the Thirty Years' War, there's not much to see now, aside from a Gothic chapel, and, of course, the unbeatable view from the top of the hill (604m).

North through the České středohoří

All northbound trains from Prague and Litoměřice take the scenic route through the long ridge of the **České středohoří** (Central Bohemian Hills), which rise up out of the Labe basin, parting only to allow the river to slither through. Huge, flat barges plough the Labe's filthy waters, flanked by electrified railway tracks, and clusters of *chata* huddled together on either side of the valley.

On the right bank, local trains from Litoměřice skirt along the northern slopes of the range, terminating at Děčín (see below). On the left bank, international expresses heading for Dresden and Berlin pass quickly through the self-confessed *Chemické město* of LOVOSICE (Lobositz), whose assorted chimneys emit a rich and pungent bouquet of chemicals, and turn the already grimy Labe black. Twenty kilometres down the tracks, on the other side of the hills, is yet another chemical town, **ÚSTÍ NAD LABEM** (Aussig), a solidly German port until its destruction in the last war and the expulsion of its citizens. Trains usually only stop for four or five minutes, and a visit to Ústí is best left at that, unless you want to explore the ruins of **Střekov** (Schreckenstein), the "Rock of Fear", a dramatic rocky pile commanding the opposite bank. Like the Lorelei on the Rhine, this too was an inspiration for one of Wagner's operas, *Tannhäuser*.

Česke Švýcarsko

The area of sandstone rocks around Děčín is popularly known as **Česke Švýcarsko** (Bohemian Switzerland), though this nickname, first coined by artists of the Romantic movement, is misleading: the landscape, far from looking Swiss, is archetypally central European. The River Labe drives a deep wedge into the geographical defences of Bohemia, forging a grand valley through the dense forests, interrupted by outcrops of sandstone rock welded into truly fantastic shapes.

Like the other *skalí město*, or "rock-cities", in the Český ráj (see p.223) and the Broumov region (see p.233), the whole area was formed when volcanic rock thrust its way to the surface, causing fissures and cracks in the land which later widened. The result is probably the most impressive geological amusement park in the country, a dense network of mini-canyons and bluffs all covered in a blanket of woodland – spectacular stuff, and a favourite with rock climbers, but fairly easy **hiking** country for non-specialists, too.

Transport throughout the region is not great – just infrequent rural bus services to most places – though the distances are small enough to make hiking an attractive proposition as a means of getting about. In contrast to a few years ago, there's now plenty of inexpensive **private accommodation** throughout the region, making it possible for non-campers to spend more than just a day in the countryside.

Děčín

Despite being German-speaking for most of the last thousand years, **DĚČÍN** has long been the gateway to Bohemia. Its castle, which rises up to the east as you enter the country from Dresden, was once the stronghold of the Slav tribe *Děčané* (hence its Czech name). Modern Děčín is really two towns – **Děčín** (Tetschen) itself and **Podmokly** (Bodenbach) – divided by the River Labe, which has always been the driving force behind the town's economy. As a busy inland port, its attractions are limited, but, lying at the heart of Česke Švýcarsko, it does serve as a convenient base for exploring the region.

Podmokly

The main point of **arrival** is the grubby hlavní nádraží in **Podmokly**, which looks out on to the *Grand Hotel*'s mass of grey concrete and an unsightly local supermarket. It's not a great start, but then Podmokly was a late developer, only coming into existence in 1850 through the amalgamation of three villages on the left bank. Sixty years of furious building followed, funded by the town's flourishing shipping industry, the results of which are still visible in the four or five blocks west of the station, where Czechs, Romanies and Saxons while away the hours window-shopping and wolfing down ice cream.

With time to kill, and an interest in seamanship and navigation, you can spend a happy hour in the **Museum of Elbe Transport**, situated in a former hunting lodge on Zbrojnická, behind the *Hotel Sever*. Alternatively, head for the meringue-coloured mansion (lit ultraviolet at night) atop the precipitous **Pastýřská stěna** (Shepherd's Rock); head down Mládeže, continue under the railway, and take the lift (*výtah*) cut into the rock halfway along Labské nábřeží – the return trip costs

four local bus tickets, which (if you have the change) you buy at the entrance. At the top there's a small **café** with an incredible view over Děčín, and, a little further back from the cliff, a small **zoo**.

Děčín

To cross the river to **Děčín** from Podmokly, take any of the buses from outside the station, or continue downstream from the above-mentioned lift until you reach the Tyršův most. Despite its superior antiquity, Děčín itself was, until recently, hampered by the fact that its showpiece, the **Schloss Tetschen-Bodenbach** (as it was known for most of its life) – a simple but beautiful eighteenth-century pile, elevated above the river on an isolated lump of rock – was a Soviet army barracks and therefore a no-go area. Although it is still out of bounds, restoration work is being carried out, and there are plans to open it to the public in the near future.

In the meantime, visitors must content themselves with a stroll round the castle's **Růžová zahrada** (May–Oct daily 10am–5pm), a truly wonderful Baroque rose garden laid out on a terrace cut into the north face of the rock. To gain access to the garden, you must walk up the sloping **Dlouhá jízda**, a 300m-long drive cut into the rock, and enter through a small, separate doorway on the right. From the gardens, you're treated to a bird's-eye view of U brany, probably Děčín's best-looking street, and the Baroque church of **sv Kříž**, its distinctive dome, twin towers and lanterns designed by Fischer von Erlach.

Practicalities

There's a choice of three **hotels** in Podmokly – the *Grand* (☎0412/270 41; ④), situated opposite the main station, and plush inside despite its dreary exterior; and the two no-frills options, the *Sever* (☎0412/232 77; ①), also by the main station, and the *Šport* (☎0412/221 66; ①), on the corner of Teplická and Prokop

Holého. In Děčín (bus #8 or #9 from Podmokly), there's just the *Pošta* (☎0412/228 31; ②) on the main square, Masarykovo náměstí, and a small **campsite** (May–Sept) on the south side of the castle rock, with an open-air swimming pool nearby; though there are some equally well-equipped sites in the České Švýcarsko itself (see below).

Those with their own transport might consider staying at the luxurious *Pension Jana* (☎0412/895 71; ②), a couple of kilometres out of town on Route 13 to Teplice. Alternatively, the whole region (though not Děčín-Podmokly itself) is inundated with **private rooms**, available on spec, or booked through *ČEDOK* (see below), or one of the accommodation agencies in town – for example *Dezka* at Teplická 61, Podmokly, or *Jatour*, Masarykovo náměstí, Děčín. If you're looking for something different on the **restaurant** front, instead of the ubiquitous hotel chefs, try the *Asia* on Teplická (closed Sat & Sun).

Daily **ferries** to Hřensko and Dresden (just 60km away), via the Labe gorge, depart from just past the Tyršův most on the Děčín side; *ČEDOK*, at Prokopa Holého 8 in Podmokly, can give you the current schedule.

Walking in the České Švýcarsko

The České Švýcarsko splits neatly in half with Děčín as the meeting point. Whichever part you're heading for, it's a good idea to get hold of the 1:50,000 *Českosaské Švýcarsko* **map**, which marks all campsites and footpaths in the area, including those on the German side. The popular **Jetřichovické stěny**, to the northeast of Děčín, is topographically more interesting and covers a much greater area than its western counterpart. At its base runs the Kamenice river, accessible in parts only by the popular boat trips. The smaller range to the west, the **Děčínské stěny**, is less spectacular, but doesn't suffer from the same human traffic jams and, what's more, can be easily reached from Děčín itself on a hiking day trip.

Jetřichovické stěny

The only way to get to the Jetřichovické stěny and the Kamenice gorge is by bus, since the railway line from Děčín follows the left bank, which falls into German territory. Three or four weekday **buses** make the roundabout journey to Jetřichovice, via Hřensko, Tří prameny, Mezní Louka and Mezná, or you can take one of the two morning **boats** (May–Aug), which run from Děčín to Hřensko.

Despite its dramatic mountainous setting, **HŘENSKO** (Herrnskretchen), at 116m above sea level, is, in fact, the lowest point in Bohemia. It's a pretty village on the right bank of the Labe, dotted with half-timbered houses and redolent of Saxony, which faces it on the opposite bank. Today, Hřensko makes its living out of the German day-trippers flocking to the nearby rocks, and with their former East German neighbours now flush with Deutschmarks, business is booming, with several **hotels** to choose from, but often precious few spare rooms. The rather splendid *Hotel Labe* (☎0412/981 88; ①), right by the river front, is very good value, as is the *Lípa* (☎0412/981 17; ①), further up the River Kamenice.

By far the most popular destination is the **Pravčická brána**, at 30m long and 21m high the largest natural stone bridge in Europe. It's a truly breathtaking sight, though not one you're likely to enjoy alone unless you get there very early or out of season. It's a two-kilometre hike up from Tří prameny, a clearing (and bus stop) 3km up the road from Hřensko. The German border is less than 1km away, but the red-marked path that appears to head towards it actually rejoins the road 4.5km further east at **MEZNÍ LOUKA**, whose **hotel** (☎0412/981 89; ①) of the same name stands opposite a **campsite** (May–Sept) with cheap bungalows for rent. If you get no joy in Mezní Louka, **VYSOKÁ LOUKA**, another 5km along the road, is littered with **private accommodation**.

From Mezní Louka, the red-marked path continues another 14km to Jetřichovice, meandering through the southern part of the complex of mini-canyons, taking in the **Malá Pravčická brána**, a smaller version of the bridge, and a couple of very ruined border castles. **JETŘICHOVICE** itself is an old Saxon hamlet made up of huge wooden farmsteads typical of the region, their present-day Czech owners keeping up Germanic standards of cleanliness and domesticity. There's a pension in the centre of the village, and, just to the south, across a ford, a **campsite** and swimming pool (open in high season only).

The Kamenice gorge

Another option from Mezní Louka is to walk the 2km southwest to **MEZNÁ**, an unassuming little village that basks in a sunny meadow above the River Kamenice. From the village green, a green-marked path plunges a hundred feet down to the cool, dank shade of the river, traversed by means of the wooden Mezní můstek bridge. Here, you have a choice of heading up or down the **Kamenice gorge** to the landing stages, from where boatmen will take you on a short but dramatic boat trip down (or up) the river. The trips (May to mid-Sept) are justifiably popular, so be prepared to wait a couple of hours at least in high season. The downstream trip drops you at the edge of Hřensko (see above), while the upstream one unloads its passengers close to Dolský Mlýn. If you're keen to do some more walking, take the latter trip and continue along the yellow-marked path up a shallower gorge to Jetřichovice, about 3km east.

Děčínské stěny

If your sole aim is to see the rocks, it's simplest to catch a bus from Děčín to Tisá; or take the train to LIBOUCHEC station and walk the 2.5km north to Tisá. If, however, you're intent on a day's walking, follow the red-marked path from the Tyršův most in Děčín for 10km to **Děčínský Sněžník** (728m), a giant rock plateau that has thrust itself up above the decaying tree line. At the summit, there's an old tower that you can climb for a great view over the flat, forested landscape towards Dresden, and back over to the Jetřichovické stěny. If you're in a hurry to get to Tisá, follow the tarmacked road, rather than the red-marked path which swings north to OSTROV, the last village before the border, before returning to the main road (the nearest border crossing is the 24hr one at Petrovice, on the other side of Tisá).

From the village of **TISÁ** itself, the **Tiské stěny** are hidden from view, but climb the hill and the whole "sandstone city" opens up before you. Sandy trails crisscross this secret gully and it's fairly simple to get to the top of one or two of the gigantic boulders without any specialist equipment. You could spend hours here, exploring, picnicking and taking in the panoramic views. Via Děčínský Sněžník, it's a full day's walk from Děčín, so if you want to hole up here for the night, there's private accommodation in the village, and a **motel** and **campsite** (open all year) just off the road northwest to Nový Dvůr.

On from the České Švýcarsko

If you've got your own transport, **ČESKÁ KAMENICE** (Böhmisch Kamnitz), 18km east of Děčín, is a possible alternative base for exploring the České Švýcarsko. For a start, it's a lot more pleasant to rest up in than Děčín, with its interesting blend of nineteenth-century Habsburg edifices, and the odd wooden folk building. There's just one hotel, the *Slavie* (☎0412/95 21 22; ①) on the main square, but it's rarely full.

Five kilometres east of Česká Kamenice, on the other side of KAMENICKÝ ŠENOV, is another, much rarer geological phenomenon: the **Panská skála**, a series of polygonal basalt columns that's basically a miniature Giant's Causeway, minus the sea. They are the result of a massive subterranean explosion millions of years ago, during which molten basalt was spewed out onto the surface, and cooled into what are, essentially, crystals. Without a doubt, they make a strange, supernatural sight in this unassuming rolling countryside, but are too small to be really awe-inspiring. Unlike Ireland's major tourist attraction, the Panská skála are easily missed, even though they're only 500m south of Route 13; ask the bus driver to tell you when to get out.

Another 5km east is one of the numerous glass-making towns in the region, **NOVÝ BOR** (Haida). What makes it stand out from the rest is its **Glass Museum** (Sklenarské muzeum; Tues–Sun 9am–noon & 1–4pm), which contains a particularly rich collection of glassware, including a functionalist tea set by Adolf Loos and a great Art-Deco *vitraille*. The museum is on the main square, itself a typical mixture of folk cottages and late nineteenth-century industrial wealth.

Liberec and around

Lying comfortably in the broad east–west sweep of the Nisa valley, framed by the Jizera mountains to the north and the isolated peak of Ještěd to the south, **LIBEREC** (Reichenberg) couldn't hope for a grander location. The town itself, made prosperous by its famous textiles, can't quite live up to its setting, but it's lively and bustling, with a smattering of interesting buildings and a couple of fairly good museums, all of which could keep you happily amused for the best part of a day.

The Town

From Liberec train station, jump on tram #1, #2 or #3, or walk for five minutes down 1 máje to the town's sublime brown and orange giant department store on Soukenné náměstí. From here, it's a short steep walk up the bustling cobbles of Pražská to the main square, náměstí dr E. Beneše.

Liberec's cathedral-like **Rathaus**, totally dominating the main square, is probably the most telling monument the chauvinistic *Reichenberger* could have bestowed on the city. Purposely designed to recall Vienna's own town hall, its lofty trio of neo-Renaissance copper cupolas completes the effect with an impressive Flemish flourish. Several cafés now spread their tables out onto the square, from which you can contemplate this great German edifice, and soak in the scene.

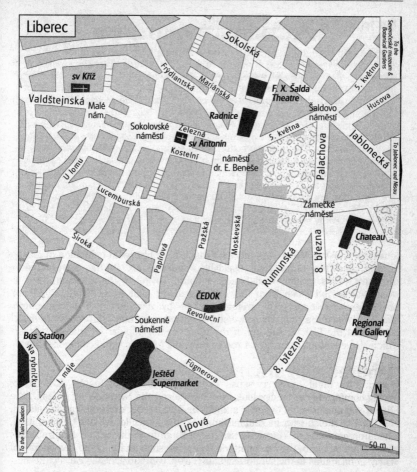

As for the rest of the town, there's an offbeat collection of paintings and sculpture at the **Regional Art Gallery** (Oblastní galerie; Tues–Sun 10am–6pm), a white nineteenth-century building off 8 květná that has been a gallery since 1873. Its unusually large collection includes a series of nineteenth-century French landscapes and some much earlier Dutch and Flemish masters, all of which were bequeathed to the gallery by the local German industrialist Johann Liebig, but none of which is outstanding, with the exception of the one and only Rembrandt. In addition, there's now a fairly wide range of modern Czech paintings and sculptures, including two striking female portraits by the Impressionists Jiránek and Hudeček, a room of Cubist and Fauvist canvases, containing Josef Čapek's much reproduced *Woman Over the City*, and a new, uncensored postwar section.

Across the newly replanted formal gardens is the town's rouge and cream sixteenth-century **chateau**, previously owned by the Clam-Gallas family, but now converted into a trade centre concentrating on promoting the local glass industry.

KONRAD HENLEIN IN REICHENBERG

Had Liberec been a little further northwest, it could have lived on in the postwar world as Reichenberg. Sited just the wrong side of the historical borders of Germany, the *Reichenbergers* made up for this geographical oversight with their ardent Pan-Germanism. It was the home town of the First Republic's ultimate fifth columnist, **Konrad Henlein**, born in the nearby village of Reichenau (Rychnov) in 1898 and destined to become the leader of the pro-Nazi Sudeten German Party (SdP). Henlein played an unheroic role in World War I, and after a spell as a bank clerk in Reichenau he became a gym teacher in the pure German town of Asch (Aš) in West Bohemia. The combined effects of the slump and the events in the neighbouring German Reich excited the Sudeten Germans, who proclaimed Henlein their *Führer* at a huge rally outside Saaz (Žatec) in 1933. When the newly formed SdP won roughly two-thirds of the German vote in the 1935 elections (thus becoming the largest single party in the country), Reichenberg became a centre of pro-Nazi sentiment. However, few of the Germans survived the postwar expulsions and Liberec (unlike Cheb) was swiftly repopulated and successfully Czechified after the war.

Intruders aren't welcome, but there's a much finer historical exhibition of glass-making, and the other local speciality, clothmaking, in the **Severočeské muzeum** (Tues 1–5pm, Wed–Sun 9am–5pm). To get to the museum, itself a wonderful period piece from the 1890s, walk or take tram #1, #2 or #3 up Masarykova, a long, leafy avenue flanked by decadent turn-of-the-century mansions, once the property of wealthy *Reichenberger*, now converted into flats, clinics and the like. At the top of the road are the popular botanical gardens, which also encompass the oldest **zoo** in Bohemia (if that's any recommendation).

Ještěd

Liberec's top hotel – in every sense – sits on the summit of **Ještěd** (1012m) or *Jeschken*, from which you can look over into Poland and Germany on a clear day. Even if you don't decide to stay the night, be sure to check out the bar-cum-diner and the restaurant with its crazy mirrors, either of which wouldn't look out of place in an episode of *Thunderbirds*. To get there from the centre of town, take tram #3 to the end of the line and then follow the signs to the **cable car** (*lánovka dráha*), which runs to the summit and hotel from 6am to 10pm all year.

Practicalities

ČEDOK, at Revoluční 66 (Mon–Fri 9am–4.30pm, Sat 9–11.30am) are still probably the best source of **information**, though they're unlikely to be able to speak anything but German and Czech.

Česká Beseda, Na rybničku 14 (☎048/231 61). Next door to the bus terminal, and one of Liberec's rock-bottom hotels. ①

Dům rekreace, Šaldovo náměstí. Modern red-brick hotel, but very centrally located. ③

Imperial, 1 máje 29 (☎048/280 51). Top-notch but fairly reasonably priced with it. Close to both train and bus stations. ③

Ještěd, Horní Hanychov (☎048/340 21). Unbeatable location, view and decor, for – all things considered – bargain prices. ③–④

Praha, Železná 2 (☎048/289 53). Very comfortable new hotel on the main square, with a hint of its Art-Nouveau origins. ⑤

Camping Stadión Pavlovice, Letná (☎048/364 06). Flash campsite, complete with heated swimming pool, in the midst of a half-built housing estate (bus #22 to the end of the line). Open mid-April to mid-Oct.

Eating and drinking

As for **restaurants**, the *Radnická restaurace* (daily 10am–10pm) serves up typical Czech meals and *Budvar* under the high vaulted ceiling of the town hall cellars. For something a bit more special, check out the *Pošta*, across the road from the town theatre, on the corner of Mariánská. Decorated inside in white and gold Neoclassical style, with dazzling chandeliers, it conjures up turn-of-the-century Reichenberg beautifully. At the other end of the scale, try the seedy *Sadovna* on Sokolovské náměstí (Mon–Fri 3–11pm), which doles out *Velkopopovický kozel*. On Pražská, it's worth exploring the terrace of *U zlatého džbánu* (closed Sun), half-way down on the right, or the pizza place at no. 10.

Jablonec nad Nisou

JABLONEC NAD NISOU (Gablonz) starts almost before the southwestern suburbs of Liberec end. It began life as a small Czech village but was cut short in its prime by the Hussite Wars, when the whole area was laid waste by the neighbouring Catholic Lusatians. Apocryphally, the only survivor was the large apple tree (*jabloň*) that stood on the village green and gave the subsequent town its name. From the sixteenth century onwards, it was better known as Gablonz, the name used by the Saxon glassmakers who began to settle in the area, but it wasn't until the late nineteenth century that the town's **jewellery trade** really took off.

By the turn of the century Gablonz was exporting its produce to all corners of the globe, and its burghers grew very rich indeed, building themselves mansions fit for millionaires and endowing the town with lavish public buildings. In 1945 that all changed – almost the entire (German) population of 100,000 was expelled – and threw the local glass industry into a crisis that lasted for decades. Meanwhile, uniquely for German refugees from Eastern Europe, nearly a fifth of the exiled townsfolk resettled in a suburb of Kaufbeuren, in Bavarian Swabia, which they named Neugablonz after their Bohemian hometown.

The Town

The main reason for venturing into Jablonec is to visit the engaging **Glass and Jewellery Museum**, one block east off the main square down U muzea (Tues–Sun 9am–noon & 1–4pm), which traces the history of the two intertwined industries. Chandeliers and garnets are the two Bohemian specialities to look out for, as is the superb collection of turn-of-the-century and Art-Deco pieces.

Outside, despite the obvious former wealth of the town, the turn-of-the-century houses have generally not been well looked after. A prime example is the potentially graceful Secessionist **Starokatolický kostel** (open for services only) 500m or so east of the centre, just off Route 4 to Tanvald. The town also boasts a number of dour 1930s structures, which have lasted a bit better, most notably the **Nová radnice**, whose slimline clock tower dominates the skyline. Up the hill from the town hall, local boy Josef Zasche was the architect responsible for the gargantuan brick-built **Church of the Sacred Heart**, which towers over náměstí Rudé armády.

Practicalities

You can reach Jablonec on tram #11 from Liberec, which winds its way scenically up the Nisa valley. If you'd prefer to stay here rather than Liberec, there's a wide choice of cheap **hotels**, starting with the *Corso* (☎0428/243 23; ①) on the main square, Radniční náměstí. One block west, the *Zlatý lev* (☎0428/239 42; ①), a converted seventeenth-century blacksmiths on Kostelní, is a more attractive prospect. *Na baště*, by Zasche's church, is currently under reconstruction, but should be open again soon.

On warm summer days, the people of Jablonec head out to the nearby **Mšeno lake** for a spot of sunbathing and swimming; should you wish to join them, take bus #1 or #7 from the centre of town.

The Jizera Mountains and Frýdlant

Northeast of Liberec, and reachable by tram #3 or #4 from the town, the **Jizera Mountains** (Isergebirge) form the western edge of the Krkonoše range which, in turn, makes up the northern border of Bohemia. Like their eastern neighbours, they have been very badly affected by acid rain, compounded by the proximity of the Bogatynia power station just over the border in Poland. The mountains rise suddenly from Liberec's northern suburbs to over 1000m high – and that's part of the problem, since at such a height they soak up every cloud of filth that floats by. The upper reaches, once covered in thick pine and even the odd patch of virgin forest, are now desolate and depressing. The Czechs and Germans, seemingly unperturbed, flock there still, but it's best to steer clear of the mountains themselves altogether.

Frýdlant

> *It was neither an old stronghold nor a new mansion, but a rambling pile consisting of innumerable small buildings closely packed together and of one or two storeys; if K had not known that it was a castle he might have taken it for a little town.*
>
> Franz Kafka, *The Castle*

The hybrid sprawling *Schloss* at **FRÝDLANT** (Friedland), a town on the north side of the frontier mountains, forty minutes by train from Liberec, was one of the models for Kafka's novel *The Castle*. Like his fictional character *K*, Kafka came here on business, not as a land surveyor but as an accident insurance clerk, a job he did for most of his brief life. In Kafka's time the castle was still owned by the Clam-Gallas clan, but its most famous duke was Albrecht von Waldstein, whose statue still stands in the town's main square.

The **castle** (daily April, Sept & Oct 9am–noon & 1–3pm; May–Aug 8am–noon & 1–4pm) is ensconced on a rock over the river, a short walk from the town centre along a pretty tree-lined avenue. The two-hour guided tour might be a bit too much for some people, but the interior is, for once, richly furnished and in good condition, having been a museum now for almost two hundred years.

If you want to stay in the area, there's a large, friendly **campsite** by a bend in the river below the approach to the castle, or the *Valdštejn* **hotel** (☎0427/212 88; ①) on Míru. Otherwise, you could try the nearby village of HEJNICE, 10km southeast (30min by train; change at RASPENAVA), where the *Perun* (☎0427/933 51; ①), within sight of the village's towering pilgrimage church, usually has rooms. There's a Polish border crossing 13km north of Frýdlant at Habartice-Zawidów, on the road to Zgorzelec/Görlitz.

travel details

Trains

Connections with Prague Bohušovice (9 daily; 1hr 10min–2hr); Děčín (18 daily; 1hr 40min–3hr 30min); Teplice (3 daily; 2hr); Liberec (3 daily; 2hr 45min).

From Litoměřice to Děčín (5 daily; 1hr 10min); Mělník (9 daily; 30–45min); Ploskovice/Úštěk (11 daily; 12min/35min); Liberec (7 daily; 3hr 15min).

From Liberec to Frýdlant (up to 11 daily; 40min); Jablonec nad Nisou/Železný Brod (8 daily; 30min/ 2hr); Turnov (16 daily; 50min).

Buses (ČSAD only)

Connections with Prague Terezín (up to 12 daily; 1hr 10min); Litoměřice (up to 20 daily; 1hr 15min); Liberec (up to hourly; 1hr 40min).

From Teplice to Litoměřice (7 daily; 1hr 10min); Děčín (up to 6 daily; 1hr 20min).

From Děčín to Liberec (up to 3 daily; 2hr 10min).

From Liberec to Vrchlabí (up to 6 daily; 2–3hr); Hradec Králové (up to 5 daily; 1hr 50min).

CHAPTER FIVE

EAST BOHEMIA

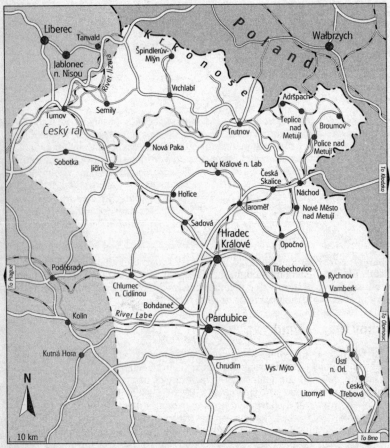

East Bohemia (Východní Čechy) is probably the most difficult Czech region to categorise. It has none of the polluting industry of its immediate neighbours, though it has suffered indirectly from their excesses; it contains some of the flattest landscape in Bohemia, but also its highest peaks; it has been historically predominantly Czech, though pockets of German settlement have left their mark in the culture and architecture. Lastly, though the region has never had fixed borders, the confusion is heightened by the administrative borders currently in operation, which have arbitrarily added on parts of Moravia.

For variety of scenery, East Bohemia is hard to beat. Along the northern border with Poland, the peaks of the **Krkonoše** and the **Orlické hory** form an almost continuous mountain range. However, the havoc wreaked by acid rain is depressing and unavoidable on the summits: only in the valley bottoms, and the foothills, are its effects less noticeable. The **Český ráj**, to the south, and the area around **Broumov** to the east have escaped the worst of the damage – both are archetypally Bohemian landscapes, rocky sandstone regions covered in thick forest. Further south still, the terrain on either side of the River Labe – the *Polabí* as it is known – is flat, fertile and, for the most part, fairly dull. But the towns of the river basin do much to make up for it – **Hradec Králové**, the regional capital, and its historic rival, **Pardubice**, both boast handsomely preserved historic centres.

Český ráj

Less than 100km from Prague, the sandstone rocks and densely wooded hills of the **Český ráj** (Bohemian Paradise) have been a popular spot for weekending Praguers for over a century now. Although the Český ráj is officially limited to a small nature reserve southeast of Turnov, the term is loosely applied to the entire swathe of hills from Mnichovo Hradiště to Jičín. **Turnov** is the most convenient base for exploring the region, but there's little incentive to stay there. Infinitely more appealing is **Jičín**, which has preserved its seventeenth-century old town intact. But more interesting than either of the towns is the surrounding **countryside**: ruined fortresses, bizarre rock formations and traditional folk architecture, all smothered in a blanket of pine forests.

From Turnov, local **trains** run roughly every two hours to Jičín; local **buses** from both towns infrequently wind their way through the otherwise inaccessible villages nearby. Generally, though, the distances are so small – Turnov to Jičín, for example, is just 24km – that you might as well buy the *Český ráj Poděbradsko* map and **walk** along the marked footpaths.

Turnov and around

TURNOV (Turnau) is somewhat short on excitement. Aside from the **Český ráj museum**, containing an interminable collection of semiprecious stones dug out of a nearby hillside, and temporary exhibitions of nature photography, there's nothing to see here except grimy streets. If you're spending your days walking, though, you may find it convenient **to stay** overnight here; *Hotel Sport* (☎0436/636; ①), near the football stadium, or the cheaper *Slavie* (①), just off the main square, occasionally have vacancies. Alternatively, *ČEDOK* (on the main square) may be able to rustle up a hostel bed or a hotel room in a nearby town.

One place worth heading for, on the outskirts of Turnov, is the chateau of **Hrubý Rohozec** (Tues–Sun April, Sept & Oct 9am–noon & 1–4pm; May–Aug 8am–noon & 1–5pm), high up on the left bank of the Jizera river, just off Route 10 to Železný Brod. A Gothic castle, redesigned in the Renaissance, it is a welcome contrast to the rest of the town, its hour-long guided tour dishing out some great views, and a series of handsome Renaissance chambers. On the road up to the chateau there are some **private rooms** to rent – probably the best accommodation in Turnov.

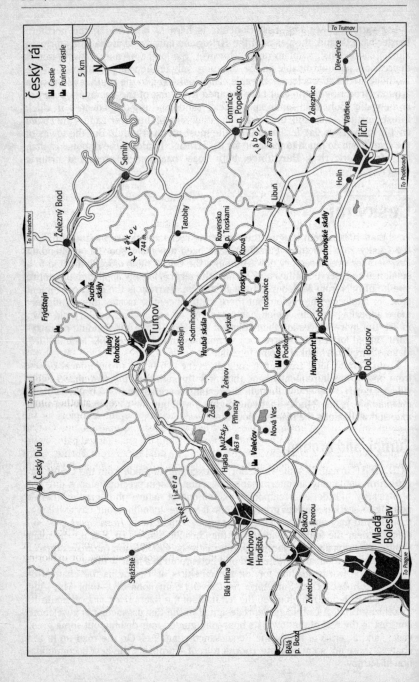

Valdštejn and Hrubá skála

Two kilometres through the woods from the Turnov-město railway station (one stop down the Jičín line) is the former Gothic stronghold of **Valdštejn** (May–Sept 15 Tues–Sun 9am–4.30pm), the ancestral castle of the Waldstein family for many years. Already in ruins by the late sixteenth century, it was occupied by vagrants, and later attempts to restore it never came to fruition, though its position remains impressive – as does the eighteenth-century stone bridge, flanked by Baroque statues.

Another 2km southeast, the first (and arguably the best) of Český ráj's *skalní město* or "sandstone cities", **Hrubá skála** (also, confusingly, the name of the nearby village), unfolds amidst the trees. It's easy to spend hours clambering up and down the bluffs and dodging the crevices, whose names – *Myší díra* (Mouse Hole), *Dračí věž* (Dragon's Tower) and *Sahara* – give some idea of the variety of rock formations to be found here. Various viewpoints, like *Zamecká vyhlídka* or *Mariánská vyhlídka*, range high above the tree line, with the protruding stone slabs emerging from the pine trees like ossified giants.

The nearby **chateau** is a colossal nineteenth-century reconstruction of the original Gothic castle: very popular with Czech film crews, but closed to the public. From here, a green-marked path descends through the *Myší díra* and the *Dračí skály*, zigzagging down to a large lakeside **campsite** (April–Oct) near the Karlovice-Sedmihorky station on the Turnov–Jičín line.

Trosky

The spectacular ruined castle of **Trosky** (which means literally "rubble"), 5km southeast of Hrubá skála, is the Český ráj's number-one landmark. Its twin Gothic towers, *Bába* (Grandmother) and *Panna* (Virgin), were built on volcanic basalt rocks which burst through the sandstone strata millions of years ago. You can climb *Bába* for a far-reaching view of the Jizera basin, but *Panna*, the higher of the two, is suitably out of bounds. Although the brooding ruin is officially only open at the weekend (April–Sept), it's easy enough to gain access at other times. There's a flash new **hotel** (☎0436/91290; ①) and restaurant complex by the castle car park, with cheap doubles, and two very basic **campsites**, one a short distance to the south, the other 2km northwest along the red-marked path, by the Vidlák lake. Getting to Trosky, three or four daily **buses** run from Turnov, but it may be quicker to take the train to Ktová station on the Jičín line, and walk 2km uphill.

Sobotka and around

Compared to Turnov or Jičín, **SOBOTKA** is off the beaten track: 13km from either place, hotel-less, and only accessible by train from Jičín (50min; change at Libuň). Unless you're camping (and hiking), it's no good as a base for exploring the region, though it does harbour some good examples of the local brightly painted half-timbered architecture and – just northwest of the town, on a strange conical hill – the striking seventeenth-century **Humprecht hunting lodge** (April–Sept Tues–Sun 8am–noon & 1–5pm), named for its eccentric aristocratic instigator, Jan Humprecht Černín. It's a bizarre building, worth a peek inside if only for the central *trompe l'oeil* dining room, a windowless 16-metre-high oval cylinder with the acoustics of a cathedral. On the other side of the hill from Sobotka is a rudimentary **campsite** (mid-June to Sept) and swimming pool.

Podkost

One bus daily (at around 1pm) covers the 3km northwest from Sobotka to **PODKOST**, a small settlement by a pond at the edge of the Žehrov forest. The village is dominated in every way by **Kost** castle (April, Sept & Oct Tues–Sun 9am–noon & 1–4pm; May–Aug 8am–noon & 1–5pm; 50min guided tour), which sits on top of a gigantic sandstone pedestal and sports a characteristic rectangular keep. Thanks to a fire in 1635 – after which it was used as a granary – Kost retains the full flavour of its fourteenth-century origins. The late Gothic art exhibition is well worth seeing, too, but to do so you have to sign up with a tour, and since Kost is by far the best preserved castle in the Český ráj, tour groups congregate early. Down in the village, *Hotel Podkost* (☎0433/931 27; ①) is good for a bed or a beer.

Around Mužský

You're more likely to find available accommodation another 4km northwest along the scenic red-marked path through the woods of the Žehrovský les, at **NOVÁ VES**, a tiny village by the **Komárovský lake**, which has three campsites and a hotel on its banks. North of the lake lies a matrix of paths that crisscrosses the complex rock systems, leaving the forest after 3km at the hotel and campsite in **PŘÍHRAZY**. Paths spread out west from here, back into the woods, emerging only to ascend **Mužský** (463m), but otherwise continuing for 2km to the prehistoric burial ground of Hrada and the rocky viewpoint at Drábské světničky. The truly amazing sight of **Valečov**, a ruined fort cut into the rock, lies another 2km to the south at the southwestern edge of the woodland. On a day's hike, you could easily do a round trip from Nová Ves or Příhrazy by heading east from Valečov, or else continue for another 3km west to the station at MNICHOVO HRADIŠTĚ, on the main railway line to Prague.

Jičín and around

At the southeastern tip of the Český ráj, where the fertile plain of the River Labe touches the foothills of the Krkonoše, **JIČÍN** (Gitschin), an hour by train from Turnov, is easily the most rewarding stop in the region. Its location, close to some of the Český ráj's most dramatic scenery, makes it a convenient base for some easy hiking, while its Renaissance chateau and arcaded main square make it by far the most attractive place to stay.

The Town

The town is closely associated with the infamous **Albrecht von Waldstein** (better known as Wallenstein), who, during his brief and meteoric rise to eminence (see p.162), owned almost every chateau in the region. Waldstein confiscated Jičín early on in the Thirty Years' War, and chose this rather unlikely town as the capital of his new personal empire, the Duchy of Friedland. In the 1620s he rebuilt the main square – now named **Valdštejnovo náměstí** after him – in stone, in a late Renaissance style, full of light touches.

One side is still dominated by Waldstein's **chateau**, which now contains the town museum and, in the converted riding school, an art gallery, as well as the great conference hall in which the leaders of the three great European powers, Russia, Austria and Prussia, signed the Holy Alliance against Napoleon in 1813. A covered passage connects the chateau's eastern wing with the Jesuit church next door, allowing the nobility to avoid their unsavoury subjects while en route to mass. But this steeple-less Baroque church is eclipsed by the mighty sixteenth-century **Valdická brána** (Tues–Sun 10am–6pm) close by, whose tower gallery offers a panorama over the town.

One of Waldstein's more endearing additions to the town is the **lipová alej**, an avenue of lime trees, 1200 in all, planted simultaneously in two dead straight lines, 2km long, by Waldstein's soldiers. At the far end is the once princely garden of **Libosad**, now an overgrown spinney but still worth a wander. The melancholy of its Renaissance loggia, last repaired at the end of the First Republic, is easily over-shadowed by the horror of one of the country's most brutal Communist prisons in nearby **VALDICE**. Originally a seventeenth-century Carthusian monastery, it was converted into a prison by the Habsburgs, and used after 1948 to keep the regime's political prisoners in a suitably medieval state of deprivation.

Practicalities

At present, **accommodation** in Jičín is limited to the *Start* (☎0433/233 63; ②), a modern hotel 1km down the lime tree avenue that leads to Valdice – that is, until the *Astra*, east off the main square, is reopened. *Sportcentrum*, at no. 2 on the main square, can book you a room in its sports complex, 4km north of Jičín, off Route 35 to Turnov. Two kilometres down Route 16 to Mladá Boleslav, there's also a **motel**, *Rumcajs* (☎0433/214 00; ①), with a **campsite** and wooden **chalets** (May–Sept).

There are two new **restaurants** to choose from in the old town: *U Valdštejna*, in the arcades along from the chateau, and *U Rynečku*, down Chelčického – both closed on Sundays – plus the old beery faithfuls, *Hotel Praha* on Husova and *U anděla* on the main square. Given the dearth of public transport in the region, you might want to make use of the **bike rental** service offered at *Cyklocentrum*, between the centre of town and the above-mentioned motel.

Prachovské skály

Despite the very real attractions of the town, the reason most people come to Jičín is to see the **Prachovské skály**, a series of sandstone and basalt rocks hidden in woods 6km to the northwest. There's an occasional local bus, but it's a gentle walk, via the *Rumcajs* campsite, to the rocks. They lack the subtlety of the Hrubá skála formations, but make up for it in sheer size and area; their name derives from the dust (*prach*) that covers the forest floor, forming a carpet of sand. In high season, swarms of climbers cling to the silent, grey rocks like a plague of locusts, but out of season it's possible to find a tranquil spot; try the green-marked path.

Železný Brod and Malá Skála

Heading northeast from Turnov, the railway follows the course of the Jizera river to **ŽELEZNÝ BROD** (Eisenbrod), one of the many centres of Bohemia's world-famous glass-making industry. It's a town of contradictions, its factories and high-rises spread along the banks of the river, while half-timbered cottages in the tradi-tional Český ráj colours cover the hillside. The tiny main square is a typical mix of styles: one side is taken up by two wholly uninspiring 1950s buildings – the glass and crystal factory, and the *Hotel Cristal* – while the other side shelters the nine-teenth-century town hall and the timber-framed local **museum**, which displays local arts and crafts. Up the hillside by the town church, which sports a nifty little wooden belfry, are some outstanding examples of **folk architecture**, usually confined to more inaccessible villages.

Six kilometres back down the valley towards Turnov (and also accessible by train) is the village of **MALÁ SKÁLA**. A steep red-marked path leads from the village to the **Suché skály** (Silent Rocks) and a number of rock caves, used during the Counter-Reformation as safe houses for persecuted Protestants. Alternatively, there's a red-marked path that follows a ridge on the other side of the river; the view across the valley to the ruined castle of Frýdštejn is the reward you get for your pains. Should you wish to stay the night, there's a **campsite** on the right bank of the river, and a **hotel**, the *Jizera* (☎0428/772 02; ①), on the same side of the river, up a hillside 500m further north.

The Krkonoše

The **Krkonoše** (Giant Mountains) are the highest mountains in Bohemia, and formed part of the historical northeastern border of its ancient kingdom. They remained uninhabited until the sixteenth and seventeenth centuries, when glass-making and ore-mining brought the first German and Italian settlers to the Riesengebirge, as they were then known. The mountains' undoubted beauty ensured an early tourist following, and, for resorts like Špindlerův Mlýn, it's now the sole industry. Despite being one of the few protected national parks in the country, since the war thousands upon thousands of trees have become fatally weakened by **acid rain** (the annual level of rainfall here is among the highest in the country). Once the trees are badly affected, insects do the rest, transforming them into grey husks, devoid of foliage. Extensive felling has been the government's hopelessly inadequate response so far, aimed at stopping the spread of the destructive insects – rather like a smoker removing a set of lungs to prevent cancer.

For many people, the fate of Bohemia's ancient forests is the most damning indictment of the Communists' forty years of mismanagement, and as if to rub the matter in, despite the irretrievable damage, the focus over the last ten years has been on new hotels and chairlifts rather than environmental measures. Since 1989, though, all the political parties have paid lip service to the importance of environmental issues, but the Right, in particular, has clearly stated that the country cannot afford the luxury of (expensive) green policies in the switch to a market economy.

Czechs will reassure you that things here are nowhere near as bad as in the Krušné hory (see p.203), and it's true: if you stay in the largely unspoiled valley bottom, or come here in winter, when the snow obscures much of the damage, it's possible to be lulled into a false sense of security. In summer, though, when walking is the main mode of transport, it's well-nigh impossible to ignore the rain's effects. Basically, the situation is worse the further west and the higher up you go, so if you want to avoid the badly hit areas, keep east, and keep low.

Some practicalities

These grim realities fail to deter the coachloads, which makes **accommodation** difficult to obtain at the height of summer. That said, the cheap and abundant **private rooms** that have sprung up all over the region make life a lot easier. The main *ČEDOK* office in Vrchlabí still has some influence with the **hotels** in the resorts. Theoretically, you can also stay at one of the **bouda** (chalets) dotted across the mountains, originally hideouts for the fleeing Protestants of the seven-

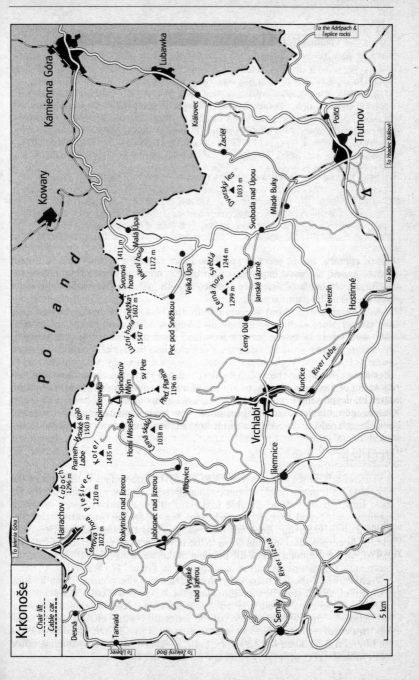

Krkonoše

- - - Chair lift
--- Cable car

To Jelenia Góra

To the Adršpach &
Teplice rocks

P o l a n d

Kamienna Góra

Kowary

Lubawka

Král</
Žacléř

Poříčí

Trutnov

To Hradec Králové

Dvorský les
1033 m

Svoboda nad Úpou

Mladé Buky

Svorová 1411 m
Jelení hora
Malá Úpa
1172 m

Černá hora
1299 m

Janské Lázně

Terezín

Hostinné

To Jičín

Luční hora Sněžka
1547 m 1602 m

Pec pod Sněžkou

Velká Úpa

Čemá hora světlá
1244 m

Čemý Důl

Kunčice

River Labe

Vrchlabí

sv Petr

Špindlerův
Mlýn

Před Planina
1196 m

Špindlerovka

Vysoké kolo
1503 m

K o t e l

Pramen
Labe

Harrachov Luboch
1296 m

Plešivec
1210 m

Čemá skála
1038 m

Horní Mísečky

1435 m

Rokytnice nad Jizerou

Jablonec nad Jizerou

Vítkovice

Ilemnice

Čemova hora
1022 m

Vysoké
nad Jizerou

River Jizera

Desná

Tanvald

Semily

To Liberec

To Železný Brod

N

5 km

To Jelenia Góra

HIKING AND SKIING IN THE KRKONOŠE

A detailed **map** of the mountains, showing the network of colour-coded marked paths, is a must if you intend doing any serious **hiking**. No matter what the season, you should take **warm clothing** even on a hot summer's day – the summits are battered by wind almost every day, and have an average annual temperature of around freezing point. Persistent **mist** – around for about 300 days in the year – makes sticking to the marked paths a must. In winter, most of the high-level paths are closed, and recently, even in summer, several have been closed to give the mountains a rest. To find out the latest details, try the **National Park Information Centre** (May–Sept daily; Oct–April Mon–Fri only), on the Špindlerovka road out of Špindlerův Mlýn.

The Krkonoše is also one of the most popular regions in the Czech Republic for **skiing**, since it receives by far the longest and most reliable snowfall in the country. Queues for lifts can be long and slow, but are more than compensated for by the cheapness of the ski passes and accommodation. It's best to bring your own equipment, since renting gear once you get here is still relatively difficult to do.

teenth century, but in practice you'll be lucky to find a vacancy at any except *Labská bouda*, the most expensive. **Camping** is one way of ensuring a place for the night, although facilities are restricted, with just two sites within the strict boundaries of the national park.

As for transport, **hiking** is undoubtedly the best way of getting around (see box above), since each valley is basically a long, winding dead end for motor vehicles, with pretty hefty car parking fees (and often queues) at the end, aimed at dissuading drivers from bringing their vehicles into the park. **Trains** can get you as far as Harrachov, Vrchlabí and Trutnov; **buses** do actually run right the way to *Špindlerova bouda*, on the Polish border; and there are numerous **chairlifts** that operate even in summer. There are now three **border crossings into Poland**: Harrachov-Jakuszyce and Královec-Lubawka are both 24-hour crossings; Pomezní Boudy-Przelecz Okraj on Route 296 from Trutnov, is for cyclists and pedestrians only, and operates shorter hours (10am–6pm) from October to April.

Vrchlabí

If you can talk in such terms, then **VRCHLABÍ** (Hohenelbe) is the hub of the Krkonoše for transport and accommodation. Reservations are essential for the six daily **buses** from Prague (double that number on a Friday), some of which continue on to Špindlerův Mlýn (see below), but not for the two **trains** a day that make it here (with the *Krakonoš* express, you must change at Kunčice, 4km south). **Accommodation** boils down to the newly renovated *Hotel Labuť* (☎0438/229 64; ③) on the main street; the pension at the zimní stadión (①), south of the centre; and the **campsite** with swimming pool on Route 14 to Semily.

Vrchlabí itself, though marred by the amount of traffic pouring down its long main street, which stretches for 3km along the banks of the Labe, does contain a number of traditional wooden arcaded folk buildings. Aside from some low-key "attractions" – the gardens and zoo of the sixteenth-century chateau, and a small **folk museum** – the town's most important asset is its *ČEDOK* office (☎0438/31 80; Mon–Fri 8–11.30am & 12.30–4pm, Sat 8.30–11.30am), the only **tourist office** that can deal direct with every hotel and *bouda* in the Krkonoše.

Around Špindlerův Mlýn

No doubt **ŠPINDLERŮV MLÝN** (Spindlermühle), 15km north up the Labe valley, was once an idyllic, isolated mountain hamlet. Successive generations, however, have found it difficult to resist exploiting a town where seven valleys meet, and countless private pensions and ugly hotels lie scattered across the hillside (the hotels are likely to be full, but the chances of finding some **private accommodation** are much greater). It's possible to see huge tracts of dead forest from Špindlerův Mlýn itself, but should you want a closer look, there's a chairlift to just below the summit of **Medvědín** (1235m); it's north of the centre, on the way to the **campsite** (mid-May to Sept), and must be approached from the left bank.

The **River Labe**, which flows into the North Sea (as the Elbe) near Hamburg, has its source in the Krkonoše. It takes about three hours to reach the source, the *pramen Labe*: a long, boulder-strewn walk along the valley, followed by a short, sharp climb out of the forest to the modern *Labská bouda* (☎0438/932 21; ②) – more a **hotel** than a *bouda*. Characteristically for the Krkonoše, the summit is disappointingly flat and boggy, and the source itself (500m from the Polish border) no great sight. If you're carrying your pack with you, continue for three hours along the blue-marked track to Harrachov (see below). Otherwise, it's around two hours back to Špindlerův Mlýn, via Horní Misečky and Medvědín. For a **glimpse of Poland**, you should catch a bus from Špindlerův Mlýn to *Špindlerova bouda*, where dead trees, Polish border guards and the odd grazing sheep provide the entertainment.

Harrachov

Five buses and one train a day (change at nearby Tanvald) make the journey from Prague to the westernmost resort in the Krkonoše, **HARRACHOV** (Harrachsdorf), whose cottages are scattered about the Mumlava valley. A glassworks was established here in 1712, and the local **glass museum** has a small sample of its wares throughout the ages. Otherwise, your time is best spent in the surrounding mountains.

Harrachov's **hotels** are usually full, with the possible exception of *CKM*'s moderate *Juniorhotel Fit Fun* (☎0432/92 93 76; ① for *IYHF* members and students, ③ for non-members). This should present few problems, though, since the area is literally swarming with **private accommodation**; to save yourself the legwork, go to the *HIC* (daily 9am–6pm), the information centre near the main road, who can book hotel and private rooms in the area. Alternatively, there's a **campsite** up the road towards the Polish border. For cheap thrills, Harrachov's brand new **chairlift** sends you over the dry tobogganing course to the top of **Čertova hora** (1022m), high enough to view the pollution damage all around.

Pec pod Sněžkou and Janské Lázně

PEC POD SNĚŽKOU (Petzer) is the main hiking base for climbing **Sněžka** (Schneekoppe or Snow Peak), at 1602m the highest mountain in Bohemia, and the most impressive in the entire range. Its bleak, grey summit rises above the tree line, relieving walkers of the painful sight of gently expiring pines, and making for a fine panorama. If you don't fancy the six-kilometre ascent, take the **chairlift** from the village, which will take you right to the top. The border, signified by discreet white and red stone markers, divides the rounded summit; on the

Czech side there's a restaurant (of sorts). But unless Czech–Polish relations take a dramatic turn for the worse, the Polish border guards are unlikely to use the Kalashnikovs that swing nonchalantly at their sides.

Many Czechs use the chairlift as a launching pad for further **hiking**. To the east of the summit, a path follows the narrow mountain ridge (which also marks the border) for 2.5km to another peak, Svorová hora (Czarna Kopa to the Poles). To the west, there's a steep drop, again along the ridge, to *Slezská bouda* (on the Polish side). To reach Špindlerův Mlýn from here (3hr 30min), follow the blue markers (via *Luční bouda*), and not the red and blue ones, which veer into Polish territory.

There are regular **buses from Prague** to Pec pod Sněžkou, plus the occasional one to Janské Lázně (see below), and the *Úpa* express from Prague ends at Svoboda nad Úpou, 3km east of Janské Lázně. As for **accommodation**, Pec has no campsite and little likelihood of vacancies in any of the hotels, so you may have to rely on locals touting private rooms, or on finding a secluded spot where you can pitch your tent.

Janské Lázně

JANSKÉ LÁZNĚ (Johannisbad), hidden away in a sheltered, fertile valley on the southern edge of the national park, has a different atmosphere from the other resorts. Visitors come here to take the cure rather than climb the surrounding peaks (although even the lazy can reach the top of Černá hora by the hourly cable car). On a hot summer's day all the classic images of spa life converge on the central stretch of lawn: a brass band plays "oom-pah-pah" tunes in slightly lackadaisical fashion, while the elderly and disabled spill from the tearoom on to the benches outside. The *Lesní dům*, *Praha* and *Zátiší* are Janské Lázně's **hotels**, in ascending order of price – all fairly cheap (①–③) and usually full, but worth a try.

Trutnov

The modern factories and housing complexes that ring Bohemia's easternmost textile town, **TRUTNOV** (Trautenau), signal the end of the national park, though the town is a useful fall back for the Krkonoše in the height of summer, and makes an equally good base for exploring the Adršpach and Teplice rocks (see below).

The busy arcaded main square, downstream and uphill from the railway station, has been beautifully restored and is closed to vehicles. Alongside the plague column, there's a fountain depicting *Krakonoš* (*Rübezahl* to the Germans), the sylvan spirit who guards the Giant Mountains and gave them their Czech name. All this can be best appreciated from one of the cafés under the arcades of the main square. If you've got some time to kill, there's the odd exhibition at the **museum** in the former *stará škola*, just off the old town square. Trutnov's most recent claim to fame is that, for some time in the early 1970s, **Václav Havel** used to work in the local brewery, which produces a very good beer called *Krakonoš*. His experiences later provided material for *Audience*, one of three plays centred around the character *Vaněk* (a lightly disguised version of himself).

Trutnov's **accommodation** is out of town: the *Horník* (☎0439/69 61; ③) is 1km east towards Poříčí, the *Motel Horal* (☎0439/48 51; ②) 2km out on Route 14 to Vrchlabí, and the nearest **campsite** (mid-June to mid-Sept) is by a small lake, 3km southwest of Trutnov – take the blue-marked path from the centre of town.

East to Broumov

Between Trutnov and Broumov, some 30km east, lie two seemingly innocuous hilly strips smothered in trees, which only on much closer inspection reveal themselves to be riddled with sandstone protrusions and weird rock formations on the same lines as those in Český ráj (see p.223). Distances here are small and the gradients gentle, making it ideal for a bit of none too strenuous – but no less spectacular – **hiking**. If you're thinking of exploring the rocks, get hold of the extremely detailed *Teplicko-Adršpašské skály/Broumovské stěny* map before you get there, which shows all the colour-coded footpaths and the campsites. The local **buses** will get you to the more out-of-the-way places like Broumov, but it's also worth taking advantage of the slow but scenic **train** service from Trutnov to Teplice nad Metují, via Adršpach.

The Adršpach and Teplice rocks

The **Adršpach and Teplice rocks**, 15km east of Trutnov, rise up out of the pine forest like petrified phalluses. Some even take trees with them as they launch themselves hundreds of feet into the air. It's a region that has been popular with German tourists since the nineteenth century, though nowadays they are outnumbered by Czech rock-climbers and ramblers. The rocks are concentrated in two separate *skalní město*, or "rock cities": the Adršpach rocks, just south of the village of the same name, and the Teplice rocks, 2km south through the woods. The latter can also be approached from the villages of Janovice or Teplice.

ADRŠPACH (Adersbach) train station (one stop on from Horní Adršpach) lies at the northern extremity of the rock system, though you can't really miss it, since some of the rocks have crept right up to the station itself. Once you enter the **Adršpašské skalní město**, the outside world recedes and you're surrounded by new sensations – sand underfoot, the scent of pine, boulders and shady trees. Most of the sandstone rocks are dangerous to climb without the correct equipment and experience, so you'll probably have to content yourself with strolling and gawping at the rocks, best described by their nicknames: *Babiččina lenoška* (Grandmother's Armchair), *Španělská stěna* (Spanish Wall) and the ironic *Trpaslík* (Dwarf). After the initial burst of bold and dramatic formations, the green-marked path leads to the Adršpach lake, where Czech kids call out to *Krakonoš* three times, and a waterfall "miraculously" bursts into life.

A couple of kilometres southeast of the Adršpach lake, down the yellow-marked path, you should come to the *Hotel Orlík* on the edge of the woods. An easy approach is from Teplice nad Metují-skály station, just across the river from the hotel, or from Teplice nad Metují itself (see below). Right by the hotel, a blue-marked path heads west to the Anenské údolí. After 1km, you need to switch to the green-marked path, which threads its way through the main valley of the **Teplické skalní město** – another theatrical burst of geological abnormalities.

Teplice nad Metují

Just 1km east of the woods' edge, **TEPLICE NAD METUJÍ** (Wekelsdorf) provides a functional base for the rocks, with a supermarket, a cinema, and a couple of cheap hotels in town, besides the *Orlík* (☎0447/933 66; ①) by the rocks. There's no official campsite, but people are bound to be camping nearby: try attaching yourself to one of the more legitimate-looking clusters of tents. If you're a keen rock-climber, then the annual **festival of mountaineering** held here in early September may be of interest. It's basically an excuse for a lot of boozing and showing off, but specialist climbing films are also shown. It attracts people from all over Europe, who come to share their experiences, many demonstrating their skills on the local formations.

The Broumov walls

The **Broumov walls** (Broumovské stěny) make up a thin sandstone ridge that almost cuts Broumov off from the rest of the country. From the west there's no indication of the approaching precipice, from which a wonderful vista sweeps out over to Broumov and beyond into Poland, but from the east the ridge is clearly spread out before you. The best place to appreciate the view is from Dientzenhofer's chapel of **Panna Marie Sněžná**, situated in among the boulders at the edge of the big drop. The best rock formations are 9km south of here, close by the highest point of the wall, **Božanovský Špičák** (733m), only a few hundred metres from the Polish border.

You can approach the Dienzenhofer chapel from either POLICE NAD METUJÍ, 5km to the southwest, or BROUMOV (see below), 6km to the east. To get to the rocks around Božanovský Špičák, take the bus from Police to MACHOV, and walk the final 3.5km; alternatively, there's the train from Broumov to Božanov, followed by a walk of 3.5km. **Accommodation** is available in Police at the *Ostat* (☎0447/943 44; ①) on the main square, or at the small, basic **campsite** in Machov.

Broumov

BROUMOV (Braunau), 30km due east of Trutnov, is itself no great attraction: a thoroughly German town before the war (a feeling it still retains), it's stuck in the middle of nowhere, and there's no real reason why you should end up here unless you're hiking along the Broumov wall, or wish to visit the unusual **wooden Silesian church** on the Křivinice road out of town. Besides, the town is at its most impressive from a distance, with its colossal Baroque monastery – used by the Communists to incarcerate much of the country's priesthood after 1948 – perched on a sandstone pedestal above the river. Should you need to stay the night, there are two **hotels**: the *Městský hotel* (☎0447/218 53; ①) and the *Praha* (☎0447/213 94; ①), both near the main square.

With a car and a passion for Baroque churches, you could happily spend a more profitable morning exploring the local **Stěnava valley**. In the eighteenth century, Kilian Ignaz Dientzenhofer, Bohemia's foremost ecclesiastical architect, was chosen by the local abbot to redesign the Broumov monastery. He was also commissioned to build numerous **village churches** in the area (and in the Klodzko region, over the border in Poland), in an attempt to Catholicise the staunchly Protestant Silesian Germans who used to live here. With each church, he experimented with a different design – a simple oval plan at VERNEŘOVICE (Wernersdorf), an elongated octagon at RUPRECHTICE (Rupperdorf), a crushed oval at VIŽŇOV (Wiesen). Most are now down to their bricks and mortar and firmly closed, but the key is usually easily traceable, and the effort well rewarded.

Náchod and around

Cowering at the base of its large lordly seat, built to guard the gateway to Bohemia from Silesia, **NÁCHOD** is one of the few Czech border towns that has been predominantly Czech for most of its life. Even the Nazis stopped short of annexing it when they marched into the Sudetenland in 1938, since at the time there were only four German-speaking families in the whole town. Nowadays, most people just stop off in order to break the journey and spend their last remaining crowns en route to Poland – the border is a couple of kilometres east of the town centre.

In fact, Náchod is a lot better looking than your average border town: the main square, in particular, **náměstí T. G. Masaryka**, has had a new lease of life following its recent restoration. Its two most appealing buildings are the fourteenth-century church of **sv Vavřinec** (St Lawrence) at the centre, sporting two comically large wooden onion domes, and, to one side, the Art-Nouveau **Hotel U Beránků**, which looks stunning in its gold trimming. Peeking out of the foliage, high above the town centre, and a very stiff climb through the woods, is the town's unassailable sgraffitoed **chateau** (April–Oct Tues–Sun 9am–noon & 1–4pm). The original Gothic castle of the Smiřický family survives only in the single round tower; everything else you see is the result of successive building projects during the Renaissance. Inside there's an interesting hotchpotch of furnishings and exhibits, accrued over the centuries by the Piccolomini family, plus an art collection courtesy of the Duke of Kurland.

You can **stay the night** at the aforementioned *Beránek* (☎0441/217 52; ②), and as a last resort, at the *Hron* (☎0441/207 52; ①) on the Dobrošov road, or the **campsite** (mid-May to mid-Sept) 2km east at BĚLOVES, by the Polish border.

Nové Město nad Metují

In many ways **NOVÉ MĚSTO NAD METUJÍ**, 9km south of Náchod, is an archetypal Bohemian town, divided into two mutually exclusive historical areas. While its bustling modern quarter sprawls unattractively northwards, the preserved medieval part sits quietly (and extremely prettily) on a high spur hemmed in by a tributary of the River Labe. Restored sixteenth-century houses line each side of the rectangular arcaded main square, no doubt once a busy market place, now

---

THE COWARDS IN NÁCHOD

The exiled writer **Josef Škvorecký** was born and bred in Náchod – a "narrow cleavage between the mountains", as he characteristically dubbed it. During his wartime adolescence he was joined by film-director-to-be Miloš Forman, then only a young boy, who came to stay with his uncle when his parents were sent to a concentration camp from which they never returned. Later, in the cultural thaw of the 1960s, before they were both forced to emigrate, the two men planned (unsuccessfully) to make a film based on *The Cowards*, Škvorecký's most famous novel. Set in "a small Bohemian town" (ie Náchod) in the last few days of the war, the book caused a sensation when it was published (briefly) in 1958 because of its bawdy treatment of Czech resistance to the Nazis. Škvorecký also set the action of a later novel, *The Miracle Game*, in the nearby village of Hronov. In both novels, the name of the main character is Danny Smiřický, supposedly a descendant of one of the most powerful aristocratic families in the region, the Smiřickýs.

maintaining a museum-like silence only occasionally disturbed by the arrival of coach parties.

What makes Nové Město's old town extra special is its remarkable seventeenth-century **chateau** (April & Oct Sat & Sun 9am–noon & 1–4pm; May–Aug Tues–Sun 8am–noon & 1–5pm; Sept Tues–Sun 9am–noon & 1–5pm), which looks out across the Labe basin (known as the *Polabí*) from the northeast corner of the square. After piecemeal alterations over the centuries, it fell into disrepair in the nineteenth century, until the industrialist Josef Bartoň bought the place in 1908. Bartoň commissioned the quirky Slovak architect **Dušan Jurkovič** to entirely redesign the place – which he did, most notably with the timber-framed structures, redolent of his native land, in the terraced gardens, and the bizarre wall-to-wall leather vaulting of the *Žebrový sál* (Ribbed Hall). The other rooms are lavishly furnished in every period from the original Renaissance to highly unusual works by Czech Cubists like **Pavel Janák**. Along the bridge across the moat, and on the wall of the terrace, Bartoň placed a set of dwarves by the Baroque sculptor Braun. Bartoň eventually died here in 1951, at the ripe old age of 98. In an uncharacteristically magnanimous gesture, the Communists had allowed him and his wife (and their cook) to live out their last days in three rooms at the top of the chateau.

The town is a beautiful eight-kilometre **walk** from Náchod down the winding River Metuje (yellow-marked path, followed by red), for those with the time and inclination. If you arrive here by **train**, you'll end up 2km northwest of the chateau, in Nové Město's new town; town (and *ČSAD*) buses link the old town square with the station. If you arrive by **bus** from Náchod or Hradec Králové, you can get off at the old town square itself. If you want to stay the night, the only **hotel** in town is the *Metuj*, Klosova 60 (☎0441/720 37; ②), off Komenského, the main street running north to south through the new town.

The Babiččino údolí

Ten kilometres west of Náchod by train, the town of **ČESKÁ SKALICE** marks the beginning of the Úpa valley, better known as the **Babiččino údolí** after the novel that made it famous – *Babička* (Grandmother) by **Božena Němcová** (1820–1862). Forced to marry at just seventeen to a man more than twice her age, she wrote "the years of my childhood were the most beautiful of my life. When I married I wept over my lost liberty, over the dreams and ideals forever ruined". It's statements such as these, and the stories of personal conduct that caused outrage at the time, that have endeared her to the hearts of many Czech women. Nowadays, she is still very much a household name, and one of the few Czech women to have entered the country's literary canon.

There are now three museums-cum-memorials to Němcová in the area, two in Česká Skalice itself. The first is in her old school house, the Baruncina škola, northwest off the main square up B. Němcové; the second is in the former pub, *U českého lva*, in which she got married, next door to the town's textile museum, further up B. Němcové and across the river. The last one is in the **chateau** at RATIBOŘICE, 2.5km north of Česká Skalice, where Němcová's father was equerry. An alternative to visiting one of the above is to pick up a copy of the novel, and set out up the valley, which was her childhood haunt and the main inspiration for the novel, and is, in any case, a very beautiful place in its own right. Be sure not to miss the modern statue group by Otto Gutfreund, sitting on the edge of the fields 500m north of the chateau.

Hradec Králové

Capital of East Bohemia and the largest city on the fertile plain of the *Polabí*, **HRADEC KRÁLOVÉ** (Königgrätz) is a typically attractive Bohemian town, with a handsome historical quarter paid for by the rich trade that used to pass through en route to Silesia. But there's another side to the town, too. To the west of the medieval centre is one of the great urban projects of the interwar Republic, built by some of the best modern Czech architects of the time. The two towns don't really blend in with one another – in fact, they barely communicate – and these days, the staré město is little more than a museum piece. Even if you don't particularly take to the new town, it's a fascinating testimony to the early optimism of the First Republic, and gives the whole of Hradec Králové a unique, expansive and prosperous atmosphere.

Hradec Králové spreads itself out on both banks of the Labe: on the left bank, the **staré město** (old town) sits on an oval rock between the Labe and the Orlice rivers; the **nové město** (new town) begins as soon as you leave the old town, straddling the river and then composing itself in fairly logical fashion between the river and the station to the west. By **train** or **bus**, you arrive in the nové město; to reach the staré město, take a #5, #6, #8, #11, #15 or #20 bus from the station down the main street, Gočárova, into town.

The staré město

The **staré město** was entirely surrounded by zigzag red-brick fortifications in the eighteenth century, though they've now been replaced by a modern ring road that keeps traffic out of the old quarter. With most daily business being conducted over in the new town, a small supermarket and a couple of bookshops are all that remain to disturb Hradec Králové's two adjoining medieval squares, **Velké náměstí** and the much smaller **Malé náměstí**. At the western end of Velké náměstí, the skyline is punctuated by five towers. Two of them belong to the church of **sv Duch** (Holy Ghost), one of Bohemia's few great brick churches, a style more commonly associated with neighbouring Silesia. Given its grand Gothic scale, the whitewashed interior is a letdown, despite Petr Brandl's *St Anthony* and a superb stone tabernacle dating from 1497.

The church's twin towers are outreached by the once-white **Bílá věž**, built in the sixteenth century from the profits of Bohemian–Silesian trade. Also in this corner of the square is the town **brewery**, invisible but for the terrace of Baroque former canons' houses that lead to its gate, bristling in their bright new coats of paint. To the east, where the two sides of the square converge, the older Renaissance houses on the north side have kept their arcades, while, opposite, the Jesuits built their Baroque "barracks" and church – the latter beautifully maintained, its Baroque altarpiece providing a suitable repository for Brandl's work.

The Gallery of Modern Art

Hradec Králové's **Gallery of Modern Art** (Tues–Sun 9am–5pm), opposite the Jesuit church, currently houses the best permanent collection of twentieth-century Czech art in the country. The building itself – designed by Osvald Polívka in 1910–12, the genius behind much of Prague's finest Art-Nouveau structures – is a treat: five-storeys, with a large oval shaft at the centre that sheds light onto the corridors and the glass-roofed foyer.

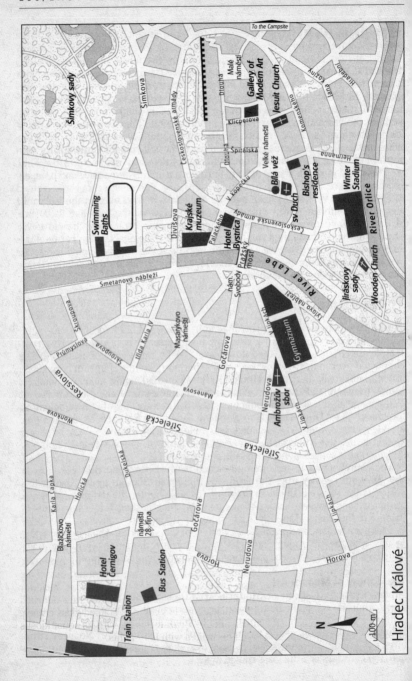

Hradec Králové

The ground floor is given over to temporary exhibitions, while on the first floor, the collection of works by turn-of-the-century artists is entirely in keeping with its surroundings. Among the highlights are a couple of lesser-known **Mucha** drawings, an early **Kupka**, and a whole series by **Jan Preisler**, including a study for the mural which now adorns the *Hotel Bystrica* (see below). The unexpected pleasure is **Josef Váchal**'s work, in particular the mysterious *Satanic Invocation* (*Vzývači ďabla*), which spills over onto its carved wooden frame. Several wood sculptures by **Bílek** and three bronze reliefs by **Sucharda** make for a fairly comprehensive overview of Czech Secessionist art. The floor ends with the beginnings of the Czech obsession with Cubism, most famously **Emil Filla**'s own version of "Les Demoiselles d'Avignon", *Salome's Dance*.

The second floor is almost wholly devoted to Czech Cubist and Fauvist painters, interspersed with a few from the Realist and Surrealist school who gained prominence in the 1920s. **Josef Šíma**'s semi-surreal work is probably the most original (he was a member of the avant-garde group, *Devětsil*), though sadly only two canvases and a pen-and-ink sketch are displayed here. Postwar art up to 1968 is the subject of the third floor, and is interesting, if only because many of the artists, like **Mikuláš Medek**, have only recently been exhibited in public galleries. The balcony views from the top floor should be sufficient incentive to get you up there, and again there's plenty of previously censored post-1968 material to feast your eyes on, like the psychedelic *Přátelé*, though patently political works like *Červená zeď* (Red Wall) are the exception. Surrealism was always frowned upon, the reason why artists like **Jiří Kolář**, two of whose classic collages are shown here, are much better known in the West.

The nové město

Most of what you now see outside the old town is the result of an architectural master plan outlined between 1909 and 1911, though much of the work wasn't carried out until the 1920s. Building began on a grand scale with the **Krajské muzeum** (Tues–Sun 9am–noon & 1–5pm) on the leafy waterfront, designed by the father of the Czech modern movement, **Jan Kotěra**. With the rest of central Europe still under the obsessive hold of the Viennese Secession, Kotěra's museum, crowned with one of his characteristic domes, represents a shot across the bows of contemporary taste, finished in what was at the time an unconventional mixture of red brick and concrete rendering. The entrance is guarded by two colossal sphynx-like janitors, but otherwise the ornamentation is low-key – as is the exhibition inside, a straightforward though attractive display of nineteenth- and twentieth-century arts and crafts, books and posters.

Close by, on the inner ring road, is another work by Kotěra, the **Hotel Bystrica** (originally called, simply, the *Grand Hotel*), built immediately after the museum. It's difficult to see beyond the pollutant-caked rendering to appreciate the subtleties of the facade, and unfortunately, at the time of writing, the whole interior was undergoing a thorough restoration. If and when it reopens, head for the Art-Nouveau restaurant – the fruit of an earlier work by Kotěra – adorned with murals by Jan Preisler and František Kysela's graceful stained-glass cranes. Kotěra is also responsible for the distinctive **Pražský most**, with its squat kiosks at either end, and wrought-iron arch decorated with fairy lights.

Before crossing the river into Gočár's new town, there are a couple of minor attractions that might appeal. The **Jiráskovy sady**, which occupies the slip of land at the confluence of the rivers Labe and Orlice, boasts a colourful rose garden, and a sixteenth-century **wooden Uniate church** (invariably closed) brought here from Sub-Carpathian Ruthenia in 1935. Alternatively there are some **swimming baths**, designed in the 1920s, with an artificial wave machine, at the opposite end of the Labe embankment.

Gočár's new town

Kotěra died shortly after World War I, and it was left to one of his pupils, **Josef Gočár**, to complete the construction of the new town. Gočár had been among the foremost exponents of Czech Cubist architecture before the war, but, along with Pavel Janák, he changed tack in the 1920s, and attempted to establish a specifically Czechoslovak style of architecture, which incorporated prewar Cubism. Dubbed "Rondo-Cubism" because of its recurrent semicircular motifs, few projects got off the ground, but elements of the style are reflected in the appealing homogeneity of the new town. On a sunny day, the light pastel shades of the buildings provide a cool and refreshing backdrop; bad weather brings out the brutalism that underlies much of Gočár's work.

This brutalism is most evident in his largest commission, the **Statní gymnázium** on the right bank, a sprawling series of buildings with an L-shaped four-storey red-brick structure, fronted by an atypically slender bronze nude by Jan Štursa, as the main entrance. Up the side of the school, on V lipkách, is a later, still more uncompromising work, the Protestant **Ambrožův sbor**, built in functionalist style on a striking angular site. But by far Gočár's most successful set-piece is **Masarykovo náměstí**, which basks in the sun at the heart of the new town, shaped like a big slice of lemon sponge, with a pivotal statue of Masaryk back in its rightful place after a forty-year absence.

Practicalities

Accommodation can be hard to find, particularly when there's a big match on at the ice hockey stadium, so it might be worth enquiring about vacancies at ČEDOK, Gočárova 63 (☎049/325 86), before trekking round the hotels yourself. **Private rooms** are now beginning to appear in town: the most central ones are above the new café on V kopečku, the little street leading up to the old town from opposite the *Bystrica*.

Alessandria, SNP 733 (☎049/415 21). High-rise luxury hotel, very definitely in the wrong part of town; impossible to miss on bus route #6, #12, #21 or #22 from the train and bus stations. ④

Bystrica, Čs. armády (☎049/242 01). The interior of Kotěra's hotel has changed a great deal, all except for the adjoining restaurant. Centrally located, but sadly closed at the time of writing.

Paříž, Baťkovo náměstí (☎049/326 31). Cheap hotel in the new town, at the northern end of Mánesova. ①

Zimní stadión, Komenského 1214 (☎049/239 11). Much better than it looks from the outside, and centrally located, right by the ice hockey stadium. ②

Camping Stříbrný rybník (mid-May to mid-Sept). Popular summer campsite, due to its adjacent lake; you can even rent **bicycles**. To get there, take bus #17.

Eating and drinking

The best place in town for **eating** is Kotěra's *Bystrica* hotel restaurant (at the time of writing closed for restoration); otherwise, there are several *pivnice* in the old town which serve plain but filling Czech food, and good beer – try *Pod věží* on Velké náměstí, or *Na hradě* on Špitálská. In the new town, there's *Pizzeria Pinocchio* (daily 9am–midnight), perfectly positioned for admiring Gočár's Masarykovo náměstí, or *Bašta*, the café/restaurant on Ulrichovo náměstí (open till midnight).

Around Hradec Králové

The flat expanse **around Hradec Králové**, known as the *Polabí*, is a fertile region whose hedgeless cornfields stretch for miles on end. It's pretty dreary to look at, baking hot in summer and covered in a misty drizzle most of the winter, but there are several places within easy reaching distance of Hradec Králové which merit a day trip or overnight stop.

Jaroměř

JAROMĚŘ, 36km northeast of Hradec Králové and accessible by train, is a grey and uninviting town for the most part, blighted by the proximity of the Josefov barracks (see below). The only sight worth writing home about is one of Gočár's early works, the **Wenke department store** (Mon–Fri 9am–4pm, Sat & Sun 9am–noon), situated on Route 33, the busy main road from Hradec Králové to the Polish border. In this exceedingly unpromising street (now called Husova), Gočár undertook one of the first self-conscious experiments in Cubist architecture in 1911. It's an imaginative, eclectic work, quite unlike the much plainer Cubism of Prague's Vyšehrad villas or the nearby spa of Bohdaneč, the plate-glass facade topped by a Neoclassical top floor, and the monochrome, geometric interior still intact, though no longer packed with goods. Instead, it now serves as the venue for displays of local school exam work and the like, but upstairs there's a tiny art gallery with exhibits by all three of Jaroměř's home-grown artists: the sculptors Otakar Španiel and Josef Wagner, and the *Devětsil* painter Josef Šíma, whose wilfully optimistic painting of Jaroměř is, sadly, the only example of his work on show.

Josefov

One kilometre south of Jaroměř, where the Labe and the Metuje rivers converge, is the fortress town of **JOSEFOV** (Josefstadt). In the 1780s the Habsburgs created three fortified towns along the northern border with their new enemy, Prussia: Hradec Králové (which has since lost its walls), Terezín and Josefov – the last two purpose-built from scratch and preserved as they were. Terezín was put to terrible use by the Nazis during World War II, but Josefov remains the great white elephant of the Empire, never having witnessed a single battle. Their mutual designs are unerringly similar: two fortresses (one large, one small), identikit eighteenth-century streets, and a grid plan whose monotony is broken only by the imposing **Empire Church** on the main square. Again like Terezín, Josefov is still a garrison town, packed with soldiers and posses of military police cruising around in jeeps. All in all, it's not a great day out, but the thick zigzag trail of red-brick fortifications, now topped by beautiful tree-lined paths, is eminently strollable, with far-reaching views across the wheat fields of the *Polabí*.

Kuks

The great complex of Baroque spa buildings at **KUKS**, just 5km north of Jaroměř, on the banks of the Labe, was the creation of the enlightened Bohemian dilettante Count Špork. Work began, largely according to Špork's own designs, in 1695, and by 1730 he had created his own private **spa resort**, kitted out with a garden maze, a hospital, a concert hall (complete with its own orchestra) and a racecourse (surrounded by statues of dwarves). For a while, Kuks' social life was on a par with the likes of Karlsbad; then, in 1738, the impresario died, and two years later, on December 22, 1740, disaster struck when the river broke its banks, destroying all the buildings on the left bank, and – worse still – the springs themselves.

All that remains now of the original spa is an overgrown monumental stairway leading nowhere, and, on the right bank, the hospital building fronted by **Matthias Bernhard Braun**'s famous terrace, now the chief reason for visiting Kuks. Špork invited Braun to Prague in 1710, and became the Tyrolean sculptor's chief patron in Bohemia, commissioning from him a series of **allegorical statues** intended to elevate the minds of his spa guests: to the west, the twelve *Vices* culminate in the grim *Angel of Grievous Death*; to the east, the twelve *Virtues* end with the *Angel of Blessed Death*. Over the years the elements have not been too kind to Braun's work, whose originals, including a few surviving dwarves, have had to retreat inside the hospital building and now provide the highlight of the 45-minute guided tour (May–Sept Tues–Sun 9am–noon & 1.30–5pm; Oct Sat & Sun only). Also included in the tour are the beautifully restored eighteenth-century pharmacy and Špork's gloomy subterranean mausoleum.

There's no accommodation in amongst the wooden cottages of Kuks village on the left bank, but it's easy enough to come here on a day trip from Hradec Králové. Buses will either drop you at the main road, a short walk north of the village, or in the village itself; the **train station** lies to the south of the hospital building and gardens (follow the blue-marked path).

Betlém

One stop along the tracks, or a pleasant three-kilometre walk up the river from Kuks, is **Betlém** (Bethlehem), Braun's outdoor sculpture park, again sponsored by Špork. It's an unlikely, ingenious location, deep in the midst of a silver birch wood, and used to include several working springs, including one that shot water high up into the foliage, but centuries of neglect and weathering have taken their toll. What you see now are the few survivors of what would once have been a remarkable open-air *atelier* – exclusively the ones that Braun hacked out of various boulders he found strewn about the wood. In contrast to Kuks, the theme is more explicitly religious here, with the best-preserved sculptural groups depicting *The Coming of the Magi* and the *Nativity*. The dishevelled-looking man crawling out of his cave, and looking very much like a 3D representation of William Blake's *Fall of Man*, is in fact an obscure Egyptian hermit called Garinus.

The zoo at Dvůr Králové nad Labem

Familiar to postwar generations of Czech kids as the site of the country's largest **zoo**, at **DVŮR KRÁLOVÉ NAD LABEM**, 8km northwest of Kuks, is hardly a must on most visitors' itineraries, but if you're travelling with children, it's a stopoff that's pretty much guaranteed to please. As underfunded eastern European zoos go, Dvůr Králové has tried harder than most to make life bearable for the animals, but a "safari park" it is not, despite its persistent claims to the contrary. For a start, you don't drive through, and although there is a short bus ride round part of the site, the animals are not allowed to roam about freely. All the usual beasts are here – lions, elephants, monkeys, polar bears, etc – and there's a *dětský koutek* (kids' corner), where children can touch and stroke the more domesticated animals.

Dvůr Králové **bus station** is on 17 listopadu; to get to the main square, walk north two blocks, then left down Švehlova. The **train station** is 2km southwest of the centre; follow 5 květná, which becomes 28 října before crossing the river, after which it's due north up Riegrova and Revoluční to the main square. The zoo is 1km west of the town, on Štefánikova, and is well signposted. The town itself has a fairly good-looking arcaded main square, with a **restaurant** and *vinárna* in the cellars of its sixteenth-century radnice. Further up on the same side of the square, *Hotel Central* (☎0437/24 75; ①) can provide cheap **rooms**.

Hořice

Just about every Czech sculptor of the last hundred years was trained at the School of Masonry and Sculpture founded in 1884 at **HOŘICE**, 23km northwest of Hradec Králové. As a result, the town now boasts easily the richest collection of sculpture in the country after Zbraslav in Prague (see p.113), and plays host to an annual **International Symposium of Contemporary Sculpture**.

There are sculptures all over town, and exhibitions of contemporary works in the town museum (Tues–Sun 9am–noon & 1–4pm) on the main square, but the largest collection is in the **Gallery of Modern Sculpture**, halfway up the sv Gothard hill to the east of town (five minutes' walk down Janderova). Half the gallery is given over to temporary exhibitions, but the permanent collection is still impressive. All the leading lights of Czech sculpture are represented here, even Šaloun, famous for his Jan Hus Monument in Prague, and Bílek, neither of whom actually studied here, as well as one of the few extant works by Otakar Švec, the man responsible for Prague's since-dynamited Stalin Monument. In the meadows and orchards to the north of the gallery is the **symposium area**, with this year's exhibits out on show. To the west, the **Smetanovy sady** are dotted with mostly nineteenth-century sculptures of leading figures of the Czech *národní obrození*.

Despite the town's enormous artistic treasures, it sees very few visitors, so finding **accommodation** at the *Hotel Beránek* (☎0435/25 98; ①), just south of the main square on Husova, should present few problems. There are also no fewer than three **campsites** in the area – the nearest being the *U věže* site (April–Sept), 1km north of town on the road to Dvůr Králové. The **train station** (Hořice v Podkrkonoší) is 1km south of town down Husova (there's a connecting bus).

Chlumec nad Cidlinou

At **CHLUMEC NAD CIDLINOU**, 29km west of Hradec Králové, in the middle of the featureless dusty *Polabí*, is one of Bohemia's most exquisite provincial chateaux, **Karlova Koruna**. Built in 1721–23 to a design by Giovanni Santini, it stands on a rare patch of raised ground to the northwest of the town, south of the train station. Santini's ground plan is a simple but intriguing triple-winged affair, dominated by a central circular hall whose pink and grey marble dome fills two storeys, with a grand staircase leading to the upper balcony. For the last twenty years or so, this modest Baroque pleasure house has been filled with copies of Braun's statuary. However, at the time of writing, the whole place was closed to the public, following the return of the property to its previous owners. It remains to be seen what will happen to it in the future.

Pardubice

There's always been a certain amount of rivalry between the two big towns of the *Polabí*. **PARDUBICE**'s historical core is more immediately appealing than Hradec Králové's, but its new town lacks the logic and cohesion of its neighbour – which means that, on balance, there's slightly less to see here. You could easily come on a day trip from Hradec Králové (it's only 30min away by train); not a bad idea when you consider the fact that Pardubice is also the capital of the country's chemical industry and not the healthiest of places to spend the night.

The Town

The **train** and **bus stations** lie at the end of Palackého in the new town, a busy thoroughfare and the beginning of Pardubice's seemingly endless parade of shops. It's a good ten-minute walk from here (or a short ride on trolley bus #2) to the old town, much of it along **Míru**, a busy commercial street that contains an arresting threesome of late Secession buildings on the left-hand side, with *U lva* at the centre, distinguished by the two tiny lion heads on its gable. Opposite, the glass-roofed 1920s Pasáž, decked out in lime green and cream, is worth strolling down, even if does need sprucing up.

Míru comes to an end at **náměstí Osvobození**, which marks the transition from the new town to the old. At one end, the seriously striking Art-Nouveau **theatre** is a deliberately Czech structure, designed by Antonín Balšánek (who collaborated with Polívka on Prague's Obecní dům), its magnificent facade flanked by multicoloured mosaics: Libuše founding Prague on one side and a blind Žižka leading the Hussites into battle on the other. The other truly arresting building on the square is the church of **sv Bartoloměj**, originally Gothic but more memorable for the Renaissance additions to its exterior, which makes up for its lack of a tower with a syringe-like central spike. Gočár worked in Pardubice, too: the squat grey *Statní banka* and the *Hotel Grand* opposite, the hub of all Pardubice's nightlife, are both his.

SEMTEX

Pardubice is the home of the most famous Czech export, **Semtex**. This plastic explosive became a firm favourite with the world's terrorists during the 1980s because of its ability to avoid detection by electronic means in customs halls. Approximately 1000 tons of the explosive is reckoned to have gone to Libya alone (and from there – it seems – into the hands of the IRA). It's still produced at the huge chemical complex in the village of Semtín (from which it gets its name), a few kilometres northwest of Pardubice – until recently the village was etched out of all maps. Selling arms and explosives is not at all new to the Czechs, but it sits ill with the republic's new squeaky clean image, and the company has pledged to tag all future exports of the explosive so that it can be easily spotted by airport X-ray machines.

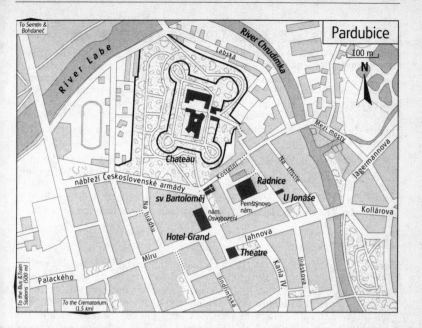

The soaring Gothic gateway, with its twisted uppermost tower and wonderful baubled spikes, makes for a memorable entrance to the old town. The main square, **Pernštýnovo náměstí**, is an intimate affair, an effect made all the more pronounced by the tall three-storey buildings on each side, handsome gabled sixteenth- and eighteenth-century houses for the most part. The sculptural decoration throughout the old town is remarkable and at its most striking on **U Jonáše**, whose plasterwork includes an exuberant depiction of Jonah at the moment of digestion by the whale (currently under repair). What little else there is of the staré město spreads north from here, either down the buttressed beauty of Bartolomějská or the crumbling facades of Pernštýnská. Both lead eventually to the romantic embankment, Wernerovo nábřeží, its drooping willow trees providing a perfect spot for the town's budding artists, music wafting across the courtyard from the almost chic *bistro* at no. 100. At this point, all that's left of the old town is the **chateau** (Tues–Sun 10am–5pm); an impressive series of walls, gates and barbicans lead to a rather colourless courtyard, with an art gallery housed in one of the wings.

Practicalities – and horse-racing

Pardubice's **hotels** are much of a muchness, but if it's functioning again after its recent modernisation, the *Hotel Grand* is the most central. In the interim, the *Zlatá štika*, Štrossova 127 (☎040/51 62 82; ②), is probably your best bet. There are several **restaurants** to choose from on the old town square: *U bílého koníčka*, which boasts a garden out the back, and a *vinárna* that stays open until 3am; *U černého vola*, which serves up the local brew; and *Pizzeria U dušičků*.

Pardubice has the best **steeplechase course** in the country (and the most difficult in the world after Liverpool's Aintree course), and races take place every other weekend. The traditional big race (which was first run in 1874) is the *Velká Pardubická* in early October, at which time it is impossible to find anywhere to stay in town. The racecourse (*závodiště*) is 2km out of town; take bus #4 or #14.

Chrudim

Twelve kilometres south of Pardubice, the otherwise provincial town of **CHRUDIM** springs into life in early July when it hosts its annual **Puppet Festival**. At other times of the year, it's still worth the short train ride to visit its marvellous **Puppet Museum** (Muzeum loutkářských kultur; daily 9–11am & 1–5pm) in the sixteenth-century Mydlářovsky dům, just off the main square. The Czech Lands have a long tradition of puppetry, going back to the country's peasant roots, and the museum acts as a repository for marionettes and puppets donated from all over the world. Down the hill from the square, you'll find Chrudim's two **hotels**: the *Centrál*, Husova 246 (☎0455/39 63; ①), is the cheaper; the modern high-rise *Bohemia*, on Masarykovo náměstí (☎0455/30 51; ②), has the better restaurant.

Litomyšl

LITOMYŠL (Leitomischl) sits on the border between Bohemia and Moravia in a kind of no-man's-land between the two provinces. The **train station** is five minutes' walk northwest of the old town, a pleasant stroll along (and across) the River Loučná. Everything there is to see is close at hand. The picturesque main square, strung out like a juicy fat Czech sausage, is lined with almost uninterrupted arcades, a pastel parade of Baroque and Neoclassical facades. The sixteenth-century **U rytířů** at no. 110 (now an art gallery) is the finest, decorated with medieval knights and merchants holding bags of money, clinging rather mischievously to their carved columns.

To the east, a knot of ramshackle backstreets, punctuated by churches in need of, or undergoing, repair, leads up to the Pernštejns' **chateau** (Tues–Sun April, Sept & Oct 9am–noon & 1–4pm; May–Aug 8am–noon & 1–5pm), a smart, sgraffitoed affair that bursts into frivolous gables and finials on its roof, and boasts Bohemia's finest triple-decker loggia inside. It used to house a fascinating exhibition of old musical instruments, which has now been replaced by porcelain and period furniture, and retains its late eighteenth-century theatre intact, including all the original scenery.

The inspiration for the original museum came from the brewery next door, where the composer **Bedřich Smetana** was born in 1824, one of the eighteen children of an upwardly mobile brewery manager. The family's stay at Litomyšl was uneventful, and when Bedřich was seven his father got a job in Jindřichův Hradec. Catalysed by the events of 1848, Smetana became a leading figure in the Czech *národní obrození* (despite German being his mother tongue), helping to found the National Theatre in Prague, and promoting the nationalist cause through works like *Ma vlast* ("My Country"), a symphonic poem inspired by Czech legends. Like others before him, Smetana became deaf towards the end of his life (during which time he composed some of his most famous works), and ended his days in a mental asylum, driven insane by syphilis. Jan Štursa's effete statue of the composer stands on the main square, and every year in his honour, the town puts on a **festival** of Smetana's music at the end of June.

The ugly but moderate *Zlatá hvězda* (☎0464/23 38; ①) on the main square should be able to provide **food** and **accommodation**, but if not, the no less ugly *Dalibor* (☎0464/21 11; ②) near the station will oblige. There's a **campsite** (May–Sept) 2km east of the town centre.

travel details

Trains

Connections with Prague Pardubice (up to half-hourly; 1hr 10min–2hr 20min); Jičín (4 daily; 1hr 50min); Turnov (3 daily; 4hr); Trutnov (3 daily; 4hr); Vrchlabí (1 daily; 3hr 30min).

From Turnov to Jičín (11 daily; 50min–1hr 10min); Železný Brod (16 daily; 20min); Hradec Králové (up to 16 daily; 2–3hr).

From Hradec Králové to Jaroměř (20 daily; 20–30min); Kuks (10 daily; 40min); Dvůr Králové (13 daily; 40min–1hr); Hořice (10 daily; 50min); Chlumec nad Cidlinou (15 daily; 20–40min); Pardubice (26 daily; 30min).

From Pardubice to Chrudim (15 daily; 30min).

Buses (ČSAD only)

Connections with Prague Harrachov (up to 5 daily; 3hr); Vrchlabí/Špindlerův Mlýn (up to 7 daily; 2hr 30min/2hr 40min); Náchod (up to 6 daily; 3hr); Litomyšl (up to 6 daily ; 3hr 30min).

From Hradec Králové to Jaroměř (up to hourly; 25min); Kuks (up to 10 daily; 30–40min); Trutnov (up to 14 daily; 1hr 10min); Pec pod Sněžkou (up to 8 daily; 2hr); Náchod (up to 6 daily; 1hr); Nové Město nad Metují (up to 5 daily; 1hr 20min); Litomyšl (5 or more daily; 1hr 10min).

CHAPTER SIX

SOUTH MORAVIA

At first sight, the landscape of **South Moravia** (Jižní Morava) appears little different from that of much of Bohemia – rolling hills, dense forests and cultivation – only as you move south towards Vienna does the land become noticeably more plump and fertile, with the orchards and vineyards continuing into Austria itself. **Brno** is the most obvious starting point: an engaging city, whose attractions are often underrated due to the heavy industrial base and housing estates that surround it. Brno is also within easy reaching distance of a host of sights, most notably Moravia's karst region, the Moravský kras, which boasts the most spectacular **limestone caves** in the Czech Lands. South of Brno a whole string of Germanic medieval villages, towns and chateaux punctuate the **River Dyje** as it meanders along the Austrian border.

By contrast, the **Bohemian-Moravian Uplands** or *Vysočina*, which separate Bohemia and Moravia, are poor and sparsely populated, viewed by most travellers only from the window of their coach or train to Brno. If you do stop off in the *Vysočina* – and parts of it are definitely worth visiting – make sure you go further than **Jihlava**, the area's most convenient starting point. To the south, **Telč** and **Slavonice** are arguably the country's most perfect architectural set-pieces, and even if you're not a devotee of Santini's Baroque-Gothic confections, the pilgrimage church at **Žďár nad Sázavou** is something special.

To the east of Brno, the landscape around the **River Morava** is – visually, at least – pretty uninspiring, and for most travellers the wine is the one (very good) reason to stop. That said, some towns on and around the river stand out on their own merit: the provincial treasure house and graceful gardens of **Kroměříž** and, at the other end of the scale, the modernist aesthetics of **Zlín**, where the multinational Baťa shoe empire has its roots.

Transport is fairly good throughout Moravia, though the **train system** is not quite as comprehensive as that of Bohemia, petering out in the *Vysočina*, and degenerating into a series of overcomplex branch lines along the more industrialised River Morava. In such instances, **buses** are invariably quicker and more direct. **Accommodation** should present few problems, with the situation in the big towns like Brno and Olomouc a vast improvement on the difficulties of Prague.

Brno

BRNO (Brünn) "welcomes the visitor with new constructions", as one ČEDOK brochure euphemistically puts it. In fact, the high-rise tenements that surround the city play a major part in discouraging travellers from stopping here. But as the second largest city in the Czech Republic, with a population of over 400,000, a couple of really good museums and galleries, a handful of other sights and a fair bit of nightlife, it's worth a day or two of anyone's time. As yet, though, the city receives few visitors outside the annual trade fairs. This has its advantages, of course: tourists here are welcomed rather than alternately shunned or ripped off as in Prague, and life still maintains some of the endearing (and infuriating) affectations of a provincial Vienna, itself only an hour or so away by car.

Brno was a late developer, being no bigger than Olomouc until the late eighteenth century. The town's first cloth factory was founded in 1766, and within fifteen years was followed by another twenty, earning Brno the nickname of *rakouský Manchestr* (Austrian Manchester). With the building of an engineering plant early in the next century, the city began to attract Czech workers, along with Austrian, German, English and Jewish entrepreneurs, making it easily the second largest city in the Czech Lands by the end of the nineteenth century. Between the wars Brno enjoyed a cultural boom, heralded by the 1928 Exhibition of Contemporary Culture, which provided an impetus for much of the city's **avant-garde architecture**. After the war, the city's German-speakers (some 25 percent of the population) were rounded up and ordered to leave, on foot, for Vienna. Following the 1948 coup and the subsequent Communist centralisation, state funds were diverted to Prague and Bratislava, pushing Brno into third place – where it has remained. However, with the recent switch to a more decentralised economy, the city's fortunes seem to be looking up at last.

Arrival, information and accommodation

Arriving at Brno's main **train station** is no longer the ordeal it once was, since the scaffolding was stripped off in 1989 for the 150th anniversary of the Brno–Vienna railway. Nowadays, as you leave the fresh and creamy late nineteenth-century splendour of the station, it only serves to point up the rot and decay that has been the lot of the rest of the city's buildings. Brno's main *ČSAD* **bus station**, situated five minutes' walk south of the train station, is a lot less impressive, but easy to escape: simply follow the overhead walkway which descends into the train station. *ČEBUS*, the private bus company, uses the old *ČSAD* station opposite the *Grand Hotel*.

Getting around

Most of Brno's sights are within easy walking distance of the train station, although **trams** will take you almost anywhere in the city within minutes. Tickets, which are half the usual width and currently cost 3kčs, must be bought beforehand from news kiosks or yellow ticket machines, and validated in the punching devices on board. The red machines dispense day tickets, which currently cost 15kčs – only really worthwhile if you're going to be whizzing about in the suburbs for some obscure reason. Some trams run all night (signified by a red number on the tram stop), gathering together in front of the station on the hour, every hour. The same tickets are valid for the city's **buses** and **trolley buses**, though you're unlikely to need to use them unless you're staying right out in suburbia.

Information

Train (and other sorts of) **information** is now relatively easy to obtain from the new office inside the station, which also sells various maps and guides to Brno. There's a tourist information office at Radnická 4 (Mon–Fri 8am–6pm, Sat 9am–6pm), by the old town hall, but it's not as comprehensive as those in Prague or

The Brno area telephone code is ☎05

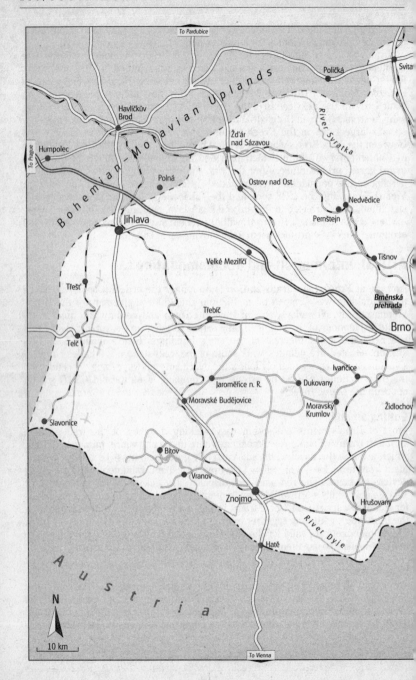

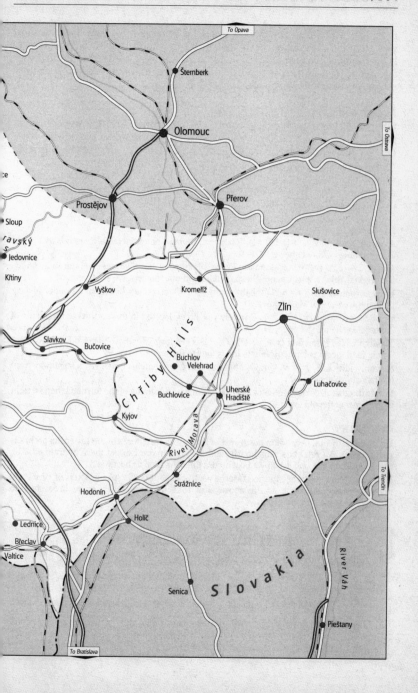

To Opava

Šternberk

Olomouc

Přerov

To Ostrava

Prostějov

ce

Sloup

ravský

s

Jedovnice

Křtiny

Vyškov

Kroměříž

Slušovice

Zlín

Slavkov

Bučovice

Chřiby Hills

Buchlov

Velehrad

Buchlovice

Uherské Hradiště

Luhačovice

Kyjov

River Morava

To Trenčín

Strážnice

Hodonín

Holíč

Lednice

Břeclav

Valtice

Slovakia

River Váh

Senica

Piešťany

To Bratislava

Bratislava. *ČEDOK* at Divadelní 3 (Mon–Fri 9am–6pm, Sat 9am–noon), a short walk from the train station, is always worth a try, otherwise your best bet are the hotel receptionists at the *Grand* or *International*, who are used to dealing with foreigners. The 24-hour snack bar *Taxatour,* near the train station, is another useful source of information on all aspects of the city.

Accommodation

Compared to Prague, finding **accommodation** in Brno is relatively easy, though prices are fairly high thanks to the expense-account business people who come here for the various trade fairs. *ČEDOK* on Divadelní can arrange cheap **private rooms**, but *Accomodea*, on Rašínova (Mon–Fri 8am–8pm), can probably get you something cheaper and is open longer hours. In July and August it's possible to stay in one of the city's **student dorms**; to find out the latest addresses and information, go to the *CKM* office on Skrytá (Mon–Fri 10am–noon & 1–5pm).

HOTELS

Astoria, Novobranská 3 (☎225 41). Revamped *Morava* hotel, incredibly central, with some cheap doubles without showers. ②–④

Avion, Česká 20 (☎276 06). Bohuslav Fuchs slimline functionalist hotel, though sadly minus the original fittings; again, some cheap doubles without showers. ②–④

Evropa, Jánská 1/3 (☎266 21). Slightly tatty turn-of-the-century hotel, but a wonderful location on the corner of Masarykova. ③

Kozák, Horova 30 (☎74 41 89). Privately run hotel, located in the northwestern suburb of Žabovřesky, hence the price. ②

Myslivna, Nad Pisárkami (☎38 32 47). Take bus #68 from Mendlovo náměstí for a secluded, scenic (and inconvenient) location in the woods to the west of town. ④

Slovan, Lidická 23 (☎74 55 05). Comfortable and unpretentious hotel, just a step away from the Janáčkovo divadlo. ④

U Jakuba, Jakubské náměstí 6 (☎229 91). The most welcoming of the top notch hotels, right in the heart of the old town. ⑤

CAMPSITES

Veverská Bítýška, over 15km northwest of the city on the shores of the Brněnská přehrada (Brno Dam). A *ČSAD* bus runs hourly, and in summer you can get there by tram #3, #10, #14, #18, #20 or #21, followed by a boat across the dam, then a short walk.

Bobrava, 10km south at Modřice (March–Oct). Situated on the plains south of Brno, and not nearly as picturesque as the above site. Take the local *osobní* train three stops to Popovice (last one around 11pm).

ACCOMMODATION PRICES

Each place to stay in this chapter has a symbol which corresponds to one of seven **price categories**:

① Under 500kčs   ② 500–750kčs   ③ 750–1000kčs   ④ 1000–1500kčs
⑤ 1500–2000kčs   ⑥ 2000–3000kčs   ⑦ 3000kčs and upwards

All prices are for the cheapest **double room** available, which usually means without private bath or shower in the less expensive places. For a **single room**, expect to pay around two-thirds the price of a double.

Masarykův okruh, 15km west of Brno (summer only). You'll need your own transport to camp (rather uncomfortably) at the Grand Prix circuit; take the motorway in the direction of Prague to the Kývalka exit, then follow the signs. Buses between Brno and the circuit are laid on during the Grand Prix.

The City

One of the nicest things about Brno is that its historical centre is compact and almost entirely traffic-free. The city's main action goes on within the small egg-shaped old town, pedestrianised for the most part, and encircled by a swathe of parks and the inner ring road. Around **Zelný trh** and **náměstí Svobody** you'll find most of the city's shops and markets. In the southwestern corner of the old town are the quieter streets around Petrov, the lesser of Brno's two hills, topped by the **Peter and Paul Cathedral**. Further west, the squat fortress of **Špilberk** looks down on the old town to the east and Staré Brno to the south, site of the original early medieval settlement. Worth a visit, but still further from the centre, are Brno's modern architectural sights, the exhibition grounds of **Výstaviště** and – on the opposite side of town – Mies van der Rohe's **Tugendhat Haus**.

Masarykova and Zelný trh

Every tram in Brno congregates in front of the station, and there's an infectious buzz about the place in the early afternoon, after work. A steady stream of people plough up and down **Masarykova**, a somewhat hazardous cocktail of cobbles, steaming manholes and tram lines, which leads to náměstí Svobody (see below). Don't let that stop you from looking up at the five-storey mansions, laden with a fantastic mantle of decorations, some grotesquely disfigured by pollutants.

To the left as you head up Masarykova is **Zelný trh** (literally "cabbage market"), the chaotic vegetable market on a sloping cobbled square, now beginning to return to the brisk trade of its prewar days, and somewhat ill-served by the mishmash of buildings which line its edges. At its centre is the petrified diarrhoea of the huge *Parnassus* fountain by Fischer von Erlach: in the good old days, when it worked properly, live carp was sold from its waters at Christmas. At the top of the square, the plain mass of the Dietrichstein Palace conceals an intimate arcaded courtyard that forms the entrance to the **Moravian Museum** (Tues–Sun 9am–6pm). Brno is at the centre of quite an extensive area of early human settlement, and the museum contains an impressive collection of prehistoric finds from the surrounding region (there are more in the Anthropos annexe, see below), including the famous *Venus of Věstonice*, plus a large section on the Great Moravian Empire.

Much more interesting, if only for their macabre value, are the **Capuchin tombs** (Tues–Sat 9–11.45am & 2–4.30pm, Sun 11–11.45am & 2–4.30pm), to the far south of the square: a gruesome collection of dead monks and top nobs, mummified by chance in the crypt of the Capuchin church. Until the eighteenth century, Brno's moneyed classes forked out large sums to be buried here in the monks' simple common grave, in the hopes of finding a short cut to heaven – righteousness by association, perhaps. The bodies lie fully clothed, some with the hollow expressions of skeletons, others still frozen in the last painful grimace of death. Just to drive the point home, signs in Czech chime in with "What we are, they once were, what they are, we will be". Not an experience for the faint-hearted.

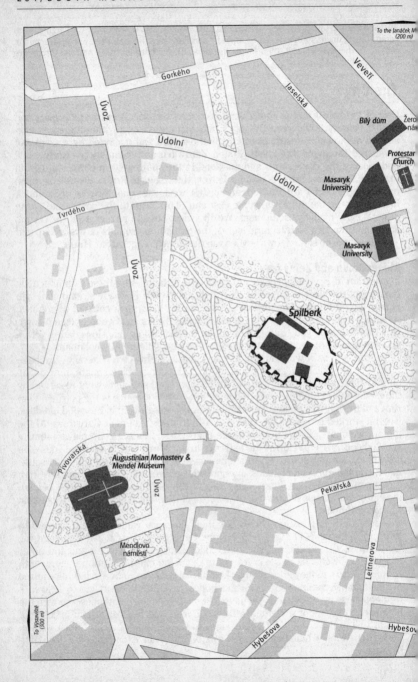

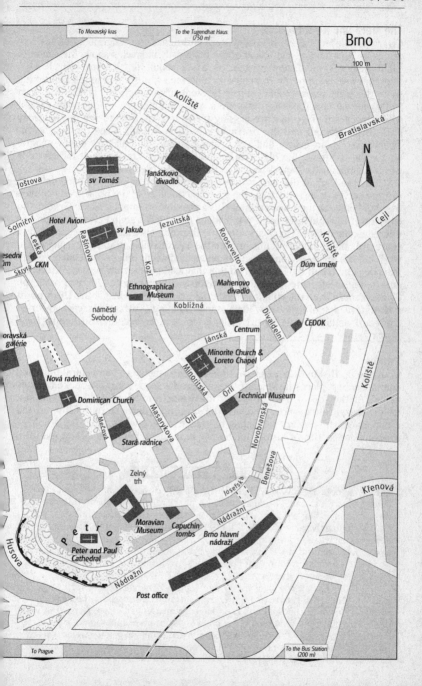

To Moravský kras

To the Tugendhat Haus (750 m)

Brno

100 m

N

Koliště

Bratislavská

Cejl

Koliště

Joštova

sv Tomáš

Janáčkovo divadlo

Solniční

Hotel Avion

Jezuitská

Rooseveltova

Dům umění

Česká

Rašínova

sv Jakub

esední ím

Skrytá CKM

Kozí

Ethnographical Museum

Mahenovo divadlo

náměstí Svobody

Kobližná

Centrum

ČEDOK

oravská galérie

Jánská

Minorite Church & Loreto Chapel

Divadelní

Koliště

Nová radnice

Minoritská

Orlí

Orlí

Technical Museum

Dominican Church

Masarykova

Orlí

Novobranská

Mečová

Stará radnice

Benešová

Zelný trh

Josefská

Křenová

Nádražní

Petrov

Moravian Museum

Capuchin tombs

Brno hlavní nádraží

Husova

Peter and Paul Cathedral

Nádražní

Post office

To Prague

To the Bus Station (200 m)

The stará and nová radnice

Clearly visible from Zelný trh is the **stará radnice**. Anton Pilgram's Gothic door-way is its best feature, the tallest of the five thistly pinnacles above the statue of Blind Justice symbolically twisted, as if it's about to fall onto your head – Pilgram's testament to the corrupt town aldermen who shortchanged him for his work (he went on to build Vienna's St Stephen's Cathedral). Inside, the town hall's courtyards and passageways are a confusing mixture of styles, jam-packed with whatever tour groups are passing through town, here to see the *Brněnský drak* (Brno dragon) and the *Brněnské kolo* (Brno wheel) – see the box below. There's also an art gallery and a café; and if you're still a bit hazy on the geography of the old town, the **observation gallery** (daily 9am–5pm) of the tower is worth a climb for the panorama across the city's red-tiled rooftops.

Round the back of the stará radnice, the cobbled square below the Dominican Church serves as a car park for the grey functionaries of the present city council who hold office at the **nová radnice**. It's a passable attempt by Mořic Grimm, the city's chief Baroque architect, "a provincial talent but a sound craftsman" as one critic described him. There are a couple of pretty sundials in the echoing first courtyard, and a modern fountain from the 1928 Exhibition in the second court-yard, but otherwise nothing much to get excited about unless someone's getting married. The handful of cobbled streets that lead south from here to Petrov hill are the nearest Brno gets to a secluded, intimate spot. As you walk up Dominikanská from the cobbled square, take a quick look inside the **Dům pánů z Kunštátu**, one of Brno's few Renaissance buildings, with an attractive galleried courtyard; until recently an art gallery, it's soon to become the luxury *Hotel Baron Trenck*.

Petrov

Continue up Biskupská to **Petrov**, the smaller of the city's two central hills, and one of the best places in which to make a quick escape from the choked streets below. At the top of the hill stands the **Peter and Paul Cathedral**, whose needle-sharp Gothic spires dominate the skyline for miles around. Close up, the crude nineteenth-century rebuilding has made it a lukewarm affair, but it holds a special place in Brno's history for having been instrumental in saving the town

---

THE BRNO MASCOTS

Countless local legends surround the **Brněnský drak** (literally "Brno dragon", though in fact it's a stuffed alligator), which hangs from the ceiling of the town hall entrance rather like a cheap inflatable space shuttle. The standard version is that the marauding beast was tricked into eating a carcass stuffed full of lime, and having eaten it, rushed down to the River Svratka and drank so much it burst. The most likely origin of the creature is that it was a gift from the Turkish Sultan to Archduke Matthias, who in turn bequeathed it to Brno in an attempt to ingratiate himself with the local aristocrats.

The other town mascot displayed here is the **Brněnské kolo** (Brno wheel), made in 1636 by a cartwright from Lednice, who bet a friend that he could fell a tree, make a wheel and roll it to Brno (some 50km away) all before sunset. He won the bet and the wheel has been given pride of place in the stará radnice ever since, though the story goes that following his great feat people began to suspect that the cartwright was in league with the Devil: his business fell off and he died in poverty.

from the Swedes during the Thirty Years' War. After months besieging the town during the course of 1645, the Swedish general Tortennson decided to make one last attempt at taking the place, declaring he would give up at midday if the town hadn't surrendered. In a fit of inspiration, the bell-ringer, seeing that the town was on the brink of defeat, decided to ring the midday bells an hour early. The Swedes gave up their attack, the city was saved, and as a reward the Habsburg emperor switched the Moravian capital from Olomouc to Brno (well, so the story goes).

Inside the lofty nave, there's a valuable fourteenth-century *Madonna and Child*, but the most intriguing art treasures are the aluminium *Stations of the Cross*. Constructed in the 1950s, these get progressively more outrageous and abstract as the story unfolds, until the final relief is no more than flailing limbs and anguished metal. Other than this, it's not really worth venturing into the cathedral, despite its recent facelift, unless you're in need of sanctuary from the heat of the day.

The cathedral is not the only reason to climb Petrov: from the nearby **Denisovy sady**, tucked into the city ramparts, there's a far-reaching view over the great plain south to Vienna, and an interesting angle on the cathedral itself. In among the trees, a slender white obelisk commemorates the end of the Napoleonic Wars (the Battle of Austerlitz took place just outside Brno – see p.267), lining up perfectly with the avenue of Husova which leads to the red-brick Protestant Church, and, beyond it, the bright white former Party headquarters, known affectionately as the **Bílý dům** (White House). When this was at the planning stages in the 1950s, the more committed cadres wanted to remove the offending Protestant Church, which blocked the view up Husova. Fortunately, aestheticism triumphed over atheism and the plan was somehow foiled.

Náměstí Svobody

Back down on Masarykova, follow the flow north and you'll end up at **náměstí Svobody**, nominally the city's main square and focus of the November 1989 demonstrations for Brno's citizens. Far short of magnificent, it's nonetheless the place where most of Brno come to meet up, chat and shop. In summer, you can sit and drink coffee in the shadow of the square's golden plague column (see box below) – and admire the square's three finest buildings, which together span almost four centuries. The earliest is the **Dům pánů z Lipé** (just out of view if you're actually sitting at the café), with an ornate Renaissance facade in need of a cleaning. Opposite, and totally lacking in such subtlety, is **Dům u čtyř mamlasů**, belonging to one of Brno's richest nineteenth-century Jewish industrialists, whose four muscle-bound employees (the "four stupid boys") struggle to hold up both his building and their loincloths. And in the northwest corner of the square, Bohuslav Fuchs' functionalist **Moravská banka** (now simply the *Komerční banka*) has turned a rather nasty green since its inception in the 1930s.

Heading north from náměstí Svobody, a steady stream of people flows past the concentration of book and record shops, pubs and cafés on **Česká**, wolfing down takeaways and *zmrzlina* on the way and, at the top, waiting for the trams and buses that congregate on Joštova, which marks the end of the old town. On the northeast corner of the square is the **Ethnographical Museum** (Tues–Sun 9am–6pm), which contains a large permanent collection of Moravian folk costumes, ceramics, painted easter eggs and an album of old photos, as well as occasionally hosting exhibitions on ethnographic themes from other countries.

PLAGUE COLUMNS

Plague columns are a frequent feature of Catholic towns and cities, an expression of civic gratitude for having been delivered from the Black Death; many were in fact erected in thanks for the town's liberation from the Protestant "plague". In the Czech Lands, they came to be regarded by Czech nationalists as symbols of the Austro-Hungarian hegemony, and a number were torn down during the celebrations following the foundation of the Czechoslovak Republic in 1918, including the one which used to grace Prague's old town square. Brno's column was erected in 1648 after the unsuccessful Swedish (Protestant) siege of the city.

East of náměstí Svobody

The Grimm brothers' finest architectural work in Brno (there really were two of them) is the **Minorite church** on the corner of Minoritská and Jánská, whose vivacious frontage makes the most of its cramped site. The right-hand portal leads to the main gilded nave, whose recently renovated interior is much the best Baroque in town, high to the point of giddiness, an effect that's intensified by the false perspectives of the frescoes. Linked to the church next door by double doors in the north aisle is an equally stunning chapel, with a steep altar staircase that must be ascended on bended knee, and full-size colour terracotta statues of Jesus and the two robbers looking down from the gallery above. The greater part of the church is taken up with a **Loreto chapel**, its outer walls smothered in grisaille depictions of the miracle (see p.68 for the full story); the atmospheric red-brick interior holds the standard *Black Madonna and Child* set against a rich marble backdrop.

Further along Minoritská and into Josefská, the **Technical Museum** (Tues–Sun 9am–6pm, Sun 9am–2pm), housed in an old nunnery, boasts a wonderful stock of old trams, bicycles and cars from which to stage its temporary exhibitions. One permanent exhibit worth seeking out is the **Panorama** (for which you need a separate ticket), a large wooden stereoscope built in 1890 and designed to allow several viewers to see its rotating slides simultaneously. Usually it's loaded with old photos of Czech and Slovak towns (but the slides are changed every fortnight or so). Backtrack for one block and walk down to the bottom of Jánská, where the department store **Centrum**, built in 1928 by the shoe magnate Tomáš Baťa, still cuts a bold figure sixty years on.

Brno's finest nineteenth-century building is the **Mahenovo divadlo**, a forthright structure exuding the municipal confidence of its original German patrons in its Corinthian columns and pediment. Its insides are suitably smothered in gold sculpturing and glittering chandeliers, and it has the distinction of being the first theatre in the Austro-Hungarian Empire to be fitted with electric light bulbs. In total contrast to the flamboyant Mahenovo is Bohuslav Fuchs' squat functionalist **Dům umění** (art gallery; Tues–Sun 10am–6pm), which puts on some of the city's most innovative art exhibitions, theatre performances, and even the occasional gig. A little further up Rooseveltova from the Mahenovo is the grey and fairly unappealing **Janáčkovo divadlo**, built in the 1960s as the city's – indeed the country's – largest opera house.

The Moravská galérie

On Husova, which forms the western limit of the old town, can be found one of the best collections of modern applied art in the country, the **Moravská galérie**

(Tues–Sun 10am–5pm), a neo-Renaissance pile built as a museum by one of Brno's many wealthy Jewish industrialists. The richly decorated ground and first floors (and the garden) are used for consistently good temporary exhibitions of anything from avant-garde photomontages to the work of the local art school. The gallery's permanent applied arts collection is located on the top floor, and ranges from the Gothic period to the present day. German and Austrian craftsmanship predominates, as it did for much of Brno's history, but there are works from all over Europe.

The section from the Art Nouveau period onwards is particularly interesting in terms of the development of Czech applied arts. A curving Gaillard sideboard stands alongside a standing *bufet* by Brno's own Jan Kotěra. Pavel Janák's Cubist ceramics and Josef Gočár's angular furniture are just some of the specifically Czech highlights. Also on display are the few surviving pieces of original furniture from Mies van der Rohe's Tugendhat Haus (see below). Finally, there is a whole room of 1960s and 1970s gear, which will appeal to lovers of kitsch.

Špilberk and the Augustinian monastery

Skulking on a thickly wooded hill to the west of Husova and barely visible through the trees, the ugly squat fortress of **Špilberk** (Spielberg) acquired a reputation for being one of the most god-awful prisons in the Habsburg Empire. As you walk up through the castle grounds, a monument of Romulus and Remus commemorates the many Italians who died here, having been incarcerated fighting for their country's freedom in the northern borders of what is now Italy. The testimony of one Italian inmate, the poet Count Silvio Pellico, so shocked the Austrian middle classes that the prison was closed down in 1857. Less than a hundred years later, it was put back into use by the SS who confined, tortured

---

JANÁČEK IN BRNO

Although he was born in Hukvaldy, in northern Moravia, **Leoš Janáček** moved to Brno at the age of eleven and spent most of his life here, first as a chorister and then teacher and choirmaster at the local Augustinian monastery. Battling against the prejudices of the German town administration, he managed to drag Czech music out of the pubs and into the concert hall, eventually founding the Brno Conservatoire and Organ School in 1882. As a composer he remained virtually unknown outside Moravia until well into his sixties, when he began the last and most prolific creative period of his life (for more on his life and works, see p.308). For much of this century, Janáček has been overshadowed by his compatriots, Smetana (whom the Communists were particularly keen on) and Dvořák (whom the western world has always revered), but recently his music has become increasingly popular.

Across the park from the opera house named after him, at the junction of Kounicova and Smetanova, there's a modest memorial **museum** (Mon–Fri 8am–noon & 1–4pm) in the former Organ School, where you can sit back and relax to the composer's music. Unlike his predecessors, Smetana and Dvořák, Janáček chose not to be buried in Prague's illustrious Vyšehrad cemetery, opting instead for Brno's municipal cemetery. If you're on the Janáček trail, bus #62 from the train station terminates at the main entrance; or else tram #6, #7, #8, #9 or #15 will take you to within walking distance – the cemetery is easy enough to spot thanks to the bright white pinnacles of Arnošt Wiesner's strikingly modern crematorium.

and killed thousands of prisoners during the war. Being aware of this, the tour round the dimly lit dungeons is depressingly evocative, though the place is now undergoing a lengthy overhaul not due to finish until 1994. As a consolation, stroll around the brooding battlements or visit the castle's swish *vinárna*.

The area south of the Špilberk hill, where the first settlements sprang up in the early Middle Ages, is known as Staré Brno. Few traces of these survive and nowadays there's nothing particularly old or interesting about this part of town, with the exception of the fourteenth-century **Augustinian monastery** on Mendlovo náměstí. Despite its unpromising locale – the square is little more than a glorified bus terminal – it's one of Brno's finest Gothic buildings, its pillars and walls smothered in delicate geometric patterning.

The monastery is best known for one of its monks, **Gregor Mendel** (1822–1884), whose experiments in the abbey gardens with peas and bees eventually led to the discovery of the principles of heredity and, subsequently, genetics. Despite the publication of several seminal papers outlining his discoveries, his work was ignored by the scientific establishment and in 1868 he gave up his research to become the monastery's abbot. Only after his death was he acknowledged as one of the greats of modern biology, and following the 170th anniversary of his birth in 1992, several rooms in part of the monastery have been dedicated to him as the **Mendel museum** (Mon–Fri 9am–4pm). In addition, the Augustinian library, Mendel's beehives and the garden he used for his experiments are all now open to the public.

Výstaviště and around

To the southwest of the city centre, where the River Svratka opens up to the plain (tram #1 or #18 from the station), is the **Výstaviště Exhibition Ground**. The main buildings were laid out in 1928 for the city's Exhibition of Contemporary Culture, and most of the leading Czech architects of the day were involved in the scheme, which prompted a flurry of functionalist building projects across the city's burgeoning suburbs. The most arresting (and largest) building on the site, the circular crystal and concrete **Z pavilion**, is actually one of the postwar additions, but one which kept to the spirit of the original concept. The only building which predates the complex is the **Zámeček**, which features an interior by Brno-born arch-minimalist Adolf Loos. Even if you've no interest in modern architecture, the various fairs and exhibitions staged here between March and November are the largest in the country, and often interesting in their own right. Once the showpieces of socialism, they're now more an opportunity for foreign companies to try and sell their goods.

The part of the 1928 exhibition which really caused a sensation was the **Nový dům** settlement, worth a look if you're keen on Bauhaus-style architecture. Inspired by the *Weissenhofsiedlung* built a year earlier in Stuttgart, Bohuslav Fuchs and various others designed a series of boxy white concrete villas by the woods of the Wilsonův les, north of Výstaviště, up Žabovřeská (tram #18 or #20), in the streets between Šmejkalova and Bráfova. The brief for each architect was to create modest two-storey houses for middle-income families, using standard fittings and ordinary materials to keep the unit cost down. Now grey, peeling and overrun by vegetation, it takes a leap of imagination to appreciate the shock of the new which these buildings must have aroused at the time.

There are two other sights worth visiting, close, but entirely unrelated, to Výstaviště. The first, visible from the main trade ground entrance, is a Louis XIV summer palace, **Letohrádek Mitrovských**, an unusual sight in this part of the world. Napoleon stayed here the night before the Battle of Austerlitz (see p.267), while his opposite number, the Russian general Kutuzov, stayed in the Dietrichstein Palace on Zelný trh. Nowadays, the palace serves as a temporary exhibition space. On the opposite side of Výstaviště, over the River Svitava, is **Anthropos** (Tues–Sun 8.30am–5pm), an annexe of the Moravian Museum, which concentrates on Ice Age geology and fauna, including remains of mammoths, Neanderthals and early Homo sapiens. As well as fossil bones and replicas of prehistoric cave paintings, the museum contains numerous paintings by Zdeněk Burian, a Czech painter who specialises in scientifically authentic illustrations of Stone Age life.

The Tugendhat Haus

On the opposite side of town, in the northeastern suburb of Černá Pole, modernist guru Mies van der Rohe built the **Tugendhat Haus** (Černopolní 45; tram #5, #9, #17 or #21) in the same functionalist style as the above-mentioned Nový dům settlement, but to a very different brief: the Tugendhats, an exceptionally rich Jewish family who ran a number of the city's textile factories, wanted a state-of-the-art house kitted out in the most expensive gear money could buy. Completed in 1930, the family had barely eight years to enjoy the luxury of the place before fleeing to South America (with most of the period furniture) in the wake of the Nazi invasion. For the last fifty years it has been put to many uses – both the Nazis and Communists were particularly partial to it for exclusive social functions – and only recently has it been possible to gain access to the place (by appointment only; phone ☎576 909). Entering through the top floor, the main living space is actually downstairs, open-plan for the most part, and originally decked out in minimalist monochrome furnishings (a few surviving pieces are on show in the Moravská galérie) offset by colourful Persian carpets. The Communists' "modernisation" after the war was depressingly thorough and the huge unbroken front window, which looked out over the garden and the whole cityscape beyond it, has been replaced by a series of much smaller panes, being all the Communists' glassworks could muster.

FUCHS AND FUNCTIONALISM

Although Brno produced two great modern architects in Adolf Loos and Jan Kotěra, they spent most of their time in Vienna or Prague, and it was left to another Moravian, **Bohuslav Fuchs**, who began working here in 1923, to shape the face of modern Brno. Fuchs and his functionalist cohorts turned their hand to everything from the town's crematorium to the Protestant church on Botanická, its interior decoration as "low-church" and prosaic as you can get. Fuchs' own hand is everywhere in the city, in the now gloomy arcade off Jánská, in the slimline *Hotel Avion* and in Výstaviště itself. His most famous works are the open-plan boarding school and Vesna girls' school (on Lipová, just north of Výstaviště), two simple four-storey functionalist buildings, way ahead of their time *at* the time, but already gone to seed in the intervening years. Perhaps the best way to appreciate Fuchs' work is to head out to the outdoor swimming pool he built in the city's eastern suburbs, just off Zábrdovická (tram #2, #8, #16, #19 or #21 down Cejl), where you can laze by the pool and take in the culture at the same time.

Eating, drinking and entertainment

There's no shortage of good places **to eat and drink** in Brno: the restaurants have an old-fashioned air of good service, while the pubs have, on the whole, kept their traditional decor and low prices – though most close around 10pm, leaving only a few drinking holes open after midnight. As for **nightlife**, classical music and opera are well catered for, and, with a large contingent of students, there's usually something a bit less formal going on during term time. One word of warning: Brno (and many of its pubs and restaurants) tends to close up shop for much of the weekend, so, if you want to experience city life to the full, come on a weekday.

Eating

Česká is a good place to look for **takeaways** like *bramborák* or *hranolky* and, of course, ice cream. If you need provisions, there's a daily **vegetable market** in Zelný trh, and the **bakery** on Josefská is worth heading for. One of the best **stand-up eateries** is the new *Care* bufet, opposite the station; for fish specialities, try *Rybena* on Běhounská.

The choice of sit-down **restaurants** has improved in the last year or so. For traditional **Czech food**, the pubs listed below are likely to be the cheapest, followed by hotel restaurants like the *Slovan* on Lidická, or the *Astoria* on Novobranská. Surprisingly enough, the renovated Habsburg-style *restaurace* at the station is actually not a bad choice. The *Academická* on Gorkého, and *U Luzerna* on Slovákova, are both close to the university and inexpensive. For something a bit more formal, *U Jakuba* is still a good bet, as is the small and intimate *Černý medvěd* on the opposite side of Jakubské náměstí.

Several **ethnic** restaurants have recently added a bit of variety to Brno's culinary scene. The *Italia*, on Zamečnická, serves really good thin-base Italian pizzas, *gelati* and real cappuccino; the *Shanghai*, on Pekárská, en route to Mendlovo náměstí, serves passable Chinese food; while the Greek restaurant near the trade fair ground is worth checking out.

Cafés and pubs

Brno is better for pubs than **cafés**, though of course you can get a coffee in either. During the summer, outdoor tables abound at the various cafés around náměstí Svobody and Zelný trh. More specifically, the *Kapucín* by the Capuchin tombs is OK; and the *Kabinet můz*, on Kozí, and *Ambrosiana*, on Jezuitská, are both trendy arty venues to hang out in. As for **pubs**, the local brew is *Starobrno* but the best places are actually the ones which don't serve it. *Špalíček* at the top of Zelný trh is a good bet, with tables outside in summer and lashings of *Gambrinus* from Plzeň. *Stopka* on Česká, once the best *pivnice* and restaurant in town, has hiked up its prices after a revamp, though downstairs is still OK for a jar of dark beer or *Pilsner Urquell*. If you're keen to taste the local beer, try the renovated Gothic vaults of *U tří knížat*, Minoritská 2, which opens at 8am, or better still rough it at *Pivovarská*, right by the brewery itself on Mendlovo náměstí.

Entertainment and nightlife

Ballet, opera and orchestral concerts are the most accessible of the **classical** arts for those without any Czech, and the Mahenovo and Janáčkovo divadlo, both off Rooseveltova, share the load. It's true that the best Moravian singers are eventually lost to Prague, but they make their reputations here as much as anywhere, and productions are usually competent if a little conservative. There's a lively fringe theatre scene, but unless you chance upon a particularly physical, visual show, the language is going to be an insurmountable barrier. Tickets for all shows can be bought in advance from the **box office** at Dvořákova 11 (☎263 11), or (much more cheaply) from the venue itself, half an hour before the performance starts.

It's not that there aren't any **clubs** in Brno – there just aren't that many. One of the better **live venues** is the *Vysokoškolský klub*, Gorkého 43, which specialises in indigenous folk, jazz and anything in between – check out the monthly posters dotted round town. *U labutě*, Dukelská 100 (tram #3 or #12), is primarily a café (open daily from 1pm), but has live bands some nights. *Harlem* is a serious all-night **club** on Spolková (which used to be called Marxova) in one of the Romany-dominated suburbs, Zábrdovice (take any tram heading up Cejl). *Studio Boleslava Polívky* is a new jazz club on Šelepova (tram #12 or #22, Klusáčkova stop) with regular gigs. The last few years have also seen an **International Music Festival** take place in late June at the village of Lelekovice, 10km north of Brno and home of Moravian modern folk guru Iva Bittová, with an eclectic mix of bands from Britain's own Fred Frith to the likes of *Půlnoc*.

Listings

Books and prints A bizarre collection of books in English grace the shelves of *Orbus Pictus*, náměstí Svobody 18.

Bike rental Tyršova 5, Královo pole; tram #13, #16 or #22.

Car rental *Brnocar* at Solniční 6 (☎240 39).

ČEDOK Main office for foreign tourists is at Divadelní 3 (☎254 66).

Chemists All-night service at Kobližná 7 (☎222 75).

Currency exchange *ČEDOK* will only accept credit cards and foreign cash. All other matters are dealt with by the *Komerční banka*, náměstí Svobody 21. 24-hour exchange at the *Taxatour* snack bar near the main train station.

Hospital Bratislavská 2; emergency medical attention ☎155.

Motorcycle Grand Prix Brno hosts the grand prix at the end of August at the Masarykův okruh. Special buses are laid on during the competition, otherwise take bus #65 and walk westwards for five minutes.

Newspapers The *tabák* on the east side of Masarykova sells a good selection of foreign newspapers.

Police The main police station is at Kounicova 46.

Post office The central post office is next door to the train station. It runs a 24-hour telephone exchange.

Supermarket Brno's biggest supermarket lies between the bus and train stations. Late-night shopping Thursdays.

Taxis The main taxi ranks are outside the station and on Solniční, or dial ☎245 04, ☎256 06 or ☎272 65.

Around Brno

Brno has plenty to keep you occupied, but if you're staying any amount of time, follow the advice of the health authorities (and the example of most of its citizens) and get out of the city at the weekend. One of the few good things about living in Brno's drab concrete suburbs is that you can walk straight out into the woods and bump into a deer. If that doesn't take your fancy, the most popular day trip is to the limestone caves of the **Moravský kras**, closely followed by the castle of **Pernštejn** and the battlefield at **Slavkov** (Austerlitz). Potentially more interesting than any of those is the Renaissance chateau at **Moravský Krumlov**, which houses a museum of the work of the Art-Nouveau painter Alfons Mucha.

The Moravský kras

Number one destination for all tour groups passing through Moravia is the limestone **karst region** of the **Moravský kras**, just over 25km northeast of Brno. It's definitely worth a visit, but unless you're part of a coach tour (you can book yourself on one at *ČEDOK* in Brno), it's not that easy to reach the caves. The best thing to do is to get the morning train from Brno out to BLANSKO (get off at Blansko-Macocha station), and then walk 200m south to the nearby bus terminal. From Blansko bus station, there are buses around 8am and 11am, which will drop you at Skalní Mlýn, near the Kateřinská jeskyně; a couple of buses make the return journey at 2.20pm and 3.20pm. The alternative, if you miss the last bus, is to hitch or walk the 5km back through the woods along the green-marked path.

The most popular tour target is the **Punkevní jeskyně**, the largest cave system and the deepest part of the gorge – get there early if you want to avoid the queues. Daily tours run every fifteen minutes (April–Sept 7am–4.30pm; Oct–March 7.30am–2.30pm) and take around fifty minutes. It's pointless cataloguing the fantastic array of stalactites and stalagmites; suffice to say it really is worth the hassle of getting there. After a series of five chambers, you come to the bottom of the **Macocha Abyss**, a gigantic 138-metre mossy chasm created when the roof of one of the caves collapsed. The first man to descend into the abyss and return alive was Father "Lazerus" Erker in 1728, almost two hundred years before the caves themselves were properly explored. From the abyss, you're punted half a kilometre along the slimy underground Punkva river which gives the cave its name.

KARST TOPOGRAPHY

Named after the Karst, the barren limestone plateau around Trieste, **karst** landscapes are formed by the action of rainwater on limestone. Rain picks up small amounts of carbon dioxide from the atmosphere, which, when it falls on limestone rock, slowly dissolves it. Gradually, over millions of years, the action of rain attacking the rock causes hairline cracks in the limestone, which are steadily enlarged by running water. In its early stages, karst scenery is characterised by thin, narrow ridges and fissures; as these grow and deepen, the dry limestone is raked into wild, sharp-edged fragments – practically bare of vegetation since any topsoil is blown away – and bleached bright white, like shards of bone. Karst scenery is found throughout the Czech and Slovak Republics, particularly in **Moravia** and **Slovakia**.

Rivers do odd things in karst landscapes: they disappear down holes where the limestone is weakest, and flow for miles underground, suddenly bursting from rocks when the geology changes. If an underground river widens and forms a cavern, the drips of rainwater percolating through the soil above will deposit minuscule amounts of the calcium bicarbonate that the rain has dissolved from the limestone above. Over millions of years these deposits form stalactites hanging from the roof of the cavern; the drips on the floor form columns called stalagmites. Traces of other minerals such as iron and copper colour the stalactites and stalagmites, and the whole process forms cave systems like the **Punkevní jeskyně**.

The two other caves open to the public are only slightly less spectacular, but with the added advantage that the queues are correspondingly smaller. The **Kateřinská jeskyně** (30min tour; April–Sept 7.30am–3.30pm; Oct–March 8.30am–3.30pm), one and a half kilometres before the Punkevní jeskyně at the point where the Punkva river re-emerges, is basically one huge "cathedral" of rock formations, a hundred metres long and twenty high. The smallest of the lot is the **Balcarka jeskyně** (April–Sept 7.30am–3.30pm; Oct–March 8.30am–3.30pm), which lies 2km east of the Macocha Abyss. A fourth cave system called Sloupsko-šošůvské jeskyně sits on the southern edge of the village of SLOUP, but is really only worth visiting for the occasional concerts that take place there.

Křtiny, Jedovnice and Senetářov

The whole karst region boasts some dramatic and varied scenery, all smothered in a thick coating of coniferous forest and riddled with marked paths. In other words, it's great **walking country**, and if you're not in a hurry three churches deserve a visit, providing a more relaxed alternative to the crush along the Punkva river. If you're serious about heading off into the hills, try and get hold of the elusive *Okolí Brna východ* map.

You can avoid all the crowds by getting off the Blansko train one stop after ADAMOV and walking east up the **Josefovské údolí** (the blue-marked path follows the road), a steep craggy valley with remnants of the original primeval forest cover and open-air stalagmites. After 3km, at the top of the valley, there's a special nature trail round a mini-karst region of around five caves, none of which is actually accessible. Another 3km further east along the blue path, and out of the woods, leaps the enormous dome and tower of the unfinished pilgrimage church of **KŘTINY**, started by the Baroque genius Giovanni Santini. One of the doors is usually open to let you inside, where the nave has been handed over to a series of frescoed domes which fuse into one, giving the church a Byzantine feel. Only one set of curvaceous cloisters to the south was completed, now filled with the gifts and remembrances of a thousand pilgrims.

Taking the yellow-marked path, skirt the edge of the woods to the northeast, which rise gently past the understated peak of Proklest (574m). Six kilometres on from Křtiny, you emerge from the trees at the small lake which accompanies the village of **JEDOVNICE**, no beauty itself thanks to a fire in 1822 which also torched the late eighteenth-century village church. From the outside the latter looks hurriedly restored, but a group of Moravian artists redesigned the interior in the 1960s, filling it with symbolic art, stained glass and, as the centrepiece, the striking **altar** painting by Mikuláš Medek, *persona non grata* in Czechoslovakia in the 1950s for his penchant for surrealism and social comment. His choice of colours is didactic: a blue cross for hope, and red for the chaos of the world. Unless it's a Sunday, you'll have to get the key from the *kaplan* who lives opposite the church, and who can also furnish you with an *anglický text*.

There's no escaping the modernity of the concrete church at **SENETÁŘOV**, 4km down the road to Vyškov; it's built in the shape of a ship, its "mast" visible as you approach from the plateau – though as a concept, its symbolism is reminiscent of the work of Santini. It's an uncompromising building, with huge plate-glass panels at the west end through which you can clearly see Medek's vivid blue altarpiece. But it's his *Stations of the Cross*, lost in a corner of the north wall and difficult to see without getting inside, that are the church's masterpiece.

Starting with a deep red crown of thorns, the pictures progress in bold simple colours and symbols, fusing into one long canvas and signalling a new and original working of an otherwise hackneyed theme.

On a completely different score, there's a minute **folk museum** (April–Oct Sat & Sun 8am–6pm) in a thatched cottage opposite the church, with a mock-up display of a typical Moravian home around the end of the last century.

PRACTICALITIES

A regular **bus** service runs from Brno and Blansko to Jedovnice, passing through Křtiny and occasionally continuing to Senetářov, making all the above places relatively easy to visit on a day trip from Brno. If you want to **stay** the night, try the *Dukla* (☎0506/50 01; ②) or *Macocha* (☎0506/10 10; ①) in Blansko, but get ČEDOK in Brno to ring through to check vacancies for you. Alternatively, in Jedovnice you can choose from the *Riviera* (☎0506/932 09; ③), private accommodation and the lakeside *Olšovec* campsite (May–Oct 15). There's a good restaurant called *U lišky bystroušky* (☎05/654 39) in BÍLOVICE, halfway between Brno and Blansko on the main railway line; otherwise, the local *hostinec* in each of the villages will provide you with plenty of beer and food.

Brněnská přehrada and Pernštejn

Just as Brno's housing estates peter out to the northwest, you come to the long, snake-like **Brněnská přehrada** (Brno Dam), a favourite place for Brno's inhabitants to go on a sunny weekend (tram #3, #10, #14, #18, #20 or #21). The further you get from the lake's bulbous southern end, the thinner the crowds and the thicker the woods along the shoreline. In the summer, boats zigzag their way to VEVERSKÁ BÍTÝŠKA, passing the thirteenth-century cliff-top fortress of **Veveří**, currently undergoing a lengthy restoration. There's a pretty path through the spruce on the left bank, should you miss the boat back.

Pernštejn

The Gothic stronghold of **Pernštejn** is a lot of people's idea of what a medieval castle should look like, and consequently is one of the most popular targets around Brno. The train up the Svratka valley takes just over an hour from Brno, making it one of the easiest and most rewarding day trips. It's a picturesque train journey, and if you have to change at TIŠNOV, be sure to check out the remarkable Romanesque portal at the town's former Cistercian monastery. The nearest station to Pernštejn is at the village of NEDVĚDICE – from the platform, the castle is immediately visible on the cusp of a low spur to the west. As you approach by the yellow-marked track, it becomes increasingly intimidating. After a series of outer defences, the **castle** (April & Oct Sat & Sun 9am–4pm; May–Aug Tues–Sun 8am–5pm; Sept Tues–Sun 9am–5pm) proper is a truly dramatic sight, kestrels circling the dizzying sheer walls. Originally built in the thirteenth century, various reconstructions have left it a jumble of unpredictable angles and extras, including a death-defying covered wooden bridge which spans the castle's main keeps. The hour-long guided tour is short on specific treasures, but makes up for it in atmosphere and spectacular views across the mixed woodland of the nearby hills. Should you wish to stay, the *U sokolovny* (☎0505/22 67; ①) near the station in Nedvědice might have rooms.

Moravský Krumlov

MORAVSKÝ KRUMLOV, squeezed into a tight bend of the Rokytná river southwest of Brno, and reachable by bus and (almost) by train, is worth making the effort to see. The train station is actually 2km east of the town, which, like a lot of small Moravian towns, has the feel of a mud-spattered working farmyard – there's just one **hotel**, the *Jednota* (☎0621/23 73; ①), on the main square. The local **chateau** to the west of town is similarly earthy, despite its lofty Italianate pretensions. Its delicate arcaded loggia from 1557 now resounds with the noise of the fifteen-year old railway workers who learn their trade here, and you'll have to sneak past the foreman to get a look.

If you haven't got the nerve, content yourself with the **Mucha gallery** (April–Oct Tues–Sun 9am–noon & 1–4pm), housed in one of the outbuildings, which contains the paintings and drawings of one of the better-known Czech artists, **Alfons Mucha** (1860–1939). Mucha was actually born in the even grubbier mining town of Ivančice, a few kilometres to the north, an odd starting point for an artist who is best known for his graceful Art-Nouveau posters. In the West he is known solely for the work he did while in Paris, where he shared a studio with Gauguin (there's a photo of the latter playing the piano with his trousers down just to prove it). In fact, Mucha came to despise this "commercial" period of his work, and when the First Republic was declared in 1918, he threw himself into the national cause like no other artist, designing its stamps, bank notes and numerous posters.

However, it was left to an American millionaire to commission him to do what he saw as his life's work: a cycle of twenty monumental canvases called the *Slovanská epopej* (*The Slav Epic*), which constitute the bulk of the work on display here. In Czech terms they're well-worn themes – Komenský fleeing the fatherland, the Battle of Vítkov – but they were obviously heartfelt for Mucha, and in these damp and badly lit rooms, his gloomy, melodramatic paintings take on a fascination all of their own. In the end he paid for his nationalism with his life: dragged in for questioning by the Gestapo after the 1939 Nazi invasion, he died shortly after being released.

Slavkov

Twenty kilometres by train across the flat plain east of Brno, **SLAVKOV** (Austerlitz) would be just another humble ribbon village, were it not for the great mass of Martinelli's late Baroque **chateau** (Tues–Sun April, Sept & Oct 9am–noon & 1–4pm; May–Aug 8am–noon & 1–5pm) and accompanying Neoclassical church. Like so many chateaux close to the Austrian border, its contents were quickly and judiciously removed by their owners before the arrival of the Red Army in 1945, but the 45-minute guided tour is still worth it for the incredible acoustics of the central concave hall. Every whisper of sound in the giant dome echoes for a full ten seconds, while outside not one word can be heard.

On December 2, 1805, in the fields between Slavkov and Brno, now peppered with simple crosses, the Austrians and Russians received a decisive drubbing at the hands of the numerically inferior Napoleonic troops in the **Battle of Austerlitz** (also known as the "Battle of the Three Emperors"). The Austrians and Russians committed themselves early, charging into the morning fog and attacking the French on both flanks. Napoleon, confident of victory, held back until the enemy had established its position and then attacked at their weakest point, the central commanding heights of the Pratzen Hill, splitting their forces and throwing them into disarray. It was all over by lunchtime, with over 24,000 troops dead. After the battle, all three emperors signed a peace treaty, marking an end to Napoleon's eastern campaign until the fateful march on Moscow in 1812. There's a graphic description of the battle in Tolstoy's epic novel *War and Peace*.

Just over one hundred years later, on the strategic Pratzen Hill (known in Czech as the Pracký kopec) 8km southwest of Slavkov, the **Mohyla míru** (Monument of Peace) was erected on the instigation of a local pacifist priest, and paid for by the governments of France, Austria and Russia, who within three years of pledging the money would once again be at war with one another. The battlefield round about is now just another ploughed field, dotted with the odd little Calvary, but the tent-like stone monument designed by the Art-Nouveau architect Josef Fanta contains a small **museum** (May–Sept daily 8/8.30am–3.30/ 5pm; Oct–April closed Sun), including the obligatory toy soldier mock-up of the battle. Military enthusiasts without their own transport will have to walk the 2km from PONĚTOVICE station (25min) to the battlefield. If you happen to be here on the anniversary of the battle, the Friends of the French Revolution treat onlookers to a chilly re-enactment of it.

Bučovice

Ten kilometres further east, and accessible by train from Brno, the **chateau** (April & Oct Sat & Sun 9am–noon & 1–4pm; May–Aug Tues–Sun 8am–noon & 1– 5pm; Sept Tues–Sun 9am–noon & 1–4pm) at **BUČOVICE** gets a fraction of the visitors who turn up at Slavkov. Part of the explanation must lie with its unpromising exterior: a dull grey fortress with four ugly squat towers. None of it prepares you for the subtle, slender Italianate arcading of the courtyard's loggia, with each set of supporting columns topped by a different carved motif. At the centre of the courtyard a stone fountain was added a few generations later – "a little too robust" as the guide puts it, and out of keeping with the rest of the masonry. The towers, the gardens and countless rooms once matched the charm and elegance of the courtyard, but the Liechtensteins, who obtained the house through marriage in 1597, soon turned the place into little more than a storage house for the family records, scattering its original furnishings among their many other Moravian residences.

The only things they couldn't remove were the original sixteenth-century **ceiling decorations**, a fantastical mantle of sculpture and paint which coats just five or so rooms, none more than twenty feet across. The first few are just a warm up for the thick stucco of the **císařský sál**, with the bejewelled relief figures of Mars, Diana, a half-naked Europa and, most magnificent of all, the Emperor Charles V trampling a turbaned Turk into the paintwork. But the decoration of the **zaječí sál** (The Hall of Hares) is the real star turn, an anthropomorphic work reckoned to be one of the few of that period still in existence. It's a comical scene, with the hares exacting their revenge on the world of man and his closest ally – the dog. The aftermath of the hares' revolution sees them sitting in judgement (wigs and all) over their defeated enemies, as well as indulging in more highbrow activities – hare as Rembrandt, hare as scholar and so on.

Along the Austrian border

Historically, the land on either side of the River Dyje (Thaya), which either forms, or runs parallel with, the border between Moravia and Austria, has for centuries been German-speaking, its buildings designed by Austrian architects and its sights set firmly on Vienna, just 60km to the south. But, as in the rest of the country, the ethnic German population was forcibly removed from South Moravia after 1945 and their private vineyards handed out to the demobilised Czech heroes of the liberation. The region's viticulture is one of the few industries that kept going on private plots even after nationalisation in 1948, but in every other way the last forty years have driven a great wedge between two previously identical regions on either side of the river. The neat, prim and wealthy Austrian Weinviertel to the south now seems worlds apart from the shabby, unkempt and dirt-cheap Moravian side of the Dyje, but there are one or two real high spots that make this a region worth exploring. The recent reopening of the border may yet bring a greater parity, as Austrian *Schillings* begin to filter through, and the region begins to wake from its enforced forty-year slumber.

Mikulov and around

Clinging on to the southern tip of the Pavlovské vrchy, the last hills before the Austrian plain, **MIKULOV** (Nikolsburg) is one of South Moravia's minor gems. Slap bang in the middle of the wine-producing region, it's been a border post for centuries – hence the narrow streets and siege mentality of much of the architecture. The town still functions as a busy crossing point between the two countries; if you're driving from Vienna, it's a great introduction to the country and, given its strategic locale, surprisingly tourist-free.

Raised above the jumble of red rooftops is the **castle** (April–Sept Tues–Sun 8am–4pm), an imposing complex that sprawls over a rocky hill on the west side of town. Close up, it's a plain, rather characterless building: used by the Gestapo to hoard confiscated art objects, it was blown to smithereens by them in the last days of the war in a final nihilistic gesture. It was rebuilt in the 1950s to house the town museum, which covers the history of the town (minus the controversial episodes), viticulture, and dishes out amazing views into Austria.

In 1575 castle and town fell into the hands of the fervently Catholic Dietrichsteins, who established various religious edifices and institutions here. They're also responsible for the hint of Renaissance in the town – the occasional arcade or pictorial sgraffito – and the main square itself, appealingly misshapen and huddled below the castle. Later, behind the oversized plague column, they built the church of **sv Anna**, originally intended to be the family mausoleum, now a strange, monstrous and half-finished building which looks a bit like the Karlskirche in Vienna, with its combination of smooth classical columns and stumpy Baroque towers. On the exposed limestone hill to the east of town, the family also set up a series of chapels. It's a bleak, windblown outcrop, but well worth the sweat of the climb for the view across the vineyards to Vienna.

Mikulov boasted a thriving **Jewish community** until the advent of the Nazis: in the mid-nineteenth century, it was the second largest in the Czech Lands, and the seat of the Chief Rabbi of Moravia from the sixteenth century until 1851. The old Jewish ghetto lies to the west of the castle, where the town's seventeenth-century **synagogue**, on Husova, is slowly being renovated; there are plans to resume services and turn the place into a museum of Jewish culture (due to open some time in 1993). Round the corner in Brněnská, a rugged path leads to the town's overgrown medieval **Jewish cemetery** (židovský hřbitov), with finely carved marble tombstones dating back to 1618. To get into it, you'll need to pick up the key from Brněnská 28, but failing that there's a hole in the wall towards the top of the cemetery.

The town is rarely busy, the majority of visitors pausing for a couple of hours at the most before moving on, since until recently there was no accommodation – there is now just one **hotel**, the *Brichta*, Husova 8. Being in the wine region, the best time to come here is after the grape harvest in late September, when the first bouquet of the year is being tried and tested in vast quantities at the local *sklepy* (wine caves) on the edge of town.

Pavlovské vrchy

Mikulov is the starting point for hiking and exploring the **Pavlovské vrchy**, a big, bulging ridge of limestone hills, rugged and treeless in a thoroughly un-Czech way. Since the damming of the Dyje and the creation of the artificial Nový mlýn lake, the rare plant life on the Pavlovské vrchy has suffered badly. In a rather belated and empty gesture, the authorities declared the region a protected landscape region. With or without its original vegetation, it's good gentle **hiking country**, with wide-angle views on both sides and a couple of picturesque ruined castles along the ten-kilometre red-marked path to DOLNÍ VĚSTONICE. Archaeological research has been going on here since 1924, when an early Stone Age settlement was discovered. Wolves'-teeth jewellery and a number of clay figurines were found here, and the best stuff is now displayed in the Slovak National Museum in Bratislava, including the voluptuous *Venus of Věstonice*, a tiny female fertility figure with swollen belly and breasts. From Dolní Věstonice you can either walk another 4km to the station at POPICE, or catch one of the hourly buses back to Mikulov.

Valtice and Lednice

To the southeast of Mikulov, nose to nose with the Austrian border, are the twin residences of the Liechtenstein family, one of the most powerful landowners in the country until 1945 (see box below). Both chateaux are laid out in one magnificent stately park, the Boří les, and in many ways this delightful setting is the best feature of the whole area.

At **VALTICE** (Feldsberg), the family's foremost residence, the **chateau** (Tues–Sun May–Aug 8am–5pm; Sept 9am–4pm) was cleaned out just before the end of the war, and its endless rooms are relentlessly bare. The whole place has recently been renovated, and its east wing has been converted into a swish hotel and restaurant which does a brisk trade with holidaying Austrians. Valtice only became part of the Czech Lands during a minor border adjustment in 1918, and from the end of the garden, you used to be able see the watchtowers of the Iron Curtain in amongst the chateau's vineyards which produces a good Moravian red. A red-marked path from the train station leads you on a scenic wander through the woods of the **Boří les**, which the family's nineteenth-century heirs took pleasure in embellishing with the odd quasi-historical monument – here a triumphal arch, there a temple to Apollo. The path skirts one of the two fifteenth-century fishponds, eventually winding up in Lednice (3hr).

Although just 7km northwest of Valtice, the family's summer residence at **LEDNICE** (Eisgrub) couldn't be further away in style. Part of the family estate since 1243, it was one of the last to be subjected to a lavish rebuild job in the 1840s, which turned it into a neo-Gothic extravaganza. In contrast to Valtice, there's plenty to look at, romantic interiors crowding every one of its wooden-panelled rooms. Bear in mind, though, that Lednice is one of the most popular Czech chateaux (April & Oct Sat & Sun 9am–4pm; May–Aug Tues–Sun 8am–5pm; Sept Tues–Sun 9am–4pm), so if you want to avoid the tour groups, try the orangerie – or better still head off into the chateau's watery grounds, home to numerous herons and laughing gulls. Piqued by local objections to their plan for a colossal church, the Liechtensteins decided to further alienate the village by building the largest minaret outside the Islamic world: it dominates the view of the park from the chateau, but apart from a few resident swallows, there's nothing to see inside.

PRACTICALITIES

Valtice is just twenty minutes by **train** from Mikulov, and Lednice is served by the occasional train from Břeclav, but travelling between the two, you'd be better off hitching or walking, than waiting for the infrequent bus. As for **accommodation**, there's the *Hubertus* (☎0627/945 37; ②) in the chateau at Valtice, and the *Zámecký hotel* (☎0627/982 20; ①), both of which tend to be swiftly booked out each summer, particularly in August when there's a Baroque Music Festival at Valtice.

Other than camping at the *Apollo* **campsite** (May–Sept) by the Lednice fishpond, the only alternative is to stay in the rather drab town of BŘECLAV, 8km east of the two chateaux (and accessible by the occasional train from Lednice), which has three cheap hotels to choose from.

THE LIECHTENSTEINS

The **Liechtensteins** (of Grand Duchy fame) were for many centuries one of the most powerful families in the Czech Lands and, in particular, Moravia. At their peak they owned no fewer than 99 estates – one more and they would have had to maintain a standing army in the service of the empire. The one who made the most of all this wealth was Prince-Bishop Karl Eusebius von Liechtenstein-Kastelcorn, who came into the family fortune in 1627 and whose motto – "Money exists only that one may leave beautiful monuments to eternal and undying remembrance" – can be seen in practice all over Moravia.

Like nearly all the ethnic Germans who used to live in Czechoslovakia, the Liechtensteins were forced to leave in 1945 on grounds of collaboration with the Nazis. For the last 45 years, it looked like the long history of the Liechtensteins in the Czech Lands had come to an end. Then in 1990, the new government passed a law of *restituce* (restitution), which meant that all property confiscated by the Communists from 1948 onwards was to be handed back to its original owners. Despite having had their property taken from them in the earlier appropriations of 1945, the Grand Duchy has formally requested that at least some of its former residences, which comprise something like 1600 square kilometres of land – ten times the area of present-day Liechtenstein – be returned. Negotiations look likely to continue for some time to come.

Znojmo and around

Further up the Dyje valley, approximately 45km west of Mikulov, **ZNOJMO** (Znaim) is not as immediately appealing as Mikulov. It's a much bigger town, with the last hundred years' industry and suburbs spreading in unsightly fashion to the north and east, which means a stiff hike from the station to the old town: up Rudoleckého, left up Lidická to náměstí Republiky, then up Kollárova to the old town square. Initial impressions of **Masarykovo náměstí** do nothing to dispel the gloom: the sloping market square has a weary air about it. Damaged in the last war, its cobbles have literally gone to seed and the Capuchin buildings at the bottom of the square are as uninspiring as the concrete supermarket that squats at the opposite end.

Hope rears up at the top of the square, in the shape of the **radniční věž**, all that's left of the old town hall, burnt down by the Nazis in the closing stages of the war. A soaring romantic affair, which twists its uppermost gallery at an angle to the main body, the view through its wooden hatches is little short of spectacular – and it's a good way to get your bearings and a feel for this decidedly run-down old town. To climb up the tower, enter through an alleyway on the opposite side of the street, which also serves as the starting point for touring the warren of *podzemí* or **underground tunnels** that run for miles under the old town. A minimum of ten people are needed for a tour, but the armless guide is open to persuasion, since he seems to relish his task of getting visitors lost and confused in this medieval labyrinth, originally built for defensive purposes, later used for storing wine.

At this point you can head off in a number of directions, but the most interesting is the narrow lane of Velká Mikulášská, which leads to the oldest part of Znojmo – a tight web of alleyways woven round the church of **sv Mikuláš**, a plain Gothic hall church sporting an unusual panelled gable. Set at a right angle to it is the much smaller **chapel of sv Václav**, now handed over to the Orthodox community and invariably locked. Nevertheless it's a curious building, on a north–south axis and tucked into the town walls, from which you get a commanding view down the Dyje valley as it blends into the Austrian plain.

"Better a living brewery than a dead castle" goes one of the more obscure Czech proverbs, and as far as Znojmo's **castle** goes it's not difficult to agree. More of a tragedy is the fact that the most valuable twelfth-century paintings in the country, including contemporary portraits of the Přemyslid princes, which adorn the walls of the rotunda of **sv Kateřina**, should have festered in the brewery forecourt for so many years. The murals are currently closed off for restoration, but should be accessible to the public again in the near future: the nearest you'll get, for the moment, is Přemyslovců at the end of Velká Františkánská, where the former **Minorite monastery** (May–Sept daily 8am–4pm; Oct–April Mon–Fri only) puts on the occasional contemporary art exhibition and classical concert in the cloisters.

The location of Znojmo's old town, perched high above the deep gorge of the Dyje to the south, means that leaving the safety of the town walls at the end of Přemyslovců plunges you straight into thickly wooded countryside. It's a gentle wander round the foot of the castle to the chapel of sv Václav, but for a longer walk, take the path down to the dam, and keeping on the same side of the river, climb up to the village of HRADIŠTĚ for an unbeatable vista of Znojmo and the Dyje.

Architecture buffs may want to take a look at the huge yellow colossus of the **Premonstratensian convent** at LOUKA (Klosterbruck), now a suburb of Znojmo (10min walk down the road to Vienna). It was begun but never finished by the Baroque architect Johann Lukas von Hildebrandt, and soon afterwards turned into a barracks, its precious library carried off to Prague's Strahov monastery. From a distance it still manages to make an impression, but, on closer inspection, the smashed windows, and the watchtowers of the Czech Army who currently use it, are a miserable end for such a place.

Practicalities

Trains run fairly frequently from Mikulov to Znojmo, taking around an hour; trains from Brno often take over two hours, with a change (but no wait) at Hrušovany. If you're heading into Austria, the 24-hour border crossing is at HATĚ, 12km southeast on Route 38 (the occasional bus goes there). The cheapest **hotel** in town is the *Černý medvěd* (☎0624/42 71; ①) on the main square. If it's full – or, more likely, closed – try one of the new private hotels, like the *Kárník*, Zelenářská 25 (☎0624/68 26; ①), in the old town, before falling back on the town's characterless luxury hotels. The **campsite** is 3km from the train station at SUCHOHRDLY (bus #1). As for **food**, the old town's northernmost square is a good place to head for *zmrzlina* or *langoše*, but for more substantial fare, try the hot and beery *Znojemská Libuše* behind the main supermarket. Aside from wine, **pickled gherkins** (*kyselá okurka*) are Znojmo's speciality, though you needn't feel any compulsion to join in.

Vranov and Bítov

Twenty kilometres west of Znojmo, the River Dyje has been dammed just above the village of Vranov (see below), and whatever the implications for the equilibrium of the ecosystem, it provides a summer playground for large numbers of holidaying Czechs and Austrians, with a couple of interesting chateaux and some great opportunities for swimming and generally lazing around. Without your own transport, getting around can be a time-consuming business, so it's best to plan to spend at least one or two days in the area.

VRANOV (Frain) itself is a regular South Moravian village, entirely dominated by its cliff-top **chateau** (April & Oct Sat & Sun 9am–4pm; May–Aug Tues–Sun 8am–5pm; Sept Tues–Sun 9am–4pm), magnificently poised on a knife's edge above the Dyje. Originally a medieval stronghold, it was converted into a beautiful Baroque chateau by the Viennese genius Fischer von Erlach after a fire in 1665. There's no alternative to the one-kilometre hike up the steep road which leads round to the back of the castle. Nothing in the rest of the sprawling complex can quite compare to Fischer's trump card at the far end – the real reason for trekking out here. The truly awesome overall effect of the cavernous dome of the **Ancestors' Hall** is as much due to Rottmayr's wild frescoes as to Fischer's great oval skylights: its frenzied, over-the-top paintings depict the (fictitious) achievements of the Althan family who commissioned the work.

At the weekend **buses** run regularly from Znojmo to Vranov, less frequently during the week. Alternatively, you could take the more frequent **train** to ŠUMNÁ station and walk the 4km to Vranov. From Vranov, where there are several cheap **hotels**, it's only a fifteen-minute walk to the *přehrada* (dam) and the sandy beach known as Vranovská pláž; to get there, take the shuttle boat across the lake. From May to September there's a fair bit of life here: camping, chalets, boat rental, a couple of shops and a **daily boat service** up the lake to Bítov and beyond. The sun-worshippers are shoulder to shoulder on the beach in the high season, but it's easy to lose the crowd by picking a rocky spot further upstream.

The village of **BÍTOV**, 8km west up the lake, is more geared to vacationing Czechs than Vranov, and of its two **campsites**, the *Kopaninky* site to the south-east is the more secluded. The only way to get from Vranov to Bítov – apart from hitching – is to take the boat. Even buses from Znojmo to Bítov are infrequent, but connections with Jihlava (see below) are much better. The ruined castle which can be seen from the village is a fourteenth-century defence fort; Bítov's wholesome **castle** (July–Sept Tues–Sun 9am–5pm) is 1.5km further upstream. Like Vranov it boasts a classic defensive location on a spit of grey rock high above the river, which the flooding of the valley has diminished only slightly. For this reason alone, it's worth clambering up to enjoy the view, but inside it's not a patch on Fischer's genius touch at Vranov; contrived neo-Gothic decor and soulless, unlived-in rooms fail to come alive in the tedious guided tour.

Jaroměřice nad Rokytnou

One hour northwest by train from Znojmo, and a convenient place to break the journey to Jihlava, the village of **JAROMĚŘICE NAD ROKYTNOU** is completely overwhelmed by its gargantuan russet and cream Baroque **chateau** (April & Oct Sat & Sun 9am–noon & 1–4pm; May–Sept Tues–Sun 8/9am–noon & 1–4/5pm), built over the course of 37 years by the wealthy and extravagant Johann Adam von Questenberg. For the most part it's the work of Dominico d'Angeli, but the two darlings of Vienna, Jakob Prandtauer and Johann Lukas von Hildebrandt, also appear to have been involved at various stages. The highlights of the hour-long guided tour are the elegant Rococo halls, the *hlavní sál* and the *táneční sál*, where Questenberg used to put on lavish classical concerts.

Alternatively, you could skip the tour and spend the morning exploring the great domed chapel or pottering around the formal gardens, or, even better, come during July and August, when the chateau stages a festival of classical music. Should you wish to stay the night, the moderate concrete **hotel**, *Opera* (☎618/972 30; ①), will no doubt oblige.

Jihlava

When silver deposits were discovered in the nearby hills in the 1240s, **JIHLAVA** (Iglau) was transformed overnight from a tiny Moravian village into one of the biggest mining towns in central Europe. Scores of German miners came and settled here, and by the end of the century Jihlava could boast two hospitals, two monasteries and, most importantly, the royal mint. The veins of silver ran out in the fourteenth century, but the town continued to flourish from the cloth trade, reaching its zenith around the latter half of the sixteenth century when over 700 master spinners worked in the town.

For all its history there's not that much to see in Jihlava. This is partly due to a fire in 1523 and the ravages of the Thirty Years' War, but most of all to the expulsion of ethnic Germans from this "language-island" in 1945. This move signalled the end of an era or, as Czech guidebooks prefer to put it, "the beginning of a new stage in the development of Jihlava". In reality the town has been in decline ever since, plagued by an ignorant Communist council who in their comparatively brief forty-year rule have left the most indelible mark on the town – the mud-brown multistorey car park/supermarket complex plonked in the middle of Jihlava's huge main square in place of a block of medieval houses.

The Town

If you can look beyond Jihlava's most glaring addition, the main square, **náměstí Míru**, is actually a wonderfully expansive space, lined with restrained Baroque and Rococo houses, sporting two fountains, a couple of outdoor cafés and plenty of street life to soak in. At the top of the square is the **town museum** (Tues–Fri & Sun 9am–5pm, Sat 9am–1pm), worth a visit for the interior alone, being one of the few Renaissance houses to survive the 1523 fire. Its covered inner courtyard with an arcaded gallery and diamond vaulting is perfectly preserved and peculiar to Jihlava. You can see different kinds of interior design in the small **art gallery** diagonally opposite, on the main square.

MAHLER IN IGLAU

"I am thrice homeless, as a native of Bohemia in Austria, as an Austrian among Germans and as a Jew throughout the world. Everywhere an intruder, never welcomed." **Gustav Mahler**'s predicament was typical of the Jews of *Mitteleuropa*, and it only exacerbated his already highly strung personality. Prone to Wagnerian excesses and bouts of extreme pessimism, he would frequently work himself into a state of nervous collapse when composing or conducting. It was this Teutonic temperament, more than his German-speaking background, that separated him from his more laid-back Czech musical contemporaries.

Born in 1860 in the nearby village of Kalischt (Kaliště), on the Bohemian side of the border, Mahler's parents took advantage of the 1860 law allowing the free movement of Jews within the Empire, and moved to Pirnitzergasse (Malinovského) in Iglau (Jihlava), where there had been a strong Jewish community since the mid-fourteenth century. Mahler's father Bernhard, "a man of humble origins", ran a distillery and a couple of pubs, drunken dives by all accounts and certainly too much for a sensitive vegetarian like Mahler. These business ventures nevertheless failed to drag the family out of their interminable poverty, which caused the untimely deaths of eight out of his thirteen brothers and sisters. Mahler went to Iglau's German Gymnasium (some fifty years after Smetana), and at the age of ten made his first public appearance as a pianist at the town's municipal theatre, then in a converted church on Komenského. A local farmer persuaded Bernhard to send his boy to Vienna, where he was accepted as a student at the conservatoire. After a fairly stormy career as a conductor that included stints at Olomouc and Prague, Mahler finally settled in Vienna, the place with which he is most closely associated.

For over fifty years now there's been little mention of the town's greatest son, and the only place with any kind of memorial is HUMPOLEC, 25km northwest of Jihlava, a Bohemian town with precious little connection with the composer. Here, a local teacher has single-handedly amassed the largest collection of Mahleriana in the world, now on display on the ground floor of the town museum. Bear in mind, before you get too excited, that it is the remarkable achievement rather than the exhibition itself that's worthy of admiration.

The Jesuit church of sv Ignác is the only church that intrudes onto náměstí Míru, all the town's other churches comply with medieval requirements and are set back from the square. The most attractive of these is the church of **sv Jakub** (St James), east of the square, and best admired from afar where its two plain stone towers and steeply pitched roof rise majestically above the burgher houses around. There's little to get excited about inside, but if you want a closer look you'll have to ask round for the key, or hope a tour group arrives. The town walls run round the back of the church and in the valley below are the woods of the Březinovy sady, which contain a rather sad zoo. On a hot day, they're a cool and pleasant place for a stroll.

For a town originally built on silver, Jihlava lacks the vestiges of prosperity which grace, for example, Kutná Hora. Just one fine gateway guarding the road from the west is all that's left of the town's five gates, along with a few finely carved portals, the remnants of fifteenth-century frescoes, and, in between, a lot of rubble.

Practicalities

If you arrive at the main **train station**, hop on trolley bus A rather than walk the 2km into town; from the **bus station**, it's only five minutes' walk up into town. It hardly seems worth staying the night in Jihlava, but should you need to, the *Grandhotel*, on Husova (☎066/235 41; ③–④), is an option, as is the recently renovated *Zlatá Hvězda* (☎066/294 21; ③), in the sgraffitoed corner house at the bottom of the main square. If you're camping, the lakeside *Pávov* **campsite** (open all year) is 4km north of Jihlava, not far from the motorway; a local bus goes there. In the evenings, there's drinking and dancing in the *Zlatá Hvězda* cellars until 3am; or else you could check out the alternative *AMC Rock Club*, near the bus station. Another option is to go watch the town's army ice hockey team *Dukla Jihlava*, one of the best in the country; they play at the *zimní stadión*, on Tolstého, again near the bus station.

Žďár nad Sázavou

The highest point in the Bohemian-Moravian Uplands or *Vysočina* is around 40km northeast of Jihlava, though you'd hardly realise since the whole range is more like a high plateau. This is and always has been a poor region, but one really good reason for venturing into the hinterland is to visit **ŽĎÁR NAD SÁZAVOU**, originally a small settlement pitched not far from its Cistercian monastery, and established in the thirteenth century.

Since the war the population has increased tenfold, making it one of the largest (and bleakest) towns in the region. The **monastery** complex, which is the only thing worth seeing, is a three-kilometre walk north through the grey new town of Žďár – instructive if nothing else. As you approach the woods and fishponds, there's a small bridge decorated with the familiar figures of eighteenth-century saints. More of a building site than a House of God, the great rectangle of ragged outbuildings which spreads over a muddy paddock to your right is undergoing a slow restoration. You'll need to get the keys from the priest (who speaks some German) to get into the Zelená hora pilgrimage church – worth doing if you've made the effort to come here.

The whole complex is the work of **Giovanni Santini** (who also had a hand in the monasteries of Plasy and Kladruby near Plzeň), perhaps the most gifted architect of the Czech Counter-Reformation. His two great talents were marrying Gothic and Baroque forms in a new and creative way, and producing buildings with a humour and irony often lacking in eighteenth-century architecture. The monastery church isn't a particularly good example, but the **Zelená hora** (Green Hill) pilgrimage church, up through the wooded hill to the south of the monastery, undoubtedly is. It's a unique and intriguing structure: zigzag cemetery walls form a decagon of cloisters around the central star-shaped church, a giant mushroom sprouting a half-formed, almost Byzantine dome, dedicated to sv Jan Nepomucký (St John of Nepomuk). Details of his martyrdom (for which see p.62), symbolic and numerical references to the saint and the Cistercians fill the church. On the pulpit, a gilded relief depicts his being thrown off the Charles Bridge in Prague by the king's men, while everywhere in macabre repetition are the saint's severed tongue and the stars that appeared above his head: above the pulpit, on the ceiling, in the shapes of the windows, and in the five side chapels. Back in the main part of the monastery, there's a book museum and a small exhibition dedicated to Santini (April & Oct Sat & Sun 8am–4pm; May–Sept Tues–Sun 8am–4pm), housed in the stables he himself designed with swirling zigzag patterning on the ceiling. The exhibition traces Santini's influences and is packed with plans and photos of his other works in the Czech Lands.

Practicalities

Žďár is only an hour's fast train ride from Brno; the town centre is 1km north of the train station, and another 2km from the monastery. It's easy to get a room in the town, whose **hotels** include the *Bílý lev* (☎0327/39 82; ②), on the main square, and the huge *Hotelový dům* (☎0327/241 46; ①), just below the square. There's a decent *hostinec* by the monastery, and, fifteen minutes' walk north up the road, a lakeside **campsite** (June 15–Sept 15).

MORE SANTINI

For further exposure to Santini's work, a number of his more lighthearted minor buildings are dotted about the Žďár region. The first, a couple of hundred yards further north of the Cistercian monastery in Žďár, is the graveless and eerie **dolní hřbitov** (lower cemetery), whose three simple chapels symbolise the Trinity. The cemetery walls form gentle ripples that enclose the bare space, inhabited by a lonesome angel calling the tune for Judgement Day.

Down the road at **OSTROV NAD OSLAVOU** (7min by train), using a similar design to the one he employed in the chateau at Chlumec nad Cidlinou, Santini built a *hostinec* (pub) in the shape of a "W" in memory of his local patron, the Abbot of Žďár, Václav Vejmluva (in German his initials read as W.W.). It's seen a lot of use and abuse over the years, and is not in great shape today, but it's still the local village boozer: buy a pint and appreciate the architecture at leisure.

Just 2km northeast of Ostrov and within easy walking distance, the local church at **OBYČTOV** is another Santini design, built in the shape of a turtle, one of the Virgin Mary's more obscure symbols. Four chapels mark each leg, a presbytery the neck, and the west onion-domed tower the distorted head. Ask around for the key to the whitewashed interior, which features more turtle symbolism.

Telč and Slavonice

Telč and Slavonice are two of the most beautiful Renaissance towns anywhere in Europe. Yet while Telč is a popular stopoff on whirlwind tours of the country, Slavonice – every bit as perfect – is invariably deserted. Both are feasible day trips from Jihlava, even on the ridiculously slow *osobní* **trains**, which take up to an hour and a half to reach Telč and slightly over two hours to get to Slavonice (change at Kostelec for both). On the other hand, **buses** to Telč take just 45 minutes (there's even a direct service from Brno), but there's no direct service to Slavonice from Jihlava.

Telč

It's hardly an exaggeration to say that the last momentous event in **TELČ** (Teltsch) was the great fire of 1530, which wiped out all its wooden Gothic houses and forced the town to start afresh. It is this fortuitous disaster that has made Telč what it is: a perfect museum-piece sixteenth-century provincial town. Squeezed between two fishponds, the Štěpanický to the east, the Ulický to the west, the **staré město** is little more than two medieval gate towers, one huge wedge-shaped square and a chateau. Renaissance arcades extend the length of the square, lined with gentle pastel-coloured houses (including, oddly enough, a Renaissance fire station) that display a breathtaking variety of gables and pediments, none less than two hundred and fifty years old.

At the narrow western end of the square, the **chateau** (Tues–Sun April, Sept & Oct 9am–noon & 1–4pm; May–Aug 8am–noon & 1–5pm) in no way disturbs the sixteenth-century atmosphere of the town – it too was badly damaged in the fire, and had to be rebuilt in similar fashion. Like the chateau at the nearby Bohemian town of Jindřichův Hradec, it was the inspiration of Zacharias of Hradec, whose passion for all things Italian is again strongly in evidence. It's not exactly packed with treasure troves, but the period ceilings are exceptional and the whole place is refreshingly intimate and low-key after the intimidating pomposity of the Baroque chateaux of the region. At the end of the tour you'll be let loose on the cloistered garden and the art gallery squeezed into the chateau's east wing.

Most tour groups come here for a couple of hours and then leave, so it's often relatively easy to get a bed in the *Černý orel*, perfectly situated on the main square (☎066/96 22 21; ②). Another possibility is the new *Pod kaštany* hotel on Štěpanická (☎066/96 24 31; ①), just north of the Ulický fishpond, or the various **private rooms** on offer in the old town.

Slavonice

SLAVONICE (Zlabings), 25km south of Telč and a stone's throw from the Austrian border, is in many ways even more remarkable. It's a crumbling monument to a prosperity that lasted for just one hundred years, shattered by the Thirty Years' War which halved the population, and then dealt its deathblow when the post road from Prague to Vienna was rerouted via Jihlava in the 1730s. To make matters worse, the forced removal of the German-speaking inhabitants in 1945 emptied Slavonice, and when the Iron Curtain wrapped itself around the village, road and rail links with the west were severed, border guards stalked the streets and the arrival of any visitor was treated with deep suspicion.

Even now, the **staré město** – not much larger than the one at Telč – has a strange and haunting beauty. The impression is further enhanced by the bizarre biblical and apocalyptic sixteenth-century "strip cartoons" played out on the houses in monochrome sgraffito, many of which have been restored to their former glory. Slowly, though, life is returning to Slavonice: the border crossing has now reopened, albeit for pedestrians and cyclists only (daily 8am–8pm), and the Cold War paranoia has gone – there's even a trendy art gallery/café on the main square, and Austrians (some of whom no doubt once lived here) are gradually rediscovering the town.

Despite Slavonice's attractions, it's difficult to kill more than an hour or so here. For a start, pick up an ice cream at the local *cukrárna*, if only for a closer look at the obligatory diamond vaulting in the entrance hall. Alternatively, go for a quick walk across the former Iron Curtain, a few hundred metres south of the station, to the Austrian village of Fratres. There's a **pension** on the main square should you get stranded or wish to stay. If you don't fancy the slow train journey northwards, Slavonice is well connected by bus to Jindřichův Hradec and points west.

Up the River Morava

What the Labe basin is to the Bohemians, the **River Morava**, 50km east of Brno, is to the Moravians, who settled in this fertile land around the late eighth century, taking their name from the river and eventually lending it to the short-lived Great Moravian Empire, the first coherent political unit in the region to be ruled by Slavs, and the subject of intense archaeological research (and controversy) over the last forty years. For the visitor, it's a dour, mostly undistinguished landscape – flat, low farming country, with just the occasional factory or ribbon village to break the monotony – and most people pass through en route to more established sights. In summer this can be a great mistake, for almost every village in the area has its own folk festival, and in early autumn the local wine caves are bursting with life and ready to demonstrate the region's legendary and lavish hospitality.

Geographically the Morava (along with the River Odra) forms a natural corridor between east and west, difficult to defend against intruders, and consequently trashed by numerous armies marching their way across Europe, from the Turks to the Tartars. Nowadays, at various different points, it forms the border between Slovakia and Austria, then, moving north, Moravia and Slovakia. The surrounding area is known as *Slovácko*, a grey area where Czechs and Slovaks happily coexist – the local dialect and customs virtually indistinguishable from West Slovakia.

Hodonín

As the River Morava cuts across country northeast from the Slovak–Austrian border, the first place of any size is **HODONÍN**, (Göding), an industrial town whose only claim to fame is **Tomáš Garrigue Masaryk**, the country's founding father and first president, who was born here in 1850. His mixed parentage – his mother was German-speaking, his father a Slovak peasant – was typical of the region in the nineteenth century. His statue, which had graced the main square since the foundation of the Republic in 1918, was removed by the Communists, and naturally enough it's back with a vengeance, unveiled by Havel himself shortly after the beginning of his own presidency.

Strážnice and around

For most of the year **STRÁŽNICE** (Strassnitz), 17km upriver, sees perhaps a handful of visitors, but for one weekend at the end of June, thousands converge on this unexceptional town for the annual **International Folk Festival**, held in three purpose-built stadiums in the chateau grounds. During the festival, all hotels are booked solid for miles around and the only thing to do is to bring your own tent and try and squeeze onto the castle campsite (open all year round), or just crash out somewhere in your sleeping bag.

If you're here at any other time of the year, there's only enough to keep you occupied for an hour or two: the chateau, though no work of art itself, contains an exceptionally good **folk museum** (May–Oct Tues–Sat 8am–5pm, Sun 9am–6pm) that belongs to the Institute of Folk Art housed in the same building, and in a field to the south there's a newly established **skansen** (same times as above) with thatched cottages and peasant gear from the outlying villages. Outside of the festival, it should be easy enough to stay at the *Černý orel* on Malinovského, or get a table at the *Zámecká vinárna* in the chateau, which serves up the local wine and features live music at the weekend.

Wine caves in and around Petrov

Strážnice also makes a good base for visiting one or more of the private *sklepy* or **wine caves** that survived collectivisation and now provide the focus of village life in the summer months before and after the grape harvest. Perhaps the easiest *sklepy* to visit for those without their own transport are the Plže caves at **PETROV**, a thin settlement strung out along the main road from Hodonín, one stop down the railway line from Strážnice. Hidden from sight, on the other side of the railway track, are around twenty or so whitewashed stone caves, over two hundred years old, some beautifully decorated with intricate floral designs, others with just a simple deep blue stripe. Most days around late September, there are one or two locals carefully overseeing their new harvest, who'll happily show you around and no doubt invite you to sample (and of course buy) some of their wine. During the rest of the summer, merrymaking goes on in the evenings at weekends. Those with their own transport and a taste for the stuff could check out POLEŠOVICE, 12km north, or MUTĚNICE, 15km west, or better still the thatched *sklepy* at PRUŠÁNKY. There are countless other festivals in the area, as in VLČNOV and HLUK at Whitsuntide, and pilgrimages to places like BLATNICE; check the listings in the local press for forthcoming events.

Uherské Hradiště and around

UHERSKÉ HRADIŠTĚ (Ungarisch-Hradisch), like many towns on the Morava, has sold its soul to industry, and the only time travellers stray into its shapeless centre is in their search for the **Památník Velké Moravy** (April–Oct Tues–Sun 8am–noon & 1–4pm), suspected site of the capital of the Great Moravian Empire. It's actually north of the centre, across the Morava in a part of town known as Staré Město (10min by foot, or bus #1 or #4 to the second stop after the bridge), the archaeological remains housed in what looks like a concrete bunker from the last war. The foundations of a ninth-century church, discovered in 1949, are on display, along with a lot of bones and broken crockery. A more accessible load of old rocks can be viewed, along with a good selection of folk costumes and such-

VELKA MORAVA – THE GREAT MORAVIAN EMPIRE

At its peak under the Slav prince Svätopluk (870–894), the territories of **Velká Morava** (the Great Moravian Empire) extended well into Slovakia, Bohemia, and parts of western Hungary and southern Poland, and arguments over the whereabouts of its legendary capital *Veligrad* have been puzzling scholars for many years. At first the most obvious choice seemed to be Velehrad in Moravia, but excavations there have proved fruitless. Opinion is nowadays divided among Nitra in West Slovakia, Mikulčice, right on the Slovak border southeast of Hodonín, and Staré Město, now part of Uherské Hradiště. The Slovaks, in particular, see themselves as the true descendants of the Great Moravian Empire, while Staré Město is the site pushed for by most Czech archaeologists. Whatever the truth, the whole lot had been laid waste by the Magyar hordes by 906, not long after the death of Svätopluk, and Slovakia remained under Hungarian rule for the next millennium.

like, at the **Slovácké muzeum** (times as above) in the Smetanovy sady to the east of town.

The obligatory Jesuit church aside, the town's only other sight as such is the late Baroque apothecary *U zlaté koruny* on the main square. It's still functioning as a *lékárna* (pharmacy), but the service area has been brusquely modernised and you can only peep through into the frescoed back room. On the same square is the town's oldest and cheapest **hotel**, the *Slunce* (☎015/34 40; ①), best approached before trying the *Morava* (☎015/26 73; ①) on Šafaříkova, or *Grand* (☎015/30 55; ①) on Palackého náměstí; there's also **camping** at the *Kunovice* site (bus #2).

Velehrad

The **Cistercian monastery** at **VELEHRAD**, just 9km across the fields from Uherské Hradiště, is one of the most important pilgrimage sites in the Czech republic. It's an impressive sight, too, the twin ochre towers of its **church** (daily 9am–5pm) set against the backdrop of the Chřiby hills, a low beech-covered ridge which separates Brno from the Morava basin. There's no accommodation here – other than a campsite (April–Sept), 1.5km up the road to SALAŠ – but the village is served by regular buses from Uherské Hradiště.

The monastery's importance as an object of pilgrimage derives from the belief (now proved to be false) that it was the seat of Saint Methodius' archbishopric, the first in the Slav lands, and the place where he died on July 5, 885 (see box below). The 1100th anniversary of this last fact attracted over 150,000 pilgrims from across Czechoslovakia in 1985, the largest single unofficial gathering in the country since the first anniversary of the Soviet invasion in August 1969 (July 5 is now a national holiday). More recently, when Velehrad entertained Pope John Paul II on his light-ning tour of the country in April 1990, half a million people turned up.

There's certainly something about the place that sets it apart: its historical associations, the sheer magnificence of its Baroque detailing, or its strange limit-less emptiness outside of the annual pilgrimage. The gigantic scale of the church is borrowed from the original Romanesque church on the same site, which after being sacked by marauding Protestants several times, burned down in 1681 (you can visit the remains of the Romanesque crypt). Inside, the finer points of the artistry may be lacking in finesse, but the faded glory of the frescoed nave, suffused with a pink-grey light, and empty but for the bent old women who come here for their daily prayers, is bewilderingly powerful.

THE APOSTLES OF THE SLAVS

The significance of Saints **Cyril** (827–69) and **Methodius** (815–85) goes far beyond their mere canonisation. Brothers from a wealthy family in Constantinople, they were sent as missionaries to the Great Moravian Empire in 863 at the invitation of its ruler, Rastislav, less for reasons of piety than to assert his independence from his German neighbours. Thrust headlong into a political minefield, they were given a hard time by the local German clergy, and had to retreat to Rome, where Cyril became a monk and died. Methodius meanwhile insisted on returning to Moravia, only to be imprisoned for two years at the instigation of the German bishops. The pope eventually got him released, but dragged him back to Rome to answer charges of heterodoxy. He was cleared of all charges, consecrated Bishop of Pannonia and Moravia, and continued to teach in the vernacular until his death in 885.

More important than their achievements in converting the local populace was the fact that they preached in the tongue of the common people. Cyril in particular is regarded as the founder of Slavonic literature, having been accredited with single-handedly inventing the Glagolithic script, still used in the Eastern Church and the basis of the modern Cyrillic alphabet that takes his name, while Methodius is venerated by both Western and Eastern Christians as a pioneer of the vernacular liturgy and a man dedicated to ecumenism. After Methodius' death, his followers were duly chased out and forced to take refuge in Bulgaria. The Czech Lands and most of Slovakia came under Rome's sway once and for all, and had to wait until the end of the fourteenth century before they once more heard their own language used to preach the gospel.

Buchlovice and Buchlov

Four kilometres west of Velehrad, still just out of reach of the Chřiby hills, is the village of **BUCHLOVICE** (Buchlowitz), easily accessible by bus from Uherské Hradiště. The reason for being here is to see the Berchtolds' pretty little eighteenth-century **chateau** (40-min guided tour every half-hour Tues–Sun; April & Oct 9am–4pm; May–Sept 8am–5pm), a warm and hospitable country house with a lovely arboretum bursting with rhododendrons, fuschias and peacocks. The house, composed of two symmetrically opposed semicircles around a central octagon, has been recently renovated, and the smallish suite of rooms still holds most of its original Rococo furniture, left behind by the family when they fled to Austria in 1945. Another prize exhibit abandoned in haste was a leaf from the tree beneath which Mary Queen of Scots was executed.

A stiff three-and-a-half-kilometre climb up into the forest of the Chřiby hills, the Gothic hrad of **Buchlov** (times as above) couldn't be more dissimilar. In bad weather, as the mist whips round the bastions, it's hard to imagine a more forbidding place, but in summer the view over the treetops is terrific and the whole place has a cool, breezy feel to it. Founded as a royal seat by the Přemyslids in the thirteenth century, it has suffered none of the painful neo-Gothicising of other medieval castles – in fact the Berchtolds had turned it into a museum as early as the late nineteenth century. Heavy, rusty keys open up a series of sparsely furnished rooms lit only by thin slit windows, and dungeons in which the Habsburgs used to confine the odd rebellious Hungarian. If you're on for a bit of hiking, the stillness and extraordinary beauty of the surrounding beech forests are difficult to match, but make sure you stock up with provisions, as there are few shops in the area. The only place to stay is the *Smraďavka* campsite (open all year), 2km southeast of Buchlovice.

Luhačovice

Twenty-seven kilometres east of Uherské Hradiště, **LUHAČOVICE** is decidedly lush after the rather demure aspect of the Morava valley, but as a rather genteel spa town it can't hope – nor does it try – to compete with the pomp and majesty of the west Bohemian spas. Although the springs are mentioned as far back as the twelfth century, nothing much was done about developing the place until it was bought up in 1902 and the first of Dušan Jurkovič's quirky half-timbered villas, which have become the spa's hallmark, were built.

The largest of these buildings, the **Jurkovičův dům**, dominates the central spa gardens which spread northeast from the train station. The beams are purely decorative, occasionally breaking out into a swirling flourish, and the roof is a playful pagoda-type affair – all in all a uniquely Slovak version of Art Nouveau. The blot on Luhačovice's copybook is the new colonnade, a graceless concrete curve, but nevertheless a good place to sit and watch the patients pass by, sipping the waters from their grotesquely decorated mugs. The rest of the spa forms a snake-like promenade boxed in by shrubs and trees, with overly quaint bridges spanning the gentle trickling river. Soon enough you hit another cluster of Jurkovič buildings, one of which is the open-air natural spring **swimming pool**, good for a cheap unchlorinated dip. The villas continue into the leafy surburbs, but unless you fancy a hike into the surrounding woods or are staying at the lakeside **campsite** a kilometre up the main road (mid-April to Sept), there's no reason to continue walking.

Practicalities

To get to Luhačovice from Uherské Hradiště by train, you need to change at Uherský Brod; buses run direct, though less frequently. The **bus** and **train stations** are at the southwestern end of the spa and the two **hotels** open to non-patients are within a few hundred metres of each other: the more expensive *Alexandria* (☎067/93 33 11; ③), which runs a "traditional" variety show in its nightclub, and the down-to-earth *Litoval* (☎067/93 30 40; ①). Check with ČEDOK, near the train station, for any other possibilities. Although buses from all over the country run regular services to Luhačovice, it's still a bit out on a limb, stuck halfway up the Šťávnice valley leading nowhere. If you're planning to continue into Slovakia, however, the scenic train journey from Uherský Brod through the White Carpathians to Trenčianska Teplá is as good a way as any to get there.

Zlín

Hidden in a gentle green valley east of the Morava, **ZLÍN** is one of the most fascinating Moravian towns. Despite appearances, it's not just another factory town, it is *the* factory town – a museum of functionalist architecture and the inspiration of one man, **Tomáš Baťa** (pronounced "Batya"). When Baťa set up his first factory at the turn of the century, Zlín's population was just 3000. Now, with suburbs trailing for miles along the River Dřevnice, it is approaching 90,000. Its heyday was during the First Republic when Baťa planned and started to build the ultimate production-line city, a place where workers would be provided with good housing, schooling, leisure facilities and a fair wage. All along the approach roads to

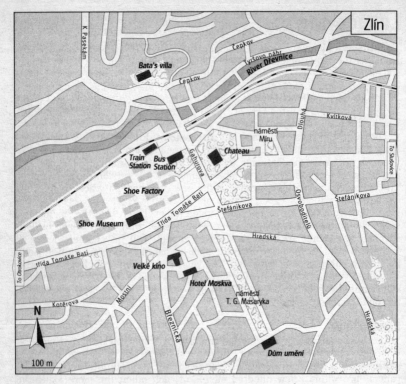

the town centre you can see the red-brick shoe-box houses which Baťa constructed for his workers as "temporary accommodation" – houses which have lasted better than anything built after 1948. The combined effects of Allied bombing, nationalisation and economic stagnation have left only a hint of the model garden city Baťa had in mind. Zlín can't hope to appeal to everyone's aesthetic tastes, but it does present an entirely different side of the country from the usual provincial medieval staré město.

A little history

Son of a local cobbler, Tomáš Baťa worked his way up from nothing to become the First Republic's most famous millionaire. He grew rich supplying the Austro-Hungarian army with its boots during World War I, and between the wars quickly became the largest manufacturer of shoes in the world, producing over 50 million pairs annually. Baťa died in a plane crash in 1932 at the peak of his power, and although his work was continued by his son (also called Tomáš), the family and firm were forced to leave the country in 1938. Tomáš Junior elected to go to Canada, taking his own management team (100 families) and shoemaking machinery with him. There, he quickly set about building another model factory town, known as Bataville, just outside Ottawa, and the company continued to expand into the vast multinational it is today.

Nationalisation in 1948 robbed Baťa of the company's spiritual home. When the Communists fell from power in November 1989, Tomáš Junior paid his first visit to Zlín for over forty years – the whole town turned out to geet him. After tough negotiations with the government, Baťa has regained a foothold in shoe production and retailing, with around a fifteen percent stake in the market. Property returned to the firm includes the flagship store, Dům obuvi, on Wenceslas Square (though not, in fact, the factory at Zlín). Other Baťa shops are now reopening, most housed in their renovated modernist buildings – at least one industry in the former Czechoslovakia looks set to survive the difficult times ahead.

The Town

Baťa was a longstanding patron of modern art, art which would reflect the thrust and modernity of his own business. In 1911 he had his own **villa** built, on the north side of the river, by the leading Czech architect of the time, Jan Kotěra; a very understated affair, virtually devoid of ornamentation, it's now a *dům maldeže*. In the late 1920s Le Corbusier was called in to design the town, but after an abortive sketch of the place, the job fell to local architect **František Gahura**, who had studied under Kotěra and was now given the chance of a lifetime – to design and build an entire city.

Unlike every other town in the country, Zlín does not revolve around the local chateau or marketplace but around the **Shoe Factory** itself, its sixteen-storey offices designed by one of Gahura's assistants, Vladimír Karfík. The style – concrete frame, red-brick infill and plate-glass windows – is typical of all the town's original 1930s buildings, slavishly copied and barbarised by undistinguished postwar architects. Baťa's own office was a huge air-conditioned lift capable of visiting every floor. As well as serving as the corporation's administration office, it now houses Zlín's main "sight", the **Shoe Museum** (Obuvnické muzeum; Mon–Fri 8am–4pm, Sat 8am–2pm), which used to work the same shift as the rest of the factory: Monday to Friday 6am to 2pm. Even if you're not a foot fetishist, it's a wonderful 1930s-style museum, with shoes from all over the world from medieval *boty* to the latest sad attempts of the Zlín factory (renamed *Svit* after nationalisation in 1948), plus a recently "revised" final section on Baťa himself.

From out of the factory grounds rises the obligatory red and white striped chimney, industriously spewing black smoke over the town – in its own way a reassuring guarantee of further employment. When the siren goes at 2pm for the end of the dayshift, the workers pour out of the factory gates and onto the trolley

ZLÍN – GOTTWALDOV

On old maps of the country and on the odd signpost on the roads leading to Zlín, you might see mention of **Gottwaldov**, the name given to the town by zealous local Party hacks in 1949 after the country's notorious first Communist president, Klement Gottwald, known as the "Stalinist butcher". It was no doubt seen as a just revenge on Baťa, who rid his shop floor of Communists by decree in the 1920s. Not long into the Velvet Revolution, the idea of reverting to the original name became a local obsession. Banners were draped out of windows saying "ať žije Zlín" ("Long live Zlín"), and sure enough, by 1990, the town once more became officially known as Zlín.

buses, as if part of some strange Orwellian dumb show. Directly opposite the main entrance, across třída Tomáše Bati, is Karfík's plate-glass department store which naturally includes a shoe shop (the country still leads the world in one respect – shoe consumption, which stands at an annual rate of 4.2 pairs per capita). Beyond here, further up the slope, lies the faded white 1930s **Velké kino** which holds 2000 movie-goers, and the eleven-storey **Hotel Moskva**, built by Karfík and Lorenz in 1933.

Gahura's master plan was never fully realised and much of the town is accidental and ill-conceived. Only the sloping green of the **Masarykovo náměstí**, flanked by more boxy buildings, gives some idea of the trajectory of Gahura's ideas. The first block on the left is Gahura's Masarykovy školy, where Baťa pursued his revolutionary teaching methods still admired today. At the top of this leafy space is the **Dům umění**, designed by Gahura in 1932 as a memorial to Baťa, where his statue, some memorabilia, and the wreckage of the biplane in which he crashed used to stand. For the moment it serves as the concert hall for the town's orchestra and for exhibitions of contemporary art – appropriate enough given Baťa's tireless patronage of the **avant-garde**, which he not only utilised in his photographic advertising, but also produced in the film studios that were built here between the wars, which still produce many of the animation films for which the country is renowned. The only other place of interest is the modest country **chateau** (Tues–Fri 9am–5pm, Sat & Sun 10am–6pm) set in the park opposite the factory, which contains a museum, art gallery and café.

SLUŠOVICE

It is no mere coincidence that the region that produced Baťa and Zlín should be home to **JZD Agrokombinát Slušovice**, less than 10km east of Zlín and probably the most thrusting and successful company of the Communist era. Reports of the scope and range of its activities have always been a mixture of fact and myth, but, having started out as just another farming cooperative in the 1950s, it ended up in the 1980s producing everything from computers to cucumbers, running its own national chain of supermarkets, restaurants and hotels (including one in Vietnam), an international airport, and even its own football team. If you've got your own transport, a quick spin up the newly resurfaced roads that surround Slušovice is a salutary experience. The white and yellow of JZD AK turn up everywhere: on garden fences, on the special bus stops, and across the roofs of factories. Slušovice has also become something of a centre for the surrounding districts, hosting shambolic flea markets as well as horse-racing, cycling and football events – at the weekend the place is often packed.

The key to the co-op's success was that it enjoyed the enthusiastic patronage of the Party, but the real driving force behind Slušovice's meteoric success was **František Čuba**, the co-op's founder. Čuba's style of management was nothing if not controversial, combining a Thatcherite disregard for labour laws and pay differentials with a head-hunting recruitment policy which, perhaps uniquely for the former Eastern Bloc, was not based wholly on Party membership. The events of 1989 witnessed fairly vitriolic attacks against his autocratic practices, but Čuba seems to have ridden out the storm despite blunt statements like "democracy ends at the gates of the enterprise", landing himself the largest piece of the shareholding cake in the company's foreign trade section. However, the future is uncertain even for this most modern of companies, which basically knew all the loopholes of the old system but now has to meet the challenge of a market economy.

Lastly, and a propos of nothing in particular, Zlín is the birthplace of two unlikely bedfellows, the not so avant-garde playwright **Tom Stoppard**, and New York magnate's ex-wife, Ivana Trump (see below). Stoppard's father was a Czech doctor by the name of Eugene Straussler, but barely two years after his birth, the family fled from the Nazis to Singapore, where his father died. His mother later married a major in the British army (named Stoppard) and settled in England. These two snippets explain two otherwise puzzling points: why Stoppard has a slight foreign accent and why the Tom Stoppard Prize is given to Czech or Slovak authors in translation. **Ivana Trump** (Trumpová to the Czechs), was born here as Ivana Zelníčková, and rose to fame in her home country in the 1972 Czechoslovak Olympic ski team. Her shocking blond hair and formidable physique allowed her to pursue a modelling career in Canada, before making the headlines as wife (and now ex-wife) of the tycoon, Donald Trump.

Practicalities

Arriving at Zlín's **train** or **bus station**, you're just a few minutes' walk from the centre and everything there is to see. **Accommodation** in Zlín is expensive, catering mostly for business clientele. *The* hotel to stay at is Gahura's high-rise *Moskva* (☎067/2312; ⑤), though it's also the centre of the town's nightlife, with a casino, disco and its fair share of prostitutes. Otherwise, there's the *Sole* (☎067/ 277 85; ④), 1km out on the road to Slušovice (bus #31 or #54), or *Ondráš* on Kvitkova (☎067/232 09; ③). For **food**, the hotel restaurants are your best bet, or alternatively the vegetable market around náměstí Míru. The nearest **campsite** (open all year) is 12km west in Napajedla, on the River Morava.

Kroměříž

KROMĚŘÍŽ (Kremsier), 30km or so up the Morava from Uherské Hradiště, and seat of the bishops of Olomouc from the Middle Ages to the nineteenth century, is one of Moravia's most graceful towns. Its once-powerful German-speaking population has long since gone, and nowadays the town feels pleasantly provincial, famous only for its Moravian male-voice choir and folk music tradition. Quiet though it is, Kroměříž is definitely worth a day trip, if only for the chateau's rich collections and the town's very beautiful and extensive gardens.

Savagely set upon by the Swedish army in the Thirty Years' War, Kroměříž was rebuilt by order of **Prince-Bishop Karl Eusebius von Liechtenstein-Kastelcorn**, a pathological builder (see p.270), and a member of the richest dynasty in Moravia at the time. Vast sums of money were spent not only hiring Italian architects, but also enriching the chateau's art collection and establishing a musical life to rival Vienna. Liechtenstein founded a college for choristers, maintained a thirty-piece court orchestra and employed a series of prestigious *Kapellmeisters*, though aside from the chateau's extensive archives there's little evidence of courtly life extant today.

The old town

Standing on the southwest side of the River Morava, the centre of the **staré město** is the former marketplace of Velké náměstí. A broad, gracious square, its sea of cobblestones is interrupted only by the four bushy lime trees that surround

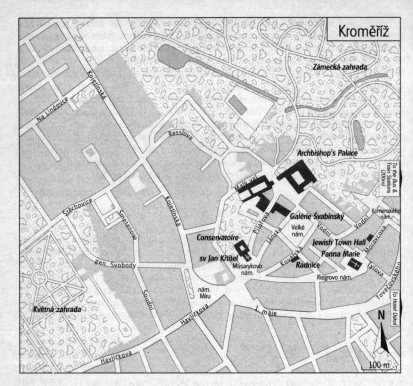

a plague column and fountain (there's an even better column and fountain ensemble on Riegrovo náměstí). Arcades have survived here and there round the square, and the radnice has a fine white Renaissance tower, but the houses themselves have suffered over the years. Jánská, just off the square, hides the town's finest ensemble: a flourish of terraced canons' houses with bright Empire frontages in primary colours.

The Archbishop's Palace

The houses at the northern corner of Velké náměstí part to reveal the **Archbishop's Palace** (1–2hr guided tour; April & Oct Sat & Sun 9am–5pm; May–Sept Tues–Sun 9am–5pm), a Baroque fortress whose severity is relieved only by the fifteenth-century lanterned tower, sole survivor of the Swedes' rampage in the Thirty Years' War. Inside, the chateau is actually a more gentle Rococo than its uncompromising exterior might at first suggest. The dark wood and marble decor of the small *manský sál* where the bishops held court is overwhelmed by Maulbertsch's celebratory frescoes, which bear down on guests from the unusually low ceiling. The archbishop's bedroom rather alarmingly contains a double bed – the official story being that it was for his parents when they came to visit.

The showpiece of the palace is the fiddly white and gold excess of the **sněmovní sál**, as high and mighty as anything in Prague, and a perfect setting for the concerts that still take place here. In the first three months of 1849, delegates from all parts of the Empire met to thrash out a new constitution in the face of the revolutionary events of the previous year. The "Kremsier Constitution" that came out of these brainstorming sessions acknowledged "equality of national rights", only to be unceremoniously ditched by the Habsburgs who launched into their final bout of absolutism a few years later.

If you want, you can skip the tour entirely and just visit the **Chateau Gallery** (Zámecká obrazárna), which contains what's left of the Liechtensteins' vast collection, still the best selection of sixteenth- and seventeenth-century European paintings in Moravia. There's plenty of bucolic frolicking supplied by the Flemish masters, including an earthy Breughel, and a more sober portrait of Charles I of England and his wife Henrietta by Van Dyck. Others worth noting are Veronese's awestruck *Apostles*, Cranach's *Beheading of St John the Baptist* (with a mangy dog lapping up the spillage), and, the gallery's prize possession, Titian's gruesome *Apollo Punishing Marsyas*.

The rest of the old town

Like Olomouc (see Chapter Seven), Kroměříž is a place as rich in gardens as in buildings. The watery **Zámecká zahrada** (daily 7am–6.30pm), established by one of the green-fingered Chotek family who held the archbishopric in the 1830s, stretches right down to the Morava, covering an area twice the size of the old town. Having long since lost its formality, it's now a pleasantly unruly park, reeking of wild garlic and hiding an aviary, a deer park and a few stalking peacocks. Ten minutes' walk west of the chateau is the **Květná zahrada** (daily 7am–7pm), more formal but also more beautiful and generally in a better state of repair. The garden was laid out by the Liechtensteins in the 1670s, "ten years and no expense spared" as the Latin inscription reminds you. Its finest vista and one much snapped by photographers is the Neoclassical colonnade along the gardens' north side, with its parade of columns, 46 in all, each topped by a Roman bust.

Other than the bishop's palace and its two gardens, there's not much else on offer in Kroměříž. The **Galérie Švabinský** (Tues–Sun 8am–noon & 1–5pm) on the main square is mostly dedicated to the work of Max Švabinský, a turn-of-the-century artist and graphicist who was born here in 1872. There's no denying his skill nor his prolific output, but he's a mite too gushy and romantic for today's tastes, and the drawings of nudes and tigers displayed here are unlikely to make many new converts. Of the town's churches, the Gothic sv Mořic is the oldest, but its innards were ripped out by fire in 1836 and rebuilt without much feeling. A better bet is the Baroque church of **sv Jan Křtitel** at the top of Jánská, whose sensuous lines and oval dome represent one of the showpieces of Moravian Baroque.

Lastly, it's worth wandering round to Moravcova in the easternmost corner of the old town, which was formerly the Jewish ghetto. Jewish communities in places like Kroměříž, Uherské Hradiště and Prostějov were among the largest in the Czech Lands before World War II, and since they provided many essential services the local bigwigs left them alone. The **Jewish Town Hall** (the only one outside Prague) in Moravcova is remarkable not for its architectural beauty but for its mere existence, the result of a magnanimous gesture by the prince-bishop for services rendered in the Thirty Years' War; today it serves as a local cultural centre and gives little hint of its previous life.

Practicalities

The **train** station is across the River Morava; as you walk into town, pay a quick visit to *ČEDOK* on Komenského náměstí, who hand out free sketch-maps of the town. The **accommodation** scene in Kroměříž was pretty dire at the time of going to press; the *Straka* (☎0634/217 15) on Komenského náměstí, once the cheapest option in town, is currently under reconstruction, as is the *Haná* (☎0634/204 68) on the main square; which leaves only the *Oskol* on the street of the same name (☎0634/242 40; ③), a modern hotel in an unprepossessing part of town, and a short walk east of the main square.

travel details

Trains

Connections with Prague Brno (hourly; 3hr 15min–4hr 30min); Žďár nad Sázavou (12 daily; 2hr 30min–3hr 30min); Jihlava (10 daily; 2hr 20min–4hr).

From Brno to Žďár nad Sázavou (hourly; 1hr–1hr 40min); Jihlava (up to 11 daily; 2hr–2hr 40min); Blansko (up to 16 daily; 25–40min); Slavkov/Bučovice (up to 12 daily; 25–40min/40–50min); Znojmo (6 daily; 1hr 40min–2hr 20min); Olomouc (up to 20 daily; 1hr 30min–2hr 40min); Bratislava (up to 20 daily; 1hr 45min–3hr 30min); České Budějovice (2 daily; 4hr 30min); Liberec (2 daily; 6hr 40min); Poprad/Košice (2 daily; 11hr 15min).

From Znojmo to Mikulov/Valtice (11 daily; 1hr 10min/1hr 30 min); Jaroměřice nad Rokytnou (12 daily; 45min–1hr 15min); Jihlava (3 daily; 1hr 45min).

Buses (ČSAD only)

Connections with Prague Brno (hourly; 2hr 35min); Znojmo (up to 4 daily; 3hr); Kroměříž/Zlín/Luhačovice (1 daily overnight; 6hr/6hr 30min/7hr 15min).

From Brno to Křtiny/Jedovnice (up to 10 daily; 45min/1hr); Znojmo (up to 11 daily; 1hr 10min); Mikulov (up to 14 daily; 1hr 20min); Hodonín (up to 8 daily; 1hr 20min); Buchlovice/Uherské Hradiště (up to 10 daily; 1hr 10min/1hr 20min); Zlín (up to 16 daily; 2hr–2hr 40min); Kroměříž (up to 14 daily; 1hr 30min); Luhačovice (up to 4 daily; 2hr 10min).

From Uherské Hradiště to Velehrad (up to 14 daily; 25min); Buchlovice (up to 15 daily; 20min); Strážnice/Hodonín (up to 4 daily; 45min/1hr); Luhačovice (up to 5 daily; 40min); Zlín (up to 16 daily; 40min–1hr); Kroměříž (up to 6 daily; 1hr); Trenčín (up to 6 daily; 1hr 15min).

CHAPTER SEVEN

NORTH MORAVIA

North Moravia (Severní Morava) is not the never-ending conglomeration of factories that its critics would have you believe, though it certainly has more than its fair share of ecological disaster zones, in particular the industrial belt in the Odra (Oder) basin, now in the grip of a severe depression. At the same time the north also boasts some of Moravia's wildest and most varied countryside, including the **Jeseníky**, the region's highest peaks, which form part of what is still – nominally at least – known as Czech Silesia. As with the Sudetenland regions of Bohemia, Silesia's long-standing German community was forcibly expelled after the last war, leaving many villages and towns visibly underpopulated even today.

To the east, near the border with Slovakia, the traditional communities in the nether reaches of the **Beskydy** hills have fared much better. Wooden houses and churches are dotted along the valley, and a whole range of folk buildings have been gathered together and restored in the republic's largest open-air museum in **Rožnov pod Radhoštěm**. In addition to its folk culture and hiking potential, the Beskydy is endowed with some intriguing museums: a large car collection at the *Tatra* plant in **Kopřivnice**, a hat museum in **Nový Jičín**, and two memorials to famous local boys – Sigmund Freud, who was born in **Příbor**, and Leos Janáček, who lived and worked in **Hukvaldy**.

The region's two largest cities typify North Moravia's contradictions. **Ostrava**, the country's largest mining and steel town in the north, is a place no Moravian would ever recommend (with some justification); **Olomouc**, on the other hand, the medieval capital on the banks of the River Morava, is probably Moravia's most attractive and vibrant city after Brno, and a definite target in the region.

Olomouc

For the last twenty years or so, the only foreigners to be seen on the streets of **OLOMOUC** (pronounced "Olla-moats" and known to the city's sizeable prewar German community as *Olmütz*) were Soviet soldiers from the nearby garrison, easily picked out by their flying-saucer hats and tightly fitting riding boots. Happily, this episode in the city's life is now over, and its reputation as Moravia's most immediately appealing city is surfacing once again. With a well preserved staré město, sloping cobbled squares and a plethora of Baroque fountains, not to mention a healthy quota of university students, Olomouc has a great deal more to offer than most Moravian cities.

Occupying the crucial Morava crossing point on the road to Kraków, Olomouc was actually the capital of Moravia from 1187 to 1641, and the seat of the arch-bishopric for even longer. All this attracted the destructive attention of Swedish troops in the Thirty Years' War, and their occupation in the 1640s left the town for dead. During this period, the capital was moved to Brno, in reward for the latter's heroic stand against the Swedes, and only the wealth of the church and its

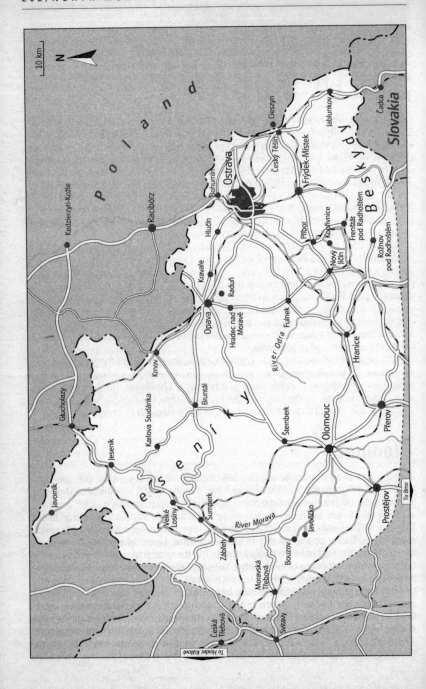

strategic trading position kept Olomouc alive. Meanwhile, the military threat from Prussia confined the town within its eighteenth-century red-brick fortifications; only after these were finally torn down in 1888 did the city begin to evolve into the industrial centre it now is.

The City

Despite being a quarter the size of Brno, Olomouc has the same exciting buzz of life, its main arteries chock-a-block with shoppers in the afternoon rush. The **staré město** is a strange contorted shape, squeezed in the middle by an arm of the Morava. **Train** and **bus** terminals are 1.5km east of the old town – and too far to walk – so on arrival, take any tram heading west up Masarykova and get off after three or four stops (get on at the front and drop the fare into the machine).

Horní and Dolní náměstí

In the western half of the staré město, all roads lead to the city's two central cobbled main squares, which are hinged to one another at right angles. The lower of the two, Dolní náměstí, is more or less triangular, but the upper one, **Horní náměstí**, is thoroughly irregular, at its centre an amalgamation of buildings and styles that make up the **radnice**. From its creamy rendering the occasional late-Gothic or Renaissance gesture emerges – a freestanding flight of steps, the handsome lanterned tower soaring up to its conclusion of baubles and pinnacles and a lonely oriel tucked round the back. Most people, though, stare at the north side with its crude arcade of shops and astronomical clock, which, like its more famous successor in Prague, was destroyed in the war. The rather soulless workerist remake chimes all right, but the hourly mechanical show is disappointing.

Far more action-packed is the monumental, polygonal **Holy Trinity Column**, erected in the first half of the eighteenth century to the west of the radnice, big enough to be a chapel and easily the largest plague column in either republic. It's a favourite place for meeting up, eating your lunch, or just sitting and soaking it all in. Set into the west facade of the square is the **Divadlo Oldřicha Stibora**, previously the *Olmützer Stadttheater* where the young Gustav Mahler arrived as the newly appointed *Kapellmeister* in 1883. The local press took an instant dislike to him, according to his own words, "from the moment I crossed the threshold . . . I felt like a man who is awaiting the judgement of God". No doubt there was a strong element of knee-jerk anti-Semitism in his hostile reception, but this was not helped by Mahler's own autocratic style, which caused a number of the local prima donnas to live up to their name. He lasted just three months.

Olomouc makes a big fuss of its sculpture, like that adorning the Edelmann Palace (no. 28 – now a bookshop), and even more of its **fountains**, which grace each one of Olomouc's six ancient market squares. Horní náměstí boasts two of them: Hercules, looking unusually athletic for his years, and, to the east of the radnice, a vigorous depiction of Julius Caesar – the fabled founder of the city – bucking on a steed which coughs up water from its mouth. Jupiter and Neptune can be found in **Dolní náměstí**, which has a dustier feel to it, sloping down to the characteristically low-key church of the Capuchins, with the single Renaissance oriel of the **Haunschild Palace**, on the corner with Lafayettova, standing out amongst the subdued Baroque facades. The city's main **art gallery** is – temporarily at least – at no. 7 on the east side of the square (Mon–Fri 9am–noon & 1–5pm, Sat noon–5pm, Sun 9am–noon).

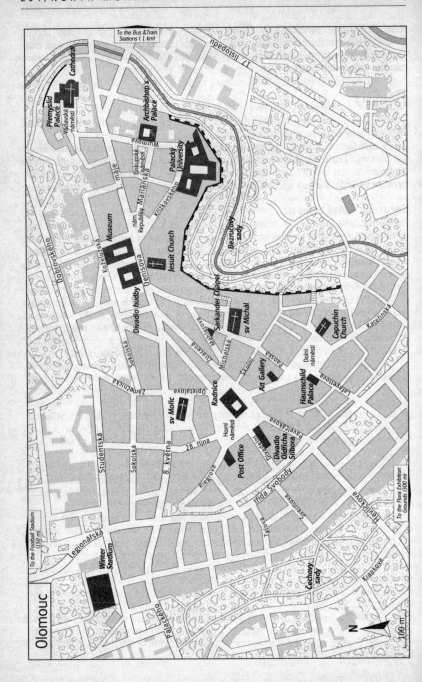

Olomouc

To the Bus &Train
Stations (1 km)

17. listopadu

To the Football Stadium
(150 m)

Legionářská

Winter
Stadium

Palackého

Čechovy
sady

Krapkova

Hálíčkova

To the Flora Exhibition
Grounds (300 m)

Kateřinská

Lafeyettova

Dolní
náměstí

Capuchin
Church

Pavelčákova

Haunschild
Palace

panská

Art Gallery

Divadlo
Oldřicha
Stibora

třída Svobody

Škrétova

Tylova

Kateřinská

Dobrovského

Sokolská

Studentská

Sokolská

8. května

Křížová

Litovelská

Pekařská

Stolní

Michalská

Malinská

Žerotína

Ztracená

Opletalova

28. října

Horní
náměstí

Radnice

sv Mořic

Post Office

Divadlo

Sarkander Chapel

sv Michál

Zámečnická

Koželužská

Divadlo hudby

Museum

Jesuit Church

Denisova

Křížkovského

nám.
Republiky

Mariánské

Biskupské
náměstí

Wurmova

1 máje

Archbishop's
Palace

Palacký
University

Bezručovy
sady

Přemyslid
Palace

Václavské
náměstí

Cathedral

N

100 m

The central sidestreets

North of Horní náměstí is the church of **sv Mořic**, an oddly mutant building from the west at least, and defensive like a Norman fort, but inside overcome by a thick coat of pink paint that makes the original Gothic interior difficult to stomach. It does, however, boast the largest organ in either republic, an ugly dark wooden affair with 2311 dirty grey pipes – it sounds better than it looks. Back out through the west door, you're confronted with a typical socialist supermarket, which has muscled its way into the historic part of town with the connivance of the philistine Communist council.

Two of the city's best-looking backstreets, Školní and Michalská, lead southeast from Horní náměstí up to the long slope of Žerotínovo náměstí, which features an appealing ensemble of lime trees, streetlamps and Baroque statuary at its upper end. Overlooking them all is the church of **sv Michál**, plain enough on the outside but inside cool, spacious and clad in the masterly excess of Baroquification. Three octagonal domes rise up in Byzantine fashion, raised up by Roman pilasters with Corinthian capitals so large their acanthus leaves bear fruit. It's like some neo-Romanesque basilica, and in the middle of Moravia, frankly quite disorientating. Romany families have been moved into the dilapidated streets round about, and as the bedclothes get aired and the sun beats down, there's a Mediterranean feel to the quarter.

Close to sv Michál on Univerzitní, the exuberance of the turn-of-the-century **Vila Primavesi** is well hidden behind dense foliage and a coat of blackened pebbledash. It's now a health clinic, but it's worth climbing the stairs – a blaze of gold and blue mosaic – to check out the Art-Nouveau decor of the waiting room. More obviously accessible is the mini-dome of the neo-Baroque **Sarkander Chapel**, which replaced the old prison on the corner of Na hradě and G Mahlera at the beginning of this century. It's hardly big enough to kneel in, though this is perhaps its main charm.

From the University to the Cathedral

Firmly wedged between the two sections of the staré město is the obligatory **Jesuit Church**, deemed to be particularly necessary in a city where Protestantism had spread like wildfire among the German community during the course of the sixteenth century. Jutting out into the road, the church signals the gateway to the less hectic eastern part of the town. The great mass of the former Jesuit College, now the **Palacký University**, dominates the neighbouring square, **náměstí Republiky**. Opposite is the town **museum** (Tues–Sun 9am–5pm), housed in the former convent and cloisters of sv Klara, with a pretty tame permanent display but the occasional worthwhile temporary exhibition of contemporary art.

The trams and cars hurtling across the cobbles make this one of Olomouc's least accommodating squares, and, apart from the Bernini-esque Triton fountain, you'd be as well to slip down Mariánská to the leafy **Biskupské náměstí**, closed in on all four sides by fine Baroque buildings erected after the destructive occupation of the Swedes, including the Archbishop's Palace financed by the multimillionaire archbishop Liechtenstein in the 1660s. It's one of the most peaceful spots in town, popular with students easing their brains from a session in the library. Also popular is the **student centre** in the main university building, up Wurmova, which has a suntrap terrace café.

On the other side of the tramlines, the **Cathedral of sv Václav** started life as a twelfth-century Romanesque basilica, but, as with Brno and Prague, the current structure is mostly the result of a nineteenth-century neo-Gothic restoration, which included the addition of the 100-metre eastern spire. However, the secluded cathedral close on which it stands – a less famous Václavské náměstí (Wenceslas Square) – is a cut above its counterparts. The nave, too, is bright and airy, its walls and pillars prettily painted in imitation of the great Romanesque churches of the West, and the **crypt** has a wonderful display of gory reliquaries and priestly sartorial wealth. Next door, the scanty remains of the original twelfth-century **Přemyslid Palace** (Přemyslovský palác; Tues–Sun 9am–12.30pm & 1–5pm) are on display in the chapterhouse. The Gothic frescoes and Romanesque stonework are quite impressive and the guides enthusiastic, but it's all a bit too earnest and specialised for most people. Right by the entrance is the Baroque chapel of sv Anna and, set back from it, the deanery where the teenage King Václav III, the last of the Přemyslids, was murdered in mysterious circumstances in 1306, throwing the country into a bloodletting war of succession.

Beyond the staré město

The Habsburg defences to the west of the staré město were completely torn down in the late nineteenth century to make way for what is now a long, busy thoroughfare known as **Svobody**. Starting in the north with the cinema, a late Secession building decorated with caryatids worshipping Edison light bulbs, it continues with the familiar trail of Habsburg bureaucracy. Halfway down on the right, a leftover water tower is the only survivor on a square that contained a synagogue until the Nazis burnt it down in 1939, and where a statue of Stalin and Lenin subsequently stood. The former (and only the former) was defaced badly towards the end of the 1980s, apparently by an outraged Gorby-supporting Soviet soldier; neither survived the iconoclasm of November 1989.

If you're tired of Olomouc's uneven cobbles, the best places to head for are the **parks** which practically encircle the town. A couple of blocks of *fin-de-siècle* houses stand between Svobody and the long patchwork strip of crisscross paths, flowerbeds and manicured lawns. It's just a small sample of what goes on show at the annual **Flower Festival**, a mammoth international gathering of florists, held at the beginning of May in the special Flora Exhibition Grounds (there's a smaller affair some time in August or September). Another pleasant walk is out of the southern end of Dolní náměstí and left into the tiny Malé náměstí, which has a flight of steps leading down to the Bezručovy sady, once the city moat, where the local youth like to hang out.

Practicalities

The revamped *ČEDOK*, on the corner of Horní náměstí and 28 října, can book **hotel and private rooms** for you; someone there usually speaks German and occasionally English. Out of office hours, try the centrally located *Morava*, Riegrova 16 (☎068/296 71; ②), the nineteenth-century *Národní dům*, 8 května 21 (☎068/251 79; ③), or, if you must, the *Palác*, 1 Máje 31 (☎068/240 96; ②). Alternatively, you can fork out a lot more for the likes of the *Hotel Flora*, Krapkova 34 (☎068/232 41; ④). A word of warning: rooms can be hard to come by in May when the Spring Music Festival follows the Flower Festival. See "North to Šternberk", below, for details of the nearest **campsites**.

For **restaurants**, try the *Národní dům* or any of the other larger hotels. The *Hanacká restaurace* on the lower square is more of a traditional Moravian establishment, and the posh-ish *Orient* right at the end of Divadelní serves "Asian" food (Tues–Sat evenings only). For lighter snacks, typically Czech pizzas and other takeaways can be found in the Divadelní arcade, and a good range of cakes in the *cukrárna* next to *ČEDOK*; if you're assembling a picnic, don't forget to pack some of the local, extremely pungent *Olomoucký sýr* (cheese).

In the **evenings**, there's a bit of life in the two big squares, but inevitably most people head for a *pivnice*/restaurant like the *Opera* by the main theatre, or a café/bar like the *Café Corso* on the other side of the square, and the *Viktoria*, Školní 2a, which serves an excellent range of cocktails. The *Divadlo Oldřicha Stibora* puts on a good selection of opera and the city's philharmonic orchestra regularly performs here. In late May, Olomouc has its own *Hudební jaro* (Spring Music Festival), when concerts are spread evenly around the town's venues and churches. The youthful *Divadlo hudby* at Denisova 47 puts on a more adventurous programme of **gigs**, films and video – anything from Jan Švankmajer to U2. The subsidiary *S-Klub* advertises its gigs and events here, which take place at the student college on 17 listopadu 43; you could also try the *Rockový club*, which takes place nightly at náměstí Republiky 1. There are several cinemas to choose from, but the *Kinokavárna Jas* in the Divadelní arcade is the one to go for, an old-style **café cinema** where you can order drinks and smoke during screenings.

Around Olomouc

Olomouc sits happily in the wide plain of the **Haná region**, famous for its multifarious folk costumes and songs reflecting the fertility of the land. Naturally enough in a strongly agricultural area, the harvest festivals (*Hanácké dožínky* or *dožínkový slavnost*) are the highlight of the year. If you're in the region in the second half of September, you'll see posters up everywhere advertising them. All the places covered below are situated in the Morava plain, and are easily reached by bus or train on day trips from Olomouc, with the exception of the area round Bouzov, which is really only accessible to those who have their own transport.

North to Šternberk

If you're **camping**, the nearest site to Olomouc is *Dolní Žleb*, 14km north in Šternberk. En route, to the east the ridge of the Jeseníky foothills drifts imperceptibly towards you, broken only by the twin towers of the Baroque pilgrimage church at **KOPEČEK**. Perched 200m above the plain and flanked by its whiter-than-white convent wings, the site and scale are truly spectacular. Close up, it doesn't live up to expectations – it's only really worth making your way up here if you want to see the adjoining **zoo**; bus #11 from Olomouc train station will take you there. You can enjoy just as good a view from the heights above **ŠTERNBERK** (Sternberg), where the annual *Ecce Homo* motor race is held in mid-September over the lethal switchbacks on the road to Opava. The town itself, a long two-kilometre haul from the train and bus stations, is not much more than its giant Baroque church and **chateau** (April & Oct Sat & Sun 9am–4pm; May–Sept Tues–Sun 8am–5pm), the latter rebuilt in Romantic style in the late nineteenth century, and worth a visit not for the overlong guided tour of its rooms, but for its **clock museum**, which houses a fabulous collection of timepieces and watches from ancient Chinese alarm clocks, through the wild excesses of the Baroque era, to the substandard work churned out by the old state watch manufacturers, *Prim*, who are based in the town.

Přerov and Prostějov

Twenty-three kilometres southeast of Olomouc, and twenty minutes by train, **PŘEROV** (Prerau) is an ungainly town dedicated to the chemical and engineering industries. Aside from a brief annual Jazz Festival in late September, its single redeeming feature is the endearing old town square, a tight semicircle of colourful houses centred around a typically melodramatic statue by František Bílek, which depicts the sixteenth-century religious reformer Jan Blahoslav brandishing his Czech translation of the New Testament. The straight side of the square is taken up by the sixteenth-century **chateau** (April–Sept Tues–Fri 9am–noon & 2–4pm, Sat 2–4pm, Sun 9am–noon), whose museum commemorates Blahoslav's more famous successor in the Protestant Unity of Brethren, **Jan Ámos Komenský** (aka John Amos Comenius; see box).

Twenty kilometres and half an hour by train from Olomouc, the big textile town of **PROSTĚJOV** (Prossnitz) has a more grand and spacious old centre, but the real highlight is Jan Kotěra's 1908 **Národní dům**: close to the last remaining bastion of the Gothic town walls, this now houses a theatre and restaurant. As in his museum at Hradec Králové, Kotěra was moving rapidly away from the "swirl and blob" of the Secession, but here and there the old elements persist, in the sweep of the brass door handles, and the pattern on the poster frames. Apart from its furniture, the restaurant has been left unmolested, and the bold Klimt-like relief of the *Three Graces* above the mantlepiece is still as striking as ever.

Five kilometres west of Prostějov, two good lakeside **campsites** (May–Oct) provide plenty of opportunities for swimming, and on a high mound above the westernmost reservoir stands the imposing slab of the chateau at **PLUMLOV** (Plumenau), another of the Liechtensteins' fancies. Designed by Prince-Bishop Karl Eusebius von Liechtenstein-Kastelcorn himself, only one wing out of the

---

COMENIUS

Jan Ámos Komenský was born in 1592, in a village close to Uherský Brod, but his Latin schooling took place at the Unity of Brethren's school in Přerov. He served as a Protestant minister in Fulnek from 1616 to 1621, before being forced to flee the Czech Lands after the victory of the papal forces at the Battle of Bílá hora. Komenský and the Brethren set up an academy in the Polish city of Leszno, until forced to move on once more by the Swedish Wars of the 1650s. Of his many writings, Komenský's graded and pictorial Latin textbooks (the first of their kind) have proved more influential than his religious treatises, and he was called to put his educational theories into practice in Sweden, Hungary, Holland and England. He even received invitations from the Protestant-loathing Cardinal Richelieu in France, and from Harvard University, which wanted him as its president; he is buried in Naarden in Holland. Throughout the eastern part of Moravia, the Brethren rode out the Counter-Reformation to emerge in significant numbers once Austrian liberalism began to take effect in the late eighteenth century. They were later transformed into the Moravian Church, a body which continues to have an influence out of all proportion to its size, particularly in the Czech Lands and the USA.

four planned got off the drawing board, and it's been under reconstruction for a long time now, but it makes a good piece of scenery beneath which to swim.

Around Bouzov

The northernmost tip of the Drahanská vrchovina around Bouzov – an extension of the hills of the Moravský kras – has enough to keep you occupied on a lazy weekend. **BOUZOV** itself is nothing but its **castle** (hour-long guided tour; April & Oct Sat & Sun 9am–4pm; May–Sept Tues–Sun 8am–5pm), a stunning thirteenth-century Gothic fortress right on the high point of the *vrchovina*, and perfectly suited as a base for its former proprietors, the Teutonic Knights. Predictably enough, it also took the fancy of the Nazi SS, who based their Czech headquarters here during the last war. Whether because of this last fact, or just because of the usual pompous neo-Gothicising, the guided tour might be considered worth skipping for a walk in the surrounding hills instead.

Four kilometres south at **JAVOŘÍČKO**, the local SS burnt the village to the ground and shot 38 of the inhabitants in the last days of the war. This futile and tragic act aside, the reason for coming here is to visit the **Javoříčské jeskyně**, limestone karst caves on a par with the ones near Brno, but without the crowds and queues. Five kilometres east of Bouzov, **BÍLÁ LHOTA** has an eighteenth-century chateau worth visiting for its beautiful arboretum. The **Mladečské jeskyně**, a more extensive and popular limestone cave system another couple of kilometres on, is just off the main Olomouc–Prague road and at the end of the most twig-like of branch rail lines from **LITOVEL**; **accommodation** might be possible at the *Záložna* hotel (☎0644/22 90; ①) on the main square. Given that there are no official campsites in the area, the only other place you might be able to stay is the *Hotel Bouzov* (☎0644/932 06; ①), below the castle of the same name.

The Jeseníky mountains

The **Jeseníky mountains** are the highest mountains in what is now Moravia. Sparsely populated since the postwar expulsion of its German-speakers, it's a region that's worlds apart from the dense network of industrial centres in the north and east of the province, or even the vine-clad hills of the south, having more in common with the Bohemian Krkonoše (of which it is a natural eastern extension). The highest reaches rise up to the northwest between Šumperk and Jeseník, but the peaks have been damaged by acid rain and are worth avoiding; to the south, the hills drift into a gentle high plateau. Perhaps the best areas to head for are the foothills on either side of the big peaks, which harbour some low-key spa resorts like Lázně Jeseník and the historical remains of Czech Silesia.

Around Šumperk

ŠUMPERK (Schönberg) is the gateway to the upper Jeseníky, though it actually gets surprisingly few visitors. It has the feel of a mountain town, despite the fact that the shift from plain to hills is much less dramatic here than at Šternberk. For the last two centuries it was a thriving German textile town, at the vanguard of the language frontier. The original German inhabitants may have gone but the town still relies on its cloth-making tradition.

Unlike most provincial towns, there's no obvious centre to Šumperk; its neo-Renaissance radnice stands on the quiet and insignificant náměstí Míru, while the action – so to speak – goes on along the town's long shopping mall, Hlavní třída, and the park that lies to the north of the train station. Unreconstructed street names were a feature of most towns under the Communist regime, but Šumperk topped the lot with a Stalin Square, a Stalingrad Street and a statue of the man himself in a car park by the old town walls – all intact right up to November 1989. This last attraction having gone, there's not much to see here, but if you end up staying over, details of the current entertainments on offer are available from ČEDOK, 100m east of the *Grand Hotel*.

Finding a **room** should be easy enough; there's the *Grand* (☎0649/21 41; ②) by the park, the *Moravan* (☎0649/35 91; ①) at Odborářů 3, and various **private rooms** on offer in the surrounding area. For a change from the usual Czech fare, try **eating** at the *Pizzeria Riviera* in the *Kavárna Opera* by the main theatre on Hlavní, or the Asian restaurant, *Sam Pan*, on Husitská. If you don't fancy stopping off at Velké Losiny, Jeseník is a scenic two-hour train ride from Šumperk.

Velké Losiny

One good reason for staying in Šumperk is to visit the Renaissance chateau in the tiny Moravian spa of **VELKÉ LOSINY** (Gross-Ullersdorf), twenty minutes away by train. One of the last oases of civilisation before you hit the deserted heights of the Jeseníky, the **chateau** (45-min guided tour; April & Oct Sat & Sun 9am–noon & 1–4pm; May–Sept Tues–Sun 8/9am–noon & 1–4/5pm) is set in particularly lush grounds beside a tributary of the River Desná. It's a three-winged, triple-decker structure, opening out into a beautifully restored sixteenth-century arcaded loggia, and for once the guided tour is really worthwhile. The chateau was the northernmost property of the extremely wealthy Žerotín family, but inhabited for less than a hundred years. Strong supporters of the Unity of Brethren, the Žerotíns were stripped of their wealth after the Battle of Bílá hora and the chateau left empty – except as a venue for the region's notorious witch trials during the Counter-Reformation.

The **train station** is in the spa itself, and it's a pleasant one-kilometre walk south to the chateau, along the blue-marked path through the verdant gardens peppered with the familiar faded ochre spa buildings. The *Praděd* (☎0649/94 92 15; ①), at the crossroads by the station, serves food and may even have a bed for the night if it isn't closed for reconstruction.

Over the pass to Jeseník

The railway and the River Desná peter out before the real climb into the mountains begins. A bus from Šumperk runs roughly every two hours via the last train station, KOUTY NAD DESNOU, to the saddle of Červenohorské sedlo (1013m) and beyond. The ascent by road from Kouty is a dramatic series of hairpins, but the top of the pass is a disappointment. The tourist board may prefer to talk of "mountain meadows and pastures" but the reality is low-lying scrub and moorland: any spruce or pine trees that dare to rise above this are beaten down by acid rain. There's the possibility of a beer and some food at the restaurant by the roadside, and an impromptu **campsite**, 500m away to the northwest. If you want to enjoy a better view, it's a 45-minute walk north to **Červená hora** (1333m) and another hour and a half to **Šerák** (1351m), which looks down onto the

Ramzovské sedlo, the much lower pass to the west that the railway from Šumperk to Jeseník wisely opts for. There's a chairlift to take you down to the campsite at RAMZOVÁ should you so wish. Two hours in the opposite direction take you to **Praděd** (1491m), the highest and most barren peak in the range. From there you can easily drop down to **KARLOVA STUDÁNKA** on the River Bílá Opava, the nearest the Jeseníky get to an old Silesian mountain resort. Accommodation options in the area have greatly improved, thanks to the increasing availability of **private rooms**. There are, however, still very few **hotels**, the two in Karlová Studánka being your best bet: the *Džbán* (☎646/932 38; ②) and *Opava* (☎646/932 30; ①). Rough **camping** in these parts is fairly acceptable, especially if you manage to befriend a passing hiking group.

Jeseník and around

On the other side of the pass, the road plunges down with equal ferocity to **JESENÍK** (Gräfenberg), a town that's pleasant without being at all picturesque. There are a couple of reasonably priced hotels, including the *Stařič*, on Lipovská (☎26 70; ①), which should make finding a room fairly easy, after which you should head up to **LÁZNĚ JESENÍK** (Bad Gräfenberg), 2km above the town, where local farmer Vincent Priessnitz established one of the many famous Silesian spas in the nineteenth century. There's a wonderful Art-Nouveau monument to the spa's founder in the spa gardens, presiding godlike over the skinny and ill on his right and the "cured" (or at least plump) on his left. The Russian writer Gogol took the cure here, but such days are only really recalled in the grand-ish Priessnitz Sanatorium. The natural springs are actually scattered about the surrounding countryside, providing hot and sulphuric refreshments on the obligatory constitutionals. If you'd prefer to get clean away from people, and particularly sickly spa patients, the viewpoint from the summit of Zlatý chlum, 2km east of Jeseník, fulfils the requirements. There's a **campsite** with swimming pool less than 2km along the valley towards another spa resort, LIPOVÁ LÁZNĚ.

If you're serious about a bit more **hiking**, two long but gentle hikes are possible around here. Follow the blue-marked path from Lázně Jeseník over the hills to Velké Špičák (12km), where weird rocky outcrops and a mini-karst cave system can be explored (the local train will take you back to Jeseník); or take the red-marked path from Lázně Jeseník over to ŽULOVÁ (13km), where the local fortress has been converted into a church. At Žulová, the countryside flattens out as it slips into Poland, but you might consider hopping on the train (30min) to JAVORNÍK (Jauernig), where the local chateau features a collection of historical pipes and ornate smoking devices.

Opava and around

Hard by the Polish border and on the road from Jeseník to Ostrava, **OPAVA** (Troppau) is one of the oldest towns in the country, an important trading centre on the Amber Road from the Adriatic to the Baltic Sea, but perhaps better known as **Troppau**, capital of Austrian (and later Czech) Silesia (see box on p.302). Badly damaged in the last few weeks of the war, when ninety percent of the town was reduced to rubble, and then depopulated by the expulsion of the town's majority of Germans, it remains a big, busy, if fairly nondescript town. Much has been rebuilt since 1945, and while Opava may not merit a detour, it's a good place to break a journey or do a bit of chateau-seeing.

Nothing too spectacular remains of the town's Silesian days: the huge fourteenth-century church of **Nanebevzetí Panna Marie**, built in the northern German red-brick Gothic style, has survived more or less intact in the old fish market – now a car park for the spanking new red-brick monstrosity of the *Kamyšin* nightclub-cum-hotel complex. Behind this rises the tall **Městská věž**, symbol of the town's forgotten prosperity, and, close by, another object of civic pride, the neo-Baroque theatre. The **Silesian Diet** used to meet in the old Jesuit seminary at the top end of Masarykova třída – Opava's best-looking street, boasting a couple of Baroque palaces – and later moved to the Minorite monastery further down on the left. It was here that the Troppau Conference took place late in 1820, when the "Holy Alliance" of Austria, Russia and Prussia met to thrash out a common policy towards the revolutionary stirrings of post-Napoleonic Europe. Lastly, the grand nineteenth-century **Silesian Museum** (Tues–Sat 9am–noon & 1–4pm, Sun 9am–noon & 2–4pm), set in the town's pretty semicircle of parks, has been painstakingly restored since the war and houses a large but uninspiring exhibition that manages to avoid all the most controversial aspects of Silesian history.

There are several good medium-range **hotels** to choose from: the *Koruna*, náměstí Republiky 17 (☎0653/21 69 15; ②), the *Parkhotel*, by the Městské sady (☎0653/21 37 45; ③), and, of course, the *Kamyšin* (☎0653/21 69 15; ④). The recent founding of a (Czech) Silesian University in Opava should bring some excitement to an otherwise dead nightlife.

Hradec, Raduň and an arboretum

There are three Silesian chateaux of varying interest within easy reach of Opava. The mock-Gothic chateau of **Hradec nad Moravě** (currently no admission), 8km away at the end of its own little branch rail line, was visited by Beethoven, Liszt and Paganini, and every June there's a Beethoven music competition held here. Since 1982 the chateau and park have been undergoing a slow restoration programme and the furniture and exhibits have been transferred to the chateau of **Raduň** (April & Oct Sat & Sun 9am–3pm; May–Sept Tues–Sun 9am–4.30pm),

SILESIA

From 1335 onwards **Silesia** (*Slezsko* in Czech) was an integral part of the Historic Lands of the Bohemian Crown. In the 1740s, the majority of it was carelessly lost to the Prussians by the young Habsburg Empress Maria Theresa. The three remaining Duchies – Troppau (Opava), Jägerndorf (Krnov) and Teschen (Těšín) – became known as Austrian Silesia, with Troppau as their capital, separated from each other by the Moravian salient around Ostrava. The population, though predominantly German, contained large numbers of Czechs and Poles – a mishmash typical of the region, and one which caused interminable territory disputes. In 1920 – after a few bloody skirmishes – the new state of Czechoslovakia lost part of Těšín to Poland and gained part of Hlučín from Germany, and, in 1928, Silesia was amalgamated with Moravia. This last act, in particular, annoyed the violently irredentist prewar German population. However, like the majority of the country's German-speaking minority, they were expelled in 1945, making the whole issue of a separate Silesia fairly redundant. Nevertheless, following the downfall of the Communists in 1989, the newly formed Moravian nationalists teamed up with their Silesian counterparts (HSD-SMS) and have since scored some surprise election victories that have put the whole issue back on the agenda.

6km southeast of Opava (15min by bus). If you'd rather skip the period interiors entirely, or you're here in the winter, head out to the vast **arboretum** (daily April–Oct 8am–6pm; Nov–March 8am–4pm) at NOVÝ DVŮR U OPAVY, 8km west of Opava by bus, which contains trees and shrubs from all over the world.

Krnov and Bruntál

The nearest border crossing into Poland from Opava is 25km away at **KRNOV** (Jägerndorf), famous for the organs manufactured here since 1873. It, too, was flattened in the last war, and lost most of its population in the postwar expulsions, but should you wish to stop over before heading into Poland, there's an offbeat and pricey hotel, the *Morava*, in the former Augustinian monastery.

On the main road from Olomouc to Krnov, **BRUNTÁL** (Freudenthal) is only worth a mention for its Baroque **chateau** (Tues–Fri 8am–noon & 1–5pm, Sat & Sun 10am–noon & 1–5pm), another hang-out of the Teutonic Knights, which, if you're passing through, doles out all the usual attractions – an arcaded courtyard with loggia, "valuable furnishings" – without actually pulling off any surprises.

Ostrava

If you told a Czech you were going to **OSTRAVA**, they'd probably think you were mad. The city is regularly shrouded in a pall of pungent sulphurous smog, and although efforts have been made in the last ten years to clean up the centre, they can't cover up the fact that it's coal and steel that have made the town what it is – rich and dirty. It is, however, the Czech republic's third largest city (population 330,000, a large proportion of whom are Polish) and the main gateway into Poland (though the Polish side is little better). Should you end up having to stay in the North Moravian coal basin, Ostrava is as good a place as any, with a goodish cultural and sporting life.

The City

Ostrava divides into three distinct districts: **Slezská Ostrava** to the east, where the first black coal deposits were discovered back in the 1760s, **Vítkovice** to the south, where the first foundry was set up in 1828, and what used to be **Moravská Ostrava**, the central district where most of the town's "sights" are located. If you've any sense you'll spend your time exclusively in this third, largely pedestrianised part of town, where Ostrava's shops and department stores bunch up around the old marketplace and main square, **Masarykovo náměstí**. Though hardly an architectural masterpiece, it's still able to vaunt a handful of swanky turn-of-the-century facades put up by the rich German and Austrian capitalists who owned the mines here until nationalisation in 1945. Until recently the square was known as náměstí Lidových milicí (People's Militia Square) – a once-proud reference to the city's strong working-class traditions and staunch postwar support for the Communist Party (the Party still gets its highest percentage of the vote here). This largely unspoken alliance ensured high wages and well stocked shops, and for the last twenty years the commercial district was always crowded with Poles and Soviet soldiers gaping in awe at what to them was an unbelievably wide range of products.

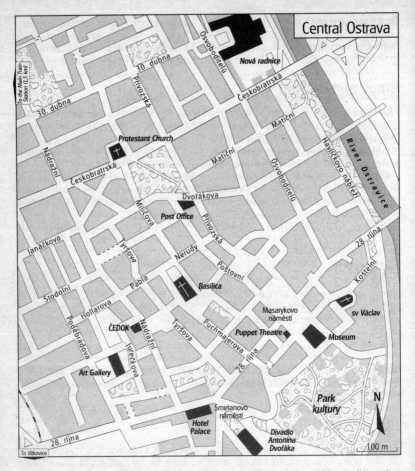

Ostrava's most lavish museum was the one dedicated to the working-class movement, on Nádražní – it has now reverted to its original function as a bank. The sixteenth-century **stará radnice**, on the main square, one of the oldest buildings in the city, houses the local **museum** (Mon–Fri 9am–5pm, Sat 8am–noon), but contains few thrills. By contrast, the city's functionalist **art gallery** (Tues–Fri 10am–noon & 12.30–6pm, Sat & Sun 10am–3pm) on Jurečkova, one block west of Nádražní, houses an impressive collection of nineteenth- and twentieth-century Czech art.

The Karolina coking plant, just south of the centre, was pulled down a few years ago, having spewed out lethal carcinogenic filth over the city's main shopping district for over a century. Even now, antiquated pitheads, silver snaking pipes and red and white striped chimneys are very much a part of the cityscape: an awesome sight, lit up at night like proverbial satanic mills, their immediate future – like that of the city itself – looks very bleak indeed.

Practicalities

Ostrava's main **train station**, Ostrava hlavní nádraží, is north of the city centre (tram #2, #8 or #12), while the local station, Ostrava střed, and bus terminal are just a few minutes' walk west of the centre. **Hotels** are on the cheap side, but tend to be booked up by a combination of people on business, long-distance travellers and Polish migrant workers, so if you're here during office hours go straight to ČEDOK, Nádražní 9 (Mon–Fri 8am–noon & 12.30–5pm). The cheapest and most central hotels are the *Brioni*, on Stodolní (✆069/23 19 66; ①), and, rather surprisingly, the *Palace*, 28 října 59 (✆069/23 21 22; ①).

  Eating options include some great thin-based pizzas from the *Domino* pizzeria and steak restaurant on the far side of the main square. Standard Moravian food and the local brew are available from the *Českočeská pivnice* by the *Palace Hotel*, or go for the same food washed down with *Radegast* beer at *U jelena*, on the main square. For something a bit more upmarket, try the *Moskvanka* on the ground floor of the *Hotel Imperial*, Tyršova 6.

  With big state funds once backing it, Ostrava boasts a good **philharmonic orchestra** and a range of opera, ballet and theatre based at the *Divadlo Antonína Dvořáka*; while Janáček, who died in Ostrava, is the subject of the city's **May Music Festival**. The city that produced Ivan Lendl is also one of the republic's most important sports centres after Prague. Predictably enough, as a working-class city *par excellence*, Ostrava's strongest tradition is in **football**, with both *Baník Ostrava* and *Vítkovice* enjoying long stretches in the *první liga* (First Division). A large number of the country's big sporting events are held here, too, so check the listings in ČEDOK and on fly-posters around town for the latest fixtures.

The Beskydy region

Despite the short distance between them, the hilly **Beskydy region** couldn't be further from the apocalyptic filth of the Ostrava coal basin. In the foothills there's a whole cluster of interesting sights not far from (and including) **Nový Jičín**. Further south and east, into hiking country proper, the old Wallachian traditions of the region have been preserved both *in situ*, in the more inaccessible villages, and at the *skansen* at **Rožnov pod Radhoštěm**.

WALLACHIAN CULTURE

As far as anybody can make out, the **Wallachs** or **Vlachs** were semi-nomadic sheep farmers who settled the mountainous areas of eastern Moravia and western Slovakia in the fifteenth century. Although their name clearly derives from the Romanian Vlachs, it is thought that they arrived from eastern Poland and the Ukraine, and the name Vlach is simply a generic term for sheep farmer. Whatever their true origins, they were certainly considered a race apart by the surrounding Slav peasants. Successive Habsburg military campaigns against the Vlachs in the seventeenth century destroyed their separate identity, and nowadays Wallachian culture lives on only in the folk customs and distinctive wooden architecture of the region.

Nový Jičín

NOVÝ JIČÍN (Neu-Titschein) is a typical one-square town on the main road from Olomouc to Ostrava. That said, it's a particularly fine square, with wide whitewashed arcades tunnelling their way under a host of restrained late Baroque facades painted over in pastel colours. The **radnice** is an unusual white boxy affair rebuilt in the 1930s, its wonderfully jagged gable a reminder of its seventeenth-century origins; but one building stands out (literally) from the rest, the **stará pošta**, with a pretty two-storey loggia dating from the town's boom time in the sixteenth century when it bought its independence from the Žerotín family.

The chief attraction of the town is now its **Hat Museum** (Kloboučnícké muzeum; Tues–Fri 8am–noon & 1–4pm, Sat & Sun 9am–noon), laid out in the Žerotíns' old chateau, through the covered passageway of Lidická, which claims to be the only such museum in the world. Thankfully, the present exploits of the old state hat enterprise *Tonak* (based in the town) are only lightly touched on, leaving most of the museum to a wonderful variety of hats produced in Nový Jičín since 1799 by the original firm of *Hückel*. The bit that gets the Czechs going is the array of hats worn by famous national personages – a bit esoteric for non-Czechs, though some might be stirred by the sight of Masaryk's topper.

Nový Jičín has two **train stations**, both located at the end of obscure and inconvenient branch lines, making the **bus** by far the easiest way to come and go. *ČEDOK* are at the end of ulica 28 října, off the main square, but it should be no hassle getting a **room** in the *Praha*, opposite the hat museum on Lidická (☎0656/ 209 11; ①), a big old nineteenth-century hotel that retains at least a hint of its opulent past.

Hodslavice

One place you can reach by train is the village of **HODSLAVICE**, 8km south of Nový Jičín and birthplace of **František Palacký** (his house is now a memorial), one of the chief political figures of the nineteenth-century *národní obrození*. More exciting than this last fact for most people is the village's sixteenth-century **wooden church** of sv Ondřej, a first hint of the local Wallachian culture.

Štramberk

Eight kilometres east of Nový Jičín, acessible by the occasional bus, or an easy two-hour walk away, the smokestack settlement of **ŠTRAMBERK** is actually one of the best places to take your first dip into Wallachian culture. Clumped under the conic Bílá hora (not to be confused with *the* Bílá hora in Prague) like an ancient funeral pyre, Štramberk feels very old indeed, yet many of its wooden cottages were built as recently as the first half of the nineteenth century. Its virtue is in seeing Wallachian architecture *in situ*, the cottages simply constructed out of whole tree trunks, unpainted and free of tourists rather than cooped and mummified in a sanitised skansen. Despite being no more than a village, Štramberk does have a nominal main square with three stone buildings in "folk Baroque" at one end and an old Jesuit church at the other, beside which there's a small **museum** (April–Oct only) displaying archaeological findings from the nearby Šipka cave, where remains of Neanderthal Man were discovered. You can see the galleried wooden tower of the original church, halfway up the walls to the castle, laid to waste by the Tartars and never rebuilt. Its one remaining round tower, **Trúba** (April–Oct Tues–Sun 8/9am–4/5pm), is now a tourist lookout post, with a restaurant nearby. *Hotel Šipka*, on the main square, lets out cheap rooms (☎483 14; ①).

Kopřivnice

On the other side of Bílá hora from Štramberk (and an easy half-hour walk), **KOPŘIVNICE** is an ugly sprawling factory town, but nevertheless worth a quick visit for its **Tatra Museum** (April–Nov daily 8am–4pm; Dec–March Mon–Fri only), situated in the hangar-like building next door to the train station. Even if spark plugs don't fire your imagination, there are some wonderful old cars here. Unlike the popular and ubiquitous Škoda, Tatra cars have always aimed to be exclusive: the first model, which came out in 1897, was called the *President* and from 1948 onwards that's exactly who rode in them. The silent and powerful black Tatra, looking like something out of a gangster B-movie, became the ultimate symbol of Party privilege. Ordinary mortals could buy any colour they liked – as long as it *wasn't* black – the colour reserved for Party functionaries. When you've seen the Tatra 87 and the 603, it's a slighty hysterical and somewhat frightening thought to imagine the country's top Stalinists cruising around in these cars, which were succeeded in the 1970s by the more modern Tatra 613. The post-Communist leadership has tended to avoid the stigma of the Tatra, and with the Party no longer in a position to pay for its usual bulk order, the firm has recently enlisted the help of the Italian truck company *IVECO* in order to modernise its Tonka-tough trucks, and continue production of its line in super-luxury cars.

Kopřivnice's other **museum** (Tues–Sun 9am–4pm) contains some of the factory's earliest horse-driven carriages, and a small tribute to the famous Olympic medallist and long-distance runner of the 1950s, **Emil Zátopek**, who was born in the town in 1922. One thing the museum doesn't tell you is that his wife, Dana Zátopková, was also an Olympic record holder in the javelin. The museum also features a tame section on the controversial subject of Lachian culture (see "Frýdek-Místek", p.310).

Příbor

Five kilometres and one train station north of Kopřivnice, **PŘÍBOR** (Freiberg) appears at first to be a scruffier rerun of Nový Jičín – which it is – except that it has a much greater claim to fame as the birthplace of **Sigmund Freud**. Although the family's financial problems forced them to leave for Vienna when Sigmund was only four, it's difficult to resist the chance to visit the place where Freud went through his oral and anal phases. The town **museum**, situated in the former monastery on Lidická, has only one room out of four devoted to the man (Tues & Thurs 8am–noon & 1–4pm, Sun 9am–noon) and sadly, there are no pictures of baby Sigi, only dull official photos of learned and bearded men (including Jung) at conferences on psychoanalysis. In the rest of the town, few associations present themselves, apart from Freud's bust, which sits on a plinth by the local supermarket.

> ### FREUD IN FREIBERG
>
> Born in 1856 to a hard-up Jewish wool merchant and his third wife, Freud had no hesitation in ascribing significance to events which took place during the family's brief sojourn in the ten-metre-square rented room above Zajík the blacksmith at Zámecnická 117 (now a locksmith's). "Of one thing I am certain," Freud wrote later, "deep within me, although overlaid, there continues to live the happy child from Freiberg [Příbor], the first-born child of a young mother who received from this air, from this soil, the first indelible impressions." Things were not always so idyllic, and Freud later used a number of events from his early childhood to prove psychoanalytical theories. The family maidservant, "my instructress in sexual matters" in Freud's own words, was a local Czech woman who used to drag him off to the nearby Catholic church and in Freud's eyes was responsible for his "Rome neurosis". She was eventually sacked for alleged theft (and for encouraging baby Sigmund to thieve, too) and sent to prison. Things weren't too bad on the Oedipal front either, Freud suspecting his half-brother of being the father of his younger sister, Anna.

Hukvaldy

Moravians hold Janáček much dearer to their hearts than Freud, and the village of **HUKVALDY**, 6km east of Příbor, has become a modest shrine to the composer. Born just two years before Freud, **Leoš Janáček** was the ninth of fourteen children, too many for his impecunious father who taught at the local school. Thus at the age of eleven Janáček was sent to Brno to be a chorister and from then on he made his home in the city, battling against the prejudices of the powerful German elite who ruled over the Moravian classical music scene. When at last he achieved recognition outside Moravia, through the success of the opera *Jenůfa*, he was already in his sixties. Having bought a cottage in Hukvaldy, he spent his last, most fruitful years based here and in Brno, composing such works as the *Glagolithic Mass*, *The Cunning Little Vixen* and *The House of the Dead*. The music of this period was fired by his obsessive love for a woman called Kamila Strösslová, wife of a Jewish antique dealer in Písek, who had sent him food parcels throughout World War I. Although he never left his wife, Janáček kept an almost daily correspondence with Kamila for over ten years. In August 1928, he caught a chill searching for her son in the nearby woods and died in a hospital in Ostrava.

Even if you've no interest whatsoever in Janáček, Hukvaldy is a homely little village, sheltered under the woods of a thoroughly ruined castle that comes complete with a deer park. The composer's **museum**, housed in his cottage, is pleasantly low-key (May–Sept Tues–Sun 9am–noon & 1–4pm; April & Oct Sat & Sun only), containing just a little modest furniture and his lectern: he always composed standing up. Really, though, it's the gentle pastoral setting, a constant textural element underlying all Janáček's music, that remains the most instructive impression of the place. Should you wish to stay, the *Hukvaldy* (☎065897/972 17; ①) should be able to accommodate you, but ring ahead to avoid disappointment.

Into the hills of the Beskydy

Between the sparsely wooded pastureland around Nový Jičín and the Rožnovská Bečva valley to the south are the **hills of the Beskydy**. Starting off in North Moravia and entering Poland, they actually extend right over into the Ukraine, shadowing the much higher Carpathian range to the south. Spruce has gradually given way to pine, as yet not too badly affected by pollutants, though far from free of acid rain damage, and in the westernmost reaches patches of beech forest still exist. If you're planning on any serious **hiking**, get hold of the 1:100,000 *Beskydy* map, which marks all the hiking paths in the area.

Around Radhošť

FRENŠTÁT POD RADHOŠTĚM is the main resort in the hills, previously a fairly grim town dominated by the local Red Army barracks, one of the first to shut up shop in the 1990 troop withdrawals. Since it's not exactly in the thick of the Beskydy, it's only really worth staying here if **hotels** are your only option for accommodation, with the *Radhošť* (☎06565/58 80; ①) and *Sport* (☎06565/58 92; ②) in town or the highly recommended *Hotel Vlčina* (☎06565/53 51; ④), 1.5km up the hill from town on the green-marked path. **Radhošť** (1129m), which Rožnov (see below) and Frenštát both dub themselves under (*pod*), is the most famous peak – thanks to its legends – though not the tallest. Nevertheless, the view from the summit is still pretty good. Two kilometres east, there's a primitivistic totem featuring *Radegast*, the mountain's legendary pagan god (who lends his name to the famous local beer), and a fanciful wooden Uniate chapel, done out in neo-Byzantine style. With the help of a chairlift (*lánovka*), the less athletic can reach the top of the pass, where the fantastical *Tanečnica* hotel (named for the nearby mountain), and a number of other nineteenth-century timber-slat buildings survive, including a nifty, carefully balanced *zvonička* (belfry); the yellow and/or green-marked path will take you down to the campsite in PROSTŘEDNÍ BEČVA.

Rožnov pod Radhoštěm and around

Halfway up the Rožnovská Bečva valley, **ROŽNOV POD RADHOŠTĚM** is home to the biggest and most popular skansen of folk architecture in either republic. To the west the town displays its postwar industrial development, while on the other side of the river from the station, where the town's spa gardens once were, is the main entrance to the **skansen**. The museum is divided into three parts, each with different opening times.

The moving force behind the first part, the **Dřevené městečko** (Wooden Town; May, June & Sept daily 8am–6pm; July & Aug daily 8am–7pm; Oct–Nov 15 daily 8.30am–5pm; Dec 15–March Mon–Wed 8.30am–3.30pm, Sat 8.30am–1pm, Sun noon–4pm), was local artist Bohumír Jaromek, who was inspired by the outdoor folk museum in Stockholm (from which the word *skansen* derives). In 1925, Rožnov's eighteenth-century wooden radnice was moved from the main square to the site of the present museum, followed by a number of other timber buildings from the town and from neighbouring villages like Větřkovice u Příbora, which supplied the imposing seventeenth-century wooden church. There are Wallachian beehives decorated with grimacing faces, a smithy and even a couple of *hospoda* selling food and warm *slivovice*. The second part of the museum, the **Valašská dědina** (Wallachian Village; daily May 16–31 8am–6pm; June–Aug 8am–6pm; Sept 9am–5.30pm), built in the 1970s on a hillside, takes a more erudite approach, attempting to recreate a typical highland sheep farming settlement – the traditional Wallachian community, complete with live sheep and organic crops. The third section, **Mlynská dolina** (Mill Valley; daily April–May 15 & Sept–Oct 15 8.30am–5pm; May 16–Aug 8am–6.30pm) – yet to be fully completed – is centred around an old water mill.

Coach parties are frequent visitors to Rožnov, and in July and August folksy festivities are put on for the tourists, making the chances of finding a vacancy in one of the town's **hotels** slim. **Campsites**, however, are also thick on the ground, with one on either side of the road to Prostřední Bečva and a third 3km up the road in DOLNÍ BEČVA.

If you want to see Wallachian folk architecture in its natural habitat, head further south to the villages of the Vsetínksá Bečva valley, which runs parallel to the Rožnovská Bečva. From Postřední Bečva, you can walk over the hills via the predominantly wooden hamlets of Bzové, Jezerné and Raťkov before descending into Velké Karlovice, a mixture of vernacular architecture and the new industry foisted on the region after the war.

Frýdek-Místek

Lying halfway between the Beskydy and Ostrava, and accessible by train from either, **FRÝDEK-MÍSTEK** is a rather rude re-entry into the Ostrava coal basin. Its charms are few and its soulless industrial quarter has assumed a much greater importance than its twin old towns that straddle the River Ostravice: **Místek**, on the flat left bank, where the business of the town now goes on, and **Frýdek**, on the hill opposite, somewhat neglected in comparison. Frýdek's main square is in the process of being restored, with a statue of Saint Florian superintending a waterless fountain – a sad comedown for the patron saint of firemen. For an indication of the whole town's popularity, there's just one cheap hotel, the *Beskyd* (☎0658/207 51; ①), by the train station, and one dear one, *Centrum* (☎0658/215 51; ④), on Na Poříčí. The town's landmark is its **chateau** (Tues–Fri 8am–noon & 12.30–4pm, Sun 1–5pm), which once belonged to the lords of Těšín, and now contains a small folk museum and tributes to Janáček, and the Silesian poet Petr Bezruč who stayed in Místek for a while, championing the grievances of the poverty-stricken local miners.

ONDRA ŁYSOHORSKY

The ninth child of a Frýdek miner, the poet **Óndra Łysohorsky** (whose real name was Erwin Goy) took his pen-name from the local Robin Hood rebel, Ondráš, who was imprisoned in, and escaped from, Frýdek castle back in the seventeenth century, when it was owned by the wicked Duke Pragma. The surname comes from the highest peak in the Beskydy, Lysa hora. Łysohorsky was brought up speaking German and the local Slav dialect, but, after writing his first verses in his German mother tongue, decided to change to Lachian, a written form of the local dialect which he himself invented, but which never really caught on. The dialect (or language, depending on your point of view), somewhere between Czech and Polish, survives in the towns and villages along the Polish border, and was spoken by around a million people (mostly miners) at its peak between the wars. Łysohorsky's obstinacy on this linguistic point eventually brought him into conflict with the postwar Communist authorities, who accused him of supporting the region's Polish irredentists. Apart from a brief reprise in 1958, his verse remained unpublished in Czechoslovakia, despite his being one of the country's better-known poets abroad. Łysohorsky died shortly after the upheavals of 1989 in Bratislava, and the poet's vast archives are now safely deposited in Frýdek castle. As yet there's no mention of him in the local museum, but there are plans to place a memorial alongside Bezruč's.

Český Těšín

If you fancy a quick jaunt into **Poland**, probably the easiest place to do it is at **ČESKÝ TĚŠÍN** (Cieszyn), 20km east of Frýdek-Místek. It's one of those places that found itself arbitrarily divided when the borders were drawn up following the collapse of the Habsburg Empire after World War I. Claimed by both Poland and Czechoslovakia, it was finally decided in 1920 to use the fairly insignificant River Olše (Olza) as the frontier. In this instance, the Poles got the best deal, with the majority of the town, including the staré město and the castle on the right bank, ending up in Poland. The Czech side is made up of grim, grey blocks of housing, built between the wars, and the only reason for coming here is to cross over to the Polish side, where the town's main sights are located (see *Poland: the Rough Guide* for details).

The main **border crossing**, at the end of Hlavní třída, is currently closed for repairs, so you have to use the second bridge 1km upstream (pedestrians only). Visa regulations and price disparities between the two countries have fluctuated over the years. At the height of Solidarity, during the 1980s, it was almost as difficult for Czechs to get into Poland as it was for them to travel to the West. Then the tables were turned and, with the Polish economy in free fall, the Czechs clamped down on Poles entering the country. Nowadays, people on either side of the border can cross using just their ID cards, though few Czechs do, since prices in Poland are much higher; instead they earn a bit of extra cash by selling cheap Czech beer to the hordes of Poles who pour over each day. If you need to spend the night in Těšín, keep to the Czech side, and try the *Piast* (☎0659/556 51; ②), opposite the train station.

travel details

Trains

Connections with Prague Olomouc (16 daily; 3hr 30min) ; Ostrava (8 daily; 4–5hr).

From Olomouc to Prostějov (up to 16 daily; 15–30min); Přerov (up to 20 daily; 20min); Šumperk/Jeseník (up to 10 daily; 1hr–1hr 30min/2hr 10min–4hr); Bruntál/Krnov/Opava (up to 8 daily; 1hr 30min/2hr/3hr); Ostrava (up to 10 daily; 1hr 30min–2hr 30min); Poprad (5 daily; 6hr 30min); Banská Bystrica (1 daily; 5hr 15min); Košice (4 daily; 7hr); České Budějovice (1 daily; 6hr 20min).

From Ostrava to Český Těšín (20 daily; 50min); Frýdek-Místek/Frýdlant (up to hourly; 40min/1hr).

Buses (ČSAD only)

Connections with Prague Olomouc/Nový Jičín/Ostrava (up to 3 daily; 4hr/5hr/6hr); Opava (1 daily overnight; 7hr 30min).

From Olomouc to Opava (up to 4 daily; 2hr); Nový Jičín (up to 10 daily; 1hr 15min); Příbor/Frýdek-Místek (up to 8 daily; 1hr 30min/1hr 50min); Rožnov pod Radhoštěm (2 daily; 1hr 15min).

From Nový Jičín to Štramberk (up to 19 daily; 15–40 min); Kopřivnice (up to hourly; 35min); Příbor (up to 20 daily; 25min); Frýdek-Místek (up to 8 daily; 45min); Frenštát pod Radhoštěm (up to hourly; 40min).

PART THREE

THE

SLOVAK REPUBLIC

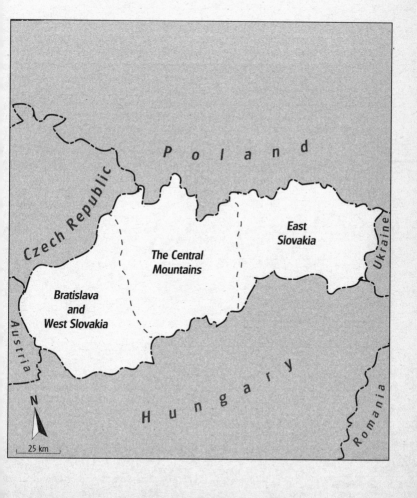

CHAPTER EIGHT

BRATISLAVA AND WEST SLOVAKIA

Despite a history of relentless cultural repression by the neighbouring Magyars, whose feudal seats, now mostly in ruins, are visible on almost every hillock in the country, the Slovaks emerged from a millennium of serfdom within the kingdom of Hungary with their language and national identity just about intact. For the first-time visitor, perhaps the most striking cultural difference on entering Slovakia from the Czech Lands is in the attitude to religion. Catholicism is almost as strong here as in parts of Poland, the churches are full to overflowing on Sundays, and even during the week there's a steady flow of after-work worshippers.

However, in many ways, the western third of Slovakia is the least typically Slovak. For a start, it's flat, fertile and fairly treeless; the only mountain range, the Small Carpathians, is too tame to compare with the more typical central mountains further east. Then there's the capital, **Bratislava**, which was for centuries a basically Austro-Hungarian city in which the Slovaks, like the Romanies and Jews, were a distinct minority. It's now one of the new European capital cities, thoroughly Slovak, but far removed from the real heart of the country in the central mountain regions. The great flat plain of the **Danube**, to the east of Bratislava, has always been (and still is) inhabited by Hungarian-speakers – well over half a million at the last count. Its two major cities – **Trnava** and **Nitra** – although now mostly Slovak, contain some of the most important religious institutions of the old Hungarian Kingdom. In the Váh valley, too, the spa town of **Piešťany** was, in its heyday, one of the favourite watering holes of the Hungarian nobility. Further up the Váh, however, the stronghold of **Trenčín** marks the beginning of the Slovak mountain region, and the real heartland of Slovakia.

A Brief History of Slovak Nationalism

It's not just today's Slovak nationalists who see their country as separate from the Czech Lands. For most of the last thousand years, it *was* a different country – Hungary. If the Slovaks have ever previously had sovereignty over their own land (and even this is debatable), it went under with the defeat of the Great Moravian Empire (much of which was in present-day West Slovakia) by the Magyars in 906. From that time on, virtually without interruption, the majority of Slovaks remained tied by serfdom to their Magyar or "Magyarised" feudal lords.

All things considered, it's hardly surprising that there was little in the way of a Slovak national revival, or *národné obrodenie*, until the **nineteenth century**, but while many of the new leaders were pan-Slavists who viewed all Slavs, be they

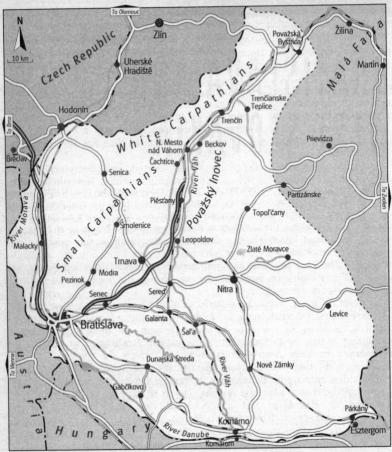

Slovak, Czech, Polish or Russian, as brothers, few singled out the Czechs for special attention. When they did, briefly in 1848 and later in 1918 with the formation of the First Czechoslovak Republic, it was on the grounds of expediency, to scupper any of the compromise plans put forward by the Hungarians. When the Czechs began behaving uncannily like their previous Hungarian masters – taking all the top jobs, and ruling by decree from Prague – many Slovaks became disillusioned with the First Republic and viewed its demise in 1938 as a blessing in disguise.

The pros and cons of Slovakia's brief period of **independence** from 1939 to 1944 under the leadership of Jozef Tiso – which in practice meant just another Nazi puppet state – are the subject of much public and private discussion at the moment. Whereas many Slovaks saw it as a genuine expression of Slovak statehood, thousands of Jews, Democrats and Communists took to the hills and fought against the state in the 1944 anti-Fascist uprising. Opinions on the issue are as divided as ever, but at least the subject is now discussed openly, something that was impossible in the black-and-white world of the last regime.

Whatever their differences over World War II, few Slovaks were happy with the **post-1945 situation**. Once more, Czech promises of Slovak autonomy, set out in 1945, were reneged upon. The Communists, by far the largest party in the Czech Lands, trailed behind the newly formed Democrats in the Slovak polls. True to form, though, the Slovak Communists were put into positions of power by their highly placed comrades in Prague. After 1948, centralisation was one of the cornerstones of Stalinist economics, putting paid to any hopes Slovak Communists might have had of running their own affairs; and in the 1950s, the victims of the show trials and purges were more often than not Slovak and/or Jewish.

In January 1968, Alexander Dubček was elected First Secretary of the Communist Party, the first Slovak to hold such a high position. Nevertheless, **the events of 1968** were primarily Prague-inspired, and while the Czechs got nothing out of the Warsaw Pact invasion, the Slovaks did at least get federalisation, a bilingual national media, and a large injection of state money to help adjust the economic imbalance between the two republics. It was a sop to the Slovak Communists – classic divide and rule tactics – and one that worked, at least for a while.

From the dissident movement of Charter 77 to the Velvet Revolution of November 1989, events over the last twenty years have been focused on Prague, but it wasn't long before old differences began to emerge, most famously in the summer of 1990, when it came to deciding on a new name for the country in what became known as the **great hyphen debate**. The Slovaks' insistent demand that a hyphen be inserted in "Czechoslovakia" was greeted with ridicule by most Czechs. Havel was one of the few who understood that what was just a hyphen to the Czechs meant a whole lot more to the Slovaks.

The electoral failure of the extremist Slovak Nationalist Party (SNS) had seemed to confirm that most people wanted the federation to stay together, but that all changed in the **June 1992 elections**. Following the victory of the new nationalist force, the Movement for a Democratic Slovakia (HZDS), under the canny leadership of populist politician **Vladimír Mečiar**, events moved very rapidly towards the break-up of the federation – to the alarm of many people, in particular the republic's Hungarian minority. On January 1, 1993, the dream of **Slovak independence** became a reality, though exactly what this will mean for the future relationship of the two republics remains to be seen.

Bratislava

Caught between the westernmost tip of the Carpathians and the flat plain of the Danube, with both Austria and Hungary tantalisingly close, **BRATISLAVA** has two distinct sides to it. On the one hand, the old quarter is quite simply a manageable and attractive slice of Habsburg Baroque; on the other, the rest of the city has the brash, crass and butchered feel typical of the old Eastern Bloc metropolises. Those who come here in search of a Slovak Prague will be disappointed: more buildings have been destroyed here since the war than were bombed out during it, not least the Jewish quarter, bulldozed to make way for the colossal new suspension bridge, most SNP, symbol of the capital's upwardly mobile thrust.

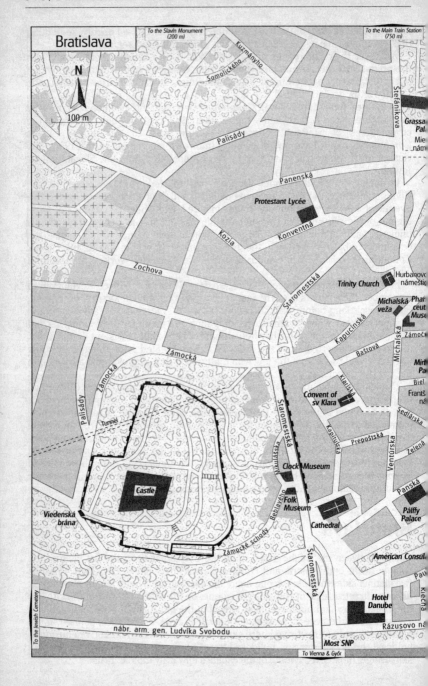

Bratislava

N

100 m

To the Slavín Monument (200 m)

To the Main Train Station (750 m)

Kuzmányho

Somolického

Štefánikova

Grassa Pal

Mie nám

Palisády

Panenská

Protestant Lycée

Konventná

Kozia

Zochova

Staromestská

Hurbanovo námestie

Trinity Church

Michalská veža

Phar ceut Muse

Kapucínska

Zámoč

Baštová

Michalská

Zámocká

Zámocká

Palisády

Mirl Pa

Biel

Klariská

Convent of sv Klara

Frantš ná

sedlárska

Tunnel

Staromestská

Kapitulská

Prepoštská

Ventúrska

Zelená

Castle

Mikulásska

Clock Museum

Panská

Viedenská brána

Folk Museum

Beblavého

Cathedral

Pálffy Palace

Zámocké schody

American Consul

Staromestská

Pau

klecha

To the Jewish Cemetery

Hotel Danube

Rázusovo ná

nábr. arm. gen. Ludvíka Svobodu

Most SNP

To Vienna & Györ

To the Bus & Nové Město
Train Stations (2,5 km)

Slovak Parliament
(200 m)

ukobystrická

Mickiewiczova

ul. 29. augusta

Kollárovo
námestie

Markušova

Špitálska

Duklianska

Obchodná

tel Fórum

Pošťova

Heydukova

Synagogue

Cintorínska

ná

To the Ondrej Cemetery
(400 m)

Post Office

Hotel Kyjev

Kolárska

nám. SNP

Post Office

Špitálska

Dunalská

ciscan
h

Ulsulinská

Klobučnika

Kamenné
námestie

Dunalská

Primate's
Palace

Hummel
Museum

Primaciálne
námestie

Laurinská

Modrý
Kostolík

Bezručova

né
stie

Stará radnica

Gorkého

ČEDOK

BIS

Slovak National
Theatre

Jesenského

Štúrova

Razinova

Suvorova

doslavovo
mestie

Palackého

Tobrucká

Mostová

otel Carlton

Reduta

Kúpeľná

Komenský
University

Šafárikovo
námestie

ovak
ational
allery

Vajanského nábr.

Slovak
National
Museum

Hydrofoil
Terminal

To Petržalka

For centuries Bratislava was *Pressburg* to the German world, who supplied around half the inhabitants until the 1945 expulsions, and *Pozsony* to the Hungarians, who used the place as their capital for several centuries, crowning their kings and queens in the cathedral and holding their Diet here until the Turks were finally beaten back from the Hungarian plain. At the turn of the century the city had barely 60,000 inhabitants, most of whom were German, Hungarian and/or Jewish, with a smattering of Romanies and Slovaks. The balance shifted with the establishment of the Czechoslovak Republic in 1918, which gave a leg-up to the Slovaks who took over the cultural and political institutions and renamed the place Bratislava after Bratislav, the last Slav leader of the Great Moravian Empire.

Over the last seventy years, the population has increased sevenfold and is now the second largest city of the two republics, with a population of over 400,000. However, the historical centre is much smaller than you'd expect, most of the population living in the city's mushrooming high-rise estates. Whatever the city's previous identity, it's Slovak through and through now, its youthful centre packed out with students and the new westernised generation of Slovakia's burgeoning population. The multicultural atmosphere of the prewar days is only vaguely echoed in the city's smattering of Magyars, Romanies and day-tripping Austrians – but there's still a ring of truth to Metternich's much-quoted aphorism, "East of Vienna, the Orient begins".

You'll need a couple of days at least to soak the city in, and with none of the sightseeing crowds of Prague, the relaxed feel of the old town, and some of the best weather in the country, you'll probably want to stay longer.

> The Bratislava area telephone code is ☎07

Arrival

The geography of Bratislava is easy to get to grips with: the **staré mesto** – where you'll want to spend most of your time – lies on the north side of the Danube; sitting on the rocky hill to the west is the city's most enduring landmark, the **castle** or *hrad*. Equally difficult to miss is the spectacular suspension bridge over the Danube, **most SNP**, leading to the vast **Petržalka** housing development, which continues as far as the eye can see on the south bank. East and north of the staré mesto, nineteenth-century residential blocks gradually give way to the postwar housing of the city's sprawling suburbs.

Points of arrival are less straightforward. A kilometre or so north of the staré mesto is the city's **main train station**, Bratislava hlavná stanica, where most international and long-distance trains pull in to. It has had a much needed facelift in recent years, and, although the architecture smacks of the old regime, it's a definite improvement on the previous chaos. Once you've made it out of the building, go down to the big tram terminus below the station and – having bought your ticket from one of the machines on the platform – hop on tram #1 or #13 into town. Buses and trolley buses leave from directly outside the station steps.

If you're arriving from, or heading for, destinations within West Slovakia by train, you're most likely to use Bratislava's **Nové Mesto train station**, situated next to the main **bus station** on Bajkalská, northwest of the town centre. To get to the city centre, turn right and walk 100m to the junction with Vajnorská, and catch tram #6 or #14 into town.

Bratislava does have an **airport** of sorts, but at present there are no direct flights to or from the West. There are, however, several domestic flights a day to Prague, as well as two to Košice and one to Poprad. Bus #24 goes from the airport to the main train station, or else you could catch the ČSA bus, which runs a shuttle service to and from the ČSA office on Štúrova, timed to coincide with the flight schedule. If you're flying in to Vienna, there's a regular bus service from Vienna airport which drops passengers at the main bus station in Bratislava (see above). Another possible arrival point from Vienna or Budapest is the **hydrofoil terminal** on Fajnorovo nábrežie, opposite the Slovak National Museum, a short walk from the old town.

Getting around and information

The best way to see Bratislava is to walk – in fact it's the only way to see the pedestrianised staré mesto and the area around the castle, where most of the city's sights are concentrated. However, if you're staying outside the city centre or visiting the suburbs, you'll need to make use of the city's cheap and comprehensive **transport system** of buses, trolley buses and trams (known as *električky* in Slovak). Tickets are standard for all types of transport: buy your ticket beforehand (from newsagents, kiosks or ticket machines), validate it as soon as you get on, and use a fresh ticket each time you change. If you're going to be using the system a lot, it might be worth buying a one-day (*24 hodiny lístok*) or two-day ticket (*48 hodiny lístok*), available from the city transport office on Štúrova 5. **Night buses** congregate at námestie SNP, every quarter to the hour.

Like Prague, Bratislava boasts a proper **tourist information office**, *Bratislavská informačná služba* or *BIS* for short, at Laurinská 1 (Mon–Fri 8am–6pm, Sat 8am–1pm), good for general queries (some English is spoken there) and getting hold of the monthly listings magazine, *Kam v Bratislave* (mostly in Slovak but with a few pages of English info); they may also be able to help with accommodation (see below). You should be able to buy a detailed *orientačná mapa* from one of the bookshops near *BIS*; try the *Slovenská kniha*, opposite.

Accommodation

Bratislava has none of the logistic problems of overcrowding that plague Prague, but nor does it have anything like the range of possibilities. Cheap hotels do exist – *ČEDOK* on Jesenského (Mon–Fri 9am–6pm; Sat 9am–noon) may be able to

---

ACCOMMODATION PRICES

Each place to stay in this chapter has a symbol which corresponds to one of seven **price categories**:

① Under 500kčs   ② 500–750kčs   ③ 750–1000kčs   ④ 1000–1500kčs

⑤ 1500–2000kčs   ⑥ 2000–3000kčs   ⑦ 3000kčs and upwards

All prices are for the cheapest **double room** available, which usually means without private bath or shower in the less expensive places. For a **single room**, expect to pay around two-thirds the price of a double.

help – but, as with Prague, at least some of those listed below are liable to close sometime in the near future for modernisation. Private rooms are not as easy to come by; try *BIS* or *ČEDOK*, or else check out the accommodation bureau based in a caravan by the *Hotel Danube* on Riačná. In July and August, there are also various hostels to choose from: *BIS* or *CKM* at Hviezdoslavovo námestie 16 (Mon–Fri 9am–noon & 1–4pm) are the best bet, and the latter should be able to give you a list of the current student hostels.

Hotels

Palace, Poštová 1 (☎33 36 56; ②). A bargain (breakfast included) right on the corner with Obchodná, and a step away from námestie SNP.

Lux, Šafárikovo námestie (☎554 71; ③). Don't be put off by the name; this is a friendly, privately run place right by the old town.

Botel Gracia, Rázusovo nábrežie (☎33 24 32; ⑤). Floating hotel moored on the main embankment. Not everyone's cup of tea, especially in summer when the mosquitoes arrive.

Carlton, Hviezdoslavovo námestie (☎582 09). This *was* one of Bratislava's more memorable hotels, but is undergoing a lengthy refurbishing that's likely to push the previously reasonable prices up.

Kyjev, Rajská 2 (☎570 82; ⑥). Sky-rise 1960s hotel near Kamenné námestie, with a reputable restaurant on the top floor.

Fórum, Mierové námestie 2 (☎348 11; ⑦). The businessperson's hotel, on the northern edge of the staré mesto and at $140 a double beyond the means of most individual travellers.

Devín, Riečná 4 (☎33 66 40; ⑦). On the river front, not quite as flash as the *Fórum*, but $100 a double nevertheless.

Danube, Rybné námestie 1 (☎34 00 00; ⑦). The newest and one of the most expensive hotels in the city, built in titanium blue and grey, just off Rázusovo nábrežie; currently charging around $115 a double.

Hostels and Camping

Youth Hostel Bernolák, Bernolákova (☎49 77 25; ①) The liveliest and cheapest hostel in the city, and only a short tram ride northeast of the centre (tram #7 or #11 from Kamenné námestie). Breakfast is included, and there's a bar and regular discos and gigs.

Sputnik, Drieňová (☎23 43 40; ③). *CKM*-run hostel-cum-hotel in Nové Mesto. *IYHF* members can get a very good deal here, but the place is often full. Some way east of the centre; bus #34 or #54.

Zlaté Piesky. Two fairly grim campsites, 8km northeast of the city centre, near the swimming lake of the same name. To get there, take tram #4 from the main train station or tram #2 from town. Motel rooms (③) and cheap bungalows are on offer all year round; tent camping May to September only.

The staré mesto

Trams #1 and #13 from the main train station offload their passengers behind the *Hotel Fórum* in Obchodná – literally Shop Street – which descends into Hurbanovo námestie, a busy whizzing junction on the northern edge of the staré mesto. Here you'll find the city's biggest shoe store, and, unmoved by the vulgar clamour of it all, the hefty mass of Galli da Bibiena's **Trinity Church**. Inside, the single-domed nave gives off a faded musty ambience, the exuberant trompe l'oeil frescoes creating a magnificent false cupola on the ceiling, typical of the Bibiena family who excelled in theatrical design. If this is your first Slovak church, though, probably the most striking feature is the constant flow of worshippers, young and old, who shuffle in and out genuflecting all the while: a far cry from the wizened penitents who form the congregations in Czech churches.

Across the road and past the functionalist shoe shop, a footbridge passes under the first tower of the city's last remaining double gateway. Below, in what used to be the city moat, is an open-air *čitáreň* reading area (Mon–Sat 1–7pm), a tiny garden which hosts the odd literary event in amongst the modern sculpture and the shrubbery, a favourite spot for mothers and their napping offspring. It belongs to the **Baroque Apothecary** called *U červeného raka* (At the Red Lobster), immediately on your left between the towers, which now houses a **Pharmaceutical Museum** (Tues–Sun 10am–5pm) displaying everything from seventeenth-century drug grinders to Slovak herbal tea bags. Upstairs, period pharmacies have been reconstructed, but if you'd rather see a fully functioning *lekáreň*, try the neo-Renaissance *U Salvatora*, Panská 35.

The second and taller of the two gateways is the **Michalská veža** (daily 10am–8pm; closed Tues), an evocative and impressive entrance to the staré město, whose outer limits are elsewhere hard to distinguish. You can climb the tower, giving a quick glance en route to the vertical **museum of arms and armaments**, for a great rooftop view of the old town. Michalská and Ventúrska – which make up the same street – are lined with some of Bratislava's finest Baroque palaces, but the talk and chatter issuing from the cafés and bars is that of students, shoppers and young politicos. On the right is the main university library, in the building that once held the **Hungarian Diet**; from here a passageway leads west to the **Convent of sv Klara**, whose chapel spire is one of the most beautiful pieces of Gothic architecture in the city. Sadly, the convent now houses another university library, and except for the occasional concert, the chapel can only be admired from its southern wall.

Back on Michalská, a few doors down, is one of three Baroque palaces owned by the Pálffy family, now known as the **Mozartov dom** (Mozart once performed here as a child). Here *Verejnosť proti nasiliu* (People Against Violence), the Slovak sister of the Czech Civic Forum, seconded what was the Institute for Political Education into their headquarters during the student strike of 1989. The building itself is strikingly beautiful; there's a relaxed atmosphere and it's a good place to meet up with people, either at the **information centre** downstairs, in the swanky **café** upstairs, or the vegetarian restaurants in the leafy balconied courtyard and in the basement.

Opposite the Mozartov dom is the **Academia Istropolitana**, the first Hungarian (or, if you prefer, Slovak) university. Founded in 1465 by Matthew Corvinus, it continually lost out to the more established nearby universities of Vienna, Prague and Kraków, and was eventually forced to close down in 1490. The buildings and the inner courtyard were modernised in the 1960s for the faculty of performing arts, who put on some interesting shows and exhibitions of their work in the chapel and crypt.

The palaces of the Austro-Hungarian aristocracy continue right into Panksá, starting with the **Pálffy Palace**, today an **art gallery** (Tues–Fri 10am–8pm, Sat & Sun 10am–5pm) with the occasional live "happening" in the basement, where temporary exhibitions also take place. The rest of the building has a mediocre collection of European paintings from the fourteenth to the twentieth centuries, only worth bothering with for the Slovak art section, which includes works by Ľudovít Fulla and Martin Benka, plus a couple of Janko Alexy's smooth pastel canvases and the occasional one-off expo on the top floor. Further down, next to the Esterházy Palace, is the **kaplnka Božieho tela** (Corpus Christi Chapel), a richly decorated intimate space packed with illuminated manuscripts, jewellery and ecclesiastical wealth.

Hlavné námestie, Františkánske námestie and around

Slightly further east are the tranquil twin main squares of the staré mesto: **Hlavné námestie**, a patch of green focused on a Roland column and fountain sporting the usual cherubs seemingly peeing out of fishes' mouths, and the shady extension of **Františkánske námestie**. It's difficult to believe that the quiet leafy park of Hlavné námestie was once the city's main marketplace – only the surrounding buildings give any hint. On the west side of the square is a sandy yellow Secessionist building, originally a bank, now a café; opposite stands the **stará radnica**, a modest two-storey building built in a lively hotchpotch of styles. Gothic in its core, Renaissance in its innards and nineteenth-century in its reconstruction, it surpasses itself in its fanciful Baroque tower, and the serene half-moon gables and fragile arcading of the inner courtyard, where summer concerts take place. Within the town hall, the **Viticultural Museum** (Tues–Sun 10am–5pm) is the scholarly tribute to the fact that Bratislava is at the centre of the country's wine industry, but it's the building and not the exhibition that wins first prize.

The Counter-Reformation, which gripped the parts of Hungary not under Turkish occupation, issues forth from the **Jesuit Church**, nicked from the local German Protestant community and filled to the brim with the usual post-Baroque kitsch. Not far from here, opposite the gaudy yellow Franciscan Church, is the **Mirbach Palace** (Tues–Fri 10am–6pm, Sat & Sun 10am–5pm; concerts Sun 10.30am), arguably the finest of Bratislava's Rococo buildings, and preserving much of its original stucco decor. That said, the Baroque art inside isn't up to much, save for the wall-to-wall miniatures set into wooden panelling, and the story of the seventeenth-century Dutch tapestries, discovered by chance during the renovation of the Primate's Palace (see below).

Round the back of the stará radnica, with the stillness of a provincial Italian piazza during siesta, is the pastel-pink **Primaciálne námestie**, dominated by the Neoclassical **Primate's Palace**, whose pediment frieze is topped by a 300-pound cast-iron archbishop's hat. The palace's main claim to fame is as the place where Napoleon and the Austrian Emperor signed the Treaty of Pressburg in 1805. When it's been fully renovated, it will house yet more of the city's art collection, including the Dutch tapestries currently on display in the Mirbach Palace.

All over the staré mesto, commemorative plaques make much of Bratislava's musical connections, but apart from the reflected glory of its proximity to Vienna and Budapest – not to mention the prewar presence of a large German population, who ensured a regular supply of Europe's best – the city has produced only one (mildly) famous composer, **Johann Nepomuk Hummel** (1778–1837), who was in any case very much an Austrian at heart. Still, it's as good an excuse as any for a **Hummel Museum** (Tues–Sun 1–5pm; concerts late afternoon Thurs), housed in the composer's birthplace, a cute apricot-coloured cottage swamped by its neighbours and hidden away behind a row of fashionable shops on Klobučnícka (Hat Street). Like Mozart, his tutor and friend for a while in Vienna, Hummel was a *Wunderkind* who began performing at the tender age of ten. Although he wrote many fine classical works, his real talents lay in his virtuoso piano-playing, which, lacking the permanence of composition, has confined his fame to the musical cognoscenti.

The Cathedral, the Jewish Quarter and the Castle

On the side of the staré mesto nearest the castle, the most insensitive of Bratislava's postwar developments took place. As if the annihilation of the city's large and visible Jewish population by the Nazis wasn't enough, the Communist authorities tore down virtually the whole of the **Jewish quarter** in order to build the brutal showpiece bridge most SNP (see below). Quite apart from the devastation of the ghetto, the traffic that tears along the busy thoroughfare of Staromestská has seriously undermined the foundations of the Gothic **Cathedral of sv Martin**, coronation church of the kings and queens of Hungary for over 250 years, whose ill-proportioned steeple is topped by a tiny gilded Hungarian crown. In all probability it was never very attractive from the outside, but with the new road missing the west door by a matter of metres, coupled with the noise and fumes, the best policy is to take refuge inside, where, against all odds, it's pleasantly cool and light, if unspectacular.

Passing under the approach road for the new bridge, two old, thin houses stand opposite one another, both now converted into museums. The first, a yellow Rococo fancy called *U dobrého pastiera* (At the Good Shepherd), is a **clock museum** (10am–5pm; closed Tues) with a display of – depending on your tastes – nauseously vulgar or brilliantly kitsch Baroque and Empire clocks; the second

---

JEWS IN SLOVAKIA

Jews probably settled in **Bratislava** sometime during the thirteenth century. Over the following centuries, they were forced to move around the city and were expelled several times, until finally in the sixteenth century, they found refuge in Podhradie (literally "under the castle"), just outside the city walls. Before World War II, Jews made up ten percent of the city's population (the vast majority Orthodox), maintaining no fewer than nineteen synagogues and prayer rooms. Bratislava was also a significant centre of Jewish **education**, in particular the *yeshivah* founded in 1806, which became one of the most famous Orthodox institutions in Europe, a tradition carried on today by the *Pressbuger Yeshivah* in Jerusalem. Its founder, Rabbi Hatam Sofer, died here in 1839 and his grave continues to attract Jewish pilgrims from all over the world; it is situated in a modern mausoleum by the western exit of the road tunnel under the castle that was built by the Nazis, and for which the original cemetery was destroyed. Today, Bratislava's Jewish community is very small, with only one working synagogue on Heydukova, and a cemetery west of the city centre on Žižkova.

Of **Slovakia**'s considerable prewar Jewish population of 95,000, only 3000 remain. Their fate under the wartime **Tiso** regime is still a potent political issue – many Slovaks reacted indignantly to the suggestion made by the Czech ambassador to the US that anti-Semitism was, and still is, "endemic" in Slovakia, arguing that several leading members of Tiso's government tried their best to prevent Jews from being deported. Yet since 1989, Slovak nationalists have attemped to unveil a plaque commemorating Tiso, Jewish cemeteries have been vandalised in several towns across the country, and the leading *VPN* politician, Fedor Gal, now living in "exile" in Prague, claims he was forced to leave Slovakia because of anti-Semitic threats made against his life. Taken together, these incidents do not necessarily confirm the widely held Czech view of Slovakia as a hotbed of anti-Semitism, but it is particularly distasteful that anti-Semitism should have become a useful political tool in a place where so few Jews remain.

is a **folk museum** (same hours) which contains a few period dining rooms and a smallish collection of national folk art objects.

Up to the Castle

From these twin museums, **Beblavého** begins the steep climb up to the castle. For many years this was one of the city's more infamous red-light districts, serving both town and barracks from its strategic point between the two, and described evocatively by Patrick Leigh Fermor, who passed through Bratislava en route to Constantinople in 1934: "During the day, except for the polyglot murmur of invitation, it was a rather silent place. But it grew noisier after dark when shadows brought confidence and the plum brandy began to bite home. It was only lit by cigarette ends and by an indoor glow that silhouetted the girls on their thresholds. Pink lights revealed the detail of each small interior: a hastily tidied bed, a tin basin and a jug, some lustral gear and a shelf displaying a bottle of solution, pox-foiling and gentian-hued; a couple of dresses hung on a nail." Like the Jewish cafés Leigh Fermor also hung out in (along with, though not necessarily at the same table as, the young Orthodox Jew, Ludvík Hoch – better known as Robert Maxwell), all this has long since gone, but there's still a hint of the bohemian about the ramshackle houses now slowly being turned into swish galleries, chic bars and restaurants.

The **Castle** itself, frequently referred to as the "inverted bedstead", is an unwelcoming giant box, built in the fifteenth century by the Emperor Sigismund in expectation of a Hussite attack, and burnt down by its own drunken Austrian soldiers in 1811. Only recently restored, it now houses around half of the vast collections of the **Slovak National Museum** (Slovenské národné múzeum; Tues–Sun 10am–noon & 2–4pm). The dimly lit treasury in the basement of the building contains various bits of jewellery, a copy of the famous *Venus of Věstonice*, a tiny fertility figure from the time of the Great Moravian Empire, but not the Hungarian crown jewels, which were transferred to Vienna in 1783 and now reside in Budapest. Numismatologists will have fun among the coins on the top floor, but the rest of the museum could happily be passed over in favour of

---

PETRŽALKA AND PETROCHEMICALS

The **Petržalka housing estate** is a symbol of the new Slovak nation, dragged forcibly into the twentieth century – but at a cost. Over a third of the city's population – an incredible 150,000 people – live on Petržalka, whose estates still retain cruelly ironic names like Háje (Woods) and Lúky (Meadows), in what is now a virtually treeless expanse of mud and high-rise, with the added bonus of being surrounded (until recently) by the barbed wire and watchtowers of the Iron Curtain. In many respects – most notably crime and drugs – it can't compete with the worst housing estates in the West, but with the highest suicide rate in the country it's not a place where anyone would choose to live.

The Petržalka problem is just one of the many social and ecological issues that were brought to light by **Bratislava nahlas** (Bratislava Aloud), a "green" booklet published in October 1987 by an officially recognised environmental organisation, but quickly suppressed by the Communists (though not before it had been passed round almost every household in Bratislava). The two biggest polluters lambasted in the report were the *Slovnaft* oil refinery, a vast petrochemical complex just 2km east of Petržalka, and the chemical works to the northeast of the city centre, which pump some 9000 litres of sulphuric acid into the Danube every year.

the view from outside the castle gates, south across the Danube plain, which is nothing short of mind-blowing. Most of the immediate foreground is taken up with the infamous Petržalka estate, which makes it virtually impossible to focus on the romantic thought that, as you gaze out over the meeting point of three countries, you are looking at the very heart of *Mitteleuropa*.

Hviezdoslavovo námestie, the waterfront and around

Between the staré mesto and the waterfront lies the graceful, tree-lined boulevard of **Hviezdoslavovo námestie**, with a swish Hungarian restaurant and a couple of cafés along one side, and the seedy splendour of the 1920s *Hotel Carlton*, an amalgamation of three hotels, on the other. Pride of place in the square and prime spot for casual loitering is the larger-than-life statue of Pavol Országh Hviezdoslav, "father of Slovak poetry", whose life as minor government official in the Orava region was pretty uneventful, but whose poetry is still a source of great national pride. At the square's eastern end, the Hungarians and Germans (who were in the majority at the time) erected two magnificent late nineteenth-century edifices: the first, fronted by an elaborate fountain depicting the mythological figure of Ganymede, is now the **Slovak National Theatre**, a top-quality Viennese-style opera house; the second, diagonally opposite, is the later, more Secessionist **Reduta Theatre**, built as a casino, dance hall and café, but now home to the Slovak Philharmonic Orchestra (the café may yet return). At the end of Mostova is Štúrovo námestie, its modern statue of **Ľudovít Štúr** and his followers – appearing to levitate – a replacement for the grandiose statue of Maria Theresa which Slovak nationalists blew up in 1919.

The River Danube and the most SNP

Beyond Štúrovo námestie and the fast dual carriageway of Rázusovo nábrežie, you can stroll along the banks of the (far from blue) **River Danube** – *Dunaj* in Slovak. At this point the Danube is fast, terrifyingly (and unnaturally) so – witness the speed to which the massive double-barges are reduced by the current and, by contrast, the velocity of those hurtling downstream. There's a regular (and hazardous) ferry service across the river, an alternative to crossing by either of the two bridges. The larger of these is the infamous **most SNP** (Bridge of the Slovak National Uprising), for which the old Jewish Quarter was ripped up. However destructive its construction, it's difficult not to be impressed by the sheer size and audacity of this single open suspension bridge. Its one support column leans at an alarming angle, topped by a saucer-like penthouse café reminiscent of the *Starship Enterprise*. The view from the café is superlative (except after dark when you can't see a thing due to the reflection of the café's lights), but the cost of the lift and a drink puts many locals off: more cheaply, there's just as good a view from the toilet. The best place from which to view the bridge is the rather forlorn funfair in the **Janko Kráľ Park** on the opposite bank – all that's left of what Baedeker described in 1904 as "a favourite evening-promenade . . . with café and pleasant grounds".

Around the Slovak National Gallery

When the Slovaks took control of Bratislava in 1918, a town in which they had previously made little impression, they set about establishing their own cultural monuments to rival those of the Austrians and Hungarians. Three such buildings were put up in the waterfront district, of which the **Slovak National Gallery** (Slovenská národná galéria; Tues & Sat 11am–6pm, Wed–Fri & Sun 10am–5pm), housed in a converted naval barracks, is probably the most rewarding. The problem with modern Slovak art is that, until the foundation of the Republic, there was no living tradition outside the skilful and infinite folk art of the countryside. Between the wars, Slovak artists began to establish themselves in much greater numbers, elevating peasant life to a subject worthy of "high art", and recording the privation which was commonplace in the rural areas of Slovakia in the 1930s. Three artists stand out: **Janko Alexy**, the only Slovak artist to have made any impression internationally; **Miloš Bazovský**, whose naive, robust portrayals of peasant life are redolent of the Mexican artist Diego Rivera; and **Ľudovít Fulla**, whose urgent, colourful canvases are the very opposite of Bazovský's calm, Expressionist technique. For those not heading further east, the relatively small section on Uniate **icon paintings** is definitely worth catching. Some, like the *Posledný súd* (Last Supper), are an untutored personal nightmare of the apocalypse, with the Devil employing a whale-like monster to gobble up the damned as they fall from grace.

Further along the quayside, past the hydrofoil launch, is the unremarkable natural history section of the **Slovak National Museum** (Tues–Sun 9am–5pm), housed in a dark and dingy 1930s building. Further east along Vajanského nábrežie stands the **Komenský University**, an equally dour building, founded along with the Republic in 1918, and like the nearby bars and cafés, brimming with young students. Otherwise, waiting around for buses is the main object of the folk milling around Šafárikovo námestie. The only specific sight around here is Ödön Lechner's sky-blue Art-Nouveau **Modrý kostolík** (Little Blue Church) on Bezručova, a lost monument to this once-Hungarian city, abandoned in the Slovak capital. It's decorated, inside and out, with the richness of a central European cream cake, and dedicated to Saint Elizabeth, the city's one and only famous saint, who was born in Bratislava in 1207. Lechner quite clearly also designed the *Gymnasium*, one block north of the church, and recently given a lick of matching bright blue paint.

Námestie SNP and beyond

At the top end of Štúrova is **Kamenné námestie**, where the whole city seems to wind up after work, to grab a beer or takeaway from one of the many stand-up stalls, jabber away the early evening, and above all catch the bus or tram home. It's not difficult to think of a more picturesque setting than under the shadow of the high-rise *Hotel Kyjev* and the city's biggest department store, but this is where the action is. Visible to the northwest, **námestie SNP** is a bit more accommodating, with at least a few trees and a host of outdoor cafés. This is where the Slovaks gathered in their thousands for their part in the 1989 Velvet Revolution, though nowadays it's a favourite spot for Slovak Nationalist Party activists. At its centre is the inevitable Monument to the Slovak National Uprising, the anti-Fascist coup against the Nazis in the summer of 1944 which cost the country so dear. A macho bronze partisan guards the eternal flame, while two Slovak women (heads suitably covered) maintain a respectful distance. To most Slovaks, it's just another of those ugly but invisible celebrations of militarism with which the city and indeed the whole republic has been "blessed" over the last forty years.

Behind námestie SNP is the brown marble and onyx abomination of the *Hotel Fórum*, which looks out onto **Mierové námestie**, one of the city's busiest intersections and nowadays little more than a cacophony of cars and lorries, though no doubt once a princely foil for the **Grassalkovich Palace**, which cowers in the top corner. Until 1989 this was the Klement Gottwald House of Young Pioneers – the Communist youth organisation, now disbanded – though only the gardens, which excel in ugly modern fountains, are open to the public for the moment. There's not much reason to be in this part of town unless you want to pay your respects to the **Slovak Parliament**, two blocks north up Banskobystrická, which occupies the former summer residence of the archbishop of Esztergom.

Devotees of totalitarian architecture might also wish to visit **námestie Slobody**, a grandiose space designed by the local Party as a monumental setting for a giant statue of the first Communist president, Klement Gottwald (since removed). The entire length of the east side of the square is taken up by the severe concrete mass of the General Post Office building, which claims to be the largest in the world. A more successful modern addition to the city is the striking inverted pyramid of the Slovak Radio building, up Mytná, east of the square.

The other side of Mierové námestie is a better place to wander, where block after block of dowdy yet colourful late nineteenth-century buildings squat under the Slavín hill. The only sight as such is the pale blue and exceedingly plain **Lutheran Lycée** on Konventa (closed to the public), outside which a tall granite column commemorates the many leading Slovak men of letters who were educated here in the nineteenth century. Surprisingly enough for a fervently Catholic peasant country, the Protestants produced Slovak leaders far in excess of their numerical strength, including the entire 1848 triumvirate of Štúr, Hodža and Hurban. The city's Lenin Museum used to reside in a nineteenth-century neo-Baroque palace three-quarters of the way up Štefánikova; to make up for this irrevocable loss, a new **Police Museum** (Múzeum Policie; Tues–Sat 10am–5pm) has now opened a little further south on the corner of Gunduličova.

The Slavín Monument

The Slavín hill is crowned by the gargantuan **Slavín Monument** commemorating the 6000 Soviet soldiers who lost their lives in the battle for Bratislava, which was ceremoniously completed in 1960 to mark the fifteenth anniversary of the city's liberation, and must now rank as the largest Soviet monument still standing in the entire country. Visible from virtually every street corner in Bratislava, every tour group in the capital is taken to see it at some point or other. It's predictably militaristic, not to say phallic, a giant ribbed obelisk thrusting into the sky, topped by an anguished Soviet soldier holding the victory banner outstretched. Not only is it in exceedingly poor taste, but it was overshadowed eight years later by the second Soviet "liberation".

The villa quarter just below the monument has always been a well-to-do suburb, settled by the German middle class in the interwar period and until recently the exclusive territory of Party *apparatchiks*; the mild-mannered **Alexander Dubček** used to live at Mišikova 46 (Mouse Street). In 1968, he became probably the only Slovak ever to achieve world fame, a feat he achieved by becoming the somewhat unlikely leader of a deeply divided Communist Party as it attempted to bring about *perestroika* twenty years ahead of its time. Crushed by the Soviet invasion, he spent his twenty years of internal exile here too, under constant surveillance, working for the Slovak equivalent of the local forestry commission.

Eating, drinking and entertainment

Eating is taken more seriously in Bratislava than in Prague, and despite the lack of new foreign ventures, a whole host of restaurants have recently opened up, greatly improving the overall choice. In addition to the usual Slovak fare, Magyar cuisine finds its way onto most menus in various shapes and forms, though authentically only in the city's handful of truly Hungarian restaurants. The preference for wine over beer lends a cosmopolitan touch to the cafés and bars, clustered around námestie SNP; draught beer is available from only a few pubs and restaurants.

Cafés

Bystrica, most SNP. The sky-high café (prices as well as location) at the top of the city's main suspension bridge, most SNP.

Charlie centrum, Špitálska 4. Cool café-restaurant at the multi-screen art house cinema; entrance behind the *Hotel Kyjev* on Rajská.

Roland, Hlavné námestie 5. Newish café in a converted bank, decorated in a kind of repro Art Nouveau. Open Tues–Sat 9am–9pm, Sun & Mon 11am–9pm.

Štefánka, Palisády 59. High ceiling and soft-seated alcoves, but 1970s kitsch decor for this café-restaurant, which overlooks Mierové námestie from the north.

U dežmara, Klariská. Student hang-out by the university library – duck down the passageway off Michalská. Open Mon–Sat 9am–10pm.

U krála Mateja, Biela 5. Standard café/bar in the old town, with an exceptionally beautiful shady courtyard round the side. Open Mon–Fri 9am–10pm, Sat & Sun noon–10pm.

Pubs

Piváreň Wolkerová, Biela 5. Traditional *pivnica* in the old town serving *Budvar* and a good selection of Czech and Slovak dishes. Open Mon–Fri 9am–10pm, Sat & Sun noon–10pm.

Pivovarská reštaurácia, Križna. The local brewery pub, with a rowdy crowd of serious drinkers, and the odd weirdo.

Smíchovský dvor, Heydukova. Prague beer and a lively clientele, situated a short walk from námestie SNP.

Stará sladovňa, Cintorínska 32. "The Old Malthouse" is probably Bratislava's most famous eating and drinking establishment. It served as the city's malthouse until 1976, when it was converted into what claims to be the second largest restaurant in Europe (it seats 1600 at a pinch). Certainly there's rarely any problem getting a seat, and the food isn't at all bad, though they stop serving around 8 or 9pm. *Velkopopovický kozel* and *Budvar* on tap, big band music towards the end of the week. Open daily noon–11pm.

Restaurants

Arkádia, Zámocké schody (☎33 56 50). Great Slovak cuisine served in this converted house, halfway up the steps to the castle – fantastic view over the Danube, too.

Flauta, in the courtyard of the *Mozartov dom*, Ventúrská 10. Cheap and tasty dishes ranging from soya goulash to veggie burgers, not to mention delicious puddings (tables outside in summer). Open 11am–11pm; closed Tues.

Gurman, Poštová 3. *McDonald's* has yet to make it to Bratislava, and until it does, you'll have to make do with this Slovak version. Open Mon–Fri 8am–9pm, Sat 8am–1pm.

Il Caleone, Palackého 18. Pricier (and even more popular) than the other pizza joints in the city but worth the extra dosh.

Maďarská reštaurácia, Hviezdoslavovo námestie 20 (☎33 48 83). Without doubt the best Magyar restaurant in town, serving superb (though none too cheap) Hungarian meals, occasionally to the accompaniment of a *cimbalom*. Open 11.30am–10pm.

Okaj vináreň, Laurinská 7 (☎33 06 71). Cheaper, less formal Hungarian restaurant, with a good selection of wines.

Pizzeria, on Obchodná, with a non-smoking branch at Špitálska 31. Cheap, smallish Slovak-style pizzas.

Rybársky cech, Žižkova 1 (☎31 30-49). Popular and reliably good fish restaurant in a former fisherman's house down by the waterfront below the castle.

U mäsiarov, Paulinyho. Self-service stand-up *bufet* with a wide selection of cheap Slovak dishes every day. Open daily 7am–3pm.

U zlatého kapra, Prepošská. Specialises in fish dishes (thankfully not pulled out of the Danube).

Vegetariánska reštaurácia, also in the *Mozartov dom*, Ventúrská 10. No smoking, no alcohol, no frills self-service vegetarian restaurant in the basement. Open Mon–Thurs & Sat 11.30am–7.30pm, Fri 11.30am–2pm.

Veľkí františkáni, Františkánske námestie (☎33 30 73). Rather too well-known wine restaurant featuring live Slovak Gypsy music (cover charge for the music). Open daily 5pm–1am.

Entertainment

Bratislava's nightlife is still heavily biased towards high culture, though most theatres and concert halls close for much of July and August. Pick up the monthly listings magazine, *Kam v Bratislave* from *BIS*, to find out what's on. In season, there's **opera and ballet** at the *Slovenské národné divadlo*, and **classical concerts** at *Reduta*, both on Hviedoslavovo námestie, as well as the more varied programme put on at the modern *Dom odborov* complex (tram #2 or #14 from the station; tram #4, #6 or #10 from town). **Tickets** are available from the *BIS* office on Nedbalova (Mon–Fri only), or from the box office (noon–8pm) behind the National Theatre, and for the *Dom odborov* from a box office inside the building itself from 3pm onwards. If a performance is sold out, you can usually get stand-by tickets, available thirty minutes to an hour before the performance.

Apart from a few discos in the flash hotels, there's a shortage of clubs in Bratislava; larger gigs and events are often forced to use the formal setting of the *Dom odborov*. However, the **rock and jazz scene** is looking up with a new regular venue for live gigs at the *New Model Club*, a small sweaty dive down the passage at Obchodná 2 (daily 8pm–4am); dancing and live music also go on at *Rock Fabrick Danubius*, Kominárska 3, just northwest of the *Dom odborov*. The *Mozartov dom* on Ventúrská puts on an interesting cultural programme, and is a good place to go for insider tips. Another place worth checking out is the *Charlie centrum*, Špitálska 4; the entrance is one block east of the *Hotel Kyjev* on Rajská. As well as a four-screen cinema, showing mostly art house movies, it has a basement café-restaurant that occasionally features live jazz. The *Černý havran* café on Biela also puts on a varied programme – anything from folk and jazz to poetry readings.

Bratislava hosts a couple of large-scale **festivals**, starting with its own Spring Music Festival in April – without the big names of Prague's, but a lot easier to get tickets for. The Bratislava Jazz Days take place in October and often headline with the same musicians who've just trundled through Prague and Kraków. In September there's an international arts festival – mostly, but not exclusively, highbrow – with groups from all over Europe taking part. There's also a biennial international festival of children's illustrations held in odd-numbered years, of interest to adults as much as kids.

Listings

Airlines *ČSA* & *Slov-Air*, Štúrova (☎33 85 71).

BIS Laurinská 1 (☎33 43 70). Open Mon–Fri 8am–6pm, Sat 8am–1pm.

Boats Various companies run hydrofoil services from the terminal on Fajnorovo nábrežie (☎595 01) to Budapest and Vienna (see box below for details).

Books Good selection of secondhand guides and English-language books at *Antikvariát*, Kamenné námestie 5.

Car rental *Eurocar*, based in the *Hotel Danube* on Rázusovo nábrežie.

Embassies and consulates At present there's just one embassy – *Finland*, Gorkého 15 (☎55 870) – and two Western consulates – *Austria*, Červeňova 19 (☎33 51 77); *USA*, Paulinyho (☎33 08 61) – but with the formal separation of the Czech and Slovak republics, there should be more representation in the near future.

Football Bratislava's premier team is *Slovan Bratislava*, the only Slovak club to have won a European competition within living memory. *Slovan*'s ground is the *Tehelné Pole* stadium, built during the last war and also used for international games. For details of how to get there, see "Sport facilities" below.

Kids The children's theatre, *Biblava*, on Dobšinského námestie, has shows every Sunday at 5pm; open-air kids' shows at 10am on Sundays at the *Detský amfiteáter Lúky* on Šášovskej (June–Aug); not to mention an open-air circus and 10am disco at the *klub detí slniečko*, on Furdeková in Petržalka.

Left luggage Lockers and 24-hour deposit at both train and bus stations.

Markets The best fruit and vegetable market in town takes place Mon–Sat in the *Tržnica* covered market hall opposite the *Dom odborov*. Early Saturday morning is the busiest and best time to go.

Newspapers Main outlet for foreign newspapers is *Interpress Slovakia*, Laurinská 9.

Pharmacies 24-hour pharmacies at Mýtna 5, Trnavská 1 and Bebravská 24.

Post office Main post office (for letters, parcels etc) is at námestie SNP 35; poste restante at booth no .5.

Sport facilities There are two main sports complexes, *Tehelné pole* and *Pasienky*, both next to one another in Nové Mesto (tram #2 or #14 from the station; tram #4, #6 or #10 from town). An ice hockey stadium, a cycle track and the big *Slovan* football stadium are just some of the facilities on offer.

Taxis Can be hailed or found in long lines outside the top hotels like the *Fórum*, *Kyjev*, *Danube* and so on. Alternatively, telephone ☎508 51 or 508 52.

Telephones International calls can be made at the 24-hour exchange at Kolárska 12, or (for a hefty surcharge) at any of the big hotels.

Out from the city

Most people find enough in the city centre to occupy them for the average two- or three-day stay, but if you're staying around for longer, or would prefer to be among the vine-clad hills which encroach on the city's northern suburbs, there are several places where you could happily spend a lazy afternoon, all within easy reach of the city centre.

Zlaté Piesky and other swimming possibilities

Out on the motorway to Piešťany, just past the city's huge chemical works, the **Zlaté Piesky** (tram #2 from the train station; tram #4 from town) is a popular destination for weekending Bratislavans. Despite its name, which means "Golden Sands", it's a far cry from the Côte d'Azur, though on a baking hot day in August,

DANUBE TRANSPORT

From mid-April to mid-October there's a twice daily shuttle service by **hydrofoil** between Bratislava and Vienna (1hr), payable in western currencies only, and often heavily booked up in advance. Between May and September, there's a less frequent service to Esztergom and Budapest (3hr 30min). All boats leave from the jetty on Fajnorovo nábrežie, near the Slovak National Museum. For this year's timetable go to the *Slovakoturist* office in the passage between Hviezdoslavovo námestie and Panská, or the ticket office at the jetty. To find out about summer sightseeing cruises on the Danube in and around Bratislava, go to *BIS*.

not even the stench from the nearby chemical factory manages to deter large numbers of sweltering Slovaks from stripping off and throwing themselves into the lake's lukewarm waters. If you'd prefer a genuinely clean swimming environment, try the outdoor pool in the sports complex on Odbojárov (tram #2 or #14 from the station; tram #4, #6 or #10 from town).

Kamzík

North of the main train station, the city immediately gives way to the vineyards and beechwood slopes of the suburb of Vinohrady (a world apart from its vineless namesake in Prague), perfect for making a quick escape from the city and indulging in a bit of aimless wandering through the undergrowth. If you need a target, follow the yellow markers from the station, which take you 2.5km up, through the woods, to the summit of **Kamzík** (440m), topped by a TV tower with a viewpoint café that serves food of sorts. If you don't fancy the walk, take bus #33 to the chairlift on the north side of the hill, or simply take the strain out of the trip by catching trolley bus #213 from Mierové námestie, or námestie Slobody to the last stop and walking along the red-marked path for 1km.

Devín

Bus #29 from beneath most SNP will get you to the village of **DEVÍN**, 9km northwest of Bratislava, whose ruined **castle** (May–Oct Tues–Sun 10am–7pm), first established in the fifth century BC, perches impressively on a rocky promontory at the confluence of the Morava and the Danube. With the West just a stone's throw away across the river, border precautions were particularly excessive on the road to Devín – a continuous twenty-foot barbed-wire fence, punctuated at regular intervals by fifty-foot watchtowers and hidden cameras that monitored all vehicles which passed along the road. Today, such Cold War images seem about as far removed from reality as the traditional Slovak legends which surround Devín .

In 864 and again in 871, the Slavs of the Great Moravian Empire gave the Germans two serious drubbings at Devín, the last of which is said to have left the Germans with so few prisoners with which to barter that they could only succeed in retrieving one half-dead hero named Ratbod. In the nineteenth century, Ľudovít Štúr and his fellow Slovak nationalists made Devín a potent symbol of their lost nationhood, organising a series of publicity stunts in and around the castle in the run up to 1848. The castle remains a popular place for weekend picnics, and Slovak nationalist events in July.

Apart from the view over into Austria, and a small **museum** (May–Oct Tues–Sun 10am–7pm) on archaeological finds in the area, there's not a great deal to see

MILAN RASTISLAV ŠTEFÁNIK

Like so many of Slovakia's nineteenth-century nationalists, **Milan Rastislav Štefánik** was the son of a Lutheran pastor. He got into trouble with the Hungarian authorities while still only a teenager, and later left Slovakia to study astronomy at the Paris Observatoire. He took part in astronomical expeditions to the Sahara and the Pacific islands, and in 1914 volunteered as a pilot for the French Air Force. Along with Masaryk and Beneš, Štefánik formed the famous triumvirate who campaigned tirelessly for an independent Czechoslovak state during the war.

On May 19, 1919, Štefánik died when his plane crashed just outside Bratislava, within sight of the airport. As he was the only true Slovak in the triumvirate, it was a devastating blow for Slovak aspirations, and rumours quickly spread that the plane had been deliberately shot down by the Czechs. Under the Communists, Štefánik suffered the same posthumous fate as Masaryk: his name was expunged from the history books and his statues taken down. Again, like Masaryk, he has returned with a vengeance – many squares and streets have been renamed and his statue is now a common sight throughout Slovkia, though his pro-Czechoslovak views are not popular with all Slovaks.

at Devín, but *BIS* have details of possible performances at the open-air amphitheatre in amongst the ruins. Alternatively, if you fancy doing some walking, it's a nice two-hour walk through the woods along the red-marked path from just above the last stop on tram #4 or #9.

Rusovce

In 1918, when drawing up the Versailles frontiers, the new Czechoslovak Republic was handed a small stretch of forested marshland on the right bank of the Danube to shore up its exposed western flank. Much of this land is now taken up with the unmissable Petržalka housing estate, but there are at least a couple more villages before the Hungarian border, one of which, **RUSOVCE**, makes a possible half-day trip by bus #116 from most SNP. Originally the Roman camp *Gerulata*, there's now a small **museum** (May–Oct Tues–Sun 10am–5pm) containing the results of extensive archaeological excavations, which have uncovered two large Roman burial sites. Nearby, a mock-Tudor **chateau** provides a neat country retreat for the Slovak Folk Ensemble, a pleasant park for picnicking and a lake for naturist swimming.

The Small Carpathians

From the Bratislavan suburbs to the gateway into the Váh valley, the **Small Carpathians** (Malé karpaty) form a thin abrasive strip of limestone hills altogether different from the soft, pine-clad hills of the Czech Lands. These are the modest beginnings of the great Carpathian range which sweeps round through the back door into Romania. A thoroughly Balkan heat bounces off the sun-stroked plains of the Danube and permeates even these first foothills, whose south-facing slopes are excellent for vine-growing. There's also a smattering of castles and a whole host of hiking opportunities, all making for a welcome release from the Bratislavan smog.

The Small Carpathians really do force their way into the city boundaries, and you could use Bratislava as a starting point for **hiking** into the hills – just get hold of the *Malé karpaty* double map. Kamzík (440m) is the first peak (see p.333), and on a clear day the view from its television tower is difficult to beat, but if you want to do some serious trekking in unmolested countryside, continue along the red-marked path (previously known as the *cesta Hrdinov SNP*) that wiggles its way along the ridge of the hills all the way to Brezová, 75km away at the end of the range. There are campsites and hotels peppered along the route and it's easy enough to drop down off the hills and grab a bed for the night before moving on.

Modra

If you're going in search of *víno*, **MODRA**, just under 30km from Bratislava and entirely surrounded by the stuff, is the most convenient place to head for. It's a typical ribbon-village with one long street lined with barn-door cottages growing fancier the nearer you get to the centre. The town's pottery factory sells its folk ware at no. 62, while the local wines are best imbibed at the co-op headquarters further down on the other side of the street. Gracing the square at its widest point is a light stone statue of Slovak nationalist Ľudovít Štúr, who is buried in the local cemetery (see box below). The nearby **Štúr Museum** (Tues–Fri 8am–4pm, Sat & Sun 10am–4pm) is predictable enough and of course makes a classic Slovak school trip, though the kids are generally more interested in the ice cream outlet judiciously placed next door. Close by, *langoše* and sandwiches are sold to the local workers and anyone else who wants them.

There are two **hotels** in Modra itself – the *Modra* at no. 95 on the main street (☎070492/2265; ①) and *Zlaté hrozno*, on Horná (☎070492/26 08; ①) – and a fancier one up in the hills at the *chata* and camping colony of PIESOK, 6km north of Modra. Quite the most rewarding peak in terms of views is **Vysoká** (754m), a five-kilometre walk from Piesok; but for a more gentle stroll, you could do worse than head 5km east from Piesok for the hulking chateau of **Červený Kameň** (Red Rock). Its defensive position and big fat bastions (designed, apparently, by Albrecht Dürer) were made to put fear into any enemies approaching from the plain, but the powerful Pálffy dynasty later transformed it into yet another luxurious family residence, adding gardens and various other creature comforts. It will eventually serve as a museum of period furniture, with a medieval torture chamber and a seventeenth-century apothecary.

Trnava

The fact that **TRNAVA** (Nagyszombat), 45km northeast of Bratislava, is one of the few towns on the plain to have survived with its walled-in medieval character intact is reason enough to visit the place. Calling it the "Slovak Rome", though, as the tourist brochures tend to, won't fool anyone. This is, however, a useful pointer to the town's rich ecclesiastical history, which took off with the establishment of the Hungarian archbishopric here in 1541 and reached its zenith during the Counter-Reformation, with the founding of a Jesuit university.

One of the oldest towns in the republic, Trnava celebrated the 750th anniversary of its royal charter in 1988, an event that provided the much-needed impetus for restoration work on the town's various monuments. The re-establishment of Trnava's archbishopric in 1990 can't hide the fact that the town's golden days are over, and, aside from a pleasant old town, a couple of fine churches and a fairly good museum, there's nothing to make you linger longer than an afternoon or so. With fast trains from Bratislava taking just 35 minutes, it's easily visited as a day trip.

The Old Town

From the bus and railway **stations**, walk over the new footbridge, which crosses over the main ring road, ulica SNP, and head north along the leafy banks of the River Trnavka, which runs parallel with the most impressive section of the old **town walls**, reinforced in the sixteenth century (and up to six metres thick in places) in anticipation of the marauding Turks. The red-brick Bernolákova brána is the only surviving gateway, popularly known as the Franciscan gate, after their nearby church of **sv Jakub**.

Soon after the church, you come to **Trojičné námestie**, the spacious main square where Trnava's institutions old and new congregate: the **mestská veža**, dating from the beginning of the town's golden age in the sixteenth century; the Neoclassical **radnica**; the salmon-pink **theatre**, the oldest theatre in Slovakia, dating from 1809; and last but in no way least, the **Dom kultury**, just one of a number of spanking new buildings in Trnava which have risen up from the rubble piled up all over the old quarter.

A short walk up Jilemnického from the square is the town's surprisingly interesting **Jesuit Church**. The typically High Baroque nave is suffused with a pink light emanating from the marble pillasters; much more startling is the deliciously decorative north chapel, with bounteous vegetative motifs and floral stucco. On the east side of the chapel is a bizarre watery grotto, with a statue of Mary, lit only by a dramatic shaft of light, the grotto's grille entirely surrounded by plaques and graffiti in Hungarian, Slovak and even Latin, thanking the Virgin for her various intercessions in answer to prayers.

The current focus of Trnava – and the anniversary showpiece – is the newly paved avenue, **Hlavná ulica**, which leads south from Trojičné námestie: a pleasant window-shopping stroll that ends at the church of **sv Helena**, the town's

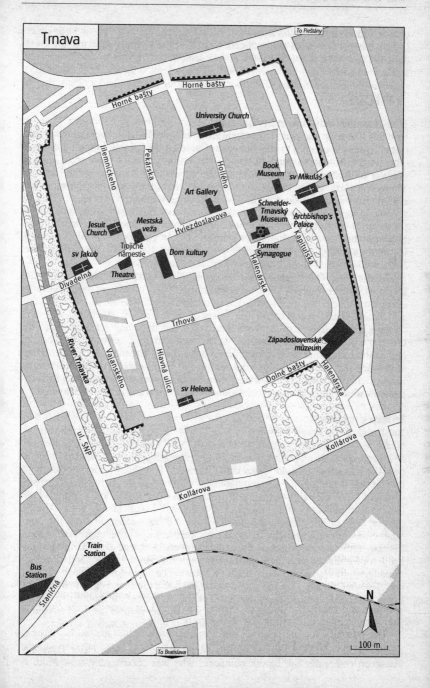

Trnava

To Piešťany

Horné bašty

Horné bašty

University Church

Pekárska

Hlemnickeho

Hollého

Book Museum

sv Mikuláš

Art Gallery

Schneider-Trnavský Museum

Archbishop's Palace

Kapitulská

Jesuit Church

Mestská veža

Hviezdoslavova

sv Jakub

Trojiché námestie

Dom kultury

Former Synagogue

Halenárska

Divadelná

Theatre

River Trnavka

Trhová

Valanského

Západoslovenské múzeum

Hlavná ulica

sv Helena

Dolné bašty

Halenárska

ul. SNP

Kollárova

Kollárova

Train Station

Bus Station

Staničná

N

To Bratislava

100 m

oldest, and in its own small way, most beguiling church, in a bare and miniature Gothic happily free from the suffocating hand of the Counter-Reformation. Next door is the town's former hospital, a Neoclassical building in an inappropriately sickly version of Imperial Yellow. South of sv Helena, a swathe of parkland has replaced the old fortifications, and boasts a working fountain and a new statue of Štefáník (see p.334).

The Cathedral and University Church

East off Trojičné námestie, the **Cathedral of sv Mikuláš** beckons with two rather clumsy but eye-catching Baroque steeples. Its Gothic origins are most obvious in the chancel, which boasts slender stained-glass windows and a fine set of choir stalls. It was promoted from a mere parish church following the Battle of Mohács in 1526, which caused the Hungarians to retreat behind the Danube: the royalty moved to Bratislava, while the archbishop transferred his see to Trnava, setting up next door to sv Mikuláš. A century later Trnava's position as a haven for Magyar cultural institutions seeking refuge from the Turks was further bolstered by the establishment of a university. In common with all Habsburg institutions of the time, it was under the iron grip of the Jesuits, and Trnava soon became the bastion of the Counter-Reformation east of Vienna.

The importance of religious over purely scholarly matters is most clearly illustrated by the sheer size of the **University church**, down Hol*lého, one of the largest and most beautiful in Slovakia. The decor is mostly Italianate Rococo, with the apricot and peach pastels of the nave offset by darker stucco vegetation. The oval frescoes appear like giant laquered miniatures, but the whole lot is upstaged by the vast wooden altarpiece, decked out in black and gold, peppered with saints, and looking more like an Orthodox iconostasis than a Catholic altar. These glory days were shortlived: with the expulsion of the Jesuit order from the Habsburg Empire and the defeat of the Turks, Trnava lost its university to Budapest, its archbishop's see to Esztergom and consequently its political and religious influence.

Trnava's museums

Kapitulská, the broad leafy street which sets off south from the archbishop's palace, is probably the prettiest street in town, with a cathedral-close feel about it. At its end, the plain off-cream mass of the seventeenth-century convent of sv Klara, now the **Západoslovenské múzeum** (Tues–Sun 9am–5pm), offers a variety of exhibitions including, for the moment, the contents of the Schneider-Trnavský museum (see below). If you've been wondering what Slovak folk ceramics look like, eight rooms of gear by local potter Štefan Cyril Parrák should put you in the picture; best of all, though, are the few bits and bobs salvaged from the now-defunct **Jewish community**. Trnava's Jews were actually expelled from the city in the sixteenth century, when, on the usual trumped-up charge of ritual murder, the Emperor Ferdinand sent them packing through the Sereď gate, walling it up with ripped-up Jewish gravestones to bar their return. For three hundred years, Trnava was *Jüdenfrei*, then in 1862 the gate was removed and the Jews began to filter back to the unofficial ghetto, located about where the car park of the main supermarket now stands. The only remaining landmark is the disused and weed-ridden Moorish **synagogue** on Havlíkova, on the brink of either restoration or collapse.

Trnava's two other museums have been undergoing restoration for the last few years. In the decaying street of the same name, the **Schneider-Trnavský Museum** celebrates the Slovak composer who was choirmaster at sv Mikuláš from 1909 until his death in 1958, but apart from confirming that he had very good taste in 1920s furniture, it's not very illuminating (exhibits are currently on display in Západoslovenské múzeum). The little-visited **Book Museum** (Múzeum knižnej kultúry; Mon–Fri 8am–4pm), opposite sv Mikuláš, has recently reopened and focuses on the many printing presses set up in Trnava by the Hungarians in the seventeenth century, and the Slovak intellectual society, here in the mid-nineteenth century.

Practicalities

If you want to **stay the night**, finding a room should present few problems at the *Slavia* on Rybná (①), or *Koliba* on Kamenný mlyn (☎0805/337 07; ①); the *Karpaty* (☎0805/246 72), at the south end of town, is currently under reconstruction. If you're very hard up, try the *Skloplast*, on Ludvika Svoboda (①) in the suburbs. If you have any problems, *ČEDOK*, across the road from the church of sv Helena, may be able to help. For **eating**, try the *Krym* on Hlavná ulica (daily 8am–10pm), an old-fashioned restaurant that has been sensitively restored, and boasts a nice shady courtyard round the back.

Nitra

While Trnava is stuck in the past, **NITRA** (Nyitra), 40km east across the plain, has effectively shed its old skin and rushed headlong into the twentieth century. The result is a clearly divided town: on the one hand, the battered and forgotten old quarter clings on for dear life at the foot of the castle rock; on the other, the ungainly sprawl of modern Nitra, agricultural capital of the nation and proverbial bustling market town, gets on with the business of the day. Sadly, there's not much to choose between the two, but the sights, such as they are, are all situated in the old town, which has a certain kudos attached to it as a centre of Slovak Catholicism, ancient and modern.

The City

The central axis of the nové mesto is the busy crossroads by the city's main **market** (*tržnica*), where the region's rich produce is sold daily. The staré mesto, and the main sights, are all north of here, except for the **Kalvária**, a kitsch mock-up of the Crucifixion which crowns the summit of a small limestone hill southeast of the train station. The brutality of Nitra's modern development serves as the apocalyptic backdrop for three ugly concrete crosses, the two robbers grey and unpainted on either side of a technicolour Jesus.

Visible to the east of the market, as you cross over Štúrovo, is the country's main **College of Agriculture**, a flying-saucer-shaped building whose research department recently invented a strain of tree that could withstand acid rain – progress indeed. On ulica pri synagóge, just off Štefánikova, the sheer size of Nitra's Moorish **synagogue** is an indication of the strength of the town's prewar Jewish community; it is due to reopen as a concert hall sometime in 1993. Farská, which leads you away from the chaos of the new town to the sights around the castle, is one of the most pleasant streets in the nové mesto, dotted with churches, little grocery stores and snack bars.

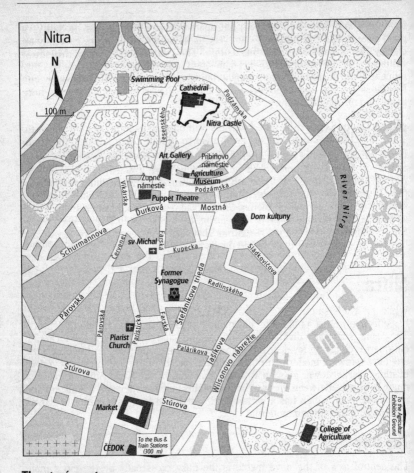

The staré mesto

Nitra's **staré mesto** is actually very small, consisting of just a handful of streets huddled under the castle. The entrance is formed by the former *župný dom* on Župné námestie, a handsome Secessionist building, now the town's **art gallery** (Nitranska státna galéria; Tues–Sun 10am–6pm), which puts on temporary exhibitions only for the time being. The right-hand arch of the building leads to the steeply sloping old town square, **Pribinovo námestie** – a very modest affair but quite pretty and totally peaceful after the frenetic activity of the lower town. At its centre stands a very recent (and fairly ugly) statue of **Prince Pribina**, the ninth-century ruler of Nitra, who erected the first church in what is now Slovakia here in 833. Though no great believer himself, he shrewdly realised such a gesture would help him keep on good terms with his German neighbours. There's also a fair amount of evidence to suggest that Saint Methodius, the first bishop of (Great) Moravia, was stationed at Nitra and not at Velehrad in the Morava valley, as was once claimed by the Czechs.

Nitra's two museums are on the lower side of the square. The **Agricultural Museum** (Poľnohospodárske múzeum), housed in the former Franciscan monastery, is the better of the two, but still a tad disappointing. Far from being an illuminating journey through the violent fortunes of Slovak agriculture, it differs very little from your average town museum, save for the odd stuffed seven-legged mutant calf.

The Castle

Nitra's **Castle** is a scruffy little hybrid, saved only by its lofty position above the river, which allows a great view north over to Mount Zobor (588m), the south-westernmost tip of the central mountains. A fortress since the time of the Great Moravian Empire (of which it may have been the capital), it provided refuge for various Hungarian kings over the centuries until being convincingly destroyed by the Turks in the seventeenth century. The walk up to the *hrad* is littered with crusty saints, a very fine plague column and two massive gateways before you reach what's left of the castle, most of which has been turned over to the Archaeological Institute and is closed to the public.

The one sight left in the complex is the **Cathedral** (frustratingly only sporadically open), an old Gothic structure which adjoins the Bishop of Nitra's cosy Baroque residence. Confusingly, you enter the south door and pass through two anti-chambers before going up some more steps to the compact main church, its Baroquised marble interior coloured in muted greys and reds. Frescoes adorn every possible space, and the modern blue stained glass in the chancel gives the whole place a memorable, magical quality. The cathedral is dedicated to two tenth-century Slovak saints, **Ondrej Svorad** and **Benedikt Junior**, both religious hermits who lived in the hills near Trenčín and spent most of their lives tending their gardens and vineyards. The locals, who had little time for able-bodied young men who wanted to devote their lives to spiritual contemplation, gave both of them a hard time. Ondrej Svorad escaped the villagers' wrath by diplomatically giving away a portion of his harvest, but Benedikt Junior failed to appease his enemies, who threw him off a nearby cliff and then drowned him in the River Váh.

Practicalities

ČEDOK (Mon–Fri 8.30am–4pm, Sat 9am–noon) have their office located next to the market, but may try to book you into the expensive high-rise *Hotel Nitra*, Slančíkovej 1 (☎087/333 96; ④). Insist instead on staying at the *Zobor* (☎087/250 60; ②) on Štefánikova, or the dorm-style *Olympia* (☎087/227 61; ①), close to the *Nitra*. The only time when finding a room might be difficult is during the agricultural fair and the music festival, which take place every August and September.

Nitra is not too bad for **eating**, with the *Nitran*, on the main crossroads in the nové mesto (open daily 7am–10pm), offering standard Slovak dishes, and the *Thurzo*, on the corner of Štefánikova and ulica pri synagóge (Mon–Fri only), a more boisterous, beery alternative. A nice place where you can hang out in the summer is the *Reštaurácia pod agátmi*, an open-air barbecue and beer joint overlooking Župné námestie. There's nowhere particularly special to sample the local white wine, *Nitria*, though *Furmanská vináreň*, on ulica pri synagóge, is as good a place as any. Another new outlet worth popping into is the *Billich cukáreň*, Farská 38 (Mon–Sat 8am–7pm, Sun 9am–8pm), a swish Italian-style ice cream parlour with coffee and chocolate to boot.

The Danube basin

To the east of Bratislava lies the rich agricultural region of the **Danube basin** (the *Felvidék* to the Hungarians), a flat, well watered expanse of land which benefits from the warmest temperatures in the country and which, since being handed over to Czechoslovakia in 1918, has formed the border between Slovakia and Hungary. It's one of the few places in Slovakia where you can go for miles without seeing a tree, and is the traditional haunt of most of Slovakia's Hungarian minority – 600,000 and rising at the last count. Sadly, it was also one of the regions that suffered badly during the last war, making one place very much like another. The only reason to come here at all is to drink, eat and lie by the region's many artificial lakes in true hedonistic fashion. The exception is **Komárno**, which, while not worth a detour in itself, has enough to make you pause en route to Hungary.

THE GABČÍKOVO-NAGYMAROS DAM

On October 24, 1992, the Slovak government threw caution to the wind, and began to divert the Danube as part of the controversial **Gabčíkovo-Nagymaros Hydroelectric Barrage** project, a megalomaniac joint project dreamed up in 1977 by the Communist old guard of Hungary and Czechoslovakia, with the cynical collusion and capital of the Austrians, who were on the lookout for cheap electricity at someone else's environmental expense. Following intense protest by the green lobby, the Hungarians withdrew from the project in 1989, and called for an EC-sponsored enquiry into the environmental effects of the dam. The Czechoslovak government, however, having invested huge sums of money, and desperate for an alternative source of energy to brown coal – the pollution from which is killing off the country's forests – pressed on and completed a scaled-down version of the scheme.

Now the whole unhappy mess looks like becoming yet another thorn in the already strained relations between the Hungarians and the new Slovak government which has inherited the dam. Hungary has threatened to take the case to the International Court of Settlement in the Hague, and is also arguing that the diversion of the river brings the whole Hungarian–Slovak border, which currently runs along the middle of the river, into question. Sadly, in environmental terms, the damage has already been done: once-perfect cropland is beginning to dry up around the construction sites, and many scientists believe that the precious underground water table, which supplies water to Budapest and Bratislava, has already been adversely – if not irrevocably – affected.

Senec

The towns of the Danube basin are probably the nearest either republic comes to seaside resorts, and in the summer the "beaches" are packed with windsurfers, canoeists and idle sun-seekers slobbing out along reservoirs, lakes, swimming pools and any stretch of water they can find. If you're staying in Bratislava, **SENEC**, 26km east and just over thirty minutes by train, is the easiest place to get to and fairly indicative of the region. The Turks left one of their few monuments here, the **Turecký dom**, and a few other odds and sods which relieve the town's monotonous concrete. The place where the crowds head is the **Slnečné**

jazerá (Sunny Lakes), a couple of reasonably warm artificial lakes within sight of the train station. There are two campsites and a hotel – the *Amur* (☎07/92 40 81; ②) – by the lake, but the whole place is full to bursting in the hot months, especially during August.

Komárno

No question about it, **KOMÁRNO** (Komárom) is a Hungarian town through and through. Even the Slovak authorities have been forced to admit this fact and erect bilingual street and shop signs. In the shops you'll be greeted with the unfamiliar *tessék* ("what do you want?") rather than the usual *prosím*, but these ethnic niceties aside, Komárno is not going to win over many people's hearts; it's only worth stopping off for should you pass through on the way to Budapest.

The Town

When the Czechoslovak border was dreamed up in 1918, the Hungarians of Komárom found their town split in two, with by far the most significant part – and what few sights there are – on the Slovak side of the border. The **train** and **bus stations** are northwest of the town's main drag, Záhradnícka, which becomes Tržničné námestie, and continues over the river into Hungary.

The town is best known for its huge **fortress** at the confluence of the Váh and the Danube, which has served as a strategic base for everyone from the Romans to the Russians, and is still in the hands of the military today. But Komárno's main "sight" is the **Podunajské múzeum** (Tues–Sun 9am–4pm) on ulica Palatínova, last right before the bridge, which pays tribute to the town's two most illustrious sons, both somewhat controversial figures. The first is the composer **Franz Lehár**, whose father was military bandmaster with the local garrison. Lehár enjoyed the dubious privilege of having written one of Hitler's favourite works, the operetta *Die Lustige Witwe*, and, despite the fact that his mother tongue was Hungarian and his own wife Jewish, he found himself much in demand during the Third Reich. The nineteenth-century Hungarian writer **Mór Jókai**, on the other hand, was an extremely nationalistic Hungarian who wrote a glowing account of the Hungarian aristocracy and would have had nothing good to say about Komárno's modern-day split nationality. You won't get much from either of the exhibitions unless you know Slovak or Hungarian.

More fascinating than either of the above is the disorientating sight of a small **Orthodox church** in the museum grounds, testifying to the Serbian colonists who settled around Komárno in the early eighteenth century in a desperate attempt to escape the revengeful Turks. Small pockets of Orthodox believers still exist in the region, and the seventeenth- and eighteenth-century Greek and Serbian icons on display here constitute one of the best collections outside Serbia.

Practicalities

ČEDOK, on Tržničné námestie, can organise **accommodation** for you in one of the town's moderately priced hotels; try the *Európa* on námestie Štefánika (☎0819/42 51; ②). Alternatively, there's a **campsite** (May 15–Sept 15) by the Danube, 6km west in NOVÁ STRÁŽ (8min by train). Basic **food** can be had in the cellars of the *Reštaurácia pri radnici*, opposite the town hall, though don't expect

THE HUNGARIANS OF SLOVAKIA

The creation of separate Czech and Slovak republics has brought into much sharper relief the rather more volatile relationship between the Slovaks and the 600,000 Hungarians who live along the southern border regions of Slovakia. Like so many ethnic disputes in Central Europe, it's an age-old conflict, one that remained fairly dormant during the Communist period but has now returned with a vengeance. For almost a millennium, Slovakia was an integral part of Hungary – Hungarians were the landlords, the Slovaks the peasantry. Slovak language and culture was suppressed with unparalled brutality right up until the foundation of the First Republic in 1918. Then, when the borders for the new republic were drawn up, 750,000 Hungarians were left on the Slovak side of the Danube. Like the Germans who once lived in the border regions of the Czech Lands, Slovakia's Hungarians have never assimilated, but unlike their Germanic counterparts, the attempt by Beneš to expel them in 1945 was successfully blocked by the government in Budapest.

In 1989, the enforced fraternal friendship of the Communist period finally came to an abrupt end with the dispute over the dam (see p.342) and the Velvet Revolution. With Mečiar's rise to power in June 1992, on the back of a tide of Slovak nationalist feeling, the Hungarian community has become understandably concerned. It is too early to predict what may or may not happen, but with nationalist sentiments high on both sides of the ethnic divide at the moment, the situation is potentially explosive. There have been accusations of Hungarian spying operations in Slovakia, and, more seriously, clear evidence of police brutality at the Ferencváros-Budapest v Slovan-Bratislava soccer match, when Slovak security forces waded into Hungarian supporters, injuring dozens of fans. One fan later died in custody, after Slovak authorities refused him medical treatment for his injuries. It remains to be seen whether Mečiar's HZDS party will seek to exploit these tensions or have the foresight to try and calm Hungarian fears.

anything more Magyar than *guláš*. The *Café Lehár*, a big nineteenth-century building in the middle of the old marketplace and not far from the Danube bridge, is the place where you can hang out in your best Budapest denim and sip a Coca-Cola. For those with the language, there's a Hungarian theatre, *Jókaiho divadlo*, down Petofího, towards the docks to the east of the bridge.

Moving on, a daily **hydrofoil** runs to **Budapest** from the launch on the island by the bridge; enquire at *ČEDOK* for the exact times of sailings. **Trains** bound for Hungary leave Komárno's Slovak station very early in the morning – more frequently from the station on the Hungarian side, a short walk from the 24-hour border checkpoint.

Štúrovo

"The Danube threads towns together like a string of pearls" wrote Claudio Magris, but it's doubtful he had **ŠTÚROVO** in mind at the time. Its major saving grace is the unbeatable view of Esztergom's great domed basilica on the Hungarian side of the river. However, the bridge linking the two towns was blown up by the retreating German army in 1944, and the replacement ferry service is open only to Hungarians and Slovaks. There are plans to construct a new bridge, to be completed by 1995, though neither government is very keen on building bridges at the moment.

As the last town on the Slovak Danube, it's not a bad place to break your journey, and, although it's still not possible to cross over and admire the treasures of Esztergom, you can hop one of the international express trains which pause here en route to Budapest. The **train and bus stations** are actually an inconvenient 2.5km west of the town, with bus #1 covering the distance only infrequently. In the summer the focus of life alternates between the two outdoor swimming pools, both fed by thermal springs: *Kúpalisko Vadaš*, by the local **campsite** (May–Sept 15) just north of the town, and the other right by the river near the car-ferry launch. If you need to stay the night, there are two cheap **hotels**, the *Dunaj* (☎0810/23 92; ①) and *Šport* (☎0810/20 80; ①).

Piešťany and the Váh valley

Finding its source in the Tatras and carving its southwesterly course right the way to the Danube at Komárno, the **Váh** is one of the great rivers of Slovakia. It's common currency in tourist office circles to talk of the "Slovak Rhine", but despite the consistent appearance of ruined cliff-top castles at every turn of the river, there's nothing which quite lives up to the magic of the Rhine valley. Heading north up the Váh from Piešťany to Trenčín, the dramatics are played down, the mountains on either side keep their distance and the whole area still has the feel of the Danube basin. Beyond Trenčín, industry, the damming of the river, and a lorry-congested highway all dampen the effects of brigand hideouts like Vršatec and Považský hrad. The best way to weigh up the relative merits of the region is on one of the fast and frequent **trains** which leave Bratislava and twist their way up the Váh valley en route to the Tatras.

Leopoldov and Jaslovské Bohunice

As you approach from Bratislava, two landmarks provide an ominous entrance to the valley proper. The first is **LEOPOLDOV**, 18km south of Piešťany, once a vital fortress in the defence against the Turks, then converted into a prison in 1854 and used by the Habsburgs and the Communists to incarcerate Slovak dissidents. It was the scene of the country's worst ever prison riot in March 1990, during which six people died. The second is clearly visible on the western horizon. Out of the flat fields to the southwest of Piešťany rise the eight cooling towers of the country's first nuclear power station at **JASLOVSKÉ BOHUNICE**, built in the 1960s and recently the cause of heated exchanges between the Austrians, who have called for the plant to be closed down immediately on safety grounds, and the Slovaks, who are trying to hold out until the new Mochovce nuclear reactor, some 50km further east, is fully operational.

Piešťany

The most convincing claim the local tourist board make about **PIEŠŤANY**, just over an hour by train from Bratislava, is that it's the largest spa town in Slovakia. If you're expecting something akin to the turn-of-the-century West Bohemian spas, it's easy to be disappointed. The place is similarly overrun with the unhealthily rich from different parts of the German-speaking world; millions of crowns have been poured into the spa facilities, but precious little has been spent on the town itself. Still, green spaces, clean swimming pools, and a host of other resources to which the public has access, make it a more pleasant place to laze in the sun than most of the "beachy" resorts further south.

The town divides conveniently into two parts: the spa island cut off from the mainland by a thin arm of the River Váh, and the rest of the town on the right bank between the main arm of the river and the **bus and train stations** to the west. It's a fifteen-minute walk into town down A. Hlinku and Štúrova (bus #3, #9 or #12) to **Winterova**, the main drag through the centre of town, a patchwork of muted turn-of-the-century and Secession buildings, decorated with balconies and lined with cafés and trinkety shops. The main spa building at no. 29 is a typical example of Piešťany's understated architecture, and now serves as the main **information centre** for those wishing to take the waters. The obligatory bandstand (performances at 3.30pm on certain days) and spanking new **Dom umenia** (which puts on plenty of Bach and Mozart for the foreign guests) are laid out in the nearby Mestský park, but the rest of the spa is on the opposite bank, a short stroll past the town's famous optimistic statue of a man breaking his crutches in two, and connected by the partly covered **Kolonádový most**, rebuilt "for the benefit of the working class" in the words of the 1950s commemorative plaque.

One place that definitely wasn't built with the latter in mind is the vaguely Art-Nouveau *Thermia Palace* hotel, which retains a hint of its bygone opulence and – if the flash cars parked outside are anything to go by – now serves the new European aristocracy. The woods and park on the spa island are decidedly verdant, with sculptures peeping out of every conceivable shrub and bush, part of the spa's annual international open-air sculpture symposium. The nearby low-lying annexes are still used for "mud wrapping and electro-treatment" to cure rheumatic illnesses (spa patients only). If you fancy a dip, the old-fashioned *Eva* swimming pool, 200m further north, is open to the public (Tues–Sun). From here the sleek, ultra-modern *Balnea* sanatorium spreads its luxurious wings the full length of the island, finishing up at the spa information centre and, behind it, the mini golf course.

Practicalities

If you haven't come here for treatment, you'll have to stay in one of the **hotels** on the right bank, of which the *Victoria Regia*, Winterova 16 (☎0838/229 91; ①), is currently the least expensive, followed by the *Eden* at no. 60 (☎0838/221 23; ②), and the *Magnolia*, Nálepkova 1 (☎0838/262 51; ④) – all of them very central. **Camping** is possible (May–Sept) at either side of the mouth of the action-packed Sĺňava lake (bus #6, #13 or #12). For cheap places **to eat**, try the pizzeria on Winterova, between the spa centre and the *Eden*, or the recently modernised *Pasáž*, hidden on Park pasáž, a side street off Winterova. Another popular choice with the locals is *Central*, a self-service *bufet* with draught beer and a patio out the back, plus a more formal restaurant.

The ruined castles at Čachtice and Beckov

Halfway between Piešťany and Trenčín, to the north, is the industrial town of NOVÉ MESTO NAD VÁHOM, not a place to hang about in if you can help it, but a necessary halt if you're changing trains or buses to get to the ruined castles of Čachtice and Beckov described below.

Čachtice

Of the two lofty piles of rubble perched on opposing sides of the Váh, the one at ČACHTICE, 8km southwest of Nové Mesto, has the edge on views and legends, for it was here that the "Blood Countess" **Elizabeth Báthori** was walled in for almost four years before her death in 1614 to pay for her crimes – which included the murder of over six hundred women (see overleaf). Čachtice was her favourite castle; "she loved it for its wildness", wrote one of her posthumous biographers, "for the thick walls which muffled every sound, for its low halls, and for the fact of its gloomy aspect on the bare hillside". There's virtually nothing left of the castle today, and the prize exhibit of the village **museum**, an impassive portrait of Elizabeth herself, was stolen in 1990 and has yet to be recovered. The quickest way to get up to the castle is actually the stiff climb from VIŠŇOVÉ train station (15min from Nové Mesto), rather than the two-kilometre haul from Čachtice village itself.

Beckov

There's substantially more of a castle above the village of **BECKOV** (presently closed for reconstruction), 5km northeast of Nové Mesto and accessible only by bus. This was another of Báthori's torture chambers, ruined by a fire which ripped through its apartments in 1729. There's a *reštaurácia* just under the rock, where you can relax and watch the rock-climbers risk life and limb on the cliff below the castle, and a small **folk museum** (Tues–Sun 10am–5pm) in which to while away half an hour.

Trenčín and around

Despite the usual high-rise accompaniments, **TRENČÍN**, 42km north of Piešťany, is the most naturally appealing of the towns on the Váh. Its central historical core sits below the most impressive castle in the valley, best known as the centre of **Matúš Čák's** short-lived independent kingdom. Čák was little more than a rebellious feudal despot who set up a mock royal court, crowning himself "King of the Váh and the Tatras". He supported the young Přemyslid Václav III in his unsuccessful quest for the Hungarian crown, and had John of Luxembourg and the Hungarian King Charles Robert on the run for a number of years. Defeated only once, near Košice, he remained in control of his fief until his death in 1321, and is now happily lauded as one of the first great Slovak heroes.

The **castle** itself – part ruins, part reconstruction – is a fiercely defensive sprawl of vaguely connected walls and ramparts on a steeply pitched and craggy site, spectacularly lit at night. Once it's fully restored it'll be a great place to explore, but as yet the only complete part is the galleried **Hodinová veža**, which gives the best view out across the valley. Slovakia's one and only **Roman inscription** of any worth is carved into the rockface below the castle, commemo-

THE BLOOD COUNTESS OF ČACHTICE

Born in 1560, **Countess Elizabeth Báthori** was the offspring of two branches of the noble Báthori family, whose constant intermarriage may have accounted for her periodic fainting spells and fits of uncontrollable rage: other Báthoris, such as Prince "Crazy" Gábor, were similarly afflicted. As a child she was intelligent and well educated, being fluent in Latin, Hungarian and German at a time when many nobles, including the ruling prince of Transylvania, were barely literate. Brought up in the family castle at Nagyecsed, a humble town near the Hungarian-Romanian border, she absorbed from her relatives the notion that peasants were little more than cattle – to be harshly punished for any act of insubordination.

As was customary in the sixteenth century, her marriage was arranged for dynastic reasons, and an illegitimate pregnancy hushed up. Betrothed in 1571 – the same year that her cousin István became Prince of Transylvania – she was married at fifteen to twenty-one-year-old Ferenc Nádasdy. Over the next decade Ferenc was usually away fighting Turks, earning his reputation as the "Black Knight", and Elizabeth grew bored at their home in Sárvár Castle. There she began to torture serving women, an "entertainment" that gradually became an obsession. With the assistance of her maids Dorothea Szentes and Anna Darvulia (who was also her lover), Elizabeth cudgelled and stuck pins into servants to "discipline" them; even worse, she forced them to lie naked in the snowy courtyard and then doused them with cold water until they froze to death. On his return Ferenc baulked at this (although he too enjoyed brutalising servants) and it wasn't until after his demise in 1604 that Elizabeth started torturing and murdering without restraint. Her victims were invariably women or girls, and – most importantly – always peasants.

Killing peasants could be done with impunity. Poor women could always be enticed into service at Beckov and Čachtice – Elizabeth's residences after she quit Sárvár, both then located within the borders of Transylvania – and, should word of their

rating Marcus Aurelius' victory over the German hordes in 179 AD, when the Romans had a fortified winter camp here, known as *Laugaricio*.

Back down the cobbled lane which leads to the castle, in the elbow of the first sharp bend is a radiant white and yellow **church** set in its own paved plateau – packed on Sundays, closed the rest of the week. A covered walkway leads down Hradná to the main square, whose young plane trees give it a Mediterranean feel. Straight ahead is the **Piarist church**, ablaze with the fury of the Counter-Reformation and definitely worth checking out if it's open. Next door in the old monastery is the **Bazovský Art Gallery** (Tues–Sun 9am–5pm), named after the Slovak sculptor and painter who died here in 1968 and whose statues stand in the courtyard. Temporary exhibitions are held here beneath the building's surviving stucco ceilings, and on the top floor there's a permanent display of works by local artists, dominated by Bazovský's beguilingly simple depictions of peasant life from the 1930s.

One side of the square is closed by Trenčín's only remaining gateway – talk while you're walking beneath it and you'll never get married, according to the locals. Once through it, take a sharp right and you'll discover the town's former **synagogue**, a Moorish hulk of a building, completely ransacked during the war, but one of the few in Slovakia to have been fully restored. Only the arcaded women's gallery and the vivid blue painted dome hint at its former life: it now serves as an exhibition hall.

deaths leak out, the authorities would hardly believe the accusations of the victims' parents against the Countess Báthori. With the assistance of Szentes, Darvulia, her son's former wet-nurse Helena Jo, and one man, the diminutive Fizcko, Elizabeth allowed her sadistic fantasies full rein. On occasion she bit chunks of flesh from servants' breasts and necks – probably the origin of the legend that she bathed in the blood of virgins to keep her own skin white and translucent.

In this fashion Elizabeth murdered over six hundred women, and would probably have continued doing so undetected had not Darvulia died. Grief-stricken, the Countess formed an attachment to a local widow, Erzsi Majorová, who encouraged her to seek aristocratic girls for her victims. Enquiries by *their* parents could not be so easily ignored by the authorities, who in any case by now had their own motives for investigating *Die Blutgräffin*. Ferenc Nádasdy had loaned the Habsburg crown 17,000 gulden, which Elizabeth had persistently – and vainly – demanded back. Should she be found guilty of serious crimes this debt would be forfeited. Others also had the knives out – notably Paul, Elizabeth's son, who had grown up apart from her at Sárvár, and one Count Thurzo, both of whom were anxious to prevent the confiscation of the Báthori estates and gathered evidence against her throughout 1610.

On December 29 Thurzo's men raided Čachtice castle, and on entry almost tripped over the corpse of a servant whom Elizabeth had just bludgeoned for stealing a pear. Thurzo secretly imprisoned the "damned woman" in her own castle immediately, so that (in his words) "the families which have won such high honours on the battlefield shall not be disgraced . . . by the murky shadow of this bestial female". Due to his cover-up the scandal was mainly confined to court circles, although when Elizabeth died in 1614 the locals protested at her burial in Čachtice cemetery. She was later reburied at Nagyecsed in the precincts of the family vault. Due to her sex (then considered to be incapable of such deeds) and rank, records of her trial were hidden, and mention of her very name subsequently prohibited by royal command.

Practicalities

The **bus and train stations** are located next to each other to the east of the old town centre, which can be reached by crossing the park adjacent to the station. As far as **hotels** go, try the *Laugaricio* on Vajanského (☎0831/378 41; ③) before resorting to the *Trenčan*, Malinovského 7 (☎0831/331 16; closed in winter; ②). The **camping site** (June to mid-Sept) is past the football stadium on an island in the Váh.

A welcome addition to the choice of **eating places** is the small vegetarian restaurant, *Malá galéria*, at Farská 10 (garden round back), at the bottom of the covered steps leading to the castle, with a limited but interesting selection of dishes. Alternatively, *Pizzeria Lemo* can be found at Hviezdoslavova 2, and there are two much more basic pubs – the *Slovenská reštaurácia*, across Štúrovo námestie from the synagogue, and the *Plzenská pivnica* in the new *Zlatá Fatima* shopping arcade off the main square.

Trenčianske Teplice

While Trenčín bakes down in the valley, **TRENČIANSKE TEPLICE**, 12km northeast, marinates in the green glades of the Teplička valley. The nicest way to get there is on the narrow-gauge train-cum-tram which trundles up the valley from TRENČIANSKA TEPLÁ, which is less than ten minutes by train from

Trenčín. Alternatively, you could hike the 9km across the hills from Trenčín following the red-marked path and ending your walk with a dip in Bohuslav Fuchs' pool (see below).

The spa itself is little more than a collection of sanatoria, ranging from the typical nineteenth-century ochre mansion of the *Sina* to the concrete *Krym*. The town's most unusual building is the stripy *Hammam* bathhouse whose Moorish interior is open only to spa guests, but you might be able to peep inside. Architecture buffs should check out the *Mahnáč* sanatorium, a top-notch Bauhaus-style building by Jaromír Krejcar; from the same period, Brno-born Bohuslav Fuchs' swimming pool complex, **Zelená žaba** (Green Frog; daily noon–5pm), has a much wider appeal. Concealed in some woods to the north of the town and cut into the curve of the hillside, it looks as good as new sixty years on, and swimming in the pool's spring water gives the weird sensation of swimming in warm lemonade. Like all spas, the strenuous stroll is an all-important part of the cure here, so for the best views and a bit of mineral refreshment halfway, continue up the valley from the Zelená žaba, and, having reached the *Baračka* restaurant, head up to **Heinrich's spring**, and then on to Kráľovec (557m) for the definitive view over the Teplička valley. The whole trip should take around two hours.

travel details

Trains

From Bratislava hlavná stanica to Trnava (14 daily; 35min); Štúrovo (7 daily; 1hr 40min); Piešťany/Trenčín (10 daily; 1hr/1hr 30min); Brno (up to 20 daily; 1hr 45min–3hr 30min); Prague (7 daily; 5hr 30min); Vienna (4 daily; 1hr 10min); Budapest (7 daily; 3hr).

From Bratislava Nové Mesto to Trnava (up to 15 daily; 35–50min); Komárno (7 daily; 2hr–2hr 30min).

Buses

From Bratislava to Modra (up to 12 daily; 35min–1hr); Nitra (up to 18 daily; 1hr 30min).

From Trnava to Nitra (up to 15 daily; 1hr–1hr 30min).

CHAPTER NINE

THE MOUNTAIN REGIONS

The great virtue of Slovakia is its mountains, particularly the **High Tatras** – which, in their short span, reach alpine heights and a bleak, stunning beauty. By far the republic's most popular destination, they are, in fact, the least typical of Slovakia's mountains, which tend on the whole to be densely forested and round-topped limestone ranges. The **Low Tatras** and **Malá Fatra**, for example, are less monumental but also somewhat less developed and lesser-known.

Geographically speaking, the region splits into two huge corridors, with the Váh valley to the north and the Hron valley to the south. The regional capital is **Banská Bystrica**, one of the many towns in the region originally settled by German miners, and still redolent of those times. Two other medieval mining towns worth visiting are **Banská Štiavnica** and **Kremnica**, set in the nearby hills. For the Slovaks, by far the most important towns historically are **Martin** and **Liptovský Mikuláš**, centres of the nineteenth-century *národné obrodenie*, both situated in and around the Váh valley.

Generally, though, the towns in the valley bottoms have been fairly solidly industrialised, and are only good as bases for exploring the surrounding country-side, which can easily be done by a combination of hiking and busing. **Railways**, where they do exist, make for some of the most scenic train journeys in the coun-try. As for the region's innumerable **villages**, from which many urbanised Slovaks are but one generation removed, they're mostly one-street affairs, it's true, but no less fascinating for that, and seemingly unchanged since the last century.

Banská Bystrica

Lying at the very heart of Slovakia's mountain ranges, the regional capital, **BANSKÁ BYSTRICA** (Altsohl), is a useful introduction to the area. Connected to the outlying disticts by some of the country's most precipitous railways, it's also a handsome historic town in its own right – although, as you arrive through the tangled suburbs of the burgeoning cement and logging industry, that may seem difficult to believe.

A prosperous royal free town in the Middle Ages, Banská Bystrica was the capi-tal of the seven "Hungarian" mining towns colonised by German miners who, in this case, extracted silver and copper from the nearby hills until the seams ran dry in the eighteenth century. Since then, the town has shaken off its Teutonic past, and is perhaps best remembered today as the centre of the 1944 Slovak National Uprising, whose history, lavishly embellished and glorified by the Communists, is now undergoing a more critical reassessment.

The Banská Bystrica area telephone code is ☎088

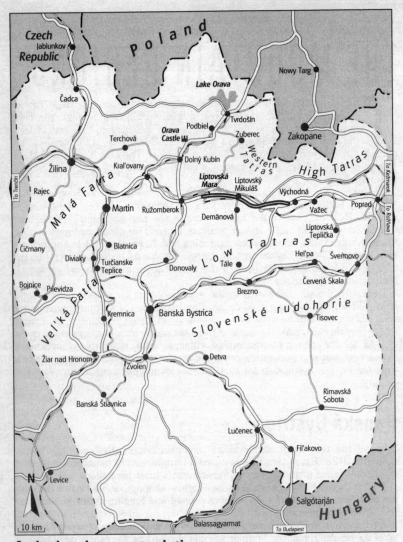

Arrival and accommodation

Banská Bystrica's main **bus and train stations** are in the modern part of town, ten minutes' walk east of the centre; if you happen to alight at Banská Bystrica mesto train station, it's only five minutes' walk north to the main square. The local *ČEDOK* office is on trieda SNP: it can book private or hotel accommodation and change money, but precious little else; you can also book rooms here or at *Slovakotour*, Hronské predmestie 12, for hotels in the southern approaches to the Low Tatras (see p.376). **Accommodation** should be easy enough to arrange on your own, however, at one of the hotels listed below.

Hotels and campsites

Junior, Národná 12 (☎233 67; ①). Centrally located opposite the main theatre, nominally run by *CKM*, and often full in peak season.

Národný dom (☎237 37; ②). Old nineteenth-century building which was modernised inside about thirty years ago.

Lux, Čs.armády (☎241 418; ④). High-rise hotel at the western end of trieda SNP, in the monumental part of town, with a nice view over the Múzeum SNP.

Urpín, J. Cikkera 5 (☎245 56; ②). Modern and unremarkable, but very central.

Autokemping, Tajovského (☎330 12). Campsite 1km west of the main square, just by the road to Tajov. Open all year.

Tajov autokemping (☎97 55). Campsite 5km west of Banská Bystrica by bus, but in a more picturesque rural setting, and a good base for hiking in the region. Open all year.

The Town

On arrival, you'll find yourself stuck in the monumental part of town, built up after the war and obviously planned as a showpiece of Communist architecture. Predictably enough, it's a thoroughly alienating space with few redeeming features, designed to culminate in a statue of Lenin (now removed), and behind him, the high-rise *Hotel Lux* (symbol of the town's inexorable progress and sophistication) and the **Múzeum SNP** (Tues–Sun 8am–6pm), looking something like an intergalactic mushroom chopped in half. For the sake of the Slovak National Uprising or SNP (see box on p.357) no expense was spared, with a lavish display of little actual substance that charted the triumphant march of Communism, from the SNP to the present day. Nowadays, the museum deals rather more sanguinely with aspects of the last war, such as the deportation of Slovak Jews, through special exhibitions on the ground floor. The main collection of militaria on the top floor remains relatively unchanged, but the two multi-projector film and slide shows (shows also in English) have been remade. The current line taken is pro-Czechoslovak and anti-Tiso, with the Communists' huge contribution to the wartime resistance now entirely ignored. If the political will (and money) is there, there may be a further swing towards a more nationalist line, but whatever the outcome, the impressive facilities create a very powerful exhibition. Outside on the grass you'll notice a collection of tanks and guns from the uprising amid the bushes and the town's last two surviving medieval bastions.

From the giddy monumental heights of the múzeum SNP, it's just a short step up Kapitulská to the more modest **námestie SNP**, the old medieval marketplace and still the centre of life in Banská Bystrica, with a couple of cafés from which to soak in the scene. The charcoal black obelisk of the Soviet war memorial and the square's revolving fountain, enthusiastically chucking water over a pile of mossy rocks, form the square's centrepiece. One or two of the Renaissance burgher houses bear closer inspection, particularly the so-called "Venetian House", **Benického dom**, at no. 16, with its slender first-floor arcaded loggia. The sgraffi-toed building opposite is now an art gallery, just a few doors down from the most imposing building on the square, the honey-coloured Thurzo Palace, decorated like a piece of embroidery and sporting some cute circular portholes on its top floor. The **town museum** (Mon–Fri 8am–4pm, Sun 9am–4pm) which now lives there houses a fair selection of folk and "high" art.

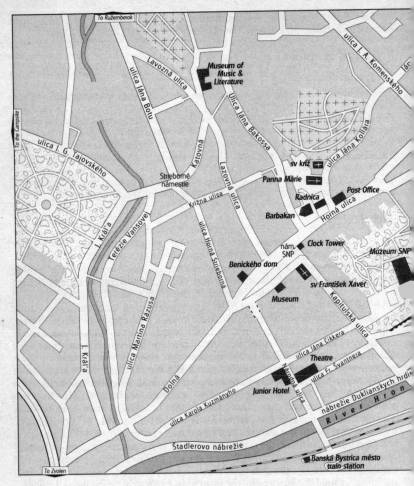

At the top end of the square, beyond the leaning clock tower, on what is now known as námestie Š. Moyzesa, there's an interesting ensemble of buildings which is all that's left of the old castle. The first building in view is the last remaining **barbakan**, curving snugly round a Baroque tower. Next door, the former **radnica**, a boxy little Renaissance structure, is now the town's main art gallery, which puts on temporary exhibitions from its extensive catalogue of twentieth-century Slovak art, including a number of works by the Slovak Jewish artist Dominik Skutecký, who spent much of his life in Banská Bystrica.

Behind the radnica is the most important building of the lot, the rouge-red church of **Panna Márie**, which dates back to the thirteenth century and contains the town's greatest art treasure, a carved late Gothic **altarpiece** by Master Pavol of Levoča, hidden away in one of the side chapels. At its centre stands the figure of Saint Barbara, the patron saint of miners, but more interesting are the

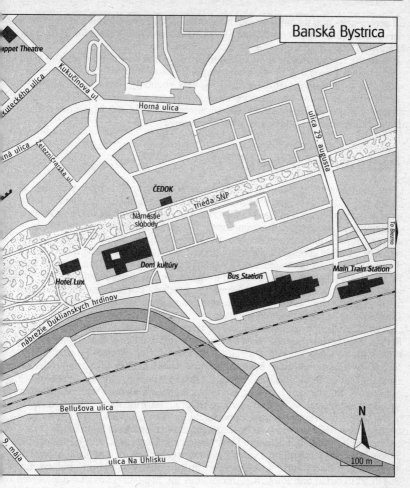

side-panel reliefs, including, among others, Saint Ursula and her posse of shipwrecked virgins. The place has been undergoing restoration, but if the work is complete be prepared also for Schmidt and Kracker's fiery German frescoes, the result of heavy Baroquification in the eighteenth century.

Eating, drinking and entertainment

Eating options in Banská Bystrica have improved greatly over the last few years: the *Kurian*, on Horná Strieborná (open till 2am), and the *Atom*, at the far end of Horná (open till 11.30pm), are both highly recommended. The *Bystrica*, an old nineteenth-century haunt on the corner of Horná, is a great place where you can hang out either in the café or the *reštaurácia*, as is the *Národný dom*, on Národná. The *Cechova*, next door to the town museum on námestie SNP, has more youthful pretensions and its outdoor café round the back is a wonderful suntrap. For a cheap and filling plate of traditional Slovak *bryndzové halušky*, head for *M Konzum* at Horná 11 (open till 8pm).

As in the rest of provincial Slovakia, **nightlife** is thin on the ground. The main opera house, *Divadlo J. G. Tajakovského*, is the town's bastion of high culture, while the local **puppet theatre** on J. Kollára regularly offers adult and kids' shows, and plays host to the occasional foreign touring company. There are a couple of youngish hang-outs on Skuteckého: the *Melod Club*, which has a disco or band most nights, and the *Omega Club* opposite.

Zvolen and around

Once the effective capital of a Hungarian *župa* or regional district stretching as far as the Orava and Liptov regions, **ZVOLEN** (Neusohl), 20km and a forty-minute train ride south of Banská Bystrica, has come a long way down the scale of importance since those halcyon days. The main reason for coming here is to see the town's four-cornered **chateau** (Tues–Sun 10am–5pm), which squats scruffily on a big mound of earth at one end of Zvolen's excessively wide main thoroughfare. Built in the fourteenth century, the chateau fell to the exiled Czech Hussite leader Jiskra of Brandýs, who for nearly twenty years ruled over much of what is now Slovakia. Later, it became the property of the powerful Esterházy family, and, as the Turks got too close for comfort, it was transformed into the stern fighting fortress it now resembles.

Nowadays, few rooms contain any of their original decor beyond some fine Renaissance portals, but one room boasts a splendid wooden coffered ceiling decorated with no fewer than 78 portraits of successive Holy Roman Emperors. The rest of the apartments have been turned into an **art gallery** displaying a decent range of sixteenth- to nineteenth-century European masters, mostly lesser-known artists save for the odd Hogarth, Breughel, Caravaggio and Veronese. Another section concentrates on Master Pavol of Levoča, easily the most original sculptor of the fifteenth century – a good opportunity to catch his work if you're going no further east – while the top floor hosts temporary exhibitions of Slovak art.

The crude, makeshift armoured train below the castle was built to protect the Slovak National Uprising in Zvolen's railway workshops. Today, Zvolen lives off its logging industry and its key position in the country's road and rail system. Polish, Hungarian and Romanian trucks litter the main street most days, as well as sundry car loads en route across Central Europe. Although small, the **museum** at no. 43 on the main street is actually better than the one at Banská Bystrica, with a good selection of folk art that includes decorated crosses from Detva (see below).

Practicalities

Zvolen is an easy day trip from Banská Bystrica, but you should find a decent meal and a hotel bed fairly easily at the *Poľana* (☎0855/243 60; ③) on the main square. As for other options, the *Grand* is now closed, and due to be converted into a theatre, which leaves only the *Rates* (☎0855/215 96; ②), south of the river by the winter stadium (bus #6 to the end), or the nearby *Neresnica* **campsite** (May–Sept). Further out of town, on the other side of the village of KOVÁČOVÁ (bus #11), there's a better campsite (May–Oct) with a swimming pool.

THE SLOVAK NATIONAL UPRISING

The **Slovak National Uprising** was probably the most costly (and ultimately unsuccessful) operation undertaken by the Czechoslovak resistance during World War II. Like the Prague Uprising of May 1945, it was portrayed in unambiguous terms by the last regime as yet another glorious (Communist-inspired) episode in the struggle to defeat Fascism. But no event in the minefield of Central European history is ever so clear cut, and the SNP is as controversial, in its own way, as the tragedy of the Warsaw Uprising.

As Hitler set about dismantling the western half of Czechoslovakia in 1938–39, the Slovaks under Jozef Tiso's Catholic People's Party established the first ever independent Slovak state. While this was an aspiration with which many Slovaks identified, it soon became clear that Tiso was bound to his governmental allies, the proto-Fascist Hlinka Guards, and that Slovakia was really little more than a Nazi puppet state. Realising this, Slovaks began to desert the army and join the partisans in the mountains, so that by 1944, partisan activity and acts of sabotage had become widespread. It was at this point that the London-based government-in-exile authorised **Lieutenant-Colonel Ján Golian** to prepare a **national coup**, to be coordinated with the arrival of Soviet troops.

By the summer of 1944, the Soviet Army was massed on the Polish-Ukrainian side of the Carpathians, busy parachuting in Soviet partisans and seemingly poised to liberate Slovakia. Golian, meanwhile, had established a secret military centre at Banská Bystrica and began forming partisan units from escaped prisoners and army deserters. But while the mountains were perfect for concealing their activities, they were not so good for communication. In the end, the uprising stumbled into action prematurely, set off by default rather than according to any plan.

On August 24, 1944, the German military attaché for Bucharest, General Otto, along with his personal entourage, was captured by Soviet partisans in Martin and shot. It was the most daring and provocative strike yet, immediately prompting Hitler to send five SS and two Wehrmacht divisions plus sundry other German troops into Slovakia. Realising they could delay events no longer, the uprising was officially declared by partisan radio from Banská Bystrica on August 29, and a Slovak National Council was set up, comprised of Communists and Democrats in roughly equal proportions.

Despite Soviet assurances of military assistance, only a few token gestures were made. As at Warsaw, the coup failed to prompt the expected Red Army offensive. The Soviets quite rightly suspected the political motives which lay behind the uprising, which smacked of Slovak nationalism, and anyway had been organised primarily from London. To be fair, though, Soviet supply lines were already stretched and breaching the Carpathians was no easy task – in the end it took the 4th Ukrainian Army over two months and some 80,000 lives to capture the Dukla Pass and reach Svidník, the first major town to be liberated. More disheartening was the Soviet refusal to allow the West to use Soviet air bases to drop essential equipment into Slovakia.

Even without Allied assistance, the Slovaks kept going for almost two months before the Nazis succeeded in entering Banská Bystrica on October 28, but apart from tying down a number of German divisions, it was a costly sacrifice to make. The reprisals went on for months and whole villages were given the "Lidice treatment" and worse – women and children were no longer considered sacrosanct. All in all, well over 30,000 Slovaks lost their lives as a result of the uprising, even though by October of the same year the Soviets had already begun to liberate the country.

Sliač and Hronsek

The wide valley that stretches between Zvolen and Banská Bystrica provides a perfect site for the largest air-force base in the country, which was, until recently, used by the Soviets. The nearby airstrip has made little impression on the sleepy hillside spa of **SLIAČ–KÚPELE**, 5km north of Zvolen by train. The springs were initially discovered back in the thirteenth century but were for years considered harmful rather than healing, since locals frequently came across the carcasses of birds and animals near the mouth of the source. Only in the eighteenth century was it discovered that fumes from carbonated waters, although therapeutic for humans, could, in sufficient concentration, asphyxiate small animals. A shot of the waters aside, there's nothing to do or see here as such, beyond a pleasant park, various mapped-out promenades and some far-reaching views across the valley basin. The **train station** lies between the village of SLIAČ and the spa, to the east, up the hill by the edge of the woods. Two stops further up the track towards Banská Bystrica is one of Slovakia's more unusual wooden churches, situated in the small village of **HRONSEK**, by the banks of the river Hron. Begun in 1726 as a Protestant church, at a time when the Counter-Reformation was still in full swing, it had to be built according to strict guidelines: wood was the only material allowed, which is why the Silesian-style timber frame is not filled in with the usual plaster, and there isn't a nail in sight. Similarly, the belfry had to be separate, and the entire building had to be finished within a year. The church is on Hronsecká cesta, west off the road to Sliač, and is normally kept locked. The interior, capable of squeezing in over 1000 worshippers, features seating rather like a theatre in the round; to get hold of the key, ask around for the local priest.

The route to Lučenec

Heading south or east from Zvolen by train takes you through the wilds of southern Slovakia to the Hungarian border, though there's no particular reason to stop. Of the two, the southbound route is the most direct (and least interesting) if you're heading for Budapest. The eastbound railway via Lučenec does, however, at least have a few morsels on offer.

Detva

Ten kilometres down the tracks, the village of **DETVA** is only really worth visiting in mid-July when the **folk festival** is on, reputedly one of the best in Slovakia. The traditional skills of the community lie in woodcarving, particularly the *fujara*, a cross between a flute and a bassoon and an instrument common in folk music right across Central Europe. Detva is also renowned for the **peasant headstones** in the local graveyard, carved in wood and looking more like totem poles than conventional Christian crosses.

Lučenec

Fifty-five kilometres southeast of Zvolen, **LUČENEC** (Losonc) is, for the most part, a scruffy, ramshackle place, typical of the border regions, with a population of Slovaks, Magyars and Romanies in roughly equal proportions. It gets few visitors, but if you're passing through it's at least worth checking out the deconsecrated **Calvinist church** (Tues–Fri 9am–5pm, Sat & Sun 10am–1pm) on what's left of the old town square. A gaudy pink neo-Gothic affair from the outside, it's been sensitively restored inside and contains a stunning selection of Art-Nouveau ceramics. Before you move on, the temporary art exhibitions at the nearby **Novohradská galéria** (same times as church) occasionally merit a closer look, as does the enormous disused **synagogue**, just off the square.

It's a good fifteen-minute walk to the church and gallery from the **bus and train stations**, but once you've hit the main drag through town, there are a few places to break your journey into town. First off is the *ČEDOK* office, where you should be able to fix up **accommodation** without too much hassle in one of the town's four moderately priced hotels. For **food and drink**, try the *Pizzeria Hacienda* on Železnická, the road leading into town from the station.

Banská Štiavnica

High above the Štiavnica river on the terraced slopes of the Štiavnické vrchy, **BANSKÁ ŠTIAVNICA** (Schemnitz), 25km southwest of Zvolen, couldn't wish for a more picturesque setting. The old town has suffered from centuries of sheer neglect, but a concerted restoration effort in recent years is slowly taking effect. The development of a modern lower town saved the place in terms of its architecture, but has turned the old town into little more than an ancient monument, as lifeless and isolated as it is beautiful.

The old town

Banská Štiavnica earned its medieval wealth from the gold and silver deposits discovered here in the thirteenth century. As at Banská Bystrica, skilled German miners were brought in to work the seams, the town was granted special privileges by the Hungarian crown and the good times rolled – as testified by the imposing sandstone Trinity column and handsome burgher houses erected on the main square, **Trojičné námestie**. Recently restored to their former glory, their names recall their German heritage: Baumgartner, Rubigall and Hellenbach. The last served as the mining court from the fifteenth century, and now houses the geological section of the town's **Mining Museum**. Of more universal interest, further up the square in a beautiful sgraffitoed building, is the Jozef Kollár **art gallery** (Tues–Sun 10am–4pm), which puts on interesting temporary exhibitions.

It's worth asking around for the key to the Gothic church of **sv Katerína**, at the bottom of the square alongside the old **radnica**, which sports a Baroque clock that tells the time anticlockwise. Lutheranism caught on fast in Slovakia during the Reformation, especially among the German communities, and opposite the radnica is one of the most impressive Lutheran churches in the country, the green-roofed bulk of the **Protestant Church**, gilded urns atop its tympanum, built shortly after the 1781 Edict of (Religious) Tolerance. Up the steps from the radnica, the fifteenth-century walled **starý zámok** (old castle), once the town's most important building, is likely to be closed for restoration for the foreseeable future. It was built on the same lines as Kremnica's castle (see below), as the town's strong box as well as a fortified residence for the local bigwigs; its central church-turned-fortress testifies to the panic which beset the Hungarian Kingdom during the peak of Ottoman expansion in the sixteenth century.

Banská Štiavnica

Below the castle, Sládkovičova leads past the **Belházyho dom**, a beautifully restored white Renaissance chateau, now a hospital, with an attractive arcaded loggia in the courtyard. Further up Sládkovičova is the seventeenth-century **klopačka** (May–Sept Tues–Sun 8am–3pm; Oct–April Mon–Fri 8am–3pm), whose wooden "clapper" used to raise the miners from their beds at 5am (nowadays it "claps" at 10am and 2pm during the tourist season only). Inside, it's a low-ceilinged building full of character, and packed with displays of miners' lamps and tools.

Out of the centre

From here the road continues uphill to the red-brick **Frauenberg Church** and the portly Baroque **Piargska brána**, one of the town's former gateways that's now stranded out on the road to Levice, giving an indication of Banská Štiavnica's original size when it was the third largest town in the Hungarian Kingdom. As further proof of this, there are no fewer than twelve cemeteries in this part of town. On a nearby hillock, the white **nový zámok** (May–Sept Tues–Sun 8am–3pm) – a turreted cross between a sugar lump and a lookout tower – was yet another attempt by the town to guard against a Turkish attack. The Turkish weaponry on display is far from gripping, but there is a map showing the proximity of the Turks at the height of their power, and a viewing gallery from which you can get a fantastic overview of the town.

For the best view of Banská Štiavnica, though, head northeast, past the imposing nineteenth-century building of the **Academy of Mining and Forestry**, which boasts one of the finest arboretums in Central Europe, to the copper-coloured hill-top church of **Štiavnica kalvária**. The green-marked path zigzags past a succession of Baroque chapels up the hill to the lower church, and on to the summit where the climactic uppermost chapel contains a gruesome, fantastical tableau of the Crucifixion.

The Open-air Mining Museum

By far the most interesting section of the town's mining museum is the **open-air mining skanzen** (Banské múzeum v prírode; Tues–Sun 8am–3pm), 2km south of town on the road to Levice. Above ground, a cluster of technical exhibits chart the technological innovations of the local mining school (information in German and Slovak only), but the highlight of the museum is the trip down the Bartolomej mine shaft in hard hat and overcoat. The tour of the narrow labyrinthine tunnel network gives a good impression of the appalling conditions medieval miners must have endured, and is not recommended for claustrophobes.

Practicalities

Bus connections to and from Zvolen and Banská Bystrica are fairly good, but the scenic **railway**, built by "voluntary brigades" of Communist youth workers back in the 1950s, is easily the most rewarding way of getting to Banská Štiavnica (1hr from Zvolen – you may have to change at Hronská Dúbrava). The station is south of the new town, with the old town a long steep hike away, so it might be worth waiting for the infrequent local bus. If you arrive by car, you'll have to pay a small entrance fee at the checkpoints on the edge of the old town, as well as a separate parking fee – the idea is clearly to discourage you from doing so.

ČEDOK have an office on Academická in the old town but with few visitors to compete with there should be no problem getting a **room** for the night at the plush *Hotel Grand*, on the main street of the old town (☎0859/211 91; ①), or in one of the private pensions around town. Campers have a wide choice of **campsites** southwest of the town, in amongst the many artificial lakes originally built in the eighteenth century as part of the town's ambitious water-pumping project, but now popular summer bathing spots. The Klinger lake is the local favourite for a dip; the nearby Štiavnické Bane campsite is also recommended. *Presso Marína* on Trojičné námestie has a nice upstairs **restaurant**, while the *Strieborna*, one of two new restaurants on the street of the same name, specialises in Italian-style dishes.

North to Kremnica

The aluminium works which stains and pollutes the whole basin around ŽIAR NAD HRONOM, 20km or so north of Banská Štiavnica, is reputedly the largest in the world, and goes some of the way to explaining the country's lethal supply of all things aluminium – from knives and forks to sculptures and buildings. It's not a place to hang around in (unless you want to get premature senile dementia from the dust particles). From Banská Štiavnica, it's simplest to catch a bus to Kremnica, but from Zvolen you also have the choice of the train; the bonus of the latter is the view as the track switches back and forth through the hills, climbing over 460 metres in just 14km, and depositing you above Kremnica itself, about a kilometre southeast of the centre.

Kremnica

KREMNICA (Kremnitz) isn't really what you'd expect from a wealthy gold-mining town. Sitting in a half-hearted plateau, midway up the Rudnica valley, it's a modest place, little more than its duo of castle and square, and certainly no match for the wealth and beauty of Banská Štiavnica – though it attracts a few more visitors thanks to the extra pull of its gold mint. Accommodation can be something of a problem, so it's probably best to come here on a day trip, especially since one of the town's main attractions, its castle, looks likely to remain closed for some time.

Founded by the Hungarian King Charles Robert in 1320, Kremnica's gold seams were once the richest in medieval Europe, keeping the Hungarian economy buoyant and booming throughout the Middle Ages. The thick walls and bastions that still surround the town and castle were built to protect what was effectively the Bank of Hungary – the royal mint. Yet **Štefánikovo námestie**, the steeply pitched main square on which the mint stands, is now little more than a provincial village green, dotted with ornamental beech trees, park benches and a particularly ornate **plague column** which, topped with a flash of gold, is the only obvious reference to the town's wealth. The tatty fortifications of the **castle complex** above the square are now overwhelmed by fruit orchards, and the castle itself is almost wholly taken up by the late Gothic church of sv Katerína, once the castle's main tower. At present it's closed to the public, undergoing badly needed restoration.

Back on Štefánikovo námestie, there's a **Museum of Coins and Medals** (Múzeum mincí a medailí; Tues–Sat 7.30am–3.30pm) which has been attracting visitors from all around the world since 1890. From Stalin to Churchill, they've all had anniversary *Kremnitzerducats* minted for them in their time. As well as some exceptionally beautiful Renaissance coins, there's a whole room of paper money, which, during the First Republic, became an art in itself, with designs by top Czech artists like Alfons Mucha and Max Švabinský. The mines still produce a small amount of gold, and the odd commemorative coin is sporadically struck at the **Štátná mincovňa** (State Mint; no admission) on the northwest corner of the square. As an unlikely accompaniment to the coin museum, the **Ski Museum** (Tues–Sat 7.30am–3.45pm) at the bottom of the square has a collection of antique skis, tins of dubbin and a whole range of ski memorabilia.

The Turiec valley

From Kremnica, the railway climbs another 18km or so before hitting the mill-pond flatness of the **Turiec valley**. Having climbed this far up a valley which gets progressively narrower and more dramatic, it comes as something of a surprise to find yourself in such a wide plateau: but for the cool mountain air and the Veľká and Malá Fatra in the distance, you could be back down in the Danube basin.

Turčianske Teplice

TURČIANSKE TEPLICE is the first stop on the railway as it romps its way across the valley floor to Martin. A modern and uninspiring spa town despite its fourteenth-century origins, it boasts very hot natural springs and a striking Bedouin-blue bathhouse, the Modrý kúpeľ. Theoretically, you could use the spa as a base for exploring the Veľká Fatra (the yellow-marked path from the station heads off into the hills) but, unless you're camping, there's nowhere for non-patients to stay. The nearest **campsite** (June 15–Sept 15) is 2km north by train at DIVIAKY, across the river from the pink seventeenth-century country house (closed to the public).

Martin

A town of considerable historic importance for the Slovaks, **MARTIN** and its industrial baggage occupy the last seven kilometres of the banks of the River Turiec before it joins forces with the mighty Váh. Perhaps unfairly, it's best known nowadays for its *ZTS* engineering works, which once had a monopoly on Warsaw Pact tank production but which is now trying desperately to survive in the post-Cold War era. Yet there's more to Martin than a five-minute drive through the town's confusing one-way system might suggest: for example, the country's most encyclopaedic folk museum, a better than average Slovak art gallery and an open-air folk museum on the outskirts of the town. There's also the possibility of a day's hiking in the less visited southern range of the Malá Fatra, the Lúčanská Fatra.

A brief history

Established back in the fourteenth century, Martin remained the extremely unex-ceptional town of Turčiansky Svätý Martin until well into the nineteenth century. Then, in 1861, a group of Slovak intellectuals and clergy gathered here to draw up the **Martin Memorandum**, which declared boldly that the Slovaks "were as much a nation as the Magyars" and asked the Austrian Parliament to establish a North Hungarian Slovak District (which would remain an integral part of Hungary) with Slovak as the official language. Their demands caused outrage among the Magyars and were studiously ignored by the Austrians.

Nevertheless, a number of important Slovak institutions were founded in the town, of which by far the most important was the **Matica slovenská**, set up to promote the embryonic national culture through education, literature and the arts. It was short-lived. The infamous *Ausgleich* of 1867, which effectively gave the Hungarians a free hand in their half of the empire, ensured that all Slovak institu-tions of higher education were closed by the mid-1870s.

HIKING IN THE VEĽKÁ FATRA

To the east of the Turiec valley lie the **Veľká Fatra**, a line of craggy mountain tops surrounded by a sea of uninhabited, undulating forest. The ridge of brittle lime-stone peaks from Krížna (1574m) to Ploská (1532m), via the highest of the lot, Ostredok (1592m), is the most obvious area to aim for, but the thin craggy valleys leading up to the mountains are actually much more enthralling to walk along: the two most accessible and geologically exciting are the **Gaderská dolina** and the **Blatnická dolina**. The return trip along either, including ascending at least one of the big peaks, is a full day's hike (6–7hr); it's a good idea to get hold of a *Veľká Fatra* hiking map. Both valleys begin at **BLATNICA**, one of the most idyllic villages in the Turiec valley. Half-timbered cottages spread along both sides of the village stream, while at their centre, the local manor house is now a **museum** (Tues–Sun 8am–4pm) dedicated to the great grandfather of Czechoslovak photography, **Karol Plicka**, whose images of the Slovak countryside are reproduced in countless coffee-table books. The only accommodation is a **campsite** (June 15–Sept 15) 1km south of Blatnica, and even that can be packed out in the summer season.

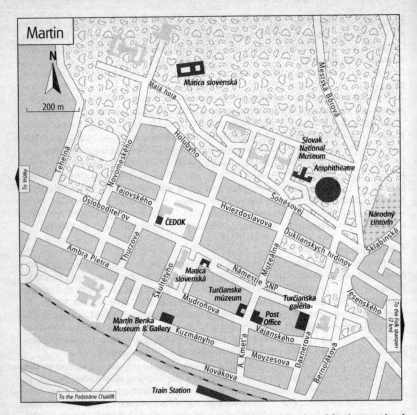

During the next forty long years of fanatical Magyarisation, Martin remained the spiritual centre of the Slovak nation, and on May 24, 1918, Slovak nationalists of all hues gathered for the last time at Martin to sign the **Martin Declaration**, throwing in their lot with the Czechs, and scuppering the Hungarians' various proposals for a "Greater Hungary". At this point Martin was still seriously under consideration as the potential Slovak capital: it was centrally located, less exposed to attack and infinitely more Slav than the Austro-Hungarian town of Pressburg (Bratislava), the other main contender. Having lost that final bid for fame, the town has never really recaptured the limelight, though the Matica slovenská is still based in the town, and has re-established itself since 1989 as a hotbed of Slovak nationalism, not to say chauvinism.

The Town

There's not much to choose aesthetically between what might nominally be called the old town in the south and the industrial estates to the north, but the sights – such as they are – are all located in the south. From the train station, Martin's modern chessboard street-plan becomes quickly apparent as you hit the first major crossroads, on which stands the **post office** and the restaurant *Hotel Slovan*, along with the **Turčianske múzeum** (Tues–Sun 8am–4pm) – paradise for your average botanist, geologist or zoologist, but of limited appeal to anyone else. Of more general interest is the **Turčianska galéria** (Tues–Fri 9am–5pm, Sat 9am–noon), which houses a good range of Slovak artists in its permanent collection on the first floor. Works by Miloš Alexander Bazovský, Ľudovít Fulla and Mikuláš Galanda are all featured, while the seminal Martin Benka, who lived and worked in Martin, has a whole room devoted to him – his simple form of Expressionism became a hallmark of much of Slovak art between the wars. Temporary exhibitions are held on the second floor and in the garden.

Straight ahead, two or three blocks up tree-lined Muzeálna, is the barracks-like mass of the **Slovak National Museum** (Slovenské národné múzeum; Tues–Sun 8am–5.30pm), which commands a great view of the Malá Fatra from its steps. The museum currently houses the country's Institute of Ethnography and one of the best and most extensive folk collections in the country. Richly decorated costumes from every region of Slovakia are displayed here, along with every folk artefact you might expect to find in an average Slovak village – exhaustive stuff. On the other side of the open-air amphitheatre, to the south, is the **Národný cintorín**, which, like the Slavín cemetery in Prague, contains the graves of most of the leading Slovaks of the *národné obrodenie*. It's nothing like as impressive as the Slavín, not least because of the subdued artistry of the headstones, as demanded by Lutheranism, the religion of many of those buried here. Using the master plan near the entrance, you can find the graves of Andrej Kmeť, Janko Kráľ, Janko Jesenský, Martin Benka, Andrej Švehla, Karol Kuzmány and Svet Hurban-Vajanovsky, all leading figures in the Slovak society of the nineteenth century.

Neither the old nor the new buildings of the **Matica slovenská**, founded in 1863, are anything to get excited about: the former, on Osloboditeľov, has been nicely restored, while the latter, which looks like a giant domestic radiator, is easily spotted to the north of the Slovak National Museum.

Perhaps the most rewarding place to visit in Martin, though, is the **folk skanzen** (Múzeum slovenskej dediny; May–Oct 9am–3.30pm), 2km south of town (bus #15, #41 or #56, then follow the signs), which gives some idea of the kind of place Martin was during the nineteenth century. It's also one of the biggest open-air museums in the country (after Rožnov in North Moravia) and contains buildings from all over Slovakia.

Practicalities

Trains from Bratislava do not pass through Martin, but stop only at **Vrútky train station**, in a working-class suburb 7km north (numerous buses go from here to the centre of Martin); Martin's own train station is on a branch line to Turčianske

---

WALKING IN THE LUČANSKÁ FATRA

The southern ridge of the Malá Fatra (see below), the **Lúčanská Fatra**, rises swiftly and dramatically from Martin's westernmost suburbs, making the town a possible base for ascending the five big bare peaks of the southern Malá Fatra. If you're staying in town, a chairlift (*lánovka*) from PODSTRÁNE, 3km west of town (bus #40), deposits you just over 1km below the highest peak, **Velká lúka** (1476m). If you choose to walk, it'll take nearly four hours to reach the top, though perhaps only half that to walk the 10km north along the ridge to the ruins at Strečno (see below). If you're camping at VRÚTKY, Martin's northernmost suburb, the nearest peak is the northernmost summit of **Minčol** (1364m).

Teplice. For **accommodation**, there's the *Turiec* (☎0842/386 03; ②) near the town's Catholic church, or the *Patrik*, on ulica Timravy (☎0842/319 59; ②), over the river in the suburb of Podháj. Alternatively, try the *Podstráne* (☎0842/389 18; ①) in the nearby village of the same name (see below); the nearest **campsite** (May 15–Sept 15) is in the woods west of Vrútky.

The Malá Fatra

The **Malá Fatra** are the first real mountains on the road from Bratislava, and one of the most popular and accessible of the Slovak ranges. Severed in two by the sweeping sabre-like meanderings of the Váh, the northern ridge is by far the most popular, having the highest peaks and the most spectacular valley, Vrátna dolina. The southern ridge, including the Lúčanská Fatra, is less geographically pronounced and drifts rather vaguely southwestwards, but contains a couple of non-hiking attractions. Most people use **Žilina** as a base simply because it's on the main line from Bratislava, though in fact it's just too far from the mountains to be really convenient. Accommodation in the area is now much easier to come by, but if you're serious about hiking, you'll solve a lot of logistic problems by bringing your own tent.

Žilina and around

Throughout the summer season **ŽILINA** (Sillein) is awash with coach parties, school kids and backpackers, all heading for the mountains of the nearby Malá Fatra. Few bother to venture far from the bus and train stations, though the town itself has a pleasant enough old quarter, originating from the fourteenth century when the town was colonised by Germans settlers. The whole place suffered badly during the Thirty Years' War, and only really began to recover with the industrial development of this century.

Between the stations and the old town to the west is námestie Andreja Hlinku, unintentionally presided over by the back end of the Trinity church, with a low-key market and a gaggle of takeaway food outlets below. At the top of the Farské schody, the old town's main square, **Mariánské námestie**, is really quite pretty, arcaded for the most part and dominated by the big yellow frontage of the Jesuit church. A fully functioning fountain, flanked by lofty trees, and a couple of cafés have livened the place up no end. Next door to the church, the old monastery has been converted into a relaxing exhibition space, **Považská galéria** (Tues–Fri 10am–5pm, Sat & Sun 11am–5pm) – unfortunately it's mostly given over to the sculpture of Rudolf Pribiš, whose sycophantic devotion to all things post-1948 ensured him a gallery of his own.

Žilina practicalities

Few people come to Žilina to sightsee, but a lot of people end up staying here – so many in fact that it may not be easy to get a bed in high season. *ČEDOK*, on the main square south of the old town, may be able to help you with **accommodation** (including private rooms) in town, or in the mountains themselves. The *Metropol*, opposite the station (☎089/329 00; ①), is a good place to try, before resorting to more expensive "international" hotels like the *Slovakia* (☎089/456 71; ④). If you've got your own transport, the *Motel Šibenice* (☎089/486 73; ②), on

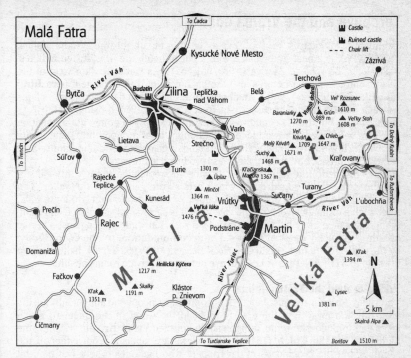

Malá Fatra

the road to Strečno, is another possibility. **Eating out**, the *Fontana* (daily until 9pm), on the main square, is quite a find – a vegetarian restaurant, offering various soya-based and even Mexican-style dishes – or else there's a new arty café-restaurant, *Atelier*, just off námestie A. Hlinku on Republiky.

Budatín and Strečno

Two kilometres north of the town centre, on the right bank of the Váh (bus #22 or #30), stands the attractive chateau of **Budatín**, a characteristically hybrid Slovak affair, now whitewashed over and housing the **Považské múzeum** (Tues–Sat 9am–5pm), which specialises in carved wooden furniture.

Infinitely more impressive in scale and setting are the fourteenth-century ruins of **Strečno** castle, which crown the summit of a 200-foot cliff 11km east of Žilina, commanding the entrance to the Váh valley as it squeezes through the Malá Fatra to Martin. You can climb up to the castle from the nearby train station, though for the last few years it has been covered in scaffolding while being converted into a museum. Nearby is a monument to the **French partisans**, escaped POWs from a camp in Hungary, who took part in the 1944 Slovak National Uprising.

There's a **campsite** (July & Aug only) in VARÍN, on the other side of the river: if you don't have your own transport, it's a more convenient base for ascending the northern peaks of the Malá Fatra than Vrátna dolina. Alternatively, you could try the *Chata pod Suchým* hostel, a two-kilometre walk from Strečno along the red-marked path via the Váh gorge's other ruined castle, **Starý hrad** – it's over 1000m above sea level, so expect a chilly night but don't count on there being vacancies.

Terchová and the Vrátna dolina

Twenty-five kilometres east of Žilina, at the mouth of the Vrátna dolina, **TERCHOVÁ** is a neat little village with a cheap hotel, the *Jánošík*, ten minutes' walk along the road to Zázrivá (☎089/951 85; ①), a campsite 3km west of the village, and a supermarket. It's also the birthplace of the Slovak folk hero **Juraj Jánošík** (see opposite), and a small **museum** (Tues–Sun 8am–4pm) draws links between Jánošík and the partisans who took part in the 1944 uprising. All the texts are in Slovak, but there's enough local folk art to keep you going, not to mention Jánošík's celebrated brass-studded belt (thought to bring good luck) and jaunty hat. On the low hill overlooking the town stands a giant futuristic aluminium statue of the man himself, one of the many mass-produced in the region.

The **Vrátna dolina** actually owes its winsome reputation to the gritty cliffs of **Tiesňavy**, the sharp-edged defile which acts as the gateway to the valley. The occasional bus goes this way from Terchová, or it's a gentle twenty-minute walk. After such a dramatic overture, the valley itself is surprisingly sheltered and calm. A short distance away is LÚKY, a major ski resort in winter, set against a scenic backdrop of thickly forested hilltops. For **accommodation**, try the *Chata Vrátna* by the chairlift, the more luxurious *Hotel Boboty* (☎089/952 27; ③), halfway down the road to ŠTEFANOVÁ, or keep an eye out for any private rooms on offer.

Hiking around the Vrátná dolina

The valley forks in two just before Lúky with most people heading south for the **chairlift** 3km away (get there early to avoid the worst of the queues), which takes you to Snilovské sedlo, a high saddle between **Veľký Kriváň** (1709m), the highest peak, and **Chleb** (1647m). The views are fantastic from either of the summits, but the coachloads of day-trippers who make it up here can be a bit overwhelming. Basically, the further you get from the chairlift, the more you'll lose the crowds. If you're out for the day from Žilina, you could descend Chleb's southern face, tracking the blue-marked path that runs via the Šútovský vodopád (waterfall) to ŠÚTOVO, fifty minutes by train from Žilina. Otherwise it's over six hours across the peaks to Strečno (see above).

In many ways a preferable alternative to the congestion of the chairlift and the peaks around Chleb is to turn left at the Vrátna dolina fork for Štefanová (2km) which lies under the shadow of **Veľký Rozsutec** (1610m), whose sharply pointed rocky summit is arguably the most satisfying to climb. Follow the yellow-marked path to Podžiar, where you should change to the blue path up **Horné Diery**, an idyllic wet ravine which has to be traversed using ladders and steps. The ravine ends at sedlo Medzirozsutce, the saddle between Malý and Veľký Rozsutec. The ascent takes around four hours, the descent via sedlo Medziholie about half that.

South of Žilina

Just south of Žilina, the cement works of LIETAVSKÁ LÚČKA coat the valley with a grey-white dust, before a bend in the River Rajčanka brings you into the verdant wooded spa town of **RAJECKÉ TEPLICE**, thirty minutes by train from Žilina. Two hotels, two beautifully placed campsites – one in town and another more primitive one 3km back along the valley (get out at Poluvsie station) – and a couple of thermal swimming pools make this a convenient base for a series of day **hikes** in the surrounding hills.

JÁNOŠÍK

Juraj Jánošík (1688–1713) is the most famous of the many Robin Hood figures who form an integral part of the songs and folklore of the Slovak mountain regions. Most originate from the turn of the seventeenth century when the central authority of the Habsburgs was at a weak point, worn down by the threat of Turkish invasion. Like many of the rural youth of his generation, Jánošík joined up with the anti-Habsburg army of the Hungarian rebel Ferenc Rákóczi II in 1703. When they were finally defeated by the Austrian Imperial forces at Trenčín in 1711, large numbers fled into the hills to continue the fight from there. Jánošík, however, opted for the priesthood and left for Kežmarok to complete his religious training. While he was away, his mother fell ill and died, and his father – who had absconded from work in order to build a coffin for her burial – was given a hundred lashes, which proved fatal for the old man. Both parents dead, Jánošík finally took to the hills and gathered round him the obligatory band of merry men, indulging in the usual deeds of wealth redistribution.

Sadly – though this, too, is typical of Slovak folklore – the crucial difference between Robin Hood and characters like Jánošík is that the latter nearly always come to a sticky end. In March 1713 Jánošík was captured by the lords of Liptov and sentenced to death in the central square of Liptovský Svätý Mikuláš, where he was hung by the ribcage. It's impossible to overestimate the importance of Jánošík to both the oral and written Slovak literary tradition. More poems, novels and plays have been inspired by his exploits than by any other episode in Slovak history – except perhaps the Slovak National Uprising.

The most obvious is across the valley via the early twentieth-century chateau of **Kunerad** (closed to the public) and up Veľká lúka (1476m), which overlooks Martin and the Turiec valley. The blue-marked path is an alternative route back to the spa, and the whole trip is a full day's walking. A more leisurely afternoon's hike north along the green-marked path from the station takes you to the ruined castle of **Lietava**, a shade less spectacular than Strečno but still an impressive pile, some 300 feet above the village of the same name. The most popular destination, though, is across the hills to the **Súľovské skaly** (3hr on the yellow-marked path via ZBYŇOV), a "rock city" made up of contorted slabs of limestone, with the ruined castle of Súľov at its centre.

Čičmany

ČIČMANY is probably one of the most hyped villages in the whole of Slovakia, and with good reason. Lying in a wide, gently undulating valley, it's a Slovak village *par excellence*: a cluster of typical wooden cottages-cum-farms haphazardly strewn about the banks of the River Rajčanka, which at this point is little more than a mountain stream. What makes Čičmany special, though, is the unique local tradition of **house-painting**. Each cottage is smothered in a simple, largely abstract decorative mantle of white snowflakes, flowers and crisscrosses, a feature entirely confined to the isolated Čičmany region. Electricity, telephone cables and the odd tractor are the only signs of modernity; the occasional tour groups break the spell, but even they don't stay longer than it takes to visit the small folk museum. The disadvantage with Čičmany's isolated position is its inaccessibility, with only infrequent **buses** covering the 38km from Žilina. You could try hitching, although the traffic is light, especially on the last 7km from the main road. Somewhat remarkably there's a **hotel** in the village, the *Kaštieľ* (①), should you make it out here.

The Orava region

Despite its wonderful mountainous backdrop and winding river valley, the **Orava region** that lies northeast of the Malá Fatra and flush with the Polish border is generally fairly bleak. For centuries it remained an impoverished rural backwater on the main road to Poland, so poor that when the Lithuanian army marched through in 1683 en route to Vienna, they burned most of the villages to the ground (including the former capital of Velična) in disgust at the lack of provisions. Emigration to America was widespread during the late nineteenth and early twentieth centuries, and only after World War II was industry hastily foisted onto the region in an attempt to save it from extinction. As a consequence, the towns are short on excitement and long on eyesores, but the artificial **lake** to the north is recommended if you want to get some relatively clean swimming, and the **Western Tatras** provide a uniquely unspoilt alpine experience.

Accommodation can be a problem, so it's worth booking ahead from Dolný Kubín, the largest town in the region. Transport relies heavily on the branch line which stretches the length of the Orava valley from Kraľovany on the Váh to Trstená by the Polish border; elsewhere you're dependent on buses or hitching.

The Orava valley

As an introduction to the Orava valley, the giant alloy plant and its attendant quarry at **ISTEBNÉ** (20min by train from Kraľovany) leave a lot to be desired. Until a few years ago, the level of dust in the atmosphere was intolerable, regularly blackening the skies over the valley at midday. Only in the mid-1980s, when the local population threatened to move out en masse, were dust separators finally fitted onto the factory chimneys. Miraculously, the pre-industrial settlement still exists, tucked into the hills to the north, fifteen minutes' walk from the bus and train station. Among its few remaining wooden buildings, it boasts a **wooden Lutheran church** with a richly patterned interior, one of only four in the country, built in 1696 on slightly raised ground above the village.

DOLNÝ KUBÍN, the regional capital, is not much better. True, its hilly locale is faultless and manages to lend a kind of surreal beauty to the gleaming white high-rise blocks which house most of the town's residents; but apart from a dull museum dedicated to the mild-mannered "father of Slovak poetry", Pavol Országh Hviezdoslav (1849–1921), who was born in nearby Vyšný Kubín, the only reason to stop here is to book some **accommodation** for further up the valley at the local *ČEDOK* office, or grab a bite to eat in the excellent new restaurant, *Marina*, on Hviezdoslavovo námestie.

Orava Castle

Eleven kilometres upstream from Dolný Kubín by train, **Orava Castle** (Tues–Sun May, Sept & Oct 8am–4.30pm; June–Aug 8am–6pm) is one of Slovakia's truly spectacular cliff-top sights. Perched like an eyrie more than 100m above the village of ORAVSKÝ PODZÁMOK (literally "Below Orava Castle"), it's an impressive testament to the region's feudal past. Whoever occupied Orava Castle held sway over the entire region and made a fortune taxing the peasants and milking the trade into Poland. Before you get persuaded into signing up for a tour, though, be warned that it takes over an hour and a half and that there have to be at least 25 people outside the gates to coax the guides into action. If you do get inside, you'll be treated to hearty dollops of medieval kitchenware, instruments of feudal justice and wood-panelled dining halls. If you're unsuccessful, content yourself with the **mini-museum** of local artefacts in the village and then head on up the valley.

Podbiel

At **PODBIEL**, thirty minutes by train from Oravský Podzámok, a collection of traditional wooden cottages has been converted into tourist accommodation. You could turn up at the *recepcia* at no. 101 during office hours on the off chance, but it's better to try and book in advance through ČEDOK in Dolný Kubín. Quite frankly, you'll be lucky to get in there before the tour groups. In any case, the only reason to stop at Podbiel is to hitch, walk or catch one of the very few local buses going east up Studená dolina, the valley which leads to the Western Tatras, impressively arrayed on the horizon.

Into the Western Tatras

Thirteen kilometres east up the **Studená dolina**, just after ZUBEREC, lies the **Orava folk museum** (Jan–April Mon–Fri 8am–3pm; May–Oct Tues–Sun 8am–4pm), a skanzen of about twenty traditional wooden buildings from the surrounding area, including a fifteenth-century **wooden Catholic church** from Zábrež, one of the few to escape the pillaging of the local Protestants. Its barn-like exterior gives no indication of the intricate seventeenth-century folk panel paintings inside. You're supposed to go round only with a guide, for which there must be at least fifteen visitors ready and waiting, but you could try pleading that you've come a long way – most countries seem exotically far away from Orava.

HIKING IN THE WESTERN TATRAS

From **Oravice**, two main trails cover the 6km to the Polish border of which the blue-marked one is the gentler. After a couple of very flat kilometres, a yellow path leads off to the right to **Osobitá** (1687m), a two- to three-hour climb from Oravice which gives a sweeping vista of the Western Tatras, weather permitting. Previously, only Polish and Slovak walkers were permitted to use the path along the border, but it's worth checking to see if these restrictions have now been dropped. That being the case, once you reach the border, follow the blue-marked path up onto the ridge between the two countries which climbs up to **Volovec** (2063m) and **Ostrý Roháč** (2084m), 1km from the border. It could easily take four hours to reach the more spectacular scenery around Volovec, which makes a return trip a full day's hike. If you're carrying a pack, it's possible to drop down onto the blue-marked path to the twin tarns of Jamnicke plesá, and then continue for 8km to the Račková dolina **campsite** (May–Oct) or a little further to the *Esperanto* **hotel** in PRIBYLINA, probably the quickest way there is of approaching the High Tatras from the Orava region.

From **Roháčska dolina**, everything happens much more quickly. As you head down the valley the brooding grey peaks begin to gather round and by the end of the road (8km from the skanzen; 3km from the final car park) it's only a steep kilometre-long walk on the green path to the still, glacial waters of **Roháčske plesá**, hemmed in by the Tatras' steep scree-ridden slopes. A punishing 2.5km (reckon on about 2hr) along the blue path leads to the Smutne sedlo ("Sad saddle"– sad because it's the mountain's cold north face) which lies on the main Roháč ridge. Ostrý Roháč is less than an hour to the east, while **Baníkov** (2178m) is the same distance west, but the king of the lot, **Baranec** (2184m), lies a good two hours' walk to the south.

The Western Tatras

With the High Tatras increasingly reaching saturation point during most of the climbing season, the **Western Tatras** (Západné Tatry) present themselves as a refreshingly undeveloped alternative. They boast the same dog-tooth peaks and hand-mirror lakes, but with half the number of climbers. Unless you've managed to pre-book from Dolný Kubín, you may find the *chata* or chalet-cum-hostels full. The only alternative is to find some private accommodation, pick a discreet spot to pitch your tent in the neighbouring forests or make your base further north, at ORAVICE, the only official **campsite** (July & Aug) on this side of the mountains. The main problem is getting to Oravice, which either means catching one of the few buses from TRSTENÁ (the last station on the Orava rail line) or walking 7km from the Orava village museum. Whatever you do, don't let the logistics get you down – you'll encounter similar problems in the other parts of the Tatras. More importantly, get hold of the *Orava* or better still the *Západné Tatry – Roháče* hiking map, plus the requisite camping gear and you'll have a smooth trip. Don't, however, undertake any mountain climbing if you've no experience, and always get a weather check before you start on a long walk that goes above 1500m. For more **information** on hiking and climbing, and important **safety hints**, see p.382.

Around Lake Orava

Back at Podbiel, the rail line continues to the village of **TVRDOŠÍN**, which boasts a fifteenth-century wooden church containing some fantastic primitive altar paintings contemporary with the building of the church itself. The last stop on the line is **TRSTENÁ**, 6km from the Polish border, which has two reasonable hotels; if you're moving on to Poland, there's enough traffic to make hitching feasible.

What was once the Orava plain became **Lake Orava** in 1954 when five villages were submerged by the damming of the river. The wooded western shore has a fair smattering of *chata* settlements and two **campsites** (June 15–Sept 15). One of the lost villages, **SLANICA**, was the birthplace of an early pioneer of the Slovak language, the Catholic priest Anton Bernolák (1762–1813). Only the village church, hidden in the trees, still rears its head above water, and has been converted into a museum of folk art and ceramics as well as a memorial to Bernolák. To reach it, take the boat from either campsite, or from NÁMESTOVO, the big new town to the far west of the lake (and thankfully out of sight from the main recreational area).

The Liptov region

The **Liptov region**, to the south of the Orava region and the Western Tatras, offers a similar cocktail of traditional Slovak villages, depressed industrial towns and a backdrop of spectacular mountains. **Ružomberok**, the first town you come to, at another T-junction on the River Váh, offers very little except accommodation, and easy access to the surrounding peaks. East of Ružomberok, the Váh valley widens into a vast plain, now partially flooded, whose main town, **Liptovský Mikuláš**, is similarly uninspiring but the best placed for exploring the Low Tatras.

As in the Orava, the traditional way of life in these parts has disappeared over the last two generations. But while few mourn the demise of subsistence farming as a way of life, more lament the fact that it was destroyed by forced collectivisation and industrialisation. Some things survive – the patchwork fields and terraces, the long timbered cottages, and of course the mountains – but give it a few more decades and the songs, dances and costumes will be of historical and folkloristic interest only.

Ružomberok and around

RUŽOMBEROK (Rosenberg), like so many big towns on the Váh, has more than its fair share of industrial suburbs and ungainly high-rise estates, not to mention a persistent smell of synthetic fabrics. Aside from the **Ľudovít Fulla Gallery** on Májekova (Tues–Sun 9am–5pm), devoted to Ružomberok's talented painter of the same name, the parish church is the place to head for, pleasantly aloof from the rest of town. Before the war, the local priest was **Andrej Hlinka** (see overleaf), spiritual leader of Slovak separatism, *persona non grata* under the Communists, but recently rehabilitated by Slovak nationalists; the church is on raised ground in the centre of town, on a square which is now named after him. On one corner of the square is another curiosity – a monument in honour of the Scottish academic, R. W. Seton-Watson, "for defending the Slovak nation", erected in 1937 and miraculously still standing today.

Practicalities

The **train station** is northwest of the town centre, on the other side of the River Váh (bus #1 or #8). Cheap **rooms** are available at the *Liptov* (☎0848/225 09; ①) – the only other downtown hotel, the *Kultúrny dom* (☎0848/224 19), is currently closed for renovation – both are situated on the main drag through town. If you want to stay in either of the two out-of-town (and up in the hills) hotels, it's best to book through *ČEDOK*, also on the main drag, to save a wasted journey. Take bus #3 or #4 from the town centre, both of which run regularly to *Hotel Hrabovo* (☎0848/267 27; ③), Ružomberok's poshest hotel, which has a grassy banked lake in which to swim. Behind it, a four-seater cable car will take you, on the hour, to *Hotel Malina* (☎0848/250 70; ①), a cheaper option with an even better view (and another swimming pool).

Around Ružomberok

One of the few redeeming features of Ružomberok is its proximity to the surrounding hills and villages. It's only a three-kilometre walk to the conic peak of **Sidorovo** (1099m) or 5km to **Malinné** (1209m), both of which are accessible via the cable car behind *Hotel Hrabovo*, and guarantee extensive panoramas over the Váh and Revúca valleys. Dropping down off the fell on the south side, head for the ribbon village of **VLKOLÍNEC**, set in a peaceful shallow valley south of Ružomberok (also reachable by bus #2 or #7 from Ružomberok to Biely Potok, then a 2-km walk). This is one of the best environments in which to see Liptov wooden folk architecture, though as ever there's a note of melancholy about the place. It was badly damaged by the Nazis in September 1944 in retaliation for the Slovak National Uprising, but those cottages that remain now form a natural skanzen of timber structures.

With your own transport, you could explore the villages east of Ružomberok, starting with **ĽUDROVÁ**, 5km southeast, a beautiful village in its own right, but one whose white stone church is now a museum of Gothic art (you'll have to ask around for the key). The whitewashed manor house at nearby **LIPTOVSKÁ**

ANDREJ HLINKA

Born in the neighbouring village of Černová in 1864, **Andrej Hlinka** served most of his life as a Catholic pastor of Ružomberok. He became a national martyr in 1906 when he was arrested by the Hungarian authorities and sentenced to two years' imprisonment for "incitement against the Magyar nationality", topped up by another eighteen months for "further incitement" in his inflammatory farewell address to the local parishioners.

Although at the time still in prison, he was also viewed by the authorities as the prime mover behind the peaceful demonstration of October 27, 1907, popularly known as the **Černová Massacre**, the "Bloody Sunday" of Hungarian rule in Slovakia. When the local Slovaks protested against the consecration of their church by a strongly pro-Magyar priest, the Hungarian police opened fire on the crowd, killing fifteen people and wounding countless others.

Not long after the foundation of Czechoslovakia in 1918, he began campaigning for Slovak independence, and, having travelled to Paris on a false Polish passport to press the point at the Versaille Peace Conference, wound up in a Czechoslovak prison for his pains. He was only released after having been elected leader of the newly founded **Ľudová strana** (People's Party), strongly Catholic, vehemently nationalistic and the largest single party in Slovakia between the wars. While by no means openly fascistic, its slogan "Slovakia for the Slovaks" by implication excluded the Jews, Gypsies, Hungarians and Rusyns who made up much of Slovakia's population. Hlinka's death in August 1938 was the only thing that saved him from the ignominy of participating in the Nazi puppet government, although his name lived on posthumously in the **Hlinka Guards**, the Slovak equivalent of the SS. Jozef Tiso, Hlinka's successor in the People's Party, went on to become the Slovak Quisling, and was eventually executed as a war criminal in 1947.

Since November 1989, Slovak nationalists have conducted a concerted campaign to rehabilitate Hlinka, Tiso and company. Many Slovaks are very much in sympathy with such moves: town councils across the republic have successfully renamed streets and squares after Hlinka. However, when a plaque in honour of Tiso was unveiled in his home town of Bánovce nad Bebravou, above the Catholic teacher training college he founded, it provoked outrage in many quarters and was eventually removed. It remains to be seen whether the new independent Slovak government will take a more lenient line on such gestures.

STIAVNIČKA, though closed to the public, is also worth a look for its shingled turrets and onion domes. Five kilometres east, the **SLIAČE** villages – Nižný, Stredný and Vyšný – are also well known for their excellent folk architecture.

Liptovský Mikuláš and around

As in Orava, the broad sweep of the main Liptov plain east of Ružomberok has been turned, for the most part, into a vast lake, whose beautiful sandy shoreline is set against the distant backdrop of the Western Tatras. Quite why it deserves the title Liptovská Mara (Liptov Sea) while the one in Orava is simply a lake remains a linguistic mystery, but a similar number of villages bit the dust in the name of "progess". On its easternmost edge sits **LIPTOVSKÝ MIKULÁŠ**, which, like Martin and Ružomberok, once played a part in the Slovak national revival or *národné obrodenie*. Nowadays, it's really only worth coming here if you're intending to explore the Low Tatras.

The Town

The first rumblings of the Slovak *národné obrodenie* in Liptovský Mikuláš occurred in the late 1820s when a Slovak reading room was founded, followed much later by the *Tatrín* literary society established by the Lutheran pastor Michal Miloslav Hodža, one of the leading lights of 1848. Hodža's house, at Tranovského 8, is now a not terribly enthralling **museum** (Tues–Fri 9am–noon & 1–4pm), which also touches on the events of May 10, 1848, in Mikuláš, when in response to the Hungarian uprising against the Habsburgs various leading Slovaks published the "Demands of the Slovak Nation" and quickly fled the country to avoid arrest.

A slightly better taste of the literary milieu of nineteenth-century Mikuláš can be had at the **Janko Kráľ Museum** (Tues–Fri 8.30am–3.30pm, Sat & Sun 9am–noon), housed in a Baroque building on the main square (the same one in which Jánošík was sentenced to death in 1713). Local boy Kráľ was the foremost Slovak poet of the Romantic movement, "a lawyer who preferred the company of shepherds", or the Slovak Lord Byron as some would have it. Needless to say he was a fervent nationalist, and only just escaped being executed for his beliefs in 1848.

At **PALÚDZKA**, a kilometre west of Mikuláš town centre (bus #2 or #7 from Štúrova), is the *kaštieľ*, which contains **Janošíkovo väženie** (Janošík's dungeon; Tues–Fri 9am–noon & 1–4pm), where the rebel hero was held before his public execution on Mikuláš's main square. The largest **wooden church** in Slovakia used to stand opposite, but was transferred in the 1970's to the nearby hamlet of SVÄTÝ KRÍŽ, 5km to the southwest. It's a remarkable barn-like structure built in 1774 for the local Lutheran community, and comfortably seating over two thousand worshippers.

Practicalities

The **bus** and **train stations** are next door to each other, a ten-minute walk from the town centre (or any bus except #5 or #7). *ČEDOK*, on the main square, will readily book you into the multistorey *Jánošík* (☎0849/227 26; ①) by the river on Jánošíkovo nábrežie, the *Bystrina* (☎0849/221 83; ①), 5km south of town at the mouth of the Demänová dolina (bus #5 then walk or take the *ČSAD* bus), or the newly modernised, Greek-owned *El Greco* (☎0849/227 13; ②), a gleaming white Art-Nouveau building on Štúrova. Back down the price scale, there's the *Kriváň*, Štúrova 5 (☎0849/224 15; ①), whose restaurant serves cheap food and draught beer. The nearest **campsite** is the lakeside site at LIPTOVSKÝ TRNOVEC (20min by bus; June 15–Sept 15) on the northern shores of the Liptovská Mara, but if you're aiming to hike in the Low Tatras, you'd be better off at PODTUREŇ, 8km east (10min by train), or the Demänová site (mid-May to Sept) by the *Bystrina* (see above).

Východná and Važec

The annual **Slovak folk festival** held in July in **VÝCHODNÁ**, 15km east of Liptovský Mikuláš and thirty minutes by train, is in every way equal to Strážnice's international affair (see p.280), attracting groups from every region of Slovakia. There's no accommodation in the village (a pleasant two-kilometre hike north from the station), but during the festival there's a makeshift campsite, with many more people crashing out in the haylofts and barns of the local farmers (ask first). At any other time of the year, Východná is a modest little village whose succession of nondescript facades hide more interesting wooden buildings behind.

VAŽEC, one stop further on, once renowned for being one of the most beautiful villages in Slovakia and built almost entirely from wood, without a brick or nail in sight, was destroyed by a catastrophic fire in 1931. Luckily, it was also a photographers' dream and you can get an impression of how things used to be from the small exhibition in the village **folk museum**. The purpose of most visits, though, is the **Važecká jaskyňa** (Tues–Sun April to mid-May & mid-Sept to Oct tours at 9am, 11am and 2pm; mid-May to mid-Sept hourly 9am–4pm), a limestone cave system discovered back in the 1920s but only recently opened to the public. To get to the cave from the train station, walk to the other side of the village; the *Hotel Važec* is another 500m further.

The Low Tatras

The impact of the **Low Tatras**' rounded peaks is nothing like as immediate as the sharp craggy outline of the High Tatras visible on the northern horizon, but they do constitute a more extensive range, in parts much wilder and less explored. The crudest development has gone on either side of the two tallest central mountains, **Chopok** and **Ďumbier**, but, particularly to the east, the crowds are thin and – with the aid of a *Nízke Tatry* map – the countryside is yours for the taking. If you're not planning on doing anything so strenuous as hiking, you could happily spend a day or two visiting some of the **caves** in Demänovská dolina, swimming at the foot of the mountains at Tále or simply riding the chairlift to the top of Chopok and effortlessly soaking up the view.

On the practical front, **accommodation** is now no longer a problem, with plenty of private rooms available and several campsites, though still very few hotels. **Transport** is also fairly good, with two rail lines serving the Váh and Hron valleys and buses taking you the rest of the way into the mountains: of course, to get the most out of the region, you'll need to walk – preferably armed with the map mentioned above and a stout pair of walking boots.

Demänovská dolina and the caves

Extremely overloaded buses wend their way fairly regularly up **Demänovská dolina**, by far the most popular valley on the north side of the mountains. Not far past the massive military training centre on the outskirts of Mikuláš, there's a brand new *Slovakotour* **accommodation bureau** (daily 8.30am–7.30pm), which can book hotels and private rooms for you.

As soon as you enter the narrow, forested part of the valley, signs point off to the left to the **Demänovská ľadová jaskyňa** (May 16–Sept 15 Tues–Sun 9am–4pm), one of Slovakia's two "ice caves". After a sweaty fifteen-minute walk up through the woods to the entrance, it's an extremely chilly thirty-minute guided tour through the cave. The first part leads through a vast hall-like chamber of mini-stalactites and stalagmites, its walls covered in eighteenth-century graffiti testifying to the early discovery of the caves. The second part descends into the claustrophobic **ice chamber**, where the temperature even in summer is well below zero. Best time to visit, though, is in the spring, when the ice formations are at their best, creating huge stalactites of frozen water which drip down onto a massive frozen lake. Two kilometres further on, signs indicate the **Demänovská jaskyňa Slobody** (Tues–Sun May 16–Sept 15 8am–4pm; Sept 16–May 15 tours at

HIKING AROUND CHOPOK

Most people start walking from **Chopok** (2024m), the second highest peak in the range, reached by two consecutive (and extremely popular) chairlifts from Jasná (closed May, Oct & Nov). It's about two hours across the bare fell to the top of **Ďumbier** (2043m), king of the Low Tatras and the easternmost limit of this central ridge. From Ďumbier, it's six or more hours for each of the following routes: via Krupova hoľa, back down the yellow-marked path to the campsite at the bottom of Demänovská dolina; down Jánska dolina on the blue-marked path to the campsite in Podtureň, or further east to the campsite at MALUŽINÁ (turn right either at sedlo Javorie or Pred Bystrou). Westwards, it's about five hours along the ridge to the isolated hamlet of MAGURKA, which has a *chata* but no official campsite; otherwise it's a good ten hours' walk to the campsite and hotel at DONOVALY, at the top of the pass from Banská Bystrica over to Ružomberok.

9am, 11am & 2pm), used for storage by frostbitten partisans during World War II – hence its name, "Cave of Freedom". It's an iceless cave (though no less freezing), much larger and more impressive than Demänovská ľadová jaskyňa when it comes to the variety of rock formations.

A little further on, the road swings violently to the right and begins to climb steeply for about 1.5km until it reaches **JASNÁ**, a major ski resort for this part of the world, with sundry chair- and skilifts, as well as a smattering of hotels, from the very reasonable *CKM Juniorhotel* (☎0849/915 71; ②) to the more expensive *Družba* (☎0849/915 55; ③) and *Liptov* (☎0849/915 05; ③); try enquiring about vacancies at *Slovakotour* or *ČEDOK* in Liptovský Mikuláš. It's also worth knowing that non-guests can use the *Liptov*'s sauna. As for **food**, the *Tri domky*, by the main car park, offering trout, and garlic soup, is probably the least pretentious option.

Approaching from the Hron valley

If you're coming from Banská Bystrica and the Hron valley, you'll end up approaching the Low Tatras from the south. The Hron valley as far as BREZNO has been marred by industry, and the latter only has its three cheap hotels to recommend it. The main approach to Chopok from this side is via **Bystrá dolina**, the flipside valley of Demänovská dolina. At its base, by the neat village of BYSTRÁ (5-km walk or bus from Podbrezová station), are the **Bystrianska jaskyňa** (Tues–Sun May 16–Sept 15 9am–4pm; April–May 15 & Sept 16–Oct tours at 9am, 11am & 2pm), the only underground cave system on offer on this side.

Two and a half kilometres up the valley is the main area of development, known as **TÁLE**, with various private rooms, and a fully equipped campsite (mid-May to Sept), swimming pool, a motel, and a hotel called the *Partizán* (☎0867/951 31; ③). Buses will drop you (and a whole load of others) outside the *Hotel Srdiečko* (☎0867/951 21; ②) and the more expensive *Trangoška* (☎0867/951 30; ③) at the end of the valley. From here, a chairlift rises in two stages to the top of Chopok, stopping just outside the *Hotel Kosodrevina* (☎0867/951 05; ③). To avoid disappointment, you should **book in advance** for the above hotels, through *ČEDOK* in Banská Bystrica. If you're walking from Tále to the main ridge, it'll take you three to four hours along the yellow-marked path to the top of **Dereše** (2003m).

The eastern peaks

East of the central Chopok ridge, the real wilderness begins. The peaks are even less pronounced and rarely raise their heads above the turbulent sea of forest where Slovakia's last remaining wild bears, lynx and chamois hide out. Meanwhile, the villages in the **Hron valley** – which forms the southern watershed of the Low Tatras – are still a world of shepherds and horses and carts. Wooden houses survive here and there, but for the most part stone, brick and cement have now replaced them; naturally enough, there's virtually nothing in the way of conventional tourist facilities. If this has only whetted your appetite, the best thing to do is book your accommodation through *ČEDOK* in Banská Bystrica or Brezno – or pack a tent and provisions and start walking.

The **railway** which climbs the Hron valley is one of the most scenic in the whole country, and if you pick the right train you can travel from Banská Bystrica through the Slovenský raj, finally coming to a halt at Košice, in three to four hours. The slower trains take significantly longer, stopping at even the most obscure villages, such as HEĽPA (1hr by slow train from Brezno), which has just one cheap hotel, *Hotel Heľpa*. To get the magnificent view from the top of **Veľká Vápenica** (1691m), follow either the yellow- or the blue-marked tracks from the station (2–3hr). One stop further on, **POHORELÁ** lies on the footpath to the next peak along, **Andrejcová** (1519m). The only campsite (mid-June to mid-Sept) in the region is close by the next station along, Pohorelská Maša, but camping rough in the hills – while officially discouraged – is unlikely to cause any problems.

A lot of the slower trains pause for breath at ČERVENÁ SKALA, not a bad place to start one of the **best hikes** of the eastern range. Take the road to the village of ŠUMIAC, which sits on the broad sweep of the mountainside with a panoramic view west and south over the valley; then follow the blue-marked path up to **Kráľova hoľa** (1948m), the biggest bare-topped mountain east of Ďumbier. It's another three hours to **LIPTOVSKÁ TEPLIČKA**, once one of the most isolated communities in the Slovak mountains. If you want to remain in the Hron valley, there's a moderate hotel and the *Penzión u Hanky* (☎0867/941 18; ③) in TELGÁRT (4km from Kráľova hoľa; get out at Švermovo-penzión zástavka), where the railway doubles back on itself before climbing to its highest point (999m) shortly before Vernár station, on the edge of the Slovenský raj (see p.397).

The High Tatras

Rising like a giant granite reef above the patchwork Poprad plain, the **High Tatras** are for many people the main reason for venturing this far into Slovakia. Yet even after all the tourist board hype, they are still an incredible, inspirational sight – sublime, spectacular, saw-toothed and brooding. A wilderness, however, they are not. At the height of summer, visitors are shoulder to shoulder in the necklace of resorts that sit at the foot of the mountains, and things don't necessarily improve much when you take to the hills. The crux of the problem lies in the scale of the range, a mere 25km from east to west, some of which is shared with the equally eager Poles, and a lot of it out of reach to all but the most experienced climber. Part of the problem, though, is the saturation tactics of the tour operators, a logical extension of the region's overdevelopment. Yet when all's said and done, once you're above the tree line, surrounded by bare primeval scree slopes and icy blue tarns, nothing can take away the exhilarating feeling of being on top of the world.

Practicalities

Most fast trains to the Tatras arrive at the **main train station** in Poprad (known as Poprad-Tatry), which is adjacent to the **bus station**. If your budget is tight, it might be worth considering staying in Poprad (for which see overleaf); otherwise, you might as well get straight onto one of the little red electric trains which connect all the main resorts. From Poprad's tiny **airport**, west of the town (bus #12 or *ČSA* bus), there's just one flight a day to and from Prague via Bratislava – obviously a great deal more expensive than the train and heavily booked up during the summer (make your reservation in Poprad at the *ČSA* office next door to the *Hotel Gerlach*).

Accommodation in the High Tatras

Sorting out **accommodation** should be your first priority, since finding a place to stay can sometimes be difficult. As far as **hotels** are concerned, if you haven't booked in advance, you'll probably simply have to take whatever's on offer (within reason) – you may even find yourself farmed out to towns like Kežmarok (no bad thing – see p.390). The *ČEDOK* offices in Poprad and Starý Smokovec deal with all hotel bookings in the Tatras; both offices can also book **private rooms**, though the Poprad office deals just with Poprad, and Starý Smokovec has only a limited number. The easiest thing to do, if you've got your own transport, is to drive round and look out for the numerous *Zimmer Frei* signs in the area.

The situation with **hostels** is pretty dire, with the *Juniorhotel CKM* (☎0969/26 61) in Horný Smokovec the region's only official *IYHF* youth hostel. It's worth asking about this and the other hostels in the area at *ČEDOK* in Starý Smokovec on the off chance. A better bet are the **mountain chata** dotted across the mountains, which are aimed primarily at walkers, and therefore often only accessible on foot. To find out the latest on their availability, go to *Slovakoturist* in Starý Smokovec. To take advantage of anything they offer, you'll have to be pretty flexible about your itinerary, and plan your hiking around your accommodation; prices are uniformly low, and most *chata* also serve a limited selection of food in the evening.

The cheapest and most reliable option (providing the weather is warm enough) is **camping**, though having said that, the big swanky international sites are among the most expensive in either republic. The best of the dear ones is the *Tatracamp pod lesom* (mid-May to Sept) in DOLNÝ SMOKOVEC (get off at Pod lesom station), with bungalows, hot showers, kitchen facilities and a good restaurant. The two camps – *Eurocamp FICC* (open all year) and *Športcamp* (June 15–Sept 15) – just south of TATRANSKÁ LOMNICA (get off at Tatranská Lomnica-Eurocamp FICC station) are similarly priced but don't offer kitchen facilities, just takeaway roast trout instead. The TATRANSKÁ ŠTRBA site (May–Sept) is the grottiest of the lot, while the cheapest and most basic is 1km south of STARÁ LESNÁ (June 15–Sept 15). If you can get there with your own transport, the *Šarpanec* site (May 15–Oct 15) is relatively secluded, and to the east, the VRBOV site (June–Sept) has many unforeseen advantages (see "The Spiš region", p.392).

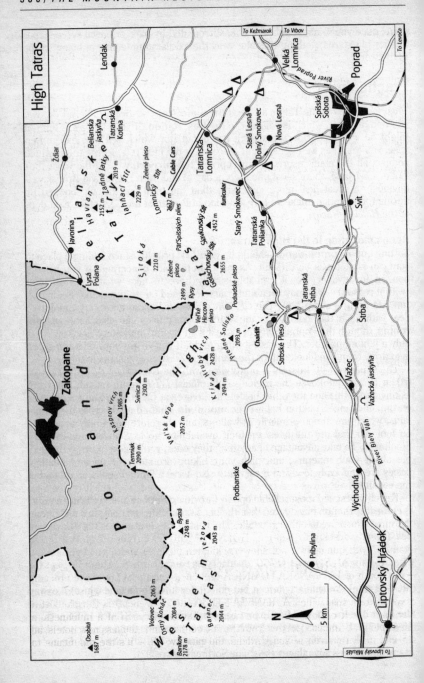

High Tatras

To Kežmarok
To Vrbov
To Levoča

Lendak
Ždiar
Javorina
Belianska jaskyňa
Tatranská Kotina
Žiadné laťky 2152 m
Havran 2019 m
Jahňací Štít
2229 m
Zelené pleso
Cable Cars
Lomnický Štít 2632 m
Tatranská Lomnica
Stará Lesná
Dolný Smokovec
Nová Lesná
Velká Lomnica
River Poprad
Spišská Sobota
Poprad
Svit
Belianské Tatry
Lysá Polana
Široka 2210 m
Zelené pleso
Par'Spišských plies
Kôprovský Štít
Sławkovský Štít 2452 m
Gerlachovský Štít 2655 m
funicular
Starý Smokovec
Tatranská Polianka
Podradské pleso
Tatranská Štrba
Zakopane
Poland
Kasprov vrch 1985 m
Świnica 2300 m
Rysy 2499 m
Velké Hincovo pleso
Pleśné Solisko
2093 m
Chairlift
Štrbské Pleso
Štrba
Važec
Vážecká jaskyňa
Velká kopa 2052 m
Krivaň 2494 m
Hruby vrch 2428 m
High Tatras
Temniak 2090 m
Bystrá 2248 m
Vežová 2043 m
Baranec 2044 m
Podbanské
Vychodná
River Biely Váh
Western Tatras
Osobitá 1687 m
Volovec 2063 m
Ostrý Roháč 2084 m
Baníkov 2178 m

N
5 km
To Liptovský Hrádok
To Liptovský Mikuláš

Poprad and around

It would be difficult to dream up a more unprepossessing town than **POPRAD** (Deutschendorf) to accompany the Tatras' effortless natural beauty. A great swathe of off-white housing encircles a small, scruffy old town centre to the accompanying backdrop of spectacular snowcapped peaks. That said, it's refreshingly free of tour groups and a lot less pretentious than the higher resorts. It's also not a bad place to stay: *ČEDOK*, at one end of the main square, opposite the town's big supermarket (Mon–Fri 9am–noon & 1–6pm, Sat 9am–2pm, Sun 9am–1pm), can book private rooms; or else you could try the *Hotel Európa* (☎092/327 44; ①), next to the train station, with a friendly, sleazy *kaviareň* and a slightly more upmarket restaurant, or the *Gerlach* on Hviezdoslavovo námestie (☎092/337 39; ②).

Poprad was originally one of the twenty or so Spiš towns (see p.390), though the only hint of this is on the long village-like main square, **námestie Duklianskych hrdinov**, five minutes' walk south of the train station, and useful for picking up provisions if you're planning any hiking. There's a good bakery and a small vegetable market on the north side of the square, while the south side is taken up with a host of new shops, including a bookshop where you might be able to pick up relevant **maps** – look out for the invaluable *Tatranské strediská* map which contains street plans of all the major resorts (excluding Poprad, which has its own map).

Spišská Sobota

If you do end up staying in Poprad, the village of **SPIŠSKÁ SOBOTA** (Georgenberg), just 2km northeast (bus #2, #3 or #4), makes for an enjoyable cloudy afternoon's outing. Only a handful of the thousands of visitors who pass through Poprad make it here, yet it couldn't be more different from its ugly, oversized neighbour. Except during Mass on Sundays there are few signs of life in its leafy square, and the only clue that this was once a thriving Spiš town is the two-storey burgher houses, distinguished by their stone facades and the wooden gables whose eaves hang six feet or so over the square. At the eastern end of the square, an entire row has been recently renovated and smartly whitewashed, while in the centre huddle the old radnica, the obligatory Renaissance belfry and the church of **sv Juraj** (St George), whose origins go back even further than its present late-Gothic appearance. Its vaulting is incredibly sophisticated for this part of the world, as are the font and a couple of the smaller chapels, but the real treat is the main **altar** carved by Pavol of Levoča in 1516, which includes a reworking of the famous *Last Supper* predella from the main church in Levoča. The **museum** (Mon–Sat 9am–4pm) at no. 33, opposite the south door of the church, is worth a look if only for the opportunity to see the inside of one of the typical town houses.

The Tatra National Park (TANAP)

Cute red tram-like trains trundle across the fields, linking Poprad with the string of resorts and spas which nestle at the foot of the Tatras and lie within the **Tatra National Park** or **TANAP**. To be honest, they're all much of a muchness, a mixture of half-timbered lodges from the last century and tasteless new hotels, all set in eminently civilised spa gardens and pine woods – it's the mountains to which they give access that make them worth visiting.

Štrbské Pleso and around

Founded in 1873 by the local Hungarian lord, József Szentiványi, **ŠTRBSKÉ PLESO**'s life as a mountain resort began in earnest some twenty years later, with the building of the rack railway which climbs 430m in just 5km from Štrba on the main line below. At 1351m, it's the highest Tatran resort. It's also the brashest, with reams of takeaway *gofry* stands and eyesore hotel hoardings, though this has more to do with its having hosted the 1970 World Ski Championships than anything else. The ski resort part of town is north of the *pleso*, the second largest of the glacial lakes from which the spa gets its name; swimming in the lake is forbidden.

In summer, the only working lift is the chairlift to Solisko, from where the climb to the top of **Predné Solisko** (2093m) takes well under an hour. As with all such lifts in the Tatras, book your ride well in advance to avoid the giant snake-like ticket queues that have usually formed by mid-morning. If you want to explore a whole ring of mystical glacial lakes which in folk legends used to be known as "the eyes and windows of another sea", the trek over **Bystré sedlo** (2314m), which skirts the jagged Solisko range, is a round trip of around eight hours – it's a one-way path, so you have to do it anticlockwise, heading from east to west.

HIKING, SKIING & CLIMBING IN THE HIGH TATRAS

It is as well to remember that the High Tatras are an alpine range and as such demand a little more respect and preparation than Slovakia's other mountains. Most of the trails described in the text are far from easy walking, and many involve the use of chains to traverse rock screes. The whole area is part of the **Tatra National Park (TANAP)**, whose often quite strict rules and regulations are designed to protect what is a valuable, fragile ecosystem – you may find that you have to pay a small fee to use some of the trails, so be sure to take some small change with you. The most important rule is to stick to the marked paths; before setting out, get hold of a *Vysoké Tatry* map, which shows all the marked paths in the TANAP.

In the summer months, the most popular trails and summits are literally chock-a-block with Czech, German and Slovak walkers, and in some ways, the best thing for the mountains would be if everyone gave them a rest for a few seasons. One of the reasons for the summer stampede is that many of the most exhilarating treks are only open from July 1 to October 30. This is primarily due to the **weather**, probably the single most important consideration when planning your trek. Rainfall is actually heaviest in June, July and August; thunderstorms and even the occasional summer snowstorm are also features of the unpredictable alpine climate. It may be scorching hot down in the valley, yet below freezing on top of Rysy.

Hiking: the golden rules

• Watch the **weather forecast** (easy enough to read even in Slovak – look for *počasie* in the paper).

• Set out **early** (the weather is always better in the morning), and tell someone when and where you're going.

• Don't leave the **tree line** (about 2000m) unless visibility is good, and when the clouds close in, start descending immediately.

• Bring with you: a pair of **sturdy boots** to combat the relentless boulders in the higher reaches; a **whistle** (for blowing six times every minute if you need help); and a flask of water.

A gentle one-hour walk through the forest along the red-marked path to **Popradské pleso** is all many people manage on a lightning Tatra tour. It's a beautiful spot to have a picnic, although given its popularity, by no means tranquil. Those with sufficient stamina can try the punishing climb to the **sedlo pod Ostrvou** (1959m), which gives a fantastic bird's-eye view of the lake. This red-marked path, known as the *Magistrála*, skirts the tree line all the way to **Zelené pleso**, 20km away in the far east of the range. If you don't have such boundless enthusiasm for walking, stroll along the yellow-marked track to the **symbolický cintorín** of wooden crosses set up to commemorate the considerable number of people who've lost their lives in the mountains.

One of the most popular climbs in the Tatras is **Rysy** (2499m) on the Slovak–Polish border, which Lenin himself once climbed. If you're planning on doing Rysy, you won't have time to picnic by the lake, since it's a good six hours' return trip from Popradské pleso via *Chata pod Rysmi*, at 2250m the highest (and coldest) of the mountain chalets, just below the first peak of Váha (2343m). If you can find a place to sit down on the often crowded summit, it has to be one of the best views in Europe. Another possible climb from Popradské pleso is the eight-hour sweep over **Vyšoké Kôprovské sedlo** (2180m) via the largest lake of the lot, **Veľké Hincovo pleso**.

Skiing

The High Tatras are as popular for **skiing** in winter as they are for hiking in summer. The first snows arrive as early as November but the season doesn't really get going for another month. By the end of March, you can only really ski on the higher slopes reached by chair- (as opposed to ski-) lifts. The main ski resort is ŠTRBSKÉ PLESO, which hosts the occasional international as well as national events; Hrebienok (near Starý Smokovec) and Sklanaté pleso (near Tatranská Lomnica) are the other two main ski areas. Queues for the lifts can be pretty horrendous – if so, head out to the quieter pistes around ŽDIAR or even JEZERSKO in the **Spišská Magura** hills.

Wherever you go, you'd be best advised to bring your own equipment, although gear can be rented from *Hotel Patria* in Strbské Pleso. If you've got the cash to spare and want to have it all planned out before you go, international branches of *ČEDOK* organise skiing holidays to the High and Low Tatras – see "Information" in *Basics*.

Climbing

To go **rock-climbing** in the High Tatras you need to be a member of a recognised climbing club and be able to produce a membership card. Otherwise, you are required by law to hire a guide from the *Horská služba* (see below), which costs a fair amount, though up to five people can share the cost of one guide. It's possible to climb throughout the year, but as with skiing you should beware of avalanches. Note that *Cesta uzavretá – nebezpečenstvo lavín* means "Path Closed – Beware of Avalanches". The most popular climbs are in the vicinity of Lomnický štít, but since **Gerlachovský štít**, the highest peak in the Tatras, can only be ascended by legitimate climbers, it too is high on the hit list.

For **advice** on where and where not to climb, tips on the weather and emergency help, contact *Horská služba*, the **mountain rescue service** next door to *ČEDOK* in Starý Smokovec (☎0969/28 20 or 28 55). As with skiing, it's best to bring your own gear with you.

Kriváň (2494m), the westernmost Tatran peak (and, in comparison, relatively easy to climb), is a short, sharp eight-hour return journey from Štrbské Pleso via Jamské pleso. In 1841, Slovak nationalists Štúr and Hurban staged a patriotic march up the mountain, a tradition which is continued to this day at the end of August. Like Rysy, it's a popular route, and at the height of summer, the top of the mountain can be difficult to spot under the great mass of walkers. If that sounds like your idea of hell, try some of the trails around PODBANSKÉ or even further afield in the Western Tatras (see p.371).

Tatranská Lomnica

TATRANSKÁ LOMNICA, 5km northeast of Starý Smokovec, is a smaller version of the latter; people come here on bad weather days, or to go up **Lomnický štít** (2632m), the third highest mountain in the Tatras, accessible by a hair-raising cable car which sets off from beside the *Grand Hotel Praha* (aptly described by one local guide as "visibly ripe for restoration"). It's difficult to fault the view from Lomnický štít, but purists may disapprove of the concrete steps and handrails built to prevent the crowds from pushing each other off the rocky summit. If you find difficulties obtaining tickets for the cable car, try the chairlift to Lomnický sedlo, the craggy saddle 500m below Lomnický štít.

Hiking options are not so good from Tatranská Lomnica, and most treks are best started from other resorts. Otherwise, cloudy days can be filled with horse-racing (Sundays only), outdoor chess and the **TANAP museum** (Mon–Fri 8.30am–noon, Sat & Sun 9am–noon), whose smart displays of stuffed Tatran animals and plants accompany a brief history of the region. It was only explored for the first time in the late eighteenth century when a Scotsman, Robert Townson (see p.403), who was botanising his way round Hungary, ascended Kežmarský štít and a number of other peaks, against the advice of the local guides.

Hikes around Starý Smokovec

The old Saxon settlement of **STARÝ SMOKOVEC** is the most established and most central of all the spas. Along with neighbouring settlements of Nový, Horný and Dolný Smokovec, it makes up the conglomeration known as **Smokovce**. The spa's old nucleus is the stretch of lawn between the half-timbered supermarket and the copper-coloured *Grand Hotel*, a sight in its own right. Built in 1904 in a vaguely alpine neo-Baroque, it's worth having a drink in the hotel café, if only to check out the wonderful 1920s decor. There are also two **wooden churches** worth seeking out in Smokovce: the neo-Gothic parish church behind the *Grand Hotel*, and, in Dolný Smokovec, the turn-of-the-century chapel perching on arcaded stilts.

The cheapest **hotel accommodation** available through *ČEDOK* (Mon–Fri 8am–7pm, Sat & Sun 9.45am–3pm) is the *Šport* (②), 200m to the east; the *Grand Hotel* is much pricier (☎0969/25 01; ⑤), but without doubt the finest guesthouse around. You can book yourself into a **mountain chata** through *Slovakoturist* (Mon–Fri 8am–4pm), a couple of minutes' walk east of the main train station; they can also arrange **private rooms** in Nová and Stará Lesná. The remarkably unpretentious *Tatra* restaurant, a short step from the train station and next door to *ČEDOK*, is a good place to have a large lunch or an early supper – open until 8pm.

If the weather's good, the most straightforward and rewarding climb is to follow the blue-marked path from behind the *Grand Hotel* to the summit of

Slavkovský štít (2452m), a return journey of nine hours. Again from behind the *Grand Hotel*, a narrow-gauge funicular climbs 250m to HREBIENOK (45min by foot), one of the lesser ski resorts on the edge of the pine forest proper. The smart wooden *Bilíkova chata* (☎0969/24 39; ①) is a five-minute walk from the top of the funicular. Just past the *chata*, the path continues through the wood, joining up with two others, from Tatranská Lesná and Tatranská Lomnica respectively, before passing the gushing waterfalls of the **Studenovodské vodopády**.

At the fork just past the waterfall, a whole variety of trekking possibilities opens up. The right-hand fork takes you up the **Malá Studená dolina** and then zigzags above the tree line to the *Téryho chata*, set in a lunar landscape by the shores of the **Päť Spišských plies**. Following the spectacular, hair-raising trail over the Priečne sedlo to *Zbojnicka chata*, you can return via the Veľká studená dolina – an eight-hour round trip from Hrebienok. This is a one-way hiking path, so you have to do it this way round; note that it involves a 100ft rock climb on a fixed chain, and is not recommended for the fainthearted. Alternatively, you could continue from the *Téryho chata* to JAVORINA, nine hours away near the Polish border, and return by bus.

Another possibility is to take the left-hand fork to the *Zbojnicka chata*, and continue to Zamruznuté pleso, which sits in the shadow of **Východná Vysoká** (2428m); only a thirty-minute hike from the lake, this dishes out the best view there is for the non-climber, of **Gerlachovský štít** (2655m), the highest mountain in Slovakia. To get back down to the valley, either descend the Poľský hreben and return to Starý Smokovec via the *Sliezsky dom* (9hr round trip without the Východná Vysoká ascent), or continue north and track the Polish border to LYSÁ POĽANA, the Slovak border post (10hr one way), returning by bus to Starý Smokovec.

Tatranská Kotlina, Ždiar and on to Poland

The overkill in the central part of the TANAP makes trekking from the relative obscurity of **TATRANSKÁ KOTLINA** an attractive alternative. Most people, however, come here not to walk, but to visit the **Belianska jaskyňa** (Tues–Sun mid-May to mid-Sept 9.30am–3.30pm; mid-Sept to mid-May tours at 9.30am, 11am & 2.30pm), fifteen minutes from the main road, whose pleasures include rock formations whimsically named the *Leaning Tower of Pisa* and *White Pagoda*, and an underground lake; another bad-weather time-filler.

The **Zelené pleso** makes a good hiking target, surrounded by a vast rocky amphitheatre of granite walled peaks including the mean-looking north face of Lomnický štít. To get there, take the blue-marked path from the southwest end of Tatranská Kotlina, and turn right onto the green trail which ends at the ruined *chata* by Biele pleso (2–3hr). From here it's half an hour to the fully functioning *Brnčalova chata* which sits by the green tarn itself. If you've still got time and energy on your hands, traverse the ridge to the north and mount the summit of Jahňaci štít (2–3hr round trip).

The mountains of the **Belianske Tatry**, which form the final alpine ridge in the north of the TANAP, are out of bounds to everyone except the native chamois, but you can skirt round their southern slopes via the Kopské sedlo (30min on the blue trail from Biele pleso) and then on to Javorina (2–3hr).

On the other side of the Belianske Tatry, slightly off the main road to Javorina (and to Zakopane in Poland) is **ŽDIAR**, a traditional rural community founded in the seventeenth century, which still lives off the land although it is now struggling to survive under the ever-increasing pressures of the neighbouring tourist industry. In all, there are numerous wooden cottages in varying stages of modernisation, a half-timbered cinema and an unremarkable brick church. One of the houses has been converted into a modest folk museum, the **Ždiarska izba** (Mon–Fri 9am–4pm, Sat & Sun 9am–noon), while another will provide you with a meal and possibly a bed. So far, the place still resembles a muddy working village more than a tourist skanzen – and it's all the better for it.

If you're continuing your journey **into Poland**, there's a daily bus service which will take you as far as LYSÁ POĽANA, 12km west of Ždiar. From there you can walk across the border into Poland and catch a bus to the main Polish Tatra resort of Zakopane (see *Poland: the Rough Guide* for details).

travel details

Trains

Connections with Bratislava: Zvolen (5 daily; 3hr 20min–4hr); Banská Bystrica (1 daily; 4hr 30min); Žilina (14 daily; 2hr 20min); Ružomberok (9 daily; 3hr); Liptovský Mikuláš (11 daily; 3hr 30min); Poprad (11 daily; 4hr 15min–5hr).

From Banská Bystrica to Zvolen (up to hourly; 20–40min); Martin (6 daily; 1hr 50min); Brezno (11 daily; 55min–1hr 30min); Červená Skala (5 daily; 1hr 40min–2hr 30min).

From Zvolen to Detva (9 daily; 40min); Lučenec (15 daily; 1hr–1hr 30min); Kremnica (9 daily; 1hr); Turčianske Teplice/Martin (10 daily; 1hr 20min–1hr 50min/1hr 40min–2hr 15min).

From Žilina to Strečno/Šútovo (up to 12 daily; 15min/45min); Rajec (9 daily; 45min); Vrútky/Kraľovany (up to 20 daily; 30min/40min); Ružomberok (19 daily; 1hr); Liptovský Mikuláš (22 daily; 1hr–1hr 30min); Poprad (21 daily; 2hr 10min).

From Kraľovany to Istebné/Dolný Kubín/Oravský Podzámok/Podbiel/Trstená (13 daily; 16min/35min/55min/1hr 30min/2hr).

From Poprad (Poprad-Tatry) to Starý Smokovec/Štrbské Pleso (up to hourly; 45min/1hr 40min); Tatranská Lomnica (up to 15 daily; 25min).

Buses

From Banská Bystrica to Banská Štiavnica (up to 6 daily; 1hr 30min); Ružomberok (up to 8 daily; 1hr 20min); Martin/Žilina (up to 6 daily; 1hr 15min/2hr).

From Žilina to Terchová/Vrátn dolina (up to hourly; 45min/1hr); Čičmany (up to 6 daily; 1hr 20min).

From Liptovský Mikuláš to Demänovska dolina/Jasna (up to hourly; 40min).

From Poprad to Ždiar/Lysá Poľana (up to hourly; 1hr/1hr 30min); Zakopane (1 daily; 2hr 15min).

CHAPTER TEN

EAST SLOVAKIA

Stretching from the High Tatras east to the Ukrainian border, the countryside of **East Slovakia** (Východné Slovensko) is decidedly different from the rest of the country. The obligatory forests of pine and spruce give way gradually to acres of beech forests in the east, at their best in September and October when the hills turn into a fanfare of burnt reds and browns.

Ethnically, East Slovakia is probably the most diverse region in the country, different groups coexisting even within a single valley. A third of the country's **Romanies** live here, mostly on the edge of Slovak villages, in ghettoes of almost medieval squalor. In the ribbon-villages of the north and east, the **Rusyn** minority – hill-dwelling peasants whose homeland became part of the Soviet Ukraine after 1945 – struggle to preserve their culture and religion, while large numbers of **Hungarians** live along the southern border. Even the **East Slovaks** themselves are thought of as some kind of separate race by other Slovaks; indeed, before 1918 there was a movement to create a separate state for them.

A short train ride east of the High Tatras, the intriguing medieval towns of the **Spiš region** constitute East Slovakia's architectural high point, while to the south, the **Slovenský raj** offers some highly unorthodox hiking possibilities. Further south still, along the Hungarian border, the karst region of the **Slovenský kras** boasts one of the longest cave systems in the world. Along the northern border with Poland, **Carpatho-Ruthenia** – where the country's remaining Rusyn population lives – is a fascinating, isolated landscape, riddled with wooden Uniate churches, among the few monuments in the region to have survived the destruction of the last war. After spending time in the rural backwaters, **Košice**, the East Slovak capital, can be a welcome, though somewhat startling return to city life, containing enough of interest for a stopover at least before heading east towards the Ukrainian border and the deserted beech forests of **the Vihorlat**.

The stream of tourists who make it as far as the High Tatras becomes a mere trickle east of Poprad (see p.381), which means extra difficulties as regards both transport and accommodation outside the two main areas: the Spiš region and Košice, the regional capital. It's not that the hotels are full or the railways slow, it's just that they barely exist. The best advice is to take a tent as a fall-back, and be prepared to be flexible about your itinerary.

ACCOMMODATION PRICES

Each place to stay in this chapter has a symbol which corresponds to one of seven **price categories**:

   ① Under 500kčs   ② 500–750kčs   ③ 750–1000kčs   ④ 1000–1500kčs
      ⑤ 1500–2000kčs   ⑥ 2000–3000kčs   ⑦ 3000kčs and upwards

All prices are for the cheapest **double room** available, which usually means without private bath or shower in the less expensive places. For a **single room**, expect to pay around two-thirds the price of a double.

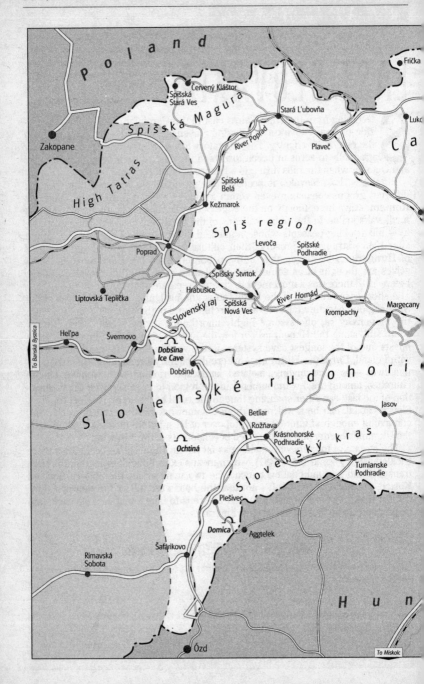

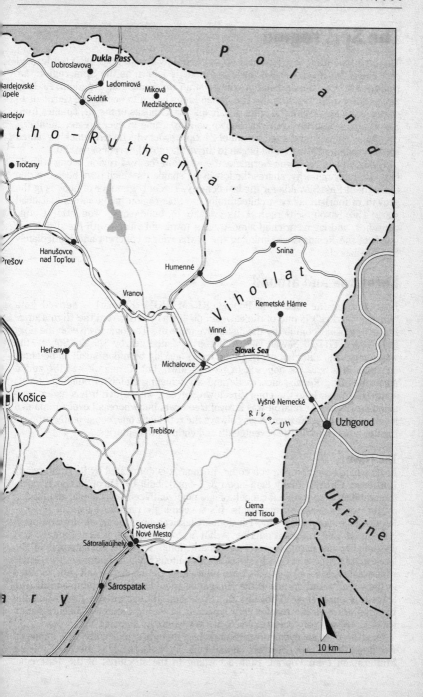

The Spiš region

The land that stretches northeast up the Poprad valley to the Polish border and east along the River Hornád towards Prešov is known as the **Spiš region**, for centuries a semi-autonomous province within the Hungarian kingdom. As long ago as the twelfth century, the Hungarian kings began to encourage Germans to colonise the area. With the whiff of valuable ore deposits in the air, families from Saxony (to whom the area was known as *Zips*) came in ever greater numbers, eventually establishing a federation of 24 Zips towns which were quickly granted special trading privileges and began to thrive like no other region around.

Today, minus its ethnic Germans, the whole of the Spiš region, along with its large Romany minority, shares the low living standards which have been the rule throughout East Slovakia for the last century. The only glimmer of hope is in the growth of tourism, since architecturally the Spiš region has a substantial head start. The Saxon settlers had the wealth to build some wonderful Gothic churches, and later enriched almost every town and village with the distinctive touch of the Renaissance, imbuing the towns with a coherent and immediately likeable aspect.

Kežmarok and around

Just 14km up the road from Poprad, **KEŽMAROK** (Käsmark – derived from "Cheese Market") is one of the easiest Spiš towns to visit from the High Tatras. It's an odd place, combining the distinctive traits of a Teutonic town with the dozy feel of an oversized Slovak village. If you've visited nearby Spišská Sobota, the wooden gables, shingled overhanging eaves and big barn doors will all be familiar signs of a Spiš (as opposed to Slovak) town, but Kežmarok has the added attractions of a Renaissance castle and a fascinating clutch of buildings on its southern fringe. Like the chief Zips town, Levoča, with which it has had a long-standing rivalry, Kežmarok was a royal free town, but whereas Levoča remained loyal to the crown, Kežmarok was always the rebellious one, consistently supporting the rebel cause in the seventeenth and eighteenth centuries.

The Town

From whichever direction you come, Kežmarok is dominated by its giant, gaudy **Lutheran Church** (daily 8am–noon & 1–5pm), built by Theophil von Hansen, the architect responsible for much of late nineteenth-century Vienna, and funded by the town's wealthy merchants. It's a seemingly random fusion of styles – Renaissance campanile, Moorish dome, Classical dimensions, all dressed up in grey-green and rouge rendering – but a concoction of which Hansen, and presumably his patrons, were particularly fond. If you're accustomed to the intense atmosphere of Czechoslovakia's ubiquitous Catholic churches, the simple whitewashed hall looks like it's been ransacked. On the right-hand side, swathed in the wreaths and sashes of the Hungarian tricolour, sits the tomb and mausoleum of **Count Imre Thököly**, the Protestant Hungarian rebel who had the Imperial army on the run for eight years or so during the anti-Habsburg Kuruc revolt of 1678, before being exiled to Turkey where he died in 1705.

Next door is an even more remarkable, though significantly less imposing **wooden Protestant church**, again built by a German – this time Georg Müttermann from Poprad. Built according to the strictures of the 1681 edict which stipulated that Protestant churches could only be erected outside the town walls, and constructed entirely out of wood, it couldn't be further from the Viennese cosmopolitanism of its neighbour. By all accounts, it's a work of great carpentry and artistry inside, capable of seating almost 1500 people. Having said that, it's currently closed for an extensive restoration.

One more building here deserves mention – the **Lutheran Lycée**, architecturally fairly nondescript but soon to be restored and transformed into a museum of Slovak literature. Lutheranism, which was rife in the nether regions of the Hungarian empire, especially those parts colonised by Germans, was also the religion of most of Slovakia's leading nationalists. Men like the Czechophile Pavol Šafárik, the poet Martin Rázus, and the writer Martin Kukučín all studied here before the Hungarians closed it down in the 1860s.

The old town itself is little more than two long leafy streets punctuated by a mixture of plane and fir trees, which set off from the important-looking boxy central radnica to form a V-shaped fork. The town's Catholic church, **sv Kríž** (Mon–Fri 9am–noon & 2–5pm), is tucked away in the dusty back alleys between the two prongs, once surrounded by its own line of fortifications, now protected by an appealing Renaissance belfry whose uppermost battlements burst into sgraffito life in the best Spiš tradition. It's currently under restoration, but if the work is complete, it's worth having a look at the side altars by Pavol of Levoča.

The **castle** (Tues–Sun 9am–4pm), at the end of the right-hand fork, is the main reason the occasional stray Tatran tour group makes it here. It was the property of the Thököly family for many years, until the Habsburgs confiscated it as punishment for the family's support of the aforementioned Kuruc revolt. To be honest, though, the museum of historical artefacts that now occupies its bare rooms doesn't really justify the hour-long guided tour.

Finally, if you've time to spare, you could do worse than take a quick turn under the sycamore trees of the local **cemetery**, just off the old *Ringstrasse* (at this point called Toporcerova, and the main road from Poprad). It's a fascinating testament to the diverse nationalities which have inhabited the region over the last century. The remaining Slovak peasantry continue to honour their dead with simple wooden crosses, while the vestigial German community stubbornly stick to their own language; *Ruhe Sanft!* (Rest in Peace) is something you'll see written on the more recent headstones, not just on the ornate (and uncared-for) turn-of-the-century graves belonging to the now displaced German and Hungarian elite.

Practicalities

Arriving in Kežmarok by train is by far the most pleasant introduction to the town, thanks to the yellowing nineteenth-century *Bahnhof* (there's also a regular bus service from Poprad). Kežmarok is near enough to the High Tatras to figure as a possible base for exploring the mountains, providing you have your own transport. That few people bother to do this is to your advantage, since **accommodation** is, as a result, fairly easy to find. *ČEDOK*, on the northern edge of the old town, can book cheap private rooms for you; otherwise there's the *Lipa* on Toporecova (✆0968/20 37; ②), or the *Štart* (✆0968/29 15; ①), which lies in the woods to the north of the castle, a good twenty-minute walk from the train station. The place where all the coach parties come **to eat** is the *reštaurácia* in the castle cellars, but if that's booked you'll do little worse at any of the hotel restaurants.

Vrbov

If you're a camper but also a hedonist, the hot sulphur springs at **VRBOV**, 5km south of Kežmarok, are the place to head for. Without your own set of wheels, you'll have to rely on hitching or the infrequent bus service from Kežmarok and Poprad. The village itself is no more than a couple of grubby streets and the obligatory Romany ghetto, but continuing on the road south, there's a hotel and restaurant which go by the unlikely name of *Hotel Flipper* – no prizes for guessing it's a fish restaurant, and a very good one at that. The rather dubious smell of bad eggs emanates from the nearby sulphurised **natural spring swimming pool** (daily 8am–10pm). It's an extremely popular spot, and in the evening, the pool becomes something of a floodlit social centre, as the locals immerse themselves in the fizzy, steaming, therapeutic water. Should you wish to stay, there's a **campsite** (mid-June to mid-Sept), beyond the pool, but it's not the best of sites, not least because of the steep bank on which campers must try to pitch their tents.

Stará Ľubovňa and the Pieniny

From Kežmarok, the railway draws a wide semicircle as it follows the Poprad river round to STARÁ ĽUBOVŇA, a scruffy, somewhat forlorn town, but marginally better placed for approaching the **Pieniny** than Kežmarok. As early as the 1930s, the Polish and Czechoslovak governments declared this small eruption of fissured limestone rocks which straddles the Dunajec river the **Pieniny national park** or **PIENAP**. Today, despite the continuing isolation of the nearby Zamagurie region (Zamagurie means literally "Behind the Spišská Magura hills"), tourism in the Pieniny on both sides of the border is flourishing, particularly the ever-popular **raft trips** down the Dunajec (see box below).

Stará Ľubovňa

If you've an hour or so to spare in **STARÁ ĽUBOVŇA** waiting for the next bus, head in the direction of the mostly ruined castle which occupies a high spur over-

---

RAFT TRIPS IN THE PIENINY

Raft trips (daily June–Sept) are becoming big business for people on both sides of the Dunajec, which means that organisationally the whole thing couldn't be simpler. As soon as you arrive at ČERVENÝ KLÁŠTOR, the touts begin their hard sell, relieving you of your money and giving you a departure time and ticket. The *plti* (rafts) themselves are not much more than a series of mini-kayaks tied together, punted downstream by locals dressed up in the traditional rafters' costume. The rapids the rafts float down are positively benevolent compared to the brittle white cliffs which rise up on either side. River meanderings make the whole trip about an hour in length, but if you'd prefer to do your own thing, the trip can be made on foot by following the red-marked path 10km along the tree-lined river bank.

At the end of the gorge, either try hitching a ride with one of the buses shipping people back, or else walk 3km along the road to LESNICA, then 5km across the hills back to Červený Kláštor, where there's a **campsite**, should you wish to stay over. In addition to the regular raft trips there's a canoe slalom competition on the river here every September, and a folk festival in mid-June. If you've time to spare at any other time of the year, pop into the fourteenth-century former **Carthusian monastery** near the campsite, now a museum of the region.

looking the town, 2km to the west. From the fifteenth to the eighteenth century, it was the main residence of the local Polish despot, who lorded it over the thirteen Zips towns pawned to the Polish crown by the Hungarians in the fifteenth century. Certain sections have remained intact and now serve as a **museum** (Tues–Fri 8am–4pm, Sat & Sun 9am–5pm) commemorating those who were tortured in the castle by the Nazis.

Far more interesting than the above, however, is the **folk skanzen** (Tues–Sun 10–11.30am & 12.30–4pm), set up in the grassy meadow below the castle in the late 1970s to preserve the precious wooden architecture of the Zamagurie region to the west of Stará Ľubovňa. In the late nineteenth century, here as in other rural parts of East Slovakia, malnutrition was the norm and starvation by no means exceptional. People emigrated in droves to other parts of Europe and in particular to the United States. Many of the cottages brought here from the surrounding villages were simply abandoned, and some of them now contain mementoes and personal details of the last owners (in Slovak only). It's a well thought out museum, and includes an early nineteenth-century wooden Uniate church whose richly decorated interior can be viewed on request of the key (*kľúč*).

In the unlikely event of your needing a place to stay, try the *Vrchovina* (☎0962/ 233 11; ①), across the river and up the hill from the train and bus stations; and for food, the *vináreň* on the main square. If you're heading north into Poland, two slow trains a day crawl across the border to Muszyna (change at Plaveč on the Slovak side).

Levoča and around

Twenty-five kilometres east from Poprad across the broad sweep of the Spiš countryside, the walled town of **LEVOČA** (Leutschau), positioned on a slight incline, makes a wonderfully medieval impression. Capital of one of the richest regions of Slovakia for more than four centuries, its present-day population of around 11,000 is, if anything, less than it was during its halcyon days. The town's showpiece main square is hit by the occasional tour group from the Tatras, but otherwise its dusty backstreets are yours.

The first attempts at founding a town here were completely trashed by the Tartars. Then, in the thirteenth-century wave of Saxon immigration that followed, Levoča became the capital of the Zips towns, a position it maintained until its slow but steady decline in the eighteenth and nineteenth centuries. This led to a kind of architectural mummification, and it's the fifteenth and sixteenth centuries – the golden age of Levoča – that still dominate the town today.

The old town

The Euclidian efficiency with which the old town is laid out, chessboard-style, means that wherever you breach the walls, you'll inevitably end up at the main square, **námestie Majstra Pavla**, itself a long, regular rectangle. Most of Levoča's treasures are located here, not least the threesome of the Protestant church, town hall and Catholic church, which dominate the central space. To the north, by the small park and bandstand, is possibly the least distinguished but most important building on the square, the former *Waaghaus* or municipal **weigh-house** (now a school), which was the financial might behind the town during its trading heyday. In 1321 King Charles Robert granted the town the Law of Storage, an unusual medieval edict which obliged every merchant passing through the region to hold up at Levoča for at least fourteen days, pay various taxes and allow the locals first refusal on all their goods. In addition, Levoča merchants were later exempted from such laws when passing through other towns. Small wonder then that the town burghers were exceptionally wealthy.

Of the three freestanding buildings on the main square paid for with these riches, it's the Catholic church of **sv Jakub** (May–Sept Tues–Sat 8am–5pm, Sun 1–4pm; Oct–April Tues–Sat 8am–4pm) that contains the most valuable booty. Every nook and cranny of the building is crammed with medieval religious art, the star attraction being the early sixteenth-century wooden altarpiece by **Master Pavol of Levoča**, topped by a forest of finials and pinnacles, which, at 18.6m in height, make it reputedly the tallest of its kind in the world. At the time, the clarity and characterisation of the figures in the predella's *Last Supper* must have seemed incredible: they were modelled on the local merchants who commissioned the work (Pavol and his apprentices can also be seen behind the figure of Saint James in the central panel). The disciples are depicted in various animated poses – eating, caught in conversation, or in the case of Saint John, fast asleep across Christ's lap. Only Judas, thirty pieces of silver over his shoulder, has a look of anguish, while Christ presides with serene poise. The work took over ten years to complete, and is only one of the many Gothic altars in the church which deserve attention.

To the south of the church is the most attractive of the central buildings, the former **radnica** (same times as above), built in a sturdy Renaissance style. Downstairs, the local administration still holds sway, along with a few tables and chairs for ice-cream eaters; upstairs (where you get your ticket) there's a museum on the Spiš region and some fairly dubious contemporary art exhibitions on the top floor. Close by the southeastern corner of the town hall stands the **Klietka hanby** (Cage of Disgrace), a rather beautiful wrought-iron contraption erected by Protestants in around 1600 as a pillory for women. The third building in the centre of the square is the oddly squat **Lutheran church**, which replaced its wooden predecessor in the early nineteenth century in an uncompromisingly Neoclassical style, its bare pudding-basin interior not worth the search around for the key.

The square is otherwise lined with some fine sixteenth-century burgher houses, at their most eye-catching in the **Thurzov dom** – at first glance a flamboyant Renaissance structure, though in fact its most striking feature, the sgraffito decoration around the windows, dates from the restoration work of 1824. Further down on the east side of the square is a simple two-storey building which historians reckon to be the **House of Master Pavol of Levoča** (Tues–Sun 10am–5pm). All that's known about Pavol is what little can be gleaned from the town hall records: he was born around 1460, sat briefly on the town council, died in 1537, and his son was murdered by a man from Kraków. Even this much is missing from the house's exhibition, which concentrates more on the Kotrba brothers who made good the woodworm of the centuries in the 1950s. Unless you're a real fan of his work it hardly seems worth the effort, since it contains only later copies of the same work displayed in the church.

The rest of the town's grid plan is made up of one-storey hovels, once the exclusive abodes of Saxon craftsmen, now crumbling homes to the town's Slovaks and Romanies. You could spend an enjoyable hour wandering the streets and doing the circuit of the rundown walls, but other than the curiosity value of the nineteenth-century German *gymnasium* in the southwest of the town, there's nothing specific to see.

THE MARIAN PILGRIMAGE

Once a year, Levoča goes wild. As the first weekend of July approaches, up to 250,000 Catholics have been known to descend on the town to attend the biggest of Slovakia's **Marian pilgrimages** which takes place in (and inevitably around) the church on Marianska hora, the sacred hill 2km north of the town. Families travel – in some cases walking – for miles to arrive in time for the first Mass, which takes place around 6pm on the Saturday evening. The party goes on throughout the night, with hourly Masses being given in the church and singing and dancing (and drinking) going on outside in the fields until the grand finale of High Mass at 10am Sunday morning, generally presided over by someone fairly high up in the church hierarchy. If you've never witnessed a Marian festival, this is the place to do it, though it only marks the beginning of a whole host of festivals which take place over the next two months in villages all over Slovakia. The main Greek-Catholic (Uniate) pilgrimage takes place some 40km northeast of Levoča, near the village of Ľutina, on the third weekend in August.

Practicalities

Since Levoča lies at the end of a poorly served branch line that begins at Spišská Nová Ves, most people arrive at the **bus station**, close to the Košická brána in the northeast corner of town. Outside the annual pilgrimage (see above), **accommodation** shouldn't be hard to find, though the choice is limited to the *Faix* (☎0966/25 59; ①) on the main road, and the **campsite** (June–Sept), a two-kilometre walk north of Levoča, in the woods by LEVOČSKÁ DOLINA. Two good places to grab a bite to eat are the cellars of the *Breurova pivnica*, below a glass and crystal shop on the east side of the square, and the meatier option of *U 3 Apostolov*, above a butchers further along on the same side.

Spišský Štvrtok

Easy to spot on the road between Poprad and Levoča, but not necessarily reason enough to get off the bus, is **SPIŠSKÝ ŠTVRTOK** (Donnersmarkt), whose splendid thirteenth-century church sits atop the village hill, its masonry tower topped by an impressive wooden spire with four corner pinnacles. The perfect French Gothic side chapel from 1473 which emerges from the south wall was commissioned by the Zápoľskýs to be the family mausoleum, and is, without doubt, one of the most surprising architectural sights in East Slovakia.

Spišská Nová Ves

Thirteen kilometres south of Levoča, **SPIŠSKÁ NOVÁ VES** (Neudorf) is the modern-day capital of the Spiš region, a relatively industrious town with a population of around 35,000, whose origins are as old as Levoča's, but which has borne the brunt of the changes wrought on the region over the last century. Pawned to the Poles at the height of the Hussite Wars, along with twelve other Spiš towns, it fell to the Habsburgs in 1772, who immediately made it the Spiš capital, a fact which played a significant part in the demise of its old rival, Levoča. As a mining town, it was virtually guaranteed to get itself on the main Košice–Bohumín railway line when it was built in the nineteenth century. What that means today is that it's a good place from which to visit both the Slovenský raj and Levoča by train, but otherwise has only a few residual pleasures.

The main square is an excessively broad leafy avenue in the style of Prešov and Košice, dotted with important-looking buildings, not least the municipal theatre in grand turn-of-the-century mood – definitely *the* place to hang out once its refurbishment is complete. The yellow Gothic church contains a couple of minor works by Master Pavol of Levoča and there's a small museum – through an arch in the best-looking building on the north side of the square – which laboriously documents the mining history of the town. Other than this, you'll probably be most interested in the hotels, *Metropol* on the main square (☎0966/21 41; ②), and *Šport*, by the ice hockey stadium (☎0966/222 17; ①).

East to Spišský hrad

The road east from Levoča takes you to the edge of the Spiš territory, clearly defined by the Branisko ridge which blocks the way to Prešov. Even if you're not planning on going any further east, you should at least take the bus as far as Spišské Podhradie, for arguably the most spectacular sight in the whole country.

En route, you might spot the palatial neo-Baroque chateau at SPIŠSKÝ HRHOV peeping through its half-tamed grounds (only the latter are open to the public). There's no point in stopping off, at least until just past the village of KLČOV, at which point you get your first glimpse of the **Spišský hrad**, its chalk-white ruins strung out on a bleak green hill in the distance – an irresistibly photogenic shot, and one which finds its way into almost every tourist brochure in the country. Predictably enough, the ruins themselves don't live up to expectations close to (May–Oct Tues–Sun 9am–5pm; last entry 4.15pm), though it's difficult to resist the impulse to get nearer, and the view from the top is undeniably good. If you do wish to wander round the castle, stay on the bus until SPIŠSKÉ PODHRADIE (literally "below the castle") and then follow the signs to the *hrad*.

If you've time to spare, and energy to expend, there's a small folk skanzen below the castle. Alternatively, you could take the path from Spišský hrad towards Dreveník, the limestone hill southeast of the ruins, and continue as far as the village of ŽEHRA. The lure here is the perky thirteenth-century church sporting a wonderfully oversized shingled onion dome and matching white perimeter walls, which contain faded frescoes contemporary with the church, and an interior decor of Byzantine richness.

Spišská Kapitula

More rewarding than a wander round Spišský hrad is a closer inspection of the walled, one-street city of **SPIŠSKÁ KAPITULA** (Zipser Kapitel), once the ecclesiastical capital of the Spiš region, whose plain monastic towers are often featured in the foreground of the aforementioned photographs. From the front, the **Cathedral of sv Martin** is clearly a Romanesque church, built as a defiant outpost of Christianity shortly after the Tartar invasions. To get inside, you must first retrieve the key from the caretaker, who hangs out in the bishop's residence opposite the north door of the cathedral; he can also give you a brief guide to the church in Slovak or German, should you so wish. The interior was originally decorated with colourful fourteenth-century frescoes celebrating the coronation of the Hungarian king Charles Robert. Here and there these have been restored after their whitewashing by Protestants during the Reformation. Outside, a couple of graceful cypress trees stand at the top of the town's single street, lined with decrepit canons' houses, some inhabited by people, others only by bats and rats. With the recent re-establishment of a Catholic seminary here, however, the whole place is beginning to wake from its forty-year religious slumber.

Practicalities

If you're in need of **accommodation**, there are a couple of cheap hotels in the vicinity: *Hotel Spiš* (☎0966/85 21; ①) in Spišské Podhradie, and *Hotel-Sivá Brada* (①), near the village of NEMEŠANY, 6km west of Spišské Podhradie on the Levoča road. The latter hotel takes its name from the nearby **artificial geyser** of Sivá Brada, which shoots mineral water twenty feet up in the air.

The Slovenský raj

After the upfront post-glacial splendour of the High Tatras, the low-key pine forests of the **Slovenský raj** (pronounced "rye" – meaning "paradise"), 20km or so to the southeast of Poprad, might seem more than a little anticlimactic at first glance. No hard slog hiking or top-of-the-world views here, but, if your inclination is towards more frivolous outdoor pursuits, such as scrambling up rocky gorges and clinging on to chains and ladders beside shooting waterfalls, then the Slovenský raj may not be far from nirvana after all.

Covered in a thick coat of pine forest, the terrain – covering just twenty square kilometres – is typically karstic: gentle limestone hills that have been whittled away in places to form deep hairline ravines, providing a dank, almost tropical escape from the dry summer heat of the Poprad plain. To the north, the Hornád river has made the deepest incision into the rock, forming a fast-flowing, snaking canyon flanked by towering jagged bluffs which attract some of the country's dedicated rock-climbers. The most dramatic ravines climb up to the grassy plateau of the Veľká poľana at the centre of the region. To the south, the geography becomes more conventional in the hills around Dedinky and in winter the whole area turns into a popular ski resort.

Practicalities

It's perfectly possible to do the area from Poprad (see p.381), by taking the **local train** to VYDRNÍK, LETANOVCE or SPIŠSKÉ TOMÁŠOVCE. Poprad being no great place to be, though, it might be more pleasant to hole up at ČINGOV, where you can stay at the *Flóra* (☎0965/911 30; ②), or in some of the cheap hostel accommodation available. You could even use Spišská Nová Ves as a base (see p.395). If you've got a tent, the PODLESOK **campsite** (mid-May to Sept) is the most convenient, the one at Čingov (June 15–Sept 15) more basic but less crowded. Between June 15 and September 15, you can also camp at the makeshift Klaštorisko site in the middle of the forest.

Transport to the south of the region is likewise okay, with buses from Poprad and the picturesque Hron valley railway from Banská Bystrica. Dedinky is, however, only useful as a base for visiting the Dobšiná ice cave and less than useless for exploring the ravines, which are clustered in the north. To get from north to south, there's nothing to take you except your own feet – it's not much more than 10km cross-country from Podlesok to Dedinky, but take adequate provisions with you. **Walking** is also the only way of seeing the canyons and it's not a bad idea to try and get hold of the detailed *Slovenský raj* map, which marks

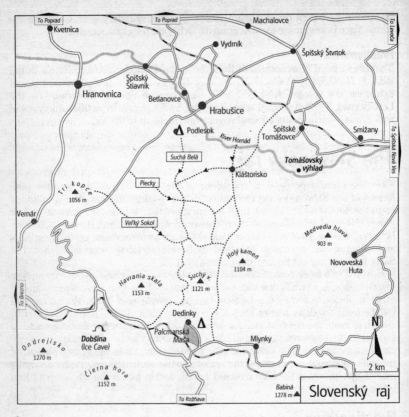

all the one-way paths, before you arrive in the area. The most exhilarating tracks are those designated one-way – a strange concept to get your head round until you've been up one – and it's important to stick to the direction indicated. However much you're walking, it's best to bring a pair of sturdy boots, preferably with a good grip and at the very least splash-proof – it's extremely wet and slippery underfoot all year round. Bear in mind, too, that if you're at all scared of heights, you might encounter a few problems with some of the deeper canyons. Note that occasionally some of the one-way paths are closed off to walkers, either for repairs or to give the ravine a rest.

Dedinky and the Dobšiná ice cave

Since the creation of the nearby lake, Palcmanská Maša, **DEDINKY** has become a thriving little tourist spot all year round, and with good reason. Nestling below Gačovská skala (1106m), whose spruce trees spill down to the grassy banks of the lake, it's the ideal recreational centre, with plenty of opportunities for swimming, rowing, cycling, hiking and of course visiting the great Dobšiná ice cave itself. Besides the lakeside **campsite** (June 15–Sept 15), there's the *Priehrada* (☎0942/

981 62; ①), and the *Geravy* (☎0942/932 27; ①), 1km northeast up the red-marked path, or a choice of **private rooms** in MLYNKY, 3km east of the lake.

Dobšina ice cave

The most obvious day trip from Dedinky is the **Dobšiná ice cave** (Dobšinská ľadová jaskyňa; May 16–Sept 15 Tues–Sun 1hr guided tours at 9am, 11am, 1pm & 3pm), by far the most impressive of Slovakia's two ice caves (the other is in the Low Tatras). It's basically one vast underground lake frozen to a depth of over 20m and divided into two halls, the biggest of which, the *Veľká sieň*, is over 100m across. Although the ice formations are a long way from the subtleties of your average limestone cave, it rarely fails to impress by the brute force of its size and weight.

From Podlesok, it's a three-and-a-half-hour hike, mostly through the forest, or a short but very chancy hitch along the road. From Dedinky, simply take the train two stops in the direction of Brezno, after which it's a twenty-minute walk into the hills. It's worth bearing in mind that the caves are very popular (so get there early) and very cold (so take something warm to put on). Should you wish to stay over, the *Hotel Ľadova* has cheap rooms (☎0942/989 19; ①); ask at the kitchen.

HIKING ROUTES IN THE SLOVENSKÝ RAJ

With the 1:50,000 *Slovenský raj* hiking map, you can plan your own routes. If you're staying at Podlesok and follow the green markers, you immediately enter the **Suchá Belá**, one of the most exciting river beds to explore, but also one of the most accessible and therefore extremely popular at the height of the season, causing the occasional queue at crucial ladders. With so many obstacles en route, it takes nearly everyone a full two hours to stumble up this one-way ravine to the top. Similarly breathtaking stuff can be experienced up the gladed ravine of **Piecky**, which starts from 3km along the green-marked track to the Dobšinská ľadová jaskyňa.

Should you need a rest after the morning's exertions, head down to **Kláštorisko**, whose sunny sloping meadow is perfect for picnicking and sunbathing. If you've forgotten your packed lunch, the small *reštaurácia* at the top of the field might oblige. At the bottom of the clearing is an ongoing archaeological dig where the local panic-stricken Slavs built a monastery to give thanks for their safe deliverance from the Tartar invasions of the mid-thirteenth century.

If you continue for another half an hour past the bottom of Piecky, you come to the deepest one-way gorge of the lot, **Veľký Sokol**, another succession of wooden ladders slung over rock pools and rapids, up the side of waterfalls and riverine gulleys. From the top, you can either walk north across the Veľká poľana plateau to Kláštorisko (1hr 30min) or head west to the top of the Malý Sokol, which swings round to join the last two-way quarter of the Veľký Sokol gorge.

The third main area to head for is the **Prielom Hornádu**, a sheer-sided breach (*prielom*) in the limestone rock forced by the Hornád river. Until recently it was impossible to enter the gorge except on ice-skates in winter or by kayak in summer. Now, in keeping with the vaguely vandalistic tendencies of the nation's trekkers, steel steps have been jammed into the rocks and rope bridges slung across the river, and the whole trip takes just three and a half hours from Podlesok to Čingov. If you're doing a round trip, take the yellow-marked path on the way back, which follows the limestone ridge high above the Hornád. The views are amazing, especially from the **Tomášovský výhlad**, a stick of exposed rock some 150m above the Prielom Hornádu.

Moving on

Dedinky lies on the wonderful Banská Bystrica–Margecany branch line, one of the prettiest **train journeys** in Slovakia. It's a slow run if you're going all the way to Košice (3hr 30min), but the fast midday *rýchlik* takes an hour off the usual running time. If you're heading south to the Slovenský kras, you'll have to walk or bus the 4km to the old German mining town of DOBŠINÁ – either way, it's a spectacular thousand-foot drop from the Palcmanská Maša. Most buses continue from Dobšiná to Rožňava, but if you prefer there are seven trains a day which also cover the route.

The Slovenský kras

Like the Moravian karst region north of Brno, the **Slovenský kras** boasts some of the finest limestone caves in Central Europe, the highlight of which are the Domica caves, stretching right under the border into Hungary (where they're known as the Aggtelek caves). Even now, the surrounding hills are still plundered for their ores – copper, iron and once upon a time gold – and the largest town in the area, Rožňava, continues to make its living from the local mines, even if the original intrepid German miners have long since gone. The towns and villages are for the most part dusty, characterless places; people are by far the dominant feature of the landscape – large communities of Hungarians and Romanies living side by side, with the Slovaks very much in a minority.

Rožňava and around

Once the seat of a bishopric and a flourishing German mining centre, **ROŽŇAVA** (Rozsnyó) is now a sleepy, mostly Hungarian-speaking town, though an undeniably useful base when it comes to making excursions into the karst region and the nearby aristocratic haunts of Krásna Hôrka and Betliar. All **transport** in the region has to pass through Rožňava at some point, although three train stations still seem a mite excessive; the main one, called simply Rožňava, is a two-and-a-half-kilometre walk from town (infrequent bus #1 or #6 from the station, #2 from the nearby petrol station on the main road); the bus station is just east of the centre. Accommodation should be straightforward at either of the town's two **hotels**: the *Gemer* (☎0942/28 29; ①) – whose *reštaurácia* serves up lashings of goulash – and the *Kras* (☎0942/22 93; ①).

The town does have a couple of other redeeming features: it once boasted a mint, a cathedral and an episcopal palace. Of the three, only the former **cathedral** (now just a parish church) is worth bothering about, largely on account of its sixteenth-century altarpiece depicting the life of the local miners; you'll find it just to the northwest of the expansive main square. Secondly, there's the **Mining Museum** (Banícke múzeum; Tues–Sat 9am–4pm, Sun 9am–1pm), set in a long *fin-de-siècle* block (no. 43) on the road to Šafárikovo, and run by a lively retired Hungarian miner who does his best to make up for the lack of information in English. Ask to see the reconstructed (and somewhat over-clean) mine shaft tucked round the back of the building (along with an iron statue of the Hungarians' hero, Kossuth), bearing the traditional, though rather ominous inscription *ZDAR BOH* (Good Luck).

Krásnohorské Podhradie and around

Plenty of buses run the 5km to **KRÁSNOHORSKÉ PODHRADIE** (literally "Below Krásna Hôrka"), the village sitting under the gaunt and seemingly unapproachable fortress of **Krásna Hôrka** (Tues–Sun April–Sept 8am–noon & 1–4.30pm; Oct–March 9am–2.30pm), built on top of the nearby limestone col, in order to protect the trade route between the Spiš region and Košice. The original owners, the Bebeks, fell from favour when it was discovered that they had been conterfeiting money. The castle was subsequently confiscated and handed over to the Andrássy family. Such was the wealth of the Andrássys, that they were able to turn the whole place into a family museum in 1910, having a number of other places in which to actually live. And that's basically what it is now, give or take the odd three-piece suite. However, with compulsory guided tours lasting an hour and twenty minutes, it's of limited appeal.

A better bet down in the village is the original Rožňava mining museum, a fabulous Secession building from 1906, which has been recently restored and turned into the **Andrássy galéria** (Tues–Sat 9am–noon & 1–4pm, Sun 9am–4pm). The main glass-roofed hall now contains portraits of the Andrássy family, including the two buried in the mausoleum described below, plus a large, dramatic canvas by the Hungarian painter, Ferenc Paczka, depicting the death of Attila the Hun, and an unusual painting of an elderly prisoner breast-feeding from the Virgin Mary.

Within sight of both castle and village, and without doubt the most beautiful Art-Nouveau building in Slovakia, is the **Andrássy Mausoleum** (Tues–Sun 8am–noon & 1–5.30pm). It was built in 1903–04 at great expense by Count Dionysus Andrássy, in memory of his wife, the celebrated Czech opera singer Františka Hablavcová, who died in 1902. Dionysus himself was disowned by the family for marrying below his station, an action which no doubt stiffened his resolve to build an even more extravagant resting place for his lover. Set in its own carefully laid-out gardens with sombre wrought-iron gates and characteristic angelic janitors, the mausoleum itself, a simple dome structure, has an austere classicism. Inside, though, it bursts into an almost celebratory orgy of ornamentation: Venetian gold for the cupola, coloured marble from every corner of the globe, and as the centrepiece, two white Carrara marble sarcophagi in which Františka and Dionysus (who died not long after the building was completed) are buried.

If you're looking for a place to stay, there's a **motel** (☎0942/238 38; ①) right by the mausoleum, and a **campsite** to the north of the village.

Betliar

The frivolous hunting chateau at **BETLIAR**, 5km northwest of Rožňava by train, couldn't be further from the brooding intensity of Krásna Hôrka, though it was owned by the same aristocratic family. It was adapted as late as the 1880s in an "indefinite style", as the local tourist brochures put it, to accommodate the Andrássys' popular hunting parties. A fairly standard array of period furniture, historical portraits and (naturally enough) reams of hunting trophies and stuffed animals greets those who sign up for the guided tour, but the large, well-groomed park steals the show, dotted with playful, folksy rotundas and mock-historic edifices. The only **accommodation** in the village is in the bungalows at the nearby campsite (June to mid-Sept).

Zádielska dolina and the caves at Jasov

One of the more bizarre karstic features of the Slovenský kras is the forested sheets of **planina** or tableland which rise above the plains like the coastal cliffs of a lost sea. In fact, the opposite is the case, the rivers having whittled down what would otherwise be a featureless limestone plateau. Mostly, these erosions form broad sweeping valleys, but in a few cases cracks appear in the more familiar form of riverine crevices. The most dramatic of these is the **Zádielska dolina**, a brief but breathtaking three or four kilometres of sky-scraping canyon. To get there, take the train or bus to DVORNÍKY, 25km east of Rožnava and 1km south of the Hungarian-speaking village, ZÁDIEL (Szádelö), at the entrance to the *dolina*. There's none of the Slovenský raj assault course on this hike, just a gentle yet magnificent stroll between the two bluffs. For something slightly more death-defying, return along the blue-marked track which ascends the right-hand ridge and shadows the canyon back to Zádiel, then dropping down 2.5km east of Dvorníky near the cement works of TURNIANSKE PODHRADIE. For a longer hike (15km), you could follow the blue-marked path over the hills to Jasov, or take the green-marked, then red-marked track to Pipitka (1225m), 10km away, returning to Rožnava by bus from the Úhornianske sedlo down below.

Jasov

The Premonstratensian monastery at **JASOV** (Jászó) is visible across the fields long before you reach the town. It's actually much older than its thoroughly Baroque appearance would suggest, but is undergoing restoration work by the Polish restorers *PKZ*. Whether, once the work is done, the public will be able to view Kracker's fiery frescoes and suchlike is anybody's guess. The main motivation for visiting Jasov in the meantime is the **Jasovská jaskyňa** (Tues–Sun May 16–Sept 15 9am–4pm), the least hyped caves in the karst region, though no less enjoyable for that, specialising in forests of "virgin stalactites" and containing some amazing graffiti scrawled on the walls by fugitive Czech Hussites in 1452. The only accommodation is the lively campsite and bungalows near the monastery, but if you're coming from Košice, Jasov can be done easily enough as a day trip.

The Gombasek, Domica and Ochtina caves

The majority of the cave systems in the Slovenský kras lie to the south and west of Rožnava, though without your own transport, it's difficult to get there and back in the same day. As one of the prime tourist destinations in Slovakia, a separate pricing system has been introduced for foreigners and it's possible that you may have to queue to get in the more popular caves.

Gombasecská jaskyňa

The most impressive of the cave systems, the **Gombasecská jaskyňa** (Tues–Sun April–May 15 & Sept 16–Oct tours at 9am, 11am & 2pm; May 16–Sept 15 9am–4pm), is also one of the most accessible. To reach the caves, you can catch a direct bus from Rožnava, or take the train one stop south of Rožnava to Slavec Jaskyňa station, whence it's 2km further south. There's a **campsite** near the caves, and every June the nearby village of GOMBASEK (Gömbaszog) is the venue for the largest annual Hungarian folk bash in Slovakia.

A JOURNEY THROUGH THE DOMICA CAVES

The following is an extract from Robert Townson's "Travels in Hungary", published in 1793. Townson, a Scottish scientist, botanised his way around the old kingdom of Hungary, staying with a lot of good-humoured Calvinists on the way, and in the passage quoted below recounts a visit to the Domica caves, long before the days of safety barriers and electric lighting.

I descended rapidly for a short distance and then I found myself in an immense cave . . . where large stalactites, as thick as my body, hung pendant from the roof, and I was shown others where the sides were ornamented in the manner of the most curious Gothic workmanship. In some the stalactites were so thick and close together that we were in danger of losing one another if we separated but a few yards. Here aged stalactites, overloaded with their own weight had fallen down, and lay prostrate; and there an embryo stalactite was just shooting into existence.

After I had wandered about for three or four hours in this awful gloom and had reached the end of the caverns in one direction, I thought it time to come out, and I desired my guide to return. After we returned, as we thought, some way, we found no passage further; yet the guide was sure he was right. I thought I recognised the same rocks we had just left, and which had prevented our proceeding further, but the guide was positive he was in a right direction. Luckily for us I had written my name on the soft clay of the bottom of the cave, which had been the extent of our journey; on seeing this the guide was thunderstruck, and ran this way and that way and knew not where he was, nor what to do. I desired him not to be frightened, but to go calmly to work to extricate us from this labyrinth.

As the wood which we burnt instead of lamps was nearly exhausted, and as I never adverted either to one of the guides whom we had left above, who by being charged with wood could not to get down the funnel-like hole, being so near; nor to the people of the village being acquainted with our being in the cavern, who no doubt would have taken every possible means of coming to our assistance had we stayed much longer than usual, I was a good deal alarmed for our safety and there was good reason; had our torches gone out, we should never have been able to find our way out; nor, had any accident have happened to our guide, could we by ourselves, though we had lights, have had any hopes of extricating ourselves. After wandering about till all our wood was nearly exhausted, we found a great stalactite from which, on account of its remarkable whiteness, I had been induced to knock off a specimen as I came by: I recollected how I stood when I struck it: this at once set us right, and after walking a little further we made ourselves heard to the other guide, from whom we got fresh torches, and we continued our route homewards without further difficulty.

So complete a labyrinth as these caverns are in some places, is not I am sure to be found in similar caverns: large open passages proved cul de sacs, whilst our road was over and under, through and amongst grotto work of the most intricate nature. I finally believe that though a man should have lights and food enough to last him a month – he would not be able to find his way out.

The Domica caves and Silická ľadnica

Ten kilometres due south of Gombasek, hard by the Hungarian border, are the **Domica Caves** (daily May 16–Sept 15 tours at 9am, 11.30am, noon, 2pm & 3.30pm; Sept 16–May 15 9am, 11pm & 2pm): at 22km in length, one of the longest cave systems in the world. The short passage from Robert Townson (see above), one of the caves' earliest explorers, should give you an idea of the gushing prose they often excite. The tours last for less than an hour and include a quick boat trip on the underground river. It should soon be possible to continue on a longer tour over the border into Hungary, where most of the cave system lies, something that's already possible from the Hungarian side.

Given Domica's inaccessibility, perhaps the easiest and most rewarding way of getting there is to follow the yellow-marked track from Gombasek up onto the *planina* and through the oak trees via the **Silická ľadnica** cave (1hr). The cave itself is closed to the public but its ominous entrance is impressively ice-encrusted throughout the summer, melting to a dribble by late autumn only to be replenished when the first cold spell of November arrives. Keep following the yellow markers east for 500m or so, then hang a right when you hit the red-marked path, whence it's a two-hour trek across the pockmarked tableland to Domica.

Ochtinská jaskyňa

Of all the cave systems, the **Ochtinská jaskyňa** (Tues–Sun April–May 15 & Sept 16–Oct tours at 9am, 11am & 2pm; May 16–Sept 15 9am–4pm) is without doubt the thinking person's cave. Set apart from the others geographically and geologically, its unique feature is the spiky aragonite "flowers" which form like limpets on the cave sides – breathtakingly beautiful but by no means as spectacular in scale as the other limestone caves. From Plešivec, there's an infrequent train service to OCHTINÁ (35min), after which the cave is a three-kilometre walk uphill along the blue-marked path; from Rožňava, there are equally infrequent buses (40min).

Carpatho-Ruthenia

Carpatho-Ruthenia* is one of those places where people come from rather than go to. The infamous media mogul, Robert Maxwell, and his cousin, set off on foot, Andy Warhol's parents went by boat, and over a million others left this far northeastern corner of Slovakia by various means to seek fame and fortune elsewhere, mostly in North America, in the late nineteenth and early twentieth centuries.

They left to escape not so much the unerring provinciality of the region, but the grinding poverty and unemployment whose stranglehold on the area has only quite recently abated. Even in the 1950s, an estimated 41 percent of Rusyn villages were still without electricity, and by 1968, enjoyed living standards of less than half the national average. Today, the villages are still visibly poorer and more isolated than their western counterparts. It's hardly an exaggeration to say that some villages have seen few visitors since the Russians passed through in 1945 (and again in 1968). Some things have changed, though not always for the best: the whole area took a hammering in the last war, wooden buildings, once the norm, are gradually being replaced by concrete and brick, traditional costumes are now worn almost exclusively by the over-fifties, and the industry which was crudely implanted here by the Communists to try and stem the continuing emigration is now deeply depressed.

---

*Carpatho-Ruthenia (*Podkarpatská Rus* in Slovak) was the name for the easternmost province of Czechoslovakia which existed between the wars, but was taken as war booty by the Soviet Union in 1945. The term is here used loosely to refer to the East Slovak districts of Prešov, Bardejov, Svidník and Humenné, which border Poland, where the Rusyn minority still predominate.

From a visitor's point of view, **Prešov** and **Bardejov** are both easy to reach and immediately appealing. Further afield, transport becomes a real problem (as it is to the local inhabitants), since the north–south axis of the valleys only hinders the generally eastbound traveller. Nevertheless, it's worth persevering, if only to visit the region's most unusual sight, the Andy Warhol Modern Art Museum in **Medzilaborce**.

Prešov

Capital of the Slovak Šariš region and cultural centre for the Rusyn minority, **PREŠOV**'s present-day split personality is indicative of its long and chequered ethnic history. Over the last few years it has been treated to a wonderful facelift, and although there's not much of interest beyond its main square, it's a refreshingly youthful and vibrant town – partly due to its university – beyond all expectations this far east.

The Town

The lozenge-shaped main square, **Hlavná ulica**, is flanked by creamy, pastel-coloured, almost edible eighteenth-century facades, topped by some exceptionally winsome and varied gables and pediments, all beautifully preserved. Next door to *ČEDOK* (no. 1), at its southern tip, is the **Uniate Cathedral** (Grécko-katolícka katedrála), in many ways a perfectly normal Rococo/late-Baroque church, except for the paraphernalia of orthodoxy, including a fabulously huge iconostasis. For the first time since the imprisonment of Pavol Gojdic (see box overleaf), the cathedral and the bishop's palace next door actually have an extant Uniate bishop and are enjoying a cultural renaissance.

Further along, on the same side of the square, the town's **art gallery** (Tues–Fri 9am–5pm, Sat & Sun 10am–2pm) has a good collection of Slovak art. Nearby is Prešov's **radnica**, from whose unsuitably small balcony Béla Kun's Hungarian Red Army declared the short-lived Slovak Socialist Republic in 1919. Searching desperately for a socialist tradition that simply never existed in this deeply religious country, the Slovak Communists made much of this brief episode in Prešov's history. In fact, it used to be the main subject of the town museum, situated in the dogtooth gabled **Rákociho dom** at no. 86 (Tues–Fri 10am–5pm, Sat & Sun 11am–3pm) – the Czechoslovak Legion's military victories that contributed to the downfall of Kun's Bolshevik government would be an appropriate replacement.

Prešov's Catholic and Protestant churches vie with each other at the widest point of the square. Naturally enough, the fourteenth-century Catholic church of **sv Mikuláš** has the edge, not least for its modern Moravian stained-glass windows and its sumptuous Baroque altarpiece. Behind sv Mikuláš, the much plainer **Protestant Church**, built in the mid-seventeenth century, bears witness to the strength of religious reformism in the outer reaches of Hungary at a time when the rest of the Habsburgs' lands were suffering the full force of the Counter-Reformation. In the 1670s the tide turned, and a wave of religious persecution followed, culminating in the "1684 Blood Tribunal" in which 24 leading Lutherans were publicly hanged in Prešov's main square. The prime mover behind the trial was **Count Caraffa**, the papal nuncio in Vienna, whose moustached figure, flanked by a hooded executioner, stands above the grim memorial on the corner of the Protestant Lycée, next door to the church.

THE RUSYNS

The **Rusyns** or Ruthenians are without doubt one of the great lost peoples of central Europe. Even their name is a subject of some debate, since *Rusyn* is often taken to mean Little Russian or Ukrainian, but in the Hungarian kingdom simply referred to any non-Catholic Slav. As to their political history, the picture is equally confusing. If they ever were an integral part of the Ukraine – whose language they speak, albeit a western or Lemkian dialect – the mountains in which they had settled soon became a permanent political barrier, dividing their territory between Hungary and Poland.

Meanwhile, their great cultural institution, the Orthodox church, underwent a series of crises and schisms resulting in the Act of Union of 1596, which established the Greek-Catholic or **Uniate church** as part of the Roman Catholic Church. This unique religion, tied to Rome but with all the trappings of eastern Orthodoxy, became (and still is) the carrier of the Rusyn national identity. In every other way – dress codes, mores and folklore – they were hardly distinguishable from their Magyar and Slovak neighbours. Throughout this period, they remained, as they still do to a great extent, hill-dwelling peasants with no political or economic influence.

The first national leaders to emerge in the nineteenth century were, predictably enough, Uniate priests, and – like many Slovaks at the time – fiercely Russophile and pro-Tsar. They played little part in the downfall of the Habsburg Empire, and when, in 1918, Ruthenia became a province of the new Czechoslovak Republic, it was largely due to the campaigning efforts of a handful of Ruthenian emigrés in the USA. The Slovaks laid claim to all the land west of the Už river, an area containing around 100,000 Rusyns, while the actual province of Ruthenia, to the east, contained not only 370,000 Ruthenians but large numbers of Hungarians, Jews, Romanies, Germans and even Romanians. Following "liberation" in 1945, the Už river became a permanent border, with the annexation of Ruthenia by the Soviet Union.

On the surface, the Rusyns who remained in Czechoslovakia have been treated better than any other minority since the war. Scratch this surface, however, and things begin to look much less rosy. Given a free choice (as they were between the wars and before 1948), the Rusyns tended to opt either for the local dialect or Russian as the language of instruction in their schools. After the 1948 coup, however, the Communist regime intervened and ruled that the term *Rusyn* was "an anti-progressive label" – all Rusyns became officially known as Ukrainians, and the language of instruction in Rusyn schools was changed to literary Ukrainian. The reaction of the Rusyns to the pedagogical chaos which ensued was to opt for Slovak schools rather than Ukrainian. Secondly, collectivisation, which disrupted all traditional peasant communities of Eastern Europe, encouraged urbanisation (and therefore Slovak assimilation). Lastly, and perhaps most cruelly of all, following the example of the Stalinist Ukrainian authorities, the Uniate church was forcibly amalgamated into the Orthodox church. Its priests and dissenting laity were, for the most part, rounded up and thrown in prison, including the church's one and only bishop, **Pavol Gojdic**, who received a life sentence and died in Leopoldov prison in 1960.

Hardly surprising then that in the last three censuses, fewer than 40,000 declared themselves as Rusyn. No one knows the real numbers, but it's estimated that between 130,000 and 150,000 Rusyns still live in East Slovakia. Since the Velvet Revolution things have begun to look up. As in 1968, when the ban on the church was finally lifted, the Uniates (who include large numbers of Slovaks) are busy arguing with the Orthodox community (reckoned to be as few as 30,000) over church property, all of which was handed over to the Orthodox church in the 1950s. Meanwhile, **Ján Hirka**, since 1968 the unofficial head of all Uniates, was ordained as a Uniate bishop in February 1990, and the martyr Pavol Gojdic canonised.

To the north of the main square, as to the south, lies "monumental Prešov", built in the optimistic days of the 1950s and presided over by the severe colossus of the Prešov district administration, which looks like something straight out of the Soviet Ukraine.

Practicalities

The **bus** and **train stations** are situated opposite one another about 1km south of the main square; any of the buses and trolley buses which stop outside will take you into town. **Accommodation** should be trouble-free, providing that the number of Russian and Ukrainian tourists doesn't increase: the *Šariš*, north of the main square (☎091/463 53; ②), is significantly cheaper than the *Dukla* on the square itself (☎091/227 41; ③).

If you want to avoid **eating** at one of the big hotels, try the pizzeria on Svätoplukova (open until 7pm), or the *Slovenská reštaurácia*, at no. 13 on the main square. Drinking or eating under the glistening chandeliers of the *Hotel Savoy*, on the square, or beside the smoky mirrors of the *Vrchovina*, Svätoplukova 1, is also a favourite local pastime. Prešov also prides itself on its cultural traditions, with two large-scale **theatres** in town: the *Divadlo Jonáša Záborského*, on the main square, and more famously, the Rusyn/Ukrainian theatre, *Divadlo Alexandra Duchnoviča* or *DAD*, based in a theatre on Jarková, west off the square; plays at the latter are generally performed in Ukrainian.

Bardejov and around

Over 40km north of Prešov, not far from the Polish border, **BARDEJOV** (Bartfeld) is an almost perfectly preserved walled medieval town, comfortably positioned on its own rock with the obligatory sprawl of postwar development below. Like Prešov, it acts as a commercial and administrative centre for the outlying Rusyn villages, most obviously during the Saturday morning market. It's perfectly possible to come here on a day trip from Prešov, though given the added attractions of the nearby spa, Bardejovské kúpele (see below), you may prefer to **stay** overnight: the *Hotel Dukla*, to the north of the old town square (☎0935/27 21; ①), should have space, but if not, they can arrange private rooms easily enough.

Built by Saxon weavers who colonised the area in the fourteenth century, the **staré mesto** (five minutes' walk southwest of the bus and train stations) remains remarkably unchanged since those days, retaining most of its Gothic fortifications, including four of the original bastions along the eastern wall (and much of the original plaster, judging by their state of disrepair). The pristine cobbled main square, **Radničné námestie**, is straight out of the German Middle Ages, both in its characteristic triangular gables (many of which are still faced with wooden slats) and in the central Renaissance **radnica**. The latter forms part of the **Šariš museum** (Tues–Sun 9am–6pm), but the best exhibits are actually housed in a building on the corner of Rhódyho, at the top end of the square (same times as above). Inside, there's an impressive collection of sixteenth- to nineteenth-century icons (many in need of some serious restoration), and a fascinating series of models of the region's Uniate churches (see overleaf). Along the north side of the square is the sandy-coloured Gothic church of **sv Egídia** (St Giles), suitably vast given the burghers' wealth at the time, and stuffed full of fifteenth-century carved wooden side altars – eleven in all – plus the main *Altar of St Barbara* by Pavol of Levoča.

Bardejovské kúpele

A four-kilometre bus ride north of Bardejov, the spa town of **BARDEJOVSKÉ KÚPELE** (Bad Bartfeld) was once a favourite playground of the Austro-Hungarian and Russian nobility. A series of devastating fires in 1910–12 destroyed most of the spa's old wooden buildings, and nowadays, aside from a few surviving nineteenth-century mansions, there's nothing much to hint at its former glory. Instead, the major attraction for non-patients is the spa's **skanzen** (Tues–Sun 8.15am–noon & 12.30–4.15pm), which contains a whole series of timber-framed buildings, thatched cottages and two eighteenth-century wooden Uniate churches transferred from the surrounding Šariš region. The spa's only other claim to fame is its seated bronze statue of the **Empress Elizabeth**, wife of the Habsburg Emperor Franz Josef, who was a frequent visitor to the spa until her death at the hands of an Italian nationalist in 1898. A group of Hungarian admirers erected the statue in 1903, but wisely left the empress's name off the plinth, allowing her real identity to remain hidden during the ideological vicissitudes of this century.

Svidník and the Dukla Pass

Twenty kilometres or so due east of Bardejov and almost completely obliterated in the heavy fighting of October 1944, **SVIDNÍK** today is, not surprisingly, a characterless concrete sprawl. However, it does contain a clutch of intriguing museums and an open-air skanzen of Rusyn folk architecture, and hosts a "Ukrainian" folk festival each year in the middle of June. It's also by far the most convenient base from which to explore the wooden Uniate churches in the Rusyn villages, chiefly those near the Dukla Pass. The only **accommodation** in Svidník is at the high-rise *Hotel Dukla* (☎0937/228 39; ②).

THE WOODEN CHURCHES OF CARPATHO-RUTHENIA

In the Rusyn villages around Bardejov, Svidník and Humenné, a remarkable number of **wooden Uniate churches** have survived to the present day. Most date from around the eighteenth century, when the influence of Baroque was beginning to make itself felt even among the carpenter architects of the Carpathians. A threesome of shingled onion domes, as at Dobroslavova, is the telltale sign, though the humbler churches opt for simple barn-like roofs.

Without your own transport, the possibility of reaching many of the churches *in situ* is limited, although there's a whole cluster within easy walking distance of the main road from Svidník to the Polish border. The easiest way of having a close look is to visit one of the skanzens at Bardejovské kúpele, Svidník or Humenné, each of which contains a wooden Uniate church. If, however, you do make it out to some of the villages, you'll need to ask around for the local priest (*kňaz*) to get hold of a key (*kľúč*).

The dark and intimate interior of a Uniate church is divided into three sections (from west to east): the narthex or entrance porch, the main nave, and the naos or sanctuary. Even the smallest Uniate church boasts a rich iconostasis all but cutting off the sanctuary, with the familiar icons of (from left to right) St Nicholas, the Madonna and Child, Christ Pantocrator and, lastly, the saint to whom the church is dedicated. Above the central door of the iconostasis (through which only the priest may pass) is the Last Supper, while to the left are busy scenes from the great festivals of the church calendar – the Annunciation, the Assumption and so on. The top tier of icons features the Apostles (with St Paul taking the place of Judas).

Next door to *ČEDOK*, just off the town's main street, is the **Museum of Ukrainian Culture** (Múzeum ukrajinskej kultúry; Tues–Fri 8.30am–4pm, Sat & Sun 10am–4pm), containing a fine array of Rusyn folk gear and models of various Uniate chruches, as well as a beautiful collection of traditional painted Easter eggs. A ten-minute walk from the museum up the hill past the bus station, and clearly signposted round town is the **Galéria Dezidera Millyho**, on Partizánska (Tues–Fri 8.30am–4pm, Sat & Sun 9am–2pm), mostly given over to contemporary Rusyn artists, but with a couple of retrospective rooms devoted to Milly, one of the first Rusyn artists to win acclaim for his Expressionist paintings of local peasant life. The gallery also houses some weird and wonderful sixteenth- to nineteenth-century icon paintings, much the best collection in East Slovakia.

Looking something like the Slovak equivalent of New York's Guggenheim Museum, the gleaming white **Dukla Museum** (Dukelské múzeum; Tues–Sun 8am–4.30pm), at the beginning of the road to Bardejov, houses a fairly standard exhibition on the last war, with plenty of military paraphernalia, and a diorama of the "Valley of Death" (see "The Dukla Pass", below). About a kilometre further along the Bardejov road, a gigantic **Soviet war memorial** commemorates the many thousands who fell in the fighting. It's an exceptionally peaceful spot, disturbed only by the occasional coachload of Soviet war veterans, who stagger up the monumental staircase to lay wreaths to the sound of Beethoven's Funeral March blasting from speakers strategically hidden in the ornamental shrubbery.

On the opposite side of the road, near the local football stadium, is Svidník's brand new, open-air folk **skanzen** (times as for Galéria Dezidera Millyho). If you're not planning to visit any of the less accessible villages, this is a great opportunity to get a close look at some thatched Rusyn cottages, as well as a typical wooden Uniate church, brought here from the nearby village of Nová Polianka.

Typically, the Last Judgement covers the wall of the narthex, usually the most gruesome of all the depictions, with the damned being burned, boiled and decapitated with macabre abandon.

The following is a varied selection of some of the most interesting churches still *in situ*:

Dobroslava, 7km north of Svidník. A delightful pagoda-style church, with a wide cruciform ground plan, distinctive triplet of shingled onion domes and an amazing Bosch-style *Last Judgement*.

Ladomírová, 4km northeast of Svidník. An eccentric mishmash of pagodas, baubles and cupolas on the main road to the Dukla Pass.

Lukov, 14km west of Bardejov. Look out for the fantastic red-black sixteenth-century diag-rammatical depiction of the *Last Judgement* on the iconostasis.

Miroľa, 12km east of Svidník. One of the most perfect examples of the triple Baroque cupolas descending in height from west to east.

Nižný Komárnik, 12km northeast of Svidník. An unusual modern wooden church not in the usual Lemkian style, with the central cupola higher than the other two.

Tročany, 12km south of Bardejov. Simple cupolas like candle extinguisher caps. Renowned for its lurid, rustic icon of the *Last Judgement*.

Uličské Krivé, 2km from the Ukrainian border. Exceptionally rich in seventeenth-century icon paintings, including one depicting the archangel Michael casually pulverising Sodom and Gomorrah.

The Dukla Pass

The **Dukla Pass** (Dukliansky priesmyk), 15km north of Svidník by bus, was for centuries the main mountain crossing-point on the trade route from the Baltic to Hungary. This location has ensured a bloody history, the worst episode occurring in the last war, when over 80,000 Soviet soldiers and 6500 Czechs and Slovaks died trying to capture the valley from the Nazis. There's a giant granite memorial to the "Dukla Heroes" at the top of the pass, 1km from the Polish border, as well as an open-air museum of underground bunkers, tussling tanks and sundry armoured vehicles, strung out along the road from VIŠNÝ KOMÁRNIK, the first village to be liberated in Czechoslovakia (on October 6, 1944), to KRAJNÁ POĽANA.

Humenné

HUMENNÉ, like Prešov and Bardejov, is another basically Slovak town which serves as a centre for the neighbouring Rusyn villages. A modern and spacious place, with more charm than you'd expect from a town based on the chemical industry, the few visitors who do make it this far (mostly American emigrés) aim straight down the leafy main boulevard from the train station for Humenné's one and only sight, the stately seventeenth-century **chateau**. The museum inside the chateau is worth skipping for the enticing **skanzen** (Tues–Fri 8am–4pm, Sat & Sun 9am–1pm) round the back of the chateau gardens. Set in a pretty little meadow-cum-orchard, there's a whole series of vivid blue-painted cottages and a characteristic eighteenth-century wooden church from Nová Sedlica; ask for the information sheet in English (*anglický text*).

Medzilaborce

Although actually closer to Svidník, **MEDZILABORCE** is best approached by train from Humenné, 42km to the south. The main reason for making the long journey out here is to visit the town's spanking new **Museum of Modern Art** (Múzeum moderného umenia; Tues–Sun 10am–5pm), one of the most surreal experiences this side of the Carpathians.

The inspiration for the museum came from local Rusyn artists and relatives of **Andy Warhol** from the US and the area around Medzilaborce, following the death of the artist in 1987. Although Andy Warhol himself was born in Pittsburgh, the steel, aluminium and glass capital of the USA, both his parents hailed from the Rusyn village of Miková, 8km northwest of Medzilaborce. His real name was Andrej Varchola, while his father was a coal-miner who, like many Rusyns, emigrated to the States shortly before World War I, the rest of the family joining him in 1918. Andy and his two brothers were brought up speaking Rusyn and English, but when fame and fortune hit in the 1960s, Warhol rarely made reference to his Slav origins, either in his work or conversation – "I come from nowhere", was his favourite enigmatic response.

Since Medzilaborce is a one-street town – albeit a larger than average one – it's impossible to miss the museum, a strikingly modern white building with two giant Campbell's Soup Cans standing guard outside the main entrance. The modest collection of original screen prints, on loan from the Andy Warhol Foundation in New York, are displayed upstairs in the main hall, along with biographical details and quotes from Warhol (in Slovak, Rusyn and English); the psychedelic *Red Lenin* and *Hammer & Sickle* are particularly appropriate choices.

In the upper gallery, there are some derivative prints by Andy's brother, Paul, and his nephew, James, followed by a room of family portraits.

In addition to the Warhol stuff, the museum puts on temporary exhibitions and installations, ranging from work by other Pop Artists to contemporary Rusyn art, and organises an ambitious programme of cultural events, gigs and talks. The gallery shop sells Warhol souvenirs (including tins of Campbell soup) as well as information on Rusyn culture and language. Should you wish or need to stay over in Medzilaborce, there is one cheap **hotel**, not far from the museum.

Košice

Slovak towns often never amount to much more than their one long main square, and **KOŠICE** – despite a population of over 250,000 – is no exception. It does, however, boast a number of worthwhile museums, the best cathedral in the republic, and a lively cosmopolitanism that can be quite reassuring after a week or so in the Slovak back of beyond. Just 21km north of the Hungarian border, Košice also acts as a magnet for the Hungarian community – to whom the city is known as *Kassa* – and the terminally underemployed Romanies of the surrounding region, lending it a diversity and vibrancy absent from small-town Slovakia.

Arrival and accommodation

The **train** and **bus stations** are opposite each other, ten minutes' walk east of the old town – an egg-shaped affair, no more than five or six blocks across from east to west. Head for the fanciful **Jakabov palác** across the park from the stations, which lies on Mlynská, one of several streets that lead on to the main square.

Finding a cheap **room** should be easy enough at either the *Európa* on Mlynská (☎095/238 97; ①), the high-rise *Hutník* at Tyršovo nábrežie 6 (☎095/377 80; ①), or the *Centrum*, just south of the main square (☎095/766 27; ①). If you'd prefer something a bit more comfortable, head for the *Slovan* (☎095/273 78; ④) or ask *ČEDOK* (Mon–Fri 9am–5pm, Sat 9am–noon), situated in the *Slovan* itself, about the availability of private rooms. For information on the city's **student hostels**, open during July and August, enquire at the *CKM* office at no. 82 on the main square (☎095/278 58). The nearest **campsite** (mid-April to Sept) is 5km south of the city centre and also rents out bungalows; take tram #1 or #4, or bus #22 or #52, from the *Slovan* to the flyover, then get off and walk the remaining 500m west along Alejová, the road to Rožňava.

The old town

Almost everything of interest is situated on Košice's long pedestrianised main square, **Hlavná námestie**, lined with handsome Baroque and Neoclassical palaces but dominated by the city's unorthodox Gothic **cathedral**, its charcoal-coloured stone recently sandblasted back to its original honeyed hue. Begun around 1390, it was paid for by the riches of the salt trade, which reached their peak in the following century. It's an unusual building from the outside, with striped roof tiles like those of Saint Stephen's in Vienna, and two contorted towers. Inside, Gothic furnishings add an impressive touch to an otherwise quite plain nave, the main gilded altar depicting scenes from the life of Saint Elizabeth,

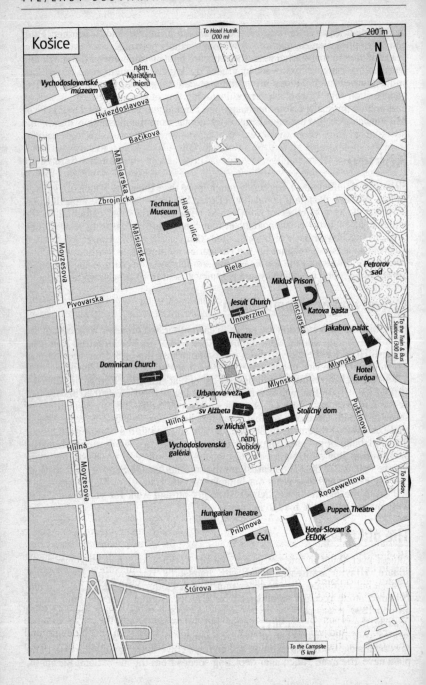

Košice

To Hotel Hutník
(200 m)

200 m

N

nám.
Maratónu
mieru

*Vychodoslovenské
múzeum*

Hviezdoslavova

Bačíkova

Mäsiarska

Zbrojnicka

Mäsiarska

Moyzesova

*Technical
Museum*

Hlavná ulica

Pivovarska

Biela

Miklúš Prison

Jesuit Church

Univerzitní

Hrnciarska

Katova bašta

Petrorov
sad

Theatre

Jakabuv palác

To the Train & Bus
Stations (300 m)

Dominican Church

Mlynská

Mlynská

*Hotel
Európa*

Urbanova veža

Mlynská

Puškinova

sv Alžbeta

Hlilná

Stoličný dom

sv Michál

Hlilná

nám.
Slobody

Moyzesova

*Vychodoslovenská
galéria*

Rooseweltova

To Prešov.

Hungarian Theatre

Puppet Theatre

Pribinova

*Hotel Slovan &
ČEDOK*

ČSA

Štúrova

To the Campsite
(5 km)

patron saint of the cathedral, despite the fact that the city had a long and bitter row with her father, Charles of Anjou, over its monopoly of the salt trade. One of the best features of the church is the intricate relief work above the north and west doors, their tympana respectively depicting the frantic scenes of the Last Judgement, and Christ and his sleepy disciples squeezed onto the Mount of Olives.

South of the cathedral is the similar, but much smaller, Gothic church of **sv Michal**, converted into a storehouse for weapons and ammunition during the sixteenth century when the threat of a Turkish invasion caused a mass exodus from the region and turned the town into little more than a military barracks. Visible from sv Michal, on the east side of the square, is the **Stoličný dom** where the postwar government was declared by President Edvard Beneš on April 4, 1945. For many observers, the fate of the country was sealed from the moment Beneš handed over four key ministries to the Communists, including the Ministry of the Interior. The Communists also saw this as a turning point, and chose the house as the venue for Košice's museum of the working class; it now contains an art gallery.

On the busy north side of the cathedral, Košice's handful of tourists dutifully climb the fourteenth-century **Urbanova veža** (Tues–Sat 9am–5pm, Sun 9am–1pm), which stands on its own set of mini-arcades, lined with gravestones discovered under the building during its nineteenth-century renovation. Lastly, the public park and fountains at the centre of the main square are a favourite spot for hanging out and make an appropriately graceful approach to the city's grand Austro-Hungarian-built **theatre** (currently undergoing a lengthy renovation).

Museums and galleries

Košice's most unusual museum is the **Mikluš Prison** (Miklušova väznica; Tues–Sat 9am–5pm, Sun 9am–1pm), down Adyho, whose original dimly lit dungeons and claustrophobic cells graphically transport you into the house's murky history as the city prison. Tickets for the prison must be bought from the geological and zoological museum ticket office diagonally opposite. Back on the main square, opposite the Franciscan Church, the **Technical Museum** (Tues–Sat 8am–5pm, Sun 8am–1pm) holds a large and eclectic selection of "technical" exhibits, from a giant pair of seventeenth-century bellows to a braille map of Europe. The emphasis, though, is on the wrought ironwork for which the region is famous – everything from gates to lampposts and church bells.

The highly recommended **Východoslovenská galéria** (Tues–Sat 10am–6pm, Sun 10am–2pm), with its permanent collection of twentieth-century paintings and sculptures by Slovak, Hungarian and Austrian artists, has moved to Hlilna 22, west of the main square. At the northern tip of the main square is námestie Maratónu mieru, a space dominated by the bulky nineteenth-century **Východoslovenské múzeum** (Tues–Sat 9am–5pm, Sun 9am–1pm), worth a look inside for its basement collection of extremely valuable fifteenth- to seventeenth-century **gold coins** – 2920 in all – minted at Kremnica, but stashed away by city burghers loyal to the Habsburgs when Imre Thököly's rebel force took Košice briefly in the 1670s. They were discovered by accident in 1935 by builders renovating no. 74 on the main square, appropriately enough the city's Finance Directorate. And just for good measure, if you haven't yet seen one, hidden round the back of the museum is a wooden Uniate Church, brought here from Carpatho-Ruthenia.

THE ROMANIES

As a foreigner, it's difficult to comprehend the animosity and racism expressed by most Czechs and Slovaks towards Gypsies, or **Romanies** (*Romy*), as they prefer to call themselves. An opinion poll published after the 1989 revolution revealed that only eleven percent of the population saw no problem in maintaining good relations with Gypsies. Yet most Czechs and Slovaks know as little about the lives of the Romanies living in their midst as the average visiting Westerner does. The prevailing media image stereotypes all Gypsies as black marketeers, pimps and alcoholics.

Like the Hungarians who inhabit the southern borders of Slovakia, the Romanies are hardly "newcomers". Originally a low-caste Indian tribe, they made their way into Central Europe via Persia as early as the fifteenth century. The Communists put a great deal of misplaced effort into forcibly integrating Romanies into Czech and Slovak society: laws were passed restricting their traditionally migratory lifestyle, families were dispersed throughout Czechoslovakia, and schools in the Romany language (an ancient tongue, closely related to Sanskrit) were not provided.

Conservative estimates put the current Romany population in the republics at around 500,000 (making this the second largest community in Europe after Romania) – in East Slovakia they account for as much as twenty percent of the population. Despite a high rate of infant mortality, caused by the insanitary conditions in which the majority of Romanies still live, the population is increasing at twice the rate of even the Slovaks. Events since 1989 have brought mixed blessings for the community: for the first time, they have begun to organise politically, and have enjoyed minor successes in local and national elections; the negative side is that rising unemployment has hit the Romanies badly, and racist attacks have greatly increased, with the police either powerless or unwilling to intervene.

Eating, drinking and entertainment

If you're looking for somewhere to **eat**, you could do worse than the *Maďarská reštaurácia* in the Levočský dom at no.65 on the main square, which features Hungarian cuisine. *U Maka* in Bočná, a side street between Vratná and Hlilná, is a new place serving draught beer and Hungarian food, definitely worth tracking down. Back on the main square, there's a pizzeria at no. 50, and opposite, the *Café Slavia*, a classy newly renovated Art-Nouveau café-restaurant. Košice's **nightlife,** such as it is, revolves around the main square and the few streets on either side. Košice's Philharmonic Orchestra play regular **concerts** at the Dom umenia on Ždanovova and inside the cathedral itself. The occasional opera is still performed at the main theatre, or at the Dom kultury while the former is closed. Those with some knowledge of Hungarian might consider an evening at the *Thalia* Hungarian theatre on Mojmirova.

One of the most unusual sights in East Slovakia is the spectacular **Herľany geyser**, 22km northeast of Košice in the foothills of the Slanské vrchy, which shoots a jet of tepid water over thirty metres into the air for about twenty minutes or so every 32 to 34 hours. *ČEDOK* will have the expected time of the next eruption, so you can time your arrival to coincide with the infrequent bus service from Košice.

Michalovce and the Slovak Sea

East of Košice lies the **Dargov Pass**, which cuts through the low-lying north–south ridge of the Slanské vrchy, gentle enough to the eye, but a natural barrier that cost the Soviet army over 22,000 men to capture in World War II. A vast **monument** at the top of the pass records the fact. Coming down from the hills, the hazy **Zemplín plain** is visible below, stretching south into Hungary's Tokaj wine region and east into the Ukraine.

Sixty kilometres east of Košice, and only 34km west of the Ukrainian border, **MICHALOVCE** is the main point of arrival for people heading for the Slovak Sea. Frequent buses run from Košice to Michalovce, but only two direct trains (1hr 30min), which leave early in the morning – otherwise you'll have to change at Bánovce nad Ondravou (2hr 30min). Other than to change buses, there's no reason to hang around in Michalovce; if you do find yourself with an hour to spare between departures, you could head for the **town museum** (Tues–Fri 8am–4pm, Sat & Sun 8–11am), housed in the chateau opposite the bus station, or sample some local Zemplín cuisine at the *Hotel Družba*, again by the bus station.

The Slovak Sea

A large artificial lake created in the 1960s for industrial purposes, the **Slovak Sea** (Zemplínska šírava) to the east of Michalovce has become an extremely popular summer destination for Slovaks in the last few years. With such a late start in life, brash cheek-by-jowl *chata* colonies are the norm in resorts that merge into one

---

HIKING IN THE VIHORLAT

The volcanic hills of the Vihorlat offer some of the most rewarding **hiking** outside the main Tatra ranges: in particular, the trek up to the glacial lake of **Morské oko**. The best time to come is in late September, when the beech trees which cover the Vihorlat turn the hills a brilliant golden brown. The most difficult part is catching a bus further than the village of REMETSKÉ HÁMRE, which you'll need to do if you want to avoid walking the 9km up to the lake. In July and August, a daily bus runs from Michalovce to the car park just below Morské oko, but it passes along the southern shore of the Slovak Sea. The bus service which stops along the northern shore runs weekday mornings only.

From Remetské Hámre, it's a gentle two-hour hike along the pockmarked road to the lake; from the car park, it's just ten minutes. Unfortunately, it's not possible to swim in the lake since the whole area has been declared a nature reserve, but you can picnic wherever you please. Alternatively, it's an hour or so from the shores of the lake to **Sninský kameň** (1005m), a slab of sheer rock which rises up above the tree line, accessible only by ladder. The view from the top is outstanding – the blue-green splodge of Morské oko, the Slovak Sea and Zemplín plain beyond are all clearly visible, and on a good day you can see over into the Ukraine, just 15km to the east. If you'd prefer not to backtrack, it's less than an hour's walk north to the village of ZEMPLÍNSKE HÁMRE, from where it's a further 5km to BELÁ NAD CIROCHOU (a short train ride from Michalovce).

If you're planning on hiking anywhere else in the Vihorlat, get hold of the hiking map *Bukovské vrchy/Laborecká vrchovina*, and ask at *ČEDOK* in Michalovce for the latest information on the area.

another along the lake's northern shores; not everyone's cup of tea, to be sure, but there are compensations – it's hotter here than anywhere else in the country, and the sun continues to shine well into October. The water is far from crystal clear, but there are plenty of opportunities for **hiking** in the hills of the Vihorlat to the north of the lake (see box overleaf).

VINNÉ, the first settlement you come to from Michalovce, isn't actually on the lake shore, but has its own swimming possibilities in the much cleaner mini-lake a short walk northeast of town, and there's even a ruined **castle** above the village (1hr 30min by foot). Otherwise, the resorts are much of a concrete muchness, though the further east, the less crowded they get. In high season, **accommodation** can be a problem unless you have a tent, although many campsites have cheap **bungalows** to rent. There's a motel in KAMENEC, and the *Merkur* hotel in HÔRKA, but failing that you'll have to fall back on Michalovce's hotel options and bus it to the beach. Of the many **campsites** along the shores, your best bet is the site just past KLOKOČOV (mid-May to mid-Sept).

INTO THE UKRAINE

Since the spring of 1992 it has been possible to obtain **Ukrainian visas** on the spot at border crossings for around £30/$50 in any hard currency, but visas issued by Russian embassies and consulates will not be accepted. The only **road crossing** between Slovakia and the Ukraine is the one at VYŠNÉ NEMECKÉ, which is open 24 hours although you should count on long delays; the rail crossing is at ČIERNA NAD TISOU, whose railway siding was the scene of the last-ditch talks between the Soviets and Dubček's reformists shortly before the invasion of August 1968. Be warned that the **customs** at UZHGOROD (Užgorod) and CHOP (Čop) on the Ukrainian side may be out to extort cash or confiscate desirable items from travellers. The reason for this becomes apparent once you enter Trans-Carpathia, a forgotten corner of Central Europe that is as poor and backward as Albania. It was known as **Ruthenia** between the wars, when it formed an integral part of Czechoslovakia.

---

travel details

Trains

Connections with Bratislava: Rožňava (2 daily; 8hr); Prešov (1 daily; 7hr 15min); Košice (10 daily; 7hr); Humenné (1 daily; 8hr 30min); Čierná nad Tisou (4 daily; 9hr 30min).

From Poprad to Kežmarok/Stará Ľubovňa (13 daily; 35min/1hr 35min); Spišská Nová Ves (up to hourly; 20min); Prešov (2 daily; 1hr 20min); Košice (12 or more daily; 1hr 30min).

From Prešov to Bardejov (up to 12 daily; 1hr 30min); Humenné (11 daily; 1hr 15min–2hr); Košice (up to 14 daily; 50min).

From Košice to Rožňava (up to 10 daily; 1hr 15min–2hr); Plešivec (8 daily; 1hr 20min–1hr 50min); Lučenec (4 daily; 3hr 10min); Čierná nad Tisou (14 daily; 1hr 10min–1hr 45min).

Buses

From Poprad to Levoča (up to 12 daily; 30–50min); Spišské Podhradie (up to 10 daily; 45min–1hr 20min); Prešov (up to 10 daily; 2hr).

From Stará Ľubovňa to Červený Kláštor (up to 10 daily; 40–50min); Prešov (up to 14 daily; 2hr); Bardejov (up to 12 daily; 1hr 20min); Svidník (up to 2 daily; 1hr 45min).

From Rožňava to Krásnohorské Podhradie (up to hourly; 10min); Ochtiná (up to 6 daily; 40min); Dedinky/Poprad (up to 8 daily; 1hr/2hr).

From Prešov to Michalovce (up to 10 daily; 1hr 45min); Medzilaborce (up to 2 daily; 2hr 20min); Uzhgorod (2 daily; 4hr).

From Svidník to Prešov (up to 3 daily; 1hr 40min); Dukla Pass (up to 4 daily; 35min); Bardejov (up to 8 daily; 1hr 5min); Medzilaborce (up to 4 daily; 1hr 30min).

From Košice to Michalovce (up to hourly; 1hr 30min); Uzhgorod (1 daily; 4hr); Miskolc (up to 3 daily; 2hr).

PART FOUR

THE
CONTEXTS

THE HISTORICAL FRAMEWORK

Czechoslovakia had been in existence for a mere seventy-four years when it officially split on January 1, 1993. Before that period, its constituent parts – Bohemia, Moravia and Slovakia – enjoyed quite separate histories: the first two under the sway of their German and Austrian neighbours; Slovakia under the Hungarian crown. Only in the early days of Slav history were all three loosely linked together as the Great Moravian Empire; later, Bohemia consistently played a pivotal role in European history, prompting the famous pronouncement (attributed to Bismarck) that "he who holds Bohemia holds mid-Europe". From the foundation of the First Republic in 1918 to the upheavals of 1989, Czechoslovakia's tragedies have been exposed to the world at regular intervals – 1938, 1948 and 1968.

BEGINNINGS

According to Roman records, the area now covered by the Czech and Slovak republics was inhabited as early as 500 BC by **Celtic tribes**: the Boii, who settled in Bohemia (which bears their name), and the Cotini, who inhabited Moravia and parts of Slovakia. Very little is known about either tribe except that around 100 BC they were driven from these territories by two **Germanic tribes**, the Marcomanni who occupied Bohemia, and the Quadi who took over from the Cotini. These later semi-nomadic tribes proved awkward opponents for the Roman Empire, which wisely chose to use the River Danube as their natural eastern border.

The disintegration of the Roman Empire in the fifth century AD corresponded with a series of raids into central Europe by eastern tribes, firstly the **Huns** who displaced the Marcomanni and Quadi, and later the **Avars** who replaced the Huns around the sixth century, settling a vast area including the Hungarian plains and parts of what is now the Czech and Slovak republics. About the same time, the **Slav tribes** entered Europe from east of the Carpathian mountains. To begin with at least, they appear to have been subjugated by the Avars. The first successful Slav rebellion against the Avars seems to have taken place in the seventh century, under the Frankish leadership of **Samo**, though the kingdom he created died with him around 658 AD.

THE GREAT MORAVIAN EMPIRE

The next written record of the Slavs in this region isn't until the eighth century, when East Frankish (Germanic) chroniclers report a people known as the **Moravians** as having established themselves around the River Morava, a tributary of the Danube, which now forms part of the border between the Czech and Slovak republics. It was an alliance of Moravians and Franks (under Charlemagne) which finally expelled the Avars from central Europe in 796 AD.

This cleared the way for the establishment of the **Great Moravian Empire**, which at its peak included Slovakia, Bohemia and parts of Hungary and Poland. Its first attested ruler, **Mojmír**, found himself at the political and religious crossroads of Europe under pressure from two sides: from the West, where the Franks and Bavarians (both Germanic tribes) were jostling for position with the papacy; and from the East, where the Patriarch of Byzantium was keen to extend his influence across eastern Europe. Mojmír's successor, **Rastislav** (850–870), plumped for Byzantium, and invited the missionaries Cyril and

Methodius to introduce Christianity using the Slav liturgy and Eastern rites. Rastislav, however, was ousted by his nephew, **Svätopluk** (871–894), who captured and blinded his uncle, allying himself with the Germans instead. With the death of Methodius in 885, the Great Moravian Empire fell decisively under the influence of the Catholic Church.

Svätopluk died shortly before the **Magyar invasion** of 896, an event which heralded the end of the Great Moravian Empire and a significant break in Czech and Slovak history. The Slavs to the west of the River Morava (ie the Czechs) swore allegiance to the Frankish Emperor, Arnulf; while those to the east (ie the Slovaks) found themselves under the yoke of the Magyars. This separation, which remained for the next millennium, is one of the major factors behind the distinct social, cultural and political differences between Czechs and Slovaks.

THE PŘEMYSLID DYNASTY

During the tenth century, Bohemia began to emerge as a coherent political unit. Although under the shadow of the neighbouring Holy Roman Empire, it was ruled over by a native dynasty of Czech princes known as the **Přemyslids**. Nothing very certain is known about the early Přemyslid rulers, though many legends survive, most famously that of the proselytising **Prince Václav** (Saint Wenceslas) who was martyred by his pagan brother Boleslav the Cruel in 929 (see p.62). By the time the latter's son, Boleslav the Pious (967–999), assumed the crown, Bohemia had officially become part of the Holy Roman Empire, its prince one of the seven electors of the emperor. During the eleventh century the Czech Lands (Bohemia and Moravia) were permanently united, though Moravia remained a separate province, usually ruled by a younger son of whoever was on the Bohemian throne.

The **thirteenth century** was the high point of Přemyslid rule over Bohemia. With the Emperor Frederick II preoccupied with Mediterranean affairs and dynastic problems, and the Hungarians and Poles busy trying to repulse the Mongol invasions from 1220 onwards, the Přemyslids were able to assert their independence. In 1212, Otakar I (1198–

1230) managed to extract a "**Golden Bull**" (formal edict) from the emperor, securing the royal title for himself and his descendents (who thereafter became kings of Bohemia). The discovery of silver and gold mines throughout the Czech Lands and Slovakia heralded a big shift in the population from the countryside to the towns. Large-scale **German colonisation** was encouraged by the Přemyslids in Bohemia and Moravia, and by the Hungarian Árpád dynasty in Slovakia. German miners and craftsmen founded whole towns in the interior of the country, where German civic rights were guaranteed them, for example Kutná Hora, Jihlava, Banská Bystrica and Levoča. At the same time, the territories of the Bohemian crown were increased to include not only Bohemia and Moravia but also Silesia and Lusatia to the north (now divided between Germany and Poland).

The beginning of the fourteenth century saw a series of dynastic disputes – messy even by medieval standards – beginning with the death of Václav II from consumption and excess in 1305. The following year, the murder of his son, the heirless teenage Václav III, marked the **end of the Přemyslid dynasty** (he had four sisters, but female succession was not recognised in Bohemia). The nobles' first choice of successor, the Habsburg Albert I, was murdered by his own nephew, and when Albert's son, Rudolf I, died of dysentery not long afterwards, Bohemia was once more left without any heirs.

THE LUXEMBOURG DYNASTY

The crisis was finally solved when the Czech nobles offered the throne to **John of Luxembourg** (1310–46), who was married to Václav III's youngest sister. German by birth, but educated in France, King John spent most of his reign participating in foreign wars, with Bohemia footing the bill, and John himself paying for it first with his sight, and finally with his life, on the field at Crécy in 1346. His son, **Charles IV** (1346–78), was wounded in the same battle, but thankfully for the Czechs lived to tell the tale.

It was Charles who ushered in the Czech nation's **golden age**. Although born and bred in France, Charles was a Bohemian at heart (his mother was Czech and his real name was

Václav): he was also extremely intelligent, speaking five languages fluently and even writing an autobiography. In 1346, he became not only king of Bohemia, but also, by election, Holy Roman Emperor. Two years later he founded a university in Prague and began promoting the city as the cultural capital of central Europe, erecting rich Gothic monuments – many of which still survive – and numerous ecclesiastical institutions. As emperor, Charles issued many Golden Bull edicts that strengthened Bohemia's position, promoted Czech as the official language alongside Latin and German, and presided over a period of relative peace in central Europe, while western Europe was tearing itself apart in the Hundred Years' War.

Charles' son, **Václav IV**, who assumed the throne in 1378, was no match for such an inheritance. He was a legendary drinker, prone to violent outbursts, and so unpopular with the powers that be that he was imprisoned twice – once by his own nobles, and once by his brother, Sigismund. His reign was also characterised by religious divisions within the Czech Lands and Europe as a whole, beginning with the **Great Schism** (1378–1417) when rival popes held court in Rome and Avignon. This was a severe blow to Rome's centralising power, which might otherwise have successfully combated the assault on the Church which was under way in the Czech Lands towards the end of the fourteenth century.

THE CZECH REFORMATION

The attack was led by the peasant-born preacher **Jan Hus**, who was the first Czech-speaker to be appointed to the influential position of Rector at Prague University in 1403. A follower of the English reformer John Wycliffe, Hus began to preach in the language of the masses (ie Czech) against the wealth, corruption and hierarchical tendencies within the Church at the time. Although a devout, mild-mannered man, as Rector Hus became embroiled in a dispute between the conservative German archbishop and clergy and the Wycliffian Czechs at the university. For political and personal reasons – Václav backed Hus, the confessor to his wife, Queen Sophie – and the Germans, who made up the majority of the students, left the university in protest.

The scene was set for an international showdown – and civil war. Widening his attacks on the Church, Hus began to preach against the sale of religious indulgences to fund the inter-papal wars, thus incurring the enmity of Václav, who received a percentage of the sales. In 1412 Hus and his followers were expelled from the university and spent the next two years as itinerant preachers spreading their reformist gospel throughout Bohemia. In 1414 Hus was summoned to the **Council of Constance** to answer charges of heresy. Despite a guarantee of safe conduct from the Emperor Sigismund, he was condemned to death and, having refused to renounce his beliefs, was burned at the stake on July 6, 1415.

Hus's martyrdom sparked off a **widespread rebellion** in Bohemia, initially uniting virtually all Czechs – clergy and laity, peasant and noble (including many of Hus's former opponents) – against the decision of the council, and, by inference, against the Catholic Church and its conservative, mostly German clergy. The Hussites immediately set about reforming church practices, most famously by administering communion *sub utraque specie* ("in both kinds", ie bread and wine) to the laity, as opposed to the Roman Catholic practice of reserving the wine for the clergy.

THE HUSSITE WARS: 1419–1434

In 1419, Václav inadvertently provoked large-scale rioting by endorsing the re-admission of anti-Hussite priests to their parishes. In the ensuing violence, several Catholic councillors were thrown to their death from the windows of Prague's Novoměstská radnice, in Prague's **first defenestration** (see p.101). Václav himself was so enraged (not to say terrified) by the mob that he suffered a heart attack and died, "roaring like a lion", according to a contemporary chronicler. The pope, meanwhile, declared an international crusade against the Czech heretics, under the leadership of the Emperor Sigismund, Václav's brother, and, since Václav had failed to produce an heir, the next in line for the Bohemian throne.

Already, though, cracks were appearing in the Hussite camp. The more radical reformers, who became known as the **Táborites**, broadened their attacks on the Church hierarchy to include all figures of authority and privilege. Their message found a ready audience among the oppressed classes in Prague and the Bohemian countryside, who went round eagerly destroying church property and massacring Catholics. Such actions were deeply disturbing to the Czech nobility and their supporters who backed the more moderate Hussites – known as the **Utraquists** (from the Latin *sub utraque specie*) – who confined their criticisms to religious matters.

For the moment, however, the common Catholic enemy prevented a serious split amongst the Hussites, and under the inspirational military leadership of the Táborite **Jan Žižka**, the Hussites' (mostly peasant) army enjoyed some miraculous early victories over the numerically superior "crusaders". The Bohemian Diet quickly drew up the **Four Articles of Prague**, which was essentially a compromise between the two Hussite camps, outlining the basic tenets about which all Hussites could agree, including communion "in both kinds". The Táborites, meanwhile, continued to burn, loot and pillage ecclesiastical institutions from Prague to the far reaches of Slovakia.

At the **Council of Basel** in 1433 Rome reached a compromise with the Utraquists over the Four Articles, in return for ceasing hostilities. The peasant-based Táborites rightly saw the deal as a victory for the Bohemian nobility and the status quo, and vowed to continue the fight. However, the Utraquists, now in cahoots with the Catholic forces, easily defeated the remaining Táborites at the Battle of Lipany, outside Kolín, in 1434.

By the end of the Hussite Wars, the situation for the majority of the population – landless serfs, and, as such, virtual slaves to the local feudal lords – had actually changed very little. The most significant development in the **social structure** was in the balance of power between the Czechs and Germans of the Czech Lands. Temporarily, at least, the seemingly inexorable German immigration had been checked. The merchant class was still predominantly German and the peasantry mostly Czech, but now, for the first time, there were additional religious differences between the two communities which only increased the mutual distrust.

COMPROMISE AND COUNTER-REFORMATION

Despite the agreement of the Council of Basel, the pope refused to acknowledge the Utraquist church in Bohemia. The Utraquists nevertheless consolidated their position, electing the gifted **George of Poděbrady** as first Regent and then King of Bohemia (1458–71). The first and last Hussite king, George (Jiří to the Czechs) is remembered primarily for his commitment to promoting religious tolerance and for his farsighted efforts in trying to establish some sort of "Peace Confederation" in Europe.

On George's death, the Bohemian Estates handed the crown over to the **Polish Jagiellonian dynasty** who ruled in absentia, effectively relinquishing the reins of power to the Czech nobility. In 1526, however, the victory of the Turks over the Hungarians at the Battle of Mohács led to the election of the Habsburg Ferdinand I as king of the Czech Lands – and what was left of Hungary (mostly Upper Hungary, ie what is now Slovakia) – in order to fill the power vacuum, marking the **beginning of Habsburg rule** over what are now the Czech and Slovak republics. Ferdinand adroitly secured automatic hereditary succession over the Bohemian throne for his dynasty, in return for which he accepted the agreement laid down at the Council of Basel in 1537.

In 1546, the Utraquist Bohemian nobility provocatively joined the powerful Protestant Schmalkaldic League in their (ultimately successful) war against the Holy Roman Emperor, Charles V. When armed conflict broke out in Bohemia, however, victory fell to Ferdinand, who took the opportunity to extend the influence of Catholicism in the Czech Lands, executing several leading Protestant nobles, persecuting the reformist Unity of Czech Brethren who had figured prominently in the rebellion, and inviting Jesuit missionaries to establish churches and seminaries in the Czech Lands.

Czechs tend to regard the reign of **Rudolf II** (1576–1611), Ferdinand's eventual successor, as a second golden age. Rudolf re-established Prague as the royal capital, in preference to Vienna, which was then under threat from the Turks. As far as the Catholic Church was concerned, however, Rudolf's religious tolerance and indecision were a disaster. In the early 1600s, Rudolf's melancholy began to veer close to insanity, and in 1611, he was forced to abdicate by his brother **Matthias**, to save the Habsburg house from ruin. Ardently Catholic, but equally heirless, Matthias proposed his cousin, **Ferdinand II**, as his successor in 1617. This was the last straw for Bohemia's nobility, and the following year conflict erupted again.

THE THIRTY YEARS' WAR: 1618–1648

On May 23, 1618, two Catholic nobles were thrown out of the windows of Prague Castle – the country's **second defenestration** (see p.63) – an event that's now taken as the official beginning of the complex religious and dynastic conflicts collectively known as the **Thirty Years' War**. Following the defenestration, the Bohemian Diet expelled the Jesuits and elected the youthful Protestant "Winter King", Frederick of the Palatinate, to the throne. In the first decisive set-to of the war, on November 8, 1620, the Czech Protestants were utterly defeated at the **Battle of Bílá hora** (Battle of the White Mountain). In the aftermath, twenty-seven Protestant nobles were executed on the Staroměstské náměstí in Prague and an estimated five-sixths of the Czech nobility went into exile, their properties handed over to loyal Catholic families from Austria, Spain and Italy.

THE DARK AGES AND THE ENLIGHTENMENT

The Thirty Years' War ended with the **Peace of Westphalia**, which, for the Czechs, was as disastrous as the war itself. The country was devastated, towns and cities laid waste, and the total population reduced by almost two-thirds. On top of all that, the Czech Lands were now decisively under the Catholic sphere of influence, and the full force of the **Counter-Reformation** was brought to bear on its people. All forms of Protestantism were outlawed, the education system was handed over to the Jesuits and, in 1651 alone, over two hundred "witches" were burned at the stake in Bohemia.

The next two centuries of Habsburg rule are known to the Czechs as the **dark ages**. Austria's absolutist grip over the Czech Lands catapulted the remaining nobility into intensive Germanisation, while fresh waves of German

immigrants reduced Czech to a despised dialect spoken by peasants, artisans and servants. The situation was so bad that Prague and most other urban centres became practically all-German cities. By the end of the eighteenth century, the Czech language was on the verge of dying out, with government, scholarship and literature carried out exclusively in German. For the newly ensconced Germanised aristocracy, of course, the good times rolled and the country was endowed with numerous Baroque palaces and monuments.

After a century of iron-fisted Habsburg rule, dispute arose over the accession of Charles VI's daughter, **Maria Theresa** (1740–80), to the throne. Maria Theresa's reign marked the beginning of the **Enlightenment** in the Habsburg Empire. Despite her own personal attachment to the Jesuits, the empress acknowledged the need for reform, and followed the lead of Spain, Portugal and France in expelling the order from the empire in 1773. But it was her son, **Joseph II** (1780–90), who, in the ten short years of his reign, brought about the most radical changes to the social structure of the Habsburg lands. His 1781 Edict of Tolerance allowed a large degree of freedom of worship for the first time in over 150 years, and went a long way towards lifting the restrictions on Jews within the empire. The following year, he ordered the dissolution of the monasteries, and embarked upon the abolition of serfdom.

Despite all his reforms, Joseph was not universally popular. Catholics – some ninety percent of the population – viewed him with disdain. His centralisation and bureaucratisation of the empire placed power in the hands of the Austrian civil service, and thus helped entrench the **Germanisation** of the Czech Lands.

THE NATIONAL REVIVALS

The Habsburgs' enlightened rule inadvertently provided the basis for the economic prosperity and social changes of the **Industrial Revolution**, which in turn fuelled the Czech national revival of the nineteenth century. The textile, glass, coal and iron industries began to grow, drawing ever more Czechs in from the countryside and swamping the hitherto mostly Germanised towns and cities. An embryonic Czech bourgeoisie emerged, and, thanks to

Maria Theresa's educational reforms, new educational and economic opportunities were given to the Czech lower classes.

For the first half of the century, the Czech national revival or **národní obrození** was confined to the new Czech intelligentsia, led by philologists like Josef Dobrovský and Josef Jungmann at Prague's Charles University. Language disputes (in schools, universities and public offices) remained at the forefront of Czech nationalism throughout the nineteenth century, only later developing into demands for political autonomy from Vienna. The leading figure of the time was the historian **František Palacký**, a Protestant from Moravia, who wrote the first history of the Czech nation, rehabilitating Hus and the Czech reformists in the process. He was in many ways typical of the early Czech nationalists – pan-Slavist and virulently anti-German, but not yet entirely anti-Habsburg.

THE SLOVAK NÁRODNÉ OBRODENIE

What the Czechs suffered in the three centuries following the Battle of Bílá hora, the Slovaks had to endure for almost a millennium, under **Hungarian rule**. For the entire duration, the territory of modern-day Slovakia was an integral part of the Hungarian Kingdom, known simply as Upper Hungary, and apart from a few German-speaking mining towns, it remained overwhelmingly rural and resolutely feudal. Those Slovaks who did rise to positions of power were swiftly "Magyarised".

The Battle of Mohács in 1526 signalled a temporary eclipse for the Hungarians as the Habsburgs assumed control of their kingdom. The eighteenth-century Enlightenment, on the other hand, boosted the **Magyar national revival**, and in 1792 Hungarian finally replaced Latin as the official state language throughout the Hungarian Kingdom. But Magyar nationalism was essentially chauvinistic, furthering the interests of the Magyarised nobility and no one else. The idea that non-Magyars might also want to assert their own separate identity was regarded as highly subversive.

With a thoroughly Magyarised aristocracy, and a feudal society with virtually no Slovak middle class, the Slovak national revival or **národné obrodenie** was left to the tiny Slovak intelligentsia that was made up mostly of Lutheran clergymen – passionately pro-Czech and anti-Magyar, but alienated from the majority of the devoutly Catholic Slovak peasantry on account of their religious beliefs. The leading Slovak figure throughout this period was **Ľudovít Štúr**, son of a Lutheran pastor, pan-Slavist but, unlike many of his contemporaries, an ardent advocate of a separate Slovak language based on his own Central Slovak dialect.

1848 AND ALL THAT

The fall of the French monarchy in February 1848 prompted a crisis in the Habsburg Empire. The new bourgeoisie, Czech, German and Magyar, began to make political demands – freedom of the press, of assembly, of religious creeds – and in the nature of the Empire, its constituent nationalities also called out for more rights. In the **Czech Lands**, liberal opinion became polarised between the Czech- and German-speakers. Palacký and his followers were against the dissolution of the Empire and argued instead for a kind of multinational federation. Since the Empire contained a majority of Slavs, the ethnic Germans were utterly opposed to Palacký's scheme, campaigning for unification with Germany to secure their interests. So when Palacký was invited to the Pan-German National Assembly in Frankfurt in May, he refused to go. Instead, he convened a **Pan-Slav Congress** the following month, which met in Prague. Meanwhile, the radicals and students (on both sides) took to the streets in protest, giving the forces of reaction an excuse to declare martial law. On June 16, the Austrian military bombarded Prague; the following morning the city capitulated – the counter-revolution in the Czech Lands had begun.

In the **Hungarian Kingdom**, the 1848 revolution successfully toppled the Habsburgs, and a liberal constitutional government was temporarily set up in Budapest. However, Hungarian liberals like Lajos Kossuth (himself from a Magyarised Slovak family) showed themselves to be more reactionary than the Habsburgs when it came to opposing the aspirations of non-Magyars. The "Demands of the Slovak Nation", drafted by Štúr, were refused point-blank by the Hungarian Diet in May 1848. Incensed by this, Štúr and his small Slovak army went over to the Habsburgs and into battle (unsuccessfully) against Kossuth's revolutionaries. Only in August 1849 was Habsburg rule reinstated, thanks to the intervention of Tsarist Russian troops on the streets of Budapest.

In both cases, the upheavals of 1848 left the absolutist Habsburg Empire shaken but fundamentally unchanged. The one great positive achievement in 1848 was the **emancipation of the peasants**. Otherwise, events only served to highlight the sharp differences between German and Czech aspirations in the Czech Lands, and between Hungarian and Slovak aspirations in the Hungarian Kingdom.

The Habsburg recovery was, however, short-lived. In 1859 and again in 1866, the new Emperor, Francis Joseph II, suffered humiliating defeats at the hands of the Italians and Prussians respectively. In order to buy some more time, the compromise or *Ausgleich* of 1867 was drawn up, establishing the so-called **Dual Monarchy** of Austria-Hungary – two independent states united by one ruler.

THE CZECH LANDS

For the Czechs, the *Ausgleich* came as a bitter disappointment. The Magyars became the Austrians' equals, while the Czechs remained second-class citizens. The Czechs' failure in bending the Emperor's ear was no doubt partly due to the absence of a Czech aristocracy which could bring its social weight to bear at the Viennese court. Nevertheless, the *Ausgleich* did mark an end to the absolutism of the immediate post-1848 period, and, compared to the Hungarians, the Austrians were positively enlightened in the wide range of civil liberties they granted, culminating in universal male suffrage in 1907.

Under Dualism the Czech **národní obrození** flourished – and splintered. The liberals and conservatives known as the **Old Czechs**, backed by the new Czech industrialists, advocated working within existing legislature to achieve their aims. By 1890, though, the more radical **Young Czechs** had gained the upper hand and instigated a policy of non-cooperation with Vienna. The most famous political figure to emerge from the ranks of the Young Czechs was the Prague university professor **Tomáš Garrigue Masaryk**, who founded his own Realist Party and began advocating the (then rather quirky) concept of closer cooperation between the Czechs and Slovaks.

SLOVAKIA

For the Slovaks, the *Ausgleich* was nothing less than a catastrophe. In the 1850s and 1860s, direct rule from Vienna had kept Magyar chauvinism at bay, allowing the Slovaks to establish various cultural and educational institutions. After 1867, the Hungarian authorities embarked on a maniacal policy of **Magyarisation** which made Hungarian (and only Hungarian) compulsory in both primary and secondary schools. Large landowners were the only ones to be given the vote (a mere six percent of the total population), while the majority of non-Magyars remained peasants. Poverty and malnutrition were commonplace throughout Upper Hungary and, by 1914, twenty percent of the Slovak population had emigrated, mostly to the USA.

Given the suffocating policies of the Magyars, it's a miracle that the Slovak *národné obrodenie* (and even the language itself) was able to survive. The leading Slovak political force, the Slovak National Party, was driven underground, remaining small, conservative, and for the most part Lutheran, throughout the latter part of the nineteenth century. The one notable exception was the Catholic priest **Andrej Hlinka**, whose unflinching opposition to Magyar rule earned him an increasingly large audience among the Slovak people.

WORLD WAR I

At the outbreak of **World War I**, the Czechs and Slovaks showed little enthusiasm for fighting alongside their old enemies, the Austrians and Hungarians, against their Slav brothers, the Russians and Serbs. As the war progressed, large numbers defected to form the **Czechoslovak Legion**, which fought on the Eastern Front against the Austrians. Masaryk travelled to the USA to curry favour for a new Czechoslovak state while his two deputies, the Czech Edvard Beneš and the Slovak Milan Štefánik, did the same in Britain and France.

Meanwhile, the Legion, which by now numbered some 100,000 men, became embroiled in the Russian revolutions of 1917, and, when the Bolsheviks made peace with Germany, found itself cut off from the homeland. The uneasy cooperation between the Reds and the Legion broke down when Trotsky demanded that they hand over their weapons before heading off on their legendary **anabasis**, or march back home, via Vladivostok. The soldiers refused and became further involved in the Civil War, for a while controlling large parts of Siberia, and most importantly, the Trans-Siberian Railway, before arriving back to a tumultuous reception in their new joint republic.

In the summer of 1918, the Slovaks finally threw their lot in with the Czechs and the Allies recognised Masaryk's provisional government. On October 28, 1918, as the Habsburg Empire began to collapse, the new **Czechoslovak Republic** was declared in Prague. In response, the German-speaking border regions (later to become the Sudetenland) declared their own *Deutsch-Böhmen* (German-Bohemian) government, loyal to the Austrians. Nothing came of the latter, and by the end of the year Czechoslovak troops had gained control of the Sudetenland with relatively little resistance.

In Slovakia, Béla Kun's Hungarian Red Army proceeded to occupy much of the country, and it took an invasion by the Czechoslovak Legion to boot them out late on in 1919. In June 1920, the **Treaty of Trianon** confirmed the controversial new Slovak–Hungarian border along the Danube, leaving some 750,000 Hungarians on Czechoslovak soil.

Last to opt in favour of the new republic was **Ruthenia** (officially known as Sub-Carpatho-Ruthenia), a rural backwater of the old Hungarian Kingdom which became officially part of Czechoslovakia in the Treaty of St Germain in September 1919. Its incorporation was largely due to the campaigning efforts of Ruthenian emigrés in the USA. For the new republic the province was a strategic bonus, but otherwise a huge drain on resources.

THE FIRST REPUBLIC

The new nation of Czechoslovakia began post-war life in an enviable economic position – **tenth in the world industrial league table** – having inherited seventy to eighty percent of Austria-Hungary's industry intact. Less enviable was the diverse make-up of its population – a melange of minorities which would in the end prove its downfall. Along with the 6 million Czechs and 2 million Slovaks who initially backed the republic, there were over 3 million Germans and 750,000 Hungarians, not to mention sundry other Ruthenians (Rusyns), Jews and Poles.

That Czechoslovakia's democracy survived as long as it did is down to the powerful political presence and skill of **Masaryk**, the country's president from 1918 to 1935, who shared executive power with the cabinet. It was his vision of social democracy which was stamped on the nation's new constitution, one of the most liberal of the time (if a little too bureaucratic and centralised), aimed at ameliorating any ethnic and class tensions within the republic by means of universal suffrage, land reform and, more specifically, the Language Law, which ensured bilinguality to any area where the minority exceeded twenty percent.

The elections of 1920 reflected the mood of the time, ushering in the left-liberal alliance of the **Pětka** ("The Five"), a coalition of five parties led by the Agrarian, Antonín Švehla, whose slogan "We have agreed that we will agree" became the keystone of the republic's consensus politics between the wars. Gradually all the other parties (except the Fascist and Communist parties) – among them Hlinka's Slovak People's Party and most of the Sudeten German parties – began to participate in (or at least not disrupt) parliamentary proceedings. On the eve of the Wall Street Crash, the republic was enjoying an economic boom, a cultural renaissance and a temporary *modus vivendi* among its minorities.

THE THIRTIES

The 1929 Wall Street Crash plunged the whole country into crisis. Economic hardship was quickly followed by **political instability**. In Slovakia, Hlinka's People's Party fed off the anti-Czech resentment that was fuelled by Prague's manic centralisation, consistently polling around thirty percent, despite its increasingly nationalist/separatist position. In Ruthenia, the elections of 1935 gave only 37 percent of the vote to parties supporting the republic, the rest going to the Communists, pro-Magyars and other autonomist groups.

But without doubt the most intractable of the minority problems was that of the Sudeten Germans who occupied the border regions of Bohemia and Moravia. Nationalist sentiment had always run high in the Sudetenland, whose German-speakers resented having been included in the new republic, but it was only after the Crash that the extremist parties began to make significant electoral gains. Encouraged by the rise of Nazism in Germany, and aided by rocketing Sudeten German unemployment, the proto-Nazi **Sudeten German Party** (SdP), led by a gym teacher named Konrad Henlein, was able to win over sixty percent of the German-speaking votes in the 1935 elections, making it the largest single party in the national parliament.

Although constantly denying any wish to secede from the republic, after 1935 Henlein and the SdP were increasingly funded and directed from Nazi Germany. To make matters worse, the Czechs suffered a severe blow to their morale with the death of Masaryk late in 1937, leaving the country in the less capable hands of his Socialist deputy, Edvard Beneš. With the Nazi annexation of Austria (the *Anschluss*) on March 11, 1938, Hitler was free to focus his attention on the Sudetenland, calling Henlein to Berlin on March 28 and giving him instructions to call for outright autonomy.

THE MUNICH CRISIS

On April 24, 1938, the SdP launched its final propaganda offensive in the **Karlsbad Decrees**, demanding (without defining) "complete autonomy". As this would have meant surrendering the entire Czechoslovak border defences in the western half of the country, not to mention causing economic havoc, Beneš refused to bow to the SdP's demands. Armed conflict was only narrowly avoided and, by the beginning of September, Beneš was forced reluctantly to acquiesce to some sort of autonomy. On Hitler's orders, Henlein refused Beneš' offer and called openly for the secession of the Sudetenland to the German Reich.

On September 15, as Henlein fled to Germany, the British prime minister, Neville Chamberlain, flew to Berchtesgaden on his own ill-conceived initiative, to "appease" the Führer. A week later, Chamberlain flew again to Germany, this time to Bad Godesburg, vowing to the British public that the country would not go to war (in his famous words) "because of a quarrel in a far-away country between people of whom we know nothing". Nevertheless, the French issued draft papers,

the British Navy was mobilised, and the whole of Europe fully expected war. Then in the early hours of September 30, in one of the most treacherous and self-interested acts of modern European diplomacy, prime ministers Chamberlain (for Britain) and Deladier (for France) signed the **Munich Diktat** with Mussolini and Hitler, agreeing – without consulting the Czechoslovak government – to all of Hitler's demands. The British and French public were genuinely relieved, and Chamberlain flew back to cheering home crowds, waving his famous piece of paper that guaranteed "peace in our time".

THE SECOND REPUBLIC

Betrayed by his only Western allies and fearing bloodshed, Beneš capitulated, against the wishes of most Czechs. Had Beneš not given in, however, it's doubtful anything would have come of Czech armed resistance, surrounded as they were by vastly superior hostile powers. Beneš resigned on October 5 and left the country. On October 15, **German troops occupied Sudetenland** to the dismay of the forty percent of Sudeten Germans who hadn't voted for Henlein (not to mention the half a million Czechs who lived there). The Poles took the opportunity to seize a sizeable chunk of North Moravia, while in the "rump" **Second Republic** (officially known as Czecho-Slovakia), the one-eyed war veteran Emil Hácha became president, Slovakia and Ruthenia electing their own autonomous governments.

The Second Republic was not long in existence before it too collapsed. On March 15, 1939, Hitler informed Hácha of the imminent Nazi occupation of what was left of the Czech Lands, and persuaded him to demobilise the army, again against the wishes of many Czechs. The invading German army encountered no resistance (nor any response from the Second Republic's supposed guarantors, Britain and France) and swiftly set up the Nazi **Protectorate of Bohemia and Moravia**. The Hungarians effortlessly crushed Ruthenia's one-day-old independent republic, while the Slovak People's Party, with the backing of the Nazis, declared **Slovak independence**, under the leadership of the Catholic priest Jozef Tiso.

WORLD WAR II

In the first few months of the occupation, left-wing activists were arrested and Jews dismissed from their jobs, but Nazi rule in the Protectorate was not yet as harsh as it would become – the economy even enjoyed a mini-boom. Then in late October and November 1939, Czech students began a series of demonstrations against the Nazis, who responded by closing down all institutions of higher education. Calm was restored until 1941 when a leading SS officer, **Reinhard Heydrich**, was put in charge of the Protectorate. Arrests and deportations followed, reaching fever pitch after Heydrich was assassinated by the Czech resistance in June 1942 (see p.102). The "final solution" was meted out on the country's remaining Jews, who were transported first to the ghetto of Terezín, and then on to the extermination camps in Poland. The rest of the population were frightened into submission – very few acts of active resistance being undertaken in the Czech Lands until the Prague Uprising of May 1945.

In independent Slovakia, **Jozef Tiso**'s government met with widespread support until the extremist Hlinka Guards (the Slovak equivalent of the SS) got the upper hand and began the inexorable Nazification of Slovak society, including the deportation of Slovak Jews. The resistance movement was slow to start, but strong enough by August 1944 to attempt an all-out **Slovak National Uprising** in the central mountains (see p.357). When the hoped-for Soviet offensive failed to materialise, the uprising was brutally suppressed and any pretence at Slovak independence abandoned for full-scale Nazi occupation.

By the end of 1944, Czechoslovak and Russian troops had begun to liberate the country, starting with Ruthenia, which Stalin decided to take as war booty despite having guaranteed to maintain Czechoslovakia's pre-Munich borders. On April 4, 1945, under Beneš' leadership, the provisional **Národní fronta** government – a coalition of Social Democrats, Socialists and Communists – was set up in Košice. On May 5, the people of Prague finally rose up against the Nazis, many hoping to prompt an American offensive from Plzeň, which General Patton's Third Army had recently captured. In the end, the Americans made the politically disastrous (but militarily wise) decision not to cross the previously agreed upon demarcation line, leaving the Russians to liberate Prague, which they did on May 9.

THE THIRD REPUBLIC

Violent reprisals against suspected collaborators and the German-speaking population in general began as soon as the country was liberated. All Germans were given the same food rations as the Jews had been given during the war. Starvation, summary executions and worse resulted in the deaths of thousands of ethnic Germans. With considerable popular backing and the tacit approval of the Red Army, Beneš began to organise the **forced expulsion of the German-speaking population**, referred to euphemistically by the Czechs as the *odsun* (transfer). Only those Germans who could prove their anti-Fascist credentials were permitted to stay – the Czech community was not called on to prove the same – and by the summer of 1947, nearly 2.5 million Germans had been kicked out or had fled in fear. On this occasion, Sudeten German objections were brushed aside by the Allies who had given Beneš the go-ahead for the *odsun* at the postwar Potsdam Conference. Attempts by Beneš to expel the Hungarian-speaking minority in similar fashion, however, proved unsuccessful.

On October 28, 1945, in accordance with the leftist programme thrashed out at Košice, sixty percent of the country's industry was nationalised. Confiscated Sudeten German property was handed out by the largely Communist-controlled police force, and in a spirit of optimism and/or opportunism, people began to join the Communist Party (KSČ) in droves, membership more than doubling in less than a year. In the **May 1946 elections**, the Party reaped the rewards of their enthusiastic support for the *odsun*, of Stalin's vocal opposition to Munich, and of the recent Soviet liberation, emerging as the strongest single party in the Czech Lands, with up to forty percent of the vote (the largest ever for a European Communist Party in a multi-party election). In Slovakia, however, they failed to push the Democrats into second place, with just thirty percent. President Beneš appointed the KSČ leader, **Klement Gottwald**, prime minister of another Národní fronta coalition, with several, strategically important, cabinet portfolios going to Party members, including the ministries of the Interior, Finance, Labour and Social Affairs, Agriculture, and Information.

Gottwald assured everyone of the KSČ's commitment to parliamentary democracy, and, initially at least, even agreed to participate in the Americans' Marshall Plan (the only Eastern Bloc country to do so). Stalin immediately summoned Gottwald to Moscow, and on his return the KSČ denounced the Plan. By the end of 1947, the Communists were beginning to lose support, as the harvest failed, the economy faltered and malpractices within the Communist-controlled Ministry of the Interior were uncovered. In response, the KSČ began to up the ante, constantly warning the nation of imminent "counter-revolutionary plots", and arguing for greater nationalisation and land reform as a safeguard.

THE 1948 COUP

Then in February 1948 – officially known as **Victorious February** – the latest in a series of scandals hit the Ministry of the Interior, prompting the twelve non-Communist cabinet ministers to resign en masse, hoping thus to force a physically weak President Beneš to dismiss Gottwald. No attempt was made, however, to rally popular support against the Communists. Beneš received over 5000 resolutions supporting the Communists and just 150 opposing them. Stalin sent word to Gottwald to take advantage of the crisis and ask for military assistance – Soviet troops began massing on the Hungarian border.

It was the one time in his life when Gottwald disobeyed Stalin; instead, by exploiting divisions within the Social Democrats, Gottwald was able to maintain his majority in parliament. The KSČ took to the streets (and the airwaves), arming "workers' militia" units to defend the country against counter-revolution, calling a general strike and finally, on February 25, organising the country's biggest-ever demonstration in Prague. The same day Gottwald went to an indecisive (and increasingly ill) Beneš with his new cabinet, all Party members or "fellow travellers". Beneš accepted Gottwald's nominees and the most popular Communist coup in Eastern Europe was

complete, without bloodshed and without the direct intervention of the Soviets. In the aftermath of the coup, an estimated two million Czechs and Slovaks fled abroad.

THE PEOPLE'S REPUBLIC

Following Victorious February, the Party began to consolidate its position, a relatively easy task given its immense popular support and control of the army, police force, workers' militia and trade unions. A **new constitution** confirming the "leading role" of the Communist Party and the "dictatorship of the proletariat" was passed by parliament on May 9, 1948. President Beneš refused to sign it, resigned in favour of Gottwald, and died (of natural causes) shortly afterwards. Those political parties that were not banned or forcibly merged with the KSČ were prescribed fixed percentage representation within the so-called "multi-party" Národní fronta.

With the Cold War in full swing, the **Stalinisation** of Czechoslovak society was quick to follow. In the Party's first Five Year Plan, ninety percent of industry was nationalised, heavy industry (and, in particular, the country's defence industry) was given a massive boost and compulsory collectivisation forced through. Party membership reached an all-time high of 2.5 million, and "class-conscious" Party cadres were given positions of power, while "class enemies" (and their children) were discriminated against. It wasn't long, too, before the Czechoslovak mining "gulags" began to fill up with the regime's political opponents – "kulaks", priests and "bourgeois oppositionists" – numbering over 100,000 at their peak.

Having incarcerated most of its external opponents, the KSČ, with a little prompting from Stalin, embarked upon a ruthless period of internal bloodletting. As the economy nose-dived, calls for intensified "class struggle", rumours of impending "counter-revolution" and reports of economic sabotage by fifth columnists filled the press. An atmosphere of fear and confusion was created to justify **large-scale arrests of Party members** with an "international" background – those with a wartime connection with the West, Spanish Civil War veterans, Jews and Slovak nationalists.

In the early 1950s, the Party organised a series of Stalinist **show-trials**, the most ruthless of their kind outside the Soviet Union, including the trial of Rudolf Slánský, who had been second only to Gottwald in the KSČ before his arrest. He and thirteen other leading Party members were sentenced to death (eleven of them Jewish, including Slánský) as "Trotskyist-Titoist-Zionists". Soon afterwards, Vladimír Clementis, the former KSČ foreign minister, was executed along with other leading Slovak comrades (Gustáv Husák, the post-1968 president, was given life imprisonment).

AFTER STALIN

Gottwald died in mysterious circumstances in March 1953, nine days after attending Stalin's funeral in Moscow (some say he drank himself to death). The whole nation heaved a sigh of relief, but the regime seemed as unrepentent as ever. The arrests and show-trials continued. Then, on May 30, the new Communist leadership announced a drastic currency devaluation, effectively reducing wages by ten percent, while raising prices. The result was a wave of isolated **workers' demonstrations** and rioting, in Prague, Plzeň and the Ostrava mining region. Czechoslovak army units called in to suppress the demonstrations proved unreliable, and it was left to the heavily armed workers' militia and police to disperse the crowds and make the predictable arrests and summary executions.

So complete were the Party purges of the early 1950s, so sycophantic (and scared) the surviving leadership, that Khrushchev's 1956 thaw was virtually ignored by the KSČ. An attempted rebellion in the Writers' Congress was rebuffed and an enquiry into the show-trials made several minor security officials scapegoats for the "malpractices". The genuine mass base of the KSČ remained blindly loyal to the Party for the most part, and the following year, the dull, unreconstructed neo-Stalinist **Antonín Novotný** – later proved to have been a spy for the Gestapo during the war – became First Secretary and President.

REFORMISM AND INVASION

The first rumblings of protest against Czechoslovakia's hardline leadership appeared in the official press in 1963. At first, the criticisms were confined to the country's worsening economic stagnation, but soon developed into more generalised protests against the KSČ leadership. Novotný responded by ordering the belated release and rehabilitation of victims of the 1950s purges, permitting a slight cultural thaw and easing travel restrictions to the West. In effect, he was simply buying time. The half-hearted economic reforms announced in the 1965 **New Economic Model** failed to halt the recession, and the minor political reforms instigated by the KSČ only increased the pressure for greater reforms within the Party.

In 1967, Novotný attempted a pre-emptive strike against his opponents. Several leading writers were imprisoned, Slovak Party leaders were branded as "bourgeois nationalists" and the economists were called on to produce results or else forego their reform programme. Instead of eliminating the opposition, Novotný unwittingly united them. Despite Novotný's plea to the Soviets, Brezhnev refused to back a leader whom he saw as "Khrushchev's man in Prague" and on January 5, 1968, the young Slovak leader **Alexander Dubček** replaced Novotný as First Secretary. On March 22, the war hero Ludvík Svoboda dislodged Novotný from the presidency.

1968: THE PRAGUE SPRING

By inclination, Dubček was a moderate, cautious reformer, the perfect compromise candidate – but he was continually swept along by the sheer force of the reform movement. The virtual **abolition of censorship** was probably the single most significant step Dubček took. It transformed what had hitherto been an internal Party debate into a popular mass movement. Civil society, for years muffled by the paranoia and strictures of Stalinism, suddenly sprang into life in the dynamic optimism of the first few months of 1968, the so-called **"Prague Spring"**. In April, the KSČ published their Action Programme, proposing what became popularly known as "socialism with a human face" – federalisation, freedom of assembly and expression, and democratisation of parliament.

Throughout the spring and summer, the reform movement gathered momentum. The Social Democrat Party (forcibly merged with the KSČ after 1948) re-formed, anti-Soviet polemics appeared in the press and, most famously of all, the writer and lifelong Party member Ludvík Vaculík published his personal manifesto entitled "**Two Thousand Words**", calling for radical de-Stalinisation within the Party. Dubček and the moderates denounced the manifesto and reaffirmed the country's support for the Warsaw Pact military alliance. Meanwhile the Soviets and their hardline allies – Gomulka in Poland and Ulbricht in the GDR – took a very grave view of the Czechoslovak developments on their doorstep, and began to call for the suppression of "counter-revolutionary elements" and the reimposition of censorship.

As the summer wore on, it became clear that the Soviets were planning military intervention. Warsaw Pact manoeuvres were held in Czechoslovakia in late June, a Warsaw Pact conference (without Czechoslovak participation) was convened in mid-July and, at the beginning of August, the Soviets and the KSČ leadership met for **emergency bi-lateral talks** at Čierná nad Tisou on the Czechoslovak–Soviet border. Brezhnev's hardline deputy, Alexei Kosygin, made his less than subtle threat that "your border is our border", but did agree to withdraw Soviet troops (stationed in the country since the June manoeuvres) and gave the go-ahead to the KSČ's special Party Congress scheduled for September 9.

In the early hours of August 21, fearing defeat for the hardliners at the forthcoming KSČ Congress, and claiming to have been invited to provide "fraternal assistance", the Soviets gave the order for the **invasion of Czechoslovakia** to be carried out by Warsaw Pact forces (only Romania refused to take part). Dubček and the KSČ reformists immediately condemned the invasion before being arrested and flown to Moscow for "negotiations". President Svoboda refused to condone the formation of a new government under the hardliner Alois Indra, and the people took to the streets in protest, employing every form of non-violent resistance in the book. Apart from individual acts of martyrdom, like the self-immolation of **Jan Palach** on Prague's Wenceslas Square (see p.96), casualties were light compared to the Hungarian uprising of 1956, but the cost in terms of the following twenty years was much greater.

NORMALISATION

In April 1969, there were anti-Soviet riots during the celebrations of the country's double ice hockey victory over the Soviets. On this pretext, another Slovak, **Gustáv Husák**, replaced the broken Dubček as First Secretary, and instigated his infamous policy of "**normalisation**". Over 150,000 fled the country before the borders closed, around 500,000 were expelled from the Party, and an estimated one million people lost their jobs or were demoted. Inexorably, the KSČ reasserted its absolute control over the state and society. The only part of the reform package to survive the invasion was **federalisation**, which gave the Slovaks greater freedom from Prague (on paper at least), though even this was severely watered down in 1971. Dubček, like countless others, was forced to give up his job, working for the next twenty years as a minor official in the Slovak forestry commission.

An unwritten social contract was struck between rulers and ruled during the 1970s, whereby the country was guaranteed a tolerable standard of living (second only to that of the GDR in Eastern Europe) in return for its passive collaboration. Husák's security apparatus quashed all forms of dissent during the early 1970s, and it wasn't until the middle of the decade that an organised opposition was strong enough to show its face. In 1976, the punk rock band, *The Plastic People of the Universe* was arrested and charge with the familiar "crimes against the state" clause of the penal code. The dissidents who rallied to their defence – a motley assortment of people ranging from former KSČ memebers to right-wing intellectuals – agreed to form **Charter 77** (*Charta 77* in Czech and Slovak), with the purpose of monitoring human rights abuses in the country (which had recently signed the Helsinki Agreement on human rights). One of the organisation's prime movers and initial spokespersons was the absurdist Czech playwright, **Václav Havel**. Havel, along with many others, endured relentless persecution (including long prison sentences) over the next decade, in pursuit of its ideals. The initial gathering of 243 signatories increased to over 1000 by 1980 and caused panic in the moral vacuum of the Party apparatus, but consistently failed to stir a fearful and cynical populace into action.

THE EIGHTIES

In the late 1970s and early 1980s, the inefficiencies of the economy prevented the government from fulfilling its side of the social contract, as living standards began to fall. Cynicism, alcoholism, absenteeism and outright dissent became widespread, especially among the younger (post-1968) generation. The **Jazz Section** of the Musicians' Union, who disseminated "subversive" pop music (like pirate copies of "Live Aid"), highlighted the ludicrously harsh nature of the regime when they were arrested and imprisoned in the mid-1980s. Pop concerts, annual religious pilgrimages and of course the anniversary of the Soviet invasion all caused regular confrontations between the security forces and certain sections of the population. Yet still a mass movement like Poland's Solidarity failed to emerge.

With the advent of **Mikhail Gorbachev**, the KSČ was put in an extremely awkward position, as it tried desperately to separate perestroika from comparisons with the reforms of the Prague Spring. Husák and his cronies had prided themselves on being second only to Honecker's GDR as the most stable and orthodox of the Soviet satellites – now the font of orthodoxy, the Soviet Union, was turning against them. In 1987, **Miloš Jakeš** – the hardliner who oversaw Husák's normalisation purges – took over smoothly from Husák as General (First) Secretary and introduced *přestavba* (restructuring), Czechoslovakia's lukewarm version of perestroika.

1989 – THE VELVET REVOLUTION

Everything appeared to be going swimmingly for the KSČ as it entered 1989. Below the surface, however, things were becoming more and more strained. As the country's economic performance worsened, divisions were developing within the KSČ leadership. The protest movement was gathering momentum: even the Catholic Church had begun to voice dissatisfaction, compiling a staggering 500,000 signatures calling for greater freedom of worship. But the 21st anniversary of the Soviet invasion produced a demonstration of only 10,000, which was swiftly and violently dispersed by the regime.

During the summer, however, more serious cracks began to appear in Czechoslovakia's staunch hardline ally, the GDR. The trickle of East Germans fleeing to the West turned into a mass exodus, forcing Honecker to resign and, by the end of October, prompting nightly mass demonstrations on the streets of Leipzig and Dresden. The opening of the Berlin Wall on November 9 left Czechoslovakia, Romania and Albania alone on the Eastern European stage still clinging to the old truths.

All eyes were now turned upon Czechoslovakia. Reformists within the KSČ began plotting an internal coup to overthrow Jakeš, in anticipation of a Soviet denunciation of the 1968 invasion. In the end, events overtook whatever plans they may have had. On Friday, **November 17**, a 50,000-strong peaceful demonstration organised by the official Communist youth organisation was viciously attacked by the riot police. Over 100 arrests, 500 injuries and one death were reported (the fatality was later retracted), in what became known as the *masakr* (massacre). Prague's students immediately began an occupation strike, joined soon after by the city's actors, who together called for an end to the Communist Party's "leading role" and a general strike to be held for two hours on November 27.

CIVIC FORUM AND THE VPN

On Sunday, November 19, on Václav Havel's initiative, the established opposition groups like Charter 77 met and agreed to form Občanské fórum or **Civic Forum**. Their demands were simple: the resignation of the present hardline leadership, including Husák and Jakeš; an enquiry into the police actions of November 17; an amnesty for all political prisoners; and support for the general strike. In Bratislava, a parallel organisation, Verejnosť proti násiliu, or **People Against Violence** (VPN), was set up to coordinate protest in Slovakia.

On the Monday evening, the first of the really big **nationwide demonstrations** took place – the biggest since the 1968 invasion – with more than 200,000 people pouring into Prague's Wenceslas Square. This time the police held back and rumours of troop deployments proved false. Every night for a week people poured into the main squares in towns and cities across the country, repeating the calls for democracy, freedom and the end to the Party's monopoly of power. As the week dragged on, the Communist media tentatively began to report events, and the KSČ leadership started to splinter under the strain, with the prime minister, **Ladislav Adamec**, alone in sticking his neck out and holding talks with the opposition.

THE END OF ONE-PARTY RULE

On Friday evening, Dubček, the ousted 1968 leader, appeared before a crowd of over 300,000 in Prague, and in a matter of hours the entire Jakeš leadership had resigned. The weekend brought the largest demonstrations the country had ever seen – over 750,000 people in Prague alone. At the invitation of Civic Forum, Adamec addressed the crowd, only to get booed off the platform. On Monday, November 27, eighty percent of the country's workforce joined the two-hour **general strike**, including many of the Party's previously stalwart allies, the miners and engineers. The following day, the Party agreed to an end of one-party rule and the formation of a new "coalition government".

A temporary halt to the nightly demonstrations was called and the country waited expectantly for the "broad coalition" cabinet promised by Prime Minister Adamec. On December 3, another Communist-dominated line-up was announced by the Party and immediately denounced by Civic Forum and VPN, who called for a fresh wave of demonstrations and another general strike for December 11. Adamec promptly resigned and was replaced by the Slovak Marián Čalfa. On December 10, one day before the second threatened general strike, Čalfa announced his provisional **"Government of National Understanding"**, with Communists in the minority for the first time since 1948 and multi-party elections planned for June 1990. Having sworn in the new government, President Husák, architect of the post-1968 "normalisation", finally threw in the towel.

By the time the new Čalfa government was announced, the students and actors had been on strike continuously for over three weeks. The pace of change had surprised everyone

involved, but there was still one outstanding issue, the election of a new president. Posters shot up all round the capital urging **"HAVEL NA HRAD"** (Havel to the Castle – the seat of the presidency). The students were determined to see his election through, continuing their occupation strike until Havel was officially elected president by a unanimous vote of the Federal Assembly on December 29.

INTO THE 1990s

Czechoslovakia started the new decade full of optimism for what the future would bring. On the surface, the country had a lot more going for it than its immediate neighbours (with the possible exception of the GDR). The Communist Party had been swept from power without bloodshed, and, unlike the rest of Eastern Europe, Czechoslovakia had a strong, interwar democratic tradition with which to identify – Masaryk's First Republic. Despite Communist economic mismanagement, the country still had a relatively high standard of living, a skilled workforce and a manageable foreign debt.

In reality, however, the situation was somewhat different. Not only was the country economically in a worse state than most people had imagined, it was environmentally devastated, and its people were suffering from what Havel described as "post-prison psychosis" – an inability to think or act for themselves. The country had to go through the painful transition "from being a big fish in a small pond to being a sickly adolescent trout in a hatchery". As a result, it came increasingly to rely on its new-found saviour, the humble playwright-president, Václav Havel.

In most people's eyes, "Saint Václav" could do no wrong, though he himself was not out to woo his electorate. His call for the rapid withdrawal of Soviet troops was popular enough, but his apology for the postwar expulsion of Sudeten Germans was deeply resented, as was his generous amnesty which eased the country's overcrowded prisons. The amnesty was blamed by many for the huge **rise in crime** in the first half of 1990. Every vice in the book – from racism to homicide – raised its ugly head in the first year of freedom.

In addition, there was still plenty of talk about the possibility of "counter-revolution", given the thousands of unemployed StB (secret police) at large. Inevitably, accusations of previous StB involvement rocked each political party in turn in the run-up to the first free elections. The controversial *lustrace* (literally lustration or cleansing) law, which barred all those on StB files from public office for the following five years, has ended the career of many a politican and public figure, often on the basis of highly unreliable StB reports.

Despite all the inevitable hiccups and the increasingly vocal Slovak nationalists, Civic Forum/VPN remained high in the opinion polls. The **June 1990 elections** produced a record-breaking 99 percent turnout. With around sixty percent of the vote, Civic Forum/VPN were clear victors (the Communists got just thirteen percent) and Havel immediately set about forming a broad "Coalition of National Sacrifice", including everyone from Christian Democrats to former Communists.

THE ECONOMY

The main concern of the new government was how to transform an outdated command-system economy into a market economy able to compete with its EC neighbours. One of the first acts of the new government was to pass a **restitution law**, handing back small businesses and property to those from whom it had been expropriated after the 1948 Communist coup. Even this proved to be a controversial issue, since it excluded Jewish families driven out in 1938 by the Nazis, and, of course, the millions of Sudeten Germans who were forced to flee the country after the war. The argument over the speed of economic reform caused Civic Forum to split into two main camps: the centre-left Občánské hnutí or **Civic Movement** (OH), led by the foreign minister and former dissident Jiří Dienstbier, who favoured a more gradualist approach; and Občánská democratická strana or the right-wing **Civic Democratic Party** (ODS), headed by the finance minister **Václav Klaus**, whose pronouncement that the country should "walk the tightrope to Thatcherism" sent shivers up the spines of those familiar with the UK in the 1980s.

Klaus is currently putting the country through the most radical privatisation programme in the former Eastern Bloc. In the first stage, small businesses were auctioned off, many going for well over the 500,000kčs

any one person could have earned under the last regime – in other words, most of the buyers were either Czechs and Slovaks acting as proxies for foreign investors, ex-Party hacks who had laundered money, or black marketeers. The second stage, still in progress at the time of going to press, is the unique **coupon privatisation**. Every citizen was offered the right to buy 2000kčs worth of privatisation coupons, which would then be converted into shares in whatever business they saw fit. Potentially a quite radical democratising move, this has been watered down by the involvement of various less than scrupulous investment agencies, to which many people have pledged their coupons, and who then make the final decision as to where the money is invested. After a slow start, a staggering nine million people have now taken up the offer. However, given that an estimated forty percent of the businesses being floated are likely to go under in the first year, it remains to be seen whether this programme of privatisation will go any way to solving the country's economic malaise.

Thanks to severe devaluation, the Czechoslovak crown (though not yet fully convertible) now seems to be holding its own against the major western currencies, and inflation is stabilising, though industrial production has dropped by more than 25 percent and unemployment, particularly in Slovakia, is now a major concern. Life for someone on the national average wage is becoming more and more difficult, and society is in danger of developing into the classic Third World model of a small number of haves, set against a large number of have-nots.

THE SLOVAK CRISIS

One of the most difficult issues that needed to be resolved in post-Communist Czechoslovakia was the **Slovak problem**. Having been the victim of Prague-inspired centralisation from just about every Czech leader from Masaryk to Gottwald, the Slovaks were in no mood to suffer second-class citizenship any longer. During the whole of 1990 and 1991, feelings were running high in Slovakia, and, more than once, the spectre of a "Slovak UDI" seemed perilously close. Despite the tireless campaigning and negotiating by both sides, a compromise agreement failed to emerge.

The **June 1992 elections** soon became an unoffical referendum on the future of the federation. Events moved rapidly towards the breakup of the republic after the resounding victory of the Movement for a Democratic Slovakia (HZDS), under the wily, populist politician, **Vladimír Mečiar**, who had promised to declare Slovak sovereignty if he got into power. In the Czech Lands, Václav Klaus' right-wing ODS emerged as the largest single party. Although Klaus spoke in favour of continuing the federation, he was more pragmatic than many about the possible break-up of Czechoslovakia. He was adamant that if the Slovaks remained within the federation, they must adhere to his free-market economic reforms. Since Mečiar had been elected, in part, for his popular commitment to slow down the harsh privatisation policies which had already wrought such havoc in Slovakia, the possibility of a compromise seemed more hopeless than ever. The talks went badly, and Mečiar went ahead with his **declaration of sovereignty**. The HZDS also succeeded in blocking the re-election of Havel, who had committed himself entirely to the pro-federation cause. Havel promptly resigned, leaving the country presidentless, though he has since hinted that he may stand for the Czech presidency in 1993.

The official **break-up of the republic** took effect from January 1, 1993. However, negotiations about the exact nature of the split look set to continue over the next year or so, as the two republics attempt to disentangle themselves from their 74-year marriage. Neither republic is keen to jeopardise its relationship with the EC; a free trade agreement has already been signed, but separate currencies look inevitable in the near future. Fears of a Yugoslav-type situation arising between the Czechs and Slovaks are unfounded, but the possibility of trouble between the Slovaks and the Hungarian minority is rather more worrying (for more on this, see p.344).

BOOKS

The recent upsurge of interest in all things eastern European has had a number of positive repercussions. In addition to the eye-witness accounts of the "Velvet Revolution", several new histories of the country have appeared in print and there's a much wider choice of Czech fiction than ever before, including several previously untranslated women writers, though still precious few new Slovak translations to speak of. Nevertheless, if you're encountering any difficulties, the best source of specialist books on all things Czech and Slovak is *Collets London Bookshop*, 40 Great Russell Street, London WC1 (☎071/580 7538).

Where two publishers are given, the first is the UK publisher, the second the US.

HISTORY, POLITICS AND SOCIETY

Janusz Bugajski *Czechoslovakia – Charter 77's Decade of Dissent* (Praeger). Informative, comprehensive but rather dry account of Charter 77's background and campaigns, as well as information on a host of other dissident activities in the 1980s.

Mark Frankland *The Patriots' Revolution* (Sinclair Stevenson/IR Dee). Falls somewhere between Garton Ash's eye-witness account and Glenny's more lengthy analysis, but fails to be convincing either way.

Timothy Garton Ash *We The People: The Revolutions of 89* (Granta, Penguin). A personal, anecdotal, eye-witness account of the Velvet Revolution (and the events in Poland, Berlin and Budapest), and for that

reason by far the most compelling of all the post-1989 books.

Misha Glenny *The Rebirth of History: Eastern Europe in the Age of Democracy* (Penguin). Eight chapters in all, one of which deals with Czechoslovakia, focusing on the events of 1990 and the problems of the future rather than the Velvet Revolution itself. Correspondent for *The Guardian* and *BBC*, Glenny knows his stuff, but don't expect any jokes.

Karel Kaplan *Report on the Murder of the General Secretary* (IB Tauris/Ohio State University Press). Detailed study of the most famous of the anti-Semitic Stalinist show trials, that of Rudolf Slánský, number two in the KSČ until his arrest.

Jaroslav Krejčí *Czechoslovakia at the Crossroads of European History* (IB Tauris). Fairly breezy, lacklustre account of Czechoslovakia's history by a 1968 Czech emigré. Despite its recent publication, it contains only the briefest summary of the events of November 1989.

Zdeněk Mlynář *Nicht Frost in Prague – The End of Humane Socialism* (Hurst). Detailed account of the Prague Spring by one of its active participants.

Hans Renner *A History of Czechoslovakia since 1945* (Routledge, o.p.). General history by one of the 1968 emigré generation, finishing with the accession of Jakeš to General Secretary in December 1987.

David Selbourne *Death of a Dark Hero – Eastern Europe 1987–90* (Cape). A collection of articles by a leading journalist on eastern Europe. Several deal with the Czech and Slovak republics, mostly personal accounts of meetings with the country's leading dissidents, before and after the revolution.

R. W. Seton-Watson *The History of the Czechs and Slovaks* (Hutchinson, o.p./Transatlantic, o.p.). Seton-Watson's highly informed and balanced account, written during World War II, is hard to beat. The Seton-Watsons were lifelong Slavophiles but managed to maintain a scholarly distance in their writing, unlike the many emigré historians.

Ivan Svítek *The Unbearable Burden of History*. No prizes for guessing what inspired the title of this recent history, which starts with the crisis of 1938, and ends with the revolution of 1989.

Elizabeth Wiskemann *Czechs and Germans* (Oxford, o.p./AMS Press). Researched and written in the build-up towards Munich, this is the most fascinating and fair treatment of the Sudeten problem. Meticulous in her detail, vast in her scope, Wiskemann nevertheless manages to suffuse the weighty text with enough anecdotes to keep you gripped. Unique.

Sharon L. Wolchik *Czechoslovakia in Transition: Politics, Economics and Society* (Pinter). Dry, but detailed and well-researched sociological study of the country, published in 1991.

Zbyněk Zeman *Prague Spring; A Report on Czechoslovakia 1968* (Penguin, o.p.). Short, straightforward, and in many ways the easiest of the books on 1968, including useful background on the country's postwar history.

ESSAY, MEMOIRS AND BIOGRAPHY

After the Velvet Revolution – Václav Havel and the New Leaders of Czechoslovakia Speak Out ed Tim Whipple (Freedom House). Articles written by leading Czech and Slovak politicians (though sadly not Mečiar) during 1990.

Stephen Brook *The Double Eagle: Vienna, Budapest and Prague* (Picador). Taking the shared Habsburg tradition of these cities as a starting point, Brook's readable, personal foray gives an illuminating picture of dissident life in Prague in the late 1980s before the neo-Stalinist bubble finally burst.

Margarete Buber-Neumann *Milena* (Collins Harvill/Schocken). A moving biography of Milena Jesenská, one of interwar Prague's most beguiling characters, who befriended the author while they were both interned in Ravensbrück concentration camp.

Neil Butterworth *Dvořák* (Omnibus/Paganiniana Publications). An extremely accessible illustrated biography of the best-known Czech composer.

Jana Cerná *Kafka's Milena* (Souvenir Press). Another biography of Milena Jesenská, this time written by her daughter, a surrealist poet, whose own writings were banned under the Communists.

The Czech and Slovak Experience (Macmillan/St Martin's Press). An interesting

collection of academic papers on aspects of nineteenth- and early twentieth-century Czech and Slovak history.

Czechoslovakia 1918–88 ed Gordon Skilling (St Martin's Press). Essays by Czechs, Slovaks and western Slavists including Havel and Hájek on a range of subjects from Rusyns to Czech/German relations.

Dubček Speaks (IB Tauris). Verbatim account of Dubček's interview in early 1989 with Andras Sugar, one of Hungary's leading political writers, in which Dubček spoke for the first time in public about the events of the 1968 Prague Spring.

Patrick Leigh Fermor *A Time of Gifts* (Penguin/Viking Penguin). The first volume of Leigh Fermor's trilogy based on his epic walk along the Rhine and Danube rivers in 1933–34. In the last quarter of the book he reaches Czechoslovakia, indulging in a quick jaunt to Prague before crossing the border into Hungary. Written forty years later in dense, luscious and highly crafted prose, it's an evocative and poignant insight into the culture of *Mitteleuropa* between the wars.

Timothy Garton Ash *Uses of Adversity* (Granta, Penguin). A collection of Garton Ash's journalistic pieces on eastern Europe, written mostly in the 1980s, including several informative pieces on Czechoslovakia.

Granta 30: New Europe! (Penguin). Published at the beginning of 1990, this state-of-the-continent anthology includes Graham Swift's *Looking for Jiří Wolf*, as well as a series of brief reactions to events by a dozen or so European intellectuals.

Patricia Hampl *A Romantic Education* (Houghton Mifflin). An account of the author searching for her Czech roots in pre-1989 Prague.

Václav Havel *Living in Truth* (Faber & Faber); *Letters to Olga* (Faber/Owl Books); *Disturbing the Peace* (Faber/Knopf), *Open Letters* (Faber/Vintage). The first essay in *Living in Truth* is *Power of the Powerless*, Havel's lucid, damning indictment of the inactivity of the Czechoslovak masses in the face of "normalisation" (also included in *Open Letters*). *Letters to Olga* is a collection of Havel's letters written under great duress (and heavy censorship) from prison in the early 1980s to his wife, Olga – by turns philosophising, nagging, effusing, moving.

Disturbing the Peace is probably Havel's most accessible work yet: a series of autobiographical questions and answers in which he talks interestingly about his childhood, the events of 1968 when he was in Liberec, and the path to Charter 77 and beyond (though not including his reactions to being thrust into the role of president).

Václav Havel et al. *Power of the Powerless* (Hutchinson/ME Sharp). A collection of essays by leading Chartists, kicking off with Havel's seminal title-piece. Other contributors range from the dissident Marxist Petr Uhl to devout Catholics like Václav Benda.

High Hopes – Young Voices of Eastern Europe (Virago). A series of short personal accounts by young people across the former eastern bloc, expressing their often mixed feelings about the events of 1989.

Miroslav Holub *The Dimension of the Present Moment* (Faber & Faber). A series of very short musings/essays by this unusual and clever scientist-poet.

Heda Margolius Kovaly *Prague Farewell* (Gollancz/Penguin). An autobiography that starts in the concentration camps of World War II, ending with the author's flight from Czechoslovakia in 1968. Married to one of the Party hacks executed in the 1952 Slánský trial, she tells her story simply, and without bitterness. The best account there is on the fear and paranoia whipped up during the Stalinist terror.

Nikolaus Martin *Prague Winter* (Peter Halban). Brought up in Prague in the 1930s, Martin ended up in Terezín, Czechoslovakia's most notorious ghetto and concentration camp, because of his mother's Jewish background. This autobiography follows his life up to and including the 1948 Communist coup, after which he escaped to Canada.

New Left Review (Number 179). Contains a rare interview with leading Charter 77 spokesperson and dissident Marxist Petr Uhl, conducted during the heady first few months of the Velvet Revolution.

Jan Patočka – Philosophy and Selected Writings (Chicago UP). A collection of essays by one of the first of Charter 77's spokespeople, on subjects ranging from Charter 77 itself to Husserl and phenomenology.

Jan Šejna *We Will Bury You* (Sidgwick & Jackson, o.p.). The memoirs of Czechoslovkia's highest ranking military defector, Major General Šejna, who fled to the West in February 1968. The memoir part is the most interesting, the sections uncovering the Commies' secret plan to take over the world little short of hysterical.

William Shawcross *Dubček and Czechoslovakia 1918–1990* (Hogarth Press/Simon & Schuster). Biography of the most famous figure of the 1968 Prague Spring, updated to include Dubček's role in the 1989 Velvet Revolution.

Michael Simmons *The Reluctant President* (Methuen). The definitive (and so far the only) biography of Václav Havel, by the long-time *Guardian* reporter.

Phyllis Myrtle Clarke Sisperova *Not Far From Wenceslas Square* (The Book Guild). Autobiography of an English woman who married a Czech airman in World War II, and afterwards settled in Prague, only to be arrested during the 1950s "terror". She was released and finally returned to England in 1955 amid a blaze of publicity in the West.

Josef Škvorecký *Talkin' Moscow Blues* (Faber/Ecco Press). Without doubt the most user-friendly of Škvorecký's works, containing a collection of essays on his wartime childhood, Czech Jazz, literature and contemporary politics, all told in his inimitable, irreverent and infuriating way.

The Spirit of Thomas. G. Masaryk 1850–1937 (Macmillan). An anthology of writings on philosophy, religion, Czech history and politics by the country's founder and first president, affectionately known as TGM.

Ludvík Vaculík *A Cup of Coffee with My Interrogator* (Readers International). A lifelong Party member until 1968, and signatory of Charter 77, Vaculík revived the *feuilleton*, a short political critique – a journalistic literary genre once much loved in central Europe. This collection dates from 1968 onwards. His first novel, *The Axe* (Andre Deutsch, o/p/Northwest University Press), is *the* definitive account of the forced collectivisation of the 1950s.

Zbyněk Zeman *The Masaryks – The Making of Czechoslovakia* (IB Tauris). Written in the 1970s while Zeman was in exile, this is a very readable, none too sentimental biography of the country's founder Tomáš Garrigue Masaryk, and his son Jan Masaryk, the postwar Foreign Minister who died in mysterious circumstances shortly after the 1948 Communist coup.

CZECH AND SLOVAK FICTION

Boundaries of Twilight: Czech–Slovak Writing from the New World ed CJ Hribal (New Rivers Press). An anthology of over fifty modern Czech and Slovak emigré writers from North America.

Karel Čapek *Towards a Radical Centre* (Catbird Press); *The War with the Newts* (Picador/Northwestern University Press); *Nine Fairy Tales* (Northwestern UP). Čapek was the literary and journalistic spokesperson for Masaryk's First Republic, but he's better known in the West for his plays, some of which feature in this anthology.

Jozef Cíger-Hronský *Jozef Mak* (Slavica, US). A pro-Tiso Slovak writer, exiled in Argentina after the war. This is the simple, common story of the sufferings of a Slovak villager.

Ladislav Fuks *The Cremator* (Marion Boyars); *Mr Theodore Mundstock* (Four Walls Eight Windows). The first novel is about a man who works in a crematorium in occupied Prague, and is about to throw in his lot with the Nazis when he discovers that his wife is half-Jewish. The second is set in Prague 1942, as the city's Jews wait to be transported to Terezín.

Jaroslav Hašek *The Good Soldier Švejk* (Penguin/Viking Penguin); *The Bachura Scandal* (Angel Books). The former is a rambling, picaresque tale of Czechoslovakia's most famous fictional fifth columnist, Švejk, who wreaks havoc in the Austro-Hungarian army during World War I, by Bohemia's most bohemian writer. The latter is a collection of zany short stories on life in prewar Prague.

Václav Havel *The Memorandum* (Methuen, o.p./Grove Weidenfeld); *Three Vaněk Plays*; *Temptation*; *Redevelopment*; *Selected Plays 1963–83* (all Faber & Faber/Grove Weidenfeld). Havel's plays are not renowned for being easy to read (or watch). *The Memorandum* is one of his earliest works, a classic absurdist drama which, in many ways, sets the tone for much of his later work, of which the *Three Vaněk Plays*, featuring Ferdinand Vaněk, Havel's *alter ego*, are perhaps the most successful.

Bohumil Hrabal *Closely Observed Trains* (Abacus/Viking Penguin); *The Death of Mr Baltisberger* (Abacus); *I Served the King of England* (Picador/Vintage); *Too Loud a Solitude* (Abacus/Harcourt Brace Jovanovich). A thoroughly mischievous writer, Hrabal's slim but superb *Closely Observed Trains* is one of the postwar classics, set in the last days of the war and relentlessly unheroic; it was made into an equally brilliant film by Jiří Menzl. *I Served the King of England* follows the antihero Dítě through the crucial decade after 1938. *Too Loud a Solitude*, about a waste-paper disposer under the Communists, is also being made into a film, again by Menzl.

Alois Jirásek *Old Czech Legends* (Forest Books). A major figure in the nineteenth-century Czech *národní obrození*, Jirásek popularised Bohemia's legendary past. This collection includes all the classic texts, including the story of the founding of the city by the prophetess Libuše.

Franz Kafka *The Collected Novels of Franz Kafka*; *Letters to Felice*; *Diaries* (all Minerva/Schocken). A German-Jewish Praguer, Kafka has drawn the darker side of central Europe – its claustrophobia, paranoia and unfathomable bureaucracy – better than anyone else, both in a rural setting, as in *The Castle*, and in an urban one, in one of the great novels of the twentieth century, *The Trial*.

Eva Kantůrková *My Companions in the Bleak House* (Quartet/Viking Penguin). Kantůrková spent a year in Prague's Ruzyně prison, and *Companions* is a well-observed novel based around the characters within the prison's women's wing, the measure of their kindness, violence and despair mirroring the outside world.

Ivan Klíma *A Summer Affair* (Penguin); *My Merry Mornings* (Readers International); *First Loves* (Penguin/Norton); *Love and Garbage* (Penguin/Knopf); *Judge on Trial* (Chatto), *My Golden Trades* (Granta). A survivor of Terezín, Klíma is another writer in the Kundera mould as far as sexual politics goes, but his stories are a lot lighter. *Judge on Trial*, is one of his best, concerning the moral dilemmas of a Communist judge. His latest novel, *My Golden Trades*, is an autobiographical account of the many weird and wonderful jobs Klíma had to put his hand to while he was banned as a writer.

Milan Kundera *Laughable Loves* (Faber); *The Farewell Party* (Penguin/Viking Penguin); *The Joke*; *The Book of Laughter and Forgetting*; *Life is Elsewhere* (all Faber/Viking Penguin); *The Unbearable Lightness of Being*; *The Art of the Novel*; *Immortality* (all Faber/HarperCollins). Milan Kundera is the country's most popular writer – at least with non-Czechs. Certainly, if you can stand his sexual politics, his books are very obviously "political", particularly *The Book of Laughter and Forgetting*, which led the Communists to revoke Kundera's citizenship. *The Joke*, written while he was still living in Czechoslovakia, and in many ways his best work, is set in the very unfunny era of the Stalinist purges. Its clear, humorous style is far removed from the carefully poised posturing of his most famous work, *The Unbearable Lightness of Being*, set in and after 1968, and successfully turned into a film some twenty years later.

Arnošt Lustig *Diamonds of the Night*; *Darkness Casts No Shadow*; *Night and Hope* (all Quartet/Northwestern University Press); *A Prayer for Kateřina Horovitová* (Quartet/Overlook Press); *Indecent Dreams* (Northwestern University Press). A Prague Jew exiled since 1968, Lustig spent World War II in Terezín, Buchenwald and Auschwitz, and his novels and short stories are consistently set in the Terezín camp.

Gustav Meyrink *The Golem* (Dedalus/Ariadne); *The Angel of the West Window* (Dedalus/Dover). Meyrink was another of Prague's weird and wonderful characters who started out as a bank manager, but soon came involved in cabalism, alchemy and drug experimentation. His *Golem*, based on Rabbi Löw's monster, is one of the classic versions of the tale, set in Jewish quarter. *The Angel of the West Window* is a historical novel about John Dee, the English alchemist who was invited to Prague in the late sixteenth century by Rudolf II.

Ladislav Mňačko *The Taste of Power* (Weidenfeld & Nicolson, o.p/Praeger, o.p.). Now exiled in Israel, Mňačko is one of the few Slovak writers to have been widely published abroad, most frequently this novel about the corruption of ideals that followed the Communist takeover.

Libuše Moníková *The Facade* (Chatto/Knopf). Humorous novel about the adventures of a group of anarchic artists who cause havoc in Communist Bohemia and Siberia.

New Writing in Czechoslovakia (Penguin, o.p.). First published in 1969, this is one of the easiest collections of Czech and Slovak writing to get hold of secondhand.

Vladimir Páral *Catapult* (Catbird Press). An irreverent look at the country through the eyes of an engineer from Ústí nad Labem, which caused a stir when it was first published in Czechoslovakia in 1968.

Leo Perutz *By Night Under the Stone Bridge* (Harvill/Arcade Publishing). A Jewish-German Praguer who emigrated to Israel and wrote a series of historical novels. This one is set in Rudolfine Prague, and, among other things, tells the story of the emperor's love affair with the wife of Mordecai Maisl.

Robert Pynsent (ed) *Modern Slovak Prose* (Macmillan). Literary criticism on Slovak fiction since 1954 by Slovaks and western Slavists.

Josef Škvorecký *The Cowards* (Penguin/Ecco Press); *The Swell Season* (Picador/Ecco Press); *The Bass Saxophone* (Picador/Pocket Books); *Miss Silver's Past* (Picador, o/p/Ecco Press); *Dvořák in Love* (Hogarth, o/p/Norton); *The Engineer of Human Souls* (Picador); *The Miracle Game* (Faber & Faber/Norton). A relentless anti-Communist, Škvorecký is typically Bohemian in his bawdy sense of humour and irreverence for all high moralising. *The Cowards* (which briefly saw the light of day in 1958) is the tale of a group of irresponsible young men in the last days of the war, an antidote to the lofty prose from official authors at the time. *The Bass Saxophone* is based around Škvorecký's other great love, jazz, while *Dvořák in Love* and *The Engineer of Human Souls* are both set in and around the Czech emigré communities of the "New World", where Škvorecký has lived since 1968. *The Miracle Game* is a humorous account of the first twenty years of Communist rule.

Josef Škvorecký *The Mournful Demeanor of Lieutenant Boruvka*; *Sins for Father Knox*; *The Return of Lieutenant Boruvka* (all Faber & Faber/Norton). Less well known (and understandably so) are Škvorecký's detective stories featuring a podgy, depressive Czech cop, which he wrote in the 1960s at a time when his more serious work was banned. The later book, *The Return of Lieutenant Boruvka*, is set in Švorecký's new home, Canada.

Božena Slančiková-Timrava *An Incipient Feminist: Slovak Stories* (Slavica, US). Not strictly a feminist as such, Slančiková-Timrava tells her Slovak tales from a decidedly female perspective.

Zdena Tomin *Stalin's Shoe* (Dent, o.p./Dodd Mead, o.p.); *The Coast of Bohemia* (Picador). Although Czech-born, Tomin writes in English (the language of her exile since 1980), with a style and fluency all her own. *Stalin's Shoe* is the compelling and complex story of a girl coming to terms with her Stalinist childhood, while *The Coast of Bohemia* is based on Tomin's experiences of the late 1970s dissident movement, when she was an active member of Charter 77.

Ludvík Vaculík *The Guinea Pigs* (Northwestern UP). Vaculík was expelled from the Party in the midst of the Prague Spring in 1968; this novel, set in Prague, catalogues the slow dehumanisation of Czech society in the aftermath of the Sovet invasion.

Jiří Weil *Life With a Star*; *Mendelssohn is on the Roof* (Flamingo/Viking Penguin). A novel written just after the war and based on Weil's experiences as a Czech Jew in Prague as the Nazis occupied Czechoslovakia.

POETRY

Jaroslav Čejka, Michal Černík and Karel Sýs *The New Czech Poetry* (Bloodaxe). Slim, but interesting volume by three Czech poets; all in their late forties, all very different. Čejka is of the Holub school, and comes across simply and strongly; Černík is similarly direct; Sýs the least convincing.

Child of Europe – A New Anthology of East European Poetry (Penguin). This collection contains many hitherto untranslated Czech poets, including Ivo Šmoldas, Ewald Murrer and Jana Štroblová.

Sylva Fischerová *The Tremor of Racehorses: Selected Poems* (Bloodaxe). Poet and novelist, Fischerová is one of the new generation of Czech writers, though in many ways she is continuing in the Holub tradition. By turns powerful, obtuse and personal, as was necessary to escape censorship during the late 1980s.

Miroslav Holub *The Fly* (Bloodaxe); *Poems Before & After* (Bloodaxe); *Vanishing Lung Syndrome* (Faber/Oberlin College Press). Holub is both a scientist and scholar, and his poetry reflects this unique fusion of master poet and chief immunologist. Regularly banned in his own country, he is the Czech poet *par excellence* – classically trained, erudite, liberal and westward-leaning. *Vanishing Lung Syndrome* is his latest volume; the other two are collections.

Vladimír Janovic *The House of the Tragic Poet* (Bloodaxe). A bizarre epic poem set in the last days of Pompeii in 79 AD, and centred around six young men who are rehearsing a satyr play.

Rainer Maria Rilke *Selected Poems* (Penguin/HarperCollins). Rilke's upbringing was unexceptional, except for the fact that his mother brought him up as a girl until the age of six. In his adult life, he became one of Prague's leading Jewish-German authors of the interwar period.

Jaroslav Seifert *The Selected Poetry of Jaroslav Seifert* (Andre Deutsch, o.p./Collier Macmillan). Czechoslovakia's one and only Nobel prize-winning author, Seifert was a founder-member of the Communist Party and the avant-garde arts movement *Devětsil*, later falling from grace and signing the Charter in his old age. His longevity means that his work covers some of the most turbulent times in Czechoslovak history, but his irrepressible lasciviousness has been known to irritate.

LITERATURE BY FOREIGN WRITERS

Bruce Chatwin *Utz* (Picador/Viking Penguin). Chatwin is one of the "exotic" school of travel writers, hence this slim, intriguing and mostly true-to-life account of an avid crockery collector from Prague's Jewish quarter.

Martha Gellhorn *A Stricken Field* (Virago, o.p./Viking Penguin). The story of an American journalist who arrives in Prague just as the Nazis march into Sudetenland. Based on the author's own experiences, this is a fascinating, if sentimental, insight into the panic and confusion in "rump" Czecho-Slovakia after the Munich Diktat. First published in 1940.

Ellis Peters *The Piper on the Mountain* (Headline). Ellis Peters, whose real name is Edith Pargeter, is the author of the popular crime series *The Chronicles of Brother Cadfael*.

A woman with strong Czech connections, Peters has chosen Prague and the Slovak Tatra mountains as the setting for this modern-day detective story.

Zina Rohan *The Book of Wishes and Complaints* (Flamingo). Rohan is a British-born writer of German-Jewish and Russian-Yugoslav origin, who married a Czech. The story revolves around a young country girl, Hana, who moves to Prague and embarks upon a voyage of self-discovery against the backdrop of the 1968 Prague Spring.

ART, PHOTOGRAPHY AND FILM

Czech Modernism 1900–1945 (Bullfinch Press). Wide-ranging and superbly illustrated, this American publication records the journey of the Czech modern movement through Cubism and Surrealism to Modernism and the avant-garde. The accompanying essays by leading art and film critics cover fine art, architecture, film, photography and theatre.

Devětsil – Czech Avant-Garde Art, Architecture and Design of the 1920s and 30s (Museum of Modern Art, Oxford). Published to accompany the 1990 *Devětsil* exhibition at Oxford, this is the definitive account of interwar Czechoslovakia's most famous left-wing art movement, which attracted artists from every discipline.

Disorientations – Eastern Europe in Transition (Thames & Hudson). A self-explanatory book of photographs accompanied by text by Pavel Kohout.

Peter Hames *The Czechoslovak New Wave* (Californian UP). An intelligent and detailed history of the golden age of Czechoslovak cinema during the 1960s, but a bit mean on the stills.

Josef Koudelka (Photo Poche, o.p.). Without doubt the most original Czech photographer and purveyor of fine Prague Spring photos. This pocket-size monograph is occasionally available in secondhand art bookshops.

Miroslav Lamač *Osma a skupina 1907–1917* (Odeon, o.p./Szwede Slavic). Czech text, but with a good selection of full-colour reproductions (mostly of paintings) of the Cubist phase in Czech art.

Josef Sudek – A Photographer's Life (John Murray/Aperture). Hauntingly beautiful set of sepia photographs by the old man of Czech photography, who died in the 1970s.

LANGUAGE

The official language of the Czech republic is Czech (český), that of the Slovak republic Slovak (slovenský). Both are mutually intelligible, highly complex Slav tongues. Whether they are separate languages or simply diverse dialects of a common one is still a hotly disputed issue. However, for the non-Slav, they are sufficiently distinct to cause serious problems of understanding.

Unless you're here for some time, it's all rather academic, since you're not likely to make any great inroads into either. If you know some German already, brush up on that, since, among the older generation in particular, German is the most widely spoken second language, and as a visitor you'll be expected to know at least some. Russian, once the compulsory second language, has been practically wiped off the school curriculum, and the number of English-speakers has been steadily increasing. That said, any attempt to speak Czech or Slovak will be heartily appreciated, if a little difficult to understand for a people unaccustomed to hearing foreigners stumble through their language.

PRONUNCIATION

English-speakers often find Czech impossibly difficult to pronounce (Slovak less so). In fact, it's not half as daunting as it might first appear from the traffic jams of consonants which crop up on the page. Apart from a few special letters, each letter and syllable is pronounced as it's written – the trick is always to **stress the first syllable** of a word, no matter what its length; otherwise you'll render it unintelligible.

SHORT AND LONG VOWELS

Czech and Slovak have both short and long vowels (the latter being denoted by a variety of accents). The trick here is to lengthen the vowel without affecting the principal stress of the word, which is invariably on the first syllable.

a like the u in c**u**p
á as in f**a**ther
ä closer to the e in l**e**t than an a
e as in p**e**t
é as in f**ai**r
ě like the y in **y**es
i or y as in p**i**t
í or ý as in s**ea**t
o as in n**o**t
ó as in d**oo**r
ô like the u in l**u**rid
u like the oo in b**oo**k
ů or ú like the oo in f**oo**l

VOWEL COMBINATIONS & DIPTHONGS

There are very few dipthongs in Czech, substantially more in Slovak. Combinations of vowels not mentioned below should be pronounced as two separate syllables.

au like the ou in f**ou**l
ie like the ye in **ye**s
ia like the ya in **ya**k
iu like the u in fl**u**te
ou like the oe in f**oe**

CONSONANTS AND ACCENTS

There are no silent consonants, but it's worth remembering that r and l can form a syllable if standing between two other consonants or at the end of a word, as in Brno (Br–no) or Vltava (Vl–ta–va). The consonants listed below are those which differ substantially from the English. Accents look daunting, but the only one which causes a lot of problems is ř (Czech only), probably the most difficult letter to say in the entire language – even Czech toddlers have to be taught how to say it.

c like the **ts** in boats
č like the **ch** in chicken
ch like the **ch** in the Scottish loch
ď like the **d** in duped
g always as in goat, never as in general
h always as in have, but more energetic
j like the **y** in yoke
kd pronounced as **gd**

ľ like the **lli** in colliery
mě pronounced as mnye
ň like the **n** in nuance
p softer than the English p
r as in rip, but often rolled

ř like the sound of **r** and **ž** combined
š like the **sh** in shop
ť like the **t** in tutor
ž like the **s** in pleasure; at the end of a word
like the sh in shop

A CZECH–SLOVAK LANGUAGE GUIDE

● There are very few **teach-yourself Czech** courses available – and none for Slovak – and each has drawbacks. *Colloquial Czech* is a bit fast and furious for most people. *Teach Yourself Czech* is a bit dry for some. The best portable **dictionaries** are the *kapesní slovník* for Czech and the *vreckový slovník*, most easily purchased in the Czech and Slovak republics. Colletts produce a phrasebook called *Travellers' Czech*.

● In many instances the **Czech** and **Slovak words** for things are the same. Where they're different, we've separated them below, giving the Czech word first and the Slovak word second.

BASIC WORDS AND PHRASES

Yes	*ano/áno* or *hej*	Yesterday	*včera*
No	*ne/nie*	Tomorrow	*zítra/zajtra*
Excuse me/please/	*prosím*	The day after tomorrow	*pozítra/pozajtra*
don't mention it		Now	*hnet/teraz*
You're welcome	*není zač/nemáte začo*	Later	*později/neskôr*
Sorry	*pardon/pardón*	Leave me alone	*pusť mě/nechaj ma*
Thank you	*děkuju/ďakujem*		*osamote*
OK	*dobrá/dobre*		
Bon apetit	*dobrou chuť*	Go away	*jdi pryč/choď preč*
Bon voyage	*šťastnou cestu*	Help!	*pomoc!*
Hello/goodbye	*ahoj*	This one	*tento*
(informal)		A little	*trocha*
Goodbye (formal)	*na shledanou/ do videnia*	Large–small	*velký–malý*
Good day	*dobrý den*	More–less	*více–méně/viac–menej*
Good morning	*dobré ráno*	Good–bad	*dobrý–špatný*
Good evening	*dobrý večer*	Hot–cold	*horký–studený/*
Good night (when	*dobrou noc*		*horúci–studený*
leaving)		With–without	*s–bez*
Today	*dnes*	How are you?	*jak se máte/ako sa*
			máte?

GETTING AROUND

Over here	*tady/tuná*	By taxi	*taxíkem/taxíkom*
Over there	*tam*	Ticket	*jízdenka/lístok*
Left	*nalevo/naľavo*	Return ticket	*zpátečá jízdenka/spiatočný*
Right	*napravo*		*lístok*
Straight on	*rovně/priamo*	Railway station	*nádraží/železničná stanica*
Where is . . .?	*kde je . . .?*	Bus station	*autobusové nádraží/*
How do I get to	*jak se dostanu do Zvolena/*		*autobusová stanica*
Zvolen?	*ako sa dostanem do*	Bus stop	*autobusová zastávka*
	Zvolena?	When's the next	*kdy jde další vlak do Prahy/*
How do I get to	*jak se dostanu k univerzitě/*	train to Prague?	*kedy ide najbližší vlak do*
the university?	*ako sa dostanem k*		*Prahy?*
	univerzite?	Is it going to Brno?	*jde to do Brna/ide to do*
By bus	*autobusem/autobusom*		*Brna?*
By train	*vlakem/vlakom*	Do I have to change?	*musím přestupovat/musím*
By car	*autem/autom*		*prestupovat?*
By foot	*pěšky/pešo*	Do I have to have a	*musím mít místenku?*
		reservation?	

QUESTIONS AND ANSWERS

Do you speak English?	*mluvíte anglicky/ hovoríte anglicky?*	Why	*proč/prečo*
I don't speak German	*nemluvím německy/ nehovorím nemecky*	How much is it?	*kolik stojí/koľko stojí?*
		Are there any rooms available?	*máte volné pokoje/ máte voľné izby?*
I don't understand	*nerozumím/nerozumiem*	I want a double room	*chtěl bych dvou lůžkovy*
I understand	*rozumím/rozumiem*		*pokoj/chcem dvojposte-*
Speak slowly	*mluvte pomalu/hovorte pomalšie*		*ľovú izbu*
		For one night	*na jednu noc*
How do you say that in	*jak se tohle řekne*	With shower	*se sprchou/se sprchy*
Czech/Slovak?	*česky/ako sa to povie slovenský?*	Are these seats free?	*jsou tyto místa volná/ sú tieto miesta voľná?*
Could you write it down for me?	*můžete mí to napsat/ mohli by ste mi to napísať?*	May we (sit down)? The bill please Do you have . . .?	*můžeme/môžme? zaplatím prosím máte . . .?*
What	*co/čo*	We don't have	*nemáme*
Where	*kde*	We do have	*máme*
When	*kdy/kedy*		

SOME SIGNS

Entrance	*vchod*	Open	*otevřeno/otvorené*	No bathing	*koupání zakázáno/ zákaz kúpania*
Exit	*východ*	Closed	*zavřeno/zavreté*		
Toilets	*záchod*	Danger!	*pozor!*	No entry	*vstup zakázáno*
Men	*muži*	Hospital	*nemocnice/ nemocnica*	Arrivals	*příjezd/príchod*
Women	*ženy*			Departure	*odjezd/odchod*
Gentlemen	*pánové*	No smoking	*kouření zakázáno/ zákaz fajčiť*	Police	*policie/polícia*
Ladies	*dámy*				

DAYS OF THE WEEK

Monday	*pondělí/pondelok*	Sunday		*neděle/nedeľa*
Tuesday	*úterý/utorok*	Day		*den/deň*
Wednesday	*středa/streda*	Week		*týden/týždeň*
Thursday	*čtvrtek/štvrtok*	Month		*měsíc/mesiac*
Friday	*pátek/piatok*	Year		*rok*
Saturday	*sobota*			

NUMBERS

1	*jeden*	15	*patnáct/pätnásť*	100	*sto*
2	*dva*	16	*šestnáct/šestnásť*	101	*sto jedna*
3	*tři/tri*	17	*sedmnáct/sedemnásť*	155	*sto padesát pět/ stodpäťdesiatpäť*
4	*čtyři/štyri*	18	*osumnáct/osemnásť*		
5	*pět/päť*	19	*devatenáct/devätnásť*	200	*dvě stě/dvesto*
6	*šest/šesť*	20	*dvacet/dvadsať*	300	*tři sta/tristo*
7	*sedm/sedem*	21	*dvacetjedna/dvadsaťjeden*	400	*čtyři sta/štyristo*
8	*osum/osem*	30	*třícet/tridsať*	500	*pět set/päťsto*
9	*devět/deväť*	40	*čtyřicet/štyridsať*	600	*šest set/šesto*
10	*deset/desať*	50	*padesát/päťdesiat*	700	*sedm set/sedemsto*
11	*jedenáct/jedenásť*	60	*šedesát/šesťdesiat*	800	*osum set/osemsto*
12	*dvanáct/dvanásť*	70	*sedmdesát/sedemdesiat*	900	*devět set/deväťsto*
13	*třínáct/trinásť*	80	*osumdesát/osemdesiat*	1000	*tisíc*
14	*čtrnáct/štrnásť*	90	*devadesát/deväťdesiat*		

MONTHS OF THE YEAR

Czechs and Slovaks use completely different words to denote the **months of the year**. While the Slovaks copy the Roman calendar names, Czech uses the highly individual Slav system, in which the names of the month are descriptive nouns – sometimes beautifully apt for the month in question.

CZECH

January	*leden* – ice	July	*červenec* – redder
February	*únor* – hibernation	August	*srpen* – sickle
March	*březen* – birch	September	*září* – blazing
April	*duben* – oak	October	*říjen* – rutting
May	*květen* – blossom	November	*listopad* – leaves falling
June	*červen* – red	December	*prosinec* – slaughter of the pig

SLOVAK

January	*január*	May	*máj*	September	*september*
February	*február*	June	*jún*	October	*október*
March	*marec*	July	*júl*	November	*november*
April	*apríl*	August	*august*	December	*december*

AN A–Z OF CZECH AND SLOVAK STREET NAMES

Since 1989, many streets named after erstwhile stars of the Communist party have disappeared. It's not the first time that the sign writers have had their brushes out either: after World War II, all the Herman-Göring-Strasses were quickly renamed, and a similar process occurred after World War I. The following names are currently the most popular in the Czech and Slovak republics; remember that street names always appear in the genitive or adjectival form, eg Palacký street as Palackého or Hus street as Husova.

29 August. The day the unsuccessful Slovak National Uprising against the Nazis began in 1944.

Beneš, Edvard (1884–1948). President from 1935 until the Munich Crisis and again from 1945 until the Communist coup in 1948. Making a stronger than expected comeback.

Bernolák, Anton (1762–1813). Slovak theologian and pioneer in the Slovak written language. Author of the first Slovak dictionary.

Bezruč, Petr (1867–1958). Pen name of the Czech poet Vladimír Vašek who wrote about the hardships of the Ostrava mining region.

Čapek, Karel (1890–1938). Czech writer, journalist and unofficial spokesperson for the First Republic whose most famous works were *The Insect Play* and *R.U.R.*, which introduced the word *robot* into the English language.

Čech, Svatopluk (1846–1908). Extreme Czech nationalist and poet whose best-known work is *Songs of a Slave*.

Chelčicky, Petr (born c.1390). Extreme pacifist Hussite preacher who disapproved of the violence of Žižka and his Taborite army.

Dobrovský, Josef (1753–1829). Jesuit-taught pioneer in Czech philology. Wrote the seminal text *The History of Czech Language and Literature*.

Duklianské hrdiny (The Dukla Heroes). The name given to the soldiers who died capturing the Dukla Pass in October 1944, the first decisive battle in the liberation of the country from the Nazis.

Dvořák, Antonín (1841–1904). Perhaps the most famous of all Czech composers whose best-known work is his *New World Symphony* inspired by his extensive sojourn in the USA.

Fučik, Julius (1903–1943). Communist journalist murdered by the Nazis whose prison writings, *Notes from the Gallows*, were obligatory reading in the 1950s. Later doubts about the authenticity of the work, and general hostility towards the man, has seen his name disappear off many, though not all, streets and squares.

Havlíček-Borovský, Karel (1821–56). Satirical poet, journalist and nationalist, exiled to the Tyrol by the Austrian authorities after 1848.

Hlinka, Andrej (1864–1938). Leader of the Slovak People's Party, which went on to found the Slovak Nazi puppet state.

Horáková, Milada (died 1950). Socialist deputy who was killed in the Stalinist purges.

Hurban, Jozef Miroslav (1817–1888). Slovak writer and journalist who edited various pioneering Slovak-language journals.

Hus, Jan (1370–1415). Rector of Prague University and reformist preacher who was burnt at the stake as a heretic by the Council of Constance.

Hviezdoslav, Pavol Orságh (1849–1921). The father of Slovak poetry who lived and worked in the Orava region where he was employed as a court official until his retirement.

Janáček, Leoš (1854–1928). Moravian-born composer, based in Brno for most of his life, whose operas in particular have become quite widely performed in the West.

Jánošík Fabled Slovak folk hero, modelled along the lines of Robin Hood, who operated in the Malá Fatra range (see p.369).

Jesenský, Janko (1874–1945). Slovak poet who accompanied the Czechoslovak Legion in its long trek across the Soviet Union during the Bolshevik Revolution.

Jirásek, Alois (1851–1930). Writer for both children and adults who popularised Czech legends and became a key figure in the národní obrození.

Jungmann, Josef (1773–1847). Prolific Czech translator and author of the seminal *History of Czech Literature* and the first Czech Dictionary.

Kollár, Ján (1793–1852). Professor of Slav archaeology in Vienna and Slovak poet who wrote in Czech and opposed the formation of a separate Slovak written language.

Komenský, Jan Amos (1592–1670). Leader of the Protestant Czech Brethren. Forced to flee the country and settle in England during the Counter-Reformation. Better known to the English as Comenius.

Kráľ Janko (1822–76). A Slovak poet who wrote folk ballads, while **Fraňo** (1903–55) is a Slovak Communist poet and no relation to the former.

5 května (May 5). The day of the Prague Uprising against the Nazis in 1945.

Mácha, Karel Hynek (1810–36). Romantic nationalist poet, great admirer of Byron and Keats who, like them, died young. His most famous poem is *Maj*, published just months before his death.

Masaryk, Tomáš Garrigue (1850–1937). Professor of Philosophy at Prague University, President of the Republic (1918–1935). His name is synonymous with the First Republic and was removed from all street signs after the 1948 coup. Now back with a vengeance.

Nálepka, Ján (1912–1943). Slovak teacher and partisan in World War II who won fame through his daring antics in the Nazi-occupied Ukraine where he eventually died.

Němcová, Božena (1820–1862). Highly popular writer who got involved with the nationalist movement and shocked with her unorthodox behaviour. Her most famous book is *Grandmother*.

Neruda, Jan (1834–1891). Poet and journalist for the *Národní listy*. Wrote some famous short stories describing Prague's Malá Strana.

Opletal, Jan Czech student killed by Nazis in 1939 during demonstration.

Palach, Jan (1947–1969). Philosophy student who committed suicide by self-immolation in protest against the 1968 Soviet invasion.

Palacký, František (1798–1876). Nationalist historian, Czech MP in Vienna and leading figure in the events of 1848.

Purkyně, Jan Evangelista (1787–1869). Czech doctor, natural scientist and pioneer in experimental physiology who became professor of physiology at Prague and then Wrocław University.

Ressel, Josef (1793–1857). Fascinatingly enough, the Czech inventor of the screw-propeller.

Rieger, Ladislav. Nineteenth-century Czech politician and one of the leading figures in the events of 1848 and its aftermath.

Šafárik, Pavol Jozef (1795–1861). Slovak scholar and son of a Slovak Lutheran pastor whose major works were actually written in Czech and German.

Sládkovič, Andrej (1820–1872). Slovak poet who lived and worked in the Detva region, and whose pastoral love poem *Marína* is regarded as a classic.

Smetana, Bedřich (1824–1884). Popular Czech composer and fervent nationalist whose *Ma vlast* ("My Homeland") traditionally opens the Prague Spring Music Festival.

SNP (*Slovenské národné povstanie*). The ill-fated Slovak National Uprising against the Nazis which took place in August/September 1944.

Štefánik, Milan Rastislav (died 1919). Slovak explorer and fighter pilot who fought and campaigned for Czechoslovakia during World War I.

Štúr, Ľudovít (1815–1856). Slovak nationalist, who led the 1848 revolt against the Hungarians and argued for a Slovak language distinct from Czech.

Svoboda, Ludvík. Victorious Czech General from World War II, who acquiesced to the 1948 Communist coup and was Communist President (1968–1975).

Tajovský, Jozef Gregor (1874–1940). Slovak dramatist and short story writer whose moral ethics and identification with the underdog made him a sharp social critic of the times.

Tyl, Josef Kajetán (1808–1856). Czech playwright and composer of the Czech national anthem, *Where is my Home?*.

Vajanský, Svetozár Hurban (1847–1916). Romantic Slovak novelist whose Russophile views were as unpopular then as now.

Wolker, Jiří (1900–1924). Czech Communist who died of TB aged 24, and whose one volume of poetry was lauded by the Communists as the first truly proletarian writing.

Žižka, Jan (died 1424). Brilliant military leader of the Táborites, the radical faction of the Hussites.

GLOSSARIES

CZECH/SLOVAK WORDS

BRÁNA Gate.

ČESKÝ Bohemian.

CHATA Chalet-type bungalow or country cottage.

CHRÁM Large church.

CINTORÍN Cemetery (Slovak).

DIVADLO Theatre.

DOLINA Valley (Slovak).

DÓM Cathedral.

DŮM/DOM House.

DŮM KULTURY/DOM KULTURY Communal arts and social centre; literally "House of Culture".

HRAD Castle.

HRANICE/HRANICA Border.

HŘBITOV Cemetery (Czech).

HORA Mountain.

HOSTINEC Local pub.

JESKYNĚ/JASKYŇA Cave.

JEZERO/JAZERO Lake.

KÁMEN/KAMEŇ Rock.

KAPLE/KAPLNKA Chapel.

KAŠTIEĽ Manor house (Slovak).

KATEDRÁLA Cathedral.

KAVÁRNA/KAVÁRIEŇ Coffee house.

KLÁŠTER/KLÁŠTOR Monastery.

KOSTEL/KOSTOL Church.

KOUPALIŠTĚ/KÚPALISKO Swimming pool.

KÚPELE Spa (Slovak).

LABE River Elbe.

LÁNOVKA Funicular or cable car.

LÁZNĚ Spa (Czech).

LES Forest.

MĚSTO/MESTO Town; *staré město* – Old Town, *nové město* – New Town, *dolní město* – Lower Town, *horní město* – Upper Town.

MORAVSKÝ Moravian.

MOST Bridge.

NÁBŘEŽÍ/NÁBREŽIE Embankment.

NÁDRAŽÍ Train station (Czech).

NÁMĚSTÍ/NÁMESTIE Square, as in *náměstí Svobody/námestie Slobody* – Freedom Square.

NISA River Neisse.

ODRA River Oder.

OSTROV Island.

PAMÁTNÍK/PAMÄTNÍK Memorial or monument.

PIVNICE/PIVNICA Pub.

PLANINA Valley basin (Slovak).

PLESO Mountain lake (Slovak).

PRAMEN Natural spring.

PROHLÍDKA/PREHLIADKA Viewpoint.

RADNICE/RADNICA Town hall.

ŘEKA/RIEKA River.

RESTAURACE/REŠTAURÁCIA Restaurant.

SADY Park.

SÁL Room or hall (in a chateau or castle).

SEDLO Saddle (of a mountain).

SKÁLA/SKALA Crag/rock.

SKANSEN/SKANZEN An open-air folk museum, with reconstructed folk art and architecture.

SLOVENSKÝ Slovak.

STANICA Train station (Slovak).

STARÉ MĚSTO/STARÉ MESTO Old Town.

ŠTÍT Peak (Slovak).

SVATÝ/SVÄTÝ Saint, such as svatý Václav – Saint Wenceslas. Abbreviated to sv.

TEPLICE Spa.

TŘÍDA/TRIEDA Avenue.

ULICE/ULICA Street.

VĚŽ/VEŽA Tower.

VINÁRNA/VINÁRIEŇ Wine bar or cellar.

VLTAVA River Moldau.

VRCHY Hills.

VRCHOVINA Uplands.

VÝSTAVA Exhibition.

ZAHRADA/ZÁHRADA Gardens.

ZÁMEK/ZÁMOK Chateau.

ART/ARCHITECTURAL TERMS

AMBULATORY Passage round the back of the altar, in continuation of the aisles.

ART NOUVEAU Sinuous and stylised form of architecture and decorative arts. Imported from Vienna and Budapest from 1900–10, and therefore known as the Secession in Czechoslovakia, rather than *Jugendstil*, the German term.

BAROQUE Expansive, exuberant architectural style of the seventeenth and mid-eighteenth centuries, characterised by ornate decoration, complex spatial arrangement and grand vistas.

BEAUTIFUL STYLE Also known as the Soft Style of painting. Developed in Bohemia in the fourteenth century, it became very popular in Germany.

CHANCEL Part of the church where the altar is placed, usually at the east end.

EMPIRE A highly decorative Neoclassical style of architecture and decorative arts, practised in the first part of the nineteenth century.

FRESCO Mural painting applied to wet plaster, so that the colours immediately soak into the wall.

FUNCTIONALISM Plain, boxy, modernist architectural style, prevalent in the late 1920s and 1930s in Czechoslovakia, often using plate-glass curtain walls and open-plan interiors.

GOTHIC Architectural style prevalent from the twelfth to the sixteenth century, characterised by pointed arches and ribbed vaulting

LOGGIA Covered area on the side of a building, often arcaded.

NAVE Main body of a church, usually the western end.

NEOCLASSICAL Late eighteenth- and early nineteenth-century style of architecture and design returning to classical Greek and Roman models as a reaction against Baroque and Rococo excesses.

ORIEL A bay window, usually projecting from an upper floor.

PREDELLA Small panel below the main scenes of an altarpiece.

ROMANESQUE Solid architectural style of the late tenth to thirteenth century, characterised by round-headed arches and geometrical precision.

ROCOCO Highly florid, fiddly though (occasionally) graceful style of architecture and interior design, forming the last phase of Baroque.

SECESSION Style of early twentieth-century art and architecture based in Germany and Austria and a reaction against the academic establishment (see also "Art Nouveau").

SGRAFFITO Monochrome plaster decoration effected by means of scraping back the first white layer to reveal the black underneath.

SHINGLE Wooden roof tiles.

STUCCO Plaster used for decorative effects.

TROMPE L'OEIL Painting designed to fool the onlooker into believing that it is actually three-dimensional.

TYMPANUM Area above doorway or within a pediment.

HISTORICAL AND POLITICAL TERMS

CIVIC FORUM (Občanské fórum). The umbrella coalition which brought down the government in 1989, and won the general election of 1990 (now no longer in existence).

CZECH LANDS A phrase used to denote Bohemia and Moravia.

FIRST REPUBLIC The new Czechoslovak Republic founded by Masaryk after World War II, made up of Bohemia, Moravia, Silesia, Slovakia and Ruthenia, dismantled by the Nazis in 1938–39.

GREAT MORAVIAN EMPIRE The first Slav state covering much of what is now Czechoslovakia, which ended shortly after the Magyar invasion of 896 AD.

HABSBURGS The most powerful family in central Europe, whose power base was Vienna. They held the Bohemian throne from 1526 to 1918, the Hungarian kingdom from 1526 to 1867, and by marriage and diplomacy acquired territories all over Europe.

HISTORIC PROVINCES Land traditionally belonging to the Bohemian crown, including Bohemia, Egerland, Moravia, Silesia and Lusatia.

HOLY ROMAN EMPIRE Name given to the loose confederation of German states (including for a while the Czech Lands) which lasted from 800 until 1806.

HUSSITES Name given to Czech religious reformers who ostensibly followed the teachings of Jan Hus (1370–1415).

JAGIELLONIANS Polish-Lithuanian dynasty who ruled the Czech Lands from 1471 to 1526.

MAGYARS The people who ruled over the Hungarian Kingdom, and now predominate in modern-day Hungary.

MITTELEUROPA Literally German for central Europe, but it also conveys the idea of a multi-lingual central European culture, lost after the upheavals in post-1945 Europe.

NÁRODNÍ FRONTA Literally the National Front, the dummy coalition of parties dominated by the Communists which ruled the country until December 1989.

NÁRODNÍ OBROZENÍ/NÁRODNÉ OBRO-DENIE The Czech and Slovak "national revival" movements of the nineteenth century which sought to rediscover the lost identities of the Czech and Slovak people, particularly their history and language.

PŘEMYSLID The dynasty of Czech princes and kings who ruled over the Historic Lands of Bohemia from the ninth century to 1306.

RUTHENIA Officially Sub-Carpatho-Ruthenia, the easternmost province of the First Republic, annexed by the Soviet Union at the end of World War II.

SUDETENLAND Name given to mostly German-speaking border regions of the Czech Lands, awarded to Nazi Germany in the Munich Diktat of September 1938.

UNIATE CHURCH Formed from various breakaways from the Eastern (Orthodox) Church in the sixteenth century, the uniate church retains many Orthodox practices and rituals but is affiliated to the Roman Catholic Church.

VELVET REVOLUTION The popular protests of November/December 1989 which brought an end to forty-one years of Communist rule. Also known as the Gentle Revolution.

ACRONYMS

CKM (Cestovní kancelář mládeže) Youth Travel Organisation.

ČEDOK State travel and tourist agency.

ČSD (Československé státní dráhy) State Railways.

ČSAD (Československá státní automobilová doprava) State bus company.

HSD-SMS Movement for Democracy in Moravia and Silesia.

HZDS Movement for a Democratic Slovakia.

KSČ (Komunistická strana Československá) The Czechoslovak Communist Party (now defunct).

KSČM Communist Party of Bohemia and Moravia.

OF (Občanské fórum) Civic Forum (now defunct).

ODS (Občanská demokratická strana) Civic Democratic Party – right-wing faction of Civic Forum whose leader, Václav Klaus, is the current Czech Prime Minister.

OH (Občanské hnutí) Civic Movement – the left-wing faction in Civic Forum, now a separate political party.

SdP Abbreviation of the Sudeten German Party (Sudetendeutsche Partei), the main proto-Nazi Party in Czechoslovakia in the late 1930s.

SNS (Slovenská národná strana) Slovak Nationalist Party – extremist Slovak separatists.

StB (Státní bezpečnost) The Communist secret police.

VB (Veřejná bezpečnost) The old name for the police under the Communists.

VPN (Verejnosť proti nasiliu) People Against Violence. The Slovak partner of Civic Forum, formed during the Velvet Revolution.

INDEX

Accommodation 18–20
Acronyms 454
Adamites 149
Adamov 265
Adršpach 233
Airlines 4
American Liberation of Plzeň
  175
Architectural terms 452–453
Austerlitz, Battle of 267
A–Z of Czech and Slovak
  Street Names 449–451

Babiččino údolí 236
Banská Bystrica 351–356
Banská Štiavnica 359–361
Bardejov 407
Bardejovské kúpele 408
Baťa, Tomáš 283, 284, 285
Báthori, Countess Elizabeth
  348–349
Bechyně 151
Beckov 347
Beskydy Region 305–311
Betlém 242
Betliar 401
Bezděz 211
Bibliography 438–444
Bítov 174
Blansko 264
Blood Countess of Čachtice
  348–349
BOHEMIA,
  EAST 222–247
  NORTH 199–221
  SOUTH 144–170
  WEST 171–198
Books 438–444
Bouzov 299
BRATISLAVA 317–334
  Accommodation 321–322
  Castle 326
  Cathedral 325
  Devín 333
  Eating, drinking and
    entertainment 330–331
  Information 321
  Jewish Quarter 325–326
  Kamzík 333
  Listings 332

Most SNP 327
Námestie SNP 328
Petržalka and Petrochemicals 326
Rusovce 324
Slavín Monument 329
Slovak National Gallery 327–328
Slovak National Museum 326,
  328
Staré mesto 322–324
Brezno 377
Brněnská přehrada 266
BRNO 248–263
  Accommodation 249–253
  Eating, drinking and
    entertainment 262–263
  Listings 263
  Moravian Museum 253
  Moravská gálerie 258
  Náměstí svobody 257
  Peter & Paul Cathedral 256
  Špilberk 259
  Tugendhat Haus 261
  Výstaviště 260
  Zelný trh 253
Břeclav 271
Broumov 234
Buchlov 282
Buchlovice 282
Bučovice 268
Budatín 367
Buses 15

Čachtice 347
Camping 20
Car rental 17
Carlsbad 190–197
Carpatho-Ruthenia 404–411
Casanova, Giacomo 204
Castles 30
ČEDOK offices abroad 13
Černá v Pošumaví 165
Červená Lhota 154
Červená Skala 378
Červený Kláštor 392
Česká Kamenice 216
Česká Skalice 236
České Budějovice 156–160
České středohoří 211
České Švýcarsko 212–216
Český kras 140
Český Krumlov 160–162
Český ráj 223–228
Český Šternberk 138
Český Těšín 311
Changing Money 12
Charter 77 433

Cheb 185–188
Chlumec nad Cidlinou 243
Chods 179
Chopok 377
Chrudim 246
Chýnov Caves 151
Čičmany 369
Čierná nad Tisou 416
Cinema 34
Coaches from the UK 5
Comenius, John 298
Currency 11
Customs 9
Cycling 17

Danube Basin 342–345
Děčín 212
Děčínský Sněžník 215
Dedinky 3948
Defenestrations, first 101,
  second 63, *third* 68
Demänovská dolina 376–377
Detva 358
Directory 38–39
Disabled travellers 37
Dobšiná ice cave 399
Doksy 211
Dolní Vltavice 165
Dolný Kubín 370
Domažlice 176–180
Domica caves 403
Drink 26–27
Driving in the Czech/Slovak
  republics 16
Driving to the Czech/Slovak
  republics 5
Dubček, Alexander 329, 432,
  435
Duchcov 204
Dukla Pass 410
Dvořák, Antonín 104, 106, 127
Dvůr Králové 242
EAST BOHEMIA 222–247
EAST SLOVAKIA 387–417
Eger 185–188
Egerland 187
Electricity 38
Embassies abroad, Czech/
  Slovak 9

Felvidék 342–345
Ferdinand, Archduke Franz
  138, 207
Festivals 32–35

Flights from North America 6
Flights from the UK 3
*Flights within the Czech/
  Slovak republics* 18
Food 21–27
Frantiskovy Lázně 188–190
Franzensbad 188–190
Frenštát pod Radhoštěm 309
Freud, Sigmund 307, 308
Frýdek-Místek 310
Frýdlant 220
Frymburk 164

Gabčíkovo-Nagymaros Dam
  342
Gerlachovský štít 385
Glossaries 452–454
Goethe, Johann Wolfgang von
  180, 182, 183, 184, 196, 205
Gombasecská jaskyňa 402
Gottwald, Klement 84, 109,
  285, 430–432
Gottwaldov 285
Great Moravian Empire 281,
  421–422

Harrachov 231
Hašek, Jaroslav 104, 148, 153
Havel, Václav 85, 433–437
Health 10
Heľpa 378
Henlein, Konrad 218, 429
Herľany geyser 414
Heydrich, Reinhard 102, 141,
  207, 430
High Tatras 378–386
History of Czech/Slovak people
  421–437
Hlinka, Andrej 373, 374, 427
Hluboká nad Vltavou 158
Hodonín 279
Hodslavice 306
Holašovice 159
Holidays 29
Hořice 243
Horní Planá 165
Horní Vltavice 168
Horšovský Týn 180
Hotels 19
Hradec Králové 237–241
Hradec nad Moravě 302
Hřensko 214
Hronsek 358
Hrubá skála 225

Hrubý Rohozec 223
Hukvaldy 308
Humenné 410
Hummel, Johann Nepomuk
  324
Hungarians of Slovakia 344
Hus, Jan 79, 85, 167, 423
Husinec 167

Insurance 10
Istebné 370

Jablonec nad Nisou 219
Jáchymov 197
Jakeš, Miloš 434
Janáček, Leoš 259, 308
Jánošík, Juraj 368, 369
Janské Lázně 232
Jaroměř 241
Jaroměřice nad Rokytnou 274
Jaslovské Bohunice 345
Jasná 377
Jasov 402
Javoříčko 299
Javorník 301
Jazz Section 434
Jedovnice 265
Jemniště 138
Jeseník 301
Jeseníky Mountains 299–
  303
Ještěd 218
Jetřichovické stěny 214
Jews in Slovakia 325
Jičín 226–227
Jihlava 274–276
Jindřichův Hradec 154
Jizera Mountains 220
Jókai, Mór 343
Josefov 241

Kačina 136
Kadaň 202
Kafka, Franz 65, 81, 89, 91,
  108, 129, 180, 220
Kámen 152
Kamenice gorge 215
Karlová Studánka 301
Karlovy Vary 190–197
Karlštejn 138
Karlsbad 190–197
Kašperské Hory 169
Kežmarok 390–391
Kladno 141
Kladruby 177

Klatovy 177
Klaus, Václav 436–437
Klimt, Gustav 195
Klokoty 150
Kokořín 129
Kolín 132
Komárno 343
Komenský, Jan Ámos 298
Konopiště 138
Kopřivnice 307
Košice 411–414
Kost 226
Kralupy nad Vltavou 127
Krásna Hôrka 401
Krásnohorské Podhradie 401
Kratochvíle 159
Kremnica 362
Křivoklát 140
Krkonoše 228–232
Kroměříž 287–290
Křtiny 265
Krušné hory 203
Kuks 242
Kunerad 369
Kutná Hora 133–136

Lake Lipno 164–165
Lake Orava 372
Language: Czech/Slovak 445–
  448
Lány 141
Lázně Jeseník 301
Lázně Kynžvart 184
Lednice 271
Lehár, Franz 343
Lendl, Ivan 305
Leopoldov 345
Levoča 393–395
Liběchov 129
Liberec 216–220
Lidice 141
Liechtensteins 271
Lipnice nad Sázavou 152
Lipno nad Vltavou 164
Liptov Region 372–376
Liptovská Stiavnička 373–374
Liptovská Teplička 378
Liptovský Mikuláš 374–375
Litoměřice 208–210
Litomyšl 246
Litvínov 203
Loket 197
Louka 273
Louny 201

Low Tatras 376–378
Lučenec 358
Ľudrová 373
Luhačovice 283
Lysá Poľana 386
Łysohorsky, Óndra 310

Mahler, Gustav 275, 293
Malá Fatra 366–369
Malá Skála 228
Maps 13
Marian Pilgrimage at Levoča 395
Mariánské Lázně 180–184
Marienbad 180–184
Martin 363–366
Marx, Karl 195
Masaryk, Jan 68, 142
Masaryk, Tomáš Garrigue 142, 279, 427–429
Matica slovenská 363
Maxwell, Robert 326, 404
Mečiar, Vladimír 317, 437
Medzilaborce 410–411
Mělník 128
Mendel, Gregor 260
Metric Weights and Measures 39
Mezná 215
Mezní Louka 215
Michalovce 415
Mikulov 269
Milevsko 151
Mladá Boleslav 130
Modra 335
Modrava 169
Money 11
MORAVIA,
NORTH 291–311
SOUTH 248–290
Moravský kras 264–266
Moravský Krumlov 267
Most 203
Mount Kleť 159
MOUNTAIN REGIONS, THE 351–386
Mozart, Wolfgang Amadeus 73, 83, 113
Mucha, Alfons 267
Museums 31
Music 33

Náchod 235
Navrátilová, Martina 139

Nelahozeves 127
Němcová, Božena 236
Newspapers 28
Nitra 339–341
Nízke Tatry 376–378
NORTH BOHEMIA 199–221
NORTH MORAVIA 291–311
Nová Ves 226
Nové Město nad Metují 235
November 17, 1989 demonstration 98, 434
Nový Bor 216
Nový Dvůr u Opavy 303
Nový Jičín 306

Ochtinská jaskyňa 404
Olomouc 291–297
Opava 301–303
Opening Hours 29
Orava Castle 370
Orava folk skanzen 371
Orava Region 370–372
Oravský Podzámok 370
Orlík 146
Ostrava 303–305

Package Tours from North America 8
Package Tours from the UK 4
Palach, Jan 90,
Palúdzka 375
Panská skála 216
Pardubice 244–246
Párkány 344–345
Pavlovské vrchy 270
Pec pod Sněžkou 231
Pelhřimov 152
Pernštejn 266
Petrol 17
Petrov 280
Phones 28
Pieniny 392
Piešťany 346
Pikarts 149
Písek 147
Plastic People of the Universe 433
Plasy 176
Ploskovice 210
Plzeň 171–177
Podbiel 371
Poděbrady 131
Podkost 226
Pohorelá 378

Police 36–37
Police nad Metují 234
Poprad 381
Post 27
Prachatice 166
Prachovské skály 227
Praděd 301
PRAGUE 43–126
  Accommodation 53–56
  Arrival and information 47–50
  Astronomical Clock 79–80
  Bílá hora 112
  Cemeteries:
  • Military 108
  • New Jewish 18
  • Old Jewish 89
  Olšany 108
  Charles Bridge 75–77
  Charles University 83
  Churches:
  • Bethlehem Chapel 84–85
  • Convent of sv Anežka 82
  • Emmaus Monastery 103
  • Loreto 68
  • Na Karlově 104
  • Nejsvětější Srdce Páně 107
  • Panna Marie pod řetězem 72
  • Panna Marie Sněžná 98
  • Panna Marie Vítězná 72
  • St Vitus Cathedral 60–63
  • Strahov Monastery 68–69
  • sv Cyril and Metoděj 101
  • sv František 77
  • sv Jakub 82
  • sv Jiljí 85
  • sv Kliment 78
  • sv Martin ve zdi 84
  • sv Mikuláš (Malá Strana) 69–70
  • sv Mikuláš (Staré Město) 80
  • sv Salvátor 77
  • Týn Church 80–81
  • Vlašská kaple 77
  Eating and drinking 114–119
  Entertainment 119–124
  Getting around 51–53
  Holešovice 109–111
  Hradčany 57–69
  Hus Monument 79
  Hvězda 112–113
  Jewish Quarter 86–91
  Josefov 86–91
  Kampa Island 73–74
  Klementinum 77
  Listings 125
  Malá Strana 69–74
  Museums:
  • Bertramka (Mozart Museum) 113

- Bílek Museum 110
- Comenius Museum 71
- Dvořák Museum 104
- Kafka Museum 91
- Museum of Military History 66, 109
- Museum of Modern Sculpture 113
- Náprstek Museum 85
- National Museum 96
- Police Museum 104
- Smetana Museum 85
- Technical Museum 111
- UPM 90–91
National Theatre 99
Nové Město 91–104
Obecní dům 100
Palaces:
- Archbishop's Palace 66
- Buquoy Palace 73
- Černín Palace 67–68
- Golz-Kinský Palace 80
- Lobkovíc Palace (Hradčany) 65
- Lobkovíc Palace (Malá Strana) 71
- Šternberk Palace 66–67
- Valdštejn Palace 71
Petřín Hill 74
Prague Castle 57–65
Slavín 105–106
Slovanský ostrov 101
Smíchov 113
Staré Město 75–86
Staroměstské náměstí 78–81
Střelecký ostrov 102
Troja 112
Vinohrady 107
Vyšehrad 105–107
Výstaviště 111
Wenceslas Square 94–96
Žižkov 108
Zbraslav 113
Pravčická brána 214
Přerov 298
Přerov nad Labem 130
Prešov 405–407
Příbor 307
Prices 11
Příhrazy 226
Princip, Gavrilo 207
Private rooms 19
Prostějov 2948
Průhonice 137
Public transport 16

Rabí 168
Racism 39
Radio 29

Radnošť 309
Raduň 302
Rajecké Teplice 368
Reichenberg 216–220
Řevnice 139
Rohe, Mies van der 261
Rožmberk nad Vltavou163
Rožňava 400
Rožnov pod Radhoštěm 309
Rusyns 406
Ružomberok 373
Rysy 383

Saint Benedikt Junior 341
Saint Cyril 282
Saint Methodius 282
Saint Ondrej Svorad 341
Santini, Giovanni 277
Sázava 137
Schiele, Egon 162
Sedlec 135
Semtex 244
Senec 342
Senetářov 265
Silesia 302
Silická ľadnica 403
Slanica 372
Slavkov 267
Slavonice 278
Sliač 358
Škoda 131, 173
Škvorecký, Josef 235
Slovak National Uprising 357
Slovak Sea 415
SLOVAKIA,
CENTRAL 351–386
EAST 387–417
WEST 315–350
Slovenský kras 400–404
Slovesnký raj 397–400
Slušovice 286
Small Carpathians 334–336
Smetana, Bedřich 65, 85, 105, 154, 247
Smokovce 384
Sněžka 231
Sobotka 225
Soos 190
SOUTH BOHEMIA 144–170
SOUTH MORAVIA 248–290
Špičák 170
Špinlerův Mlýn 231
Spiš Region 390–397

Spišská Kapitula 396
Spišská Nová Ves 395
Spišská Sobota 381
Spišské Podhradie 396
Spišský hrad 396
Spišský Štvrtok 395
Sport 35–36
Srbsko 140
Srní 169
St John of Nepomuk 62, 76
Stará Ľubovňa 392
Starý Smokovec 384
Štefánik, Milan Rastislav 334
Stifter, Adalbert 165
Stoppard, Thomas 287
Štramberk 306
Štrbské Pleso 382
Strakonice 168
Strážnice 280
Strečno 367
Střekov 211
Štúr, Ľudovít 333, 335, 426
Štúrovo 344–345
Šumava 163–170
Šumiac 378
Šumperk 299
Sušice 169
Svidník 48
Švihov 178

Tábor 148–151
Tále 377
Tatra National Park 381–386
Tatranská Kotlina 385
Tatranská Lomnica 384
Telč 278
Temelín 147
Teplá 184
Teplice nad Metují 233
Teplice-Šanov 204–205
Terchová 368
Terezín 206–208
Theatre 34
Theresienstadt 206–208
Time 39
Tisá 215
Tiské stěny 215
Tourist Information Offices 12
Trains 14
Trains from the UK 3
Transport 14–18
Travel agents in North America 7

Travel agents in the UK 4
Třeboň 154
Trenčianske Teplice 349
Trenčín 347–349
Trnava 336–339
Troppau 301–303
Trosky 225
Trstená 371
Trump, Ivana 287
Trutnov 232
Turčianske Teplice 362
Turnov 223
TV 29
Tvrdošín 372

Uherské Hradiště 280
Ukrainian visas 416
Úštěk 211
Ústí nad Labem 211

Valtice 270
Važec 376
Vegetarians 25
Velehrad 281
Velké Losiny 300
Veľký Kriváň 368
Veltrusy 127
Velvet Revolution 94, 95, 96, 97, 434–435

Vihorlat 415
Vimperk 168
Vinné 416
Visa requirements 9
Vladštejn 225
Vlkolínec 373
Volary 165
Vranov 273
Vrbov 392
Vrchlabí 230
Východná 375
Vysoká Louka 215
Vysoké Tatry 378–386
Vyšší Brod 164

Walking 17
Wallachian Culture 305
Warhol, Andy 404, 410–411
Wenceslas, Good King & Saint
61, 62, 95, 422
WEST BOHEMIA 171–198
WEST SLOVAKIA 315–350
Western Tatras 371–372
*Women and sexual
harassment* 38
Wooden Churches 30
Bardejovské kúpele 408
Dobroslava 409
Hronsek 358
Istebné 370

Ladomírová 409
Lukov 409
Miroľa 409
Nižný Komárnik 409
Palúdzka 375
Stará Ľubovňa 393
Svidník 409
Tročany 409
Tvrdošín 372
Uličské Krivé 409
Zuberec 371

Youth Hostels 19

Zádielska dolina 402
Žatec 202
Zátopek, Emil 307
Žďár nad Sázavou 276–277
Ždiar 385
Žehra 396
Železná Ruda 170
Železný Brod 227
Zemplínska šírava 415
Žiar nad Hronom 361
Žilina 366
Zlatá Koruna 160
Zlín 283–287
Znojmo 272–273
Zuberec 371
Zvíkov 146
Zvolen 356

ROUGH GUIDES – THE FULL LIST

EUROPE
- Amsterdam
- Barcelona and Catalunya
- Berlin
- Brittany and Normandy
- Bulgaria
- Crete
- Czech and Slovak Republics
- Eastern Europe
- Europe
- France
- Germany
- Greece
- Holland, Belgium and Luxembourg
- Hungary
- Ireland
- Italy
- Paris
- Poland
- Portugal
- Prague
- Provence and the Côte d'Azur
- The Pyrenees
- Scandinavia
- Sicily
- Spain
- Tuscany and Umbria
- Venice

Forthcoming:

☐ Cyprus ☐ St Petersburg

NORTH AMERICA
- California and West Coast USA
- Florida
- New York
- San Francisco and the Bay Area
- USA
- Canada

CENTRAL AND SOUTH AMERICA
- Brazil
- Guatemala and Belize
- Mexico
- Peru

AFRICA
- Egypt
- Kenya
- Morocco
- Tunisia
- West Africa
- Zimbabwe and Botswana

ASIA & AUSTRALASIA
- Hong Kong and Macau
- Israel and the Occupied Territories
- Nepal
- Turkey
- Thailand

Forthcoming:

☐ Australia

ROUGH GUIDE SPECIALS

- Mediterranean Wildlife
- Women Travel: Adventures, Advice and Experience
- Nothing Ventured: Disabled People Travel the World

Forthcoming:

☐ World Music: the Complete Handbook (large format, fully illustrated)

For mail order enquiries please write to:
Marketing Dept. RG, Penguin Books, 27 Wrights Lane, London W8 5TZ, England

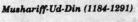

You are
A STUDENT

You travel
THE WORLD

You want
TO SAVE MONEY

Here's how

The International
Student Identity Card

Entitles you to discounts and special services worldwide.

BEFORE YOU TRAVEL THE WORLD, TALK TO AN EXPERIENCED STAMP COLLECTOR.

At STA Travel we're all seasoned travellers so we should know a thing or two about where you're headed. We can offer you the best deals on fares with the flexibility to change your mind as you go – without having to pay over the top for the privilege. We operate from 120 offices worldwide. So call in soon.

74 and 86 Old Brompton Road, SW7, 117 Euston Road, NW1. London.
Manchester. Leeds. Oxford. Cambridge. Bristol.
North America 071-937 9971. Europe 071-937 9921. Rest of World 071-937 9962
(incl. Sundays 10am-2pm). **OR 061-834 0668 (Manchester)**

WHEREVER YOU'RE BOUND, WE'RE BOUND TO HAVE BEEN. STA

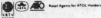 Retail Agents for ATOL Holders

STA TRAVEL